HG29　　　　　　　　68-6909
P7　　　Powell
Ev　　　Evolution of the
　　　　money market

Date Due	
JUL	2000
JUN	2004
JUL X X 2015	

THE EVOLUTION OF
THE MONEY MARKET 1385-1915

THE EVOLUTION
OF
THE MONEY MARKET
1385-1915

*An Historical and Analytical Study of the
Rise and Development of Finance as a
Centralised, Co-ordinated Force*

ELLIS T. POWELL

CUMBERLAND COUNTY COLLEGE
LIBRARY P.O. BOX 517 VINELAND N.J.

REPRINTS OF ECONOMIC CLASSICS

Augustus M. Kelley, Bookseller
New York 1966

Published by Frank Cass & Co. Ltd.,
10 Woburn Walk, London W.C.1
First published by The Financial News in 1915

Published in the U.S.A. by A. M. Kelley,
24 East 22nd Street, New York, U.S.A.

First Edition	1915
Second Impression	1916
Third Impression	1966

Printed in Great Britain

TO
MY VALUED COLLEAGUES OF
THE FINANCIAL PRESS
AS WELL AS TO
THE CITY EDITORS AND
CITY FINANCIAL WRITERS GENERALLY
THIS STUDY OF THE GIGANTIC PROCESS
WHICH THEY CHRONICLE WITH UNDEVIATING ACCURACY
AND INDEFATIGABLE VIGILANCE
IS MOST CORDIALLY
DEDICATED

FOREWORD

No intelligent student of modern events can possibly have overlooked the vast change which the last fifty years has wrought in the enhancement of the influence of finance as a social factor overshadowing all other contemporaneous forces, with the exception of religion and love. Contemplating the ceaseless and irresistible advance of the financial power, and the simultaneous weakening of those authorities which base their claims on political predominance, tradition, custom, precedent, convention, expediency, and the cognate origins, the philosophic watchman could hardly avoid reflecting that finance must increase, while these must decrease. But still, with the scholarly dubiety which is ever humble in the presence of such a complex of concurrent influences as the modern social organism presents to its would-be scrutineers, the observer might well hesitate to affirm the consciously separate existence of the force whose operations he discerned. He might hardly dare to believe that the golden thread of the Money Power, so to speak, might be extracted from the warp and woof of the social texture, and subjected to detailed examination as a thing apart.

And yet, long before the German war crisis of 1914, the present writer had formulated for himself the theory that the ever-increasing stability and potency of modern finance were attributable to something in the nature of organic development, operating by means of Natural Selection, and therefore completely in accordance with the main postulate of the Darwinian theory. At first blush, perhaps, the attempted application of the biological theory of evolution to the mechanism of notes and gold, cheques and Stock Exchange securities, may seem a fanciful extravagance. Still, since physico-chemical research has brought us at least to the *suspicion* that the evolutionary principle extends beyond the living world and operates upon the " elements," there is really nothing very extravagant in the suggestion that it can also be discerned in the processes of the economic mechanism which are carried on by living men, are dominated by Mind, and depend for their successful operation upon the most deeply ingrained of human instincts. At any rate the writer of the present essay was bold enough to believe that the process, and the force behind it, might be isolated sufficiently for the purpose of separate study. The idea had, indeed, occurred to other observers, but it had not commended itself. " The subject " (of Darwinism), says Professor Cannan,[1] " has not been much discussed by economists of any school, because the analogy between industrial competition and the struggle for existence among the lower animals is too imperfect to be of much service." Undeterred, however, by opinion so authoritative, the present writer set himself to subject his theory to the test of research, and to trace the operation of the great biological principle in one of the most important and conspicuous departments of the organic and super-organic worlds. Mr. Darwin, remarked Bagehot,[2] " has shown how one *vera causa*, ' natural selection,' would account for an immense number of the facts of nature : for *how* many, no doubt, is controverted, but, as is admitted, for a very large number. . . ." To discover whether or not the same *vera causa* would account for some, or all, of the facts of finance, was one of the purposes

[1] In the *Encyclopædia of Political Economy*, Art. "Darwinism."
[2] *Economic Studies*, p. 16.

FOREWORD

of the investigation whose results are offered in the present volume. A large portion of the study had been written and some of its leading arguments published in essay form[1] when its conclusions were suddenly and unexpectedly submitted to the supreme test of the German war crisis of 1914. Whether or not they were equal to the strain the reader will judge for himself.

The survey extends over the period from about 1385 to 1915. It begins with the rule of Richard II. and ends in the reign of George V. For the period between 1385 and 1694—the date of the establishment of the Bank of England—the treatment of the subject is not more detailed than is necessary to exhibit the origins and nature of all the factors of the Money Market in their proper focus, by way of preparation for the subsequent scrutiny of their gradual gravitative response to the inexorable authority of a centripetal sway. After the date of the establishment of the Bank of England the essay becomes rather more elaborate in its recital of fact and inference. In other words, Part I. is simply introductory to the main topic. No phenomenon, be it spiritual, intellectual, physical or financial, will ever be properly understood without some knowledge of the sources whence it was originally produced, and of the forces by which its early development was encompassed. The rest of the study is, in effect, a brief history of the first hundred years of the modern Money Market.

There have been woven into the essay a number of quotations, in support and illustration of the text. This plan has the advantage of exhibiting the facts exactly as they presented themselves to the living observers or later critics. The verbatim citation adds vividness to the presentation of the fact, the scientific deduction, or the generalisation. It is more candid to quote than to para-

[1] In *The Financial News*.

phrase. Perhaps it may also be said that illustrative quotation from authoritative sources strengthens the reader's faith in the soundness of the argument which he is following.

Some criticism may, perhaps, be directed to the amount of detail here and there introduced, and especially to the extended notes, such as those upon Negotiable Instruments, Unlimited Liability, the Clearing-House, and so forth. But in this respect the writer had in his mind's eye the needs of the younger men who are qualifying in many City offices for ultimate control of a branch bank, a financial organisation, a City column, or for the occupancy of the editorial chair, or the management of one of the editorial departments, of a financial newspaper. When these aspirants first approach the subject of finance as a whole, or, say, the history of banking as a department thereof, it presents the same disheartening appearance of arbitrariness and disconnection as is offered by the English law during the first year of a budding lawyer's study. It is not until considerable progress has been made that the student begins to see the various legal principles in their proper proportion and perspective, and to discover that what seemed to him a wilderness of anomaly is only highly organised complexity. Therefore if the notes are criticised as occasionally very copious, the reply is that they have been deliberately made so, in an effort to clear away the difficulties from the beginner's path, so that he may see finance not as a confused labyrinth, but as an organic entity, wherein every part has its place and function clearly defined. The general scheme of the book, with its exposition of the organic growth of finance, is auxiliary to this device. There is an almost inestimable intellectual value in the discernment and definition of some principle, operative from age to age, around which the various phenomena can be grouped as they come one by one within the survey. Disconnection means imperfect intellectual assimilation, whereas a demonstrated and consistent relationship means exactly the reverse, because of the mnemonic co-operation and stimulus which it affords at every stage. The copiousness of the notes, further, has enabled the inclusion of a good deal of information and explanation which was worthy of incorporation, though its full insertion in the text might now and then have interrupted the flow of the argument.

It would be too much to hope that a survey of so wide a field, including such a multitude of factors, involving the consultation of a myriad authorities, and extending over more than five centuries of time, should be wholly free from blemishes. The friendly indication of them will be welcomed. Impatience of criticism is incompatible with the spirit of earnest search for truth in which all our great scientific problems should be approached, dissected and discussed.

CONTENTS

PART I
INTRODUCTORY HISTORICAL SKETCH

CHAPTER I
THE EMBRYOLOGY OF THE MONEY MARKET . . PAGE 3

CHAPTER II
THE EARLY MONEY-MARKET—DECLINE OF ANTI-USURY SENTIMENT—BEGINNINGS OF BANKING . . . 38

CHAPTER III
THE SUPREMACY OF THE GOLDSMITH-BANKERS . . 94

CHAPTER IV
THE BANK OF ENGLAND—EXTENSION OF BANKING ENTERPRISE 114

CHAPTER V
THE STOCK EXCHANGE (1500–1815) 142

CHAPTER VI
THE JOINT-STOCK COMPANY—TRANSFERABLE SHARES AND LIMITED LIABILITY—INSURANCE . . . 163

PART II
THE NUCLEUS OF ORGANISATION

CHAPTER VII
THE PRESTIGE OF THE BANK OF ENGLAND . . 197

CONTENTS

PART III
THE RISE OF THE MODERN MONEY MARKET

CHAPTER VIII
THE MODERN MONEY MARKET — THE BIOLOGICAL ANALOGY ELABORATED 243

CHAPTER IX
THE AGGREGATION OF CAPITAL—THE ABSENCE OF BANKING PRINCIPLES 269

CHAPTER X
THE RISE OF THE JOINT-STOCK BANKS . . . 299

CHAPTER XI
THE PANIC OF 1825 AND THE " PRESSURE " OF 1836–1839 322

CHAPTER XII
THE BANK CHARTER ACT AND THE 1847 PANIC . . 343

CHAPTER XIII
THE 1857 PANIC—THE WIDENING ARENA AND THE " NEW SPIRIT " IN FINANCE 364

CHAPTER XIV
THE OVEREND-GURNEY CRISIS AND THE END OF ISOLATION AND DISUNION 395

CHAPTER XV
NATURAL SELECTION AMONG THE BANKS—ABSORPTION AND AMALGAMATION 411

CHAPTER XVI
THE FINANCIAL TRUSTS—" INVESTMENT BY PROXY " AND ITS EXTENSION 464

CONTENTS

PART IV
THE STRUGGLE TOWARDS CONSOLIDATION

CHAPTER XVII
FINANCIAL CONFEDERACY "IN A FLOOD" . . . 481

CHAPTER XVIII
THE BARING CRISIS, 1890 521

CHAPTER XIX
THE STOCK EXCHANGE AS A FUNCTION OF THE MODERN MONEY MARKET 533

PART V
CONFEDERACY, THE GREAT AVOWAL AND THE SUPREME TEST

CHAPTER XX
POST-BARING EVOLUTION—BANKERS' COUNCIL AT THE BANK OF ENGLAND 637

CHAPTER XXI
SUMMARY AND CONCLUSION 682

INDEX 709

PART I
INTRODUCTORY HISTORICAL SKETCH

THE EVOLUTION OF THE MONEY MARKET

CHAPTER I

THE EMBRYOLOGY OF THE MONEY MARKET

An endeavour to describe and analyse the evolution of the Money Market must begin with its embryology. But even that starting-point involves, as Maitland would have said, the making of a rent in a seamless robe. Economic phenomena are in the most profound degree mutually dependent, each the last portion of a chain that stretches back, link by link, beyond the time when our sun first hurled his satellites into their eternal orbits. There is no date in our island history since the Christian era at which we might take for granted the absence of *every* element of a money market, and set ourselves to discern the gradual advent of the various factors which compose it. Unless, indeed, we begin with Cæsar, we are constrained to make a more or less arbitrary selection of a starting-point, and to take for granted the result of the previous evolutionary workings. Inasmuch as the idea of a money market suggests a concomitant money-economy, the best choice of a date is probably that (about the end of the fourteenth century) at which we can observe, with a fair degree of certitude, the influence of money—in the shape mainly of cash, but reinforced by a rudimentary credit—upon society. If it be objected that this date is unduly remote, the answer is that the aggregation of money, and the extended use of credit instruments are characteristic pheno-

4 EVOLUTION OF THE MONEY MARKET

mena of the fifteenth century, just as the transformation of the goldsmith-banker from a mere bailee or depositary into the debtor of his client is a sixteenth-century symptom of rapidly progressing economic change. To initiate a survey of the evolution of the money market at a date subsequent to the appearance of these phenomena would be almost as futile as the writing of a history of the ascent of man by beginning with Shakespeare at the summit instead of with the anthropoid apes and the cave-dwellers at the base. The rigidity of a feudal régime had been relaxed, and the flexibility of a money-economy had begun to manifest itself when Richard II. succeeded to the throne in 1377. The money-solvent had then been at work upon the crystalloid fabric of feudalism for nearly two centuries, if we reckon from the first traceable commutation of the feudal dues into money. The process had been slow in operation upon a society mainly voiceless, economically ignorant, without national self-consciousness, or the power of united initiative. But its results are plain as we study the growing social instability which characterises the uneasy periods of Richard II. and Henry IV., as we watch the gradually gathering storm that culminated in the Wars of the Roses, and as we ultimately witness the close of the long mediæval drama when the night fell over Bosworth Field.

THE MONEY-SOLVENT AT WORK—COMMUTATION

The operation of the money-solvent upon feudal society was aided by a long series of calamitous epidemics. The greatest and most disastrous was the Black Death of 1348–1349. A second pestilence came in 1361, a third in 1368, a fourth in 1381, and a fifth in 1396. But the Black Death was immeasurably the most disastrous visitation. If Stow is to be believed (but probably his figures are exaggerated), he had seen an ancient monument which recorded the mortality in London during the Black Death at 50,000—about half the total population. We have the names of the six wardens of the Hatters' Company on December 13, 1347. All were dead before July of 1350.

Four of the wardens of the Goldsmiths' Company died in 1349. Whole villages were depopulated, entire monastic establishments left without a single inhabitant. Meanwhile, under an elementary money-régime, personal relations, once not easily alterable at will, had become liquefied. The square man was no longer forced to continue in the round hole. Labour had begun to follow capital. But a large proportion of the labour dues and obligations were commuted before there was a gold coinage, and at a time when money was extremely scarce, and prices consequently very low. By the year 1381, personal property (as distinguished from real) had been augmented to an enormous extent, and the gradual increase in the supply of currency, however irregular and unsystematic it may have been, had raised prices and changed the whole character of the conditions under which commutation had taken place, or was soon to be arranged. The tenants at Great Tew, in Essex, for instance, commuted on the basis of paying a halfpenny for each day's winter labour owed by them, and a penny for each day's autumn labour. But by the end of the fourteenth century the labourer who did the tenant's commuted work was getting threepence a day for it; so that the change in money values had placed the landlord in the position of buying for threepence what he had sold for a halfpenny or a penny. He was like a landowner who lets a farm for a long term at a fixed rent in an era of rising prices. He even had to hire, instead of being able to command, the labour for cultivating his own demesne (i.e. the land which he personally occupied for his own use). Not unnaturally, he tried to undo the bargains into which his ancestors had entered with their tenants. He demanded the labour itself instead of the money commutation.

It is easy to understand how odious was the demand for a reversion to the feudal services made upon men born and bred under the new conditions. Such a requirement, addressed to freeholders, copyholders, and cottars, who had so long paid the money instead of yielding the labour —who had, in fact, neither experience nor recollection of any other state of affairs—was bound to produce dissatis-

faction and resentment. Those results need not of necessity
have followed under the earlier régime, where the relationship between the landlord and his legal inferiors was of the
domestic and paternal type. But the conditions were
vitally and fundamentally changed when the paternal was
exchanged for the pecuniary nexus. These bonds breed
totally different sentiments, not likely to co-exist side by
side. The dissolution of the ancient tie of sentiment between owner and tenant was in one aspect the displacement
of personal in favour of impersonal obligation—an innovation destined to produce, in a wider and different arena,
immeasurable changes in the economic history of the world.
From one point of view it may have been a loss, but in
the strictly economic sense it was a gain. A man who
deems himself free of the obligation to labour for the benefit
of another, and who has risen to the dignity of his free
position, is not likely to submit tamely to an intimation
that for the future he must yield to the landlord the ancient
toll of days of severe manual toil. When he can earn more
as a settler in a town, or at all events swell his resources by
occasionally disposing of his labour there, he will not listen
patiently to the intimation that he and his are *adscripti
glebæ*. His resistance to such demands is likely to be all
the more desperate where the defendant must plead in
the manor court itself before an officer whose every interest
is that of the plaintiff. The unexpected reappearance of
an ancient obligation to labour, and the endeavour to
enforce it upon men whose ancestry, for four or five
generations, had yielded no such service, are among the
social incidents which (to use one of Huxley's metaphors)
beat gunpowder hollow as an explosive. They produced the
tremendous concussion of 1381.[1] Its results have been

[1] These views, which are substantially those of Thorold Rogers, are
challenged by Ashley, *Economic History* (i. 265, and see note p. 289), who
believes that it was rather the humiliating incidents of the tenures (e.g.
the tenant's obligation to pay a fine on his daughter's marriage) than
the essential conditions, which precipitated the upheaval. But so far as
commutation is concerned, Ashley himself notes its widespread operation. The Stoneleigh Register, he says (criticising Vinogradoff, *Economic
Review*, Vol. III. p. 173 n.), " dates only from 1392, and Domesday enters
most of the tenants as villeins and only a few as socmen. The appearance
three hundred years later of a greater number of socmen is most easily

MONEY MARKET EMBRYOLOGY

palpable down to our own day. If it had not happened, there would have been no money market.

The Black Death had laid the train for the explosion. Multitudes attempted to fly from the stricken land with such money as they could collect, and had to be stopped by royal proclamation (December 1, 1349). Jurors summoned to value mills and farms declared them worthless, since no miller or labourer could be found to tend them. Such labour as could be (and must be) obtained for harvest work was paid at amazing rates. The reaper, according to Knighton, got 8d. a day and the mower 12d. (in each case with food), and this at a time when a cow could be had for 12d. (the mower's daily wage) and a fat sheep for 4d. The inevitable result (there being no such national food reserves as modern capital resources, operating in the field of international trade, would ensure) was that prices rose, in the words of Professor Thorold Rogers, " to the extent of 50, 100 and even 200 per cent.," while some of the commonest articles of food became so dear as to be entirely out of the reach of ordinary consumers. Another inevitable consequence, then as in our day, was to inflict great hardship on all persons with fixed incomes. Commodities had doubled and trebled in price, whereas the means of paying for them remained a fixed quantity. The demands of the parish priests for increased fees were granted by statute in 1362. In our day, in the case of the railways permitted to increase statutory rates as compensation for the payment of higher wages, we have an instance of the same trouble, with the application of the same remedy. With the price of food greatly enhanced, and with the population reduced to one-half its previous numbers, wages rose in spite of legislation forbidding the

explained by commutation." Elsewhere Ashley says that "the revolt brought about no sudden change; but in the years which closed the fourteenth century and during the early decades of the fifteenth, commutation went on much more rapidly than before, and that on terms favourable to the peasants " (*Economic Organisation of England*, p. 52). As to the date of the ultimate extinction of services, Ashley's view is that " by about the middle of the fifteenth century, that vitally important feature of the manorial system, the services of the customary tenants for the cultivation of the lord's demesne, had almost entirely passed away, and their place had been taken by *money payments* (*ibid.*, p. 45).

labourer to demand or the employer to pay anything beyond the old rate. An attempt was made to reaffix the labourer to the soil, not by the cancellation of commutation agreements, but by forbidding him to quit the parish where he lived, in search of better employment. " Every man or woman," said the Statute of Labourers (1351), " of whatsoever condition, free or bond, able in body, and within the age of threescore years . . . and not having of his own whereof he may live, nor land of his own about the tillage of which he may occupy himself, and not serving any other, shall be bound to serve the employer who shall require him to do so, and shall take only the wages which were accustomed in 1346, or the six or seven years previous to be taken in the neighbourhood where he is bound to serve." The Legislature makes no attempt to revive the personal services which had been commuted or were in course of commutation. It simply endeavours to re-enact the old rate of wages. But labour seems to have defied the legislator, because it had the relentless pressure of economic law upon its side. The statute was impotent to suppress the working of human nature and the economic principle behind it. Statutory impotence and economic power will come into still more brilliant and instructive contrast as we proceed. As for the employer, he had either to accede to the demands of his workmen or see his crops rotting on the ground. The peasant's chance was a sudden and unexampled opportunity of betterment, and the fact that he took it has altered the whole course of England's economic history. Where efforts were made to enforce the legislation by imprisonment, such labourers as could escape fled ad silvas et boscos—to the woods and thickets. Many got away to distant manors (where their presence was welcome enough for the manner of their coming to be winked at) and were transformed from native to free labourers. Others went to the towns—progenitors of the nineteenth-century industrial workers, ready material for the use of the fifteenth and sixteenth century capitalist. Inside the town the worker was a craftsman ; outside he might be little better than a serf. Outside, he was the fixed portion of a rigid fabric; inside he could enter into a multitude of new relationships, every one of them a stimulus to individual pride and self-respect.

LAND SOLD BY RETAIL

To all intents and purposes, villeinage by tenure and villeinage by blood had disappeared before the end of the fifteenth century. Services were defined—standardised so to speak—and their character inscribed on the roll of the manor as the beginning of copyhold tenure. Mr. Page's researches have shown that of 81 specified manors before the Plague, all labour services had been commuted on 6. Partial commutation had taken place on 31, and there had been no commutation on 34. But on 182 manors in 1440, there had been complete commutation on 101, and partial commutation on 71, and no commutation only on 8, and even on these the team work was commuted. Society on a basis of *status*, as Sir Henry Maine would have said, was evolving rapidly into society on a basis of *contract*. The revolution in agricultural method resulting from the introduction of capitalistic policy, and the ever-increasing demand for labour in the capitalistic industries of the towns, represented a combined influence too strong for the manorial lords to resist.

Naturally, the tenants, finding themselves under the necessity of paying double the old rate of wages to their labourers (and realising that if the villeins were defeated their own turn would be the next to come), insisted upon concessions by the landlords. These latter were flatly told that unless they did reduce the rents the tenants would abandon their holdings. They had, in fact, no option in the matter. At a subsequent inquest upon certain of the Christ Church manors near Oxford, it was ascertained that " in the time of the mortality or pestilence which was in the year 1349, there remained hardly two tenants in the said manor (Ensham), and these had wished to leave, had not brother Nicholas de Upton, then abbot of the said manor, compounded anew with them, as well as with the other tenants who came in." The fall in the incomes of religious foundations (partly due to the reduction of rents and partly to the falling off in the yields of tolls at the fairs) rendered the great monastic communities less able to relieve indigence, and set in motion the sentiments and forces which ultimately led to the Elizabethan Poor Law. Some of the individual landlords, despairing of the situation, began to sell small holdings; so that by the end of the fourteenth century there was a fairly free market in them. While the realty went as an aggregate to the eldest son (in accordance with the practice of primogenitary devolution, which is the rule in mediæval England, at all events after the time of the so-called Leges Henrici Primi), the personalty was distributable. As long as there was but little personalty, such a policy was ineffective as a social solvent; but as soon as the practice of commutation increased the available resources in personalty the inheritor of the realty was left with less capital at his command for working it. The contingency forced him into the position of a seller by retail. He discovered buyers without much trouble among the rising capitalist class. All over the country, the successful trader was to be found, ready and willing to pick up cheap land. Sometimes he bought as an investment, becoming a capitalist sheep farmer, whose specialised activity required the employment of much less labour than was the case with his genuinely agricultural predecessor. He stocked the land with sheep, but spent no money on the soil itself, save, possibly, in fencing. It was not until the advent of the Tudor epoch that he bought for investment, and endeavoured, by judicious improvements, to augment values. In other instances, he bought less as an investment than as a means of enhancing his social status. It was a tremendous innovation—the sale, by retail, of a commodity essential to human existence, and yet hitherto only sold wholesale (and that to a very limited extent) or not sold at all. The land market was no longer monopolised by a national nobility. In modern market parlance, the " little man " was there, exerting a disintegrating influence upon all that survived of the antique feudal fabric.

NEW CLIENTS FOR THE GOLDSMITHS

The change was almost cataclysmic in comparison with that ideal evolved by the newly-formed courts of Henry II., according to which each military fee descended as an impartible whole. When he got his money, the seller proceeded to secure it in the only non-landed investment then easily available—plate and jewellery. Thus a trading class which originally consisted in the main of men engaged in dealing in food and clothing, came to be reinforced by the goldsmiths, the pioneers of the banker and the financier. This trading class possessed the ready money, while the landed class, influential though they might be, possessed only limited resources. For the next couple of centuries, this contrast between fixed and liquid assets was destined to become more and more conspicuous, and ultimately to throw a huge share of political influence into the hands which held the money, in contrast with those which held the land. When the land was sold, and the proceeds in effect hoarded in the shape of plate, the pace of rural development was slowed down in comparison with the rate of social advance in the towns. The modification of the economic focus not only checked agricultural progress by the direct diversion of capital and labour to other objects, but by training national ambition to look to commerce for its triumphs. The result was that the agricultural industry certainly remained stationary during the fifteenth and sixteenth centuries. The sweeping assertion has even been ventured that there was little advance in English agriculture between Henry III. and George III.

CAPITALISM AS A POLITICAL POWER

It is a very suggestive fact that the insurgents in this Peasants' Rising of 1381 were supported by the belief that they were acting on the command and at the wish of the King. If, as a matter of fact, the King really was behind the movement, we should be better able to understand why it was that certain of the country gentry favoured it, and, as Mr. Edgar Powell points out,[1] the sudden and peculiar

[1] *The East Anglia Rising*, 1381, p. 59.

ease with which the rebels transferred their allegiance to the King on the death of Wat Tyler would need no further explanation. The main suggestiveness of the idea, however, lies in its pointing to a very early royal realisation that in the organised peasantry, as well as in the new capitalist class, there was a force which might be arrayed in the interest of the monarchy against the feudalists. The availability of the capitalist power against the landed classes was very obvious indeed, to the keen political observation of Henry VII. and Henry VIII. They united it with the monarchical power for the final destruction of feudalism. But if Richard II. really was in the background of the peasants' rebellion in 1381, we must give him credit for a greater measure of economic discernment than has hitherto been attributed to him. Such ideas would explain his own endeavour, after he had crushed the outstanding manifestations of revolt, to bring about some compromise between the landowners and those whom they still called their "serfs." But Parliament, largely composed of the landowning class, would have none of it. The serfs, said the landlords, were part of their property, and could not be taken from them save with their own consent—which, they declared, they would never give. The landed interest remained for years to come insistent in its attempt at the frustration of the labourer's struggle towards a better destiny. By 7 Henry IV. cap. xvii. a father was prohibited from apprenticing his son or daughter to any trade unless he were possessed of the then large annual income of £20 in land or rent. Such legislation was a renewed effort to pin the peasant to the land, and, but for the insuppressible influence of the money-solvent, it might have been effective. The heads of the Norfolk worsted industry, by 11 Henry VII. cap. xi. and 12 Henry VII. cap. i. succeeded in obtaining exemption from these provisions. Ultimately, under the pressure of Tudor capitalism, this short-sighted policy of repression was altogether abandoned, and 39 Eliz. cap. iii. proceeded to enact the very system of apprenticeship which the earlier statutes had sought altogether to prohibit.

Whether or not Richard II. had fully discerned the change, the passage of the power of the purse from feudal magnate to town merchant became unmistakable during the reigns of his immediate successors. With his wages in money the labourer can move to a more promising or congenial environment, and—far more important—capital can be extracted from one species of enterprise and made to flow into another. In England the first form of differentiation is the appearance of the trader in cloth side by side with the maker of it. This type of specialisation is one of the commonest in our modern commercial system; and that, perhaps, is all the more reason why we fail to comprehend its transcendent importance when it makes its appearance simultaneously with a wider and more pervasive money-economy, and instantly expands the orbit of every mode of commercial enterprise. It introduces, moreover, the possibility of financial co-operation. Capital which is *adscriptus formæ suæ* cannot be detached from its position to co-operate with other capital similarly placed; but two masses of free capital, like mutually-attracted chemical elements, rush impetuously together. The amalgamated force may conquer where the separate entities would not venture to attempt. By their merged energy they can better discharge that which is the primary function of all capital—the economising of human effort by spending it a long way ahead of the end to which it is ultimately directed. The larger the capacity for preparation, the more economically advantageous the result. The beginnings may have been humble. The weaver who saved enough to buy another loom would only require to carry his thrift a stage further in order to accumulate the resources for paying a worker to operate it. This beginning of great things is actually on record as having occurred at Coventry early in the fifteenth century, when masters and journeymen agreed that there should be no restriction on the number of looms worked in a cottage, nor yet upon the number of apprentices which the weaver might take. But an understanding of this kind, and the state of affairs which brought it into being, must inevitably have led to the craft guilds becoming associations of small capitalists, every one of whom aspired to increase his resources, so as to develop his business on a larger scale.

WHENCE CAME EARLY CAPITAL ACCUMULATIONS?

Since the existence of some amount, however small, of free capital must have prefaced the rise of capitalism, it is of vital moment to inquire whence came these first supplies. The most likely answer seems to be that one class or other of those concerned with the cloth manufacture—the weaver, or the finisher, perhaps—began (in modern parlance, if we may use it in advance of its period) to finance the whole process of production and to hold a stock of cloth ready for the customer who called to buy it. This is an advance upon the almost entirely " bespoke " trade of earlier times. Experience will tell us that business would readily flow in the direction of a trader who had in this way anticipated the needs of his customers and could supply them on demand. He measured, and faced, the risks of fluctuations in the larger market where he operated. The London butcher began to buy cattle and sheep as far away as Nottingham. Such a trade, with its more adequate adjustment to the needs of a changing society, would grow, and would need to be financed upon a more ambitious scale. Intelligent conjecture would lead us to suggest a probable husbanding of the trader's own augmented resources, for the purpose of fostering his growing business, as well as an application, to some external source, for further capital supplies. Money was, for instance, tempted to leave its lairs in hoards. No doubt, many of these early capitalists got their original start by the practice of the severest self-denial,[1] and occasionally by less reputable means—the tricking of " country folks " who sold them corn,[2] the peddling of nondescript and petty wares, short weight, cloth-stretching, coin-clipping, lending small sums

---

[1] In this respect Senior's term "abstinence," as applied to the source of capital, would have almost completely fitted fifteenth-century conditions.

[2] See Riley, *Liber Albus*, p. 229, for a London instance as early as temp Edw. I.

at usurious rates, fining their workpeople, and paying them in truck :—
" Lytyll thei take for theyre labour, yet half ys merchaundise. Alas ! for rewthe, yt ys gret pité."[1]

Again, as the foreign trade expanded there would be more extensive supplies of capital which were capable of being turned back upon the home industry itself, so that a circle of influences would be set in operation. In 1437 one single English merchant sold to the Albertine Company wool to the value of £12,000. If the consequently enhanced accumulations could find no adequate outlet in the industry whence they had originally been garnered, they would seek opportunities in other directions, precisely as profit made in one department of the Stock Exchange tends to flow into another as soon as there is a slackening of the movement which led to the accumulation of the original profit. Some of the money, as we shall see, went abroad ; but the temperamental nervousness of its proprietors would also keep some at home, precisely as it does to-day. Elsewhere a hoard was tempted from its lair ; a retired trader ventured his savings in backing the younger man ; a wife brought in her husband the portion which enabled him to widen the area of his venture ; and every addition to the store stood for another potential surplus and a greater power of accumulation. The great and striking difference between this and the earlier age is that money in the period we are considering was to a great extent lent and used for reproductive purposes, instead of being advanced, as had been the case in previous centuries, for consumption of an utterly unproductive kind, like warfare and ostentation. In every direction, capital was springing into activity : so that it soon becomes possible to say that the small retail trader, as the representative of a class " freed, in great measure, from the tyrannous restrictions which had made business a virtual monopoly enjoyed by a privileged few . . . is certainly the most significant of all the signs of the times."[2] All through the

[1] Wright, *Political Songs*, Vol. II. p. 285.
[2] Hall, *Custom-Revenue*, p. 105.

reign of Henry VII. we shall see the rapid advance of this section of the community (the progenitors of the middle class; the pioneers of the army of small investors; the advance guard of the *clientèle* which created and supports modern banking) into comfort and comparative affluence.

TYPICAL INSTANCES OF AGGREGATION

It will be useful to illustrate these considerations by some typical instances. In 1482 we have the Leather Sellers' complaint that the ex-apprentice sets up in business at once on his own account, taking one or two apprentices of his own, and goes into debt for his stock and maintenance. That is a sign of available credit, possibly lent by the older man to the younger—and in some cases, there is good reason to suppose, taken by the younger man without permission. Here and there, as we grope among the scanty records of the century, we can discern the money on its way from the hoard into business; but the vast majority of the transactions have vanished in the oblivion of the years. Sir William Plumpton's servant tells him, in 1464, that there is a " young man, a mercer in the Chepe, the which a Michaelmas purpose to sett up a shop of his owne . . . what he is worth in goods I cannott wytt; mercers deals not at all with their own proper goods." However, a certain Jeffrey Dawne " hath proferred to lend him for iiij. yeare a hundreth merce, the which mony is ready in a bag if they agre." The money in a bag was obviously one of the myriads of hoards existing under a social system which knew nothing of the branch bank. The ambitious mercer had offered to " find surety that if he die," the lender is " to have Cli. besides her part of his goods after the custome of the Cittie."[1] When Paston, in 1474, told his uncle that he hoped to find a friend who would lend him £100, " he axed me, who was that ? I answered hym, an olde marchaunt."[2] When once the start was made, progress might well be rapid. Tyece, the Romney vintner, beginning business in a small way in 1387, is a big enough

---

[1] *Plumpton Correspondence*, Camden Soc., 11 and 12.
[2] *Paston Letters*, Ed. Gairdner, Vol. III. p. 114.

man to be sent on a deputation to the Archbishop in 1394. In 1398 he was Jurat, and in 1414 held such a quantity of land that it was ultimately made into a separate ward. No sooner did the struggling capitalist possess a small surplus than he augmented it by lending to other strugglers. This was at the beginning of the period of transformation. If we seek another instance, at a more advanced stage, we may find it in the early struggles of one of the greater statesmen of the Tudor age. Thomas Cromwell had seen the establishment of the Frescobaldis at Florence, in the course of his early and dubious wanderings, and had, years afterwards, helped Frescobaldi himself to collect a sum of 15,000 ducats owing to him in England.[1] It seems clear that he utilised his financial experience and such money as he had accumulated; for the malleus monachorum, before he entered Wolsey's service, combined the business of draper and money-lender.[2] Between 1518 and 1529 he had accumulated so much that it was necessary for his servant to be commissioned to buy him an iron strong box when he was next in Flanders.

The worst feature of this development lay in the fact of its placing a huge power over the lives and happiness of their fellow creatures in the hands of men who possessed ability and the capacity of self-denial, but who knew nothing of culture, and therefore, nothing of the duties of consideration and self-restraint. Hard upon themselves in their struggle for advancement, they developed an unrelenting hardness upon others when the struggle had been won. Capitalism, as it felt its power and became more or less free from control, occasionally offered an excessive and mischievous allegiance to the belief that money might be made to any extent, and employed in any

[1] See Foxe, v. 392, where the story is quoted from Bandello.
[2] Fairly early in his career as usurer, Cromwell removed from his residence "by Fanchurch" into a house at the junction of Throgmorton Street and Broad Street, "against the Austin Friars' Gate." This point is, in our time, almost the exact centre of the financial district, and immediately contiguous to the Stock Exchange. Have we in this removal from "Fanchurch" (still outside the financial district) some hint of the centripetal force of finance as already operative in the City? The combination of money dealing with another business was to be characteristic of the embryo financial system for the next 250 years.

way by its fortunate possessors, without moral responsibility for the results. More had these men in his mind when he wrote that the " rich are ever striving to pare away something further from the daily wages of the poor by private hand and even by public law." Even in the nineteenth century, as we shall be unmistakably reminded at a later stage, unorganised and undisciplined capitalism was blind to many of its obligations.

ENGLISH MONEY VENTURES ABROAD

Allusion has been made to the fact that English money began to be sent abroad. Accumulation had already gone so far even in the time of Henry VI., that Englishmen were beginning to send surplus capital, to be deposited in Italian banks and share in the profits of their business. When the Albertines failed in 1437 the Florentine merchants wrote to Henry VI.[1] acknowledging (the careful reader will note the italicised words) that integra fide et incorrupta probitate hactenus se gesserunt. Nunc autem, supervenientibus et erumpentibus in illa Societate variis morbis atque occultis et jam pridem conceptis, tandem in manifestam ruinam prolapsi sunt. Nos igitur dolentes, ut diximus, de casu illius societatis ; maxime propter damna et incommoda hominum vestri regni, *qui eidem Societate pecunias crediderant, sub spe futuræ munerationis ac restitutionis* omnia fecimus ac facturi sumus pro justitiæ complemento, tam erga creditores ipsos, qui suum procuratorem huc destinaverunt, quam erga Alexandrum de Ferrantinis et Ludowicum de Cavigianis, ejusdem societatis gubernatores.[2] Almost simultaneously there appear the

[1] *Bekynton's Correspondence,* Rolls Series, p. 248.
[2] Henry replied with a recital (p. 250) of the case of one Wolley, who had sold wool to the company, but, in spite of a verdict in his favour at Florence, had been unable to get his money. He went on to argue that if the company had failed, its members were solvent. Postremo ; quod in vestris prædictis literis inscripsistis, societatem prædictam in manifestam ruinam fuisse prolapsam, ostensum nobis est, satis notum fuisse et esse, quod Benedictus ille, de quo supra meminimus, antequam moreretur, ad summam xxii.ml librarum vel circiter, secundum compotum monetæ Angliæ, testamento reliquit : et quod dominus Franciscus de Altibianco neque in mobilium neque immobilium quidem possessione pauper consensus sit. Wherefore he demanded satisfaction without further delay,

MONEY MARKET EMBRYOLOGY 19

first traces of advances by the ordinary investor, as distinguished from the professional lender and the corporate body. In 1438 a loan of £40, and in 1443–1444 another loan of £50 were made to the King by the burgesses of Canterbury. In this and similar cases the editor of the Appendix to the Ninth Report of the Historical MSS. Commission [1] sees the first outlines of a national debt. He adds that " private individuals advanced the money—that is, purchased the stock—in various amounts, some speculating largely, others more timidly, and it may be assumed that they received certificates promising interest and redemption at par." If the certificates were negotiable, here is the embryo Consols stock certificate.

THE PRINCIPLE OF NEGOTIABILITY

What Brunner calls the Inhaberklauseln are discoverable in the ninth century. The *alternative* Inhaberklausel is tibi aut eidem homini qui hunc scriptum pro manibus abuerit, or else mihi seu ad hominum illum apud quem brebem iste in manu paruerit. The pure (reine) Inhaberklausel has the phrase ad hominem aput quem iste scribtus paruerit.

The principle of negotiability [2] was indeed developing

[1] p. 139.

[2] EARLY HISTORY OF NEGOTIABLE INSTRUMENTS
The principle of negotiability implies that an instrument (a bill of exchange, bond, or promissory note, for example), when it is in that state in which, by law and the usage of trade, it is accustomed to pass from one man to another by delivery, carries with its transfer, like a coin, all the property in it, provided that the transferee has been guilty of no fraud in taking it. The negotiable instrument is impersonal as distinct from indebtedness between two people who know each other; it evidences indebtedness between the creator of the obligation and any person in the whole world who acquires the instrument. Its holder can always sue the person or authority bound by the obligation to which it constitutes a title, in his own name, provided, of course, that they are accessible by methods within the jurisdiction which can be invoked by the plaintiff. He can do this centuries before a similar extension of legal conception enables him to sue upon the rights which purport to be transferred by the assignment of shares in a joint-stock company. The struggle for the general right to transfer shares by deed is reviewed in connection with the evolution of the joint-stock company with limited liability and transferable shares (p. 163).
As late as the reign of Queen Victoria we shall be told that shares are not transferable, save in the case of a corporation or joint-stock company specially created by Royal Charter or specific Act of Parliament. The

20   EVOLUTION OF THE MONEY MARKET

apace. There is a fifteenth-century decision at Lübeck, then an important banking centre in rivalry with Italy,[1] which points clearly to the wide acceptance of the doctrine of the negotiability of a money bond. Defendants made answer, to a plaintiff suing on the bond, that the latter

[1] Jenks, *Law Quarterly Review*, Vol. IX. p. 80.

utmost that assignment can do by common law, equity, or statute is to bind the party chargeable to the assignee, provided notice is given to him, and " subject always to the rule that a man cannot give a better title than he possesses in himself " (Anson, *Law of Contract*, 13th ed. p. 282). *Nemo dat quod non habet*. If the assignor is in possession on a vitiated title, or on no title at all, he can convey nothing better to his assignee. But the negotiable instrument is a document evidencing a contract, the benefit of which is assignable in such a manner that the promise may be enforced by the assignee of the benefit without previous notice to the promisor, and without running the risk of being met by defences which would have been good as against the assignor of the promise. What we get in the negotiable instrument as distinguished from the assignable contract, are four features : (1) title by delivery ; (2) creating a claim of which no notice need be given to the party liable, so that (3) the *assignor's* title is immaterial, and (4) the holder, if he has bona-fide given value, is not prejudiced by defects in the title of his assignor—the claim passes free of all equities (Anson, *op. cit.*, 283 ; and see Colonial Bank *v.* Whinney, 11 Ap. Cas. 426). All negotiable securities are assignable, but not all assignable securities are negotiable.

It is obvious that the theory of negotiability had been struggling towards legal and commercial recognition long before the eyes of the legal and mercantile communities were opened to its real significance. As early as 1036 (see Jenks' " Early History of Negotiable Instruments," *Law Quarterly Review*, Vol. IX. p. 80) the guardianship of a widow appears to have been negotiable, passing from certain specified individuals illi viro cui scriptum in manu paruerit. Jews were charged in England with having operated in the exchange (cambivisse) as early as 1181. Macpherson (p. 367) gives instances of general letters of credit, as remote as the year 1200. The prohibition (temp. Henry III.) of the sale to Christians of land bonds originally granted to Jews indicates the principle at least of transferability, if not of negotiability, as operative. In 1275 (see *Select Pleas in Manorial Courts*, p. 152) a merchant of Bordeaux sues in an English manorial court on a bond which contains a promise to pay to him " vel cuicunque de suis scriptum obligatorium portanti." Here, however, the negotiability is limited ; only the merchant's associates (de suis) are to be recognised as assignees of the obligation. Elsewhere in France the transition stage was further advanced. Mr. Jenks adduces a document of 1247-1248 from the archives of Marseilles, of which the material words for our purpose are : " Ego W. . . . confiteor et recognosco vobis Guidaloto . . . et Rainerio. . . . me habuisse et recepisse ex causa permutacionis seu cambii a vobis £216 . . . renunciancis [money not counted, etc.] : pro quibus £216 . . . dicte monete promicto vobis per stipulationem dare et solvere vobis vel Dono de Piloso vel Raimachi de Balchi consociis vestris *vel cui mandaveritis* £100, etc." This form is half-way on the road toward negotiability. About the same time Edward I. (1272-1307) was borrowing money from Italian merchants, on the security of the Customs, against assignments certis attornatis eorundem mercatorum—to the merchants or their assigns, clearly (Hall, *History of the Customs Revenue*, p. 22). In

had no authority from the original holder of the instrument; but this plea was overruled, and the negotiability thus distinctly asserted. A " memorandum that I owe [without naming anyone] ten pounds to be paid at Michaelmas and subscribing his name I. S. is a good obligation."[1]

[1] Note to Core's Case, Dyer 226. The case is temp. Henry VIII., but the note is of Elizabethan date.

1339, at Canterbury, we have a money bond given pro negotiis nostris et ecclesie nostre expediendis (*Hist. MSS. Comm.* IX. p. 85). This anticipates the modern form " for value received." The first statutory reference to bills of exchange, as " letteres d'eschange," occurs as long ago as 1379 (3 Ric. II. c. 3). An ordinance of March 18, 1394, by the magistrates of Barcelona, makes it clear that acceptance was at that time familiar in connection with bills of exchange. It is concerned with the form of the acceptance of bills (y sobre la forma de la aceptacion de las letras de Cambio). (Quoted in Jenks' " Early History of Negotiable Instruments," *Law Quarterly Review*, Vol. IX. p. 71).

Byles has a conjecture that the original bill was an order from a merchant in one country to his debtor, a merchant, in another, to pay the debt to a third person, the bearer of the letter. The safety and convenience of the transaction even as a mere means for the transmission of money, as distinct from the creation of credit (see p. 24) need no emphasis. At first, no doubt, the order was incorporated in a more general communication, but as it became occasionally desirable to transfer it to a third party, the personal element was separated from the business instrument, which gradually sank to the dimensions of the slip now in use. The assignee, desirous of assuring himself that the bill would be paid, showed it to the drawee (very much as we, nowadays, may get a cheque " marked "), and obtained his assurance, verified by signature, that it would be met. This was the original basis of the modern process of " acceptance." The early bills have four parties : (1) drawer, (2) drawee, (3) payee, and (4) presenter, or recipient on behalf of the payee. The last has vanished from modern commercial practice, leaving the parties at a total of three. Up to the time of James I. a bill was not made negotiable by endorsement, but was drawn to the payee and his assigns, or, as we have seen, to bearer.

Professor Sombart (*The Jews and Modern Capitalism*, p. 79) argues that the whole principle of negotiability (which undoubtedly owes its most effective development to Jewish agency) is itself an actual offshoot of the Jewish law. Sombart asserts that the Jewish law has no term for obligation ; it knows only debt and demand. Consequently the relationship between debtor and creditor is impersonal. The claim is really against things, rather than against persons, and therefore the original obligation may be imagined as referring as much to mankind in the aggregate as to the original specified individual. Jewish law, says Sombart, can conceive of an impersonal standardised legal relationship, which neither Roman nor Teutonic law is capable of doing. Sombart adduces a passage from the Talmud : " In the court of R. Huna a document was once produced to this effect : ' I, A. B., son of C. D., have borrowed a sum of money from you.' R. Huna decided that ' from you ' might mean ' from the Exilarch, or even from the King himself.' " But more to the point is a passage quoted from Rabbenu Asher (1250–1327), which has a direct reference to negotiable instruments. He says : " If A sends money to B and C, and notes in his bill ' payable to bearer by B and C,' payment must be made accordingly." This is practically the full doctrine of negotiability.

22 EVOLUTION OF THE MONEY MARKET

With regard to one special form of negotiable instrument, in 1462 there is an ordinance of Louis XI. which makes it obvious that remittance by means of bills of exchange had become a common and usual method of transferring money in any direction. The bank note, as distinguished from

Further, Sombart argues that the growth of the doctrine was materially assisted by the making of insurance policies to "bearer" by Jewish merchants of Alexandria. Jewish ships ran the risk of capture by Christian pirates, and the fleets of His Catholic Majesty, who regarded the property of Jews and Turks as legitimate booty. Therefore the Jewish merchant inserted in his policy some fictitious Christian name or bearer (" et quævis alia persona " or sometimes the form " sive quamlibet aliam personam "), and based his own title upon the alternative thus created. To the discovery and utilisation of this principle in their dealings with each other was due the fact that Jews so quickly recovered from the raid upon their property made by some royal or baronial vampire. It meant that Jewish wealth, being largely in the form of negotiable securities, could not be effectively plundered. As soon as A had reason to apprehend a raid upon his property, his securities were handed over to B, who would, if the necessity arose, pass them on to C. The Jews learnt, from a sympathy bred of their common oppression, to respect each other's rights. (See also the note on Bearer *Bonds*, as one form of modern securities, *post*, p. 560.)

The evolution of full negotiability, involving, as it did, the conveyance of a title absolute and unchallengeable, except in case of fraud by the holder, was doubtless assisted by the currency of a system, applicable to loan business, of renouncing all technical defences in advance. In early loan transactions, owing to the strong religious sentiment against usury, reinforced by the provisions of the canon law, the interest is generally in the form of a penalty for delay in payment. This is not an innovation, but only the utilisation of an old practice for a new purpose. No legal transaction at that time was completed without a penal stipulation. It is an essence of contract—a relic of the period when contract itself was a compromise between litigants secured by oath, pledges [i.e. sureties], and hostages. A loan to the Abbot of Rievaulx stipulates that in respect of every delay of two months in the repayment of the money the lenders are to receive one mark on every ten—that is to say, 60 per cent. per annum, " pro recompensatione, interesse, et expensis." But the debtor had also to renounce in advance " every possible ' exception ' that civil or canon or customary law might give him. The cautious Lombard meant to have an instrument that would be available in every court, English or foreign " (Pollock and Maitland, *Hist. Eng. Law*, Vol. II. p. 225). Further, the debtor is bound to pay the money, not only to the original lender, but, in the alternative, as we have already seen, to any attorney or mandatory of his who shall produce the bond. In these two provisions, (a) the renunciation in advance of all technical defences and (b) the obligation to pay the creditor or his attorney or mandatory, we have another of the many concurrent influences which resulted in the emergence of the principle of negotiability into the light of day. Like the Archæopteryx among fossils, they mark the advent of a new type, as distinct from the purely personal obligation as Archæopteryx, the earliest of birds, from his reptilian ancestry. They denote an epoch in financial palæontology. Bonds with such characteristics were, in effect, bonds to bearer. They were not only the *evidence* of the contract ; they *were themselves the contract*. The obligation is embodied in the document ; and whosoever possesses the latter enjoys to the full all the benefits of the former. " It has been

the bill, probably originated in the deposit receipt. As soon as the receipt has reference only to a given sum, and not to a specific deposit by a given person, the bank note is in existence. Sombart[1] thinks that the personal deposit receipt gave place to the impersonal bank note in Venice about the beginning of the fifteenth century. Within a century from that date we can distinguish the vogue of a freely negotiable promissory note. The bill became the exception to the maxim otherwise applicable to all personal obligations—assignatus utitur jure auctoris. The risks of the operation of negotiability were deliberately incurred, as the price of greater celerity.[2] One of the principles underlying the doctrine of negotiability—viz. freedom and safety of commercial intercourse, without the apprehension that a purchase can be subsequently challenged owing to the latent rights of third parties of which the purchaser was totally ignorant when he bought—was consistently applied in other directions. It gave us the rule (now nearly "eaten up by the exceptions," as Lord Campbell said in Sims v. Marryat) that there is no warranty of title in a sale of a personal chattel, as well as the other and scarcely less important doctrine that a sale in market overt will pass the property, even if effected by a non-owner.

[1] *Jews and Modern Capitalism*, p. 69.
[2] Is it possible that bribes were sometimes paid in instruments readily transformable into coin, corresponding to an open bearer cheque ? Louis XI. paid Lord Hastings 2000 crowns a year to " keep him sweet." But de Commines (Bk. VI., chap. I.) says that Hastings refusèd to give a receipt, and told the messenger from Louis that if he meant to leave it he " might put it in his sleeve." What sort of a sleeve was it which could hold 2000 crowns ? Was the expression merely figurative, or was the money really in the form of a bill, readily negotiable ?

acutely remarked [by Savigny] that the assignability of a negotiable instrument is due to its being, in point of fact, a material object, and so capable of actual delivery. The written document is thus, as it were, the embodiment of what would otherwise be an intangible, and therefore untransferable, claim " (Holland, *Jurisprudence*, 10th ed. 305). The money will be paid either to the original lender, " vel suo certo attornato has litteras deferenti." The instrument of credit has ceased to stand for a personal nexus. It is beginning to represent an impersonal relationship. This is the first stage in the evolution of the negotiable security. The second—the advent of a market in these securities—was bound to evolve ultimately.

BILLS OF EXCHANGE

The merits of the bill of exchange, as a rapid means of assigning a debt, authenticating the amount, and affording a title which could be maintained without evidence of the original transaction, could not remain unrecognised in a society which was becoming immersed in trade. The bill is one of the most powerful, as it is one of the most legitimate and safe, of the aids to economic progress—a " most wonderful and magical instrument of credit."[1] When it began to be found that, by the addition of machinery which we call discount, credit to the buyer could be combined with ready money to the seller, and that this beneficent transaction spread its circle of gratification even so far as a third party—the discounter—the simple but pregnant invention was established as part of the running gear of the commercial mechanism. The mutuality of confidence necessary for the operation of the bill of exchange was itself a new economic phenomenon, endowed with infinite potentiality. " The first symptom of a correlation of the behaviour of an organism with that of others may be taken as an indication of a new synthesis, whereby the organism will enter, as a constituent, into a higher organism."[2] It is true that the early policy of the law was one of discouragement—of tolerance of the bill system, that is to say, only as between merchants; but judicial sentiment has long ago changed, and is now prepared " industriously to remove every impediment, and add all possible facilities to the wheels of the vast commercial system."[3] The vogue of the Bill became steadily wider throughout the period between 1400 and 1600. The foreign merchant was especially skilful in these exchange and bill transactions.[4] He occasionally accom-

[1] Hartley Withers, *Money Changing*, p. 91.
[2] Hobhouse, *Development and Purpose*, p. 359.
[3] *Byles on Bills*, pref. to First Edition.
[4] The Act 3 Henry VII. c. 6 provides for the restriction of the business of exchange to those possessing the king's licence : and proceeds to enact that " all unlefull chevysaunce and usurye be dampned " on pain of forfeiture of the money. Even divers " englisch brokers and estraungers brokers whieh be named and assygnet to occupie lefull brocage " are to cease being " ynducers and bargeyne makers of unlefull chevysaunce and

modated the English trader out of what was really his own money :—

> " And thus they wold, if we will beleve,
> Wypen our nose with our owne sleve." [1]

Nicander Nucius,[2] a learned Greek who visited England in the time of Henry VIII., speaks of bills as a recognised part of the commercial machinery, daily utilised for remittances to all parts of the Continent, in order to defeat the attacks of pirates by sea and robbers by land. The wide general recognition of their utility is evident from Richard Porder's denunciation of them in his Whitsun Monday sermon at St. Paul's in 1570. " When money is delivered by exchange betwixt place and place," said he, " as from London to Hamborough, etc., to bee payde two, three or fower monthes after the deliverie thereof, and in respect of that time contracted and given any greater or more price to be taken upon the pound or hundreth pounds, than the price is at sight [note the modern technical term already familiarly known] by the market, and more than the deliverer would have taken to have had payment with all possible speeds at sight (as they call it) that overplus or greater price taken for ye times forbearance is usurie forbidden, and that deliverer is an usurer." As such instruments became more and more familiar, it was impossible to maintain, without exception, the ancient common law rule that a debt is not assignable and that chattels personal cannot, except by sale in market overt, be transferred to a vendee, however innocent, by a party who has himself no title to them. The maintenance of the rule intact would have been fatal to the inchoate doctrine of negotia-

[1] *Libel of English Policy,* Rolls Series Political Poems, Vol. II. p. 176.
[2] *Travels,* p. 10.

---

usurie," on pain of losing their occupation, in addition to fine and imprisonment.

Endeavours to maintain fixed and definite rates of exchange were abandoned early in the seventeenth century, and the attempt by Charles I. in 1627 to appoint an official for the regulation of the exchanges was met by the goldsmiths' company with the reminder that the office was obsolete and long out of use " although endeavoured to be revived two several times in the reign of the late King James."

bility, to every custom dependent upon it, and ultimately to the evolution of London into the money centre of the world. The rising equity jurisdiction recognised the new principle (which will be discussed in detail at a later stage, when we analyse the working of the Stock Exchange), so vital to the very existence—nay, to the birth—of an organised disciplined international money-power, working with its own cosmopolitan currency. At the very end of the transition period comes the first judicial decision on a Bill of Exchange—Martin v. Boure.[1] Within a few years—in 1622-1624—the Monte dei Paschi non Vacabile at Siena was issuing five per cent. bonds of 100 scudi each, which lacked only one element of complete negotiability. The right of proprietorship in these bonds was complete and unchallengeable in their owner for the time being, with the single limitation that certain rights of pre-emption were retained by the bank. The former secretary of the Monte dei Paschi told H.M. Consul in 1883[2] that these bonds were the first examples of negotiable mortgage bonds met with in Europe, and, as they are "anterior by nearly a century and a half to the Pfand-Briefe invented by Wolfgang Büring in Berlin in 1767, the merit of this useful invention should be placed to the credit of Italy." But if the rights of pre-emption were enforced, these bonds were not negotiable in the full sense of the word, since there was an inalienable " clog " upon the freedom of transmission.

The wide acceptance of the principle of negotiability has more than justified the foresight of its discoverers by adding immensely in magnitude and celerity to the financial potentialities of the modern world. Its boundless utility as a quickener of the flow of the life-blood through the arteries of the body politic, will again and again confront us as we proceed. It represents such an advance upon the older, clumsier and slower modes as does the twentieth-century Derby winner in comparison with his ancestor Eohippus, eleven inches high, far away in the Eocene ages. The evolution of the horse is wrapped up with the evolu-

[1] 1603, Cro. Jac. 6.   [2] Consular Reports, 1883, IX., 1356-7.

MONEY MARKET EMBRYOLOGY

tion of the plains. The evolution of the bearer bond is wrapped up with the evolution of social necessity and financial capacity. We are able, as Mr. Jenks says, " to trace in the clauses of early mediæval documents the germs from which the limbs of the negotiable instrument, so startlingly different from the orthodox forms of legal anatomy, were developed ; for we may be quite sure that negotiable instruments were not an invention, but a development." Under the mantle of the economic investigator, we find the palæontologist. Without the principle of negotiability the modern banking system would have been an impossibility. Without the assignability of a chose in action there could have been no Stock Exchange. Without both, cosmopolitan finance must have been a mere academic theory. The evolution of the assignability of a *chose in action* is treated at a later date (pp. 143, 177).

EARLY NEWS SERVICE

The international dealings thus facilitated by the negotiable instrument early gave birth to a system of news-service, designed to keep the rudimentary financial community *au fait* with events that might affect its interests. Next to judgment in the acquisition of a negotiable security comes adequate appreciation of the nature and scope of influences affecting its value and prospects. The Jews, as Bagehot used to say, " have shown a marked excellence in what may be called the commerce of imperceptibles . . . the exchange of money between country and country is a business of fine calculation which prepared them for other fine calculations." The extreme sensitiveness of the modern money market—one of its most essential characteristics, inestimable as a protective agency—depends upon this principle of exact and recent knowledge. The Jews organised an intelligence system—at first, in the case of ordinary messages, by means of letters sent by travellers and merchants (there being no objection to Christians or Mahommedans) and marked with a characteristic device cautioning the bearer against opening them, and later by a special organisation. At a very early stage in mediæval Jewish financial history, the European Governments were accustomed to rely on the Jews for early intelligence, and to use their machinery for its transmission. The Jewish merchants have almost always combined finance with mercantile business. Hence the cosmopolitanism of modern finance has, without doubt, been, at all events in a considerable degree, the consequence of the dispersion of the Jewish people. More important, however, than the creation of an international news service is the growth of international business law.

THE LAW MERCHANT

There was a special code of law applicable to mercantile dealings. Indeed, all law itself, as Loria says, is " simply the necessary outcome of economic conditions." In spite of minor differences, the Law Merchant was really the private international law of the Middles Ages. As the towns consolidated and rose to power, the Law Merchant became the Law of the Town, or, at all events, an inseparable portion thereof. Edward I., while he enacted, in the Carta Mercatoria, that all plaints of foreigners should be decided according to the Law Merchant, recognised the necessity of inquiry about the usages and customs of the fairs and market towns where the contract had originally been made. In Littleton's day (1402–1481) we hear that the proper court for aliens who had come here under the King's safe conduct is the Court of Chancery. " They are not bound to sue according to the law of the land . . . but shall sue in Chancery, and the matter shall be determined by the law of nature."[1] The local customs may have varied slightly, but the Law Merchant, in its broad lines, was brought into being for the sake of a commerce whose routes traversed many jurisdictions, and was therefore internationally uniform. It was a customary law to be declared, where there was a doubt, by the merchants themselves, even as in our own day expert evidence is admissible to prove a commercial custom. It was the origin of the Law Merchant in mercantile custom which

[1] Pollock and Maitland, *Hist. Eng. Law*, Vol. I. p. 466.

made it so thoroughly adaptable (especially in its swiftness of operation) to the necessities of commerce, and which enabled it to evolve concurrently with commercial needs, as in the development of the principle of negotiability. What Loria[1] calls "the law's absolute independence of national character, and its exclusive dependence upon the economic structure of society," was never better exemplified than in this gradual, yet reluctant, adjustment of legal sentiment to the financial exigencies of the age, and this in advance of specific legislation. The Law Merchant had its most characteristic vogue in the markets and fairs.[2] To the latter, which lasted for several days, flocked merchants from all parts of Europe. "The dealings of the merchants necessitated the use of simple rules : no technical jurisprudence peculiar to any country would have been satisfactory to traders coming from many different countries."[3] A law which was international tended to produce facility of negotiation in instruments that were largely handled by a scattered and cosmopolitan people who "had the exceptional interest of a common religion destitute of a political centre."[4]

The Law Merchant made its way inexorably into general acceptance and recognition. The *Lex Mercatoria* of 1622 emphasised the advantage to be derived from the ready transfer of commercial paper as in vogue in Amsterdam, Middleburg and Hamburg. The author of the *Lex Mercatoria* gives a form for a bill :—

I., A.G., merchant of Amsterdam, do acknowledge by these presents to be truly indebted to the honest X.Y., English merchant dwelling at Middelburgh in the sum of one hundred pounds, current money, for merchandize, which is for commodities received of him for my contentment,—which sum

[1] *Economic Foundations of Society*, 83.
[2] The fair has its own jurisdiction over visitors, in the court of pie powder—Curia Domini Regis pedis pulverisati tenta apud civitatem A., coram majore et duobus convicibus secundum consuetudines civitatis. These courts applied the Law Merchant, not the common law. They were gradually superseded by the common law courts, however, as the fairs died out. Their effective existence ceased with the sixteenth century, and all claims to a separate jurisdiction of this kind were finally abolished by the Municipal Corporations Act of 1835.
[3] Smith, *Mercantile Law*, Ed. 1890, lxix., lxx.
[4] Abrahams, *Jewish Life in the Middle Ages*, p. 4.

D

aforesaid I do promise to pay to him, the said X.Y., or the bearer hereof within six months next after the date of these presents. In witness whereof I have subscribed the same at Amsterdam, this tenth day of July, 1622.

The author adds the remark that " the civil law and the Law Merchant do require that the bill shall declare for what the debt groweth, either for merchandise or money, or any other lawful consideration." The courts, when the usages had been proved to them " have adopted them as settled law, with a view to the interests of trade and public convenience . . . proceeding herein on the well-known principle of law that, with reference to transactions in the different departments of trade, courts of law, in giving effect to the contracts and dealings of the parties, will assume that the latter have dealt with one another on the footing of any custom or usage prevailing in the particular department."[1] " When a general usage has been judicially ascertained and established," said Lord Campbell,[2] " it becomes a part of the Law Merchant which courts of justice are bound to know and recognise. Such has been the invariable understanding in Westminster Hall for a great many years, . . . and justice could not be administered if evidence were required to be given *toties quoties* to support such usages, and issue might be joined upon them in each particular case."[3] Mellish, L.J., put it more

[1] Cockburn, C.J., in Goodwin v. Robarts, L.R., 10 Excheq., p. 346.
[2] Brandao v. Barnett, 12 Cl. and F., p. 805.
[3] Lord Campbell instanced the general lien of bankers, the negotiability of bills of exchange and the days of grace allowed for their payment. It now appears to be the law that if there be an established usage of the mercantile world to treat certain instruments as transferable in this country like cash, by delivery, and if such instruments are, from their nature, not incapable of being sued upon by the holder for the time being, then they are negotiable. Even if an instrument is not strictly negotiable, yet if it purports to be so, and is deposited with an agent who passes it to a bonafide holder for value, the holder will be estopped from denying that the security is, what it appears to be, negotiable (Smith's *Mercantile Law,'* Vol. I. p. 241). " Each bond, according to its tenor," said Lord Watson, speaking of cedulas in London Joint Stock Bank v. Simmons (1892, App. Cas. p. 212), " appears to me to represent that the document will pass from hand to hand, and that any bona-fide holder will be entitled to claim fulfilment of its terms from the Buenos Ayres Bank by whom it was issued. Then there is direct testimony to the effect that, on the London Stock Exchange, the bonds do pass from hand to hand by delivery only, and are treated as negotiable securities."

broadly still : " The law should be so interpreted as to be in accordance with the customs of trade." These principles represented great advances upon the dictum (described by counsel in Grant v. Vaughan as " peevish ") in the course of Clerke v. Martin,[1] " that the continuing to declare upon these notes upon the custom of merchants proceeded from obstinacy and opinionativeness." In this case, Holt decided that a goldsmith's note, payable to J.S., or order, was not negotiable ; adding that the " maintaining of these actions upon such notes were innovations upon the common law, and that it amounted to the setting up a new sort of specialty, unknown to the common law, and invented in Lombard Street, which attempted, in these matters of bills of exchange, to give laws to Westminster Hall." The Statute 3 and 4 Anne c. 8 was passed[2] to remedy Holt's error, and to bring the judiciary again into line with financial interests and principles.

THE PREVALENCE OF HOARDING

Simultaneously with the liberation of commercial usage from the pressure of the dead hand of antique prejudice, another process was taking shape and gathering impetus. All unconsciously, throughout the fifteenth and sixteenth centuries the foundations of modern banking were consolidated by the growing influence and wealth of the goldsmiths. In one single street, says the author of the " Italian Relation,"[3] about the end of the fifteenth century, " there are fifty-two goldsmiths' shops, so rich and full of silver vessels, great and small, that in all the shops in Milan, Rome, Venice, and Florence put together I do not think there would be found so many of magnificence that are to be seen in London." The explanation lay in the universal tendency to invest surplus funds in gold and silver plate, chains, jewels, brooches, and girdles, as well as in garments of satin, damask, silk, velvet, and fur, at a time when other investments were only to a compara-

[2] Ld. Raym. 757. [2] So Byles hints, *Bills*, first ed., 1829, p. 8.
[3] Camden Soc., p. 43.

tively small extent available. The mediæval safe—a wooden chest with half a dozen locks—will be found to contain the Royal charters,[1] which had established and successively widened the bounds of municipal or corporate liberty,[2] rather than bonds and share certificates. The capable and energetic man used his money in trade, or, as we have seen, sent it abroad at interest. But the more conservative and nervous people hoarded it, either as specie or as plate and jewellery. Precisely the same system of financial natural selection can be seen in our own day. The nervous man hoards his surplus money, or leaves it in the bank. The more progressive owner buys Dominion, Provincial or Municipal bonds, while the most enterprising of all pits his skill against the market by operating in mining, oil, and rubber shares. This early habit of hoarding was—to resume—doubly objectionable from the economic point of view. It drew the metal from circulation, and involved expense in the watch and ward necessary for its safe custody. In those days the man with treasure must pay watchmen to look after it : nowadays the watchmen, called bankers, pay *him* for that privilege. Moreover, looking at all the circumstances, we may be sure that the amount spent upon these investments was far more than their realisable value as assets of the owner's estate. They were earning a negative interest. A hoard is a waste of potential wealth in a far truer sense than a run-down clock, a steamless locomotive, or a waterless mill. In the fifteenth century " no one who has not in his house silver plate to the amount of at least £100 sterling is considered by the English to be a person of any consequence.[3] The Pastons stored nearly 16,000 oz. of silver plate. An inventory of their holdings occupies nearly four pages[4] of

---

[1] "Some of the deeds in the Barnstaple records of the time of Edward IV. (*Hist. MSS. Comm.* IX. p. 208) are sealed through rush rings, such as were used by the peasantry in plight of matrimonial troth. The editor of the report hazards the conjecture that the ring, " the familiar symbol of perpetuity," may have been used to " heighten the solemnity of the ceremony and indicate the perpetuity desired for the decision and testimony of the instrument.'
[2] Mrs. J R Green, *Town Life in the Fifteenth Century*, p. 12.
[3] *Italian Relation*, Camden Soc., p. 29
[4] Vol. III. pp 270–274.

Mr. Gairdner's edition of the family letters. At the other end of the social scale is the Bristol grocer who bequeaths 350 oz. of silver plate to be divided among his children.[1] In the sixth year of Edward IV. Sir John Howard delivered to his wife[2] a huge aggregate of goods, among which are two gold rings with diamonds, a gold ring with a ruby, an " owche " of gold set with a sapphire, a device of gold with fourteen links set with four rubies, three diamonds, and seven pearls ; another, also with fourteen links, but with seven rubies and seven pearls, a girdle of cloth of gold and the harness of gold, a collar of gold with thirty-four roses and suns, three owches of gold garnished with three rubies, a sapphire, an amethyst, an emerald, and fifteen pearls, three Agnus Dei of gold, a great signet of gold, five other gold rings, and a chain of gold with a lock of gold. Again, when Richard III., on his way to the fatal field of Bosworth, slept at the Blue Boar at Leicester, he brought with him his own bedstead, which had a false bottom, and in which he had concealed £300, say £5000 of our money.[3] There the treasure lay unsuspected for a century after he was gone. In the reign of Elizabeth the inn " was kept by one Clarke, whose wife, hastily making the bed, a piece of gold dropped out, which led to the discovery of the rest : some, the King's own coin."[4] Probably hoarding tended to become more general in the early sixteenth century, before the goldsmiths were really bankers. On the one hand, the Spanish exploitation of Mexico and Peru had increased the supplies, while, on the other, there were as yet no facilities for investment available to the man in the sixteenth-century street. People of larger means, if they realised the fatuity of buying plate and jewellery, could lend their money at interest, or add it to the fund which some community or corporation was advancing to a prince.[5] But the ordinary man did not enjoy these chances. Even as late as the death of Gresham,

[1] Hunt, *Bristol*, p. 108.
[2] *Hist. MSS. Comm.* VII. p. 537.
[3] Gairdner, *Richard III.* p. 293.
[4] Thorsby, quoted by Hatton, *Bosworth Field*, p. 49
[5] Ashley, *Econ. Hist.*, I. ii. p. 430.

in 1579, it was found that his money had been largely invested in gold chains. The crucial point is that this species of investment, by encouraging the art of the goldsmith, served to foster the prosperity of a craft which was ultimately to evolve the banker and, after him, the financier.

Thus monarch and subject alike were the victims of this economically-benumbing habit. In 1559 the " chest of a clothear " in " Bredstret " was broken up by thieves who " toke out xl.lb., and after cryd fyre! fyre!"[1] The xl.lb., no inconsiderable sum, was the clothier's hoarded savings, doubtless. When Henry VII. died, £1,800,000 in gold and silver was found in his coffers—a hoard, equal from the economic point of view, to the withdrawal of £20,000,000 from the modern circulating medium of the country. The official account of the gold plate stolen from the monasteries by the plunderers of the sixteenth century gives the total as 14,531 oz. of gold plate, 129,520 oz. of gilt plate, and 67,600 oz. of silver.[2] Probably not more than a third of the full amount ever came within the official cognisance and found a place in the public accounts. How immense these private hoards of silver and gold plate had been we can infer from the fact that when, on June 10, 1642, the Commons issued propositions for the bringing in of money, plate, arms, and horses for " the defence of the King and both Houses of Parliament," Clarendon[3] says that within ten days, such a vast proportion of plate was brought in that there were hardly men enough to receive it or places to lay it in. Doubtless hoarding was further stimulated by the knowledge that where the trader's assets consisted of personalty, there was, in the absence of investments, the greatest difficulty in making provision for a family. An ordinary citizen would find trustees; but the trustees could discover no investments. As early as the time of Richard II. municipal authorities were assuming the guardianship of orphans,

[1] Henry Machyn, *Diary*, p. 219.
[2] Gasquet, *English Monasteries*, Vol. II. p. 535.
[3] *Rebellion*, I. p. 651.

but they were, at this time, in no better a position than the private trustee when it became necessary to invest the money. As late as 1522 the sum of £66 13s. 4d. (apparently trust money) is stated to be " put into the chest at Goldsmiths' Hall," being part of £833 6s. 8d. for the use of the children of Robert Latham, deceased, and a receipt given for it.

SCARCITY OF READY MONEY

The striking fact, as illustrating the limited financial evolution of the age, is this—that in the absence of credit facilities, the owner—even if he were royal—of all these hoarded treasures was frequently at his wits' end for a mere trifle of ready money. " In times past," says an English writer of 1581,[1] " and within the memory of man, he hathe been accoumpted a rich and wealthy man which (all things discharged) was clearly worth xxx. or xl. li." Edward III. pawned the crown itself. The royal attitude towards the social factors of constitutional development was necessarily modified when the King began to be a constant and insistent borrower from the trading community as distinct from the feudal landed class which had, in earlier days, been his main source of aid. The accession of a still more rigorous and wholesome business sentiment became obvious, when, as at Sandwich, in 1435, the commonaity refused to lend, or when, as in the instance of Norwich, legal action was taken against the royal borrower (much to his amazement) for the return of an overdue loan. The transactions were mainly small ; to our eyes, they wear an almost trifling aspect. Richard II. himself borrowed such a meagre amount as 40 marks from Barnstaple, and gave an acknowledgment with promise to repay.[2] Lynn lent money to the King upon the deposit of a golden circlet, and in 1428 agreed to permit its redemption by the executors of Henry V. for £100, because no greater amount was obtainable. The simple Croyland chronicler refers to one collection of taxes (1475) as having produced a mass of money " the like of which was never

[1] Quoted by Cunningham, *Modern Times,* Vol. I. p. 162.
[2] *Hist. MSS. Comm.* IV. p. 212.

before seen at one time, and probably never will be seen in future." Yet it was doubtless far short of £100,000. But the significance of these transactions, which were being continually arranged in all directions, frequently in consideration of an inspeximus or analogous favour, lies rather in their character than in the actual sums of money. Royal eyes were turned to the trader rather than to the feudal magnate as the source of the money which was power. Among other classes of non-trading society there was the same extraordinary scarcity of ready money resources. Sir John Paston is found pawning his coat in London. When, as a brilliant inspiration, he bethought him of raising money on the security of the pall which had covered his father's corpse, he found that his mother had already hypothecated it for a loan. Lady Berkeley, in 1449, found herself so short of money in London as to contemplate pawning her horse and walking home to the vast landed estates of which she was the mistress.[1] Sir William Plumpton, ordering his servant, in 1464, to buy certain supplies of velvet, was informed that the money receivable for the marriage of the Plumpton heiress to Henry Suthill had not been paid. Consequently, the velvet could not be purchased.[2] The members of the county families borrowed from their relatives and neighbours if they could, pledging realty and personalty *en masse*, and were driven to every kind of desperate shift if the loans were recalled. As one instance from the scanty literature of this uneasy period, we have Margaret Paston's letter of November 5, 1471, to her son. She says,[3] " Mine Cosyn Clere hathe sent to me for the C. marc that I borwed of her for your brother. It fortuned so that a frend of her of late hath loste better than CCC. marc, and he sent to her for money and she had non that she myght comyn by : and ther for she sent to me for the seyd C. marc : and I know not how to do therfor, for by my trowth I have it not, nor can I not make shyft therfor and I shuld go to

[1] *Lives of the Berkeleys*, Vol. II. p. 83.
[2] *Plumpton Correspondence*, Camden Soc., p. 10.
[3] *Paston Letters*, Ed. Gairdner, Vol. III. p. 23.

preson : therfor comune with your brother her of and send me word how that he wull make shyft ther for in hast." Courtiers " paid on their pawns when their pence lacked " (so, at least, says " Richard the Redeless "), and the pile of obligations went on accumulating until death dissipated the store of dead assets in the shape of plate, jewellery, and gorgeous garments, and in that fashion at last appeased the creditor. In such circumstances as these arose the opportunity for the burghers in the town on his estate to bargain with the landed proprietor for the abolition, or perhaps the control, of tolls arising from markets and wharfages. They did not fail to take it.

CHAPTER II

THE EARLY MONEY-MARKET — DECLINE OF ANTI-USURY SENTIMENT—BEGINNINGS OF BANKING

THE origin[1] of the money-market (including in that term both the banking and the Stock Exchange factors) must be looked for in the assemblies at cross-roads, and in churches and churchyards, at the monastery gates, and in the synagogue. These were the first markets,—fairs first, and markets[2] afterwards—and around some of them the market towns grew up. In their essential characteristics there is really no difference between these gatherings and a modern Stock Exchange. The existence of a Gothic church was the signal of settlement and progress, just as truly as the Stock Exchange and the branch banks indicate to us the growth of economic complexity and the direction in which it is moving. The ancient market and the modern Stock Exchange are both of them simply convenient and prearranged meeting-places, where men foregather for the purpose of trafficking with one another, to gossip, to buy and sell produce, and to adjust bargains generally. In the Middle Ages it was the *day* that was agreed upon for the assembly; now it is the *hour*. Then

[1] i.e. The *ultimate* origin that is. The Stock Exchange, as a group of specialist dealers, did not greatly antedate the Bank of England. As an accepted and recognised institution it only slightly antedated Waterloo. Before then it was potent, but taboo.

[2] Held at shorter intervals, and occupying a more confined and definite area, the market excluded the fair, which rapidly declined, and at length assumed the form in which alone the present generation has known it—that of an assemblage of merry-go-rounds and shooting galleries. Stately market crosses began to be set up, distinguishing a centralised commercial intercourse, which, in another form, evolved in the early sixteenth century into the daily assemblage of merchants in Lombard Street, and was the prototype of the Stock Exchange, the Metal Exchange, and the Baltic.

BEGINNINGS OF BANKING 39

there was a bell; now, frequently, a "call."[1] To the ancient market comes the latest news, as in our time to the analogous institution—the Stock Exchange. Then it was the tale of a strayed sheep; in these days it is the number of a lost bond, the rumoured passing of a dividend, the terms of a new loan, or the imminence of an important prospectus. The mediæval gossips of the market heard a proclamation by the bailiff of the latest penalties in the manor court; now it is the sharp, stern sentence of a Stock Exchange Committee upon some offending member which they see on the notice-board. The pandemonium of the early assembly is frequently reproduced, especially under conditions of mining or "Yankee" excitement, in its modern Stock Exchange anti-type. In the early days the goods themselves were dragged through miry lanes, and massed around the cross. The modern market is less concerned with the goods themselves than with the documents of title to them. The mediæval vendor had a "standing" in the market: the modern jobber announces his "stand" in the official Stock Exchange Directory. The town broker can be traced at work in the fifteenth century, conducting bargains on behalf of the whole community, in return for a commission on the goods which passed through his hands, but sworn to make no private profit otherwise. The market began as the arena around the market cross or under the churchyard wall, and has now been expanded, by rapidity and facility of communication, up to the point where it includes continents, and enables buyer and seller to deal at a distance of 5000 miles from each other. The earlier evolution of the market was capitalistic; the later stages have been guided and energised by finance.

EARLY "STREET" DEALINGS

There may, possibly, have been the germ of an Exchange in the London of Norman times. The name of a London

---

[1] Canterbury cooks are to " by no pultry botir, ne none other vytaile, coming to the market at Canterbury for to be sold, before vii. of the bell, and that openly in the market thereto assignyd, and that they forestall not the market in no manner wyse of soche maner vytile." (*Hist. MSS. Comm.*, Vol. IX. p. 172).

Portreeve in 1158—Gaufridus Bursarius—was thought by Mr. Loftie[1] to indicate the existence of some institution like the Royal Exchange. There was a bourse at Bruges; and, since the invention of that species of market is attributed to the Jews, and many Jews came to England in the train of the Conqueror, the conjecture has much to support it. But, at any rate, in the early Tudor period the Stock Exchange itself is almost discernible in the shape of a regular and organised assemblage for the transaction of money-business. It was cosmopolitan in character. The influx of foreign capital must have been very large, as we can gather from many scattered hints. Money gravitates towards stability, and the strong Tudor rule was, for that period, a firmly established régime. Foreign capitalists not only sent their money, but came here themselves to employ it, as the advance guard of the many foreign banking houses which are now clustered around the Bank of England. In the early sixteenth century it was the custom of the merchants to meet twice a day, in the open, in Lombard Street, for the transaction of business. These daily assemblages of the London merchants, and the extensive "barterings and traffic," impressed the learned Greek traveller Nicander Nucius, who saw them.[2] Stow says that "the merchants and tradesmen, as well English as strangers, for their generall making of bargaines, contracts, and commerce . . . did usually meete twice every day"—at noon, and in the evening; "but their meetings were unpleasant and troublesome, by reason of walking and talking in an open narrow street, . . . being there constrained either to endure all extreamities of weather—viz., heat and cold, snow and raine, or else to shelter themselves in shoppes." About the year 1534 King Henry VIII. suggested that the meetings should take place in Leadenhall. This proposal was declined at a meeting of the Common Council. Gresham's servant, Richard Cloughe, provides us with a vivid sarcasm at the expense of the peripatetic London merchants, who preferred the open street to a roofed building. " Consyder-

[1] *Historic Towns—London*, p. 35.   [2] *Travels*, p. 10.

yng," he says,[1] " whatt a sittey London ys, and that in so many yeres they have nott founde the menes to make a Bourse ! but must wallke in the raine, when ytt raineth, more lyker pedlers then marchants ; and in thys countrie, and all other, there is no kynde of pepell that have occasyon to meete, butt they have a plase meete for that pourpose. In dede, and yf your besynes were done, and that I myghtt have the lesure to go about hytt, and that you wyll be a menes to Mr. Secretary to have hys favore therein, I wyll nott doutt butt to make so fere a bourse in London as the grett bourse is in Andwarpe, withoutt molestyng of any man more than he shulld be well dysposyd to geve." The modern analogy of the Street market in Americans, which is conducted under the open sky to this day, will readily occur to the mind. The modern stock and share-dealer is as conservative as his sixteenth-century ancestors, and would probably be as difficult to persuade to avail himself of offered shelter elsewhere.[2]

COSMOPOLITAN FINANCE AMONG US

After Gresham's new structure, originally called the Bourse, was renamed, by the Queen, as the Royal Exchange, in 1571, it rapidly became a replica of the Bourse at Antwerp. The " merchants of Amsterdam, of Antwerp, of Hamburg, of Paris, of Bordeaux, of Venice, and Vienna, distinguishable to the eye by the dress of the nations they represented, and to the ear by the differences of language, conducted their exchanges with English merchants and with each other,"[3] so that, as Dekker said, " at every turn a man is put in mind of Babel, there is such a confusion of tongues." Cosmopolitan finance, the beginning of the all-embracing modern Money-Power, was in our midst. Malynes alleges that the foreign bankers had practically cornered the supply of the circulating medium,

[1] Burgon, *Life and Times of Gresham*, Vol. I. p. 409.
[2] But for the efforts of the late Lord Swaythling, the Royal Exchange would probably still be open to the sky. His persistent efforts resulted in the building being roofed in, and in the consequent abolition of the ancient and picturesque spectacle of the heads of leading financial houses adjusting foreign exchange business on a wet day under the open sky.
[3] *Memorials of Old London*, Vol. II. p. 29.

and could manipulate the exchanges to suit their own books. If that be correct, these were the beginnings—albeit sinister rather than salutary—of cosmopolitan financial co-operation. The proclamation of September 20, 1576, is directed at this alleged abuse, which is said to have grown by " the corrupt dealing of sundry merchants and brokers, as well strangers as English." Stow, writing of the later years of Elizabeth's reign,[1] says it was argued that the aliens, when in England, included many rich men " that lived obscurely, to benefit themselves by usury and exchange of money." There was a suggestion, it seems, that they sometimes " stole away " out of the country " with other men's goods, without any notice given thereof." Possibly the chronicler means that they lent money against pawned goods, with a wide margin, and then decamped with the security.

The influx of the cosmopolitan factor was not confined to those engaged in the discharge of purely monetary functions. The commercial capitalists came in increasing numbers. John Vanhulst, a brewer and denizen of obvious Dutch origin, protests, in January, 1600,[2] that he cannot lend £500 to the Queen as required to do by Privy Seal. He once lent £100 to the Queen, he adds, " and it has not been repaid, nor has other money lent by Privy Seal." On December 20 there is another effort to borrow from " aliens of ability resident in London." A form of demand, accompanied by a menace, transmitted by Privy Seal letters, is set forth,[3] in draft, and bears Cecil's corrections. In January of 1601 (?) there are[4] lists of Low Country residents in London from whom loans are required—23 to pay £5100 ; 11 free denizens, £1800 ; six born in England, £1700. A further list of 18 Low Country residents prescribes loans of £2000 to £3000 from each of them—a total of £10,500 to be repaid to them in six months. In February of 1601 we have a list of 107 strangers and denizens, who had been required to lend an aggregate of £23,200 in sums

[1] *Survey*, Vol. V. p. 406.
[2] S. P. D., Eliz., 1600, Vol. CCLXXIV. p. 28.
[3] S. P. D., Eliz., 1600, Vol. CCLXXV. p. 143.
[4] *Ibid.*, Vol. CCLXXVIII. 6, *et seq.*, 27 and 124.

BEGINNINGS OF BANKING

of £50 to £2000 each. The "Merchant Goldsmith" is traceable among the aliens in London in 1618.[1] But even with the advent of the cosmopolitan banker and capitalist, the yoke of the foreign financier was not completely shaken off ; for in 1625 we find the crown jewels and plate pawned in the Low Countries for £300,000.[2]

SIXTEENTH-CENTURY INVESTMENTS

The dealings on the Bourse were mainly in bills of exchange, as well as in tallies and commodities (and towards the end of the sixteenth century, perhaps, in lottery tickets), not in securities as we understand the term. There were few transactions of this latter species. The Bourse was quite as much a produce exchange as a financial centre. The allusion to investment suggests the reflection that Shakespeare, who represented a rather unusual combination of the romantic and the business-like, was a good typical investor (as distinguished from a capitalist entrepreneur) of the period. He was not tempted into the new trading companies, but steadily employed his surplus funds in the purchase of real property at Stratford. In 1605, Shakespeare was induced to buy for £440 the unexpired term of thirty-one years of a ninety-two years' lease of a moiety of certain local tithes. Subject to certain prior charges, Shakespeare's income from this purchase was £38 a year, or rather under 9 per cent. on the amount invested. A purchase for £100, of an annuity of £20 for three lives was held (Fountain v. Grymes, 8 Jac. I., Bulstrode I. 37) not within the statutes 37 Henry VIII. c. 9 and 13 Eliz. c. 8 against usury. There being no provision, in the contract, for the return of the £100, the transaction was the purchase of an annuity, not a loan of money. As the plaintiff was apparently a professional dealer in money, the transaction looks like a rudimentary investment and by no means a bad one. Another form of contemporary investment was the advance of a sum of money to a trader travelling abroad, with an agreement that, at his return,

[1] Huguenot Soc., *Aliens in London*, Part III. p. 205.
[2] Walter Yonge's *Diary*, Camd. Soc., p. 88.

he would account for it and for his " bestowing of it."[1] When moneyed men sought investments of these types there was not much room for the activities of an institution like a modern Stock Exchange.

MANIPULATION OF THE USURY LAWS

As we are now on the threshold of the modern banking system, we shall have to consider the gradual disappearance of the sentiment, and the co-existent legislation, against usury. If mediæval hostility to usury, which we have already noticed, had maintained its sway over the intellect of mankind,[2] modern banking, with all that it implies for the propulsion of human prosperity, would still be the visionary ideal of progressive thinkers, and not a magnificent and potent reality. The Act 37 Henry VIII. c. 9 (1545) repealed all existing statutes against usury, on the ground that they were " obscure and darke in sentences, words, and termes,"—" so framed on purpose," says Anderson, " to leave room to avoid the penalties, whilst in general words, all usury, to please the clergy, was declared sinful." The statute proceeds to prohibit the sale of goods and their repurchase within three months at a reduced price. This provision is directed at one of the ingenious methods then in vogue of evading anti-usury legislation. Under the Act 10 per cent. is to be the maximum interest on commercial loans and mortgages. The enacting portion is concerned with interest in consideration of forbearance in collecting a due debt quite as much as with interest upon an actual advance of money. This legislation was in effect a statutory recognition of usury. It was, however, a little premature, and in the next reign there was a reaction. The Act 5 and 6 Edw. VI. c. 20 after reciting the previous enactment, proceeds to state, in emphatic terms, that such " Acte was not ment or in-

[1] Hawkins v. Parker, 1613. Bulstrode II., p. 256.
[2] The distinction between the productive loan and the borrowing for mere waste was recognised by the fifth Lateran Council (1512–17) when it decreed " Ea est propria usurarum interpretatio, quando videlicet ex usu rei quae non germinat nullo labore, nullo sumptu, nullove periculo lucrum foetusque conquiri studetur."

BEGINNINGS OF BANKING

tended for mayntenance and allowaunce of Usurie as dyvers parsons [persons, not clerics], blynded with inordinat love of themselves, have and yet doo mistake the same." It was rather made and intended against all kinds of usury; but, nevertheless, it was by the Act permitted " for the avoyding of a more yll and inconvenyence that before that tyme was used and exercysed." Still, as usury is a " vyce moste odyous and detestable," and—here is the significant statement—is " dailye used and practysed " by persons who refuse to forsake such " filthie gayne and lucre," *no interest* is from May 1, 1552, to be taken on any loan.

But this did not stop a practice so essential to the wellbeing of an advancing community, and so congenial to insuppressible human instincts. John Potter in London writes to John Holmes at Doncaster,[1] asking him (1555) to get in some money that was lent out at 12 per cent.—evidently by a lady; for he adds : " I pray God send it well in agayn, for here is in London many merchants bankerowts : as I lerne my awntt will not trust no more eny merchaunts." Holmes appears to have been a financial confidant; for we have also the Earl of Cumberland writing him, in 1556, that he has received a privy seal for loan of money to the Queen, but not having enough he is forced to borrow of his friends : " Money is scarce to come by : where some time he could have borrowed £100 or £200, now he cannot borrow £20." Moreover—and these facts are more significant still—the Government was forced to disregard its own legislative principles. It borrowed incessantly, as we shall see when we come to consider the politico-financial aspects of the loans. The Act of Edward VI., consequently, was foredoomed to failure. Another attempt was therefore made, by 13 Eliz. c. 8, to deal with the whole question. The Act opens with a recital of the earlier endeavours, adding a frank and quaint admission that the Act of Edward VI. " hathe not done so muche good as was hoped it shoulde." It was evaded by " sales of wares and shiftes of interest." The

[1] *Hist. MSS. Comm.*, 3rd Rep., p. 37.

new enactment repealed the older Act as from June 25, 1571. It was then provided (Section 2) that "Tenne Pounds for the Hundred for one year" should be the maximum interest upon all "Bonds, Contracts, and Assurances, collateral [the reader will note this familiar financial term] or other." Brokers, Solicitors, and "Drivers of Bargaynes" contrary to the Act are to incur the penalties of Premunire. If a reservation of a greater interest than 10 per cent. be discovered, the excess is to be forfeited in the case of the "Lender, Contractor, Shyfter, Forbearer, or Deliverer," all these sweeping provisions, with their enumeration of the different operators, being aimed at the parties intervening at the various stages of the contract, or responsible for the various forms of evasion. But the Government was all the time embarrassed by its own legislation, so that when Elizabeth borrowed from the principal merchants and aldermen through the intermediary of Gresham, it was necessary to guard the lenders against the consequences of disobedience to the usury laws.

BEGINNINGS OF COMPLEXITY AND SPECIALISATION

These numerous intermediaries, each specialising in a separate financial function, represent the beginnings of that intricate complexity of structure which is ultimately to distinguish the financial system. Here we confront a biological principle operative in the financial sphere. "It may be summed up as a general law, universal in its application to all matter, although varying in intensity in different types of matter, and holding throughout all space as generally as the law of gravitation—a law which might be called the Law of Complexity—that matter, so far as its energy-environment will permit, tends to assume more and more complex forms in labile equilibrium. Atoms, molecules, colloids, and living organisms arise as the result of the operations of this law, and in the higher regions of complexity it induces organic evolution and all the many thousands of living forms. At still higher levels, it forms the basis of social evolution and leads to that intellectual development in individual and community which surmounts the whole and is ever building upwards."[1] To those who live amid the movement of the complex financial mechanism it will suffice to quote Professor Moore's observations, and to add si exemplum quaeris, circumspice.[2]

BIOLOGICAL SIGNIFICANCE OF DIFFERENTIATION

For, indeed, at each stage, as we advance, we see that the conditions of a higher stage are already present. Finance itself is destined to depend upon complex psychical, physical, and social relations between individuals and groups. Unorganised action, random, isolated, conflicting, blind, must give place to the unification, systemisation and co-ordination of an organic whole : and " the more complete the differentiation—the more definite and distinct the special organs, the more firm will become their dependence upon the central organism considered as a unit."[3] " By an organic whole," remarks Hobhouse,[4] " is understood one which (a) has a certain general character or individuality, while (b) it consists of distinguishable parts each with a certain character of its own, but (c) such that they cannot exist unmodified apart from the whole, while the character of the whole is similarly dependent upon them." That is, each factor is modified by the very relations which it helps to build up : and

---

[1] Moore, *Origin and Nature of Life*, p. 188.
[2] It should be added that Mr. Matthews (*Law of Moneylending*, p. 17) argues that this Act (13 Eliz. c. 8 cited in the previous paragraph) did not *legalise* usury, and cannot properly be said to fix, but only to permit, a 10 per cent. rate. There was an exception for cases where orphans are the beneficiaries of loans made out of their property. There was good reason for this. Here and there were to be found funds established, generally by the wills of deceased benefactors, for the purpose of granting financial aid to young traders, generally with stringent regulations for safeguarding the capital. In the reign of Elizabeth there was a regular system of lending orphans portions, at easy interest, to " young and towardly merchants and occupiers " within the City of London. The income provided for the maintenance of the orphans, and the system was defended by the Mayor and Corporation, before the Privy Council, in 1586 (Stow, *Survey*, Book V, Chap. XXIII). As such schemes are roughly analogous, both in method and purpose, to banking business, they would add to public experience of the utility of that species of accommodation.
[3] Ward, *Dynamic Sociology*, p. 175.
[4] Hobhouse, *Mind in Evolution*, p. 374.

therefore the greater the number of factors, and the consequent complexity, the more firm their ultimate organic consolidation. "The whole is more organic in proportion as the interdependence of the parts is more complete," because "scope of organisation is proportioned to the diversity of elements that go to build up its unity."[1] The greater the differentiation of function, the higher the organism and the more brilliant its potentialities. These generalisations, originally applied purely to biological and psychological phenomena, are equally true of finance in evolution. That is the reason why, as soon as we encounter differentiation of function in the embryonic-financial sphere, attention has been called to its significance from the point of view of the present essay.

COMMON-SENSE VIEWS OF INTEREST

These statutory dubieties and meanderings, and the simultaneous open evasions, were, in fact, the signs of the dying mediæval hostility to the receipt of interest. Stern necessity, influencing minds as stern as itself, helped to facilitate the revolution in opinion. Many of the men who fled from England to escape the religious persecutions of the sixteenth century took with them, in the shape of money, all their worldly possessions. These were apparently the class in the mind of Porder when he spoke, in 1570,[2] of those who pleaded that "they have no trade, but a stocke[3] left them, and if they shoulde not put it out for profite it would soone be consumed and other thing they have not to live upon." Porder himself thought that usury might lawfully (or, at all events, with some measure of justification) be taken from "heathen rich men." Roger Fenton, who wrote a *Treatise of Usurie*, in 1612, declared that : "Had it not been for the banished men, who, in times of persecution, fled into those parts for succour, this doctrine against usurie had never been called

---

[1] Hobhouse, *Mind in Evolution*, p. 375.
[2] Preaching from Zephaniah i., v. 2-6, on Whitsun Monday at St. Paul's.
[3] Note the word, ultimately destined to signify a standardised holding in a given security.

BEGINNINGS OF BANKING 49

into question. But these exiles, bringing stocks of money with them, and wanting skill to imploy it in those strange places, it was a pity they should have been driven to have spent upon the stocke : therefore their money was used by others who had skill (i.e. by foreign bankers), and some allowance made to them for the use. This practice, growing both common and publike, it remained, then, that the wit of man, out of a tender commiseration towards those who suffered exile for religion, must trie what it could doe, if not directlie to defend, yet somewhat to qualifie the matter. Thus pitie brought in practise, and practise must seeke apologie."

Where resources are slender, and their possessor is a stranger in a strange land, he must do the best he can for himself ; and if he lend his money at interest, both he and his co-religionists will discover themselves evolving a liberality of financial sentiment which was not theirs before. This is what actually happened. As soon as a great leader like Calvin was prepared to say that lending on mortgage was fair and right, the whole fabric of anti-usury sentiment was undermined, and the way was open for the corresponding and contemporaneous modification in the law relating to the bailment of money which opened the way for the advent of the modern banker—who is, after all, only a lender on the mortgage of negotiable instruments, as distinct from real property. In the Elizabethan period, many men who had received interest from a foreign banker during an enforced residence abroad, returned to England and exerted no small influence upon the religious and ethical tendencies of the age. The sympathies of some of them, at all events, would be with the enterprising goldsmith-bankers : and where a given function meets an obvious social and commercial need, opinion rapidly veers in its favour when once definitely shown the way by those whose views command respect.

Again, the continuous royal loans undoubtedly did a great deal to assist in familiarising public opinion with the legitimacy of interest. Obviously, if the monarch needed money there could be no objection to goldsmiths and bankers lending it. But the moment so much was attempted it became obvious that the lender had a right to be compensated for the damnum emergens or the lucrum cessans which were the inevitable consequence of his abstinence from using money profitably in another direction in order that he might accommodate his royal client. When once this principle is accepted (and especially when the lender gets his funds by means of the acceptance of small deposits at interest) the doctrine of the immorality of usury can no longer hold the field. Other people consider themselves justified in following the monarch's example, and the new system has taken a recognised and assured position in the machinery of social evolution. Those who operate it are bound to exercise great influence on the change in sentiment. Onwards from the days of King Henry VIII. there is a steady growth of independent financial opinion. Its beginnings were crude and modest. They represented, however, quite a different force from the mere right of judgment exercised by the representative body, in earlier days, with regard to the financial necessities of the King. The Angevins had dealt with a baronial land-owning Assembly. The later Tudors and the early Stuarts had to confront an organised, and to some extent an expert, financial opinion. In June, 1544, Henry VIII. obtained a loan in the City itself by the mortgage of certain Crown lands. Edward VI. borrowed 129,750 Caroline florins from the Fuggers on the security of the City of London ; so that, as Anderson puts it :[1] " Even our great monarchs frequently could not borrow beyond sea without the collateral security of our renowned Metropolis." Again, the younger men, who had built their fortune upon these credit facilities,[2] were likely to harbour

[1] *Origin of Commerce*, Chap. II, p. 78.
[2] " It shall not be lawful for all to take money at use," said Burton (*Anatomy of Melancholy*), " — not to prodigals and spendthrifts, but to merchants, young tradesmen, and such as stand in need, or know honestly how to employ it." The case of the widow and orphan—the *cestuis que trustent* of our day—again, had to be considered. 1624. Discussion about a proposition concerning the acceptance of money belonging to children, to be repaid on their attaining full age, or marriage. The court agree to accept £350, the portions of James Bollet's children, at 5 per cent. simple (not compound) interest. (*Memorials of the Goldsmiths' Company*, Vol. I. p. 140.)

BEGINNINGS OF BANKING

a sentiment favourable to them, and when the onward march of the years made them the leaders of business opinion, their views received a wider acceptance, and paved the way for a general revolution in the traditional theory with regard to the whole question of interest. The author of the *Discourse upon Usury* (1692) treats it as an established fact that " many diligent apprentices had been able to set up in business by the aid of judicious loans, whereas they would otherwise have remained journeymen or servants all their lives." Not less important is the fact that the recognition of the system involves an equal appreciation of those who work it, or, in other words, of the business of receiving money and lending it to responsible beneficiaries. This factor was to be operative for many a day to come and to exert a great influence in the creation of a sentiment favourable to the new goldsmith-bankers, at the most critical period of their evolution, that between 1550 and the foundation of the Bank of England.

Puritan views aided the change by other means. It was facilitated, we may safely infer, by the declining authority of patristic opinion. If Protestants were not bound by the doctrines of the Fathers in the matter of the mass and prayers for the dead, why should they be obliged where usury was concerned ? The same independence of mind which excluded the spiritual middle-man, was fatal also to his anti-usury tenets. Ecclesiastical authority, split up among many warring theological leaders, instead of being centred at the Vatican, was failing everywhere before the growth of strong monarchies, whose heads were vividly alive to the necessity of that species of commercial stimulus which free trade in money could supply. The intellectual justification of Protestant rebellion against the Church had been the right of private judgment. But the assertion of that right could not be limited to the spiritual sphere. If it was valid there, even against the theologian who was admittedly an expert, it must be valid in other realms of thought where the theologian could claim no special pre-eminence of knowledge. The humanism of the age widened the vogue of reasoning based upon material interest, and the anti-usury tradition could not survive the searching intellectual scrutiny. Business men, thus becoming emancipated from theological and scholastic mediævalism (in the matter of anti-usury sentiment), saw clearly enough that moderate interest was reasonable and fair, though " biting " usury might be oppressive. Borrowing became general. At the social summit were the persistent loans of the monarch—their plain lesson emphasised by the fact that statesmen were borrowing largely on their own personal account. Cecil himself, involved in extravagant outlay upon his mansion and grounds, was deeply in Gresham's debt. So it was that Richard Porder was only describing obvious phenomena when he said that usury, among the multitude, was accounted no vice, " and thought so necessary that without it men (generally) cannot live." It was a wonder past wonders " how so wicked a thing should so overflowe that the vice should come to be accounted honest trade, as now it is thought to bee." It was an evil fruit universally eaten. The preacher enumerated the classes addicted to usury—" not only moneymen,"[1] but also " merchant men, citizens, noblemen, courtiers, gentlemen, grasiers, farmers, plowmen, artificers —yea, I would the clergie were free." But we must remember that Porder, however useful he is as an exponent of the conservative opinions of his age, knew nothing whatever of the principles of credit. When people bought anything, they " ought forthwith to pay ready money for the same." It does not seem to have occurred to Porder that the general adoption of such a principle would have paralysed even the modest business commitments of the Elizabethan age. To sell wheat for immediate delivery, to be paid for at the end of a given period at an enhanced price, by way of compensation for the accommodation, was usury, he declared—not seeing that the alternative might be the withdrawal of such facilities from the intending buyer, and the consequent growth of a monopoly in the hands of those who could afford to put money down.

[1] Observe the term ; for it is in itself significant of the demarcation of a financial class.

BEGINNINGS OF BANKING

THE RISING INFLUENCE OF THE GOLDSMITHS

The goldsmiths, now becoming the goldsmith-bankers, were a numerous and influential class, capable of bold and powerful initiative where they saw their opportunity.[1] The " money-men," as Porder in his famous sermon had called them, were capable of exhibiting resentment. " I might with less damage touch and shake a hornet's nest," said he, " than deale with them." Gresham uses the same expression in describing his fruitless efforts to raise money in the Low Countries for Queen Elizabeth. He says : " I have gone through all the monnie-men by one practise or other, and specially with all them which I was wonte to deale withal."[2] It is shown by the Court Book of the Goldsmiths' Company that in 1566 there were 107 London goldsmiths, of whom 76 resided in Chepe and the remaining 31 in " Lumberde-street." In 1569 there were 89 goldsmiths, of whom 68 lived in Chepe and 21 in " Lumberde-street." Bacon, discussing the desirability of a double money-rate agrees that bankers should

[1] Burnet tells the story (*History of His Own Times*, Vol. I. p. 544) of an English merchant (obviously a merchant banker generally identified as Thomas Sutton) of London who (when the Armada was about to sail) was " well acquainted with the state of the revenue of Spain, with all their charges, and all that they could raise. He knew all their funds were so swallowed up that it was impossible for them to victual and set out their fleet but by their credit in the Bank of Genoa. So he undertook to write to all the places of trade, and to get such remittances made on that bank, that he should by that means have it so entirely in his hands that there should be no money current there equal to the great occasion of victualling the fleet of Spain. He reckoned the keeping such a treasure dead in his hands till the season of victualling was over would be a loss of £40,000. And at that rate he would save England. He managed the matter with such secrecy and success that the fleet could not be set out that year. At so small a price, and with so skilful a management, was the nation saved at that time." What happened appears to have been this—the London operator sent to the various trade centres and purchased drafts from the bankers and traders having balances or credits with the Bank of Genoa. The Bank would, of course, only keep a proportion of its deposits in liquid form, and the operator having control of such a large total of short-dated paper was enabled to engineer what practically amounted to a " run " on the institution. The effect of this was to diminish seriously the (even then) all-important item of " liquid assets," and consequently to curtail the credit facilities which the bank would otherwise have been prepared to grant in other directions. The position of the bank was badly weakened, and it became impossible for its managers to consider so considerable an undertaking as the victualling of the Spanish Fleet.

[2] Burgon, *Gresham*, Vol. II. p. 158.

54 EVOLUTION OF THE MONEY MARKET

be recognised. He says : " Let there be certain persons licensed to lend to known merchants, upon usury, at a higher rate ; and let it be with the cautions following. Let the rate be, even with the merchant himself, somewhat more easy than that he used formerly to pay : for by that means all borrowers shall have some ease by this reformation, be he merchant or whosoever. Let it be no bank, or common stock, but every man be master of his own money. Not that I altogether mislike banks, but they will hardly be brooked in regard of certain suspicions. Let the State be answered some small matter for the licence and the rest left to the lender ; for if the abatement be but small, it will no whit discourage the lender. For he, for example, that took before ten or nine in the hundred, will sooner descend to eight in the hundred than give over his trade of usury ; and go from certain gains to gains of hazard. Let these licensed lenders be in number indefinite, but restrained to certain principal cities and towns of merchandising ; for then they will be hardly able to colour other men's moneys in the country; so as the licence of nine will not suck away the current rate of five ; for no man will send his moneys far off, nor put them into unknown hands." Whatever may be our opinion of these theories, they definitely point to the existence of a banking interest. Its concern in financial business is put beyond all doubt when we find Henry Machyn noting in his Diary that in " the xj day of June [1556] was a man sett on the pelere [pillory], a goldsmith in Lumbarstrett, for raysyng of an oblygasyon, and mad yt a syngull oblygassyon falsely and deseytt for money."[1] Webster, in 1604, counted 55 signs in passing Goldsmiths'-row, towards the western end of Cheapside.[2]

CONCENTRATION IN LOMBARD STREET

The money-men were already tending towards concentration around the Royal Exchange. Lombard Street interested a German traveller in 1593 because he saw there " all sorts of gold and silver vessels exposed to sale, as well

---

[1] Henry Machyn, *Diary*, Camden Society, p. 107.
[2] Introduction to *The Malcontent*, 1604.

BEGINNINGS OF BANKING

as ancient and modern coins, in such quantities as must surprise a man the first time he sees and considers them." The allusion to "ancient and modern coins," points to another source of profit to the goldsmith, arising from the immense variety of coins of all nations which circulated in England in the later Middle Ages. Out of the deposit of these coins with the goldsmiths arose a legal difficulty, destined to be solved in a manner which was of the utmost benefit to the development of the rudimentary banking system. Within a few years Lombard Street had become almost exclusively a goldsmiths' reserve,[1] and the goldsmiths had become usurers, bankers, money scriveners (or, as we should say, billbrokers), and bullion dealers. Mr. Hilton Price's careful compilation *Signs of Old Lombard Street*, which covers, as adequately as research could compass, the period between 1464 and 1764, gives the names of 94 known goldsmiths in Lombard Street at one time or another during that period. The central settlement was complete by the time that David Jones, in his farewell sermon at St. Mary Woolnoth, Lombard Street, in 1692, warned "all ye of this Parish, whose chiefest employment is banking and usury." The careful reader will note the differentiation, even on the part of a zealot like Jones.

A WEALTHY AND POWERFUL GROUP

Early in the seventeenth century the goldsmiths (or, rather, the goldsmith-bankers, as they had by that time become) were strong enough to defy the gold and silver thread monopoly.[2] They challenged the validity of the patents, and went on making the patented commodities. No amount of success attended an effort, made on the advice of the Chief Justice (Montagu), to force the gold-

---

[1] The change brought a certain pride in the appearance of the street, and an anxiety that it should wear the dignified aspect worthy of so substantial a trade. "1610. Mr. Terry, of Lombard Street, is required to reform his glass window, etc., his shop at present becoming a barber rather than a goldsmith." (*Memorials of the Goldsmiths' Company*, Vol. I. p. 114.) There was an effort made to keep goldsmiths' shops in Cheapside and Lombard Street. In 1634 two men were bound over in £100 not to keep goldsmiths' shops elsewhere.

[2] These gold and silver lace men survived in Lombard Street down to a period almost within living memory. (Burgon, *Gresham*, Vol. I. p. 281

smiths and mercers to enter into bonds not to sell their materials to unlicensed persons. Some silk mercers were sent to gaol for refusing to submit; but the indignation in the City—indicating the existence of a community of financial opinion, of the kind which in our day enjoys so tremendous a potency—compelled the King to order their release. The prestige of the goldsmiths must have been professionally enhanced, and their financial opportunities consequently enlarged, when they were made public judges of the goodness of coin. The justices were commanded (in 1560) "to sitt in . . . oppen place or at the market cross, calling to you some goldsmith of the best knowledg that ye can gett, or some other person having best knowledg in the matter of monyes, and shall there be redy to judg and discerne of all manner of testons." Such testons, if good, were to be stamped. The base money was collected by the goldsmiths—another step in the process of centralisation out of which modern banking was to arise. Nothing could be more natural to such a powerful and wealthy group of men, confronted with the loss of a once lucrative portion of their business like that of the sale of plate, than an endeavour to persuade the nervous possessors of surplus funds to deposit them, with the understanding that a share of the profits derivable from their use should be paid, either as interest or in some other form, to the owners. If this is a correct hypothesis, the transformation of the goldsmith, with his " gold rings and silver tankards," his embossed bowls and chargers, and his jewels set for fine ladies, from a mere bullion dealer and manufacturer into a banker [1] would require (save in the matter of certain legal difficulties, which we shall examine later) no further explanation. It is obvious that, in an age of great commercial daring and enterprise, the advantage of being able to place money in safe custody and at interest, while at the same time retaining it within comparatively easy reach in case of its being required to finance

[1] " The leading bankers, themselves the descendants in trade of the old goldsmiths." (City of London Livery Companies' Commission, *Goldsmiths' Company's Return*, Vol. II. p. 325.)

BEGINNINGS OF BANKING

some new commercial operation or some money-lending transaction on the part of the depositor, would be so palpable as to attract custom from many quarters. The tendency would be stimulated when the goldsmith-banker discovered that principle of modern banking which enabled him to adjust his till money to his liabilities in such a manner as to leave the surplus available for profitable use in loans. Only the legal modification, from that of bailee to that of debtor, of the relationship between himself and his customer was wanted to open a great and effectual door of opportunity by transforming the goldsmith-bailee into the goldsmith-banker.

FROM GOLDSMITH TO GOLDSMITH-BANKER

With wealth steadily passing into the hands of the rising middle class, and out of the control of the landed gentry, the latter would be compelled in the long run to slacken and diminish the investments in gold and silver plate, which they so conspicuously favoured, since they would not possess the necessary funds. The cessation of such purchases would tend to check the prosperity of the goldsmith, by cutting off that which had hitherto been a profitable market. The early goldsmith was not a money-dealer at all; he was simply concerned with plate, as such. The business of goldsmiths, Pennant remarks,[1] was "confined to the buying and selling of plate and foreign coins of gold and silver, melting them and coining others at the mint. The banking," he adds, "was accidental and foreign to their institution." The author of the *Mystery of the New-Fashioned Goldsmiths*, in immediate allusion to the period of the Civil War, or the years just before it, declares that most of the nobility and gentry were melting down their old plate rather than buying new. The trade of plate, he adds, became of little worth.[2] But, on the other hand, the

---

[1] *London*, p. 390.
[2] "1622. The King's Majesty hath declared his great dislike of the mixture of mean trades with the goldsmiths in Goldsmiths' Row in Chepe." This was said (1623) to be due to "the general decay there and elsewhere of the goldsmiths' trade." (*Memorials of the Goldsmiths' Company*, Vol. I. pp. 134 and 136.)

rising middle class, at all events in the sixteenth century, did not invest their money in gold and silver plate to anything like the same extent as the landed gentry had been accustomed to do. They turned it over in trade, and where they had a surplus they had no scruple about employing the funds in money-lending.[1] The result of the cessation of demand would be to compel the goldsmith to look out for some other field of enterprise capable of occupying his activity as fully and as profitably as the production of the gold and silver plate had formerly done. As the older means of subsistence died out, new adaptations to environment must be discovered. In biological language, the change from goldsmith to goldsmith-banker was precisely the variation necessary to ensure survival in a modified environment.

HISTORY OF THE VARIATION

Now it is a fact that the author of the tract called *The Mystery of the New-Fashioned Goldsmiths or Bankers* (incorporated in J. B. Martin's *Grasshopper in Lombard Street*), published in 1676, gives an account of the origin of banking which completely confirms this hypothesis, save only as regards the date when the system began to be operative. The author of *The Mystery of the New-Fashioned Goldsmiths* dates the rise of the system from some thirty years before he wrote—that is to say, about the year 1646, in the middle of the Civil War. But it looks very much as if he only did this in order to obtain what in American parlance would be called a "jumping-off place." If the goldsmiths had not been largely engaged in financial business they need not have been so disturbed by the proposed revival of the office of Exchanger in 1627, nearly twenty

---

[1] The possessor of a fund of money which is entirely his own, and which he employs in the making of loans at interest, is really a money-lender, and not a banker. It is not until he begins to receive other people's money, and to manage it with a view (1) to its safe custody ; (2) to its employment as the material of credit-creation ; and (3) to the making of a profit on the transaction, that he becomes a banker in the strict sense of the word. A money-lender lends his own funds, but a banker is really a borrower of money. He has nothing to lend until he has borrowed, and he can dispense no credit until credit is bestowed upon him.

BEGINNINGS OF BANKING 59

years before 1646. In their true business as goldsmiths such a revival would not have affected them in the slightest degree. But we have seen that they had for years been trafficking largely in the foreign coins of almost myriad species which were then current in England. Their operations, by precipitating the currency crisis of the early seventeenth century, helped to accentuate the social discontent and economic malaise which precipitated the constitutional disturbance that led to the Civil War. At any rate, the author of *The Mystery* argues that the Civil War gave apprentices an opportunity of leaving their masters whenever they chose, and joining the Army. It had been a practice, he says, for many masters to entrust their apprentices[1] with the custody of their money; but they were cured of this habit and induced to entrust their money to the goldsmiths when these cashiers began to leave them in the lurch, by going off with the money to take military service in the Royal or Cromwellian forces.

This species of trouble, however, was not new. It had really manifested itself long before. Of every thousand instances we may consider ourselves fortunate if we can trace one, when we must search across the chasm of the centuries. Now, even in early Tudor days apprentices apparently took charge of their master's money, even where it consisted of " receipts which do not concern the ordinary trade " of such master.[2] Again, at a still earlier date, an apprentice, in 1450, gets into arrear to the extent of £138 10s. with his master's money.[3] Malynes[4] had denounced the same evil. The opportunity of getting credit, said he, led many apprentices to set up in business on their own account, before they had thoroughly learned their trade; they became " untimely maisters, when, as swimming with other men's bladders, they are soon drowned." It was then, he says, that merchants began

---

[1] See an illustrative case of payment to Sergeant Gaudy's clerk, where the sum received was £40, Talbot v. Godbolt, Yelv. 137, Mich. 6 Jac. 1. Merchants' servants lent their masters' money, cash at call, to the goldsmith-bankers at 4d. per cent. per diem.
[2] Rivers and Pudsey's case, Leonard, C. 63.
[3] *Hist. MSS. Comm.*, Vol. IX. p. 259.
[4] *St. George for England*, p. 39.

to put their cash into the goldsmiths' hands. The latter
were the more willing to take it because the landed gentry
were melting down what plate they had, rather than buying new. Originally, the author of *The Mystery* suggests,
goldsmiths purported to take charge of the money gratui-
tously, the customers themselves being totally unaware
how profitable the transaction was to the depositary.
The careful reader will note this point, which will prove,
as we shall shortly see, to be one of the utmost significance.
But in a very short time the goldsmiths sought to be merchants' cash-keepers, and " began to receive gentlemen's
rents . . . and, indeed, any man's money, and to allow
them some interest for it, though it lay for a month only,
or less, the Owners calling for it by a hundred or fifty
pounds at a time, as their occasions and expenses
wanted it; this new practice giving hopes to everybody
to make Profit of their money, until the hour they spent it,
and the conveniency, as they thought, to command their
money when they pleased, which they could not do when
lent at interest upon personal or reall Security; These
hopes, I say, drew a great Cash into these new Goldsmiths'
hands, and some of them stuck to their old Trade, but
every of them that had friends and credit aspired to this
new Mystery to become Bankers or Casheers; and when
Cromwell usurped the Government, the greatest of them
began to deal with him to supply his wants of Money upon
great Advantages, especially after they had bought those
Dollars whereof he robb'd the Spaniards to about the value
of 300000£. After the King's return [i.e. after the Restoration of Charles II., in 1660] he wanting money, some of
these Bankers undertook to lend him not their own but
other men's money, taking barefaced of Him ten pound for
the hundred, and by private contracts many Bills, Orders,
Tallies, and Debts of the King's, about twenty, and sometimes thirty in the hundred, to the great dishonour of the
Government." As for the rate of interest, thus taken
"barefaced," it cannot be regarded as entirely incom-
mensurate with the risk of having Charles II. for a client.

FEATURES OF MODERN BANKING APPEAR

The author of *The Mystery of the New-Fashioned Goldsmiths* then indicates, in effect, how largely the main features of modern banking could already be distinguished in his age. Having explained how the bankers got money into their coffers, he goes on to describe their experience of just such an average inflow and outflow as enables a modern banker to hit upon the precise amount of till-money which would enable him to meet his customers' demands at the counter. He says : " Having thus got money into their hands, they presumed upon some to come as fast as others was paid away, and upon that confidence of a running Cash (as they call it), they begun to accommodate men with moneys for Weeks and Moneths, upon extraordinary gratuities, and supply all necessitous merchants that overtraded their Stock, with present Money for their Bills of Exchange, discounting sometimes double, perhaps treble, interest for the time, as they found the Merchant more or less pinched." The goldsmith and the banker, financing " the luxury of a bowing courtier, the ventures of a prosperous voyager," increased the interest, so as to be commensurate with the risk, on the principle, to be so clearly enunciated by Petty, that " where the security is casual, then a kinde of ensurance must be enterwoven with the simple natural Interest, which may advance the Usury very conscionably unto any height below the Principal it self "—that is, to any rate less than 100 per cent.[1] So it began to happen that the money-lenders and the goldsmith-bankers paid 10 or 12 per cent. on deposits and used the cash as the basis of loans at 20 or 30 per cent. Porder, indeed, in his St. Paul's sermon, says they granted loans at 20 or 30 per cent. *profit*—that is to say, at 30 and even 42 per cent. ; but the assertion follows some extremely flashy rhetoric, and it would, perhaps, be unsafe to take the figures as precise percentages. That argument is confirmed by Porder's allusions, elsewhere, in two places, to usurers who take " x. or xii. pounde over-

[1] Petty, *Treatise of Taxes* ; Vol. I. p. 48, in Mr. Hull's collection.

62 EVOLUTION OF THE MONEY MARKET

plus "—10 or 12 per cent., that is to say, over the rate they are paying on deposits. Anyhow, Porder says the " rich man that taketh things at usurie will, no doubt, deliver for usurie at a more cutting rate "—which, in fact, he must do, unless he is to remain a mere gratuitous bailee. To speak of such a man as " a most pestilent spoyler of his comonwealth " is simply prejudiced exaggeration.

WIDENING EXPERIENCE AND ADAPTABILITY

It was, as we saw, suggested by the author of *The Mystery* that originally the goldsmith's customers were unaware of the profit which he made by the use of the money. They deposited it only for safe keeping, with one who held himself out as a gratuitous bailee. The goldsmith made himself into a kind of safe deposit, accepting the custody of gold and silver plate, ornaments, metal, and specie, including foreign coins of varied origin and denomination (see *post*, page 68). The goldsmith, however, had not been long engaged in this safe-deposit business before he discovered that the cash lying in his hands was not likely to be withdrawn all at once, although it had been deposited at call. Quite a brief experience of this class of occupation would bring him into contact with that law of average demand which enables the modern banker to regulate to a nicety the amount of his till-money, while he makes profitable use of the rest of his balances. Consequently—and here are the beginnings of the demarcation between the banker and the money-lender—he attracted deposits of cash by offering 4d. per cent. per day interest, which is about 6 per cent. per annum, and this, by the middle of the seventeenth century, had the effect of drawing money from all parts of the country to the Metropolis, until the rise of the country banks checked the current. Then he began to lend out the superfluous balances at interest among the mercantile community around him. The new experiments, unfortunately, were then (as they were destined to be for another couple of centuries) based upon imperfect experience. Where the

BEGINNINGS OF BANKING 63

banker locked up his loanable resources in non-liquid assets, they led directly to disaster. The goldsmith originally did not appreciate the dubious character of real estate as a banker's security, nor yet the danger of financing sanguine promoters of plausible but rotten schemes. A good deal of trouble and a great many failures had to ensue before the principles which are now fundamental in the science of banking were understood by its early exponents. But the rudimentary banking system in itself makes for public stability, as, conversely, it has its origin therein. It is not until the banker is assured of such comparative public quietude as will protect him from runs that he can venture to rely upon the operation of the law of average for the calculation of a proper supply of till-money and the use of the rest of his deposits for making advances. Moreover, he will be deterred from embarking upon that class of business as long as there is any serious chance of such civil commotion as might render the borrower unable to repay the advance. But as soon as these propitious conditions are present, and the banker becomes a power in the City or the State, his whole influence is itself thrown into the scale of order and obedience to the law. It is in reliance upon the working of this principle of civic quietude, creating and maintaining average turn-overs, that modern bankers are able to reduce their till-money to the amazingly low level of about 6 per cent. of the total liabilities (rather higher for East-End branches and about 10 per cent. at head offices), and to allow practically the whole of the remaining gigantic balances to be actively employed as an addition to the available currency, in the furtherance of financial and commercial interests, and the steadying of their movement.

A CRUCIAL PROBLEM PRESENTS ITSELF

This change in the character of the goldsmith's operations, however, must have been accompanied by a corresponding modification of the legal relationship between himself and his customer. We saw him, originally, as a bailee. But the bailee is precluded from using the bailed chattel for his own personal advantage, in any manner whatsoever, without the consent of the bailor, express or implied, unless such use be needful for its preservation (as in the giving of exercise to a bailed horse). The contract could not invariably have been a strict depositum with the banker, because then ipse de ea re, quam accepit, restituenda tenetur[1]—he must return the identical thing deposited, which would border upon the impossible in the case of coined money, especially at the period with which we are concerned, for characteristic reasons shortly to be discussed. Money has no Ear-mark.[2] One penny cannot be known from another.[3] Anyhow, if the contract were only bailment, the banker could not properly have used the money, though its employment was essential to the profit of the transaction, from his point of view. " The use of credit is that it enables debtors to use a certain part of the money their creditors have lent them." So says Bagehot,[4] and it is obvious that a debtor, as distinguished from a bailee, is the only person who can carry on this species of operation. Before we can erect the fabric of credit we must get rid of this legal quagmire under its very foundations. When, then, did it begin to be the accepted doctrine that the banker was merely the debtor, and not the bailee, much less the trustee, of his customer ? What circumstances led to this modification of his legal position and produced an economic " sport " which has changed the whole outlook of finance and added incalculably to its power ? How did the note or receipt become disconnected from the *specific* deposit, and available only against the banker generally ?

TESTIMONY OF THE LAW REPORTS

At first sight, the date and nature of the transformation appear to be as perplexing a riddle in the realm of finance as the origin of the wings of insects in the records of biological evolution. Fortunately, the development of the

[1] Justinian, *Institutes*, Lib. iii., Tit. xiv. p. 3.
[2] Lord Wright in Kendar *v.* Millward 2 Vern. 440 (1702).
[3] Fairfax, J., 15 Vin. Ab. 420.
[4] *Lombard Street*, p. 55.

BEGINNINGS OF BANKING 65

doctrine is traceable, though with great difficulty, in the law reports of the period. The *specific bailment* of money was common enough. In Lyte et Ux. v. Perry a man bailed a certain sum of money to another to the use of a third, and to be delivered upon a certain contingency. It was held that at any time before the occurrence of the stipulated event he might countermand the bailment and require the return of his money.[1] For this one instance which has come down to us there were probably thousands of which we know nothing. In Core's case, temp. Henry VIII.,[2] a sum of £20 had been handed by John Core to one George Waddye, " to bestow the said £20 in French prunes "—so ran the defendant's tale—" for the behoof and use of the said John, and to see them safely shipped, as I do my own wares." Baker, A.-G., argued that this was a bailment, to have an increase and profit of the money, and not the money back . . . " for the law is taken in our Books to be that if a man bail money to be bailed over, if it be not bailed according to the condition, no action of debt lies, but account, for he shall not receive the money to retain it." Mountague, arguing in reply, claimed that here was a specific condition to lay out the money in prunes: but admitted [and this is the important point for us] that such a case differed from that of a man who " delivers money to traffic with generally." Luke, J., emphasised this distinction by an instance where " a man bailed £20 by indenture to another to employ them in woad, if the woad please him; and if not, then to re-deliver the £20 to the bailor; there an action of debt was brought for the £20, and adjudged well maintainable, because the word ' re-deliver ' implies an obligation." That is to say, this delivery of the money was a bailment, on account of the conditions attached for its use in a specific transaction, and its re-delivery failing the condition. But aliter where there is no specific purpose in the contemplation of the parties. Here Spilman & Portman, JJ., and Fitzjames, C.J., gave an instance which is right to the point : " If I bail £20 to one to keep for my use, if the £20 were not con-

[1] Dyer, 49 b. pl. 7. [2] Dyer, 20.

tained in a bag, coffer, or box, an action of detinue doth not lie, because the £20 could not be discovered or known to be mine [i.e. the coins are not specifically identifiable], but debt and account lie at my pleasure there." Where £30 had been advanced to the defendant, who promised to pay "prædictas £30" quando requisitus esset, Yelverton in arrest of judgment argued that the word " prædictas " clearly pointed to an intended repayment of the same £30 in specie, the defendant gaining no benefit by the transaction. But the court[1] was against him. The intent of the parties, said Popham, was to have " prædictam summam £30 and not the same money in specie and eo magis quia the promise is grounded upon an accommodation, viz. a loan which implies an use of the £30 by the defendant." It being agreed that defendant should use the money (i.e. he being recognised as a banker) it was impossible for him to pay the same money in specie that he received. In the language of Holt, C.J., at a rather later date, such money was delivered ad computandum, or ad merchandizandum. But otherwise if it were in a bag sealed, so that he could not have any " Use or Imployment " of the money at all. This latter species and transaction is the mere delivery of money to keep generally without any consideration or reward. In that case, if the bailee is robbed, the bailor bears the loss.[2] This is the principle which is afterwards to support the doctrine that a banker is not a gratuitous bailee of property (other than money) left with him by a customer for safe custody.

Again, Leonard tells us[3] that at Mich. 15 Eliz., in the King's Bench, it " was said by the whole court that if a man delivereth mony to another man to buy cattel, or to merchandize with, although that the mony be sealed up in a bag, yet the *property* of the mony *is in the bailee*, and the bailor cannot have an action for the mony, but only an accompt against the bailee, although that he never buyeth the cattel or other things . . . and . . . if the bailee dieth, no action of accompt lieth against his execu-

[1] Mich. 2 Jac. 1.—Yelv 50.
[2] The King v. Sheriff of Hertford 2 Show. C. 164. Mich. 33 Car. II.
[3] Reports, C., p. 38.

BEGINNINGS OF BANKING 67

tors, *because the testator had the property of the monies.*" This was accepted and recognised law by the time of Higgs v. Holliday,[1] where Anderson, C.J., laid it down[2] that " if a man delivers money to another the property thereof is in the bailee, because it cannot be known, and he can maintain accompt only . . . for the writ of accompt proves the property of the money to be in him; for it supposeth that he is receptor denariorum of the plaintiff." When plaintiff lost the possession, " he had lost the property also, because it cannot be known "—i.e. the coins are not specifically identifiable. There is a case midway between these two principles,[3] where Walmesley said that " if money be delivered, it cannot be known and therefore the property is altered and therefore a debt will lie " : but he went on to point out that " if Portugalls or other money that may be known be delivered to be redelivered, a detinue lies." There is contemporaneously in operation the same conservative legal sentiment as regards the assignment of money as we shall see applied in respect to the assignment of shares. So Coke in Moorwood v. Dickens,[4] " If one be bound in a bond of £40 to pay £20 if the obligee command him to pay this to J. S. he ought to plead that he paid this to the obligee by the hand of J. S. but is not to plead that he paid the same to J. S. by the command of the obligee." Coke laid stress (1 Inst., 89) upon the other transaction—that of safe deposit—when he declared that " where A. leaves a chest locked with B., and taketh away the key, there A. does not entrust B. with the goods, but [it] is a deposit for safe custody only." Noy, commenting (Noy 12) on Higgs v. Holliday, said that trover[5] lay for money, " although it be not in a bagg, but otherwise for detinue ; for by that the plaintiff should have judgment to recover the thing itself . . . and if not then damages, and therefore the thing ought to be known " (i.e. identifiable).

[1] Cro. Eliz., 746.   [2] Easter, 42 Eliz.
[3] Bretton v. Barnet, Mich. 41 and 42 Eliz., Ow. 86.
[4] III Bulstrode, 149.
[5] So-called from the express averment, in the declaration, that the defendant had " found " (trouver) the goods. This was formally included, even if it were a purely fictitious allegation.

THE NEW PRINCIPLES SOLIDLY ESTABLISHED

These were the doctrines that obtained during the rise of the English banking system. When the fabric was well on the way to its modern elaboration and complexity, Lee, C.J., affirmed the rule once more. " Property," said he (1743), in Hartop v. Hoare,[1] " does not follow the possession, unless in cases where the true owner hath no marks to ascertain his property, as in money." These principles introduce us to three different classes of bailment as being within legal contemplation in the latter half of the sixteenth century :—

(1) The " bare naked bailment " to which Coke refers, i.e., where there is a deposit of a locked chest, coffer, bag, or other receptacle, and the bailee has admittedly no right either to touch or to utilise the contents. As recently as Giblin v. M'Mullen[2] Lord Chelmsford quoted the judgment of the Supreme Judicial Court of Massachusetts,[3] in which the Chief Justice (1820) said that " as far as the bank was concerned, the deposit of the gold [coins in a cask] was a mere naked bailment for the accommodation of the depositor, and without any advantage to the bank which could tend to increase its liability beyond the effect of such a contract."

(2) A bailment where there is a duty on the part of the bailee to employ the money for a specific purpose, generally in trade. This is the case outlined by Mountague (*supra*).

(3) A bailment of money, in the shape of loose and therefore unidentifiable coins, where the bailor's only action for the recovery of the money is one of debt. This is the case of the banker, and the operation of the principle must have been the more emphatic where the deposit was in an alien currency.

THE FOREIGN FACTORS IN THE COINAGE

The existence of an immense foreign element in the British currency must have been a potent factor in the production of the new legal conditions. Alien coins of every value and description seem at this time to have been in circulation in England. There was, in fact, a composite

[1] Atkyns, Vol. III., at p. 49.
[2] 1868, E.R., Vol. XVI. p. 589.
[3] Foster v. the Essex Bank, 17 Mass. Reps., p. 478.

BEGINNINGS OF BANKING 69

international currency, of which the English element was subject to a continual process of debasement at the hands of foreign coiners, while it suffered almost equally by the operations of clippers at home.[1] The English merchant could make more money by exporting gold than any other commodity. There had been established, moreover, a regular trade in the export of English coin, which ultimately brought a financial crisis in its train. A State paper, apparently about 1529 (quoted by Shaw), speaks of "disputes between English, Italian, Flemish, and Spanish merchants because of the last edict about gold. The writer knows of the importation of 100,000 crowns and £10,000 in gold, which will be exported again unless care is taken." Some of these would certainly be coins of foreign mintage. He therefore recommends special vigilance on the part of the searchers at the various ports. In the correspondence of the Cely family, Merchants of the Staple, which extends down to 1488 (Royal Hist. Soc., Ed. Malden), the learned editor finds mention of an extremely miscellaneous assortment of coins, to all of which an English value could be assigned. They were the Andrewe (Scots), the Arnoldes (Gueldres), the Carolus Groat (Charles of Burgundy), the Crown (French Ecu), the David and the Falewe (issued by the Bishop of Utrecht), the Hettinus (Westphalia), the Lewe (Louis), the Lymnyr Groat (Limburg), the Milleyn Groat (Milan), the Nemyng Groat (Nimeguen), the Phellypus (Brabant), the Plalke (Utrecht), the Postlate (a debased gold coin from Utrecht), the Ryall (English, 10s.), the Rydar (probably Scots), the Rynyshe (Cologne), the Setiller (origin uncertain), and the Gylhellmus (Holland). With all this multitude and variety of foreign currency in circulation[2] it is clear that unless the bailee of the coins were to remain a depositary pure and simple he must be at liberty to repay, not only

[1] A bag containing a pound weight of clippings from coins of Elizabeth, James I., and Charles I., was discovered by some labourers near Frome in 1884. (*Antiquary*, Vol. IX. p. 93.)
[2] The Bank of England, very early in its history, set its face against these alien factors or currency and refused to handle foreign coins, "for which reason it is impracticable with many traders to keep their cash with them." (*London Magazine*, 1737: quoted by Gilbart, Banking, 39.)

in coins other than the identical pieces which he originally received, but, what is more important, in coins of a different species, only approximated in value by agreement between himself and his customer to the original deposit. If the goldsmith bailee of a given sum in gold and silver coins of various fineness and denomination is at liberty to repay his client in English currency, and, consequently, in totally different coins, it is clear that the transaction is no longer depositum, since that which is returned is not, and cannot be, that which was deposited. Some confirmation of this hypothesis drifts across the ever-widening chasm of the centuries in the shape of a brief report in late law French—en debt sur un obligation pur payment de tant argent flemish, le pl'count sur tant en deniers Anglois : & exception prise al count, uncore rule bone per curiam.[1] So, even earlier, in Willshalge and Davidge's case,[2] it was held (Mich. 28 and 29 Eliz.) that where goods had been sold for " so many portagues and so many ducats, which in toto amounted to £700 sterling," the money may be demanded in sterling, even if the contract originally contemplated satisfaction in the other coinages.[3] Small success attended the efforts to remedy the circulation of debased gold, by anticipating the nicely-adjusted scales of the modern banker. In 1588 Sir Richard Martin—the name carries us, as by a flash of anticipation, into nineteenth-century banking—told Cecil that gold coins still

[1] Rastall v. Draper, Mich. 3 Jac. I., Moore, 775.
[2] Leonard, A. 41.
[3] See a curious dispute as to the value of a besant recorded in Heydon v. Godsole (II. Bulstrode 161). The King " certified a besant to be of the value of £100 as appears by the certification of the King, as I have seen by the record of the same : the which Sir Nicolas Bacon did shew unto me " (the Court, loq.) and another case (De Acuno v. Gifford—Bulstrode III, 159) where the King of Spain paid the defendant " decem mille ducatus monetæ for to go for him in bello against the barbarians." The defendant did not go, and the Spanish ambassador sued for the return of the money. One of the points of the case was the value of the " duckets," nominally put at 5s. 6d. each. These difficulties survived long after banking was an established business. In 20 and 21 Car. II. there was an action of " indebitatus in the debet and detinet for so many Livres French, which ought to be in the detinet only, or else count on so many Livres French of the value of so much English " (Richards v. Coho, II Keble 463.) Even experts differed. In 1614 there is a " Dispute about selling two pieces of gold, whether sovereigns or double ducats." (*Memorials of the Goldsmiths' Company*, Vol. I. p. 123.)

BEGINNINGS OF BANKING

passed mainly by weight, and that very few of the specially-constructed balances, supplied by the mint authorities, had been sold. To minimise the inconvenience arising from a number of mints throughout the country, Queen Elizabeth centralised the work in one mint, at the Tower of London.

HUGE SIGNIFICANCE OF THESE PRINCIPLES

After this examination of their gradual legal evolution, we can appreciate the significance of the modification in the legal relationship between banker and customer. Unless these doctrines had been formulated, modern banking could not have come into effective existence. The change, even when an attempt is made to trace it, is almost as obscure and quite as pregnant as that from the inorganic to the organic, from the inanimate to the animate. " The plant is the origin of all the energy possessed by living things ; but how it can convert the stable inorganic into the unstable organic, while the animal cannot, we do not know." [1] More and more as we progress will it become apparent that these undeveloped germs of Tudor money-custody contained all the potentialities of the developed banking organism which means so much to the modern world. The establishment of the new doctrines involved a relaxation of legal strictness, a mitigation of the unrelenting hardness of the law, akin to that which in another sphere, and under the inspiration of the early Chancellors, gave us their equitable jurisdiction. So thoroughly had the new principle established itself as the foundation of the banking system that when an effort was made to reopen the question, by means of litigation, something like a century ago, the argument in support of the older doctrines was treated as of the flimsiest value. The relationship between banker and customer as that of debtor and creditor, and not trustee and cestui que trust, or bailee and bailor, seems to have been regarded as an established fact—obvious, notorious, and practically unchallengeable. In the arguments (1820) in Foster v. the Essex Bank,[2] counsel for the defendants

[1] Clodd, *Story of Creation*, p. 72. Mr. Clodd is himself the secretary of a great modern bank (the London Joint Stock).
[2] 17 Mass. Reps., p. 478.

said that " in every definition of a bank or banker it is implied that they shall have the *use* of the money deposited; and it is believed that no bank in Europe receives deposits, *to be kept and returned specifically* " (except, of course, where property is deposited for safe keeping only, to be returned in specie). Counsel for the plaintiff did not put his case as high as that. He defined a bank as " a society or community who take upon themselves the charge of money of private persons, to improve it or keep it secure." The Bank of England, he argued, had no express power to receive deposits ; but with that institution, as with American banks operating under charters drawn in similar terms, " it has become part of their duty and business by usage, and it now belongs to the very nature of such institutions." Counsel urged that " banks should be held to a degree of responsibility little or nothing short of that which belongs to the class of bailees under which common carriers, innkeepers, and others are ranked." The court declined to take this view, and the decision has influenced later judicial pronouncements in this country, and has more than once been quoted as an authority. The court, in Potts *v.* Glegg,[1] laid it down, in 1833, that sums which are paid to the credit of a customer with a banker, though usually called deposits, are in truth loans by the customer to the banker. Again, in 1843, the Lord Chancellor, quoting Sir William Grant's language in Devaynes *v.* Noble,[2] said that " the balance at the banker's is a debt due to the party who deposits the money. The money is not to be returned in specie : the engagement is to be ready to pay an equal amount when called for."[3] " If," added the Lord Chancellor, " it is merely a sum of money paid to a factor or paid to an agent, the party has a right to recall it—he has a right to deal with the factor or agent in his fiduciary character. But the banker does not hold that fiduciary character." Finally, " That ordinary banking transactions constituted only a debt, and not a trust, was clear from this," said Wood, v.-c. (1866), in re **Agra**

[1] 16 Mees. and W., p. 321.   [2] 1 Merivale, p. 568.
[3] Parker *v.* Marchant, 1 Phillips, p. 361.

BEGINNINGS OF BANKING 73

and Masterman's Bank, ex parte Waring,[1] "that if you had paid into your bank £100,000 one day, and the next the banker chose to invest this sum in any speculative concern, you could not file a bill against him to restrain him from so doing."[2]

THE MONEY-LENDER STILL ACTIVE

Although (thanks partly to their own enterprise, and partly as a consequence of the greater legal latitude already described) financial business, of the type characteristic of the late Tudor age, was gradually concentrating in the hands of the goldsmiths, they enjoyed nothing approaching a monopoly as yet. The average trader in the towns was alive to the profits of usury, and freely exercised his opportunities as money-lender. He continued to do so long after banking had become, in London, a distinct business, no longer combined with that of the goldsmith or any other species of trade. He was, in fact, a progenitor of the early provincial bankers, who joined shop and bank together

[1] 36 L.J., Ch., at p. 152.
[2] The present state of the law on this subject has never been better reviewed than by Lord Cottenham, in Foley v. Hill (1848, 2 H.L.C., pp. 35–38). "Money," said Lord Chancellor Cottenham, in that case, "when paid into a bank, ceases altogether to be the money of the principal; it is then the money of the banker, who is bound to return an equivalent by paying a similar sum to that deposited with him when he is asked for it. The money paid into the banker's is money known by the principal to be placed there for the purpose of being under the control of the banker; it is then the banker's money; he is known to deal with it as his own; he makes what profit he can, which profit he retains to himself, paying back only the principal, according to the custom of bankers in some places, or the principal and a small rate of interest, according to the custom of bankers in other places. The money placed in the custody of a banker is, to all intents and purposes, the money of the banker, to do with it as he pleases; he is guilty of no breach of trust in employing it; he is not answerable to the principal if he puts it into jeopardy, if he engages in a hazardous speculation; he is not bound to keep it or deal with it as the property of his principal; but he is, of course, answerable for the amount, because he has contracted, having received that money, to repay to the principal, when demanded, a sum equivalent to that paid into his hands. That has been the subject of discussion in various cases, and that has been established to be the relative situation of banker and customer. That being established to be the relative situations of banker and customer, the banker is not an agent or factor, but he is a debtor." His Lordship pointedly guarded against the misconception arising from the use of the word "deposit" in connection with moneys paid to a banker: "If . . . a sum of money had been deposited with the banker—I will not say," he added, "deposited, but *paid to* the banker—on account of the customer."

far into the eighteenth century, as we shall see. In the Tudor Age, for instance, George Stoddard[1] watches his margin with the lynx eye of a modern banker. If the security is found to have been " reyted too highly," more margin must be instantly forthcoming, upon threat to call in the loan, enforced by legal proceedings. Stoddard lent £400 on a bond to pay £80 per annum interest during his own lifetime, the debt to be extinguished by his death. He discounted a series of bills for one Francis Ascough, at about 25 per cent., until every iota of the borrower's property was hypothecated, and, in addition, his brother had become surety for an alleged unprotected margin of £200. Then he sold up his unfortunate client, seizing even his bedsteads and cupboards. Stoddard laid himself open to the sarcasm of critics on account of the " glass windows " [blanks] in some of the documents connected with his purchase of cheap interests in land from embarrassed devisees. The blank transfer and the post-dated cheque represent the modern analogues of his methods, though they are not designed for the same bloodsucking purposes.

AMAZING PREVALENCE OF HOARDS

No sooner were the goldsmith-bankers recognised as responsible recipients of money at interest than there was initiated the working of another, and most potent, stimulus to social progress. The goldsmith-bankers began to draw money out of hoards. The amount of money continuously withdrawn from circulation, and thrust into the enforced and sterile seclusion of all kinds of hiding-places, must have been all but incalculable. This is the reason for the extraordinary revelations, in wills of the period, with regard to hoards of money contained in shoes, boxes, and barrels, wrapped up in sheet-lead, concealed among the joists of a floor, or hidden behind books and in dark corners.[2] To

---

[1] *Society in the Elizabethan Age*, p. 51.

[2] These habits are, on the whole, so foreign to our modern ideas as to seem almost inconceivable, and one good instance may be given as an illustration. Richard Bellassis, making his will on February 6, 1596–1597 (Surtees Society, Vol. XXXVIII., p. 337), after specifying that he bequeathed " six owld angelles " to his niece Ursula, goes on to bequeath £64 2s. to his " suster," Jane Hedworth. This money was all in " owld

BEGINNINGS OF BANKING 75

a certain extent, of course, it is the same instinct which prompts the modern depositor of money in a bank to hide the deposit receipt, and to die without revealing the place of concealment, thereby adding materially to the unclaimed balances of the institution of which he was a client. The activity of the goldsmith-bankers was immediately operative to combat this hoarding tendency, and their successors, the modern bankers, were destined to reduce hoarding to a minimum, and in time to abolish it practically altogether.

EARLY BANKING METHODS

At this point, having considered whence came the goldsmith-banker's supplies of money, and in what capacity he held them, we may with advantage turn to the consideration of his mode of doing business. Malynes has left us a detailed analysis of the methods of continental bankers before 1600, and therefore during the period which at the moment engages us. We may be fairly sure that, with slight local variations, the methods of the English bankers were the same. According to Malynes, a bank is properly " a collection of all the ready moneys of some province, State, or Commonwealth into the hands of some persons licensed and established thereunto by public

---

gold, viz., £20 5s. in owld ryalls, at 15s. the pece; in dwble dwcketts, at 13s. 4d. the pece, £20, one owld noble 13s. 4d. iiij owld Englische crowns, one portingewe, one pece of 30s., one pece of 20s. in gowld, all of which said somes of £64 2s. is, at this present, within a litelle poursse of silke rybben, within a littell lether bagg, which is putt within a white lether showe, and lieth in the west eynd of the heighest floore of the presser, in my stodye at Morton, where the glasses stand." In schedules the testator recites other stores of money " laid up at several places," including £500 " in currant coine of goulde of severall sorts, all which is now lapped up in one severall thinne piece of lead " ; further, £100 in " currant coine of goulde, being put within a litelle wooddeen box." There is also a sum of £200 in " currante monie " " underfote, under the boordes, betwixt two jestes and the seallinge of the chamber [at Morton] . . . under the edge of the bords of the highest steppe towards the northe wyndowe " ; a further " £200 in currant monie . . . put edgewaies into a wooddeen box . . . walled up in a hollowe place within the wall of the newe great chamber at Morton " ; £200 in the bottom of an " ould litel barrell in the store house " ; £100 " within the bottom of the table chair in my bedchamber " ; £160 in " a bagge . . . behind two books " in the presser ; £64 " thrust into an old lether shoe " in the said presser ; and £100 in " my great iron cheste." Bellassis seems to have had his house honeycombed with hoards.

76 EVOLUTION OF THE MONEY MARKET

authority of some prince, erected with great solemnity in the view of all the people and inhabitants." Malynes, indeed, contemplated the display of the actual coin in some open market-place " upon a scaffold," which, as he said, would allure the common people to bring their moneys into these bankers' hands, but must, nevertheless, have been a very perilous experiment. If, however, the common people bring their money in this way, he tells us, they may command it, and have it again at their pleasure, with the allowance of " five upon every thousand ducats or crowns, when any man will retire or draw his money into his own hands again." This, as a matter of fact, is only $\frac{1}{2}$ per cent. per annum. The bankers, he adds, have their correspondents in the chief places of trade in Christendom. They are prepared to advance money against merchandise. If a customer have occasion to pay 3000 or 4000 ducats, and he have but 1000 ducats in the bank, the bankers will make up the difference, or, in modern parlance, allow him an overdraft. Malynes, moreover, proceeds to analyse the system of credit under which this kind of thing is done. He indicates, quite accurately, that what is in one sense the grant of an overdraft to A is, from another point of view, only the depletion of B's account, in order to provide the means of granting the accommodation which A requires.[1]

BEGINNINGS OF CRITICAL SUPERVISION

Apparently sixteenth-century bankers had already initiated the beneficent policy, so extensively and successfully developed by their modern successors, of exercising a kind of skilled paternal supervision over their customers'

[1] His illustration is worth quoting in full :—
" Peter hath 2000 ducats in the bank, John hath 3000, and William 4000, and so consequently others more or less. Peter hath occasion to pay unto John 1000 ducats ; he goeth to the bankers at the hours appointed (which are certain both in the forenoon and afternoon), and requireth them to pay 1000 ducats unto John ; whereupon they presently make Peter debtor for 1000 ducats, and John creditor for the same sum. So that Peter having assigned unto John 1000 ducats, hath now no more but 1000 ducats in bank, where he had 2000 before. And John hath 4000 ducats in the same bank, where he had but 3000 before. And so in the same manner of assignation. John doth pay unto William and William unto others, without that any money is touched, but remaineth still in the banker's hands ; which, within a short time after the erection of the bank, cometh to amount

affairs. Malynes says that if the client go to the banker for actual cash, the latter will be so bold as to ask "for what purpose he demandeth the same, or what he will do with it." The sixteenth-century banker, like his modern confrère, would no doubt be quite willing to grant accommodation as long as the working of the account showed that the client was engaged in legitimate commercial operations. But as soon as it became evident that he was involved in rash and hazardous speculation, or that he was wasting his substance in riotous living, the banker would abandon his complacent mood and become much more strict in his requirements. A modern banker would do precisely the same. He would be prepared to facilitate the establishment of a legitimate trade connection, conducted upon prudent lines ;[1] but the passage through the account of a cheque for the most expensive type of motor-car, or the evidence that the client was engaged in ostentatious speculative building operations, would at once put him on the alert, and probably shut off further supplies of accommodation. Modern American bankers and insurance companies will decline to advance money on a life policy, for instance, if, to their knowledge, the client is only effecting the mortgage in order to buy himself an automobile. This silent, but ceaseless, financial censorship, which we shall study in greater detail at a later stage, is not the least of the multitudinous social services rendered by the banking system.

THE ECONOMY OF CURRENCY

If—to resume Malynes—the customer require money to pay a debt the banker will offer to do it for him, and if for the purpose of a foreign remittance the banker will give him bills of exchange. If, however, the money be

---

unto many millions. And by their industry they do incorporate the same, which may be easily understood, if we do but consider what the ready money and wealth of London would come unto, if it were gathered in some one man's hands ; much more, if a great deal of riches of other countries were added thereunto, as these bankers can cunningly compass by the course of the exchange for moneys ; the ebbing and flowing whereof is caused by their motion from time to time, as shall be declared." It would be difficult, when allowance is made for the rudimentary economics of the period, to imagine anything more lucid than this. Malynes was the Hartley Withers of his age. [1] See page 435.

merely wanted for the client's "charges and expenses," the bankers will pay it without demur, because "it is but a small sum, and in the end the money cometh into their hands again." Their payments, Malynes says, "are, in fact, by assignation and imaginative," by which he means, of course, to impress us with his central principle, that there are constant adjustments of the current accounts as between themselves, A being debited and C credited,[1] while the amount in the banker's hands remains the same. Every loan creates a deposit. This curiosity on the part of the banker, with regard to the destination of the money, is by no means so inexplicable as Malynes seems to imagine. In offering to make the payment, or remit the money to a foreign country, the banker is, after all, only serving his client's interest, since he can send it with greater dispatch than his client—or, more accurately, he can make such adjustments of his relations with other bankers as will provide for its payment at the proper time and place. The older modes of transmission died hard, no doubt; for we are a conservative people. We did not take altogether kindly to either of the great modern organisations for the transmission and distribution of capital—the banks and the Stock Exchange.[2]

CLUMSY MODES OF TRANSMITTING MONEY

The modern banker's facilities, augmented by the machinery of the Stock Exchange, were destined to oust the antiquated and clumsy methods. Such slow, tedious,

[1] These ideas of Malynes secured wide acceptance and largely influenced contemporary banking literature. Lambe's scheme for a national bank was, in the main, a project for facilitating commercial transactions by the easy transfer, on the part of the participants, of their credit with the bank. It would, he argued, prevent mistakes and fraud, and minimise highway robbery. Francis Craddocke (*Wealth Discovered*, 1661, p. 5) lays stress upon the advantage of the ready transfer of money in the books of a bank. Craddocke urges that if the credit arising from the deposit of money were feasible, there should be a similar facility of credit on the security of goods, jewels, and other pledges.

[2] When Gresham succeeded in borrowing £50,000 in Antwerp, he was instructed to send the money in such coins of gold or silver as he thought most desirable, but no more than £1000 to be sent in any one ship, though a sum not exceeding £3000 might be sent overland from Antwerp to Calais, and from Calais to London at the risk of the Crown. These precautions resulted from the fact that, although Gresham could borrow money in

BEGINNINGS OF BANKING

and laborious arrangements may be advantageously contrasted with the rapid, and, in fact, almost instantaneous, transmission of money from one point of *space* to another which has been rendered possible by the far-flung network of branch banks not only throughout the British Islands, but throughout the Empire ; and with its facile transport from one point of *time* to another, which is the business of the Stock Exchanges. The old form of transmission was clumsy, slow, and expensive ; the new is expeditious and economical ; and, because in the great majority of cases where money is concerned, the transmission merely takes place from one branch to another, and is, in effect, only a readjustment of their accounts as between themselves or with their head office, the expense is reduced to an absolute minimum, and the safety simultaneously enhanced to a maximum. Thus, as in the case of the Stock Exchange mechanism (as we shall see in due course), there is, in this rapid and facile transfer of the life-blood of the body politic from point to point, a huge consumer's surplus above and beyond the amount actually or collectively paid to the banker for it.

FURTHER USURY LEGISLATION—RATE REDUCED

The advent of the goldsmith-bankers, and the consequent increase of financial facility, brought the ancient

---

the Low Countries, he was forbidden by the local law to export it. He was, consequently, forced to propose to the Privy Council that he should buy large quantities of pepper, and secrete £200 in every bag of that commodity, so as to smuggle it over to England in that way. The proposal, as a matter of fact, was not adopted ; but it has its interest all the same. The idea of the English Privy Council borrowing money at about 12 or 14 per cent., and having to contemplate smuggling it across the Channel in bags of pepper, is not without its humorous aspect. The Duke of Northumberland's collection contains a " bill of charges for the portage " of the Earl of Northumberland's money to London from Topcliff, in co. York. The date is 1604 (?) and the amount £24 12s. 6d. (*Hist. MSS. Comm.,* 3rd Rep., p. 52.) A petition to the House of Lords in 1643 (*Hist. MSS. Comm.,* 5th Rep., p. 119) deals with the default of one Francis Sadler, a " great dealer in large sums of money between England and Ireland," who was "largely indebted to the petitioners, though they, knowing the difficulty of raising money in such distracted times, had foreborne to press him." When Charles II. received a remittance at The Hague in 1660 he was " so joyful that he called the Princess Royal and the Duke of York to look upon it as it lay in the portmanteau." (*Pepys,* by Braybrooke, Vol. I., p. 90.)

question of usury once more into prominence. Another lowering of the rate, or, at all events, an attempt in that direction, by the Statute 21 Jac. I. c. 17, began with a preamble arguing that the persistence of 10 per cent. " does not only make men unable to pay their debts, and continue the maintenance of trade, but their debts daily increasing, they are enforced to sell their lands and stocks at very low rates, to forsake the use of merchandise and trade, and to give over their leases and farms, and so become unprofitable members of the Commonwealth, to the great hurt and hindrance of the same." The statute therefore reduced the former rate of 10 per cent. to 8 per cent., with the usual penalties against evasion. By section 3 we are again reminded how extensive and complicated the financial machinery was becoming, because penalties are enacted against scriveners, brokers, solicitors, and drivers of bargains who shall receive more than 5 per cent. for arranging a loan of over 12 pence for the making or renewing of the bond or bill of the loan. Straggling traces of the lingering traditional view of usury still survived in the reservation in section 5 that " no words in this law contained shall be construed or expounded to allow the practice of usury in point of religion or conscience." Even the moderate concession—if such it can be called—represented by this statute, did its work in encouraging business. Sir Josiah Child says that in 1635, ten years after the passing of this statute into operation, " there were more merchants to be found on the Exchange of London worth each £1000 and upwards than were before the year 1600 to be found worth £100." The lowering of interest, he adds, " enables merchants to increase foreign trade, whereby home manufacturers and artificers will be increased, as also our stock of other useful people, and the poor will be employed."

This statute of 21 Jac. I. was originally a temporary Act, but was made perpetual by 3 Car. 1 c. 4. sect. 5. Cromwell enacted a 6 per cent. rate, and apparently this was further reduced in cases of hardship. " An ordinance about 1653 gave power to abate interest for the troublesome times between 42 and 48, as the circumstances required."[1] But by 12 Car. II c. 13 the statutory reduction to 6 per cent. was recognised by the Restoration Parliament. The Act, for obvious reasons, does not recite the Protector's enactment of a 6 per cent. rate; but it offers valuable indications of the changing economic opinion of the age. The abatement from 10 per cent. to 8 per cent. had been found, says the recital, beneficial to the advancement of trade and improvement of land. Moreover, the change had reduced the rate " to a nearer proportion with Forraigne States, with whom wee traffique." Attempts were being made, however, to raise the rate to 8 per cent.; but the new Act proceeds firmly to decide upon 6 per cent. from September 29, 1660.[2] This reduction did not apparently affect the rate on outstanding mortgages. " If a mortgagee receives interest upon an old mortgage, after the rate of 8 per cent., after such time as the interest is reduced to 6 per cent. by the statute, yet he shall not be obliged to allow or discount the 2 per cent. towards satisfaction of the principal."[3] But with regard to all other transactions, all bonds, contracts and assurances for a greater rate are to be utterly void. These changes produced widespread controversy, fomented by great variety of opinion. Child, giving evidence in 1669 before the Committee of the Decay of Trade,[4] attributed the prosperity of the commerce of the Dutch partly to banks, low interest, and mercantile law. The way to promote trade, said he, was by increasing the capital of the nation and by bills of exchange—which are, of course, credit capital. Child wanted low interest. In Holland, he argued, it was low without law. Mr. Titus, anticipating arguments which were soon to be invoked against the proposed Bank of England, advanced the curious proposition that " in all monarchial and aristocratical Governments the first pulling

[1] So alleged in Porter v. Hubbart, 1672, III Rep. Ch. 43. In the time of Charles I. the Chancery Courts usually allowed 4 or 5 per cent. on money (Some v. Parker II. Keble 187).
[2] Scriveners [bill-brokers] who take above 5s. for the [arranging of] the loan of £100 for the year, or above 12d. for the making or renewing of the Bond or Bill, are to forfeit £20 and "have Imprisonment for halfe a yeare."
[3] Eq. Ca. Abr. 288.   [4] Hist. MSS. Comm., 8th Rep., app. 133.

down thereof has been the lowering of interest." Mr. Lone said that " money may be brought lower by prosperity, but not by law." The Committee voted, by 13 to 1, for the introduction of a Bill to reduce interest to 4 per cent., but the House disagreed. It would be a great mistake to suppose, however, that these enactments were effective. Such expedients only brought the statute law into conflict with economic law, and the latter, happily for the world, is the more powerful of the two.[1] The fact is that when the rate fixed by statute law is less than that which the condition of the market requires, lenders and borrowers are obliged to resort to circuitous devices to evade the law, and as these devices are always attended with more or less trouble and risk, the rate of interest is proportionately enhanced. The law that interest rises as risks increase is only the financial form of the biological principle that the fertility of animals is proportionate to the perils which encompass their lives. Conversely, the low rate on first-class securities is the financial analogue of the law that the power of Regeneration diminishes as organisation advances.

The intermediaries were becoming an important and wealthy class, continuously enhancing the complexity of the financial organism. Smith has the record of Mr. Abbott, Scrivener (quite possibly a bill-broker) in Cornhill, who died, as he tells us, in 1658, " dives et probus."[2] In Hill v. Snow[3] there was a loan of £21 on condition of the payment of £30 at the end of six months if a certain ship returned or if (as was the fact) she failed to start. The action was (wrongly) against the broker, and shows, at all events, the class of business which was being done.

[1] " We lay especial stress upon this point of economic rule, for the reason that not only the resolution under which your Committee acts, but many questions to witnesses, indicated a belief that, for their own selfish ends, certain men, or a group of them, have succeeded in transcending the laws of supply and demand (which operate all over the world) and in establishing new economic laws. We venture to point out that since the beginning of organised industry and commerce, covering more than two centuries in England, France, and Germany, and one hundred years in America, men never yet have succeeded in over-riding economic law." (J. P. Morgan and Co. to the Money-Trust Committee, March, 1913.)
[2] Obituary, p. 47.   [3] 1 Keble, 358, pl. 50. (14 Car. II.)

BACON ON USURY

It is desirable in passing to note the conclusions of one of the most luminous intellects of the age with regard to this question of interest. Bacon in his *Essay on Usury*, after discussing its commodities and discommodities in a manner which was no great credit to his supposed encyclopædic knowledge, goes on to propose a legislative enactment of two separate rates of usury. He desires to see a general rate of 5 per cent., with a complete abolition of any existing penalty for accepting it. " This," he says, " will ease unfortunate borrowers in the country. This will, in good part, raise the price of land, because land purchased at sixteen years' purchase will yield six in the 100 and somewhat more, whereas this rate of interest yields but five. This, by like reason, will encourage and edge industrious and profitable improvements ; because many will rather venture in that kind than take five in the 100, especially having been used to greater profit." Bacon, however, had seen far too much of the world to be ignorant of the impossibility of tempting money from its lair into mercantile risks, for no greater reward than 5 per cent., and therefore he goes on to propose the establishment of what was, in effect, a banking system, although he confessed an utter distrust of banks. All his proposals, in effect, came to no more than a constructive regulation of the rate of interest. If Bacon had been more of an economist and less of a philosopher he would have realised that these expedients would be simply futile, in the presence of the novel financial conditions of the epoch in which he lived. Even so clear-sighted an investigator as Petty seems to have had his doubts about the legitimacy of taking interest where money was lent against ample security and was to be repaid on demand. Mediæval opinion would have justified the interest on the principle of lucrum cessans ; but Petty seems only to have acknowledged damnum emergens or periculum sortis (that is to say, the risk or peril of loss) as valid bases for the exaction of interest. But the sounder view was reinforced, with increasing emphasis, by the needs of a peculiarly helpless class.

The case of the widow and orphan, left with financial resources only, but without skill in trading, or the secured income so easily obtainable in our day, was used with increasing force, like the analogous instance of the fugitive religious leaders in the previous century, as an argument in favour of interest-bearing investment. What, asks the author of the anonymous *Discourse upon Usury* (1692), must those many widows and orphans and several others do " . . . that have nothing but money to live on, and are not in a capacity to manage trades ? They must not lend it for profit, they cannot trade with it. Why, the next thing they must pitch upon is to buy houses or land with it." But such an expedient, the author argued, would have disastrous results. " This will immediately raise houses and lands to excessive prices as to purchase, and, by consequence, to such low rents as will not answer the value of the money, nor give perhaps so much as two or three per cent. improvement." The need of solid and permanent investments must have been specially urgent in the increasing number of cases where money was left to trustees for the ultimate benefit of children, then infants, on the attainment of their majority, interest to be paid for maintenance meanwhile.[1] The solicitude which in our time evolves a statutory definition of the trustee investment, appoints a public trustee, with an advisory committee of specialists to assist him, and sedulously protects all the beneficiaries, could have but little play in an environment like this.[2]

[1] See Glide *v.* Wright, 1 Rep. Ch. 140, as an instance.

[2] Yet in a social system organised on a basis of individualism like ours, there was then, is now, and must be yet for many years, the urgent necessity for trust investments offering a security as nearly absolute as mundane conditions permit. Their absence, or the existence of only a few, tempts disaster on the one hand, or an undue concentration of purchasers on the other. Out of 7000 proprietors of the Bank of England in 1866, 3000 were trustees. Trustee buying when trust investment had only a limited list available, was in some degree responsible for the raising of Consols to 114, though, of course, there were other operative factors also : and trustee selling (in order to exchange into Dominion stocks freshly admitted to the trustee list) was largely the cause of the fall of Consols to 72 in 1913–14.

BEGINNINGS OF BANKING 85

THE PSYCHOLOGICAL FACTOR—THE SENSE OF "CREDIT"

Before we proceed to the consideration of the financial environment whence sprang the Bank of England, there are certain new manifestations, of large importance to the embryo Money Power, which require to be noticed. As the banker-goldsmith interest began to be conscious of its own existence, and as commercial responsibilities widened, very stringent legislation was invoked against the bankrupt—the disturber of the money-mechanism. However elementary a *financial*, as distinguished from a *commercial* system may be, it assuredly tends towards a greater precision, and, consequently, a higher level of business morality. Henry VIII. and Elizabeth wrote the bankrupt down a criminal. Even Porder, who thought that to defraud a usurer was to perpetrate an act which might make the very Devil dance for joy, by a curious paradox of sentiment, denounced the fraudulent bankrupt. Such a one is " worse than a theefe, and ought to die as well as the theefe." The Statute 1 Jac. I. c. 15 declares that " the practices of bankrupts of late are soe secret and soe subtile that they can verie hardelie be founde out or broughte to lighte." But there was a relaxation after the Civil War, and the rest of the bankruptcy legislation of the century shows an appreciation of the fact that a bankruptcy may be the result of misfortune, and not necessarily of roguery. Some of the unrelenting hardness of mediævalism was beginning to wear away.

Simultaneously the enlarged sphere of credit operations rendered a business name more susceptible to the assault of defamation and detraction. The early seventeenth-century merchant was extremely touchy where his credit was concerned. That has always been a tender spot with Englishmen ever since they learnt to manage credit instruments and to conduct their own financial affairs. There could be no better illustration of contemporary sentiment than such a case as this, with its odd jumble of law French, English, and Latin :

" Robert Leycroft declare que il fuit un Merchant & use le trade de merchandize, per le space de 20 ans passe . . . &

que il fuit de bon credit & reputation & ne unque Bankrupt, sed de temps en temps paye duement ses Detts & 15 Jacobi ale al Hamborough de trade come Merchant, & la continue en bon credit & al fine de 6 ans vel eo circiter scilicet en 22 Jac. il revient al Angleterre & continue postea pur use le dit trade & que le Defendant premiss non ignarus falso & malitiose dit del' dit Plaintiff al dit Plaintiff Thou camest a broken Merchant innuendo a Hamborough praedict. al Angleterre, per reason, de que il perde mult profit (& fuit en damnifie al damages de . . . .) Primes tota curia agree, que pur appell un Merchant un broken Merchant, un action sur le Case gist, car est tant, sicome il ad dit, que il fuit bankrupt.[1] "

So in Selby v. Carrier[2] the words " thou art a Bankrupt knave," were held (1615) actionable. Nor would financial opinion, embryonic though it was, tolerate any tampering with the mainsprings of credit. Strype, in recording the efforts of Edward VI. to secure the renewal of maturing loans with the Fuggers, refers to the " humble and gentle words " which the King was " fain to use to his creditors to incline them to defer his payments, and to keep up his credit with them." When Gresham was required practically to force renewals of the loans, he was furious. He writes to the Duke of Northumberland, in August of 1552, that " yt shall be no small grief unto me, that in my tyme, being his Majesty's agent, anny merchant strangers shulld be forssid to forbear their monny agaynst their willes ; wyche matter from hensforthe must be otherwayse foreseen, or else in the end the disonnestye of this matter shall hereafter be wholly layd upon my necke, yff, any thinge shuld chance of your Grace, or my Lord of Pendbrocke, otherwise than well : for that we be all mortall. To be playne with your Grace in this matter, . . . if there be not some other ways takynne for the payment of his Majesty's detts, but to force men from tyme to tyme to prolong yt, I say to you, the end thereof

---

[1] Leycroft v. Dumkin, Sir Wm. Jones's Reports 321.
[2] 1 Rolles, 22. The attempt to move in arrest of judgment, on the ground that the words were not actionable (since " thou art a theevish knave " would not be so), was overruled—pur les parols avantdits l'action gist, pur ces que les parols sont 2 nownes and nul d'eux un adjective !

BEGINNINGS OF BANKING

shall neyther be honnorable nor profitable to his Highness." Thus early can there be traced, in definite shape, that which has now become an overwhelming financial sentiment in favour of the prompt and punctual discharge of obligations.[1]

Further, when there is domestic borrowing from a united and powerful moneyed class, the necessity for royal recognition and acceptance of stricter canons of financial fair play will be the more emphatic. Elizabeth obtained £30,000 from the City in June, 1575. The money was subscribed among the wealthier citizens, and half of it was repaid in little more than a year. But when the Queen discovered in 1577 that certain money entrusted to officials had not reached the creditor for whom it was designed, she issued a proclamation requiring all her creditors to send in immediate particulars of their claims. Mr. Sharpe[2] conjectures that it was in connection with this affair that George Heton was removed from the office of Chamberlain for the City. The expression of the Common Council, removing him pro diversis magnis rebus dictam civitatem et negotia ejusdem tangentibus would fit the circumstances. Towards the end of Elizabeth's reign protests were already going forth in unmistakable language against the legal and quasi-legal devices adopted by the Queen's advisers in matters of finance. In 1596 the City replied with a dignified remonstrance to the demand, by royal letter, for ten new ships. Next year the Lord Mayor ventured to urge that money borrowed for the equipment of the Cadiz expedition had not been repaid. He added—and the incident shows the rising spirit of the money power centred in the City—that the citizens were anxious to "enter into consideration by what authority the said payments were imposed upon them by the Governors and other Ministers of State." So

---

[1] Incidentally, Gresham reminded the Duke that the good credit upon which the King had hitherto stood possessed a distinct pecuniary value for him, since he had been able to borrow at 14 per cent. whereas the Emperor was forced to offer 16 per cent. "and yet no monny to be gotten." Gresham got ¼ per cent. commission on the loans which he raised.

[2] *London and the Kingdom*, Vol. I. p. 519.

again, in November, 1641, Parliament asked for an advance of £50,000 from the City at 8 per cent. But financial opinion was united and ripe, and the City took up a very firm attitude. It would find the money, but it required, as one condition, that members of both Houses should cease granting their servants " protections " against creditors—a proceeding which could not fail to excite the ire of a commercial fraternity, fast ripening into a financial community.[1] The same wholesome sentiment was spreading on the Continent. When the bills of the Cardinal Archduke, Albert of Austria, were (1596) " returned out of Spain with protest, the cause whereof is not yet certainly known " . . . it " made a foul stir in Andwarpe among the merchants, and will crack his credit shrewdly and undo many negociants."[2]

These are illuminating episodes. They evidence the ripening sense of the inviolability of contract, which was to be the fundamental principle of the modern Stock Exchange : and the vigilant jealousy of a good commercial reputat on, combined with a determination to protect it at all costs, which was to be the ultimate genesis of the accepting house, lending its credit (but not its money) to fertilise the enterprise of the world. The leaven may not be very powerful in these early days. It is, as it were, hidden in " three measures of meal " ; but like its prototype in the ancient parable[3] it is destined to work until the whole is leavened.

RETURN OF THE JEWS

At the psychological moment, as an essential factor of the rapidly evolving financial power (and one of special significance in the City), the Jews began to return to England, after an exile of nearly three hundred and fifty years. Mr. Hall[4] thinks that the Puritan party had Judaistic leanings, and therefore sympathised with the alien, and mainly Jewish, element in its efforts to re-establish itself in this country. Certain it is that the return of the Jewish

[1] Gardiner, *Hist.* 1637–1649, Vol. II. p. 316.
[2] Gilpin to the Earl of Essex, *Cecil MSS.*, Vol. VI. p. 503.
[3] Matthew XIII. *v.* 33.   [4] *Customs*, p. 106.

infusion, so distinctly cosmopolitan in type,[1] introduced precisely the factor which was wanted to stimulate and guide the process already well begun. It was just the ingredient which must otherwise have been lacking. The supremacy of the money markets of the world was still with Holland and Italy, and only the introduction of a cosmopolitan element could have transferred it to London. " The English had not originally, and they have not now, that special liking for dealing and bargaining, nor for the more abstract side of financial business, which is found among the Jews, the Italians, the Greeks, and the Armenians ; trade with them has always taken the form of action rather than of manœuvring and speculative combination. Even now the subtlest financial speculation on the London Stock Exchange is done chiefly by those races which have inherited the same aptitude for trading as the English have for action."[2] According to a contemporary writer," if death

[1] It has been argued (by Bagehot) that in the fact of their dispersion lies the key to the prosperity of the Jewish race. They prosper *because* they are so scattered ; *because*, by acclimatisation in many regions, they have acquired singular elements of variety ; *because* the Jewish race contains within itself the principle of variability, which other nations must seek by intermarriage. Cosmopolitanism as a racial trait shows the way to cosmopolitanism as a financial force.

[2] Marshall, *Principles*, p. 33. The foresight, the finesse, the daring and the manœuvring which are among the most potent and pervasive of the market influences making for sensitiveness and therefore for steadiness (see p. 607) are almost entirely modern forces—especially on the " bear " side. Their activity, even if it had been continuously present, would have been largely cramped (say) in a fourteenth-century market, which was mainly concerned with " bespoke " commodities and with real goods as distinct from choses in action. Where every seller was in direct touch with his buyer, smartness, if it existed then, consisted simply in being early in the market. At Droitwich regraterii solebant emere privatim dum cives fuerunt apud monasterium ut venderent ad lucrandum, ita quid milites de comitatu et ipsi de Wigornia non potuerunt aliquid invenire ad vendendum circa horam primam. (*Select Pleas of the Crown*, Selden Society, I. 89.) Trading transactions of early ages were all of the ordinary mercantile type, and therefore are practically all on the " long " side. The merchant was always a bull, trying to sell again at an enhanced price. It is in the reign of Edward III. that the " bear " transaction—a much more subtly organised effort than that of the " bull "—makes its first timid appearance. The primary instance on record is that of a wool dealer who, being " short " of the commodity, spread a false rumour of war in order to give himself the chance to cover. Banishment was the penalty. It is perhaps fortunate that the device does not in our day receive such drastic punishment. If it did, the occasional large departures of detected " bears " from the City would throw an undue strain upon our railway and steamship organisations.

had not suppressed the Tyrant [i.e. Cromwell] he would have made these Jewes very instrumental to carry on his designs of furnishing Cromwel with vast sums of treasure ; Anthony Fardinando, the great Jew, told me the Jewes were to advance one Million of Money."[1] The Puritan party were keenly alive to the value of finance as a factor in political policy. Ireton believed that only two classes of persons were fit to have any share in the Government—men of landed estates and members of trading corporations.[2] In the retinue of Catherine of Braganza, bride of Charles II., came a number of Jewish financiers, among them the brothers Da Sylva, Amsterdam bankers, who were entrusted with the transmission and management of the Queen's dowry. Still later in the century the Jews assisted the movement against the unconstitutional aspirations of James II. The unsigned letters (*circa* 1684) from a spy, in Sir F. Graham's collection,[3] contain the statement that " it is whispered that the Jews in several places and countries have several times made divers overtures to help the Republicans to considerable sums of money to carry on their design," conditionally upon the grant of liberty to " exercise their religion and settle in England," as well as to trade " in what commodities they pleased." Solomon Medina and Suasso, both men of immense wealth, came over with William III. The Jews were apparently excluded from the regulated companies, and therefore, as Cunningham argues,[4] from commerce with the Levant, the Baltic, and Hamburg. The Navigation Act barred them from shipping business. We can easily understand, in these circumstances, why they employed themselves so largely as brokers and intermediaries, augmenting an inherited talent for negotiation which to-day is the mainspring of their immense financial power exercised in every quarter of the globe.[5]

[1] Violet, *Petition Against the Jewes*, p. 7.
[2] Kennedy, *English Taxation*, p. 92.
[3] *Hist. MSS. Comm.*, 7th Rep. App. 401.
[4] *English Industry (Modern)*, p. 327.
[5] See Fraser, *The Conquering Jew* (1915).

BEGINNINGS OF BANKING

THE " MAINSPRING OF FOREIGN POLICY "

So it was that under the guidance of the new finance the City of London was becoming the " mainspring of foreign policy."[1] It was within sight of the time when, as Macaulay said, " a Government, supported and trusted by London, could in a day obtain such pecuniary means as it would have taken months to collect from the rest of the island." It was on the way to that supremacy which is even in our own time acknowledged by the Premier's traditional exposition of current foreign policy at the annual banquet on Lord Mayor's Day. " The amazing growth of English commercial enterprise was due to the fact that the English middle class was enabled, by strong and skilful government, conducted mainly by men sprung from its ranks, to devote to this purpose the energies, resources, daring, and intelligence which were elsewhere absorbed by religious wars or in efforts to maintain despotic authority over rebellious subjects."[2] The tendency towards the increased political power of the monied and commercial class was accentuated by the fact that Government became more costly as civilisation progressed. " The increase of Royal authority, the greater cost incurred in the performance of public tasks, and the more frequent use of money in transactions conjoined in giving higher importance to (public) financial administration."[3] The practice of individual levies, which practically involved a canvass of each capitalist in order to ascertain the extent of his financial capacity, must have become more and more cumbrous and embarrassing as the needs of the Government increased, and some measure of celerity became essential. The increasing aggregation of the control of money in the hands of a single class would be as great a facility to the Statesman and to the community at large as had been the former agglomeration of the feudal responsibilities upon the shoulders of the great tenants-in-chief who had themselves to arrange for the

[1] Pollard, *Political History of England*, Vol. VI. p. 306.
[2] Pollard, op. cit., 307.
[3] Bastable, *Public Finance*, p. 728.

devolution of their liabilities. Only a scrutiny of our modern financial organisation in comparison with its incoherent antecedents can adequately bring this fact home to our comprehension. As Bagehot said : " A citizen of London in Queen Elizabeth's time could not have imagined our state of mind. He would have thought that it was of no use inventing railways (if he could have understood what a railway meant), for you would not have been able to collect the capital with which to make them." There was neither the bank as reservoir of the surplus stores of driving power nor the Stock Exchange as the conduit pipe which conducts them to their most effective field of operation. It follows that the concentration of the custody and management of money in the hands of a professional class, confining themselves exclusively to dealing with it and possessing a special skill in its management, opens a new era in political and social development. " It is a law illustrated by organisations of every kind, that, in proportion as there is to be efficiency, there must be specialisation, both of structure and function."[1] When this specialised class, including, as we have seen, numerous sub-specialisations, becomes, as the years go on, more and more completely absorbed in its single pursuit, and more closely organised for that purpose, its power and influence in the State (as the establishment of the Bank of England will ultimately demonstrate) are bound to be augmented by every broadening of the sphere of its operations, with its consequent enhancement of the thoroughness of their control over the supply of the various forms of money. No sooner have the feudal modes of government gone finally to the melting-pot, no sooner is the traditional spiritual authority weakened than the financial hierarchy, though as yet only in embryo form, begins to take its place, working to the common end of a united cosmopolitan force, subduing and organising the world. Exponents of the older ideals were quick to note the change. As the Duke of Sully said, " This generous body of [French] nobility is brought into comparison with the managers of

[1] Spencer, *Essays*, Vol. III. p. 439.

BEGINNINGS OF BANKING

the revenue, the officers of justice, and the drudges of business." It would have been more accurate to declare, as regards England, that the nation which had been formed in comparative secrecy, shaped and moulded in comparative isolation, was now adolescent, ready to take its part in cosmopolitan rivalry.

So it was that London, as *a* centre (but not for 150 years *the* centre) of cosmopolitan finance, steadily attracted foreign money. Mr. Titus, in the course of the proceedings of the Committee on the Decay of Trade,[1] declared that " a great part of the money used in trade and for the building of London [i.e. after the fire of 1666] is Dutch money." Child denied it, alleging that there was not £10,000 of foreign money in London. But before a Committee of the whole House it was said (though it is not clear by whom) that Bucknell, a leading banker, had above £100,000 in his hands, Meynell above £30,000, Vandeput at one time £60,000, and Dericort " always near £200,000 "—all of it being the money of foreign depositors. It was alleged that these foreign deposits were advanced to merchants at 5, 6, and 7 per cent., at a time when the regular rate for money was 8 per cent. This, if true, would indicate that altruism was then a larger factor in banking practice than is the case in our own time. Dutch merchants, however, denied the truth of these assertions. They said that the greater quantity of money in England was due to " (1) portions given with daughters, and (2) great sums with apprentices, (3) the increase of the Customs, and (4) the rise of rents, and (5) the costly building in London." It is not easy to see how any of these influences could have increased the available supply of money, unless we are to understand that the portions given with daughters and the great sums with apprentices came out of hoards.

[1] 1669, *Hist. MSS. Comm.*, 8th Rep. App. 134.

CHAPTER III

THE SUPREMACY OF THE GOLDSMITH-BANKERS

WHEN the troops had to be disbanded after the Restoration [1660], and money was required to pay them off, "none could supply those occasions," says Clarendon,[1] "but the bankers, which brought the King's ministers first acquainted with them." In that way the embryonic money-power soon reached the dignity of statutory recognition. The recital of the Act 22 and 23 Car. II. c. 3[2] (granting a subsidy for "extraordinary occasions"), asserts that "whereas severall persons, being goldsmiths and others, by taking or borrowing great summes of money and lending out the same againe for extraordinary lucre and proffitt have gained and acquired [unto] themselves the Reputacion and Name of Bankers." The language of the statute is not easily reconcilable with the view expressed by Sir James Scarlett, in a note at the foot of his opinion on the Privilege of the Bank of England 1833 :—[3]

"I apprehend that the term *Bank* was not, at the time of this statute, applied to what is now an ordinary bankers' shop : they were called goldsmiths' shops, and the word *bank* implied a something in the nature of an establishment formed by general subscription or public authority. This is illustrated by the words in the same clause (8 and 9 Will. 3, c. 20, 8, 18)

[1] *Life*, Vol. II. p. 218.
[2] In adjusting the Act to the date the reader should bear in mind that the regnal years of Charles II. are counted from his father's execution in 1649 ; not from his own Restoration in 1660. The Statutes know nothing of the Protectorates, under Oliver and Richard Cromwell, from 1649 to 1660.
[3] App. p. 449 to Report of 1875 Committee on Banks of Issue.

THE GOLDSMITH-BANKERS 95

' *company* or *constitution* ' in the nature of a bank. A private banking establishment was therefore not called a *bank*, but if it consisted of a large number of persons was called a company or *constitution* in the nature of a bank."

But apart from statutory recognition, it is certain that the English goldsmith-bankers were advancing rapidly in power. When Charles I. mortgaged certain huge tracts of land to the City corporation for £300,000, the money was raised among persons described as bankers.[1] Cromwell had an account with "Hore, at the ' Golden Bottle,' Cheapside."[2] Covill, the goldsmith, who died in 1670, was reported to have been " indebted above four hundred thousand pound, and had an estate to satisfie his creditors to a penny, and a very great estate overplus."[3] When Backwell was " ordered abroad on some private score," as Pepys says, in July, 1665, there were fears that in his absence a run on his bank might break it. Sir G. Carteret told Pepys that " the King and the Kingdom must as good as fall with that great man." The Dowager Queen (i.e. the widow of Charles I.) deposited a tally for £2000 with Backwell, in 1663. As the deposit took place in the spring, and the tally was not payable until September, we have here a case of discounting a tally for the production of a readily available fund, upon which the Queen, as a matter of fact, drew her cheques.[4] Backwell usually paid 3½ or 4 per cent. on money at call, 5 per cent. on cash at fourteen days, and 6 per cent. at twenty days ; but in 1666, for reasons suggested by the date, he was paying 5 per cent.

[1] Mayor of London *v*. Bennet, I. Rep. Ch. 24. But the word is in the head-note, which is not necessarily contemporaneous with the case.
[2] Now Hoare's Bank.
[3] Richard Smyth's *Obituary*, p. 88.
[4] Bisschop, *Rise of the London Money Market*, p. 62. Here is a glimpse at contemporary financial circumspection—" Whether it is my best to pu this money out to the East India Company or Alderman Backwell, I leave it to your discretion, as likewise concerning Dulivier's £1000 sterling. I live in expectation to know whether it will be repaid in to you there, or that I must be forced to receive it here of Piatti. I suppose my payments for the buildings are at an end, and that we shall now begin to reimburse ourselves." (Lord Fauconberg to Sir William Turner, *Wombwell MSS., Historical MSS. Commission*, p. 149.)

on money at call and 6 per cent. at fourteen days. Pepys, at the same time, was withdrawing his balance of £3000 in gold from his account with Stokes, the banker ; so that doubtless there was a concurrent strain on Backwell's resources. Backwell had the accounts of the East India Company and of the various goldsmiths. His bank was, in effect, the clearing-house of the Restoration period, and his resources would have to be extensive for the fulfilment of that function. The *Little London Directory* of 1677 enumerates 58 goldsmiths, of whom 38 are in Lombard Street. Sir Josiah Child characterised the money trade in 1689 as "that lazy way of usury by bankeering." Evelyn bore involuntary testimony to the steady growth of the rising Money-Power when he wrote (June 11, 1696) of " Duncombe, not long since a mean goldsmith, having made a purchase of the late Duke of Buckingham's estate at near £90,000," and " being reputed to have as near as much in cash." " Banks and Lotteries," added the diarist, were " every day set up." Duncombe had been warned by the Earl of Shaftesbury of Charles's intended raid on the Exchequer, and had withdrawn his money in time to avoid the calamity which ruined less well-informed financiers. Shaftesbury himself, indeed, had passed the " tip " round. He had taken " all his own money out of the bankers' hands, and warned some of his friends to do the like."[1] This shows the generality of the practice of leaving money with the goldsmiths. The author of the *Discourse upon Usury* incidentally sketched the bankers' business in replying to David Jones's sermon at St. Mary, Woolnoth, in 1692. " The upbraiding Reflexion which David Jones has quoted from Bishop Sanderson, namely, ' That a man should be born for nothing else but to tell out Money and to take in Paper,' is but weakly grounded ; for those are but the Instrumental and Subservient part of their main Business, which is, or may be, the convenient helping and supplying of other Men's Affairs, and getting reasonable Advantage to themselves." As for the safe and conservative character of the methods of the goldsmith-bankers,

[1] Burnet, *History of his Own Time*, 1724, I. p. 306.

THE GOLDSMITH-BANKERS 97

there is the testimony of Pepys, writing in September, 1667. He " had not heard of one citizen of London broke in all this war, this plague, or this fire, or the coming of the enemy among us."

THE RAID ON THE GOLDSMITHS' FUNDS

But within a few years there came an utterly crushing blow. The London merchants, in the earlier years of the century, had deposited their cash at the Tower until £120,000 was seized by Charles I. in 1640, and only repaid after violent protests and prolonged delay. After the Restoration they, as well as an increasing clientele of private depositors, patronised the goldsmith-bankers. The usual practice was for the goldsmith-bankers to deposit their surplus funds with the Exchequer, and to withdraw once a week whatever they needed to meet current engagements. The Exchequer, in effect, stood where the Bank of England stands now, being the bankers' bank. In 1672 Charles II. desired to raise £1,500,000 without the necessity of applying to Parliament. On the suggestion of Sir Thomas Clifford, he filched the money from the Exchequer balances belonging to the goldsmith-bankers. The chief sufferers were Edward Backwell, to the extent of £295,994, John Covill £85,832, John Collier £1784, Joseph Horneby £22,548, John Portman £76,760, George Snell £10,894, Jeremy Snow £59,780, and Bernard Turner £16,275. The total was £1,328,526, the property of some 10,000 depositors.[1] Sums of from £50 to £100 seem, according to Child, to have been favourite amounts of deposit. The huge sum thus appropriated was to be treated as a new debt, on which 6 per cent. was " guaranteed."

" This ' stop of the Exchequer,' " says a modern historian, " was a short-sighted as well as an arbitrary act. It shook the credit of the Government, deranged the

[1] Charles himself, with characteristic and impudent cynicism, said that, " considering the great difficulty which very many of our Loving Subjects (who putt their moneys into the hands of those Goldsmiths and others from whom we received it) doe at present Lye under, almost to their utter ruine for want of their said moneys, We have rather chose out of our princely care and compassion towards Our people, to suffer in Our Affaires than that our loving subjects should want so reasonable a Reliefe."

98   EVOLUTION OF THE MONEY MARKET

business of the capital, and caused infinite distress to the numerous depositors who had entrusted their money to the bankers."[1] No doubt it helped to ripen public sentiment in favour of the establishment of a potent central bank, too big to be attacked or controlled by the monarch. The desirability of establishing such an institution was already a subject of discussion. Yet hoarding, still so unwholesomely prevalent, must have been encouraged and perpetuated by this disastrous episode.[2] It had been giving way before the healthier sentiment ; yet an incident like the robbery of the Exchequer was calculated to put

[1] Lodge, *Political History of England*, 1660–1702, p. 109.

[2] When Macaulay, in a familiar passage, tells us how " in the reign of William old men were still living who could remember the days when there was not a single banking-house in the City of London," he adds that " so late as the time of the Restoration every trader had his own strong box in his own house, and when an acceptance was presented to him told down the crowns and the caroluses on his own counter." Many typical instances can be propounded. When Pope's father retired from business he took with him into retirement a box of gold pieces, from which, as occasion required, he replenished the means of meeting his current domestic expenditure. Richard Smyth, recording the death of the Bishop of Rochester in 1666, says that he died " plenus dierum et numorum "—full of years and coins (*Obituary*, p. 73). Child, in attacking the bankers, argues that before their advent " men that had money were forced often times to let it lie dead by them until they could meet with securities to their minds." Child's point was that the bankers kept money out of land. Sir Dudley North, returning to London in 1680, after many years' residence abroad, was followed about, on 'Change, by goldsmiths begging for the honour of his custom. He was most profoundly irritated by being asked where he kept his money. " Where *should* I keep it," replied he, " but in my own house ? " Pepys writes that in 1663 he had dinner with the Comptroller of the Mint, at the Tower, who told him that there was a vast deal of money hid in the land, as he supposed. This was inferred from the comparatively small amount of money of the older coinages which came in in response to a call, while at the same time there was not any money to be had in the City. According to the arguments placed before Pepys, the hoarded money at this time in England must have run into millions, and he naively adds, " Though I can say nothing in it myself, I do not dispute it." When Henry Balguy died, in 1685, a chest of his was found so tightly packed with guineas that they could only be got out with great difficulty (*Antiquary*, Vol. IV. p. 32). Pepys himself, in 1677, had evidently a hoard of about £1300, upon which he could lay his hands at two hours' warning and send away with his wife in the "night-bag" of the coach. He carried £300 in gold in a money belt (*Diary*, Braybrooke, Vol. IV. p. 216). A " mealman " of Uxbridge left 200 guineas hidden in a hole in the wall and £200 in silver in a box. Nowadays he would have part of it in deposit and current account and would invest the rest. Kendar *v*. Milward, 2 Vern. 440 (1702). The safe deposit was still represented (1692) by a barred chest (frequently of iron), with a strong lock, wherein, said David Jones, the usurer keeps " his God and his Scriptures (his Mammon and his Parchments)."

THE GOLDSMITH-BANKERS

back the hands of the economic clock for fifty years or more. But the establishment of the Bank of England was soon to bring into play another force hostile to hoarding, which is powerfully discouraged by a facility for obtaining credit. It had been inoperative down to the foundation of the Bank of England, because credit was scarce and dear. But, now that the development of modern banking had begun, the existence of credit machinery restricted hoarding in one way just as much as the facilities for placing money on deposit discouraged it in another. As Adam Smith said, " It is not by *augmenting* the capital of a country, but by rendering a greater part of that capital more active and productive than would otherwise be so, that the most judicious operations and banking can increase the industry of the country."

" RUNNING CASH "—THE ORIGIN OF NOTES

The goldsmith-bankers simply carried on deposit banking ; they lent coin, or credit based on coin actually in their possession. In return for the deposit of the various chattels and coins of his customers, the goldsmith gave a list specifying every article or amount deposited. This, so far as the money was concerned, was the " Running Cash Note," and the banker was the man who kept " running cashes." Whenever it was desired to withdraw any part of the deposit, the list was presented and modified accordingly, interest being credited at the same time, where it was due. It has been argued that the Running Cash Note, sometimes known as an " accountable receipt," was never part of the currency in quite the same sense as the Bank of England note in our day. It was rather a mere receipt, issued for any odd sum, and cancelled when the money had been repaid to the customer. Legally, however, the goldsmith's note was ready money, which the receiver of the note should forthwith demand. " He who delivers over the note will not be charged if the goldsmith fail."[1] The disadvantage of the Running Cash Note was the absence of standardisation. The notes were

[1] Tassel *v.* Lewis, Trin. 7 W. 3, 1 Ld. Raym. 743.

100   EVOLUTION OF THE MONEY MARKET

of varying values according to the size of the customer's balance. But by the middle of the eighteenth century the necessity of standardisation had been recognised, and the notes assumed their present form.[1] To some extent the Running Cash Note may have been analogous to a duplicate paying-in slip, such as is in use in our time ; save that the modern banker would not repay money against the mere production of the slip, which he appears to have done against the Running Cash Note.

There is some reason to suppose that these Running Cash Notes were the origin of the modern Promissory Note. As soon as the element of negotiability attached to them, they were a banker's promise to pay a specified sum. The holder of the note had the banker's security for its payment, whereas in the case of an early form of cheque he had—as he has still, in our age of universal cheque currency—nothing better than the depositor's order upon a banker. It was verified to some extent, in those days, by the production of the Depositor's List (called by the Bank of England the Note-Accountable), of the amounts standing to his credit. The Promissory Note was, in fact, a marked cheque, whereas the depositor's cheque itself, verified by the list, was no better proof of an adequate balance than would be afforded by the production of a modern pass-book to a person who had expressed some doubt about the goodness of a cheque offered to him and drawn on the account represented by the pass-book.

[1] Down to 1749 the smallest Bank of England note was £20. A banknote is but an impersonal bill of exchange, drawn for a standardised amount, and enjoying negotiability in an even wider sense than its prototype. In a discount transaction the issue of the bank-notes to the client is, in effect, the splitting of the original bill into multiples, each of which is added to the effective circulation, while the parent bill lies at the bank awaiting maturity. Viewed in its impersonal aspect the bank-note is really a refinement of the bill of exchange. The promise of payment at sight excludes all the legal limitations which may arise in the case of maturity at a fixed term, and the undertaking to pay the bearer sweeps away all possibility of complications arising from endorsements, protests, and recourse. The question of the credit of the issuer of the note can hardly arise, since, at all events in modern times, the existence of the note itself will have brought him into the limelight of the Money Market. Where, as in the £1 notes issued in August, 1914, at the time of the outbreak of war, the credit of the Government is behind the note, its vogue is still more simple and assured, but its essential character remains the same.

THE GOLDSMITH-BANKERS

THE ORIGIN OF THE CHEQUE

But how did the cheque itself originate ? Doubtless the inconvenience was early appreciated of requiring the personal attendance of the depositor and the production of the list whenever any property was withdrawn. Therefore the goldsmith became content to accept an order from the customer for the delivery of specified chattels or money. This, as Dr. Bisschop points out,[1] brought the ordinary cheque system into being. Childs have a cheque drawn upon them as far back as 1684, in the following terms :—

" Bolton, 4th March, 1684. At sight hereof pray pay unto Charles Duncombe, Esq., or order, the Sum of four hundred pounds, and place it to the account of
" Your assured friend,
" WINCHESTER."

This document is within the definition of a cheque in the Bills of Exchange Act.[2] An even earlier instance, dated April 12, 1671, is in the form of a letter requesting the addressee to pay to Phil Marsh or bearer the sum of £489. At the end of 1914 the Institute of Bankers added to its collection a cheque dated August 14, 1675. A facsimile of this document was published in *The Times* of January 5, 1915, and there described as the " oldest cheque in this country." The wording of the cheque is :—

" MR. THOMAS FFOWLES.
" I desire you to pay unto Mr. Samuell Howard or order upon receipt hereof the sums of nine pounds thirteene shillings and six pence and place it to the account of
Yr. servant,

14 Augt. 1675.   EDMOND WARCUPP.
£9. 13. 6.

For Mr. Thomas ffowles, Gouldsmith at his shop betweene the two Temple gates, Fleete-streete."

---

[1] *Rise of the London Money Market*, p. 55.
[2] Section 3 of the Act (45 and 46 Vict. c. 61) gives the definition of a bill as " an unconditional order in writing addressed by one person to another, signed by the person giving it, requiring the person to whom it is addressed to pay on demand, or at a fixed or determinable future time, a sum certain in money, to or to the order of a specified person, or to bearer." Section 73 simply adds that a cheque is a bill drawn on a *banker* and payable on demand.

102 EVOLUTION OF THE MONEY MARKET

On the back appears the following endorsement by the payee:—

"Rcd. in full of this bill the sume of nine pounds thirteen shillings sixpence. SAML. HOWARD."

The Depositor's List was subsequently replaced by a book containing a copy of the account as it stood in the goldsmith's ledger, or else the customer called periodically at the bank to examine the ledger, and to place the words " I allow this account " at the foot of the record of his own transactions. The book with a copy of the account is, of course, our modern pass-book. At the first board meeting of the Bank of England, in 1694, it was resolved, " after debate, that copies of customers' accounts should be kept either in books or on paper of their own." Dr. Bisschop argues that this is evidence of the custom among goldsmiths, since a body of City men who were not banking experts would hardly have ventured upon so startling an innovation. With regard to cheques, there was probably at this time no appreciation of their value as an addition to the currency. Attempts to modify the Bill of Exchange, so as to make it, in effect, into a cheque drawable on any fund in the hands of a custodian, were frustrated by the law courts. In Jenny v. Heale [1] it was held that a document purporting to be a Bill of Exchange drawn on the cashier of a certain company, ordering him to pay certain sums out of the cash of such company, was not a Bill of Exchange at all, " for a Bill of Exchange is not payable out of a particular fund." Cheques were simply a means of saving a customer the trouble of personal attendance at his banker's, recognised neither as a facile mode of achieving the innumerable adjustments of bank balances which are the ultimate outcome of each day's business nor yet as the supremely useful form of currency, destined to predominance over both notes and gold. Further, as Withers says,[2] the extensive use of cheques is " possible only in a community which has reached a high

[1] 8 Mod. 266, Trin. 10 Geo. 1.
[2] *Meaning of Money*, p. 32.

THE GOLDSMITH-BANKERS

stage of economic civilisation, and is also blessed with a high level of general honesty among its members "—and that stage had certainly not been attained in the pre-Bubble age. The earliest *printed* cheques are those of Child's, and are believed to date from 1762.[1] Cheque *books* began to be issued about 1781.

The new system was said, and truly said, to save both labour and money. " Two clerks, seated in one counting-house," remarks Macaulay, " did what, under the old system, must have been done by twenty clerks in twenty different establishments. A goldsmith's note might be transferred ten times in a morning ; and thus a hundred guineas, locked in his safe close to the Exchange, did what would formerly have required a thousand guineas, dispersed through many tills, some on Ludgate Hill, some in Austin Friars, and some in Tower Street."

LEGAL OBSTACLES AND ADJUSTMENTS

These adjustments of the embryo banking system to economic necessity did not proceed altogether uninterrupted by legal obstacles. The practice of payment to bearer was first legally challenged in Sheldon *v.* Hentley,[2] when (in 1680) an action was brought upon an agreement under seal, wherein defendant promised to pay to bearer the sum of £100. Defendant pleaded that the note was void, because not made payable to a specific person. But Jones, J., said that the custom of merchants made the note good, and the court added the ingenious observation that " ' Traditio facit chartam loqui,' and by the delivery he (the maker of the note) expounds the person before meant : as, when a merchant promises to pay to the bearer of the note, anyone that brings the note shall

---

[1] Hilton Price, *London Bankers*, p. 28. Other expedients followed the cheque. About 1770, Herries, a former partner of Coutts's, who had been in business in Holland and in Barcelona, invented the system of circular notes. Herries originally proposed the scheme to his then partner, Thomas Coutts, but, as the latter scouted the idea, its sponsor left the firm and started the business which, originally denominated the London Exchange Banking Company, was ultimately to be known as Herries, Farquhar and Co.

[2] 2 Show. 165.

104   EVOLUTION OF THE MONEY MARKET

be paid."[1] Some laxity of business method seems to have been the real reason of the decision in Horton v. Coggs,[2] that a goldsmith's deposit note, promising to pay £55 to " William Barlow or the Bearer," was too general, " for perhaps the goldsmith before notice by the bearer had paid it to Barlow himself." This, says the learned reporter, was " at the Bar said to be the truth of the case " ; but if that were so there must have been gross negligence on the goldsmith's part in paying away money, hypothecated against the outstanding note, which was, obviously, not in Barlow's possession. At any rate, in Crowley v. Crowther, as quoted by Mansfield in Grant v. Vaughan,[3] it was laid down that " if a bill be payable to A. or bearer, it is like so much money paid to whomsoever the note is given ; that, let what accounts or conditions soever be between the party who gives the note and A., to whom it is given, yet it shall *never affect the bearer*, but he shall have his whole money." The whole interest, added Mansfield (supra, in 1764), " is transferred to the bearer." " So where the Bank Bill is payable to A. or bearer, and A. loses the note, and the stranger who found it transfers it, for valuable consideration, to C., the money being paid to bearer discharges the drawer ; for 'tis the very terms of the note, and by course of trade these notes are looked upon as money for money ; but there is no such course of trade with respect to goods : the Property does not follow the possession, unless in cases where the owner has no mark to know his own again, as in money.[4] Hodges v. Steward[5] even went so far as to lay it down that the mere drawing of a bill made a man a merchant to a sufficient extent to shut out any defence based on the non-averment of his being one.[6] This is negotiability writ

[1] The Antwerp Custom had so decided almost a century earlier—in 1582, to be exact.
[2] 3 Lev. p. 299.
[3] 3 Burr. 1516.
[4] 4 Vin. Ab. 10, on authority of Higgs v. Holliday, Cro. Eliz. 746.
[5] Salkeld I. p. 124.
[6] " Bills of exchange," said Treby, C.J., in Bromwich v. Lloyd (2 Lutw. 1582)—and the remarks are largely true of other negotiable instruments— " were originally between foreigners and merchants trading with the English ; afterwards, when such bills came to be more frequent, when

THE GOLDSMITH-BANKERS

large : but the entire doctrine has undergone a process of still further enlargement, under the influence of the financial community. It might even have been argued, at one time, that the principle had evolved too far and too fast. Bank Post Bills had to be invented in 1738 in order to defeat the numerous robberies of bank-notes which had been taking place. A bank-note, being payable on demand, could always be cashed by the thief who was quick enough to get to the bank before the news of the robbery had been known. But the Bank Post Bill, not being payable until a certain number of days, usually seven after date, gave time for a notification of the robbery to reach the bank so as to prevent payment. The leading decision, which finally stamped all negotiable instruments as exceptions to the rule nemo dat quod non habet, is that in Miller *v.* Race (1791). This was the case[1] of a stolen bank-note, which the bank was compelled to cash for an honest plaintiff, who had given value for it.

BANKING DIFFERENTIATED FROM MONEY-LENDING

Simultaneously, there were other legal adjustments and innovations. As the real nature of banking business became apparent, the distinction between banking and money-lending began to be appreciated and defined. Wilson[2] compared the moderate usurer's (i.e. the banker's) charges to the bite of a flea, whereas the oppressor's exactions were like the bite of a dog. The money-lender, as distinct from the banker, flourished like a green bay tree. An

---

[1] 1 Burr. 452. There is a case before Mansfield on all fours with this in the *Annual Register* for 1764 (Chronicle, p. 111). It ended, moreover, in the same way, with a verdict for the plaintiff, though a special jury had originally found for the defendant.
[2] *Discourse upon Usury,* f. 66 (b).

---

they were allowed between merchants trading in England, and afterwards between any traders whatsoever, and now between any persons, whether trading or not, and therefore the plaintiff need not allege any custom ; for now these bills were of that general use that upon an indebitatus assumpsit [that form of the action of assumpsit ('he undertook '), in which it is alleged of the defendant that, ' being indebted, he undertook ' to pay a debt, evidence of a promise to do so being produced] they may be given in evidence upon the trial." (See the whole question discussed in Goodwin *v.* Robarts L.R. 10 Excheq. p. 337.)

early Restoration pamphlet is devoted to " The Way to be rich, according to the practice of the Great [Hugh] Audley, who begun with two hundred pound in the year 1605, and dyed worth four hundred thousand pound this instant, November, 1662. Rem quocunque modo Rem "—which is the classical way of saying " Get rich honestly if you can, but, anyhow, get rich." Audley's latest biographer (Mr. A. H. Bullen) recognises his real mode of business, and characterises him as money-lender rather than banker. He was " a most heartless bloodsucker " at that—notwithstanding his habit of always having a devotional book at his elbow when he received his wretched clients. David Jones declared that such usurers endeavoured to conceal their identity by describing themselves as gentlemen or yeomen in their bills, bonds, and noverints. In the words of a contemporary critic, the lender to the " poor, needy, or inferior " will cut much deeper than in the case of a loan to the rich—yea, he will " cut his throat." Lands, leases, and plate were taken in pawn to double or treble the value of the loan—or, in modern English, the lender secured himself by a margin of 100 or 200 per cent. The worse the circumstances of the borrower, the higher the interest. In such cases, doubtless, even the goldsmith-banker—albeit more merciful than the professional money-lender—adjusted the bargain to the risk, by adding a constructive insurance premium to the rate of interest.[1] Pepys is confident that Maynell, the goldsmith, will not be allowed to go on making £10,000 a year by lending money at 15 and 20 per cent., " which is a most horrid

[1] The quoted rate of "interest" only approximates to *pure interest* in such cases as that of the yield on consols, where the risk is practically non-existent. In other cases the quoted "interest" rate includes three elements :—
(1) Pure interest.
(2) Premium for incurring the risk of the transaction.
(3) Remuneration for the agencies engaged (e.g. banks, stockbrokers, solicitors, etc.) and for the services they render (e.g. organisation, willingness to wait for their money, etc.).
In the modern money market there are always six rates of interest quotable : (1) The official bank rate ; (2) the bank's discount rate ; (3) the market rate of discount (*a*) for first-class bills and (*b*) for trade bills ; (4) the banker's rate for deposits at long notice ; (5) the banker's rate for deposits at call and seven days' notice.

shame." But the working of the principle of insurance was destined, at no distant date, as we shall see later, to transform the customers of the money-lender into potential clients of the banker by the scientific estimate and elimination of the factor of risk.

Anyhow, the difference between banking and usury was becoming evident to the courts. The equity doctrine (" once a mortgage always a mortgage "), which will not permit a clog upon the Equity of Redemption, is clearly applicable, in a remedial sense, to the unconscionable bargains of a money-lender. The clog represented an insidious instrument of oppression which seems to have been turned to advantage, even against Royal borrowers. Henry VIII., at a time when the annual interest on his foreign borrowings amounted to £40,000, was required, at every renewal of the loan, to purchase jewels or commodities, and sometimes both, as a consideration for deferring the liquidation of the debt.[1] Edward VI. suffered under the same exaction, save that in his case the materials of the " clog " included copper, " gundepowder," and fustians. Equity gradually evolved a repulsion (which steadily gained in authority and acceptance) of the system. Its definite establishment, in a purely financial environment, is curiously, if not significantly, coincident with the emergence of banking as a distinct business, separate from that of the money-lender and the goldsmith. The principle is early traceable in operation upon loan transactions where stocks were the security. Where an Adventure of £1700 in the East India Company had been mortgaged, and had remained unredeemed for fifteen years, the mortgagee attempted to set up the length of time against the plaintiff's title to redeem, but was unsuccessful, and admission to redemption was ordered.[2] The principle appears more definitely in Newcomb v. Bonham (1681),[3] but is even more obviously apparent in Jennings v. Ward,[4] heard in Michaelmas Term, 1705. In this latter case a sum of

[1] Burgon, *Gresham*, Vol. I. p. 68.
[2] Newton v. Langham, II Rep. Ch. 56 (1676).
[3] 1 Vern. p. 7.
[4] 2 Vern. p. 520.

£16,000 had been lent on mortgage at 6 per cent. There was a collateral deed for the conveyance by the borrower to the lender, if the latter thought fit, of ground rents to the value of £16,000, calculated at twenty years' purchase. The Master of the Rolls decreed redemption on payment of principal, interest, and costs, without regard to the collateral agreement, which he set aside as unconscionable. " A man," said he, " shall not have interest for his money and a collateral advantage besides for the loan of it, or clog the redemption with any by-agreement." Lord Henley, in Vernon v. Bethall,[1] laid down the law as it presented itself to him in the shape of an established rule, at a date (1761) almost coeval with the beginnings of the Industrial Revolution. He said : " This court, as a court of conscience, is very jealous of persons taking securities for a loan and converting such securities into purchases. And therefore I take it to be an established rule that a mortgagee can never provide at the time of making the loan for any event or condition on which the equity of redemption shall be discharged, and the conveyance absolute. And there is great reason and justice in this rule, for necessitous men are not, truly speaking, free men, but to answer a present exigency will submit to any terms that the crafty may impose upon them." In our enlightened day, however, this doctrine became a nuisance, as tending to interfere with, and upset, bargains entered into by persons of thoroughly competent understanding, negotiating at arm's length. In Samuel v. Jarrah Timber and Wood Paving Corporation[2] Lord Macnaghten expressed his regret at being bound by the ancient precedents to decide against " a fair bargain " for a collateral advantage, entered into " between men of business without any trace or suspicion of oppression, surprise, or circumvention." Lord Macnaghten added the obvious truism that " the directors of a trading company in search of financial assistance are certainly in a very different position from that of an impecunious landowner in the toils of a crafty money-lender " —which had been one of the abuses against which the

[1] 2 Eden, at p. 113.   [2] 1904 Ap. Cas. at page 325.

THE GOLDSMITH-BANKERS

doctrine was originally directed.[1] The dicta of the law-lords, in 1912,[2] that the ancient equity doctrine has probably no application to floating charges, and the specific provision[3] that perpetual debentures or debenture stock shall not be touched by it, are interesting indications, quite as suggestive as the corresponding liberalisation of the judicial and legislative mind, a century earlier, with regard to limited liability and transferable shares (*post*, pp. 181, 184).

EMPHATIC NECESSITY FOR ORGANISATION

But to return to the goldsmith-bankers and their environment—what the embryo Money Power required, before it could play its proper part in social and political advancement, was *organisation*. Each goldsmith-banker stood by himself, an isolated financial unit. In the aggregate they were a mere indefinite and incoherent congeries which, left without a rallying point, and, consequently, without centralisation, integration, or any sense of common interest and responsibility, could never have made a Money Power. There were indeed the beginnings of a stock market, and the well-defined foundations of the gigantic fabric of joint-stock enterprise. But these isolated, self-sufficing movements, without cohesion, common cause, or scientific method, must have remained ineffective as a national and ultimately a cosmopolitan force unless there had been created a rallying point. Before all things, it was essential that the new finance must integrate and centralise ; for financial evolution must conform, in its own sphere, to the necessities of the concurrent process in biology, which is " an integration of matter and concurrent dissipation of motion, during which the matter passes from an indefinite, incoherent, homogeneity to a definite, coherent, heterogeneity, and during which the retained motion undergoes a

[1] The vague judicial misgiving about perpetuities, which was ultimately to crystallise into the Thellusson Act, may perhaps have been partly originated by the consciousness that through flux and readjustment, rather than through fixity and changelessness, lay the true path of human progress.
[2] De Beers *v.* British South Africa Co., A.C. 52.
[3] Companies Consolidation Act, 1908, s. 103.

parallel transformation."¹ We have already seen, at an earlier stage of this essay, that the differentiation of financial function, with its consequent complexity, which always signals the advance of the organism to a higher stage of development, had become so obvious as to find place and mention even in contemporary Acts of Parliament. We shall see, as we proceed, that the activity of the Money Market is the function of an organic structure, not of a mere unrelated cluster of interests. The credit-evolution, like the entire world-process of which it forms a part, is " a development of organic harmony through the extension of control by Mind operating under mechanical conditions which it comes by degrees to master."² It does not invent the harmony, the unity, and the plan. It discovers them. Ultimately—in this case about the time of the Overend-Gurney crisis—"it finds that they are already there, and have been *among the conditions operating to determine its growth from the earliest stages.* Its own purposeful activity is merely the continued operation of these conditions, completed by the unifying link of the consciousness of their significance." These words, written in no immediate allusion to the Money Market, are yet a most admirable definition of its gradual awakening to purposeful progression. Such postulates point to the necessity of a self-conscious, altruistic, centralising force, endowed with the attribute of unbroken continuity, so as to be aware, in a greater or less degree, of its own power, and capable of accumulating and transmitting stores of experience. When we come to consider the establishment of the Bank of England (*post*, p. 219) we shall see how such a force sprang into existence. Our task, in surveying the financial evolution of the next 200 years, will be largely occupied with the development of its prestige and the growth of its force, originally political and financial, but in our own time mainly moral. In 1694 the time was ripe for the advent of the Bank of England. There might be, and for a century and a half there was to be,

[1] Spencer, *First Principles*, sec. 145.
[2] Hobhouse, *Development and Purpose*, p. 372.

THE GOLDSMITH-BANKERS 111

no formal and considered recognition of the fact of leadership. There might even be (and indeed there was) a jealousy of the earlier predominance, a resentment at the later suzerainty, which only gave way when common peril compelled. Down to the Overend-Gurney crisis the supremacy of the Bank of England was rather an unconscious evolution than a definite project. Orthogenic development was the fortuitous outcome of natural selection. It took a fortunate course, but it was only fortuitous for all that. It is only after the last gleaning in the field of eighteenth-century discount methods that there is a clear, unmistakable, and even eager acceptance of the Threadneedle Street mastership. From the foundation of the Bank of England down to 1866 we shall discern the "drift" of events, and we shall meet with frequent and striking manifestations of the progress towards concentrated financial power : but we shall not be able to call it conscious or deliberate—to declare that finance sees its goal, and is struggling towards it.

It is a very striking and suggestive coincidence that the Newtonian theory of gravitation was forming in the mind of its great exponent at the very time when we can descry, in the shape of nebulous ideals, theories, and efforts, the first signs of the operation of the mighty centripetal and controlling forces which were to give birth to modern finance, even as the nebula evolves into a sun, with his attendant planetary system. The same inexorable tendencies are under observation, whether the investigator be a searcher amid seventeenth-century financial origins, or an astronomer with his telescope turned towards the great nebula in Orion. Cohesion of mass and centralisation of force are the most conspicuous phenomena in both spheres. Collisions and absorptions steadily extend the control by the larger masses—money here and matter there—until an immense central luminary,[1] with an array of attendant satellites, is evolved. Gravitation rules the

[1] It would be a very remarkable thing if (as Jevons and Bagehot believed) there should ultimately prove to be some influence exerted, by the physical controller of our planetary system, upon the pace and mode of financial evolution.

one system, and credit dominates the other. The Select Committee of 1858 actually employed the word "gravitates" in describing the tendency of the bank deposits to be attracted towards London.[1] Ever augmented complexity of structure and motion, combined with an inexorable central control, come to be the characteristics of both. The observer of the development of a central financial power will find in these twin principles the guiding star of all his studies, enabling him to understand why it is that, " as years pass, the influence of finance on ' world politics ' greatly increases."[2]

BANKING AND NOTHING ELSE

. The time was ripe for another specialisation—that is, for the establishment of banking as a separate and distinct undertaking, apart from the goldsmith's business. It was Francis Child, the inheritor of a goldsmith's business which can be traced as far back as 1559, who abandoned the goldsmith's functions, and first launched into banking pure and simple. Down to 1690 the ledgers of the firm show goldsmith's and pawnbroking accounts mixed up with banking transactions. Francis Child's innovation is the more striking because the newly established Bank of England was, almost contemporaneously, advertising its own willingness to lend money upon pawned property. It is a curious fact that the differentiation between the banker and the goldsmith, thus sharply defined by Child, is marked, even in our own day, by the survival of the frequent combination of the goldsmith's and silversmith's business with that of a pawnbroker. In the seventeenth century it would seem that practically every goldsmith was a pawnbroker. But by the end of the century there were in operation the influences which have split what was then the goldsmith's business into three sections, namely, that of the banker pure and simple, that of the goldsmith pure and simple, and the hybrid operations, partly of banking and partly of the craft of the goldsmith, known as pawn-

[1] *Post*, p. 370.
[2] Lord Goschen, Address to the Institute of Bankers, November 5, 1913.

THE GOLDSMITH-BANKERS 113

broking. A case in point is that of a firm still well and honourably known among the London banking houses. In Hartop v. Hoare[1] certain jewels were deposited in a sealed bag, for safe custody, with one Seamer. This man broke open the bag, and took the jewels (1735) to Hoare's Bank, described as an " open shop, where the defendants carried on the business of bankers and also traded in jewels, and frequently lent money on the security of jewels." Hoare's lent £300 on them, taking a promissory note as collateral. When Hoare's refused to deliver the jewels to the true owner, Hartop, he brought a successful action of trover and conversion. We shall see as we proceed that although the example of definite banking specialisation had been set by Child,[2] it was not generally followed for long years afterwards. Country banking especially was combined with other businesses almost to a date within living memory. But complete specialisation was inevitable. Since 1844 "banking has been confined to banking alone."[3]

[1] Atkyns, Vol. III. p. 43.
[2] Pennant calls him the "Father of the Profession" of banking.
[3] Seebohm, 1875 Committee, Q. 4850.

CHAPTER IV

THE BANK OF ENGLAND—EXTENSION OF
BANKING ENTERPRISE

THE scheme of a central State bank had been mooted before it was advocated by William Paterson. As long ago as the first year of Queen Elizabeth John Yonge had written a *Discourse for a Bancke of Money to be established for the Relief of the Common Necessitie.* There is among the Harleian MSS., No. 600, p. 38, a scheme relating to plans for meeting " the devices that doe fall the Exchange and keepe it farre too lowe, to the great and intollerable losse of the whole Realme of Englande." The most interesting of these remedies is the third, which suggests the desirability that " the Queen's highness should have a bank of money of £10,000 or moare in her factores hande at Antwerpe." Bacon's vague proposals have already been mentioned. Samuel Lamb (or, as Thorold Rogers says, John Lambe) had twice during the later years of the Protectorate endeavoured to persuade Cromwell to establish a national bank, but he was unsuccessful. Paterson, in the course of his *Brief Account of the Intended Bank of England,* alludes to still another scheme. Writing in 1694, he tells us that

" it was proposed some years ago that a publick transferrable Fund of Interest should be established by Parliament, and made convenient for the Receipts and Payments in and about the Cities of London and Westminster, and to constitute a Society of Money'd Men for the government thereof, who should be induced by their Interests to exchange for money the Assignments upon the Fund at every demand. In this manner it was proposed that the constitution of this Fund should in the practice answer the end of a publick transferrable

EXTENSION OF BANKING 115

Fund of Interest, of a Bank, and of a Publick Lumbard at once, and a good part of the effects of the Nation might thereby be render'd useful to the Trade and Business thereof, which would of course have lowered the Interest of Money, and prevented the drawing thereof, from the Countries and places remote from Trade."

The sum of £1,200,000 required to start the Bank was subscribed in a few hours. The charter was for eleven years from July 27, 1694. Dutch capital, as was natural, both for political and financial reasons, supported the experiment. By 5 and 6 Wm. and Mary, c. 20, no person or body corporate was to subscribe more than £20,000, and 25 per cent. was to be paid on application. The Bank was not to borrow beyond the amount of its paid-up capital of £1,200,000, except upon Parliament Funds. If this provision were disobeyed, aggrieved creditors might sue individual shareholders. If the Bank advanced any money whatever to the Crown without the special permission of Parliament, it was to forfeit treble the value of such advances.[1] The Corporation was forbidden to trade " to the intent that theire Majesties' subjects may not be oppressed by the said Corporation by their monopolising[2] or ingrosseing any sort of Goods, Wares, or Merchandises " ; but there was an exception in favour of gold and silver bullion and any goods *bona fide* deposited as security for advances by the Bank. The Bank, very appropriately, commenced operations in the Mercers' Chapel,[3] and thus might almost be said to have established a continuity between itself and the ancient trading company which dated from the days of Thomas à Becket. Only 60 per cent. of the original capital of £1,200,000 was called up ; but the balance was requisitioned in 1696 and 1697, in order to enable the Bank to meet its notes. The Bank, as a matter of fact, originally borrowed the amount of the first call

---

[1] This stipulation, in less than a century, as we shall see, brought the directors into conflict with Pitt.

[2] In 1708, the Bank was accused of having financed a corner in coffee, raising it to ten times the former price.

[3] The corner-stone of the historic Threadneedle Street building was laid on August 3, 1732, and the removal from Grocers' Hall to the new premises took place on June 5, 1734.

from its shareholders, and repaid the money out of the proceeds of the formal call, when it was made, at a little later date.[1] The analysis of the full significance of the establishment of the Bank of England may advantageously be postponed until the other financial factors have been marshalled. (See *post*, chap. vii.)

RISE OF PROVINCIAL BANKING

While the goldsmith-bankers of London were slowly being transformed into bankers only, provincial banking arose. The origin of banking was for almost any shopkeeper in a little town to become the banker of the district . . . and it has only been in the course of generations that those shopkeepers have grown into bankers.[2] The process was one of specialisation, luminously illustrated in the early history of the firm which afterwards became Smith, Payne and Smiths. The original founder of the business, in the later years of the seventeenth century (about 1688, to be exact), was a draper at Nottingham, with whom his bucolic customers from the surrounding country frequently discussed the danger of the roads. The neighbourhood was infested with footpads, and the farmers feared for the proceeds of their stock sales in Nottingham market. Smith offered to take charge of their money, to keep an account of their transactions, and to be ready, with the cash, or with goods for the value thereof,[3] at any time—just as his London prototypes had done when City traders dreaded the dishonest and fugitive apprentice. Considerable sums began to flow into the hands of the shrewd tradesman. He

---

[1] The Bank of Scotland was established in the following year, and Irish banking began to develop early in the eighteenth century. In fact Burton and Harrison appear to have been established in 1700, though the Bank of Ireland itself was not started till 1753.

[2] Seebohm, 1875 Committee, R. 4850.

[3] " This deponent acts in the nature of a Banker and returnes great sums of money to London and from thence and diverse other places in this Kingdom and also for several years past, and his father many years before him, hath used to take in and receive great sums of money of diverse persons, and upon receipt to give notes under his hand for the same, thereby promising to pay that said sum so received to the person authorised in the money or the Bearer of the note upon demand." (Thomas Smith, Nottingham, before a Commission of Inquiry, 1711. Quoted by Easton, *Banks and Banking*, p. 191.).

EXTENSION OF BANKING

became known[1] as a man who would discount a good bill anywhere in Notts or Lancashire. The profits were so sure and the returns so quick that Smith found it worth his while to attract larger supplies by offering interest to his agricultural clientèle. Then the inevitable happened. He saw, as Child had seen before him in London, that it would pay to specialise in banking, instead of in drapery, and became a regular money-dealer.[2] He never went beyond Nottingham as a centre of operations, but his successor extended the business to Hull and Lincoln, while " Smith the Third " entered into co-operation, and eventually into partnership, with a London financier named Payne. The ultimate upshot is suggested by the mere collocation of the names of Smith and Payne.

Provincial banking obviously arose, then, in humble fashion, almost precisely at the date—1740—fixed[3] as the beginning of modern history and the conclusion of the process of decay which ended mediævalism. If this be really the beginning of modern history, then it actually coincides with the commencement of the process of bringing banking facilities within every man's reach, for Burke has left it on record that when he first came to England, in 1750, there were not 12 bankers' shops out of London.[4] They are now [1796], he proceeds, " in almost every market town." One of the original 12 was doubtless Wood's Bank, at Gloucester, dating from 1716, which had originally been a candle-shop; where the banking was carried side by side with the sale of bacon, cheese, packthread, and marbles; another was the Bristol Old Bank, a third was Smith's, at Nottingham, and a fourth a Derby institution, " kept by a Jew."[5] In 1754 there were only two London banks west of Temple Bar.[6] An Irish banking firm, established in 1758, accepted

[1] Martin, *Stories of Banks and Bankers*.
[2] There exists a cheque drawn on Smith dated 1705. (Sykes' note to Gilbart, Vol. I. p. 152.)
[3] By Bluntschli, *Theory of the State*, p. 55.
[4] Regicide Peace, *Works*, Vol. V. p. 291.
[5] Evans, *Chronological Outlines of Bristol*. Quoted in *Manchester Banks and Bankers*, p. 2.
[6] *Memoirs of a Banking House*, p. 13.

deposits at seven days' notice to any account at 10d. per week per cent., the money being employed in advances at 5 per cent. But the experiment only lasted four months. There were no country banks in Scotland. Bills for the imports and exports of Perth, Dundee, Montrose, Aberdeen, and other trading towns were all negotiated in Edinburgh.[1] This apparent Scottish backwardness in the development of a species of enterprise in which Scotsmen are now pre-eminently distinguished and successful may possibly have been the result of over-caution. The early Scottish banks had to lodge with the Town Clerk of the place where the bank was established, a personal bond for the due payment of the notes. In June, 1760, in the Scottish case of Trotter v. Cochrane, the Lord President and Lord Coalston expressed their dread of paper credit and their fear that banks were dangerous institutions.[2] Adam Smith had to admit that "many people had been much alarmed" by "the late multiplication of banking companies in both parts of the united kingdom."[3] As late as 1803 the three public banks of Edinburgh had but 33 branches throughout the country. As for England, however, there had, long before that time, been a rapid increase in the number of the country banks. In 1776 there were 150, and in 1790 about 350. About 100 of these disappeared in the crisis of 1792.

Burke's declaration, in 1796, that there were banks in "almost every market town," was confirmed by Mr. John Tritton, of Barclay and Co., who told the Bullion Committee, in 1810, that there were 230 country banks in the year 1797; he added that in 1808 the number was over 600, and at the actual time when he was speaking he understood there were 721. His own firm, he said, kept the accounts of several country bankers, and their transactions had much increased within the last few years. Mr. Vincent Stuckey told the Committee[4] that there had been a very considerable increase in the number of country bankers in

[1] *Memoirs of a Banking House*, p. 3.
[2] *Scotsman*, April 5, 1826.
[3] *Wealth of Nations* (Cannan), Vol. I. p. 312.
[4] *Minutes*, p. 211.

EXTENSION OF BANKING

the west of England.[1] He went on to say[2] that the circulation of Bank of England notes in the west was very small, adding the curious reason that the people there generally preferred the notes of country bankers, "whom they conceived to be men of responsibility in the country." They had qualms about the Bank of England. Such an utterance as this shows clearly enough that if financial centralisation was proceeding steadily, financial education was lagging far behind it, though, of course, it was slowly permeating provincial opinion with the leaven of the coming financial era.

OTHER MODES OF COUNTRY-BANKING ORIGIN

There was, no doubt, another concomitant mode of origin (as Dr. Bisschop ingeniously suggests) besides that which produced Smith, Payne and Smiths and the other provincial firms. Country merchants who had business relations with London would find it extremely convenient to keep an account with a London bank. Their business associates who did not possess the same facilities would, no doubt, occasionally request the use of these London accounts for the purpose of carrying out some transaction of their own. As these requests increased in number, it would occur to the merchant that he might as well put the transactions on a business basis.[3] The next step would be the transformation of his London account from that of a mere merchant to that of a banker. It only remained for

---

[1] Conversely, there was only one firm of bullion dealers (Messrs. Mocatta and Goldsmid) at this time. Apparently, they had a practical monopoly of bullion dealings, since the clerk in charge of the Bullion Office in the Bank of England, at the time of the Bullion Committee, thought that no other broker would be permitted to act with respect to bullion at the Bank of England without orders from the Court of Directors. At this time the law forbade the export of gold coin, unless an oath were taken that it had not been produced in the melting pot from the coin of this realm. It was stated before the Committee that "the restoration of the Exchange used to be effected by the clandestine transmission of guineas, which improved it for the moment by serving as a remittance."

[2] p. 212.

[3] Mr. Maberley Phillips has conjectured that these trade bankers ultimately excited the jealousy of the London bankers, who sent down junior members of their firms to combine with local gentlemen and start new provincial banks. This, if the conjecture be sound, points to still another mode of origin.

the merchant to decide which of his activities was the more congenial and profitable, and where he elected in favour of the banking, he naturally parted company with the other portion of his commitments. When the two classes of business became separated a new country bank had been evolved and a fresh stimulus given to the concentration of money business in London. The private banker thus became, in a very real sense, a kind of unofficial cashier of his customer, and would very soon learn what were his customer's requirements in the matter of till-money, just as an official cashier would acquire the same knowledge with regard to his employer's habits and the financial needs, from day to day, of his business. Such a merchant and banker would probably also provide himself with the means of safe custody for his own and his friends' funds. Then, following the example of the sixteenth-century bankers, whose methods have been the subject of an earlier analysis, he began to employ the deposited funds in his own business. This seems actually to have occurred in the case of Ralph Carr, a merchant at Newcastle-on-Tyne, who, in 1745, found the gold with which the Duke of Cumberland paid his troops on their northward march to Culloden. This brought Carr into relationship with Coutts of Edinburgh and Campbell of London, and ten years later he blossomed out as a banker himself. In 1758 the business had so far prospered as to justify the partners in a resolution that " the sums of money advanced by us on notes and accepted bills are found insufficient to employ the cash in our hands," and therefore " we have agreed that any sums of money not exceeding £7000 be lent out."[1]

NEW SOCIAL INFLUENCES

From our present point of view, the spread of country banking meant the introduction of two sound influences, both of primary importance. It altered the state of affairs existing when, " save in a rare moment of national crisis, the horizon of peasant and yeoman, parson and squire, was bounded by cattle fairs and quarter sessions, the

[1] *Maberley Phillips*, p. 179.

EXTENSION OF BANKING

land-tax, and the price of corn."[1] It involved a widespread diffusion of financial facilities, which was bound to stimulate social and commercial development, and to draw money out of hoards into useful activity.[2] Trade became more ambitious under the stimulus of organised, if amateurish, finance. The regulated companies had kept business within defined lines, so that there was little inducement to borrow capital for the use of which no special opportunities existed. So, again, in the pre-Tudor period, the great proportion of the embryo manufacturing businesses had been worked under the bespoke system. Goods were not made till they were wanted. There was no conception of the modern mode of making the goods, and then forcing a demand for them by practically artificial means. But after the formation of the Bank of England the speculative element became much more prominent in commercial affairs. Increased facilities for borrowing money, an expanded currency, and a quicker circulation of it, all tended to stimulate speculative activity, not only on the Exchange, but in the ordinary transactions of a commerce previously conducted on routine lines. As money, managed by the bankers, became more mobile, it could be shifted with comparative rapidity to the point of more urgent demand. Seventeenth-century capitalism was largely local. Yorkshire industries were behind those more favoured regions because the West Riding had no capital of its own, and the means of attracting and transmitting it from wealthier districts did not exist. In the eighteenth century the conditions began to change, and in the twentieth the superfluous resources of one of the great banks can be moved from point to point practically instantaneously, so that a slack demand for money in East Anglia is counterbalanced by abnormal exigencies elsewhere, with the resulting profitable use of

[1] Veitch, *Empire and Democracy*, VII.
[2] The same magnetic force becomes operative in other lands as they advance towards the corresponding state of development. Mr. Kennan has pointed out that the Chinaman will entrust his money at low interest to foreign banks, of whose probity he is assured, rather than to the sponsors of native enterprises, which are simply machines for systematic misappropriation.

funds otherwise idle.[1] This process would be encouraged and stimulated at every point when, about the year 1760, the north of England began to be a great industrial centre, with a consequent incessant demand for capital.[2] From this time onwards trading on borrowed capital may be said to have been popularised, with a resulting huge increase in the potentiality of the aggregated and relatively well-distributed capital resources of the country. Industry as a whole became more dependent upon capital as it grew more complex in character. It required larger stores of capital to initiate an undertaking than had been the case in the pre-machinery era. The north developed rapidly as capital provided transport, and in turn accelerated the pace of evolution by stimulating industries with the supply of fuel. The improved transport system was as yet only the canal. But as the canal between Worsley and Manchester, e.g. reduced the cost of coal from 7d. to $3\frac{1}{2}$d. the cwt., the promotion of the Canal Acts between 1790 and 1794 need not astonish us, though it demonstrates how extensive, and how readily available, the supplies of capital were becoming. The spinning jenny, the mule, the later power-looms, and other devices tended to the concentration of the carding and spinning of wool in factories around which villages and towns grew up, and the process was again emphasised and consolidated when water power gave place to steam, during the last ten years of the eighteenth century. The cotton industry became concentrated as the woollen trade had done. As the increased population caused more urgent and larger demands for food, every effort was made to meet the

[1] See page 440 for a more extensive treatment of this topic.
[2] Observe, for instance, the interaction of bank and industry upon each other. Jones and Co. of Manchester, " Bankers and Tea Dealers," *Manchester Directory*, 1772, drew on Vere Sapte and Co. in London. But the Industrial Revolution brought a huge expansion in Manchester business, and Vere Sapte and Co. became alarmed at the magnitude of their commitments. They requested Jones and Co. to remove their account. Joseph Jones therefore went to London and established Joseph Jones and Co. at 17 Watling Street. Miss Sarah Jones married Lewis Loyd, and the firm became Jones, Loyd and Co. From the marriage sprang an only child—Samuel Jones Loyd, later Lord Overstone. From the firm itself was evolved the huge business ultimately absorbed in 1864 by the London and Westminster.

EXTENSION OF BANKING 123

changed conditions, by encouraging the home growth of wheat, by improving agriculture, and by the scientific breeding of animals. Capital devoted itself energetically to those purposes, in the effort to meet the changed conditions which it had itself created in the development of manufacturing. By the end of the eighteenth century practically the whole employing class had come to depend on borrowed capital; and it is a financial paradox that the man trading on borrowed capital can do so on better terms than he who works with his own.[1]

EIGHTEENTH-CENTURY BANKING EMPIRICISM

The eighteenth century—using that term, for the moment, to describe the period from the establishment of the Bank of England to the battle of Waterloo—proved to be ill-equipped for its banking enterprises, especially in the provinces. There was no banking science. Its elements had to be learned in the school of experience, at the inevitable heavy expense. It was recalled, at the time of the Bullion Committee, that even the directors of the Bank of England did not at once obtain a very accurate knowledge of all the principles by which such an institution must be conducted. They lent money not only on discount, but upon real securities, mortgages, and even pledges of commodities not perishable. Lottery tickets were a recognised bankers' security to such an extent that in 1751 it has been said that there were 30,000 on pledge with London bankers.[2] Other less eminent practitioners lent on farm mortgages, sank money in

[1] A classic instance is that of Bagehot, who says : " If a merchant have £50,000 all his own, to gain 10 per cent. on it he must make £5000 a year, and must charge for his goods accordingly; but if another has only £10,000, and borrows £40,000 by discounts (no extreme instance in our modern trade), he has the same capital of £50,000 to use, and can sell much cheaper. If the rate at which he borrows be 5 per cent. he will have to pay £2000 a year, and if, like the old trader, he make £5000 a year, he will still, after paying his interest, obtain £3000 a year, or 30 per cent., on his own £10,000. As most merchants are content with much less than 30 per cent., he will be able, if he wishes, to forego some of that profit, lower the price of the commodity, and drive the old-fashioned trader—the man who trades on his own capital—out of the market."

[2] See, for instance, Warner v. Jenkins (4 Vin. Ab. 6), where the transactions ran into thousands of pounds.

factories and machinery, and even financed the construction of canals—none of these undertakings being legitimate arenas of banking enterprise. The lending of money on farm mortgages for agricultural improvement was the principal cause of the failure of 240 country banks in 1814, 1815, and 1816. Experience had to be gained by many a bitter lesson. The bankers had to be taught to narrow down the individual risks which are essential to the making of their profits, so that no economic hurricane shall find the broad surface of a huge individual hazard, and be able to use its leverage for the overthrow of the larger entity. They had to learn that a banker is one thing and a partner another, and that the banker who lends money to finance a going concern, or upon a wasting asset, may find himself playing the less attractive rôle. whether he likes it or not, and without the chance of resuming his original character. Dead loans were as dangerous then as now, but far more frequent. The new country bankers did not fully understand that short capital, in the shape of notes, cannot be lent against long capital, such as long-dated bills, machinery, and canal shares—that short-dated notes or bills, once more, cannot be safely advanced against real property[1] and unsaleable interests in commercial undertakings. Douglas Heron and Co. issued notes without limit, and discounted practically anything that was offered. When difficulties arose, its leading shareholders, like the Dukes of Queensberry and Buccleuch, tried in vain to induce the Bank of England to add to the £150,000 of the tottering firm's paper which it already held. When the crash came the firm had over £801,000 of paper in circulation. Nor was the amount of circulation the most sinister of the operative factors. When, worse still, money had to be recalled, by way of preparation for stringency, the very fact of its being locked up in unrealisable assets tended to increase the stress. The early bankers—town

---

[1] By the end of the eighteenth century it is only fair to say that the country bankers, in some cases, had begun to grow wiser ; for Mr. Thomas Thompson told the Bullion Committee (*Minutes*, p. 163) that country bankers did not make advances on real security and he thought it would be extremely imprudent to do so.

EXTENSION OF BANKING

and country alike—did not appreciate the danger of filling their portfolios with purely local paper, good enough in its own domicile, no doubt, but not available in any larger arena. As Baring said in 1826, when the country bankers were getting their funds in, " they were doing so by screwing almost to destruction every farmer, manufacturer, and other customer in the country from whom they could get their money." The precarious state of some of the banks is amply evidenced by the caution, dating from about the middle of the eighteenth century,[1] to get a draft paid as quickly as possible lest the banker shall have stopped payment in the meantime. Such a state of things was doubtless exceptional. As a class, bankers were reputed wealthy and powerful. When Prescott complained in the House of Commons (1774) about the " late regulation of the gold coin " and the resulting losses to bankers, " Lord North laughed, and made the House laugh, at him, by saying he was glad the loss had fallen on those who were the best able to bear it."[2]

NOTE-ISSUE COMPLICATIONS

The note-issues demand, perhaps, a rather more extended treatment. The adolescent banking fraternity did not realise with sufficient vividness the primary necessity of keeping an adequate metallic reserve against their note-issues. They scattered the notes in their own district and sent the guineas to London with the result that when public disquietude began to disturb their locality they were hindered, both by the elementary conditions of transport and by the position of affairs in London itself, in their attempt to hurry money down to the provinces to meet the demands upon them. In the earnest endeavour to exclude this source of complication the Scotch banks discouraged, and, in effect, suspended, the convertibility of their notes by inserting in them an option between payment at sight or payment six months after sight, with interest. The notes

---
[1] Quoted by Poley and Gould, *History, Law and Practice of the Stock Exchange*, p. 9.
[2] Horace Walpole, *George III.*, Vol. I. p. 295.

K

stated that the Bank would pay " the Bearer on demand £1 sterling or, in the option of the said company, £1 0s. 6d. sterling at the end of six months after the day of demand." Such notes became depreciated in comparison with specie, so as to produce the extraordinary financial abnormality of the exchange between London and Dumfries being 4 per cent. against Dumfries, while the exchange between London and Carlisle, which is not 30 miles from Dumfries, was at par. As regards the larger notes, however, the effect of their issue in the provinces, combined with the remittance of specie to London, was to accentuate the concentration of the reserve in the hands of the Bank of England. The provincial banker then, as now, depended upon London, and London upon the Bank of England. The only difference was that in the eighteenth century the London banker was a private firm, distinct from the country client, whereas it is nowadays simply the head office of a large institution, whereof the provincial bank is a branch. In those days, moreover, the holder looked to the credit of the banker, whereas in our own time, the holder of a cheque looks to the credit of the drawer. Personal knowledge of the customer's position and business induced the eighteenth-century banker to make him a loan in the shape of notes which on the strength of the banker's name gained the currency that would have been denied to cheques signed by the borrower. Moreover, the cheques, supposing them to have existed, would have come back upon the banker, draining away his specie in their payment, whereas the notes stayed out, and in that way served the precise purpose which the Government had in view in permitting their circulation, namely that of subsidising the banker in return for the facilities which he provided. But as the specie was concentrated in London, the difference was only one of detail, since the ultimate dependence was upon the Bank of England just the same. Sinclair vainly urged Pitt to compel bankers to find and exhibit securities for the notes which they issued.[1] The refusal of the Bank of

[1] *Correspondence of Sir J. Sinclair*, I. 87.

EXTENSION OF BANKING

England to open branches was another influence operating to make banking local as distinct from national in its character. There was no sound system of distributing credit facilities from point to point, or of meeting the scarcity of credit in one part of the country by utilising a surplus from another—and this although human betterment depends as much upon the mobility of money as upon the mobility of men. We shall see as we proceed how impossible it would have been to establish a science of banking or to achieve the effective distribution of credit facilities without the modern system of branch banks centred in London. Further, any person, however impecunious, could start a " bank " and (down to 1775 at all events) issue notes purporting to be payable on demand. Every grocer, draper, tailor, and haberdasher who chose might flood the country with his " miserable rags." All this small paper currency was originally abolished in 1775 (15 Geo. III. c. 31). The preamble of the Act gives a vivid picture of the existing conditions :—

" Whereas various notes, bills of exchange, and draughts for very small sums have for some time past been circulated or negotiated in lieu of cash within that part of Great Britain called England, to the great prejudice of trade and public credit, and many of such bills and draughts being payable under certain restrictions, which the poorer sort of manufacturers [i.e. hand workers : the word had not yet reached its modern sense], artificers, labourers, and others cannot comply with, otherwise than by being subject to great extortion and abuse ; be it therefore enacted that all promissory or other notes, bills of exchange, or draughts or undertakings in writing for the payment of any sum or sums in money less than the sum of 20s. in the whole which shall be made or issued at any time from and after June 24, 1775, shall be, and the same are hereby declared to be, absolutely void."

An Act of 1777 abolished all notes under £5. When specie payments were suspended in the later years of the great war the £1 notes were temporarily allowed until 1829, when there was a re-abolition of notes under £5. Since then, until the recent crisis, they have been illegal in England.

Once more, the necessity of specialisation in banking and banking only had not yet won its way to full recognition. Coutts's, like other Scottish houses, took to banking as an auxiliary to corn, wine, lead, and fish-dealing, and continued to supply correspondents with the commodities of the grocer and the oilman long after their financial interests were dominant over other departments of their undertaking.[1] The Baring firm originated in the same way. John and Francis Baring were importers of woollen and dyed stuffs, and when the elder brother retired from the firm, Francis wound up its affairs, and began to devote himself exclusively to banking business. Twinings combined tea-dealing with banking. The tea-dealing still remains, but the banking part of the business has been bought by Lloyds Bank. Cloth-dealing, drapery, and insurance-broking and commission agency were other businesses which formed the foundation of later banking houses. Now and then, under the stress of temptation, they adventured again into other enterprises—lead-mining, paper-making, brandy, hops, rice, and tobacco, for instance, as well as the linen business (as is shown by the name of the British Linen Company Bank)—but the disastrous results of one or two speculations of this kind gave a wholesome check to the tendency. Zachary-Long and Haldimand (now Morris, Prevost and Co.) combined exchange operations with "the sale of Piedmontese and Italian silks." In 1765 "Notre comerce embrassera tout objet de change, Vente & Achats de marchandises."[2] It is not till nearly the end of the eighteenth century that we see the last of the goldsmith-bankers. Till then the combined business constantly crops up in the legal and financial records. Pennant records[3] the fact that there were bankers who kept goldsmiths' shops as late as the year 1790 ; but, he adds, "they were more frequently separated." "Banking *only*," as an article of the banker's faith, comes half a century later.

[1] *Memoirs of a Banking House*, Intro.
[2] *History of Morris, Prevost and Co.*, privately printed.
[3] *London*, p. 390.

THE BANKER AS SPECULATOR

Again, the untrained bankers regularly speculated in the market, that being a recognised device for the enhancement of their profits. A bank as an operator in the speculative markets is almost unthinkable nowadays. It was the regular thing then. The Dundee Banking Co. lost £2,140 in 1810 by jobbing in Consols and Navy Five per Cents. Its losses from the same source in 1811 were £6,228, and in 1812 £10,044; but the tide turned in 1813, and there were profits of £13,200 from Consols and £11,056 from Navy Fives.[1] As long as these operations went on the balance-sheet was adjusted annually by debiting each proprietor's capital with the due proportion of the loss, or crediting it with a corresponding share of the profit.

BANKING AS AN "OPEN" PROFESSION

Not the least potent of the many sinister influences lay in the fact that the banking profession was open to everybody, however irresponsible and incapable. As late as 1826 it was possible for Lord Liverpool to say that the law permitted any shopkeeper, however limited his means, to establish a bank. But, added he, "to persons of capital willing to engage in a similar undertaking the law said, 'Your company shall not consist of more than six persons.'" The "effect of the law at present is to permit every description of banking, except that which is solid and secure."[2] Herbert Spencer even went so far as to say that, from the first, modern banking legislation had been "an organised injustice."[3] Such conditions were not likely to "throw up a sound and solid system without the

---

[1] This tendency to speculation with the funds of bankers has persisted wherever there has been no concentrated control strong enough to put a stop to it. Although the creation of such an authority has gone far in Germany, it may be recalled that as recently as the year 1911 investigation into the affairs of two well-known German banks showed that speculation had been going on to a considerable extent, that one of the banks had lent money on its own shares, even allowing its own officials who were the holders of these shares to employ them as security for advances from its own funds. See also *post*, p. 234.

[2] Letter from Lord Liverpool to the Governor of the Bank of England, January 13, 1826.

[3] *Essays*, Vol. III. p. 335.

prelude of many errors and misfortunes." Many of the eighteenth-century bankers doubtless failed to discover the necessity of liquidity or the meaning of margin until the advent of a contingency in which the knowledge was useless to them. One of their later apologists was fain to admit in the House of Commons, that " in a body of 700 persons [the country bankers, not the House itself] there might be some fools and some knaves." It was less foolery and knavery than sheer inexperience, in an age when experience of the sort required was almost unobtainable, that disturbed early provincial banking. Moreover (and we shall consider the fact in greater detail later), each of the private bankers was " on his own." There was no unity of principle or of practice. The idea of a common cause arising out of a common responsibility, though it had been grasped, and was acted upon in the presence of a common peril, had not developed as fully as the necessities of the case demanded. Since banking is a science, its methods must be standardised, and standardisation can only be effected where there is a central authority capable of defining and enforcing its terms. Therein, as we shall most plainly see at a later stage, banking and biology enunciate the same law. " Suppose every separate cell left free to follow its own ' interests ' and *laissez faire* Lord of all, what would become of the body physiological ? "[1] An enormous number of isolated banks, belonging to an equally large aggregate of different proprietors ; carrying on a business of which the principles were only dimly understood by its practitioners ; subject to all kinds of dangerous influences, of which the real nature and menace were only imperfectly appreciated ; acting to a great extent without any sense of a unity of responsibility or of professional solidarity—could never have borne the huge burden of modern financial requirements, or adequately administered the immense authority which devolves upon the modern money power. So it is that, although we find the instinct of self-preservation prompting

[1] Huxley, *Administrative Nihilism*, quoted by Ward, *Psychic Factors of Civilisation*, p. 292.

EXTENSION OF BANKING

the country bankers occasionally to unite their forces in the presence of a pressing peril, there is nothing like the resolute consolidation of authority and resources, the community of interest in self-defence, and for the protection of the interests of the financial fabric as a whole, which we are accustomed to witness in modern times. We shall see the beginnings of solidarity, but *only* the beginnings, until we come to the period of the Reform Bill.

ATTEMPTS TO ENUNCIATE BANKING PRINCIPLES

Yet it is desirable to add that here and there attempts were made to deduce and enunciate sound principles applicable to till-money and reserves—the bases of a common theory, employed to guide and guard the common interest. Such are embodied in a document dated 1746, by one of the partners of Martin's Bank. Dr. Bisschop thinks that the ideals enshrined in this memorandum were probably derived from one of the older partners of the bank, and represent the fruit of his long experience. The first eight are sufficient for our present purpose, and are in these terms:—

" (1) Some judgment ought to be made of what sum is proper to be out at a constant interest.

" (2) A proportion of bonds, land-tax tallies, and silver to be ready on a sudden demand.

" (3) A proportion of Government securities as Navy Bills.

" (4) Not to lend any money without application from the borrower and upon alienable security that may be easily disposed of, and a probability of punctual payment without being reckoned hard by the borrower.

" (5) All loans to be repaid when due, and ye rotation not to exceed six months.

" (6) Not to boast of great surplus or plenty of money.

" (7) When loans do not offer, to lend on stocks or other securities, buy for ready money and sell for time.

" (8) When credit increases by accident upon an uncertain circulation the money may be lent to Goldsmiths, or discount bills of exchange."

Thomas Martin's maxim—" not to boast of great surplus or plenty of money "—is the real basis of the

132   EVOLUTION OF THE MONEY MARKET

policy of secret reserves. There is this to be said, too—that the country bankers, if they had none too definite ideas about employing the money scientifically, were as keen as mustard on getting it together. " Agents will keep money if permitted, and tenants will not pay if they are not obliged," says Shelburne. " This . . . is now more than ever so, on account of the number of country banks, which corrupt the whole country, by soliciting the custody of ever so small a sum, if it be but for a day."[1]

TYPICAL ARRAY OF ABSORPTIONS

The extent of the contribution of the provincial banks to the fabric of the Money Power may be the better understood by considering the list given in the *Bankers' Magazine*[2] of the old country institutions which have so far been absorbed by a typical member of the centripetal hierarchy like Lloyds, by means of the process of amalgamation :—

In 1865, Lloyds and Co., Bham. Old Bank (est. 1765).
In 1865, Moilliet and Sons, Birmingham.
In 1865, P. and H. Williams, Wednesbury Old Bank.
In 1866, Stevenson, Salt, Stafford Old Bank (est. 1737).
In 1866, Warwick and Leamington Banking Co.
In 1868, A. Butlin and Son, Rugby Old Bank (est. 1791).
In 1872, R. and W. F. Fryer, Wolverhampton Old Bank.
In 1874, Shropshire Banking Co.
In 1879, Coventry and Warwickshire Banking.
In 1880, Beck and Co., Shrewsbury and Welshpool Old Bank.
In 1884, Barnetts, Hoares and Co., London (est. abt. 1677).
In 1884, Bosanquet, Salt and Co., London (est. 1796).
In 1888, Pritchard Gordon and Co., Broseley and Bridgnorth.
In 1889, Birmingham Joint Stock Bank.
In 1890, Beechings and Co., Tonbridge Old Bank.
In 1890, Wilkins and Co., Old Bank, Brecon, etc. (est. 1778).
In 1891, Praeds and Co., London (est. 1802).
In 1891, Cobb and Co., Margate, etc. (est. 1785).
In 1891, Hart, Fellows and Co., Nottingham (est. 1808).
In 1892, Bristol and West of England Bank.
In 1892, R. Twining and Co., London (est. 1824).

[1] Quoted in *Life*, by Fitzmaurice, II. 337.
[2] Augmented from the privately printed *Lloyds Bank : its History and Progress*, 1915.

EXTENSION OF BANKING

In 1893, Curteis, Pomfret and Co., Rye (est. 1790).
In 1893, Herries, Farquhar and Co., London (est. 1770).
In 1894, Bromage and Co., Old Bank, Monmouth (est. 1819).
In 1895, Paget and Co., Leicester Bank (est. 1825).
In 1897, Williams and Co., Old Bank, Chester, etc. (est. 1792).
In 1897, County of Gloucester Bank.
In 1898, Jenner and Co., Sandgate and Shorncliffe.
In 1899, Stephens, Blandy and Co., Reading, etc. (est. 1790).
In 1899, Burton Union Bank.
In 1900, Liverpool Union Bank.
In 1900, Cunliffes, Brooks and Co., Manchester (est. 1792).
In 1900, William Williams, Brown and Co., Leeds (est. 1813).
In 1900, Vivian, Kitson and Co., Torquay Bank (est. 1832).
In 1900, Brooks and Co., London.
In 1900, Brown, Janson and Co., London (est. 1813).
In 1902, Bucks and Oxon Union Bank.
In 1902, Pomfret, Burra and Co., Ashford Bank (est. 1791).
In 1903, Hodgkin, Barnett and Co., Newcastle-on-Tyne.
In 1903, Grant and Maddison's Union Banking Co.
In 1905, Hedges, Wells and Co., Wallingford Bank (est. 1797).
In 1906, Devon and Cornwall Banking Co.
In 1908, Lambton and Co., Newcastle (est. 1788).
In 1909, David Jones and Co., Llandovery (est. 1800).
In 1911, Hill and Sons, West Smithfield (est. 1825).
In 1912, Peacock, Wilson and Co., Sleaford (est. 1792).
In 1914, Wilts and Dorset Banking Co.

THE LAST OF ANTI-USURY LEGISLATION

This succinct analysis of the origins of distinctively *modern* banking may be properly supplemented by a brief review of the decline and disappearance of anti-usury legislation. The relics of mediæval anti-usury sentiment seem to have been revived as the shadow of a coming financial event—the foundation of the Bank of England—fell across the controversial arena. The author of the introduction to a *Discourse about Trade* (the book itself is probably by Sir Josiah Child) argues that the taking of interest in England at a rate exceeding that obtainable in other lands is malum in se, and, consequently, a sin, " although God had never expressly forbid it." Cut interest down to 4 per cent., says he, and land will sell at twenty-five years' purchase, instead of seventeen.[1] David Jones, preaching in St. Mary Woolnoth, in the very heart of the financial district, as late as 1692, declared that every minister and churchwarden would be perjured and forsworn if he allowed any usurer to come to the Sacrament until he had reformed and made restitution. No matter how small the interest—even if it were less than 6 per cent., and never so moderate—it was usury. No trifling or shuffling distinctions should save the usurer from damnation. But, in contrast with these views, " Shall a rich moneyed man," said Bastwick (1692),

" lend a trader or merchant so much money, by which, through his lawful industry, that trader or merchant shall gain possibly 30 or 40 per cent., and at last, through rolling that first foundation stone, arrive to infinite riches, and after all repay his kind patron with no interest, advantage, or consideration whatsoever ? Shall the borrower grow so fat, and the lender, the founder of the feast, look on and starve ? . . . Besides, what's the money more than money's worth ? Are silver and gold more riches and wealth than sheep and oxen ? The grazier that drives his six oxen to market makes increase, for he sells 'em for more than they cost him . . . and shall money, and only money, be debarr'd that improvement ? "

But Bastwick's deadliest shaft was the quotation of Christ's reprimand[2] to the servant who hid the entrusted talent underground : " Thou wicked and slothful servant. . . . Thou oughtest . . . to have put my money to the exchangers, and then at my return I should have received mine own with usury." Locke thought that high interest was by no means incompatible with flourishing trade[3]

---

[1] This is the general contemporary touchstone of the value of money —to wit, the number of years' purchase at which land will sell.
[2] Matthew xxv. 26–27.
[3] " High interest is thought by some a prejudice to trade ; but if we look back we shall find that England never throve so well, nor was there ever brought into England so great an increase of wealth as in Queen Elizabeth's and King James I. and King Charles I.'s time, when money was at 10 and 8 per cent. I will not say high interest was the cause of it ; for I rather think that our thriving trade was the cause of high interest, everyone craving money to employ in a profitable commerce. But this I think I may reasonably infer from it—that lowering of interest is not a sure way to improve either our trade or wealth."

EXTENSION OF BANKING 135

and saw clearly enough that the legal rate cannot be forced below the market rate without either dislocating all trade which is financed by means of borrowed capital, or else compelling systematic evasion.[1] When opinions like these were in the air, and the contribution of the Bank of England to national welfare had already demonstrated the soundness of Paterson's prescience, further statutory adjustment was inevitable, even though it took a mistaken course. By 13 Anne, c. 15 the rate was once more reduced, from 6 to 5 per cent. This Act[2] recites the earlier reduction of interest from 10 per cent. to 8 per cent., and from that to 6 per cent., and adds the time-honoured reflection about the "Advancement of Trade and the Improvement of Lands." It proceeds to argue that the heavy burden of the late long and expensive war has flung landowners into debt and caused trade to be neglected. Once again, therefore, it is necessary to reduce the high rate prevailing in England "to a nearer proportion with the interest allowed for money in foreign states." A maximum of 5 per cent. is enacted. Mutatis mutandis, the Act is largely a verbal re-enactment of the earlier statute; but there is a second section which evidences the growth of financial machinery. We have seen that the bill broker and the scrivener assisted the banker in his business arrangements, as advance guard of the multitudinous individualities which now make up the marching armies of finance.[3] By section ii. an attempt is made to bring their activity within the limits of statutory regulation. Not more than 5s. per cent.

[1] *Works*, IV. 7, 69; Vol. II. p. 30 *et seq.* in folio ed. (Considerations on the Lowering of Interest).

[2] Frequently cited as 12 Anne, c. 16, stat. 2. Although this Act was passed in 1713, there is among the House of Lords papers (*Hist. MSS. Comm.*, House of Lords papers 1692-3, p. 48) a Commons draft dated March 25, 1692. This draft inserts the words "banker and bankers" after "scriveners" in sec. ii., and contains a third section, which is not in the Act as ultimately passed: "Provided always, and be it enacted by the authority aforesaid, that nothing in this Act shall extend or be construed to extend to any person or persons who shall lend to their Majesties any sum or sums of money."

[3] David Jones, in his farewell sermon at St. Mary Woolnoth, in 1692, had declared that these functionaries were only allowed to scratch where the banker himself took care to bite; but it is much more probable that then, as now, they evinced a remarkable capacity for looking after their own interests.

is to be taken by " Scrivener and Scriveners, Broker and Brokers, Solicitor and Solicitors, Driver and Drivers of bargains " for " brokage, soliciting, driving, or procuring " the loan; and twelve pence over and above the stamp duties is to be the maximum charge for "making or renewing of the Bond or Bill for Loan . . . or for any Counterbond or Bill concerning the same." The significance of this increasing complexity in the personnel of finance has already been emphasised from the biological point of view. It is an incessant and inexorable process of specialisation. Every decade of financial evolution increases the number of those whom Bagehot calls the auxiliary dealers in credit. " Under any system of banking," says he,[1] " there will always group themselves about the main bank or banks (in which is kept the reserve) a crowd of smaller money-dealers, who watch the minutiæ of bills, look into special securities which busy bankers have not time for, and so gain a livelihood. As business grows, the number of such subsidiary persons augments " —that is to say, heterogeneity becomes more pronounced— and adds to the efficiency of the processes, by concentrating the incessant attention of acute minds upon every minute detail, and always with a view to the enhancement of the possible profit, and the diminution of the potential risk.

MONEY-LENDING—FOREIGN INTEREST RATES

In spite of all the legislation, however, the private money-lender was as active and rapacious as he has been in all ages of the world. There is a case of a loan of £20, lent at 1s. 6d. per week (almost 20 per cent.) interest, among Holt's Cases, temp. 1688–1710.[2] In fact instances abound, all through the eighteenth century, where redress was claimed against those who had charged more than the legal rate. A pawnbroker was cast in treble the amount of a loan of £50, in addition to the costs of the suit.[3]

---

[1] *Lombard Street*, p. 49.

[2] Barnet *v.* Tompkins, p. 740. If, as the report suggests, repayment at £1 per week was to begin forthwith, while the twenty weeks' interest was paid in advance, the rate is considerably more than 20 per cent.

[3] *Annual Register* for 1767, Chronicle, p. 158.

EXTENSION OF BANKING

Another case will be found in 1765 (*Annual Register*, Chronicle, p. 108) where the offence was the receipt of 16s. for discounting a note of hand for £30, with six weeks to run. The penalty was £90 and costs.[1] But the inexorable pressure of economic law, which had compelled the Tudor sovereigns to disregard their own anti-usury legislation and borrow at 12 per cent., now began to be operative over a vastly wider arena. Others than the Government had to be excluded from the scope of legislation. In 1716 the usury laws were suspended so far as the Bank of England was concerned. The directors were authorised " at their own good liking " to borrow or take up money at any rate of interest they chose. More significant still was the realisation that statutes which might conceivably be expedient in their application to England were mischievous, if not impossible, where the development of an over-seas Empire was concerned. Contemporaneously with the foundation of the Bank of England we encounter the equity principle, judicially enunciated at least as early as 1702, that Irish, Turkish, and Indian interest, though outside the statutory maximum, may be exacted in England, if the debt was originally contracted in the respective countries where such rates are customary.[2] Then, as now, the credit of the over-seas components of the Empire was relatively inferior to that of the mother land—though in our day the difference is perhaps more technical than real. As it would be madness to discourage colonial enterprise by insisting on a uniformity of the interest rates with those of the mother country, Parliament was compelled to prescribe, by 14 George III. c. 79, that loans of money made in the United Kingdom, but secured upon mortgages of lands, tenements, hereditaments, *slaves*, cattle, or other things in Ireland or in any of the colonies or

---

[1] When Daniel Day, the founder of Fairlop Fair, died, in 1767, it was recalled (*Annual Register*, 1767, p. 140) that " his fortune, which was easy, he kept in the bank, as he always declared against interest for money, and used to quote a passage out of the Psalms, ' He that putteth not out his money to usury, nor taketh reward against the innocent—he that doeth these things shall never be moved.' " Day's banker was doubtless not so strict as his client in his ideas about usury.

[2] Eq. Ca. Abr. 289.

plantations, should be valid, although made at a higher rate of interest than 5 per cent., provided that such rates were lawful by the laws of the country where the transaction took place.

ANOTHER COMPLICATION

Later still, as banking rapidly spread in London and the provinces, and the modern money market came into being, another trouble arose. By 58 George III. c. 93, an endeavour was made to defeat insidious attacks on the principle of negotiability by the attempted voiding of bills or promissory notes on the allegation that they had been given for a usurious consideration. It was provided that no bill or promissory note, even if given for a usurious consideration, or upon a usurious contract, should be void in the hands of an endorsee for valuable consideration, unless such endorsee could be shown to have known, when he paid the consideration, what the original terms of the bill or note had been. As late as 1828 the alleged usurious character of the loan was pleaded in an action arising out of the issue of Guatemala 6 per cent. certificates (at 68).[1] Finally, such Acts as 3 and 4 William IV. c. 98, section 7, and 2 and 3 Victoria, c. 37, have been directed to abolish altogether any arguments or defences upon allegations that usurious interest was being charged in a transaction represented in a bill of exchange or promissory note.

There cannot be the slightest doubt that this anti-usury[2] legislation was a failure from every point of view. During the Napoleonic wars it was not uncommon for a person to be paying 10 or 12 per cent. for a loan which, had there been no usury laws, he might have got for 6 or 7 per cent.[3] The Committee of 1818 reported that the laws regulating or restraining the rate of interest had been extensively evaded and had failed to impose a maximum : that recently, owing to the market rate being above the

---

[1] Thompson v. Barclay and Powles, *Annual Register*, 1828, Chronicle, p. 14.
[2] " Usury " ultimately came to signify any rate of interest in excess of that sanctioned by the law for the time being.
[3] McCulloch, *Dictionary of Commerce*, p. 771.

EXTENSION OF BANKING

statutory maximum, they had added to the expense of borrowers on real security by compelling them to raise money on annuities for lives ; that the construction of the law had been attended with great uncertainty, embarrassment, and litigation ; and that the moment of the report, when the market rate was below the legal rate, was " an opportunity peculiarly proper for the repeal of the said laws." These are the results which all modern economic experience would inevitably lead us to expect. The prohibition against the lending of money on mortgage in Russia by Jews and foreigners has the effect, even to-day, of maintaining an 8 or 9 per cent. interest rate for loans on first mortgages.[1] This state of affairs must, however, be distinguished from high interest which is a consequence of exceptional circumstances, such as the 24 per cent. that once ruled in Dawson City as the standard bank rate for money—which, even at that price, was considered cheap.[2]

The anti-usury laws were totally repealed in 1854.[3] This was thirty-eight years after Bentham had demonstrated their futility ; but in 1854 the opponents of Benthamism were slowly gaining the ear of the public. The Money-lenders Act of 1900, which is, to some extent, a revival of anti-usury laws, is one of the most conspicuous failures in recent legislation. It has not cured, and, indeed, it has scarcely mitigated, any of the evils at which it was aimed. It utterly failed to recognise the elementary economic facts that (1) the money-lender fulfils a necessary function in lending upon security, or in circumstances which could not be contemplated by a banker, and (2) that the so-called exorbitant " interest " of the money-lender is not interest simply, but interest plus insurance for the risk he incurs in entering into the transaction. Desperate financial disease may require desperate financial remedies. The sufferers make up the clientèle of a money-lender ;

[1] Hirst, *Stock Exchange*, p. 95.
[2] Report of the Select Committee on the Revision of the Canadian Bank Act, *Journal of the Institute of Bankers*, March, 1914. Where people *must* have money, interest, even in modern times, may go to a " fancy " figure. In the American panic of 1907, as much as 125 per cent. was paid for overnight money.
[3] Dicey, *Law and Opinion in England*, p. 33.

and as long as the disease exists no legislation will prevent the absorption of the only available medicine. Probably the summit-level of the modern liberalisation of opinion in this matter of anti-usury sentiment is reached by Ruskin when he admits that " the fruit (or ' interest,' as it is called) of the labour first given or ' advanced,' ought to be taken into account, and balanced by an additional quantity of labour in the subsequent repayment. . . . We can only assume, generally, that some slight advantage must in equity be allowed to the person who advances the labour, so that the typical form of bargain will be : If you give me an hour to-day, I will give you an hour and five minutes on demand."[1] But here and there among the new communities the antique ideas still survive, and their recrudescence now and then perplexes statesmen. When the revised Canadian Bank Act was before the legislature there was an agitation for the limitation of the banks to 7 per cent. interest when making loans and discounting paper. The western clients of the banks strongly pressed for this regulation, though it was pointed out that any attempt at the artificial restriction of the interest rate would be bound to check the flow of capital into Western Canada as soon as the rate obtainable elsewhere was above the maximum statutory figure in the West. This sound economic truth was accepted and the banks were left free to obtain whatever interest their clients would agree to pay.

OTHER MONEY-MARKET FACTORS

Before we follow the development of English banking beyond the end of the eighteenth century, we must retrace our steps to consider the advent of two other important specialised functions of the Money Market, namely, the Stock Exchange and the joint-stock companies. The companies are not indeed, as a rule, reckoned among the functions of the Money Market. These latter are usually regarded as a quadruple group consisting of (1) the Bank of England, (2) the joint-stock and private banks, (3) the

[1] *Unto This Last*, p. 84.

bill brokers, and (4) the Stock Exchange. But the joint-stock company plays so important a part in modern finance that it may by now be said to have justified its title to be ranked with other factors of the Money Market as a separate specialised function. The Stock Exchange, however, will be treated first.

CHAPTER V

THE STOCK EXCHANGE (1500–1815)

ALTHOUGH there is no essential difference between the Stock Exchange and any other market, there does arise, at a very early stage in the evolution of the market, a distinction which ultimately splits the institution into two well-defined portions, the one being concerned with the commodities themselves and the other only with *titles* to them or interests in them. The commodity market has evolved into the modern shop and store, as well as into the huge municipal building, where traders assemble either constantly or on an agreed day. The other market, being a place where *titles* or claims to money or commodities, or to present or future interests in them, and not the commodities themselves, are sold, is now centralised in the money market and the stock exchanges. If we take a chose in action[1] to be (as originally it certainly was) a thing recoverable by action, as contrasted with a chose in possession (which represents ownership and possession combined), it becomes apparent that the Stock Exchange is a specialised market for choses in action,[2] and to interests in them or

[1] It has also been called a " chose in suspense."
[2] Appreciation of the real character of the Stock Exchange security, as a chose in action, can be distinguished quite early. When the Earl of Aylesbury died, in the reign of George II., he gave to his wife his house, " with all that should be in it at his death." Among its contents, when death took place, were £260 in cash and £800 in bank-notes. The court, in construing the will, agreed that both cash and notes passed to Lady Aylesbury, but took the opportunity to point out, with an economic acumen rare in that age, that bonds and securities were not money, " but only *evidence of so much money due*." They could not, therefore, pass by a bequest of " money." (Popham *v*. Aylesbury, Amb. 69.) Debentures were judicially held to be choses in action by Bacon, C.J., in *ex parte* Rensburg (4 Ch. 687). "Is this debenture a chose in action ? There can be no doubt about it : it is that and nothing else " (p. 688). Shares were similarly held in Colonial Bank *v*. Whinney (11 App. Ca. 426).

142

possibly arising out of them. The conception of the market for choses in action becomes still more refined if we remember that a shareholder's right to his proportion of a declared dividend is a separate chose in action from his shares upon which such dividend is declared.[1] Even more gossamery yet is the distinction, ultimately to be discussed, between choses in action backed by subjective and objective rights respectively.

The dislike of the early courts for representation, unless it had been modified under pressure of commercial sentiment, would have been an insuperable difficulty in the way of the assignment of a chose in action, as well as of the negotiable instrument. The holder of a bearer security, as soon as he was some person other than the original grantee, would have been regarded as a complete outsider. The early legal idea, in German as in Roman theory, was that a personal obligation could not be discharged by an attorney, and that a chose in action (such as a debt in mediæval times, and a modern bond or share) was not capable of assignment. Early law necessarily contemplated the transfer of goods themselves, and even the conveyance, by a figurative process, such as feoffment, of property which was not susceptible of being passed from hand to hand, such as a field or an estate. But its exponents could not comprehend the assignment of a mere *claim* to property, or a share or interest in property, as distinct from the transfer of the property itself. The claim was a thing incorporeal, a mere right. A chose in action does not permit of formal and corporeal transfer, which is essential to the validity of early conveyance. The representative—as assignee, for instance—could not successfully sue the original debtor. He could be defeated by the obvious argument that the debtor did not know him in the matter. That a chose in action should be conveyed from hand to hand by means of the mere delivery of a slip of paper, which was no more than a symbol of a claim, was to the early lawyers a tremendous innovation. Moreover, they may have dimly surmised that this kind of

[1] Dalton *v.* Midland Counties' Railway, 13 C.B., 474.

thing would increase the velocity of the circulation of capital, and have had misgivings about the desirability of such a novelty. In Garrard v. Hardey,[1] Tindal, C.J., made the excellent point that the purported assignment of shares could not, as alleged, be an offence at common law, since such a thing as the assignment of shares was totally unknown at the period when the common law was in course of development. But when the King began to grant dispensatory letters, permitting a party to be represented, in case of real necessity, by another, and when he could himself discharge his personal duties through such attorneys as the Judges, the idea of representation became familiar and acceptable. It advanced another stage when the King himself began to assign choses in action, and when his exceptional powers in that regard began to be the subject of legal notice. " The King, by his prerogative, may grant a thing in action."[2] The King's grantee of a chose in action may sue upon it in her (and therefore in his) own name.[3] This case is the more significant because the subject matter of the action was " certain bondes "; and the court held that " for the same reason that the King has granted the bonds, which are the substance and foundation of the actions, the law implies that the grantee shall use the means to come at the things granted." Hence arises the royal power to confer the privilege of transferable shares upon a company formed under a charter from the monarch. But such a privilege is exceptional. Benloe[4] has a case which proves, as he says, grant de chose in action per common person void.[5] Shares are still " actions " in French, as they once were in our own language. Luttrell

---

[1] 5 Man. and Gr., p. 471. See *post*, p. 182.
[2] Gorge and Dalton's case, Leonard. C., 196.
[3] Breverton's case, Dyer, 30b., pl. 208. " —l'Roy solement puit grant chose in acc." Upon the King's grant of any . . . debt to me I may sue in *my own* name. But not so upon *another man's* grant to me. (Sheppard's *Abridgment* [1675] Art. Chose in Action, p. 337.) If a man be in debt to me 20li. and another man owes him 20li. by obligation, he may assign this obligation and debt to me in satisfaction of my debt, and I may sue upon it in *his* name at my proper costs, and this will be no maintenance. (*Ibid.*, p. 338.)
[4] Pl. 79. (See his Index, s.v. " Grant.")
[5] Mich. 2 and 3 Phil. and Mar.

THE STOCK EXCHANGE (1500–1815)

refers to Bank stock as actions,[1] and Evelyn recalls how " Africa Actions fell to £30."[2] This theory of the non-assignability of a chose in action survived as recently (1828) as the appeal judgment in Duvergier v. Fellows,[3] where Best, C.J., argued that the assignee of the shares could join in no suit for a cause of action that accrued before the assignment. " Such rights of action," he said, " must still remain in the assignor."[4] Sergeant Wilde argued to the same effect (1843), in Harrison v. Heathorn.[5] Now, it is the whole business of a modern Stock Exchange to deal in choses in action—that is to say, in claims to property or to interests in it. The machinery has reached such a stage of perfection that, at five minutes' notice, an investor may purchase for himself an interest in a New Zealand estate on the other side of the world with the absolute assurance that the due proportion of the income from this property will reach him in the shape of dividends, and that his title is so secure as to be available as acceptable bankers' security, although it is only represented by a slip of paper whose intrinsic value is less than a farthing. We are so accustomed to the existence of this paradoxical state of affairs that we fail to realise what a cataclysmic revolution in legal conceptions is involved in this extraordinary simplicity of transaction as compared with the cumbrous mechanism, say, of the twelfth and thirteenth century, or the restraints imposed by royal prerogative as late as the sixteenth century. This factor of the subject will be pursued in greater detail when we are able, after the date of Waterloo, to consider the Stock Exchange as an established element of the Money Power (see pp. 579 *et. seq.*).

WHAT THE EARLY MARKET DEALT IN

The early dealers were quite as much concerned with bills of exchange, with commodities of various kinds, tallies (once called the " true money of the realm of

---

[1] IV. 16.   [2] *Diary*, p. 556.   [3] 5 Bing., 248.
[4] See the whole evolution of share-transferability reviewed, *post*, p. 177.
[5] 6 Man. and Gr., p. 81.

England"), seamen's tickets, and lottery tickets, as with the shares of such companies as were already in existence.[1] The seamen's tickets represented paper payments made to seamen, and it was out of the traffic in them that Thomas Guy, the founder of the famous hospital, made a considerable portion of his fortune. The lottery tickets themselves came ultimately to be divided into fractions, and the fractions were dealt in.[2] But the difficulty of transferring shares, owing to the prejudice of the courts against the process, must have been a powerful obstacle in the way of *share* traffic. The dealings in such interests as were familiar to the market, however, expanded rapidly with the growth of financial facilities. As early as July 13, 1694, there was a record of " time bargains " in a financial weekly called the *Collection for the Improvement of Husbandry and Trade*. The stockbrokers congregated in a specified spot in the Royal Exchange, just as they now gather at a given point in the " House," which is known as the " market " in the particular class of security there dealt in. As late as the middle of the last century it was noted that " the younger Rothschilds occupy a pillar on the south side of the Exchange, much in the same place as their sire stood before them."[3] In early days, however, practically the whole commercial activity of the Metropolis was centred in the Royal Exchange. There had been no " break away " of the commodity markets—no movement towards specialisation, away from homogeneity towards heterogeneity, so essential to the delicate adjustment of prices to values—such as is now represented by the existence of Mark-lane and the Baltic. The various points of assembly in the Royal Exchange were known as " walks," the " Brokers' Walk " being close to the statue of Charles II., which stood in the centre of the building. There were " Hamburg," " French," and " Greek " walks.

[1] Doubtless they dealt in tulips about 1636, in the days of the tulip boom. A " viceroy " bulb was quoted at 2500 florins, and a " semper augustus " at 5500 florins. (Palgrave, *Dictionary of Political Economy*, Art. " Bubble.")
[2] The modern German or Austrian lottery tout still maintains the system, and offers quarter tickets. Railway shares have been so divided (p. 561).
[3] *City Men and City Manners*, p. 99.

THE STOCK EXCHANGE (1500–1815)

The term " walk " in this connection has now gone out of use, being transferred to the round made by a bank clerk who collects the proceeds of drafts from other institutions.

A VIVID STATUTORY DESCRIPTION

The most vivid idea of the position of the Stock Market at this time, as well as of public sentiment with regard to it, is furnished by the statute passed to deal with certain alleged abuses. The Act 8 and 9 William III. c. 32, recites that sworn brokers were formerly admitted for making bargains concerning goods and commodities, as well as bills of exchange, between merchant and merchant.[1] But divers brokers and stock-jobbers, or pretended brokers, have " sett up " selling and discounting " of Talleys, Bank Stock, Bank Bills, Shares and Interests in Joint Stock and other Matters and Things," and have combined to " raise or fall from time to time " the values of the aforesaid interests. " Bank stock," Swift wrote in 1711, " is fallen 3 or 4 per cent. by the whispers about the town of the Queen's being ill, who is, however, very well." This, if not timely prevented, " may ruine the Creditt of the Nation and endanger the Government it selfe." The numbers of such brokers are " very much encreased within these few yeares and doe daily multiply "—an instructive and significant sign of the times. Therefore, from May 1, 1697, no person was to act as broker in London or Westminster or within the Bills of Mortality without a license from the Lord Mayor and Aldermen, and upon a certificate of ability, honesty, and good fame. The broker, on admittance, was to take an oath :—

" I A. B. doe sincerely promise and sweare That I will truely and faithfully execute and performe the Office and Employment of a Broker between Party and Party in all things appertaining to the Duty of the said Office and Employment without Fraud or Collusion to the best of my Skill and Knowledge and according to the Tenour and Purport of the Act intituled an Act to restraine the number and ill Practice of Brokers and Stock Jobbers. So help me God."

[1] As far as dealings in commodities were concerned, their history extended back to the reign of Edward I.

148   EVOLUTION OF THE MONEY MARKET

The broker's professional conduct was subjected, under this Act, to minute and inquisitorial regulations.[1] Many of them were from the first evaded. The stipulation in the broker's bond, for instance, that he should not speculate on his own account was disregarded almost from the passing of the Act, and was a mere dead letter by the middle of the nineteenth century. The regulations, framed at a time when the functions of a Stock Exchange were entirely misunderstood, were in fact always very irksome,[2] and ultimately became intolerable. But as the impression of a responsibility where it was most essential, and as a step in the direction of definite control, the movement was justifiable. In one form or another, the City Corporation's control over brokers lasted until the Broker's Relief Act of 1884, which on September 29, 1886, brought the ancient system to a final end.

THE REMOVAL TO CHANGE ALLEY

In deference to the persistent suggestions of the Gresham Committee, the brokers in 1698 transferred their

[1] The names of the licensed brokers were to be affixed on the Royal Exchange and in the Guildhall. Unlicensed persons acting as brokers [in commodities other than tallies, Exchequer bills, notes, stocks, and shares] were to be penalised to the extent of £500, and those employing them in such capacity to the extent of £50. Further, if the subject-matter of the dealings should be tallies, Exchequer bills, notes, stocks, or shares, the penalty was £500 and one hour in the pillory on each of three successive days. The sworn broker was to keep a register of all bargains (penalty £50); to charge not more than ½ per cent. brokerage (penalty £10); to carry with him, as proof of his license, a " silver medal of the King's Arms, with the broker's name " (penalty 40s.); and to refrain from dealing on his own account, or making any other gain above the " brokage " allowed by the Act (penalty £200 and perpetual incapacity). All option contracts, except such as are to be completed within three days, were to be void, and the option money is to be returnable. Finally, the broker was to play the part of a spy, by disclosing the name of any unlicensed person whom he should discover contravening the Act. If he failed to do so, the Lord Mayor and Corporation were to " displace and turne out such sworne Broker," who is to be for ever incapable of resuming his whilom business.

[2] In Mitchell v. Broughton (Easter, 13 Wm. III.–1. Ld. Raym. 673) Holt declined to accept the defence of a defendant who pleaded 8 and 9 Wm. 3 c. 32 (the Act against stock-jobbing), in reply to a demand that he should transfer certain stock in pursuance of a contract to do so upon request. Holt said that an Act which destroyed bargains must be taken very strictly. If certain contracts were prohibited after a certain day, a contract to do one of the prohibited acts upon request was not within the statute if the request was made before the Act came into force.

THE STOCK EXCHANGE (1500–1815) 149

activities to Exchange-alley and the coffee-houses there. Dealings in foreign stocks remained in the Royal Exchange for many years afterwards,[1] and a roaring business, known as " little-go," in allotment letters was actually established there during the railway mania of the early nineteenth century ; but the rest of the securities known to the expanding market were the subject of dealings in 'Change-alley, South Sea House, and the offices of the East India Company and the Hudson Bay Company. The first of the foreign loans to become known to Exchange-alley was a £500,000 issue, bearing interest at the rate of 8 per cent., by the Emperor of Germany. It was floated here on the suggestion of the Duke of Marlborough. An attempt to float a further German loan in this country was vetoed by Walpole, who did not foresee the immense " pull " which our huge share in cosmopolitan finance was ultimately destined to give us in the affairs of the world.[2] The first regular list of prices appeared on March 26, 1714, as the compilation of John Freake, a broker. It was to be obtained at the proprietor's office, near Jonathan's coffee-house, and contained the quotations of East India stock, Bank stock, the South Sea loan, and the African Company.

[1] Duguid, *Story of the Stock Exchange*, p. 17.
[2] There was a precedent for Walpole's veto. The *Lansdowne MSS.*, No. 104, p. 50, contains Lord Burghley's minutes of a letter from the Queen to the Lord Mayor, allowing the City merchants to lend money to the King of France on the security of the Customs of " Burdeaux and Rochell." Burghley sets out that the Queen could very well allow her subjects in the City to make contracts with the said King's Ministers, upon assignations in such form as the lenders might find profitable. The minute contains no indication of the rate at which these loans were to be negotiated. But it established the principle that royal permission must be obtained for loans of money by English capitalists to foreign potentates.
On January 19, 1914, the precedent was again followed. The Government decided to exercise a veto over new issues of capital in the United Kingdom. The Government's view was that in the war crisis all other considerations must be subordinated to the paramount necessity of husbanding the financial resources of the country. For that reason, issues in relation to domestic enterprise were only to be permitted if it were shown that they were advisable in the national interest. Issues made for the purpose of undertakings in the Overseas Dominions were only to be allowed if urgent necessity and special circumstances existed to justify them. Finally, no issues were to be permitted in connection with undertakings carried on, or to be carried on, outside the British Empire. City opinion, while regretting the necessity for these drastic provisions, was unanimous in their favour.

150 EVOLUTION OF THE MONEY MARKET

There were also a few foreign exchange quotations, and notices with regard to the transfer books of the Bank of England. The Courts were early called to settle the disputes of dealers, and to lay down principles applicable to the new factor in finance.[1]

STEADILY GROWING INFLUENCE

As can easily be deduced from the attitude of its critics, the new organisation, rudimentary and invertebrate as it was, began to make its power felt, just as City capitalism and the opinion of the goldsmith-bankers had done a century or more earlier. " The stocks are to me the signs of the times," said the Canon of Christ Church in 1722, " and sufficient ones for any business I have met in the world. I judge by their rise and fall what general apprehensions are."[2] Walpole, in 1716, directly charged the embryo Stock Exchange with boycotting a particular loan transaction. He said : " I know that the members of the Stock Exchange have combined not to advance money on the loan. Everyone is aware how the administration of this country has been distressed by stock-jobbers." Again, Edward Harley[3] alleges that " the Bank stock-jobbers, and moneyed men of the City were all engaged to sink the credit of the Government." But the whole point of the Stock Exchange opposition to this loan was the City belief that the terms were inadequate. The City was not attracted by an offer of 4 per cent., in the political and financial circumstances then existing. The Stock Exchange has never pretended to be an institution existing to finance Governments or companies on terms below the rate fixed almost automatically by existing political and economic circumstances. The truth was that, in spite of Walpole and other critics, the existence of a Stock Market

---

[1] See note 2, p. 148. Dutch v. Warren (Mich. 7 Geo. I : 1 Stra. 406) established the principle that in a contract for stock the party who has the difference in his hands is receiver of so much to the other's use.

[2] Canon of Christ Church to Edward Harley, Sept. 9, 1722. *Hist. MSS., Portland MSS.*, Vol. VII. The canon had no nerve for speculative investment. "I am afraid in my own soul now I am got into the funds, which I never was before in my life." (*Ibid.*, p. 112.)

[3] *Portland MSS.* V. 650.

THE STOCK EXCHANGE (1500–1815)   151

was of incalculable value as an auxiliary of the Bank of England in the establishment of a National Funded Debt. It provided the market facilities, without which investment, even in the best securities, would never become a thriving reality. As we have seen, some of the capitalists who financed William III. really purchased annuities. They did not expect that the sum advanced would ever be repaid, but the existence of a market for the stock enabled them to secure repayment at any time at the current market quotation. The class of willing capitalists was likely to be largely augmented by the assurance that the annuity is capable of immediate sale at any time, whereas it will necessarily be limited if the investment is a final and definite lock-up of funds which will never again be available, in their capitalised form, to the lender.[1] Lotteries,[2] in such financial circumstances as those which existed at the time,[3] were useless as a means of permanent financial amelioration. If the Government wanted assistance it must obtain it on business terms. The stipulation that those terms be observed was no boycott, but rather

[1] See this most important question discussed in detail, *post*, p. 574 ff.
[2] There were State lotteries in 1758 (31 Geo. II. c. 22) for £500,000 ; in 1759 (32 Geo. II. c. 10) for £660,000 ; in 1760 (33 Geo. II. c. 7) for £240,000, in £3 tickets ; in 1761 (1 Geo. III. c. 7) for £660,000, in £10 tickets, prizes from £10,000 to £20, blanks £6, about four blanks to a prize ; in 1763 (3 Geo. III. c. 12) for £350,000, in £10 tickets, prizes from £10,000 to £20, blanks £5, about five blanks to a prize ; in 1765 for £600,000, in £10 tickets, prizes as usual, £6 blanks, which were as four to one to the prizes ; and another in 1766 (3 Geo. III. c. 39), precisely similar in amount (Ashton, *History of English Lotteries*, p. 72). " From 1785 to 1823 not a single year passed without the issue of a lottery, the management of which was placed in the hands of the Bank of England " (Maberley Phillips, at the Institute of Bankers, Feb. 9, 1910). In fact it may be said that from 1694 onward the lotteries were (with occasional legislative lapses into a financial austerity which condemned them) recognised factors of the national revenue system. In the light of modern opinion it is the merest truism to say that these episodes introduced elements of excitement and of violent changes of fortune with no economic justification, while at the same time they encouraged the gambling proclivities, never wholly dormant, of large sections of the population.
[3] Edward Harley says that his brother, in 1711, found the Exchequer " almost empty : nothing left for the subsistence of the Army, but some tallies upon the third general mortgage of the Customs : the Queen's civil list near £700,000 in debt: the funds all exhausted and a debt of £9,500,000 without provision of Parliament, which had brought all the credit of the Government to a vast discount." In this condition the nation had to pay 255,689 men. (*Portland MSS.* V. 650.)

152   EVOLUTION OF THE MONEY MARKET

the necessary bringing of national financial method into reasonable consistency with existing economic conditions. It made for advance, not for retrogression.

THE SOUTH SEA SCHEME

In such a political and financial environment Harley's famous scheme for a South Sea Company was framed. The new company was to have a monopoly comprising the east side of South America and the west of the whole continent. The capital was to be about £9,500,000 of public debt, on which it was to receive 6 per cent. and £8000 a year for charges of management. The revenue arising from the duties on various commodities was secured to it in perpetuity. In its early days the scheme failed to " catch on." Two months after the incorporation of the company the stock stood no higher than $77\frac{1}{2}$, or a discount of $22\frac{1}{2}$ per cent. In 1717 Walpole persuaded the South Sea Co. to make a further advance of £5,000,000 to the Government, and in 1720 the company agreed to take up £32,000,000 of Government annuities, 5 per cent. till 1727 and 4 per cent. thereafter. These later developments precipitated the South Sea frenzy, which bred bubbles by the dozen. The exact origin of the change in sentiment, from suspicion to frenzy, is as obscure in this instance as it is in later episodes—a long series of speculative outbursts,—for instance, the railway mania, the Kaffir boom of 1895, and the rubber excitement of 1910.

But save during the transient, if violent, excitement of episodes like the South Sea Bubble, speculative dealings were confined almost entirely to the comparatively small clique of Whig speculators who carried them on. The number of securities permanently dealt in was small. Even on the Amsterdam Exchange (then the leading Bourse of the world), in the middle of the eighteenth century, there were only known 44 securities, of which 25 were bonds of internal loans and six were German public stocks. As for bank shares (other than those of the Bank of England), they were unknown ; and the mere idea of excited dealings in the stocks of transport organisa-

THE STOCK EXCHANGE (1500–1815)   153

tions on the other side of the Atlantic would have seemed more grotesque in 1750 than the suggestion of a rig in the shares of the Mars and Jupiter Railway would appear to us. Only occasionally was it possible to allege that—

> " . . . Stars and garters did appear
> Among the meaner rabble,
> To buy and sell, to see and hear
> The Jews and Gentiles squabble."

The main lesson of the South Sea Bubble is the necessity of a centralised financial control, capable of stopping, or at least of localising and sternly discouraging, such outbreaks. So powerful an engine of social advantage was not destined to be fully evolved for another couple of centuries. But that the market had already acquired its habit of discounting events in advance is shown by the fact that South Sea Stock fell from 310 to 290 on the news that the Bill had received the royal assent.[1] With

[1] Mr. Duguid (*Story of the Stock Exchange*, p. 39) reprints a list, now owned by a member of the Stock Exchange, called " The Bubbler's Mirrour, or England's Folly." This professes to give the prices at which the alleged bubbles were subscribed, and also the highest level reached by their quotations :—

Name of Company.	Nominal value.	Highest touched.
Westley's Actions	£2 0 0	£12 0 0
Welby's Golden Mines	0 10 0	16 0 0
Long's Melioration of Oil	5 0 0	60 0 0
British Insurance	0 2 6	3 0 0
Globe Permits	nothing pd.	50 0 0
Salt Petre	0 2 6	1 10 0
Rose Insurance	0 10 0	4 10 0
Water Engine	4 0 0	50 0 0
Coal Trade from Newcastle	0 5 0	1 1 0
Stockings	2 10 0	30 0 0
Irish Sail Cloth	0 5 0	0 14 0
Furnishing of Funerals	2 10 0	15 0 0
Insurance on Lives	0 12 6	1 0 0
Royal Insurance	5 5 0	250 0 0
London Assurance	5 0 0	175 0 0
Manuring of Land	0 2 6	2 10 0
Rock Salt	1 5 0	15 0 0
Exporting Timber from Germany . . .	0 10 0	1 0 0
Bleaching of Hair	0 5 0	1 10 0
Insurance on Horses	0 2 6	0 15 0
Sugar	0 5 0	1 0 0
Radish Oil	21 0 0	25 0 0
Pensilvania Company	5 5 0	40 0 0
Buying Seamen's Tickets	0 2 6	1 0 0
Pasteboard Manufactory	0 2 6	1 10 0
Drying Malt by Air	0 2 6	1 0 0

the widening horizon came the simultaneous necessity for a keener circumspection.

SIR JOHN BARNARD'S ACT

Contemporary opinion of an institution is seldom better reflected than in the letter and the spirit of a statute for its regulation. Through the eyes of the legislator we can see the Stock Exchange as it presented itself to public opinion about the time when Wesley was beginning to create Methodism.

Sir John Barnard's Act (7 Geo. II. c. 8) is described as " An Act to prevent the infamous practice of Stock-Jobbing." The Act recites that great " inconveniences " have arisen in consequence of the " wicked, pernicious, and destructive " practice of stock-jobbing, which operates to the discouragement of industry and the detriment of trade. It proceeds to make void all " putts and refusals " (i.e. in modern parlance, options) and all contracts in the nature of wagers (i.e. time bargains, there being no intention of delivering the stock), adding the provision that any money paid in relation to such transactions shall be recoverable by action commenced within six months of the payment, with double costs. The defendant was to be a compellable witness, subject to the plaintiff's previously providing security for costs. A penalty of £500 is enacted as the liability of persons engaging in the prohibited option transactions, and is to extend also to brokers, agents, scriveners, and other persons negotiating, transacting, or writing any contract, bargain, or agreement within the prohibition. In the case of the payment of differences the penalty is £100. The Act makes the futile stipulation that such transactions are to be completed by actual delivery of the stock, not compounded by payment of the difference. A further penalty of £500 is provided as a deterrent against the " frequent and mischievous practice for persons [i.e. bears] to sell and dispose of stocks or other securities of which they are not possessed." The broker employed in the transaction is to forfeit £100 ; and, in order to provide against any evasion or collusion on his part, he is to keep

THE STOCK EXCHANGE (1500–1815)   155

a record, to be called "The Broker's Book," in which he shall enter particulars of all transactions, under a penalty of £50 for neglect to enter or for falsity of entry. Nothing in the Act is to hinder or prevent the loan of money on stocks, or the re-delivery of the security when the loan is paid off. This Act finally disappeared under the provisions of the Statute Law Revision Act, 30 and 31 Victoria, c. 59.

PUBLIC DISTRUST OF 'CHANGE ALLEY

Clearly as we realise the utility of the stock markets as a factor of the social machinery, we should not overlook the fact that to the eighteenth-century Englishman the embryo Stock Exchange was the incarnation of financial corruption. Sombart, quite rightly, says that the view of the Stock Exchange which is entertained to-day by the petty trader and the labour leader was in the early eighteenth century that of the rich man.[1] Writers who catered

[1] Dr. Johnson's original definition stood thus :—
STOCK-JOBBER.—A low wretch who gets money by buying and selling shares in the funds.
    Davenant had heard, in 1701, that " there are known brokers who have tried to stock-job elections upon the Exchange, and that for many boroughs there was a stated price." A few more illustrative quotations may be usefully added.
    " That pernicious trick of stock-jobbing, whereby several families have been already ruined." (Petition of East India Merchants, January 22, 1695–1696. *House of Lords MSS.*, Vol. II., N.S., p. 33.)
    " This new corporation of Hell, the Stock-Jobbers." (Pamphlet of 1701.)
    " Stock-jobbers swarm [1727] in this part of the world and the vilest of them." (Letters of Stratford, Canon of Christ Church, to T. Thomas. *Portland MSS.*, Vol. VII. p. 449.)
    " One's wishes do not add a hair to the scale, except one is a stock-jobber. Such gentry coin disasters, to cheat somebody by sinking the funds without cause." (Horace Walpole to Sir Horace Mann [1782], *Letters*, Vol. IV. p. 9.) " Stocks are no longer the weather glass of fortune, but part of the mask employed to disguise the nation's own face to itself." (*Ibid.*, Vol. III. p. 143.)
    " The practice [of stock-jobbing] is much followed by Frenchmen, both in English and in the French funds, and even by Princes of the blood. It is said (I do not know with what truth) that the Russian Minister (1787) has long had an establishment for this purpose at some bank in the city ; it might, perhaps, be practicable to trace and to expose it." (Wm. Eden to Pitt, *Auckland Correspondence*, Vol. I. p. 279.)
    The alleged illegality of transferable shares, with the inference that dealing in them by a broker was a criminal act, was argued as lately as 1859 (see *post*, p. 185) and may have helped to perpetuate the hostile sentiment. As lately as 1831, when Mr. Smith was told by Baring of the Government's proposal to enact a new tax on transfers of stock he replied : " Nonsense ; you are imposed upon by some stock-jobbing lie."

for him denounced the " dangerous and wickedly ruinous trade in stocks and shares." With " stockholders' heads[1] wholly engaged in this kind of negociations," said Malachy Postlethwaite, " industrious and skilful traders are deprived of those loans of money which they were wont to have on their personal security, at the legal interest, wherewith to carry on the solid national commerce." The Stock Exchange then (and almost down to the date of the Reform Bill in 1832) was contemplated as a perplexing and annoying phenomenon, which refused to be suppressed or abolished. In Adam Smith's system " there is no niche for the study of securities, or of the Stock Exchange and its business." As an accepted and recognised factor of the economic mechanism of the world it certainly does not ante-date Waterloo. Down to that period it was tabooed[2] among cautious and " respectable " people. The brokers and jobbers " have placed themselves in a system between the Government and the Fund-holders, and also between the Public individually ; so that no party can move without

[1] Much of the share dealing was carried on at this time in the shape of the personal negotiation of bargains by the stockholder himself—a thing utterly foreign to our ideas. At the time of the Bubble, and for long after, the investor was at liberty to act as his own broker. For instance, in Mrs. Centlivre's comedy of *A Bold Stroke for a Wife* (Act IV. Scene 1), a stockbroker at Jonathan's says : " I would fain bite the spark in the brown coat. He comes very often into the Alley, but never employs a broker." The persistence of this privilege of personal dealing and the consequent postponement of the strict specialisation to which we are accustomed are clearly evidenced in the record (*Annual Register*, 1767, Chronicle, p. 68) which tells how on " Wednesday last were tried, by a special jury, two causes, in both which the Chamberlain of London was plaintiff ; one against T—— J—— and the other against J—— S—— for buying and selling Government securities for their friends, not being brokers ; in both which causes, verdicts were given for the defendants, by which it is now settled that every person is at liberty to employ his friend to buy or sell Government securities, without being obliged to be at the expense of employing a broker ; which will be a great inducement for people to lay out their money in the funds and consequently a great addition to public credit." This absence of the professional element must have made prices peculiarly difficult and " tricky." Even allowing for the excitement of a boom, a market must have been far from " perfect " in which South Sea Stock was quoted 1000 at one end of Garraway's Coffee House, and 920 at the other. (Thomas Martin, June, 1720, *Journal of the Institute of Bankers*, Vol. XXXIII. p. 158.)

[2] The late King Edward (then Prince of Wales) visited the Stock Exchange on March 2, 1885—the first occasion on which Royal cognisance appears to have been taken of its existence.

THE STOCK EXCHANGE (1500–1815)

these wolves having an interest in the transaction."[1] The bear was the bête noir of the early critics of the Stock Exchange. One of the earliest attempts to regulate dealings was an anticipation of Leeman's Act, proposing that, within a stipulated time, all transfers should be completed, that no owner of stock should be entitled to sell out until he had held it for a certain period of time, and that in no case should he sell it again until it had actually been transferred into his name. These proposals, which would have made rapid and facile dealing quite impossible, never came to legislative fruition. Rapid and facile dealings were, in fact, discouraged at a time when the registers of Government stock were kept closed by the Bank of England for six weeks at a time in preparation for the dividend distribution. Still, if we keep in mind the overwhelming prejudice against the Stock Exchange, we shall the better understand the spirit in which this short-sighted suggestion of further statutory repression was received and discussed. If it had been accepted and adopted, the characteristic duality of classification, into brokers and jobbers, which marks the membership of the London Stock Exchange, might never have been evolved.[2]

DEFINITE LOCATION OF THE STOCK EXCHANGE

The resort of the stock-jobbers to Jonathan's Coffee House, where they had formed an exclusive club, made it

---

[1] *Art of Stock-Jobbing*, Pref. vii.

[2] When Barnard introduced his Act (see p. 154) it was alleged that the dealings by foreigners on the London market alone produced commissions extending to about £80,000 a year for the fortunate stock-jobbers who were entrusted with the dealings. The distinction between broker and jobber was not as yet clearly marked. As a matter of fact, the stock-jobber, out of whom the stockbroker has been evolved, originally found his opportunity in dealing for foreign clients, who desired to take prompt advantage of market fluctuations. If it had always remained essential (as Sir John Barnard hoped) to complete the actual transfer of the stock at the same time as the contract for its sale or purchase, it would not have been possible for speculators, other than those on the spot, to deal with any advantage. But as soon as the absent principal, often on the Continent, began to employ an agent on " Change " to deal with another agent, acting for another absent principal, the stockbroker began to take the place of the stock-jobber. The concurrent exercise of *both* functions is curiously mentioned by Mortimer (*Every Man His Own Broker*, p. xix.), when he urges gentlemen to look after the financial affairs of their lady relatives,

practically the Stock Exchange. It was, in fact, judicially held to be so in Renaux v. Ferres (the latter being the name of the master of Jonathan's Coffee House), tried before Chief Justice Mansfield on June 8, 1762. The allegation was that of assault by pushing the plaintiff, a stock-jobber, out of the coffee house. But, inasmuch as it was proved that the house had been a market, time out of mind, for buying and selling Government securities, the jury gave a verdict for the plaintiff, with 1s. damages.[1] Contemporary sarcasm at the exclusiveness of the " club " entirely missed the point that the growing responsibilities of the Stock Exchange business rendered discrimination imperative in the matter of membership. In spite of many abuses, the Stock Market was too firmly established to be suppressed. A legislative attempt at the total " extirpation " of stock-jobbers in 1773 was thrown out by the House of Lords.[2] In the same year the organisation of jobbers and brokers removed from the privately owned coffee houses to one of their own, at the corner of Threadneedle Street and Sweeting's Alley, opposite the present Threadneedle Street Post Office. On July 15 it was announced that " yesterday the brokers and others at New Jonathan's came to a resolution that, instead of its being called New Jonathan's, it is to be called The Stock Exchange, which is to be wrote over the door." Daily admission to the Stock Exchange Coffee House was obtainable at the charge of sixpence, and public attention was attracted to business by lists of stocks stuck up in the windows of the brokers' offices. The place had already gained its modern cognomen of the " House." Business in foreign stocks was still partly transacted in the Royal Exchange, while dealings in British Government securities were domiciled under the Rotunda at the Bank of England.

[1] *Annual Register*, 1762, p. 89.
[2] *Every Man His Own Broker*, p. xiii.

---

and thus oust the "gentry" of the Stock Exchange. "One of their principal emoluments," he says, "arises from the management of the fortunes of women, whose ignorance, joined to a propensity for gaming (become of late years a female passion), renders them the easy dupes of stock-jobbing brokers."

Thus there were three stock markets, but all sufficiently near each other for us to contemplate the centralisation of the dealings.[1] As the more reputable stockbrokers grouped themselves, by a selective process, into an organisation distinct from the "lottery jobbers, gamblers in insurance, and miscellaneous sharpers who had given Change Alley an evil name," the ever-present English instinct of organisation and discipline, so characteristic of City habits, early strove towards a professional standard by placing the rooms under the control of a "Committee for General Purposes." Then, as since and now, the functions of the Committee could be called "judicial as regards the settlement of disputed bargains, and administrative as regards rules for the general conduct of business and for the liquidation of defaulters' accounts." This stage in the development of the great institution brings us to the Stock Exchange on its present site, and cannot be better told than in the words of Mr. Levien, addressed to the Stock Exchange Commission.[2] He said : "Early in 1801 it became apparent that the rooms did not afford sufficient accommodation for the transaction of the greatly increased business arising out of the creation of loans, hitherto unprecedented in amount, and, moreover, that the indiscriminate admission of the public was calculated to expose the dealers to the loss of valuable property." Under these circumstances Mr. William Hammond and other gentlemen, who had acquired a site in Capel Court and its immediate neighbourhood (described as " a *centrical* situation "), succeeded in raising a capital of £20,000, in 400 shares of £50 each, and in founding a new undertaking, to which the affairs of the old rooms were ultimately transferred. The first stone of the new building on a site in necessary proximity to the Bank of England was laid in May, 1801. A deed of settlement was not executed until March 27, 1802. In this document it is formally recited that " whereas the Stock Exchange in Threadneedle Street,

[1] A later attempt to establish a separate Stock Exchange for foreign bonds ended in the absorption of the rival institution by the original Stock Exchange. Endeavours to start a separate Mining Exchange have been equally unsuccessful. [2] Question 3.

where the stockbrokers and stock-jobbers lately met for the transaction of their business, having been found to be inconvenient," [largely, as we have seen, because of the irresponsibility of the habitués of an open Stock Exchange], William Hammond and others, who were appointed trustees and managers of the undertaking, "came to a resolution to erect a more commodious building for the purpose." In this deed the management, regulations, and direction of all the concerns of the undertaking were vested in a Committee, consisting of thirty members or subscribers, to be chosen annually by ballot upon March 25, while the treasuryship and management of the building were placed under the sole direction of nine trustees and managers (separate from the Committee), as representatives of the proprietors. Under these conditions the new building was opened, in March, 1802, with a list of about five hundred subscribers.

Investment and speculation soon centred in the new Stock Exchange, as banking power and control had already found their focus at the Bank of England.[1] Of course, the

---

[1] Some sidelights on the market tactics of the period may be obtained from the " Glossary explaining the Cant Terms used by The Members of the Stock Exchange," published in 1819, at the end of *The Art of Stock-Jobbing Explained*. Below are a few of the terms which have become less familiar since then :

"BAWD.—A person who lends himself to a Broker, that has a large account open, he cannot get settled in his own person without being taken advantage of : it is sold to the Bawd in a whisper under the market price, and he gets rid of it in the best way he can.

" DUSTING WIGS.—Sometimes very ludicrous scenes take place when little business is going on, or after the business of the day is over. Lately, a noted but respectable old Jew was teased by the rest of his brotherhood, with sticking pens in his ear, pulling the tail of his wig, etc. ; when Moses, getting a little irritated, took his full-powdered wig in his hand, and laid it round him with no common dexterity ; till the whole House was *whitened*, and *convulsed* with *laughter*.

"EAR-WIGGING.—When bargains are done privately in the market by a whisper ; ' I do not wish to let any person know that I am a Bull.'

" FIDDLING.—When a broker has got money transactions of any consequence, as there is no risk in these cases, he will fiddle one finger across the other, signifying by this that the Jobber must give up half the turn of the market price to him, which he pockets, besides his commission.

" OMNIUM.—The name itself is derived from the Latin, and means *of all* ; that is, of all the different Stocks of which a Government Loan is composed. Thus a Loan for £10,000,000 may consist of a portion of the three per cent. Consols, three per cent. Reduced and Long Annuities, or

THE STOCK EXCHANGE (1500–1815)   161

volume of business was modest in comparison with its aggregate in 1914. In March, 1802, the list of stocks then dealt in appears in the *Gentleman's Magazine* : Bank Stock, Consols, Navy, Long and Short Annuities, India Bonds, Exchequer Bills, Funds, South Sea Stock, Old Annuities, Omnium, Irish 5 per Cents., Imp. 3 per Cents., English lottery tickets, English prizes. An entire room had originally been devoted to British and another to Foreign Government stocks. They were the predominant feature of the market. But under the pressure of industrial enterprise—namely, mining and canal shares at first—a corner of the foreign room was allotted for this class of business. After Waterloo had brought quietude, and humanity " had time to turn round," the rehabilitation of Europe and the start of the Latin-American Republics on their journey towards constitutional freedom and commercial prosperity came to be financed from London, and a constant multitude of new enterprises began to be " known to the Stock Exchange."

At this point in the evolution of the Stock Exchange, there was probably only the very vaguest conception of its real character as a developing function of the Money Market. It doubtless presented itself as an institution having no more extended economic significance than was involved in its name, namely, a place where stock could be exchanged for money or money for stock. Of its function as a means for the incessant aggregation and continual redistribution of capital, and for the mobilisation of credit, there was probably only the very haziest idea, even if there was any idea at all. Although in a

---

any other Stock, as a portion of the three, four, and five per cents. The Loan for the service of 1815 was in Stock,

£130 Reduced 3 per Cents.
10 Four per Cents.   for every £100 Sterling.
44 Three per Cent. Consols.

" Payment to be made by the contractors at ten separate instalments of £10 per month, or a discount upon prompt payment ; thus the three different Stocks become Omnium, but may be sold separately, in which case it is then denominated *Scrip*, or subscription ; some sell Consols scrip, some Reduced scrip, as best suits their convenience ; all bear separately the name of Scrip, and all together Omnium, until it is paid up in full."

minor degree, the sensitiveness of the Stock Exchange had begun to be manifest, the value of the faculty as a crisisometer was not, and could not have been, fully appreciated. In fact, the sensitiveness of the market in the pre-Waterloo period was probably regarded more as a nuisance than otherwise. In the technical language already applied to the banks, the evolution of the Stock Exchange had so far been fortuitous and only in the slightest degree orthogenic. Indeed, so far from being orthogenic, the Stock Exchange was much more completely doliogenic than the banks. But as we proceed, we shall see that the particular Stock Exchange phenomena with which we have been occupied, become merged in, and are organically related to, and involved with, larger and larger groups of phenomena, so that it becomes as difficult to disentangle the functions of the Stock Exchange from the Money Market organism as it would be to analyse the functions of the nerves or of the heart in absolute disassociation from all their physiological surroundings. The subject of the Stock Exchange is resumed in Chapter XIX.

CHAPTER VI

THE JOINT-STOCK COMPANY—TRANSFERABLE SHARES AND
LIMITED LIABILITY—INSURANCE

THE original trading corporations[1] were mainly concerned with trade to foreign lands. Their members were established and recognised merchants. Money was at once the inspiration and the means. Before Columbus sailed Westwards the Portuguese had tried the Southern route, thrusting themselves further and further towards the south of the Dark Continent under the leadership of Henry the Navigator. With his usual swift insight into the real nature of the power behind the Throne, Professor Pollard remarks that we should now call him Henry the

[1] THE THEORY OF THE CORPORATION.—Corporate organisation in England began with the Craft Guilds, the Merchant Guilds, the view of frank-pledge with its communal responsibility, the system of agriculture on practically a communistic basis, and the quasi-corporate relationships subsisting between the Jewish financiers in various parts of the country in the twelfth and thirteenth centuries. Neither in its early nor late developments was the corporate ideal, as understood in the twelfth and thirteenth centuries, essentially, or even extensively, commercial in its ultimate inspiration. Rather was it romantic and religious in its mainsprings—an inheritance from the Roman law and the principles of early Christianity, especially as interpreted by St. Paul. The existing feudal order, the accepted Christian teaching, the palpable example of the great monastic communities, and, to some extent, of the mendicant orders also —all these phenomena tended to suggest trusteeship, rather than dominium, as the basis of the social order and the principle regulating the relationship of the various factors of society. The undying corporations survived by organised co-operation, not by conquest in a lethal internecine struggle; by intelligence, not by instinct.
The influence of the corporation now extends to every department of our national existence. Within the bounds of English corporate or quasi-corporate life (as the late Professor Maitland so admirably put it) " . . . lie Churches, and even the mediæval Church, one and Catholic, religious houses, mendicant orders, non-conforming bodies, a presbyterian system, universities old and new, the village community which Germanists revealed

164   EVOLUTION OF THE MONEY MARKET

Company Promoter.[1]   The company promoter was wanted in England as well as in Portugal. As soon as trade was transformed from the pelagic to the oceanic type, as soon as mercantile prows furrowed the Atlantic rather than the Mediterranean, the great opportunity for England had arrived. Money, though as yet comparatively unorganised, began to transform Christendom from a system of independent city States into an aggregate of closely related organic communities, the nations of the modern world. But the work was too extensive for the individual capitalist. The joint-stock method became more essentia. with every advance in the progress of national enterprisel

[1] *Factors in Modern History*, p. 36.

---

to us, the manor in its growth and decay, the township, the New England town, the counties and hundreds, the chartered boroughs, the guild in all its manifold varieties, the inns of court, the merchant adventurers, the militant ' companies ' of English condottieri, who, returning home, help to make the word ' company ' popular among us, the trading companies, the companies that become colonies, the companies that make war, the friendly societies, the trade unions, the clubs, the group that meet at Lloyd's Coffee-house, the group that becomes the Stock Exchange, and so on, even to the one-man company, the Standard Oil Trust, and the South Australian statutes for communistic villages " (*Political Theories of the Middle Age*, Translator's Intro., p. 27). The " incidents of corporateness " early recognised are a juristic personality, the right of perpetual succession, of suing and being sued, of having a common seal, of holding lands, and of making by-laws—all entirely distinct from the analogous capacities possessed by its individual components. Since the corporate personality is not capable of coming into being as the result of physical procreation, and since it possesses, in fact, no physically palpable existence whatsoever, we must obviously seek the recognition and confirmation of its juristic existence in the only quarter where there exists a competent prerogative.   The King alone can confer these unique characteristics and privileges.   So (as Madox tells us in the *Firma Burgi*, 1726) " anciently a guild, either religious or secular, could not legally be set up without the King's license.   If any person erected a guild without warrant (that is, without the King's leave) it was a trespass, and they were lyable to be punished for it." As early as 1179 the burgesses of Totnes paid a fine of five marks for setting up a guild without authority (Carr, *Law of Corporations*, p. 116). We shall see, in later analysing the evolution of the modern joint-stock company, how inept this royal prerogative was.

The economic evolution of this country has been affected in succession by six distinct types of commercial corporation, using the word " corporation " in its loose and non-legal sense :

(1) The merchant guild, regulating the trade of the town as a whole, and ultimately developing into the local administrative authority.

(2) The craft guild, regulating the production of a special class of goods at the hands of craftsmen strictly limited to that species of activity

CORPORATIONS AND COMPANIES 165

Ultimately, the fact was specifically recognised and employed as an argument for royal favour. When the East India merchants asked (in 1599) for the privilege of perpetual succession, they argued that the trade of the Indies was so remote as to be incapable of proper management without a " joint and united stock."

EARLY TYPES OF COMPANY

As late as the end of the seventeenth century there were only three chartered joint-stock corporations in existence —the East India, the Royal African, and the Hudson Bay Companies. The " regulated " companies, like the Russia,

(this second species of corporation corresponds approximately, but only so, to the modern trade unions).
(3) The livery companies, mainly concerned with the wholesale dealings in a particular class of goods in a particular city.
(4) " Regulated " companies, and
(5) Chartered companies, ultimately evolving into
(6) Joint-stock companies, such as those which, in multitudinous array, now meet us at every point of the economic horizon. In commerce, especially, the artificial personality corresponds to the pupillus of Roman law, in that it cannot act for itself, but is represented by natural persons whose acts are attributed to it (Geldart, Legal Personality, L. Q. Review, 1911, 93). There was, of course, a species of still larger commercial entity like the Hanseatic League. This was a kind of international company, whose members were towns instead of individuals. When its ambassadors were asked, in England, in 1376, to state the names of the towns which were the components of the League, they replied that there were too many for such a feat of memory to be possible. It was like asking the secretary of the Chartered Company to rehearse the list of the shareholders without reference to the register.

The corporation then ultimately gave birth to the modern joint-stock company. But the common law, while it recognised the former, knows nothing of the latter. For centuries the privilege of incorporation remained particular and did not become general. The Legislature had not taken the plunge into modern conditions, when incorporation is to be had by everybody who cares to apply for it and to pay the fees. Every association of persons formed for the sake of carrying on business and sharing profits is, at common law (as distinct from statute, that is), either a partnership or a corporation. If a partnership, it is constituted by the agreement of the partners ; if a corporation, it is brought into being by a special exercise of the authority of the Crown or Parliament. From the time in 1243 when Sinebald Fieschi (afterwards Innocent IV.) first called the company persona ficta, down to the time when anybody could create such a person at Somerset House, was a period of over six centuries. " Persona ficta," we say : but in our day Gierke has argued that the " person " is not fictitious after all. There is, he declares, a real psychic self behind the legal personality—something far more than the mere complexity of relation corresponding to that which is implied in terms like " esprit de corps," or " the soul of a people." See his theories outlined in connection with an even wider argument, *post*, p. 686.

the Turkey, and the Eastland, were unincorporated guilds, whose members enjoyed a monopoly of their specific trade in a given "district," but were originally in no sense financially associated or mutually liable for one another's engagements. The joint liability developed at a later date. No subject of the Crown could trade in a "district" where a regulated company was established without first acquiring membership by payment of a fee.[1] These companies had the shelter of the Crown against home rivalry and foreign aggression. Membership of a "regulated" company could only be obtained by the consent of the whole association, and, as a rule, only by an apprentice who had served his time. The companies met their common expenses by leviations (the word "levy" is still employed, almost in that sense, by the trade unions), just as the Cornish cost-book companies once did, and the modern companies still do, by calls.[2] Each member was at perfect liberty to advance his own legitimate interests in his own way; save that, like a barrister on circuit, he must bow to certain regulations framed in the common interest of all. The group organisation was beginning to regulate internecine rivalry. "If the struggle for existence is transferred from individual to solid *groups* of men, the individuals within the groups are lifted out of the struggle in the sense in which the parts of an organic body are dispensed from struggling with each other, though not from aiding or hindering the whole body in its struggle with other bodies."[3] The Stock Exchange of the present day, remarks Cunningham,[4] "may serve as an illustration of a regulated company: for each member conducts his business independently, though all are bound to settle fortnightly with the other members, to refrain from advertising and to abide by the other rules imposed upon the whole body." In contrast with this state of affairs the joint-stock company is a single legal entity, whose members, as such, cannot

[1] Cawston and Keane, *Early Chartered Companies*, p. 10.
[2] But, of course, there is a final limit to the calls, which there was not to the leviations.
[3] Bonar, *Philosophy and Political Economy*, p. 360.
[4] *Modern Times*, Pt. I. p. 215.

CORPORATIONS AND COMPANIES 167

compete with one another, though a shareholder in his private trading capacity may compete with the company of which he is a member. So it was that the " regulated " Turkey Company could, and did, sneer at the incorporated joint-stock East India Company, because the latter was unable to " breed up " East India merchants, seeing that " anyone who is a master of money may purchase a share of their trade and joint stock."

THE JOINT-STOCK ADVENTURE

Joint-stock characteristics, as we know them, first show themselves in the enterprise originally known and described in the gift of incorporation as " The Merchant Adventurers of England for the discovery of lands, territories, isles, dominions, and signiories, unknown and not before that late adventure or enterprise by sea or navigation commonly frequented." Originally incorporated in the reign of Queen Mary, the company had its rights confirmed by the Elizabethan Parliament, which also shortened the corporate name to the " Fellowship of English Merchants for Discovery of New Trades." According to Hakluyt, " it was thought expedient that a certain sum of money should publicly be collected to serve for the furnishing of so many ships. And, lest any private man should be too much oppressed or charged, a course was taken that every man, willing to be of the society, should disburse the portion of twenty and five pounds apiece." In 1582, when the " Merchant Adventurers, with Sir Humphrey Gilbert," was formed as a society and company,[1] it was stipulated that a subscription of £5 was to constitute a " single adventure "—that is to say, it was a £5 ordinary share.[2] In this instance, if the holder of the share chose to accompany the expedition in person, he would become entitled to 1000 acres of the land (apparently Newfoundland) to be occupied—in modern parlance, he would get a

---

[1] The articles of agreement purport to make it a corporation, but this is not done by the patent.
[2] Ordinary shares, as Savigny reminds us, are not obligations but parts of ownership, producing therefore not interest but dividends.

bonus of 1000 acres on his share—thus transformed into a participating ordinary. The joint-stock method spread, even if not invariably under legal auspices or in a legal shape. When the great expedition of Norris and Drake set sail in April, 1589, says Dr. Jessopp,[1] "it assumed the character of a mere joint-stock speculation, a huge piratical venture, to which the Queen contributed £20,000 and six ships." The evolution towards modern methods and expedients was steady, if not exactly rapid. For instance, the Venetian Adventurers found that the Turkey Merchants were overlapping them, and in 1592 we got a movement towards the centralisation of financial force in the shape of what appears to be the earliest instance of an amalgamation, the Governor and Company of Merchants of the Levant. The members were to trade in " one joint capital stock " but each acted upon his own volition as to such operations as he undertook. Membership was compulsory upon merchants trading within the area of the company's operations, and two months from the date of the charter was fixed as the period during which non-members must come in. Conversely, those who should resign (or who, as we should say, declined to join the amalgamation) had eighteen months in which to wind up outstanding commitments, and must then cease to trade within the recognised area.

As Mr. Carr points out in his admirable introduction to the *Select Charters of Trading Corporations*,[2] the form of the Elizabethan and contemporary grants survives in the charters of the British North Borneo, Niger, British East Africa, and British South Africa Companies. These grants are made upon the same species of rehearsal as appears in the early charters with regard to the petitioners' past industry and expense, as well as their worthy designs for the advancement of the commerce of the Mother Country specially and of civilisation generally.[3] The cloth merchants trading to Rouen pleaded in 1606 that they

---

[1] *Dict. National Biography*, s.v. Elizabeth.
[2] Published by the Selden Society.
[3] Carr, *Select Charters*, xiv.

CORPORATIONS AND COMPANIES 169

had spent over £25,000 in establishing a market there, " upon hope to obtain a company." The very phrases of the grants survive from the fourteenth century. *De gratia speciale* points to absolute royal bounty, and no contract with the petitioners. *Ex mero motu* suggests spontaneous recognition of good work, and is not very happily rendered by " mere motion " in the modern charter.

COMPANY ENTERPRISE AT HOME

Ultimately, company enterprise became busy at home as well as abroad. In 1561 Thurland, Master of the Savoy, brought over to England a German mining engineer named Hochstetter, with whose assistance extensive copper-mining operations were commenced in Cumberland.[1] Gresham became surety for the payment of the miners.[2] The Crown could not itself afford to engage in mining operations, or to establish factories : but the middle-class capitalist was ready then, as now, to find the means. Hochstetter succeeded, in 1565, in getting the charter of the Mines Royal from Elizabeth, in consideration of his mining skill and his large expenses in preliminary work. He had " determined to join with him in company divers others, and in that respect doth mean to make divident of the commodities and profits." There were 50 shares, one each being given to various influential people (including Cecil and the Earls of Pembroke and Leicester), for fairly obvious purposes. The charter[3] is a definite grant of incorporation to those who were, or *should become*, shareholders. This is a departure from the earlier municipal and company charters, and marks the unmistakable beginning of the joint-stock company *with transferable shares* and a corporate existence altogether independent of,

---

[1] The Duke of Northumberland intervened, on the ground that the miners were trespassers, and refused to allow them to carry away the ore. This led to the famous Case of Mines (see, for pleadings and judgment, Plowden, p. 310), in which all the justices and barons agreed that by the law all mines of gold and silver within the realm belonged to the Queen (Elizabeth) by prerogative.
[2] Hall, *Society in the Elizabethan Age*, p. 60.
[3] Carr, *Select Charters*, v.

170   EVOLUTION OF THE MONEY MARKET

non-regardant of, and separate from the personalities of the shareholders.

AN EXTRAORDINARY TRANSFORMATION

Contemporaneously with the charter of the Mines Royal, a scheme was broached by a mint official, William Humphrey by name, for " battery works." This company (incorporated by patent) initiated some of the practices which have now become commonplaces of joint-stock activity. The power to assess members is anticipatory of the " call " system. The right to borrow on bond sealed with the common seal foreshadows our modern policy of raising loans upon debentures. Shares alienated—or, as we should say, transferred—were to be noted as such in a book which is really an Elizabethan share register. No shareholder could sue another shareholder in debt or trespass—in effect the same regulation as that which is in force among the members of the Stock Exchange, as such, at the present time. This company was still in existence in 1713, when the public was asked to subscribe £20,000, in order to enable it to undertake a programme of wider activities. Then, by an amazing turn in the course of events, the charters of these ancient mining companies became available as the foundation upon which unchartered insurance companies could be sustained and endowed with legal being. This is one of the romances of joint-stock legal history. When Lord Onslow first evolved his scheme for the London Assurance Corporation (Lord Chetwynd being engaged at the same time on the Royal Exchange Assurance Corporation) the Attorney-General took an adverse view of its claims to recognition by a charter of incorporation. The London Assurance promoter thereupon adopted what many have supposed to be a specifically modern device. He bought out the old proprietors of the Mines Royal and Mineral and Battery Works, carrying on business under the charter originally granted by Elizabeth, and, on the strength of such corporate rights as were thus acquired, he proceeded to initiate a marine insurance business. Onslow and his friends were told by eminent counsel that the expedient was legally quite sound. As the London Assurance Corporation still flourishes, the advice, and the curious legal expedient with regard to which it was sought, would appear to have been justified by events.

THE ADVENT OF THE MONOPOLIES

The opening of these mines and the concurrent initiation of other enterprises was part of a considered financial and commercial policy destined to be expanded to an altogether unforeseen extent by means of the gigantic resources available to a modern joint-stock régime. In securing the assistance of the Hochstetters, and behind them, of the Fuggers, Cecil was mainly anxious to obtain organising power and administrative experience. This is the reason why a multitude of new companies were brought into being with monopolistic privileges, such as would be likely to attract the alien adventurer to this country and lead to the creation of new industries. At the beginning of the reign of James I. practically the whole field of foreign commerce was in the hands of companies. " The Russian trade was monopolised by the Muscovy Company ; the Baltic trade by the Eastland Company : the trade with the shores of the North Sea by the Merchant Adventurers : the Mediterranean trade by the Levant Company : and the trade with West Africa and India by the companies named after those regions."[1]

The companies almost invariably asked for monopolistic powers, so far as the jurisdiction of the Crown extended. In some cases the amount of money spent in preparation was offered as a justification for the request of a monopoly. The attempts of the London soap-makers to establish a monopoly involved a huge expenditure of capital. They paid £10,000 in advance to the King on account of duties on the manufactured article. They paid £40,000 to the old company as compensation, £3000 to certain interested parties, and £20,000 for the stock-in-trade of the old com-

[1] Montague, *Political History of England*, Vol. VII. p. 17.

pany. The idea of monopoly, thus vividly presented in an attractive form, led to the royal grant of exclusive trading privileges to individuals as well as to companies. Where a feudal monarch would have given an estate which had escheated to him, his Tudor successor bestowed the profits of a monopoly. Ultimately, the courts declared against the monopoly patents, on the ground that their only valid justification was not the alleged royal prerogative, but the introduction of a new trade into the realm, " or any engine tending to the furtherance of a trade that never was used before." In Allen's case, where the point was originally raised, his counsel admitted that " where there be many sellers, although they be all free of one company, as Goldsmiths, Clothiers, Merchants . . . who have settled governments and wardens and governors to keep them in order, they were never accounted a monopoly."[1]

THE COLONISING COMPANIES

James I., under the pressure of public opinion, abolished the monopolies altogether. Before the monopolies were dead, however, imperial ambition had been born to vigorous life. A series of companies, organised to exploit Virginia, Massachusetts Bay, Guiana, and the Mosquito Coast, marked the early years of the seventeenth century.[2] There were also grants of incorporation for settlement purposes, quite distinct from those of purely trading charters, which only contemplated trading stations and annual voyages. As Mr. Carr happily puts it,[3] the grant (1670)

[1] Darcy v. Allen, Noy, p. 182.
[2] The ballads of the period, with their incentives to adventure in this direction, must have done a good deal to familiarise the public mind with the joint-stock principle. In the ballad called "London's Lotterie," written with special reference to the colonisation of Virginia and printed in 1612, there are lines which would have an equal application to the joint-stock form of enterprise generally :—
"Mee thinks I see great numbers flocke
And bring in fast their coyne :
And Tradesmen how in loving sort
Their Monyes all doe joyne."
(*Royal Hist. Soc. Trans.*, 3rd Series, Vol. V. p. 57.)
[3] *Select Charters*, Introduction, p. xc.

CORPORATIONS AND COMPANIES

to the Governor and Company of Adventurers of England Trading into Hudson's Bay falls somewhere between these two classes. The Bedford level scheme, another contemporary joint-stock enterprise, is outlined in an indenture of 1631, which indicates that each participant is to find £500 per share within ten days of the call for the money being made. The shares were to be assignable—an essential provision, as we shall see,[1] though the principle was destined to meet with prolonged judicial opposition, almost to our own time. Reconstruction—a familiar and extremely important portion of the modern financial mechanism—appears almost in its modern form as early as the case of the African Company (1682), where, in proceedings concerned with a debt owing from the *old* African Company, the *new* African Company was brought to hearing.[2] The new company bought the old company's stock at the true value, and the money was to be applied in paying the old company's debts. Almost contemporaneously with reconstruction, other joint-stock characteristics (fondly supposed by twentieth-century observers to be wholly modern) begin to appear. The East India Company's charter, for instance, has a provision for disenfranchising those adventurers who do not, within twenty days, pay up their subscriptions towards the first voyage—which sounds like the modern threat of forfeiture if the amount due on allotment and the subsequent instalments are not paid at the due date. Hole-and-corner manœuvres were early in evidence. The charter of the copper miners in England, granted in the third year of William and Mary, contains a provision for notice to shareholders. The governor, deputy governor, and ten to eighteen assistants were to be annually elected, and fourteen days' notice of the function was to be given to all interested in the company. But in 1709 Queen Anne was asked to abrogate this provision owing to the wide distribution of the holdings. It had become " altogether impracticable, many of

---
[1] Assignability or transferability must be distinguished from negotiability. See *ante*, p. 20 *n*.
[2] *Vernon*, Vol. I. p. 121.

[the shareholders] being so dispersed in several parts that the petitioners know not where to find them."

CORPORATION v. PARTNERSHIP

But even when the Crown had brought the trading corporation into being, by the grant of a charter, difficulties, nevertheless, arose. The common-law result was the creation of a legal entity responsible for its debts in its corporate capacity only. The individual members were not liable for the debts contracted by it. Si quid universitati debetur singulis non debetur, nec quod debet universitas singuli debent. If the legal sentiment of the eighteenth century had prevailed this privilege of limited liability would never have been allowed to extend beyond companies formed by the special motion of the Crown. The rest of the trading corporations— the entire modern joint-stock army, so to speak, would have been corporations which could act as entities, but whose individual members were simply in the position of partners, and individually liable for the corporation's debts in accordance with the principle that si quid societate debetur singulis debetur et quod debet societas singuli debent. The early charters, by ignoring this reactionary legal ideal, gave an undoubted impulse to the joint-stock movement. But, none the less, there remained the fact that a joint-stock association, if unincorporated by special exercise of the royal authority, was nothing more than a partnership on a large scale. Unless there had been an alteration, the attraction of immense masses of capital from their lairs into the protean joint-stock activity of the nineteenth and twentieth centuries, would have been impossible, with a resulting loss of all the social and political impetus which they have created. The promoters of a pitch and tar company in 1692 put this infirmity of contemporary corporate enterprise into plain English, and thus gave the real financial reason for these incorporations. They require, they say, a joint stock so great that the same is not to be raised unless upon the establishment of a corporation, because, if such an undertaking should be

CORPORATIONS AND COMPANIES 175

carried on only by articles of partnership, the stock will be liable to the particular and private debts of the several partners, and subject to be torn to pieces upon the bankruptcy of any of them.[1] Practically the same arguments were used by the undertakers of the Bedford Level Drainage scheme. Their works were on a scale which only a corporation could fitly manipulate ; and, moreover, the shareholders would die and leave infant heirs, wives, and others, who were unfit for the conduct of the works. It was to escape the onerous conditions of partnership, said James, L.J., reviewing the development of the law in this respect,[2]

" that joint-stock companies were invented. At first they existed under the favour of the Crown . . . but there were large societies on which the sun of Royal or legislative favour did not shine, and as to whom the whole desire of the associates, and the whole aim of the ablest legal assistants they could obtain, was to make them as nearly a corporation as possible, with continuous existence, with transmissible or transferable stock, but without any individual right in any associate to bind the other associates, or to deal with the assets of the association."

The industrious promulgation of the doctrine of the individual liability of its members, and the rigorous enforcement of the law whenever the opportunity arose, were among the expedients adopted to stifle and discourage the new species of enterprise.[3] In Dr. Salmon v. the Hamborough Company[4] " the members in their private persons were made liable, the company having no goods."[5] This point appears again in the case of certain copper producers, who sought to ally themselves with the Chartered Copper Miners of England in 1720. They said they could not succeed as separate traders (doubtless on account of the magnitude of the capital required) ; but if they entered into co-partnership with each other " they would thereby

[1] Carr, *Select Charters*, xvii.
[2] 5 Ch. App. at p. 734.   [3] *Lindley on Company Law*, p. 3.
[4] Note to Harvey v. East India Company, *Vernon*, Vol. II. p. 396.
[5] The learned editor of *Vernon* (at p. 121, Vol. I.) expresses his inability to give any further particulars of the Salmon case, which he had been unable to find in the reports.

be liable to many dangerous consequences in case some or one of them should happen to fail "[1] The same peril confronted Thomas Addison when, in the closing years of the seventeenth century, he was engaged in forming corporations for lead-mining and for iron-making. A mere partnership was objectionable, Addison said, because, " in case of the bankruptcy of any of the partners, the stock in partnership would be liable to be seized." The Attorney-General agreed that, in these circumstances, a charter might reasonably be asked for, and, subject to certain safeguards, it was granted.[2]

THE COMPANY AS A " NUISANCE "

This legal distrust and dislike of the joint-stock association (even then called a company) ultimately led to these undertakings being regarded as nuisances. Hostility culminated in the Act 6 Geo. I. c. 18 (better known as the Bubble Act, and repealed in 1825), which was, in effect, an attempt to put them down altogether. This impotent statute recites that it is notorious that such enterprises tend to the " common grievance, prejudice, and inconvenience of great numbers " of the lieges :

" and the persons who continue or attempt such dangerous and mischievous undertakings or projects, under false pretences of public good, do presume, according to their own devices and schemes, to open books for public subscriptions, and draw in many unwary persons to subscribe therein towards raising great sums of money . . . and whereas in many cases the said undertakers have . . . presumed to act as if they were corporate bodies, and have pretended to make their shares in stocks transferable or assignable, without any legal authority, either by Act of Parliament or any charter from the Crown for so doing."

The Act was aimed at three *supposed* evils : (1) The unwarranted presumption of corporate existence by

[1] *Petition Entry Books*, 245, p. 522.
[2] The survival of the idea of the joint-stock company as simply partnership writ large, is curiously shown in the fact that the proprietors of the Bank of England were called together at various times in its early history to consult with the directors and to share with them the responsibility of acting in times of crisis.

CORPORATIONS AND COMPANIES 177

bodies unincorporate;[1] (2) the sale of transferable stock in such organisations ; (3) the unwarranted employment of existing charters to support the carrying on of business to which they were never meant to apply ; and (4) one *real* evil, the formation of rotten companies. For these and other reasons, it was enacted that such schemes be " effectually suppressed and restrained for the future by suitable and adequate punishments." Even brokers dealing in the shares were to be punished by a fine of £500 and an incapacity " to be or act as a broker in the future."[2] The attempt at suppression, however, proved to be an endeavour to attain the impossible. The companies were too thoroughly in accord with the needs of the time, and the advent of the Industrial Revolution did but more emphatically demonstrate their necessity to the commercial organisation.

THE STRUGGLE FOR FREE TRANSFER

The attempt to hamper the free transfer of the shares was the most pernicious of all the expedients brought into play to hamper the new joint-stock experiments. Its success must have strangled cosmopolitan financial enterprise in the very act of birth. For ten men who will invest £100 in a given security which they are permitted to assign there is only one who would risk the investment if it were to be inalienable—if, when his name were once on the list of shareholders, it were irremovable until that of his executor took its place. If the principle of free assignability had never secured statutory recognition, the Stock Exchange must have been a mere shadow of its present self, and would have largely failed to discharge its characteristic function of aggregating vast masses of otherwise inactive capital, and continuously redistributing them in

---

[1] In Harrison *v.* Heathorn (6 Man. and Gr. 107), Tindal, C.J., had to remind the court (in 1843) that it was the Bubble Act (repealed by that time) which had made it illegal to presume to act as a body corporate. Tindal expressed his incredulity about such presumption being an offence at common law ; though Best, C.J., had declared (in 1828) that it was, at all events, a " contempt of the King " (Duvergier *v.* Fellows, 5 Bing. 268).

[2] We shall see, at a later stage, a striking illustration of the working of this provision. (Page 185.)

accordance with the needs of the moment. Nervousness about the possible seizure of control seems to have been one reason for this objection to the free transfer of shares. The writer of a pamphlet called *Reasons Against the Prolongation of the Bank* in 1708 points out that " it is as possible for any one prevailing party, where shares are transferable to those that bid the highest, to engross undiscerned the whole Bank, as it is for the bankers to monopolise the whole money, or the greatest part of it." Whatever was the original genesis of the mistrust, the obstructive tactics are discernible in full operation almost contemporaneously with the rise of the modern Money Market, early in the nineteenth century. In R. v. Dodd[1] it was held (1808) that the pretence of non-liability beyond the amount of the share was a mischievous delusion. The Attorney-General denounced the creation of a large joint-stock fund by means of numerous small subscriptions. Lord Ellenborough, in his judgment (p. 527), thought that the smallness of the subscription was only a " lure to the unwary."[2] The shares, the Attorney-General argued, were only made transferable " in order to facilitate the escape of those who are in the secret, and to make redress more difficult and fruitless." Such bodies, moreover, " indefinitely numerous and having only individual (? non-corporate) existence," could with difficulty be traced. Ellenborough, in his judgment, said it was clear that each partner in such an organisation was liable for the whole of the debts contracted by the *partnership*. Finally, he warned the parties to " forbear to carry into execution this mischievous project . . . founded on joint-stock and transferable shares." But the leaven of more liberal sentiment was already working. In R. v. Webb et al.[3] (1811) there is manifest a slight weakening of the judicial antipathy. The case was that of the Birmingham Flour and Bread Company, which was to have a capital of £20,000 in 20,000 equal shares. The original indictment

[1] 9 East, 516.
[2] His lordship's views on the 2s. rubber share, as well as on such phenomena as penny and farthing shares, would be illuminating.
[3] 14 East, 406.

against the defendants was for false pretences in " (1) making subscriptions towards raising a great sum of money " for setting on foot a " new and unlawful undertaking tending to the common grievance, prejudice, and inconvenience of great numbers of the King's subjects " ; (2) presuming to act as if they were a corporate body ; and (3) making the shares transferable and assignable. The Birmingham jury found that the undertaking was, in fact, beneficial to the inhabitants of the town, though prejudicial to the bakers and millers already established there ; but they prayed the advice of the court whether it was an unlawful undertaking and public nuisance under 6 Geo. I. c. 18 *supra*). Ellenborough gave judgment to the effect that the indictment had not been made out, mainly because the acts complained of did not come within that class which the original statute had been intended to prohibit. Pratt v. Hutchinson[1] was an attempt in 1809 to bring a building society within reach of the Bubble Act, with equally futile results.

The year that witnessed the repeal of the Bubble Act (1825) saw the judicial instinct in retrograde motion again towards the policy of suppression. Josephs v. Pebrer [2] was the case of the Equitable Loan Bank, a concern formed to lend money at 8 per cent., which Abbott, C.J., said was " a larger rate of interest than the law allows in general." It had a capital divided into £50 shares, with £1 paid, issued at a premium and purporting to convey to the purchaser the benefit of any future Act of Parliament obtained for the regulation of the company. This premium appears to have been the bête noir of the tribunal which tried the action. Abbott referred to these " enormous premiums " as introducing gaming and rash speculation to a ruinous extent, and gave judgment that the association was illegal.[3] So, Abbott added, "the signs of the times require us to declare it." He said that in view of the large premium on the shares, the dealings in

[1] 15 East, 511.   [2] 3.B. and C., p. 639.
[3] *The Times* was roused into protest against this decision. See leading article, February 5, 1825.

them might possibly have amounted at common law to gaming and wagering with regard to an Act of Parliament which had yet to be obtained. Eldon, who had a great aversion to companies,[1] apparently expressed himself in Kinder v. Taylor[2] as basing his dislike upon their tendency to create monopolies and to discourage the individual efforts of small traders, in support of themselves and their families, by attracting their savings into large joint-stock undertakings. Eldon did not know that there was any objection to these companies monopolising the gold mines of Mexico, but the time seemed to be approaching " when people would neither be allowed to eat, drink, or wear clean linen except upon the terms these companies thought fit to impose." Though the coercive factor is absent, it really is in our days almost impossible to " eat drink, or wear clean linen " without enlisting the services of a joint-stock company. The greater hotels and refreshment undertakings are nearly all of them in the joint-stock form, while scores of small joint-stock laundries grace the registers at Somerset House. It is a truly fundamental transformation, which, in the face of judicial hostility such as this, has in little more than a century so completely changed public sentiment in the matter of the trading company.

After the repeal of the Bubble Act in 1825 the company cases for the next few years turned upon subordinate issues, not upon the main question of legality. Best, C.J., in giving the Appeal judgment in Duvergier v. Fellows,[3] took the opportunity of pointing out that the idea of transferable shares was unrealisable unless the company were a

[1] *Lindley*, Vol. I. p. 182. But Eldon was always prejudiced against financial development. He said he "had chosen his bankers because they were the stupidest in London and if he could find any stupider he would transfer his account."
[2] *Collyer on Partnership*, p. 917, second edition.
[3] 5 Bing. 248. By the judgment it was held (1828) illegal to form a distillery company, not for intrinsic reasons, but because the patent to be acquired by the company contained a proviso rendering it void if transferred to more than five persons; and as the proposed company was to consist of more than five individuals, it was decided that in attempting to form it the plaintiff was essaying the impossible.

CORPORATIONS AND COMPANIES 181

corporation, or else a joint-stock undertaking created by Act of Parliament. " When it is said," he observed, " that the shares were to be transferable, that must mean that the assignee was to be placed in the precise situation that the assignor stood in before the assignment; that the assignee was to have all the rights of the assignor, and to take upon him all his liability. Now the assignee can join in no action for a cause of action that accrued before the assignment. Such rights of action must still remain in the assignor, who, notwithstanding he has retired from the company, will still remain liable for every debt contracted by the company before he ceased to be a member. Indeed, the members of corporations cannot assign their interest and force their assignees into the corporation—[? force the corporation to accept them as members] —without the authority of an Act of Parliament. . . . It concerns the public that bodies, composed of a great number of persons, with large disposable capitals, should not be formed without the authority of the Crown, and subject to such regulations as the King, in his wisdom, may deem necessary for the public security."

There was, however, a reversion to the more liberal view in Walburn v. Ingilby (1832), in which Lord Brougham refused[1] to hold that an incorporated joint-stock company, with transferable shares, was illegal, although there was a distinct declaration, in the deed of settlement, that such provision would be made in all engagements entered into by the directors as would prevent any shareholder from being liable for more than the amount of his share. " To hold such a company illegal," said Brougham (p. 76), " would be to say that every joint-stock company not incorporated by Charter or Act of Parliament is unlawful and, indeed, indictable as a nuisance, and to decide this for the first time, no authority of a decided case being produced for such a doctrine." The Lord Chancellor thought that the purported limitation of liability was entirely nugatory; but it was, at all events, candid. Brougham was inclined to believe that, as between the company and strangers dealing with it, proof of the publicity of the

[1] 1 M. and K., p. 61.

announcement of the purported limitation, in a neighbourhood where they might be likely to see it, might even fix them with notice. But whoever became a shareholder on the faith of such a claim " would have himself to blame, and be the victim of his ignorance of the known law of the land." Later still (1837), in Blundell v. Winsor,[1] there was a decision by the Vice-Chancellor (Shadwell) that a joint-stock company, the shares of which purported to be made assignable at the discretion of the holders, was illegal. Shadwell specifically characterised as a false and fraudulent representation the alleged holding out of the shares as being assignable. But Lindley, commenting on the case,[2] points out that the decision cannot be supported (it was indirectly overruled in Harrison v. Heathorn—see below), and that there was not, in fact, any such holding out as the Vice-Chancellor imagined. As was usual at that time, Shadwell indulged in vague critical remarks[3] about the enterprise being " a wild project, entered into by speculating persons for the purpose of deluding the weak portion of the public of this country, who too often allow themselves to be gulled by any specious scheme that holds out a prospect of gain."

As we approach our modern joint-stock era, we may observe legal opinion to be unconsciously tinged by the liberalisation of public sentiment under financial influence. In Garrard v. Hardey[4] the plea, in an action of assumpsit, was framed (1843) in the very words of the repealed Bubble Act, and alleged the company (the Limerick Marble and Stone Company) to be an illegal association. But inasmuch as the mere general allegation, quoting the words of a repealed statute, would not have been sufficient, the defendants alleged the illegality (at common law) to consist in this—that there was a presuming to act as a corporate body, a pretence of being a trading corporation, and a similar pretence of transferring shares in the stock of the purported corporation without Act of Parliament, charter, or letters patent. Tindal, C.J., in a very brief, but lucid

[1] 8 Sim., p. 601.
[2] *Companies*, Vol. I. p. 182.
[3] 8 Sim., at p. 613.
[4] 5 Man. and Gr., p. 471.

CORPORATIONS AND COMPANIES   183

judgment, pointed out that these acts could not be offences at common law,[1] because such a thing as the raising and transferring of stock in a company was altogether unknown to the law in ancient times, when the common law was in course of development. The Bubble Act, he said, was evidently aimed at some abuse which had then recently arisen, as was obvious from the wording of its preamble. That being the case, the court could see no authority for the allegation that the mere raising and transferring of stock was " simply and per se, without any statement of the mode by which it injures or defrauds the public, an indictable offence at common law." There was no complaint of any illegal mode or means of pretence " as by usurping a common seal, or the like." Judgment was therefore given for the plaintiff.

The question was again argued in 1843. In Harrison v. Heathorn[2] there was a provision in the company's deed of settlement that a person ceasing to be a shareholder should be entitled to a certificate declaring him discharged from all liability on account of the shares formerly held by him.[3] Serjeant Wilde argued that the private partnership deed, as it purported to be carried out in the form of discharge printed below, amounted to a " representation that the persons who should assign their shares would get rid of all the liabilities attached to them ; and that the persons who should take their shares would take them just as the

[1] Lindley takes it to be clear that there is no case deciding that a joint-stock company, with transferable shares, and not incorporated by charter or Act of Parliament, is illegal at common law. The tendency of the courts at one time, as we have seen, was to declare such companies illegal ; but that tendency no longer exists, and an " unincorporated company with transferable shares will not be held illegal at common law unless it can be shown to be of a dangerous and mischievous character, tending to the grievance of His Majesty's subjects " (*Lindley*, Vol. I. p. 153).

[2] 6 Man. and Gr., p. 81.

[3]   " ANGLO-AMERICAN GOLD MINING ASSOCIATION
" CERTIFICATE OF DISCHARGE.

·" I do hereby certify that A. B., of, etc., has ceased to be a shareholder in the above-named company, and that he is discharged from all liabilities on account of the shares formerly held by him. Witness my hand this —— day of ——.

" (Trustee and Treasurer.)"

assignors held them." It was clear, however, he added, that this could not be done. Tindal, C.J., delivering judgment, emphasised his views as expressed in Garrard v. Hardey (*supra*). He said that the raising of transferable shares of the stock of a company could hardly be declared an offence at common law. No instance of an indictment at common law for such an offence could be shown, for the reason that the whole system was quite a modern proceeding. There was no evidence that the creation of these shares " had been productive of injury or inconvenience to numbers of the Queen's subjects." Again, the company was composed, " not of low and ignorant persons, likely to be imposed upon, but, as far as appeared, of men acquainted with the business of the City." Unless, therefore, the nature of the scheme were such that the court had felt bound to declare it " a public and common grievance and nuisance at common law," it was impossible to find for the defendants (in an action of assumpsit), and, as the court could not so declare, there must be judgment for the plaintiffs.

NEW POWERS OF INCORPORATION

Meanwhile in 1825 the Crown had received power to grant charters of incorporation, with a declaration that the persons incorporated should be liable for the debts of the body corporate. In 1834 the Crown was empowered to confer the right of suing and being sued (in the name of a public officer) upon companies, which, nevertheless, it did not think proper to incorporate. Failing a charter or these limited privileges, the good will of Parliament had to be invoked for a special Act, either incorporating the company or, at all events, giving it the privilege of suing and being sued. The only exception to this proposition existed in the case of banking companies, which after 7 Geo. IV. c. 46 (1826) could sue in the name of a public officer, upon compliance with certain conditions. In 1844,[1] however, we encounter a paradox. These provisions of the Act of 1826 were expanded so as to enable all companies to

---

[1] 7 and 8 Vict. c. 110.

CORPORATIONS AND COMPANIES 185

obtain a certificate of incorporation from an office in London, without the necessity of obtaining either a charter or a special Act; but, at the same time, the Legislature withdrew the analogous privileges from banks, by requiring a Crown grant of incorporation in the case of all banking companies formed after 1844. In these banking cases the liability of the shareholders was to remain unlimited. The exception, however, was only a passing qualm, the result, no doubt, of the prejudice of the older banks, including the Bank of England, against the new joint-stock institutions. It was not till 1855 that power was given to companies (other than insurance companies) to obtain a certificate of incorporation with limited liability. So that joint-stock enterprises had to wait till the middle of the nineteenth century before corporateness for any lawful purpose could be obtained by the simple process of registration, and personal liability be limited by one magic word.[1]

[1] Carr, *Select Charters*, Introduction, p. xx. It is difficult to believe that as recently as 1859—within living memory—the mere acting honestly and in the ordinary course of business as a broker, in dealing with the shares of a company, was conjectured to be possibly illegal. The Mexican and South American Company had been formed in 1835, without any deed of settlement. It was neither incorporated by charter nor Act of Parliament, nor had it been registered under 7 and 8 Victoria, c. 118. The official manager, in the winding up of the company (27 Beav., p. 474) summoned a broker who had dealt in certain stock of that company, and the following colloquy ensued :

Q. Have you ever bought any scrip certificates or shares in the Mexican Company ?
A. Never for myself ; and as I am advised the company is illegal, and that I may render myself liable to criminal or penal proceedings, I decline further to answer the question.
Q. Have you ever purchased any scrip certificates for any other person ?
A. I decline to answer, fearing the consequences, as stated above, from the illegality of the company's proceedings throughout. I have no scrip certificates or shares in this company in my possession at this time.
Q. Have you ever had any of those scrip certificates in your possession at any time since November 1, 1857 ?
A. I decline to answer the question.

On a motion for the committal of the witness for contempt it was argued that his fears were illusory, since, apart from the repealed Bubble Act, the acting or presuming to act as a corporate body was not an offence at common law. For the broker it was urged that, despite the repeal of the Bubble Act, persons who presumed to act as a corporation, without the sanction of the Legislature, were guilty of a contempt of the King, by usurping on his prerogative ; and that, it was said, " is considered as a criminal act " (27 Beav. at p. 478). That being the case, dealing in the shares might be illegal for the same reason, and " trafficking in them may

186 EVOLUTION OF THE MONEY MARKET

The continuous existence and activity of the commercial company, in one shape or another, ever since the Plantagenet age, justifies the old saying of Bacon:[1] "I confess I did ever think that trading in companies is most agreeable to the English nature, which wanteth that same general vein of a republic which runneth in the Dutch and serves them instead of a company."

By now it is clearly realised that the joint-stock movement is not ephemeral. It is growing in all directions and gathering strength with its growth. Yet the prejudice against joint-stock limited liability companies did not altogether subside for many years. " I well remember," said Professor Leone Levi in 1879, " the time when limited liability was strongly opposed in the City of London. When in 1851 I gave evidence in favour of the same before a Committee of the House of Commons, the supporters of limited liability were very few."[2] As late as the early 'seventies, the old merchant firms still looked askance at the bills of joint-stock companies, which had to be very solidly backed before there was any chance of

[1] Quoted by Anderson in his *Origin of Commerce*, Vol. II. p. 232.
[2] Gilbart Lectures, 1879.

---

have been illegal at common law" (Josephs v. Pebrer, 3 Barn and Cr. 644). The representation admittedly made at the establishment of the company, to the effect that the shares were legally transferable by delivery, might also be held, said the broker's counsel, to be a fraud upon the public, " and the trafficking in such shares an indictable offence." The Master of the Rolls took the view that there could be no proper refusal to answer the questions. He saw no proof that the company had been " acting as a corporation," in so far as that expression implied the use of a common seal, or suing and being sued under a particular name. As for the alleged illegal assignment of shares, he had " listened in vain for any case, or, indeed, for the statement of any principle, whereby at common law, and independent of any statute, a partnership between persons who agree among themselves that their shares shall be legally assignable in perpetuum, or indefinitely assignable, is absolutely void or illegal." If there were fraud it might be otherwise ; but fraud was not a factor. As for the representation of alleged transferability, it amounted, said the Master of the Rolls, to no more than this : That there was a contract to that effect between the partners themselves. The decision was afterwards affirmed by the Lords Justices. It is worthy of rehearsal and consideration, not so much for the points involved as for the significance of the fact that they should have been seriously argued on such a recent date, and as it were upon the very eve of the enactment of the great Joint Stock Companies Act of 1862.

CORPORATIONS AND COMPANIES 187

discounting them.[1] The unlimited liability[2] was a bogey until a time almost within the experience of the present City generation. It was not until the Companies Act of 1879 (42 and 43 Vict. c. 76), which specifically excludes the Bank of England, that all companies registered with unlimited liability obtained the power to register anew as limited companies, subject to proper provision for all outstanding debts and obligations. Even then a bank of issue registered as a limited company was not to be entitled to limited liability in respect of its notes.

It would be futile to deny that limited liability companies have been characterised by many abuses and have been the cause of extensive losses. Companies have been formed simply in order to sell their shares, or to create a dummy behind which some sinister figure could hide, or in order to get rid of a worthless business which was rapidly declining, or to finance utterly wild and hopeless schemes which never could have raised their capital by an appeal to shrewd capitalists. But these regrettable features of the history of limited liability do not invalidate the soundness of the general proposition that socially profitable enterprise on a vast scale has been brought into existence by its means, though it could never have been created if the persons asked to invest money had known that they would incur the unlimited financial responsibilities of partners. Nor, of course, would they have joined in these numerous enterprises if their shares had been non-assignable. Had the prejudice against

---

[1] *Bankers' Magazine*, July, 1912, p. 72.

[2] At the period of the collapse of the railway boom in 1845 " many innocent men liable for [unlimited] calls had to fly the country, as if they had committed some crime, and to live abroad for many years upon what remnants of their property they could manage to save from the general wreck and from the grasp of the law." (Duguid, *Story of the Stock Exchange*, p. 154.) In Agriculturists Cattle Insurance Co., *ex-parte* Baird [June, 1870], it was unsuccessfully attempted to establish a term of fifty years from death as the period during which the estate of a shareholder remained liable for losses incurred by the company. It was contended that here, in the case of a company formed in the year 1845, under a deed of settlement, there was nothing to limit the liability of the executors of a deceased shareholder, and that their liability was not even confined to debts incurred before the death of the testator. (Baird's Case, Ch. App. 5, p. 725)

assignability prevailed, there could hardly have been a Stock Exchange at all, in the form in which we know it.

THE FUNCTION OF INSURANCE

Finally, to complete this long survey of the components out of which the modern Money Power has been evolved, the origin, purpose, and function of the insurance group requires examination. The Sun Fire office had been opened in 1710. Life Insurance as an individual speculation is traceable in late Tudor times. In its mutual form it had become a familiar thing by the end of the seventeenth century. Simultaneously marine insurance had been developed into a scientific system by the habitués of Lloyd's coffee-house. Lloyd's comes into discernible existence about the same time as the Stock Exchange and develops upon almost identical lines. It originated in a gossiping assembly—an indoor market—in a coffee-house kept by Edward Lloyd, in Tower Street, London. The gathering was a regular and recognised institution at least six years before the foundation of the Bank of England. In 1692, when the Bank was still unborn, the centripetal tendencies of contemporary finance, already clearly observable, drew Lloyd and his clientèle to Lombard Street. There he began the publication of a modest weekly sheet of commercial and shipping news, the predecessor of *Lloyd's List*. As the business done in the coffee-house grew in volume year by year, there arose (as there was doing in Change Alley) the necessity for some central disciplinary organisation of the associating merchants and underwriters, capable of enunciating and enforcing the rules necessary for the efficient and honourable conduct of business. This was difficult of achievement in private premises. Ultimately, however, the whole body removed to the Royal Exchange in March, 1774, and there it has ever since remained. The instinct for standardisation evolved a common form of marine insurance policy, still in force, with only a few changes from its original draft. Eleven years after the Stock Exchange had framed its deed of settlement, and fixed

CORPORATIONS AND COMPANIES 189

itself on its present site, there was elected by ballot the " New Committee for managing the affairs of Lloyd's."

Meanwhile, in 1720, the London Assurance Company and the Royal Exchange Assurance Corporation had come into existence under circumstances already reviewed. These two corporations had been granted a monopoly of marine insurance, though they did not confine themselves to that species. Just as no *corporation* other than the Bank of England could issue notes, so, under the Act 6 Geo. I. c. 18 no corporation other than these two, and no partnerships, could transact marine insurance. But just as private bankers were not interfered with, so " private or particular persons " were to be at liberty to write or underwrite any policies " so as the same be not on the account or risque of a corporation or body politic, or upon the account or risque of persons acting in a society or partnership for the purpose aforesaid." The two corporations, however, did a comparatively small marine business. They preferred fire risks, and left the marine business to Lloyd's. In 1810 a Select Committee was appointed to consider the proposed repeal of the joint corporate monopoly, and reported in favour of the proposal. But Parliament rejected the resolutions of the Committee. It was not till 1824 that Nathan Rothschild, Alexander Baring, Samuel Gurney and Sir Moses Montefiore were able to secure the repeal of 6 Geo. I. c. 18 and to establish the Alliance British and Foreign Fire and Life Assurance Company. Since then an endless succession of marine insurance companies has been formed. As for other insurance undertakings, their name is Legion.

From the point of view of the present essay the advent of the myriad insurance companies[1] into the financial arena has aided the efficiency and acceleration of two main progressive influences : (1) The aggregation of funds, otherwise scattered, into vast masses available for investment, and consequently for social driving-power ;

[1] Assurance had, as already pointed out, been known long before both as an individual speculation and in the mutual form (for life).

o

and (2) the elimination, up to the utmost attainable limit, of the factors of irresponsibility, faithlessness to contracts, chance, caprice, accident, waywardness, convulsion, and irreparable ruin, which, in the absence of the invocation of the principle of average against them, would still be as great a hindrance as they were in ancient days—unless, indeed, they were slightly diminished by our better means of foresight and consequent precaution. A fire—swift and disastrous in its havoc among the wooden houses of the Middle Ages—did damage which was not reparable then, as it is in our own time, out of the proceeds of a fire insurance policy, backed by an immensity of financial resources which does not shrink from rebuilding an entire city. The labours of a lifetime might be swept away in an hour. So they may be now; but mutual foresight spreads the burden over such a multitude of shoulders that it is inappreciable by that particular pair upon which it technically falls, and might have crushed beneath its weight in the absence of the protective consolidation of risks and the concurrent creation of an indemnity fund. These principles, applied in the regions of life, fire, accident, marine, and every species of insurance, make for regularity of movement on the part of the money-mechanism. " Risk is the expression of ignorance, and decreases with the progress of science."[1] Any diminution of the burden of Insecurity stimulates the flow of capital into productive activity.

Insurance makes its appearance almost immediately after the manifestation of a plain differentiation between banker and money-lender, which we can clearly distinguish at the end of the seventeenth century. The business of a money-lender is to advance upon a large but undefinable risk, with a correspondingly liberal element of insurance included in the charge which he makes for the accommodation. The business of a banker, on the other hand, is to make advances upon securities of such a character that a risk can be measured with almost mathematical precision, so as, consequently, to reduce to a

[1] Irving Fisher, *Yale Readings in Insurance*, p. 4.

minimum the element of insurance included in the rate at which he will grant the advance. The risk,[1] and the consequent premium, cannot be altogether eliminated from the majority of a banker's transactions ; but one function of the insurance company is to bridge the gulf which separates these two classes of transaction by transforming a risk which would only be suitable for a moneylender's security into one which a banker could safely handle. This is effected by reducing the risk, as far as possible, to a mathematical basis, by the aid of experience and the doctrine of probabilities, so that although the time and the circumstances cannot be precisely predicted with regard to any given contingency that may, or must, happen, they can, in the aggregate, be brought within the law of average. " Ignorance is reduced by investment in intelligence . . . by the agency of insurance companies [we] set off one event against another, and by compounding the effects, reduce, not indeed, the Uncertainty of any event, but the amount of reserve which must be held against its occurrence."[2] Consequently the life, the interest, or the property, all of them representing values which might otherwise be injuriously affected by the possibility of the contingency, can be rendered capable of becoming an addition to the credit wealth of the community, and even to the constantly increasing international currency of modern finance. Money can be borrowed upon the mortgage of a house, when the fabric is insured against fire, at a much more advantageous rate than that which would be quoted in the absence of insurance. An individual can obtain financial accommodation on the security of a life policy on terms immensely more reasonable than those available if he had nothing but personal security, subject to the inevitable ultimate contingency of his death, to offer. A ship-owner, as the events of 1914 have demonstrated,

[1] " The monied men have a right to look to advantage in the investment of their money. To advance their money, they risk it : and the risk is to be included in the price." (Burke, Regicide Peace, *Works*, Vol. V. p. 389).

[2] Lavington, *Economic Journal*, 1912, p. 401.

may proceed with his business under the shadow of a European war, and even obtain easy financial accommodation for that purpose, when he is under the ægis of modern marine insurance. Since the scope of modern insurance extends to every conceivable casualty, the modern banker will advance even upon perishable goods under the protection of an approved policy. In each case the difference between the protected rate and the unprotected rate will be considerably greater than the amount paid to secure the protection, and the result is, in effect, a large " consumers' surplus," made available by the invocation of the laws of average and experience.

No more vivid and conclusive illustration of this transformation could be furnished than is afforded by modern dealings in reversionary interests. In our own time the value of such an interest can be measured with the utmost nicety, so that it can be made the basis of a legitimate credit transaction on the best possible terms, as a consequence of the practical elimination of the element of risk. This is the difference between seventeenth-century gambling with a money-lender, on a post-obit bond, with the probable payment of 60 per cent. for the accommodation, and raising money on an actuarially-valued reversionary interest at a figure very little above the twentieth-century bank rate. Every one of these credit transactions, whether on a life policy or with a fire policy in the background, or upon a reversionary interest, stands for an increased volume of currency, and, consequently, for cheaper and more facile credit. It would be superfluous to add, however, that the growth of these facilities, which have added immeasurably to the aggregate of assets available as a basis for the credit transaction of the community, could never have taken place if there had not been the co-operation of immense financial resources. The assumption of a huge risk, in such a manner as effectively to protect an equally huge credit transaction, involves commensurate resources adequate to meet the risk if it materialise. This could only have been created under the ægis of a disciplined Money Market. The gradual extension of these

CORPORATIONS AND COMPANIES 193

principles from life, fire, and marine insurance down to sickness, accident, hail and cyclone, plate glass, fidelity, burglary, live stock, and other species, covering the most minute, remote, and apparently unappraisable contingencies, points to an ultimate extension of the principle over the whole field of human activities; so that, as a matter of fact, the sinister operation of all that multitude of unforeseen occurrences which in ancient days did so much to delay and dislocate the progress of humanity will gradually be excluded altogether. " Whereas formerly each man bore his own risks, a new class is arising to relieve him of those risks. Instead of all traders speculating a little, the special class speculates much."[1]

There is a further and most important consideration also. We shall see, in due course, that the mechanism of banking and the machinery of the Stock Exchange provide a crisisometer[2] of the utmost delicacy, which foretells trouble long before it is palpable to the ordinary observer. And there is in the insurance companies (and the investment trust organisation) a force which automatically co-operates with the other elements (though it works in the reverse direction) to relieve any strain. A banker must keep his resources as liquid as he can. If they are not in liquid form when he experiences a sudden demand, he must convert them into that form with the maximum velocity, and this whether or not he is convinced of their ultimate soundness as investments. But the Trust and insurance companies can afford to maintain a strictly passive attitude in the face of such a contingency, provided they have no doubts about the intrinsic and ultimate soundness of their investments. A great life insurance company is never subject to " runs." It can forecast with mathematical accuracy the demands which will be made upon it within a given period. The result is that a time of depression or crisis which may possibly force the bank into selling is just the period when the insurance company

---

[1] Emery, *Speculation on the Stock and Produce Exchanges of the United States.* Quoted by F. E. Steele, *Economic Journal*, 1897, p. 590.
[2] The word " crisisometer " is explained (and apologised for) on p. 591.

can afford to buy. Having satisfied itself of the ultimate soundness of its purchases, it can venture to buy and wait. Therefore it becomes a valuable market auxiliary at the very moment when the banker by force of circumstances can render little or no assistance to the market at all. This calm self-reliance means also that in a time of sudden strain or crisis a vast aggregate of securities which might otherwise be seeking realisation remains dormant in the safes and strong-rooms of these powerful holders, so that the market is called upon to sustain a shock only of such sales as are absolutely necessary to meet the trouble. It is not placed under the additional pressure of realisations forced upon it by mere unreasoning panic. Sales for liquidation are not augmented to any serious extent by sales for realisation, inspired by sheer mob-suggestibility.

Although Lloyd's has continued to hold a very strong position, it has never established anything approaching such a centralisation of insurance business as would correspond with the centralisation of stock and share dealing on the Stock Exchange. Lloyd's to-day is prepared to take practically any risk at a price : but it is only one among a myriad purveyors. There has been organisation here and there—as, for instance, in the shape of the Life Offices Association and by the tariff offices in the matter of the rates for fire insurance. But there is as yet no dominant central authority in the insurance world, though proposals for the formation of a central jurisdiction are attracting more and more sympathetic attention. When they materialise, the consolidation of finance will have been enhanced by the bringing of many hundreds of millions of funds into more direct and manageable relationship.

Allusion has been made to the investment trust and finance companies, themselves a specialised application of principle of insurance. These, however, were a later growth, and could not, without anachronism, be introduced into the present preliminary survey. They will be treated in their proper place in the course of the succeeding **analysis.**

PART II
THE NUCLEUS OF ORGANISATION

CHAPTER VII

THE PRESTIGE OF THE BANK OF ENGLAND

ALTHOUGH the modern money market dates only from Waterloo, its components had shaped themselves long before. By the year 1725 all the basic essentials of the modern financial mechanism were in being. The Bank of England had been founded : there was a banking community around it : there were localised share dealings, companies with assignable shares, negotiable instruments, the beginnings of insurance, and an increasing national trade to whet the financial ambition and offer a field for its exercise. But if all these factors had developed without any centralisation of control and responsibility, the interaction of a mutual hostility must have prevented their attainment of the maximum scope and efficiency. To some extent, indeed, this sinister influence played an obstructive and disintegrating part, while finance was learning its business in the school of experience. Again and again, as we proceed, we shall have to witness the malign results of internecine strife, where there should only have been disciplined rivalry. The formative centripetal process is even now, in the twentieth century, not wholly complete ; but it has advanced far enough for the central sources of control to be plainly definable, and for their principles of operation to be analysed with clarity and accuracy. The gradual assumption, by organised finance, of the attraction, aggregation, guardianship, stimulation, and administration of the resources of the community was destined to place English banking in the forefront of the world, to consolidate the foundations of the cosmopolitan Money-Power, and to render it, in time, the dominant influence operative upon the progress of humanity. We have scrutinised and analysed the generative process by which the elements of this gigantic and prolific force came into being. What is to be done now is to trace the slow, but steady, formation, and then the advancing confidence and strength, of a central financial nucleus, and to indicate as clearly as may be how all the numerous economic forces and interests of modern society have grouped themselves round it.

The existence of a centripetal force is a primary necessity for the development of a central control. Organisation can only take place under a prevailing sway. The atoms will not aggregate or the system integrate around nothing. This is the process by which our own planetary system has come into being. It is itself the result of the concentration of a vast nebula which has been undergoing contraction and condensation for untold millions of years. "The tendency of the transformation was, however, always in one direction. It did at last result in a great increase of the density of the substance of the nebula, both in the central regions, as well as in the subordinate parts. In due time, this increase in density had reached such a point that the materials in the condensing centres could be no longer described as retaining the gaseous form. . . . The nebula has condensed into a vast central mass with a number of associated subordinate portions."[1] The modern financial organisation could not be more vividly described than as " a vast central mass with a number of associated subordinate portions." Modern science really began with the discovery and definition of physical gravitation, and only after a couple of centuries finds out that the same inexorable law rules in the financial realm ; but reinforced by biological and psychological tendencies of a type inoperative (or only operative in the slightest degree) in the inorganic sphere. It has been said that from the fourteenth century onwards history may be summarised by titles, in crescendo—Revival, Renascence, Reformation, Revolution, Evolution. A more picturesque and a more

[1] Sir Robert S. Ball, *The Earth's Beginning*, p. 247.

THE BANK OF ENGLAND 199

accurate presentation of the facts may be attained if we contemplate the history of the last six centuries as one of decentralisation from around religious and political centres of gravity, and recentralisation around a potent financial hierarchy. Money accumulates from all quarters to be borrowed in all quarters. As mediæval ideals and beliefs lose their grip upon mankind, and politics become less and less a serious grappling with realities, financial centralisation steps into the gap. All the divisions of caste, tribe, clan, order, party, and so forth are being liquefied in the money-crucible, and are crystallising again around new centres. Standardised cosmopolitan securities facilitate rapid liquefaction and recrystallisation. All the later reluctant, but inexorable, reforms connected with the abolition of entail, the bringing of the freehold estate within the range of liability for simple contract debts,[1] the cheapening of land transfer, registration of title, and the Married Women's Property Act, belong to the same type, and have been inspired by the same instinct for loosening the grip of dead hands and dead minds upon the world, excluding the abnormal and obstructive factors, and thus facilitating freedom and celerity of readjustment among the economic components of society. There is first the aggregation of capital by the discouragement of hoards, and then its redistribution, through the banking system, and with the aid of the Stock Exchange, over an area of unprecedented extent. The aggregation of the money is the anabolic process, the storing of latent economic energy. Its transformation into credit, and distribution over the social area, is the katabolic liberation of the economic energy, its change into the kinetic form. Simultaneously, social prestige has fallen away from the *de*-structive trophy like the scalp, from the feudal possession wrung from a slaughtered or

[1] Freehold estates were formerly not subject to simple contract debts. The creditors of the country gentleman could only obtain execution on half the profits of his real property. Romilly's Bill to remedy this abuse was lost, though his analogous measure confined to freeholders who were also traders was passed without difficulty. But in 1833 the greater anomaly was remedied by a short Act of a single section. The incident marked the end of the landed monopoly, the close of the age of privilege.

enslaved owner, to the *pro*-ductive emblem (like the bond and the bank balance) of work done and the possession of the reward achieved.

THE BEGINNINGS OF PRESTIGE

The history of the Bank of England as the destined centre of the modern Money Power, is the record of a gradually accumulating prestige. For a century and a half its prestige and its financial resources grew together. The eighteenth century witnessed nothing in the nature of any formal acknowledgment of the Bank's primacy. But the gradual permeation of the public mind by a consciousness of the social services rendered by the Bank of England was the next best thing to a definite acknowledgment of its supremacy. It is a fact, as we shall see, that all through the literature, both public and private, of the eighteenth century we can detect this appreciation of the growing influence of the Bank and of the importance of the rôle which it has played. But while the prestige of the Bank of England was gradually increasing, the process is by no means easy to trace, because it was taking place in the presence of the generation which indeed witnessed the phenomenon but did not understand its meaning. We can rather infer than demonstrate. At the era of the Reform Bill—just at the most critical stage, when the control of the mainsprings of the development of society passed from the " sporting gentry and superficially educated nobility " who disgusted Herbert Spencer—the advent of the great joint-stock banks created a powerful rivalry, and the Bank of England has long ceased to be the premier institution from the point of view of its own financial resources. But its " long-existing prestige and prescriptive leadership " (the words are Professor Dunbar's) remain, and gather fresh brilliance at every crisis through which the nation passes. Bank and nation have trodden parallel paths. Both were once practically monopolists— the one of commerce, the other of financial resources. But England, says Mr. Perris,[1] " if she has no longer any

[1] *Industrial History of Modern England.*

monopoly of the means to wealth, holds her moral primacy among the nations." Threadneedle Street, if it has no longer a monopoly of money, holds, and steadily strengthens, its moral primacy among the banks. No bank, says Professor Foxwell,[1] has "played so large and so worthy a part, not merely in the fortunes of a great nation, but also in the general financial activities of the world." The key to the enigma of enhanced financial prestige, combined with relatively diminished financial power, is to be found in the words of Jeremiah Harman, who, in 1832, summed up the whole policy of the Bank in a single phrase when he said that it had "resolved to make common cause with the country." In carrying out that plan the Bank's traditional policy has been to sacrifice profit to absolute security.

NO FINANCIAL TYRANNY

Although the whole history of *financial*[2] combination, concentration, centralisation, and unification is contained within a period of less than two hundred and fifty years, it has probably determined for all time the character

[1] Preface to Andreades, *History of the Bank of England*.
[2] The word "finance," now possessing a highly specialised significance, has its ultimate origin in the Latin "finis"—an end. It comes to us, through modern French, in the basic sense of ending a dispute, or an outstanding obligation, by a payment in settlement. The accent was on the first syllable in Dr. Johnson's day, though it is now almost invariably upon the second. The essential significance of the word—an ending, or finis—does not seem to have survived, at all events as its primary meaning, very long after its introduction to the language. It can be found in a Coventry mystery about 1400 A.D., where there is an allusion to "God, that alle thynge did make of nowthe (nought) . . . puttyst each creature to his fenaunce." The word developed rapidly into the significance of "a final settlement." We get it even in Chaucer: "There is no more, but dethe is my fynaunce"—i.e. the conclusion of all my affairs. Then follows the significance of a ransom, as in Grafton's Chronicle (1568), where it is recorded of a certain individual that "after he had lyen a certaine of tyme in prison, he was for his finance delivered." The constitutions of the vill and port of Rye (temp. Henry VI.) provide for the receipt "from every stranger, as though from a prisoner taken, payment of his finance (finantiam) for his ransom." (*Hist. MSS. Comm.*, V. p. 490.) Contemporaneously, and foreshadowing the modern meaning, is the sense of a stock of money or goods, a treasure—practically equivalent to one of the senses of the word capital. In 1502, in the *Ordinance of Crysten Men*, there is the case "yf the procurer or tuter of ony faderless chylden gyveth theyr fynaunce unto usurye."

From this point we come rapidly to the modern meaning of the word. It relates, for instance, to borrowing. "There was no money to be had

of mundane civilisation. With all this there has been no financial tyranny, or anything approaching it. The financial power is rather trustee than tyrant; it is trustee for the consumer, the wage-earner, the investor, and the commonwealth. The union which we call the Money Power is, in sociological terminology, an interest group evolving into a functional group, characterised by a permitted freedom of individual movement with a collective sanction annexed. We have not experienced the results of attempted monopoly-creation to anything like the same extent as the United States, because our financial power, as the history of the Bank of England will vividly demonstrate, has always possessed a larger endowment of public spirit, a keener realisation of public duty. The " Damn the public " theory has never obtained in Great Britain. In keeping itself alive and well the financial hierarchy has provided economic health insurance for the whole community. Its

---

at finance in Antwerp," says Strype, writing in 1721 (but not writing of contemporary conditions, of course), " under 16 in the hundred for one year." Even Caxton (1489) had approached this sense when he wrote that " a prynce . . . ought beforehande to . . . see where and how his fynaunce shall be made and taken." And hence Gibbon employs the word in 1781 of the public resources : " To their wisdom was committed the supreme administration of justice and the finances." (*Decline and Fall*, Vol. II. p. 33.) And Cowper (1766) of private funds : " My finances will never be able to satisfy these craving necessities." Meanwhile Fox had utilised the word in relation to the affairs of a company—i.e. to " the finances of the East India Company " ; while Junius had already come near the modern colloquial significance (*Letters*, XXXIX. p. 201) in alluding to " his first enterprise in finance," which reads almost like an extract from a critical City article of to-day. Thus far of the noun. The verb, apparently, was new even in so recent a period as the Overend-Gurney crisis; for *The Times*, in 1866, notes that " to finance a business— a new verb—is to supply it with capital to make a daring speculation." The old noun financy, which originally meant the same as finance, is now entirely obsolete, though once used in both singular and plural (financies). Thus far of the word " finance." The distinction between finance and capitalism will be analysed at a later stage (p. 248.) It is perhaps rather unfortunate that the word " financier " tends occasionally to be used as if it were synonymous with " shady company promoter." The verb " to finance " is also occasionally employed in a similar sense. But these are at the moment abnormal uses of the words and may probably be regarded as mere temporary aberrations. Mr. Lehfeldt (*Economic Journal*, 1910, p.554) defines a financier as " a person who, disposing of a substantial amount of capital, devotes it to businesses over which he exercises the supreme control, or a substantial share in the supreme control." But surely this is the capitalist entrepreneur as distinguished from the " pure capitalist," such as the savings bank depositor, who, with regard to his deposit, plays an entirely passive part.

THE BANK OF ENGLAND

gospel was proclaimed, consciously or unconsciously, in the declaration of the first deputy governor of the Bank of England (Michael Godfrey, who died in 1695), that " in this business one cannot do good to oneself, without doing good to others." A public sentiment, or a national ambition, which is evoked, and perhaps fanned into violent manifestations, at irregular and unfixed intervals will never do the same efficient work as that which never relaxes a steady and unchanging pressure, the outcome of intelligence and not of caprice, of calculation and not impulse, of science and not partisanship. Freeman's axiom that history is past politics, and that current politics are only present history, must be modified if we reflect that the real, the profound, and the permanent evolutionary changes in the life of a nation take place in, and as a consequence of, its economic rather than its political functions. Economic history is probably destined to evolve into a new interpretation of history in the wider sense, exhibiting it as a process which is taking us from the national to the cosmopolitan as it drew our forefathers from the clan to the city-state, and thence to the nation. The power which controls and guides the economic development will therefore be more potent in ultimate influence than that which guides a Legislature or holds the Great Seal. It will accumulate vast stores of experience. It will become endowed with an ever-augmented capacity for carrying them into effect. " The Bank of England," said the Director of the United States Mint,[1] in March, 1914,

" as the custodian of the gold reserve of the London market, has had a much greater experience with this problem than any other institution. In the course of its long career it has had every kind of situation presented, and, perhaps, made every kind of a mistake, but it has gained knowledge by its mistakes, and the whole world has profited by its experience. Certain definite principles relative to the control of credits, the management of crises, and the maintenance of a gold reserve have been evolved and established so that the world has accepted them, and one by one all nations have provided them with the equipment to carry these principles into effect."

[1] *New York Times*, March 15, 1914.

In the Middle Ages, as White says, it was the Papacy which constituted the main bond between the various nations of Europe; to-day it is the financial hierarchy which rules a realm far wider in superficies, though by no means identical in character and purpose.

But when we say that these definite principles have been " evolved and established," we are contemplating rather a deliberate, conscious, hard-won adaptation to environment than the half-unconscious lethal elimination of the unfit, with the contemporaneous survival of the better-equipped entities, which is the more usual connotation of the term " evolution." The Bank of England, and the Money Power around it, have been built in the same slow, circumspect, and experimental fashion as the English constitutional fabric itself. It was doliogenic rather than orthogenic, down to the time of the Bank Charter Act, if not as recently as the Overend-Gurney crisis. That is to say, it inherited a growing accumulation of tradition and experience, by which it continuously adapted itself to its environment, though with no such conscious purpose as it has now realised :—

" The development of the Bank of England is in no way different from the evolution and completion of all other social and political institutions in England. Their foundations have been laid piece by piece at the dictates of practical needs, instead of being planned as a whole according to abstract principles. And on these foundations the buildings themselves have been practically raised, curious in form, no doubt, and irregular, but remarkable in their solidarity, imposing in their appearance, and excellent in their practical working."[1]

NEW SOCIO-FINANCIAL RELATIONSHIP

The establishment of the Bank of England, regarded from the politico-financial point of view which alone engaged the attention of its founders and their contemporary critics, marks the opening of the final stage in one of the most fruitful developments of economic differentiation —the establishment of a specific relationship between

[1] From a review in the Greek newspaper *Nea Himera* (September 8–21, 1901) of Andreades' *History of the Bank of England*, quoted therein p. 402.

organised finance and society at large. It signalises the last phase of a process of evolution, extending from the time when the nation was represented by a King who borrowed on his own securities down to the era when the borrowing is done by Parliament and the King ceases to have any authority at all to pledge the credit of the community. Although the Commons began early in the fifteenth century to use grants of taxation as a means of obtaining concessions from the King, the long hostilities with France, followed by the Wars of the Roses, and, again, succeeded by the Tudor despotism, prevented them from using their power to its full extent. Yet the money interest is no sooner born than there are plain hints that the realm is the King's to foster and protect, but not to exploit and plunder. Even as early as Piers Plowman[1] conscience is made to tell the King that " Omnia sunt tua ad defendendum, sed non ad deprehendendum "—which, being interpreted into the modern vernacular of transatlantic constitutionalism, means " Millions for defence, but not a cent for tribute." But Parliament had little or no control over the borrowings of the monarch or of the various departments of the administration. When, at length, the Commons became awake to the real position, they found themselves face to face with a sovereign like James I., who had exaggerated ideas of the royal prerogative. Hostilities became inevitable. As soon as they were over, and the nation turned to put its house in order, we entered the closing stage of the evolution of national finance, to wit, the centralisation of the public resources in one institution—the Bank of England—destined to become the rallying point of a source of supply too delicate to be forced,[2] yet too strong to be raided. Corporation

[1] Passus xxii., p. 481.
[2] " Thus, in great Britain, some of our establishments are appointed for the support of credit. They stand, therefore, upon a principle of their own, distinct from, and in some respects contrary to, the relation between prince and subject. It is a new species of contract superinduced upon the old contract of the State. The idea of power must as much as possible be banished from it : for power and credit are things adverse, incompatible : *non bene conveniunt, nec in una sede morantur.* Such establishments are our great monied companies." (Burke, Observations on a late publication, *The Present State of the Nation, Works,* Vol. III. 68.)

P

rights are given to public creditors, in return for their financial assistance. The military tradition begins to fade, and the physically weakest no longer of necessity goes to the wall, since the world begins to need brain more than brawn. Status gives place to contract and rank to bank. The monarch no longer borrows personally; for he has no security to offer. Even if he has, the only source of financial aid to which he can apply is practically controlled by Parliament. It is specifically forbidden to lend to him without the authority of Parliament.[1] Public credit[2] is in being, though destined for the next century and a quarter to be dependent upon the Bank. Not only had the King himself lost control of the national finances, but his own private account, in time, drifted away from the Bank of England into private banks like Barclay's, Drummond's, and Coutts's. So that, as Dr. Bisschop says, "the Exchequer and the King's private purse parted company for good." The Money Power is ranged against the kingly prerogative and against what is left of the Divine Right. The change is not sudden or cataclysmic. It is not possible to say, at any given moment, that yesterday we were under feudalism and to-day we are ruled by finance. "It often happens" —we are considering an actual instance—" that a new economic environment is entered before the changes of earlier epochs have been worked out. In such cases two

[1] 5 and 6 Wm. and Mary, c. 20, s. 29.
[2] Addison had seen in the great Hall of the Bank of England " a beautiful Virgin seated on a Throne of Gold. Her Name (as they told me) was Publick Credit." With an insight that looks almost like a flash of economic inspiration he adds that she was " infinitely timorous in all her behaviour . . . and startled at everything she heard." She already betrayed that sensitiveness of which we shall have more to say. In the " twinkling of an eye she would fall away from the most florrid Complexion, and the most healthful State of Body, and wither into a Skeleton." (*Spectator*, No. 3, March 3, 1711.) As for Public Credit, compare the receipt dated 1644 " for £30, the voluntary loan of John Buxton of Tibenham towards the £100,000 agreed to be advanced ' for our brethren of Scotland towards payment of their army raised for our assistance . . . to be repaid to him with eight per cent. interest . . . for the speedy repayment whereof the *Public Faith* of both nations is engaged.' " (Buxton MSS., *Historical MSS. Commission*, p. 262.) The goldsmiths lent money (1658–1659) " for the relife of Ireland upon the *publique fayth*." (Prideaux, *Memorials of the Goldsmiths Co.*, Vol. I. p. 243.)

sets of influence are at work at the same time, each modifying the national thought in particular fields."[1] In the present case the hostility of the landed classes to the Bank of England shows how bitter was the opposition of the survivors and survivals of the feudal era. The exponents of the old feudal ideals continued to resist social progress, the offspring of the new finance, down to the time of the first Reform Bill.

It was the contemporary realisation of a change in the fundamentals of society—a change only vaguely understood, and widely misinterpreted—that made the Bank of England for years the centre of political controversy, carried on to an extent, and on a basis, almost incomprehensible to us. It stood out the more conspicuously as a financial achievement because of the failure of the French Government to establish a Royal Bank for the circulation of Mint Bills.[2] One of the principal objections put forward by the opponents of the establishment of the Bank was that banks bore the brand of republicanism : " They never met with Banks nor Storks anywhere, save only in Republicks. And if we let them set footing in England we shall certainly be in danger of a Commonwealth."[3] " Is not the hand of Joab in all this ? " had been the question posed by a pamphleteer as early as 1676, in reproach of the power of the new bankers, and in obvious allusion to the designs of Joab upon Absalom.[4] Walpole's project (1721) " is to aggrandise the Bank . . . and by that to govern the other companies and consequently the whole kingdom."[5] Critics were so far justified in their partisan attitude that the Bank proved, for at least two generations, a sturdy bulwark of Whig ascendancy.[6] It was the rallying of the moneyed men[7] to the Whig party,

[1] Patten, *Development of English Thought*, p. 14.
[2] I. S. Leadam, Finance of Godolphin, *Royal Hist. Soc. Trans.*, 1910, p. 25. [3] *Brief Account of the Intended Bank of England*.
[4] 2 Samuel xiv. 19.
[5] Stratford, Canon of Christ Church, to Edward Harley, *Portland MSS.*, Vol. VII. p. 308.   [6] Lodge, *Political History*, 1660–1702, p. 386.
[7] Paterson's allusions in the *Brief Account of the Intended Bank of England* to " Money'd Men " and " considerable persons " remind us that financial differentiation was already manifest ; there were big and little powers. So much was evident in 1692. John Bastwick (*Lombard Street*

in consequence of the foundation of the Bank of England, that made the City a traditional stronghold of Liberalism down to a time easily within living memory. It laid a deeper emphasis on the division which had already ranged the trading classes on the side of the Parliamentary army, while the landed gentry stood behind the King. In fact, the whole Tory sentiment was against the new institution. This was one of the reasons why the Tory party rallied round the South Sea Company, of which the King was president, and which, for a time, occupied a more influential position than the Bank of England. In the sturdy self-confidence which withstood all opposition there is a prototype of the unswerving struggle towards disciplinary concentration and co-ordination which has ultimately made the twentieth-century Money Market. Germinal continuity, so important a doctrine in post-Darwinian biology, has its economic application also.

NOT UNNATURAL JEALOUSY

Yet it is curious that in *Reasons Against the Prolongation of the Bank* (1708), the Bank of England is alleged sometimes to be called the "Royal Bank." Bolingbroke declares that the secret policy of the Bank was to create a class of creditors dependent on the Crown, so as to counterbalance the Tory landlords. Bolingbroke was especially bitter against the new moneyed men. "The proprietors of the land and the merchant who brought riches home by the returns of foreign trade, had during two wars borne the whole immense load of the national expenses, while the lender of money, who added nothing to the common stock, throve by the public calamity, and contributed not a mite to the public charge." Apart from mere political feeling, there was bound to be class jealousy with regard to the augmentation of the influence of the London

---

Lecturer's Farewell Sermon Answer'd : or the Welsh Levite toss'd de novo— the pamphlet is in the British Museum) says that David Jones's antiusury sermon was aimed at the "*great* bankers." By this time "the usurers, brokers and jobbers . . . distinguished themselves by the name of the Monied Interest" (quoted in the *Art of Stock Jobbing*, Pref. vi.).

THE BANK OF ENGLAND

moneyed interest at the expense of the country squires. Money was Whig and Land was Tory. The power which used to follow land, said Swift, had gone over to money. The Bank, it was urged, would favour a selected few, and ruin all the rest. The Lords were afraid that the payment of such high interest as 8 per cent. would divert money from investment in land ;[1] for 6 per cent. seems to have been considered a normal return on an investment in real property, judging from some of Bastwick's observations in 1692. Their apprehensions in that respect were deepened by the fact that the Bank was empowered to grant interest on deposits at the rate of 3 per cent.[2] Paterson vigorously argued that the Bank would not " make any alteration in our Government unless it be to make Property still more

[1] Money certainly was diverted from land ; for the writer of the pamphlet called *Reasons Against the Prolongation of the Bank*, in 1708, declares that the " value of our land has so fallen already that if a country gentleman will borrow money, he must go to London for it, and if his land lies not within 40 miles of the Bank, he must pay (one way or other) at least 8 if not 10 or 12 per cent. or return home without it. For the Bank has pretended (by advertisement in the *Gazette*) to lend at 5 per cent., yet (naming not how much, nor how long to continue it) that has only been given out as a shoing-horn, they being no way obliged to it, either from their own constitution, or the Government." But as national trade developed during the eighteenth century the new trading class began to have landed ambitions, precisely as their fifteenth and sixteenth-century predecessors had done. The successful German entrepreneur, before the war, was at a stage of evolution corresponding to that of our eighteenth-century capitalists, and suffered from the same land-hunger. But in eighteenth-century England the purchasers of land were no longer, as in the Middle Ages, seeking an investment of almost the only species available. They wanted the power and prestige which attached to landed possessions. The large fortune was a competitor in the land market : the new manufacturing industries offered opportunities to small capitals. The two forces changed the character of the agricultural population, first by driving the more capable individual into industrial life, and secondly by degrading the feebler types into small tenants or mere labourers. In our time, with the prestige of landed property again on the wane, finance no longer hankers after landed acquisitions merely as such. These considerations are interesting as showing how money and the other social forces constantly influence one another, like double stars in mutual and inseparable alliance.

[2] Money was lent on mortgage and real security at 5 per cent., foreign bills of exchange were discounted at $4\frac{1}{2}$ per cent., and inland bills and notes for debt at 6 per cent., though customers of the Bank could have this business done at 3 and $4\frac{1}{2}$ per cent. respectively. The exorbitant terms on which foreign bills were discounted by the " harpies of Lombard Street," gave way before a strong and shrewd institution which could, and would, do the business at reasonable rates—in spite of being itself dubbed the " harpy of Grocers' Hall." Money was advanced by the bank on non-perishable goods at 5 per cent.

fixed and secure and to link the People more firmly to our English Constitution, and to insure them, as it were, against the itch of change." The public itself, accustomed to see 40 per cent. paid in discounts and commissions on short loans, could not believe in the possibility of so low a rate as 8 per cent. upon a loan enjoying no fixed date of maturity. As for the goldsmiths (accused by the Bank directors of being coin-clippers on a large scale), their efforts to precipitate disaster upon the Bank, by the sudden presentation of large blocks of notes, proved vain expedients, which recoiled on their own heads.

THE UNORTHODOX RELIGIOUS FACTOR

Nor were conflict and contrast only between Whig and Tory. It is impossible to pass by this epoch without noticing the advent into the economic *mélange* of an ingredient as new-fashioned as Calvinism when it sanctioned the receipt of interest, and as Judaism when it brought us the arts of financial strategy and finesse. That ingredient is the unorthodox in religion. The original charter of the Bank of England has a special provision that any proprietor, if challenged at the court where he desires to vote, must " take the oath of stock "— that is, must swear that he is a *bona-fide* holder ; but a " declaration of stock " is to suffice " if it be one of those people called Quakers." This concession is evidence at once of the influence and the wealth of the Society— destined to furnish some of the most distinguished of British bankers—for whose benefit it was inserted. They, and all the Nonconformists, were keenly alive to the locality of their butter in relation to the bread. " If God show you a way in which you may lawfully get more than in another way, if you refuse this and choose the less gainful way you cross one of the ends of your calling, and you refuse to be God's steward." These words, incredible as the assertion seems, are those of Richard Baxter,[1] the greatest of English Nonconformist saints. Petty had noticed that " Trade is most vigorously carried on in every State and

[1] Quoted by Ashley, *Economic Organisation*, p. 158.

Government by the heterodox part of the same, and such as profess opinions different from what are publicly established."[1] That is why religious persecution, by weeding out the most independent minds and driving them to other lands, has always had so deleterious an effect upon the national morale of the persecuting nation and so invigorating an influence upon the community which receives them. "For nearly two centuries," remarked Lecky, "a steady stream of refugees, representing the best continental types, poured into England's population, blending with English life, transmitting their qualities of mind and character to English descendants, and contributing immensely to the perfection and reality of English history."[2] The advent of such racial factors stimulates, and, indeed, initiates, the tendency to variation which is so inevitably the signal of advance in man or people. No small part of the labour of leadership in English trade and finance for the last two centuries has been taken by men who, from the point of view of the English Church, were unorthodox —including, of course, the adherents of the Jewish faith. To the industrial and moneyed class, " more than to any other, may be ascribed the tempered energy, the dislike of abstractions and theories, the eminently practical spirit, characteristic of English political life ; and their influence has been especially useful in moderating the love of adventure and extravagance common to pure aristocracies."[3] But, of course, it must be borne in mind that each class has been for centuries recruited from the other—peerage from money and money from peerage, to select one instance from many. The water-tight social compartments which have found a place in Spain and Germany have been unknown here, and, consequently, money has been able not only to exert its influence, with the aid of social success, but to destroy, in a very large degree, that noxious sentiment which, in other lands, looks upon business as an inferior and debasing activity. The contrast in opinion was all the clearer because the Church, under the influence

[1] *Political Arithmetic*, p. 118.
[2] *Eighteenth Century*, Vol. I. p. 190.   [3] Lecky, Vol. I. p. 201.

of aristocratic sentiment and in alliance with the landed classes, was theoretically opposed to material, or, at all events, to mercantile and pecuniary gain ; whereas Nonconformity, mainly recruited from among the trading classes, emphasised it not only as a privilege, but a duty. If it be supposed that Baxter, writing in 1673, must have assumed an attitude of exceptional tolerance towards lucre, the answer is that John Wesley's views were just the same. " Religion must necessarily produce both industry and frugality," said Wesley, " and these cannot but produce riches. We must exhort all Christians to gain all they can and save all they can ; that is, in effect, to grow rich." Of course, Wesley went on to urge that riches must not be made a source of pride and worldliness. Those who had them must " give all they can " to the needy. But about the mere acquisition of money the founder of Wesleyanism is as definite as it is possible for words to be. Pronouncements like these, from the acknowledged leaders of a body of persons distinguished by a singular independence, not to say aggressiveness, of intellect and action, wrought incalculable good in preparing and smoothing the way for modern finance. It is to the infinite credit of the Bank that in an age when complete religious toleration was as yet afar off, it should respect the susceptibilities of a small Nonconformist body, whose propagandists had, only a few years before, been " requited by an untoward generation with hooting, pelting, and horse-whipping."[1]

THE BANK AND THE STATE

Summing up the early contribution of the Bank of England to the welfare of the State, as such, its founder said that

" The erection of this famous bank not only relieved the Ministerial managers from their frequent processions into the City for borrowing money, on the best and nearest public securities, at 10 or 12 per cent. per annum, but likewise gave life and currency to double or treble the value of its capital in other branches of the public credit, and so, under God, became

[1] Macaulay, *History*, Vol. II. p. 253.

the principal means of the success of the campaign in 1695 ; as particularly in reducing the important fortress of Namur, the first material step towards the peace concluded in 1697."

This reasoning has received the imprimatur of a greater man than Paterson. " Public credit had its origin," said Burke, " and was cradled, in bankruptcy and beggary." He was alluding to the period immediately prior to the establishment of the Bank of England, when the Government was at its wits' end for money, and national default was an imminent contingency. " Montague, the Chancellor of the Exchequer of that day," he added,[1] was "obliged, like a solicitor for an hospital, to go cap in hand from shop to shop to borrow a hundred pounds, and even smaller sums. When made up in driblets as they could, their best securities were at an interest of 12 per cent. Even the paper of the Bank, now[2] at par with cash and generally preferred to it, was often at a discount of 20 per cent." The Bank had to teach itself a new trade, and the discount of the paper was almost inevitable while experience was being acquired. The Bank Return submitted to the House of Commons in December, 1696, shows that, as against liabilities of £2,101,187, the available cash balance was £35,684, or, in other words, less than 2 per cent.—a state of things calculated to make a modern banker stand aghast. Yet there was no pause in the task of consolidation. No sooner was there a National Debt than other financial expedients became possible with the aid of the newly concentrated finance. Exchequer Bills[3] of £5 and

[1] Regicide Peace, *Works*, Vol. V. p. 290.   [2] Burke was writing in 1796.
[3] It was provided by 8 and 9 William III., c. 20, sec. 63, that in order to make the £1,500,000 of Exchequer Bills of more general use, " for the publick commerce and trade," they should not only be taken by receivers and collectors of the taxes and supplies, " but shall also passe and be current to all and every the Commissioners, Receivers, or Collectors of any Revenue, Aid, Tax, or Supply whatsoever . . . and also att the Receipt of the Exchequer from the said Commissioners, Receivers, or Collectors, or from any other Person or Persons whatsoever making any Payments there to His Majesty upon any Account whatsoever." And (by sec. 64) " to the end that all Persons may be the more willing and ready to accept and receive the said Bills in all manner of Payments . . . there shall be annexed unto, attend, and go along with the said Bills an interest after the rate of Five pence a day for every one hundred pounds contained therein . . . which said interest shall be payed or allowed to the Person who is last possest thereof to the Day hee pays the same into the Exchequer."

£10, for instance, were added to the effective currency, in place of Government tallies which had been at discounts of 40, 50, and 60 per cent. Still another achievement, rendered possible by the new conditions, and the forces at work upon them, was the currency reform of 1696, carried out by Montague under the advice of Locke, with the Mint under the mastership of Sir Isaac Newton. The Elizabethan boast of *moneta in justum valorem reducta* was carried another stage towards actual realisation.[1] Foreign observers, according to Lodge,[2] were " astounded at the comparative ease and calmness with which the country, in the middle of a great European war, grappled with so vital and so difficult a problem." Once more, as soon as the new institution commenced to become the Government Bank, the State was getting benefit in return for the use of its money, which it had failed to do as long as receivers of the revenue were temporarily lending their holdings, or depositing them with the goldsmith-bankers. The new system was not only beneficial to the State, as such, but to the money market. The contrast is all the more striking if we compare the fertility of State funds in the Bank of England with their necessary sterility while in a public treasury. As early as 1711 the Bank was requesting paymasters and receivers to keep these balances with it and not elsewhere. They ought to

[1] " It may be doubted," says Macaulay, speaking of the state of things which rendered necessary the recoinage of 1696 (and, *mutatis mutandis*, had had its counterpart in earlier centuries), " whether all the misery which had been inflicted on the nation in a quarter of a century by bad Kings, bad Parliaments, and bad Judges was equal to the misery caused in a single year by bad crowns and bad shillings. The evil was felt daily, and almost hourly, in almost every place, and by almost every class—in the dairy and on the threshing-floor, by the anvil and by the loom, on the billows of the ocean and in the depths of the mine. Nothing could be purchased without dispute. Over every counter there was wrangling from morning to night. The workman and his employer had a quarrel as regularly as the Saturday came round. No merchant would contract to deliver goods without making some stipulation about the quality of the coin in which he was to be paid. Even men of business were often bewildered by the confusion into which all pecuniary transactions were thrown. The simple and the careless were pillaged without mercy by extortioners whose demands grew even more rapidly than the money shrank. The labourer found that the bit of metal which, when he received it, was called a shilling, would hardly, when he wanted to purchase a pot of beer or a loaf of rye-bread, go so far as sixpence."
[2] *Political History*, 1660–1702, p. 394.

THE BANK OF ENGLAND

do this, said the Bank, "to cultivate a good understanding."[1] Of course the change for the better did not come all at once. More than half a century later Pitt divided his patronage, as Paymaster-General, between Threadneedle Street and certain private banks.

BANKER TO THE GOVERNMENT

The Bank of England gradually, not suddenly or by specific selection, became the banker to the Government. When another issue of Exchequer Bills took place under 5 Anne c. 13 (1707), there was a power to make them interest-bearing by indorsement, and the Bank was empowered to determine whether or not such interest should be paid, and at what rate. By 7 Anne c. 7 (1708) there was a third issue, while the second was converted into funded debt to the Bank at 6 per cent. This species of interest-bearing Government paper was in circulation throughout the century, under the management of the Bank. The Bank's credit, better than that of the Government, was behind the bills : and every man through whose hands they passed was reminded of the existence and power of the new financial institution. The Bank, as such, was in a peculiarly fortunate position to bid for Government business. Its rivals—the South Sea Company and the East India Company—were trading corporations, not banks. They could only carry out financial operations by the use of their *own* capital. Their share in the management of the Government debt could only be the administration of the individual loans which they themselves had made. Philoppovitch dates from 1751 the recognition of the fact that the Bank alone should be employed in the management of the public debt.[2] But this was only an informal recognition. There was no contract. Even in 1797 the proposal that the outstanding South Sea annuities should be managed by the Bank was not made as a matter of course. By the year 1800 the Bank was administering a public debt of £393,114,680. Finally, in 1834, as a

---

[1] Philoppovitch, *History of the Bank of England*, p. 176.
[2] *History of the Bank of England*, p. 79.

result of the recommendations of a commission appointed in 1831, various public financial functionaries were abolished, and it was provided that all public moneys were to be paid into the Bank, as a single fund known as " the account of His Majesty's Exchequer." The Bank became the central and only public treasury.

The Bank, however, has always objected to any suggestion that it ever occupied or now occupies a privileged position. The word " privilege " is entirely misplaced. " As bankers we are subject to the same law as every other banking institution, and we derive no other advantage whatever, except that we hold the Government account," said the Governor at the Bank Court, September 15, 1870.[1] The truth is that, although early Tory critics, in the eighteenth century, objected that by the arrangements between the Bank and the State the former was virtually incorporated with the latter, there never was then, and never has been since, any such union. The traditional close co-operation of Bank and Ministry should not be allowed to obscure the fact that the Bank of England is only the bank of the Government. It is not a Government bank, though Lord North once called it the public exchequer. It is purely the banker of the State, and not its cashier, and as such maintains with it the same relations as with the individuals and companies who constitute its clientèle. The Government owns no Bank Stock.

CLOSE INTIMACY WITH THE STATE

The beneficent and distinguished rôle of the Bank, in its relations with the State, was not foreseen when it was

[1] At the Bank Court held in September, 1883, this was made additionally clear by the Governor. The question was raised whether there was any duty imposed upon the Bank to inquire into the legislative authority of an instruction from the Treasury to inscribe a given amount of National Debt, say ten or twenty millions. The Governor replied that the Bank had nothing to do in such matters beyond obeying the instructions given to them by the Government as its bankers. Those instructions took the form of a Treasury Warrant, " and they were bound to follow and respect it." When the Governor was asked in 1883 whether the Board of Trade had inspired the giving of assistance to the Bank of Ireland at the time of the small run upon it (see p. 516), he replied that the Board of Trade had nothing whatever to do with it. The affair was " simply a transaction between the Bank and one of its customers."

established by the Act of 1694. The scheme, as Doubleday says, "was smuggled under the long tail of an Act of Parliament for raising money generally." Its existence was intended to cease a year after it became possible to cancel the Government debt, and there was no intention of employing the new institution in the management of the debt itself. Its share therein grew out of its intimacy with the Government: and, as it grew, enhanced the prestige of the Bank. The Bank has carried out all the Government's financial operations in place of the Treasury and the Exchequer, and, consequently, apart altogether from the handsome remuneration, the fact of being the banker to the Government, and necessarily in its financial confidence, has been one of the most powerful of the many influences which have combined to build up the primacy of Threadneedle Street. "A single movement of public moneys often carries with it a State secret," said Napoleon: and a glamour grows around those who effect it. No doubt this is the reason why its rivals at one time hoped to see it lose the Government business. When the new joint-stock banks arose it was suggested that other banks would be willing to work for the Government gratis, in return for the prestige and the profit, and thus save the money (then £257,000 a year) paid to the Bank for its services. Vague rumours of the withdrawal of the Government's account were circulated in 1869, and denied by the Governor at the Court on September 16. Anyhow, it is fairly certain that the Bank would not be the power that it is if fate had made it a purely Government institution. The strength of the British banking system is largely due to the fact that its consolidation has depended upon the intellect and energy of those who manage it, rather than upon any Government protection. The bonds between the Bank and the Government are now practically indissoluble; but, in the shape of any alliance or partnership recognisable by the law, there is no relationship whatsoever. Nevertheless, when we reach the age of Waterloo and the advent of the modern Money Market, we may say with truth that out of its relations with the Government, and by means of the funds thus commanded, the Bank built up its own prestige and the money market simultaneously.

THE WEAPON OF A NATIONAL DEBT

Even the war itself was dependent upon the new finance. Without its aid Britain would have been driven from the field of commerce in which her greatest triumphs were ultimately to be achieved. The wars of the eighteenth century were fights for trade, not mere political or diplomatic contests. The sixteenth-century Spanish war had represented the "infancy of English foreign trade. The first generation of Englishmen that invested capital put it into that war."[1] Their progeny were willing to invest more capital in the same security. "Statesmen[2] were confronted with the dangers of both a naval and military supremacy and the consequences to the trade of the country were plain enough." French mercantilism, "enforced by the joint action of Spain with France, threatening Dutch and English trade at all points, was a menace to their very existence as European Powers of the first rank. The Queen's speech announcing the declaration of war, sought to enlist the sympathies of the moneyed interest by insisting upon the commercial importance of the issue." But no insistence would have sufficed, in the absence of the means of creating and maintaining, to meet the colossal necessities of the new era, the long-dated obligations of the community called the National Debt, the real significance of which we shall examine later.[3] Without the weapon of a National Debt England could not have survived the Napoleonic wars—a fact which is said[4] to be officially recorded in the minutes of the Bank of England. "The solvency of the Bank was . . . based on the integrity of the Government, and the vigour of the

[1] Seeley, *Expansion of England*, p. 130.
[2] Leadam, *Political History*, 1702–1760, p. 5.   [3] Page 629.
[4] Correspondent of the *Bankers' Magazine*, 1870, p. 756. "The German army that conquered in Italy could not have taken the field had it not been for a voluntary loan raised here in the city in which I had £1000." (Robt. Raworth to Thos. Pitt, *Fortescue MSS.*, Vol. I. p. 28, 1706–7.) In our own time the "silver bullet" has proved the most potent projectile *against* the German army!

THE BANK OF ENGLAND

Government was conditioned by the support of the Bank, for the Government soon learnt that its power in the councils of Europe depended on the punctual fulfilment of its financial pledges."[1] Of scarcely less importance was the fact that the security of the British funds brought large sums to this country from abroad. As early as 1718 these investments were extensive enough to create the idea that we should be drained of our gold.[2]

PRESTIGE, CONTINUITY, EXPERIENCE

Its share in these achievements aided to confer an undesirable prestige upon the new institution. Power begets prestige and will increase where prestige exists. Such an aggregation of capital and influence, as was represented even in its troublous adolescence by the Bank of England, at once thrusts itself above the general level, acquiring a wholly novel and unique power of resistance to hostile forces, just as the tall trees of the tropical forest represent a successful struggle for a more ample share of the light whose advent is obstructed by the impenetrable mass of vegetation at a lower level. " Progress," said Professor Flower,[4] " has been due to the opportunity of those individuals who are a little superior in some respects to their fellows, of asserting their superiority and of continuing to live and of promulgating as an inheritance that superiority." *Mutatis mutandis*, these words are equally true of the superior capacity and ideals, in the realm of credit, which are attainable by institutions of the type of the Bank of England. Mere scattered units of money in twenties, fifties, hundreds, and such-like have no economic efficiency whatsoever. But they may attempt Archimedean tasks when they are aggregated and employed in community, especially when, as in the case of the Bank, the

[1] Thorold Rogers, *First Nine Years of the Bank of England*, p. xvii.
[2] " The exportation of bullion on account of interest due to foreigners from our funds was what I was not aware of ; that in a little time must drain us, and amounts to the same thing as a balance of trade against us, viz. : Debts due from England to other countries, nor can this have any remedy but by paying off the funds, for which I suppose we are in no condition." (Canon of Christ Church to Edward Harley, February 14, 1718. *Portland MSS.*, Vol. VII. p. 233.)
[4] Addressing the Trades Council at Newcastle in September, 1889.

institution which aggregates them has early acquired its own prepollence. Massive, coherent, and disciplined aggregates of financial facility serve the State because they not only facilitate its borrowing, but enable it to get the money on far less onerous terms. The borrowing State deals with a centralised group of willing lenders, rather than with a scattered flock of coerced and suspicious capitalists. The floating debt gives place to the funded species. The lender's confidence no longer depends solely upon the credit of the borrower, but also upon the psychological reserve force arising out of the unique position of the intermediary—armed with the capacity of stern financial resentment which waits unseen, but vigorous, in the background. The Bank of England, once firmly established, meant the persistence of an organised, coherent and centralised financial force. Continuity[1] of existence and operation must become more and more essential (and essential, too, upon a larger scale) as humanity's struggle with its environment becomes more ambitious and courageous. In accordance with the well-known economic principle, humanity tends ever to travel by the longer path towards its achievements, and the longer the journey the larger and better assured must be the available financial provision by which its labours are to be sustained. The yearning for unbroken continuity, as a guarantee of stability, had given us the hereditary principle in the royal succession and the laws of inheritance, as well as in the creation of corporations which never died. The corporation, moreover, offered continuity of existence without the identity of temperament and outlook, such as was stereotyped by a feudal economy. Continuity of financial function is essential to a society where deferred payments are so largely an element of the machinery of bargaining, and consequently form a constantly increasing factor of the driving power. " Unlike so many banks founded at the end of the seventeenth century, the

[1] The Lords Committee of 1848 pointed out that this continuity was to some extent menaced by the " system of periodical elections of governors and deputy-governors . . . by a mere rotation of seniority." See the whole passage *post*, p. 511.

THE BANK OF ENGLAND

Bank of England had not a merely ephemeral existence "[1] The activity of the Bank, and of the dependent institutions which were growing up and functioning around it, exhibited an unprecedented persistence of financial stability and responsibility, marvellous in comparison with all that had so far fallen within the experience of mankind. Even in our age of feverish political change, we have recognised the necessity of continuity in foreign policy. It is even more essential in finance. This attribute of continuity was destined to exert an endless succession of unforeseen influences in the vast realm of those activities which require a deathless personality, unfailingly responsible and solvent, for their complete fulfilment.[2] Nothing but an elaborate and consolidated credit system, upon the soundest basis, can meet the necessities of a community growing at the pace, and on the principle, which has characterised Great Britain since the Revolution.

THE BANK AS A CONSCIOUS, PERMANENT SELF

There is yet another consideration, subtle in its character, and yet of the highest importance from the point of view of the present essay. For the first time in the history of the activities which were evolving into finance, the Bank assured an incessant storage of tradition and experience in the self-consciousness of an institution which, in corporate immortality, could bid defiance to the hungry years. The corporate personality may have self-consciousness, even as the individual self possesses it. Self-consciousness begins with the Self as a Person.[3] Consciousness of some sort goes on incessantly, as one state of mind succeeds another. They must do, for quiescence in consciousness is cessation of consciousness.[4] Self becomes a vivid conception, to the exclusion of all other ingredients of

---

[1] Philoppovitch, *History of the Bank of England*, p. 42.
[2] Even when the auxiliary is available, the absence of a fixed and unfluctuating standard of value may lead to gross unfairness as between lender and borrower, debtor and creditor ; but at all events, the nominal fulfilment of the bargain is assured, even if strictly equivalent value be unattainable across the gulf of the years which divide the loan from its repayment.   [3] Bosanquet, *Psychology of the Moral Self*, p. 52.
[4] Spencer, *Principles of Psychology*, II. p. 292.

the Ego, when *we think of ourselves as thinkers*.¹ Finance develops self-consciousness when it is aware of itself as finance and realises its special individuality and function as well as the element of continuity running through them as distinct from its former lack of continuity, coherence and co-ordination. As a state of consciousness that awareness must be persistent and ceaseless. As we shall see, it produces a constantly higher degree of coherence and capacity of co-ordination, advancing as the stores of experience accumulate, and ultimately confer mastery of the very conditions out of which the awareness was originally engendered. In this way the financial self-consciousness, brought to bear upon action, " correlates the act of the moment with permanent interests and general principles."² It " grasps the continuity running through its experience, and projects it into the future. It can focus its own experience in generalisations, and learn and teach others by communication." It will be observed that this reasoning implies a suggestion that the conscious self of the bank exists as a permanent continuous being, since, as Spencer would have pointed out, " modifications in its policy prompted by variations in its experience must necessarily involve something modified." But we need not hesitate to go thus far. Gierke has expressly argued that behind the so-called legal fiction of a corporate personality, there actually is in existence a self capable of willing and of acting. " The earlier inquiries which men have made about consciousness have been of a merely ethical or legal character ;—have simply aimed at deciding whether at a given moment a man was *responsible* for his acts, either to a human or divine tribunal. . . . As soon, however, as the problem is regarded as a psychological one, . . . we come to regard consciousness . . . as conceivably the psychical counterpart of all phenomenal existence."³ These are very deep waters, in which, as yet, science has only just commenced to take soundings.

---

[1] James, *Text-book of Psychology*, p. 181.
[2] Hobhouse, *Development and Purpose*, p. 83.
[3] Myers, *Human Personality*, Vol. I. p. 37.

Finally, this corporate self-consciousness, bringing a vivid realisation of the not-self (society) outside, enforces a realisation of the larger interests which this latter represents, and brings the knowledge of an obligation which may conflict with the special and immediate aims that might otherwise wholly and exclusively engage the new individuality. The result of the whole process is seen in the intrepid and unflinching national spirit of the Bank. The standard is actually formulated, in so many words—though probably without complete cognition of their tremendous meaning—in such an utterance as that of the Chairman of the National Provincial Bank—" There were other and higher motives that prompted the directors to exert their utmost on behalf of the bank, beyond the mere question of a stake in the property."[1] So Henry Birkbeck said to S. Gurney Buxton, when the latter first entered Gurney's Bank, " You must remember that you do not come into the bank only to make a profit, but you must consider it as a trust for the benefit of Norfolk."[2] Words like these are the recognition of allegiance due to the high corporate standards of conduct which had grown up around the nucleus of tradition and ideal in Threadneedle Street. More striking still, as we shall see in due course, is the fact that by the middle of the twentieth century, the very term gravitation had been employed with regard to an observable tendency in finance, though those who used it did not realise that their metaphor was in fact the enunciation of a scientific truth. The Newtonian conception of a central gravitative force harmonises naturally with the hypothesis of a permanent psychic depositary of tradition and experience, and may easily broaden into the vague idea of a central economic power. It actually did so during the next century and a half, although articulate purpose guided by a *definite* idea does not finally emerge until a comparatively late stage of the process. For the purpose of the present study I should date that stage in the period between the 1857

[1] Meeting, May 14, 1868.
[2] Norwich presentation to Gurney and Co. after amalgamation with Barclay's.

and 1866 crises. For the moment it may suffice to indicate that, as Mr. Hobhouse says, " in the formation of any new organic type there is a synthesis of elements previously separate, and in their separateness either held ineffective by counteracting forces, or, if acting, acting mechanically for simple lack of that with which they can harmonise."[1] But their ultimate harmony is the result of the development which connects the lowest with the highest orders of being. If we ask in what development consists, we are " led to the conclusion that it consists in the growth of mind."[2] Equally, where we are concerned with corporate development, must we be led to the conclusion that it consists in the growth of the corporate mind with the consequent capacity for co-ordination and organisation. As we proceed with the present study we shall see that this conclusion presents itself in irresistible and irrefragable form. In what is, for the present, the final stage of corporate development in the realm of finance we shall find the corporate mind scrutinising the ancient biological law of doliogenic evolution[3] by lethal elimination, and resolving upon its repeal. We shall even witness the beginnings of a new economic era in which, for the first time in all the long history of humanity, its corporate courage energises man (if the expression may be permitted) to grip the eternal cosmic law by the throat, and to say " for the future *my* way, not thine ! "

INCIPIENT RECOGNITION OF LEADERSHIP

With this exposition of the " drift " of the psycho-biological argument which it is hoped to elaborate as we go on, we may return to the study of the enhancement of the prestige of the Bank of England. A recognition of financial leadership is traceable, dimly though unmistakably, almost from the foundation of the great City institution around which power was destined for the next two centuries to accumulate. " I know no man and no number of men who have so well deserved of his Majesty

[1] *Development and Purpose*, p. 359.   [2] Hobhouse, *op. cit.*, p. 369.
[3] That is to say, evolution achieved by a crafty or wily (δόλιος) policy based upon no higher allegiance than immediate self-interest.

THE BANK OF ENGLAND 225

and the Kingdom as the Bank of England has," declares an anonymous panegyrist of 1696. He admits, however, that he is a shareholder. The Act of 1697, by which the Bank secured additional privileges, alludes to " the better restoring of the credit of the nation and advancing the credit of the Corporation of the Governor and Company of the Bank of England." These words almost suggest that the credit of the Bank was better than the credit of the country at large. National credit, it seems, stands in need of " restoration," while that of the Bank wants only " advancement." Anyhow, the Bank could borrow £200,000 in Amsterdam for the benefit of the Government at 4 per cent. as early as 1695, when it was urgently needed for paying the army. Certainly there was being gradually forced upon statesmen the realisation that the national credit must be raised to the same high level as that of the Bank. Burnet saw the necessity and said, almost in as many words, that the task had been achieved. He " rhapsodises over the abundance of money and the fact that at this stage of the war the Government could command it at 6½ per cent. He adds what the State papers and ministerial correspondence shew to have been but a pious belief, that ' the Treasury was as exact and as regular in all payments as any private banker could be.' "[1] The Act 7 Anne c. 7[2] is almost obsequious in its allusions to the Bank. It recites the expedients adopted by the Governor and Company " for the better enabling themselves to supply the publick exigencies," and proceeds (sec. 8) to enact certain provisions " for the Encouragement of the said Governor and Company " ; so that they may have " a competent Recompence and Consideration." In sec. 25 there is again a return to the " Encouragement of the said Governor and Company." The monopoly of note issue (and, in effect, of joint-stock banking) given by this statute was conferred in return for a reduction of the interest upon the original capital from 8 per cent. to 6 per cent., and for a fresh

[1] E. S. Leadam, Finance of Godolphin, *Royal Hist. Soc. Trans.*, 1910, p. 23. [2] Printed as c. 30 in the " command " editions of the Statutes.

226 EVOLUTION OF THE MONEY MARKET

loan of £400,000 at 6 per cent. When the Bank issued its new shares of £100 at 15 prem. the whole amount was subscribed between 9 a.m. and noon on February 22, 1709. " Near one million more," says Anderson, " would have been on the same day subscribed, had there been room for it, so great was the crowd of people coming with their money to the books." The royal attitude was as deferential as that of Parliament towards an institution created by the party which had dictated the conditions of the tenure of the royal office. When, in 1710, the Queen[1] dismissed the Earl of Sunderland and gave the seals to Lord Dartmouth, she thought it desirable to inform her subjects, and in particular the Governor of the Bank of England, that she did not intend to make any other changes. " Evidently the good opinion of the directors of the Bank was now thought to be of some importance in political circles."[2] In 1710, when the Queen resolved to dismiss Godolphin's Whig Ministers, the Bank of England sent a formal deputation of protest, and it was with reference to their Tory successors, Harley and St. John, that John Toland said in 1711, " The moneyed people will never trust this Parliament." Even in the threat of assault it gained prominence. When a proclamation by the Pretender was distributed in 1722, it was said that the Bank was destined to be pillaged first.

THE PRESTIGE OF MONOPOLY

To this politico-financial predominance there was added the prestige of monopoly. The Act of 1708 (7 Anne c. 7 s. 66), amending the charter of the Bank of England, prohibited the formation, by any number of persons exceeding six, of any other institution in the nature of a bank. The Bank disclaimed any intention of interfering with the goldsmith-bankers : but it was imagined that private firms of six persons, or less, working with *unlimited* liability, could not imperil the supremacy of the gigantic

---

[1] Queen Anne on one occasion made a gift of £100 to a man who had paid £500 into the Bank in order to help it at a critical time.

[2] Turner, *Chronicles of the Bank of England*, p. 33.

THE BANK OF ENGLAND

new enterprise, with its limited liability. In 1742 this provision was more clearly defined, in accordance with the prevalent contemporary idea that the right of note issue was essential to the existence of a bank. Early banking was regarded largely as a method of debt transfer, carried out by means of bank-notes. "The practice of note issue was historically the beginning of banking, and it has grown into a system of keeping deposit accounts and cheques. It is now the small beginning of small banking accounts."[1] The banker's profit was derived from the use of the money which, to some extent or another, formed the basis of the notes. To put it in a different way, the banker accepted the custody of the metallic currency, which was so eminently inconvenient for the purpose of debt transfer on a large scale, and issued against the deposits another form of currency—namely, bank-notes—not open to the objections, in the matter of weight and inconvenience, capable of being urged against the metal. The theory of the Bank of England was that if it could stop the issue of bank-notes by other institutions it must, of necessity, create a monopoly of banking on its own account. If other bankers were charged for the use of bank-notes, their means of debt transfer on behalf of their customers would be primitive in the extreme, consisting merely in the transport of credit from one account to another, where that process was feasible, or in the transfer of coin from place to place, where it was not. The Act 15 Geo. II. c. 13 s. 5, therefore prohibited the issue of bills or notes, payable on demand, by " any body politic or corporate whatsoever, erected or to be erected, or . . . for any partnership exceeding the number of six persons." The misconception embodied in these provisions—that a prohibition of note issue was, in effect, an insuperable obstacle to rival banks—remained an accepted tradition till it was shattered by J. W. Gilbart.[2] This monopoly of note issue enabled the bank directors to play with the Government for many years. They did not fail, at every

[1] F. Seebohm, 1875 Committee, Q. 4627.
[2] See *post*, p. 300.

renewal of their Charter, to harp upon their privileges and the necessity for their maintenance intact.[1]

Having, as Mill said, " actually made the formation of safe banking establishments a punishable offence," the Bank of England itself refused for one hundred and thirty years to establish country branches. Its supposed monopoly prevented the establishment of strong banks. " If it had not been for this privilege we should have had a bank, perhaps, in every county in England, and probably half a dozen different banks in London."[2] If the scheme had taken the form of a system of national banks, organised and managed by the Bank of England, there might have been more stability than was evolved under the management of an incoherent array of country banks. But on the other hand, unity of organisation might have meant unity of disquietude, and of disaster, if it came. As it actually worked out, banking in the eighteenth century developed into a multitude of weak country banks, with here and there a single solid and solvent concern, in contrast with one great London institution and

---

[1] It is a curious evidence of the influence of the Bank of England over the State, that it was always able to secure the renewal of the Charter many years in advance of the date of its expiration. The original Charter of 1694 was granted for twelve years. In 1697, or when the Bank was only three years old, the Charter was renewed until 1710. Without waiting for that date, the directors, in 1708, secured a further extension to 1732, on the terms of advancing £400,000 free of interest and taking over Exchequer Bills, without interest, to the amount of £1,700,000. Then, five years after the extension in 1708, which had carried the Charter onwards to 1732, the Bank again secured an extension, this time until 1742. Then came a period during which, apparently, the pressure of the Bank upon the Government relaxed. The renewals of 1742 and 1764 took place at their due dates, and not before. The extension granted in 1764 was until August, 1786, but in 1781—five years before the expiration of the term— the Bank secured an extension until 1812, in consideration of lending £2,000,000 to the Government for three years at 3 per cent. Once more, in 1799, when the expiration of the Charter was still thirteen years distant, the Bank secured a still further extension—this time until 1833—in return for the advance of £3,000,000 for six years free of interest. The Act 33 and 34 Vict. c. 71 provides that " the Bank of England shall continue a corporation until all the public funds are duly redeemed by Parliament." It is worth while to note how these bargains have been repeated in other parts of the world in modern times. In 1862 the Austrian Government Bank bargained for a new Charter in return for an advance of 80,000,000fl. to the Government, to be repaid within a fixed period, but to carry no interest.

[2] *London Magazine*, 1737 ; quoted by Gilbert, *Banking*, p. 39.

THE BANK OF ENGLAND

a number of private metropolitan banks around it. At the end of the century (1792) it could be said that " of late a vast number of country banks have been established in various counties, which have made great fortunes with small capitals : these alarms [a threatened invasion by the French] will certainly produce a run on them and many of them will be broke."[1] Many banks had practically no capital except their notes.[2] From the point of view of the present essay the inference from these facts is obvious. Just as in the country of the blind the one-eyed man is king, so in the country of doubtful and discredited notes a glamour will gather round those which are always, or practically always, paid. At first, in the case of the Bank of England, this glamour must have been mainly visible to bankers themselves, and in the area around London where Bank of England notes were familiar. We know that in the provinces they were not popular, as against the local notes, until the nineteenth century was well advanced. But London has become the financial centre of the world, and for the enhancement of the prestige of the Bank it was London sentiment that counted.

BANK STOCK AS A MARKET BELL-WETHER

The very fact that the bank stock was one of the leading gambling counters may have added to the prestige of the new institution. Even a mining share which becomes for a time the bell-wether of the market acquires an enhanced standing from the fact. A stock which was the bell-wether of contemporary world-politics was bound to attract a lustre around itself. Thorold Rogers wrote the *First Nine Years of the Bank of England* (1694–1703) to demonstrate that the record of the movements of bank

[1] Malone to James, first Earl of Charlemont, *Charlemont MSS.*, Vol. II. p. 205.
[2] After 1772 the London bankers gave up the issue of notes in favour of the greater convenience of cheques. But the technical right of issue survived, and was employed here and there until the Bank Charter Act finally destroyed it in 1844. Up to this date, for instance, Coutts's issued bills on demand, which were practically bank-notes, in large quantities. They were the last of the London banks to give up the practice. (1875 Committee, Q. 7,019–20.)

stock in that period was practically a history of England in brief, so intimate was the interaction between political incident and the current quotation. He thought that many of Luttrell's prices of bank stock represented " time bargains," and not *bona-fide* sales and transfers.[1] But the fact of bank stock being the market bellwether, as truly as that rôle is fulfilled nowadays by Chartereds or Can. Pacs. in their respective departments, is indisputable. Godolphin and Charles Duncombe sold all their stock to produce a fall. The operation must have been more threatening than a modern bear raid (now impossible in the case of bank shares, however) since Duncombe had £80,000 of Bank Stock. The charge against Walpole of being a big operator in it—whether true or not—shows that Bank Stock was the counter in which he might be *expected* to operate, if he operated at all.[2] No doubt the extreme variation of the dividends, from $18\frac{1}{4}$ per cent. in 1716 to 6 per cent. in 1722, facilitated market manipulation. It led to the establishment of a reserve fund in the latter year, with a consequent enhancement of the attractions of the shares as an investment. The Bank itself was apparently a recognised " bull " influence. " My brother Harry," says Stephen Thompson (1755),

[1] *First Nine Years of the Bank of England*, Preface, p. ix.
[2] In the course of a debate in February, 1725-6, Shippen " recapitulated what Walpole had said against stock-jobbers, and then pointed it all directly upon him, and supposed that he had sold out on purpose to sink stocks that he might buy them, with a design to raise them and sell again. He went on with great violence and insolence, he said he would do anything to bring such a bear to the stake ; that as much as he detested a bill of pains and penalties, he would readily come into it to make such a monster spew up his ill-gotten wealth, etc. Walpole rose in a great passion and protested solemnly that he never since he had been in his place had by himself or agents sold £20 ; that if that member knew he had, he ought to accuse him. That he called upon him to do it, that he challenged him to produce anything against him, that if he knew of any such thing it was his duty to acquaint the House with it, that if he had no ground for what he said he ought to recant the injustice of his insinuations. That he himself equally detested those who could be guilty of such practices, and those who could insinuate such things against others, without any ground for their accusation. The warmth was great on both sides. Shippen made no reply, but it was once thought he would have been called to the bar. After all, it is said that Walpole did sell out £30,000 of Bank Stock, though in such a manner that legal proof cannot be made of (it)." (Letters of Stratford, Canon of Christchurch, to T. Thomas. *Historical MSS. Commission, Portland MSS.*, Vol. VII. p. 420.)

THE BANK OF ENGLAND

" who thinks like a director of the bank . . . buys stock, and Dick, in the contrary opinion, sells."[1]

BEGINNING OF SELF-PROTECTIVE UNITY

Thus political power, magnitude of resources, stock-market prominence, and the sacro-sanctity of monopoly combined, from the first, to throw almost a halo round the Bank of England. It became the symbol of solidity, the synonym for strength and security. As early as 1708 it was a recognised safe deposit. " I cannot but think," says Thomas Pitt, " that the safest place for the chest that contains my grand affair [the Pitt diamond] to stand in is the Bank of England."[2] In their hour of trial the directors of the South Sea Company, initiating a method that was destined to become traditional, appealed to the Bank for help. The fact of the appeal, from a rival which was afterwards beaten out of the field, must have been an eloquent testimony to the strength of the new enterprise. A sense of common interest, and a capacity for common action in the presence of emergency begin to be plainly discernible, though in rudimentary form, before the middle of the century. At first the self-protective efforts do not connect themselves with, much less group themselves around, the Bank of England. The two factors—centralisation and the instinct of self-protection—exist in embryo, but they do not originally coalesce. There is, to begin with, a rally—perhaps rather a huddle—of the commercial community at the onset of the financial trouble. But the rally, the co-operation, and the temporary alliance are prompted only by the imminence of the danger. As soon as the peril passes away its recurring menace is forgotten. There is no endeavour to create anything in the nature of a scientific and disciplined system that would shut out the hazard altogether. The Jacobite rising in 1745 was in no small degree checked by the refusal of the North Country capitalists to have anything to do with the movement. The Pretender had made the fatal mistake of issuing a manifesto which amounted almost to a

[1] *Du Cane MSS.*, p. 221.   [2] *Fortescue MSS.*, Vol. I. p. 36.

suggested repudiation of the National Debt; so that the historic memory of the nation had only to travel backwards for a century or so in order to recollect a raid on the Mint by Charles I. and the plundering of the Exchequer by Charles II. This kind of thing instantly arrayed the embryo money-power against its indiscreet author.[1] The levying of forced contributions at Glasgow, Manchester, and Derby only intensified this distrust in financial circles. The resulting alarm in London precipitated the first Black Friday in the history of the City. It was during this run that the City merchants held a meeting at Garraway's Coffee House, and passed a resolution which dimly foreshadowed the action of the united bankers at the time of the Baring crisis :—

" We, the undersigned merchants and others, being sensible how necessary the preservation of public credit is at this time, do hereby declare that we shall not refuse to receive banknotes in payment of any sum of money to be paid to us ; and we will use our utmost endeavours to make our payments in the same manner. September 26, 1745."

Here is, at all events, recognition of the principle of joint protective action with the Bank of England in the common interest, so successfully interpreted by the modern financial hierarchy. By four o'clock on the Friday afternoon this resolution had been signed by more than 1100 traders and Fund-holders. The new expedient proved of incalculable value to the whole community. The intimate relationship subsisting between the various European financial centres led to analogous measures being adopted when, at the end of July, 1763, there was a financial crisis in Amsterdam.[2]

THE BANK AS DISCIPLINARIAN

No long time elapsed before the Bank began to play a disciplinary, or at least a retaliatory, rôle. The opportunity came during the next crisis. When the fate of Neal,

[1] The Bank of Scotland had lost its monopoly in 1727 in consequence of its suspected penchant for the schemes of the Pretender.
[2] *Annual Register*, 1763, Chron. 102.

Fordyce and Co. was trembling in the balance, on Monday, June 22, 1772, " an universal bankruptcy was expected." The stoppage of almost every banker's house in London was looked for. The whole City was in an uproar. Francis declares that there was a report of " an immediate stop of the greatest " of banks. But this is not borne out by the evidence of contemporary witnesses, who put a totally different colour on the Fordyce failure. Horace Walpole's account is that " The Scotch had for several years been drawing vast quantities of specie into Scotland by remitting bills of England : they had carried thence £15,000 a week. This had made specie rare here. . . . The Bank of England had long beheld this practice with jealousy and were glad to take the opportunity of Fordyce's gaming, villainy, extravagance, and destruction to put an end to so ruinous a combination."[1] Walpole was impressed by the temerity which had brought so formidable an assailant into action. " The Scots," said he,[2] " have given provocation even to the Bank of England, by circulating vast quantities of their own bank's notes." But if the Bank could strike hard in the interests—rightly or wrongly understood—of discipline, it was capable also of justifying expectations of its assistance, or of refusing it where the sterner policy seemed the sounder. " Drummond was near failing. The Bank lent Sir George Colebrook £190,000 or he had failed too. . . . The Dukes of Queensberry and Buccleuch and Archibald Douglas offered their estates to the Bank of England for security for the Bank of Edinburgh."[3] In furtherance of the policy represented by these expedients, " the principal merchants assembled, and means were concerted to revive trade and preserve the national credit."[4] Thus common action was again invoked to stay the ravages of panic, and must have been in no small degree inspired by the realisation how closely the general prosperity of the country was bound up with the well-being and smooth working of the financial mechanism.

---

[1] Horace Walpole, *George III.*, Vol. I. 128.
[2] *Letters to Sir Horace Mann*, Vol. V. p. 213.
[3] Horace Walpole, *George III.*, Vol. I. p. 123.
[4] Francis, *Bank of England*, Vol. I. p. 176.

In the North, at Newcastle, co-operative self-protection seems to have become the accepted policy. The Newcastle merchants, in 1772, decided by resolution to discriminate against banks which financed speculation. They agreed

" not to keep their cash at any bank who jointly or separately by themselves or agents, are known to sport in the alley in what are called bulls or bears, since by one unlucky stroke in this illegal traffic, usually called speculations, hundreds of their creditors may be ruined ; a species of gaming that can no more be justified in persons so largely intrusted with the property of others than that of gambling at the hazard tables."[1]

These critics were somewhat in advance of their age. At this time, and for thirty or forty years afterwards, speculative operations in the public funds were considered a legitimate source of banking profits. The Newcastle pronouncement was, however, an intelligent anticipation of a principle accepted in Gilbart's time and since.[2] And the men who could criticise a menace to financial stability were quick to support genuine banking. They met in the crises of 1772, 1792, 1797–1803, 1815, and 1816, and resolved to continue accepting local bank-notes in discharge of outstanding debts—and this in spite of the fact that in 1792, for instance, Lambton's had sent two partners to scour London for gold and the Commercial Bank had stopped payment. These eighteenth-century resolutions about the unrestricted acceptance of notes are all the more remarkable because the declared policy was the soundly scientific " expansive " method of treating a panic—which, as Bagehot reminded us,[3] is " a species of neuralgia, and according to the rules of science you must not starve it." In wild periods of alarm one failure makes many ; and the best way to prevent the derivative failures is to obviate the primary collapse which causes them. A panic is, in essence, only a widespread apprehension that people will not be paid the money that is

[1] *Newcastle Chronicle*, July 25, 1772.
[2] " It is not deemed creditable for a bank to speculate in the funds or to buy and sell stock frequently, with a view of making a profit by the difference of price." (*Gilbart on Banking*, p. 285.)
[3] *Lombard Street*, p. 51.

due to them. Pay them punctually, promptly, and in full, and with every payment made the justification of the panic weakens, and confidence is simultaneously augmented. The co-operative self-protection which we have been examining—so fraught with significance, in the light of later episodes in the history of finance—was organised on these lines, and was a remarkable exhibition of financial acumen. It steadily gained in favour and acceptance among bankers themselves as a specialist class, as well as among the commercial community around them. In 1788, we find the Royal Bank of Scotland offering its assistance to Sir William Forbes's business, in order to help him and his partners in meeting any run. The understanding had become much more definite by the time of the Scottish banking crisis of 1793. Forbes tells us that an association had been formed in London, of Northumberland gentlemen, with the purpose of supporting the credit of Newcastle banks. Forbes's own firm also had been able to render help to other houses, who, he says, " had been put to a nonplus, and who, without our aid, there was great reason to fear, would have been forced to stop, whereby the evil would have been still further increased." Seeing that Forbes's Bank paid out between December, 1792, and May of 1793, no less than £263,724, its efforts in stemming the crisis must have had considerable effect. In the height of the crisis Forbes and his partners met in conclave with the cashier and deputy-governor of the Royal Bank and the treasurer of the Bank of Scotland. In order to emphasise their community of interest, Forbes tells us that : " We sent for Mr. Hog (manager of the British Linen Company), for all ceremony or etiquette of public or private banks was now out of the question, when it had become necessary to think of what was to be done for our joint preservation on such an emergency." The expedient seems to have been generally recognised from that time onwards. Alexander Blair, before the 1841 Committee on Banks of Issue,[1] could not remember a time when the Edinburgh bankers did not meet to agree

[1] Q. 1924.

upon the deposit and discount rates. It had been the practice ever since he was connected with the Bank of Scotland. We may safely assume that they would not meet for administrative purposes without employing their self-protective capacities as well, whenever the need arose.

THE BANK AS MODEL

These assaults upon the banking citadel convinced Forbes—and his inference is extremely significant, even if we had no other evidence of its soundness—that it was worth the while of a country banker to be persona grata at the Bank of England. We find him, at some point before 1780, congratulating himself and his partners upon the investment of their reserve funds in Bank Stock, because, as he naïvely says, " by holding a considerable sum of it, we arrived at a certain degree of respectability at the Bank." That, of course, was true enough. A banking institution which was a large holder of Bank Stock would naturally receive greater consideration in Threadneedle Street than one which was not. Irish banking was looking in the same direction for sound principles. The Bank of Ireland was (1782) modelling its system on that of the Bank of England, and begging for leave to examine the mode of book-keeping at Threadneedle Street, and for the services of an "active clerk" proficient in it.[1] Lord Sydney, writing to the Duke of Rutland (1785) with regard to the appropriation of certain Irish funds to the purchase of stock, suggests that "there would be no difficulty in establishing by agreement some form of certificate—for instance, from the Bank of England—to be annually laid before the Irish Parliament."[2] The English Government shared these views of the responsibility of the Bank. When Pitt proposed the systematic reduction of the National Debt (1786) he emphasised the

[1] *Fortescue MSS.*, Vol. I. p. 172. The attractiveness of English financial security still remained, however. " I am assured that an apprehension of impending confusion in this country [Ireland] is drawing much cash from it to England, and that some of our own people are sending their own cash thither as to a more secure place." (Haliday to Charlemont (1788). *Charlemont MSS.*, Vol. II. p. 394.)

[2] *Rutland MSS.*, Vol. III. p. 173.

THE BANK OF ENGLAND 237

necessity that the commissioners be persons of " rank and distinction " : adding that " the governor and deputy-governor of the Bank of England ought also to be of the number."[1] The stability of the Bank of England is " equal to that of the British Government," Adam Smith declared.[2] Thornton, in 1804, spoke of Bank of England notes as " *the coin* in which the great mercantile payments in London are effected."[3]

The Bank of England, however, had still many lessons to learn. In the crisis of 1792–1793 it acted with over-eagerness. The directors cut off supplies too suddenly, and really forced a crisis. On Tuesday evening, February 19, 1793, the Bank " threw out the paper of Lane, Son and Fraser ; and next morning they stopped payment to the amount of almost a million of money."[4] The Bank maintained its restrictive policy until an issue of £5,000,000 of Exchequer Bills was imminent, of which £2,202,200 sufficed to restore confidence. As in the case of the later expedient—the suspension of the Bank Charter Act—it was a moral, rather than a monetary tonic that was wanted. The directors then adopted the " expansive " policy and the crisis gradually subsided. Public dissatisfaction with the restrictive method, however, led to a scheme, arising out of a meeting at the London Tavern on April 2, 1796, for a board of twenty-five persons to be created with powers to issue circulating promissory notes against deposits of coin, bank bills, and commercial paper. The project never came to fruition, and Pulteney's proposal for another bank, if the Bank directors did not abandon the policy of restricting their issues, proved equally abortive. But another expedient was adopted. On Sunday, July 25, 1796, a Cabinet Council was held at Whitehall, as a result of which the Bank directors were required to suspend cash payments.[5]

[1] Tomline, *Memoirs of Pitt*, Vol. II. p. 156.
[2] *Wealth of Nations*, Ed. Cannan, I. p. 303.
[3] Quoted by G. H. Pownall, *English Banking*, p. 7.
[4] Chalmers, quoted by Francis, *History of the Bank*, Vol. I. p. 213.
[5] They gave notice of the suspension thus, on the Monday :—
" In consequence of an order of His Majesty's Privy Council, notified to the Bank last night, a copy of which is hereunto annexed, the Governor,

238 EVOLUTION OF THE MONEY MARKET

This stringency[1] was caused by the excessive demands of the Government upon the Bank. Under the original Act (section 29) the Governor, Deputy-Governor, and all other officials were to be penalised (section 29) if they should purchase any land or revenues belonging to the Crown, or make loans or advances to the Crown on security or anticipation of revenue, without the authority of Parliament. These provisions were disobeyed at an early date. Ministers acquired the habit of drawing on the Bank for fairly large sums, without the sanction of Parliament. The directors, whose patriotism was in no way coloured by subservience,[2] had misgivings, and requested an Act of

[1] The mere prospect of the Bank becoming embarrassed excited the apprehension of the foreign diplomats in this country. Thus, Count Starhemberg, the Emperor's ambassador to England, writes (1796) : " J'ai lieu de supposer, d'après ce que l'on me mande, que le courier que vous avez envoyé à M. Eden pour annoncer le nouveau retard survenue à l'occasion des embarras de la Banque, était parvenu à sa destination ; mais comme on ne me fait à ce sujet aucune plainte ni reproche, j'ai lieu d'espérer que la confiance bien placée que nous avons dans l'amitié, l'honnêteté, et les talens de nos amis, l'a emporté sur les autres considérations, et prévalu audessus de toutes les craintes que cette cruelle information aurait pû produire." (*Fortescue MSS.*, Vol. III. p. 280.)

[2] Even where transactions arising out of urgent money bills were concerned, the directors declined (1790) to meet except on their regular day. (*Hist. MSS. Comm.*, Fortescue MSS., Vol. I. pp. 563–4.)

Deputy-Governor, and Directors of the Bank of England think it is their duty to inform the proprietors of the Bank Stock, as well as the public at large, that the general concerns of the Bank are in the most affluent and flourishing situation, and such as to preclude every doubt as to the security of its notes. The Directors mean to continue their usual discounts for the accommodation of the commercial interests, paying the amount in bank-notes ; and the dividend warrants will be paid in the same manner." The Bank Restriction Act was passed on the 3rd May, 1797.

Cash payments were not actually resumed until the year 1821. Bank of England notes had meanwhile been made legal tender in 1811, and their issue thereby stimulated. The paper circulation was out of control. Between 1808 and 1809 there was an increase of £3,095,340 in country bank-notes, and about £1,800,000 in Bank of England notes. This was an excess, " of which most the unequivocal symptom is the high price of bullion," and it " is to be ascribed to the want of a sufficient check and control in the issues of paper from the Bank of England, and originally to the suspension of cash payments which removed the natural and true control." (*Bullion Committee Report*, p. 73.) In 1810 the notes were at $13\frac{1}{2}$ per cent. discount. By 1817 they were almost on a par with gold, owing to the numerous failures of country banks, which contracted the paper circulation. In 1819, when the question of the resumption of cash payments entered the field of practical politics, they were only $4\frac{1}{2}$ per cent. discount. Parliament decided upon 1823 for resumption, but the directors voluntarily resumed in May, 1821.

THE BANK OF ENGLAND

Indemnity, together with the limitation to £50,000 of any future transactions of this type. Pitt gave them the Act without the limitation. The Act 33 Geo. III. c. 32 (not 20 Geo. III. c. 32, as quoted by Dr. Bisschop) recites the original prohibition, and proceeds to indemnify the governor, deputy-governor, and all other officers of the Bank for having advanced, or lent, and by reason of advancing or lending in future, any sums of money for the purpose of " paying any bills of exchange accepted by, or by the direction or on the account of, the Lords Commissioners of His Majesty's Treasury." When Pitt applied for further advances the directors swallowed their qualms and granted the loans, but they sent a copy of a " most serious and solemn resolution," to be laid before the Cabinet.[1] The Act of Indemnity was then quite recent, and doubtless its memory may have impressed prudence upon the Bank directors. But in any case their firmness was a wholesome factor at a period when the personal influence of George III., and the system of bribery worked by the " King's friends," threatened the Constitution with degradation and impotence. It was as true then as now that the Bank " has never failed in its dealings with the authorities to assert its own essential independence."[2] At any rate there was no lack of liberal patriotism on its part, for at an open meeting of bankers and merchants in 1798, to raise funds for augmenting the militia, " numer-

[1] " They beg leave to declare that nothing could induce them, under present circumstances, to comply with the demand now made upon them but the dread that their refusal might be productive of a greater evil, and nothing but the extreme pressure and exigency of the case can, in any shape, justify them for acceding to this measure ; and they apprehend in so doing they render themselves totally incapable of granting any further assistance to Government during the remainder of this year, and unable to make the usual advances on the land and malt taxes for the ensuing year, should those Bills be passed before Christmas. They likewise consent to this measure in a firm reliance that the repeated promises so frequently made to them, that the advances on the Treasury Bills should be completely done away with, may be actually fulfilled at the next meeting of Parliament, and the necessary arrangements taken to prevent the same from ever happening again, as they conceive it to be an unconstitutional mode of raising money ; what they are not warranted by their charter to consent to ; and an advance always extremely inconvenient to themselves."

[2] *Dunbar Theory and History of Banking*, p. 222.

ous mercantile firms and private individuals contributed large sums, varying from £3000 to £10,000 : and the Bank of England the noble tribute of £200,000."[1]

At the time of stringency, when the Bank suspended cash payments, the City community had again rallied round it again by holding a meeting at the Mansion House and passing a resolution in the same terms as that of 1745, declaring the intention of not refusing bank-notes in payment for money due. This was signed by 4000 of the best people in the City, with the consequence that bank-notes circulated more freely than ever, although, as a matter of fact, they began to be subject to a process of depreciation which had reached 14 per cent. in the month of June. But, discount or no discount, the prestige of the Bank was assured. It dominated London : and, since London itself " had definitely superseded Amsterdam as the chief seat of finance—and of commerce—in the West,"[2] it held the financial primacy of the world.[3] The nucleus had been created. It remained for the cosmopolitan money market to consolidate around it.

[1] Duke of Buckingham, *Memoirs of George III.*, Vol. II. p. 386.
[2] J. H. Clapham, *Camb. Mod. Hist.*, X. 728.
[3] Financial supremacy, at the earliest post-Conquest date when we can discern it, lay in Italy. The Frescobaldi found money for Edward I., and damaged their own credit in doing so. At any rate there is a claim against Edward I., in 1306, by the Frescobaldi for liquidated damages, costs, and charges on account of injury done to their business by the true report that they had advanced money to the King. They alleged that £50,000 of deposits had been, consequently, withdrawn by nervous clients. Edward settled the claim (Ramsay, *Dawn of the Constitution*, p. 539). A modern banker who should lend money to a customer, and should then claim redress for damage done to his credit by his other clients becoming aware of the transaction and withdrawing their deposits, would imperil the current faith in his own sanity.

Italian financial supremacy was injured when Edward III. and Robert of Sicily failed to keep faith with the Peruzzi (Cunningham, *Western Civilisation*, p. 203). Henceforth the *haute finance* of the age was controlled by Italy and Germany jointly. But in November, 1596, Philip of Spain repudiated his debts and resumed possession of the lands which he had mortgaged. This ruined the Italian and German financiers from whom he had borrowed, and relieved the Dutch from the dangerous rivalry of the Fuggers of Antwerp and Augsburg. Consequently Amsterdam became the financial centre of Europe, and held the position till it was ousted by London before the close of the eighteenth century.

PART III

THE RISE OF THE MODERN MONEY MARKET

CHAPTER VIII

THE MODERN MONEY MARKET—THE BIOLOGICAL ANALOGY ELABORATED

BAGEHOT dates our modern Money Market from the resumption of cash payments by the Bank of England in 1819.[1] As this was four years after Waterloo, we may well begin from the latter event, when the National Debt was £758,000,000, and the charge for interest and annuities reached £27,652,000, our analysis of the characteristic modern force which influences the lives and destinies of all of us, " and not least those who never have understood and never will understand anything about the rules which govern it."[2] Looking back, from the centenary of Waterloo to the year of the great battle itself, it is extremely remarkable how the process of financial organisation has fallen into watertight compartments, composed of half and quarter centuries, since that date. In accordance with a well-known economic law, the conditions existing in the old pre-Waterloo era were some of them projected into the post-Waterloo period. They introduced an element of weakness and malaise which, as we shall see, brought recurring complication and disaster, until it culminated in the Overend-Gurney smash, in 1866, almost exactly fifty years from Waterloo itself. The Overend-Gurney crisis marks the final elimination of the old economic infirmities, just as truly as the Battle of Bosworth signalised the close of the Middle Ages in political and social

---

[1] *Lombard Street*, p. 47. The date, as we have seen, was really 1821. Between February 1 and October 1, 1820, the Bank was required to pay its notes in gold bullion of standard fineness, but at the rate of £4 1s. per ounce, and not in a less quantity than 60 ounces at one time.

[2] Kiddy : Address to Chartered Institute of Secretaries.

England. From the time of the Overend-Gurney crisis onwards the modern Money-Power has been gradually centralising the entire financial control of the world—and this of deliberate purpose, knowing its own aim. The passing of the Elementary Education Act, just after the Overend-Gurney crisis, began the genesis of the small investor, as it also marked the partial reversal of the biological law of Natural Selection in the economic realm. Within twenty-five years of the Overend-Gurney affair, almost to a month, we reach another milestone on the pathway of modern economic evolution when we are confronted by the Baring crisis. But in that instance, in contrast to the Overend-Gurney affair, the crash was not allowed to come. The modern Money-Power was strong enough to grapple with the difficulty, and to prevent the cataclysmic upheaval which must otherwise inevitably have occurred. Once more, practically within a quarter of a century from the Baring emergency, we found ourselves face to face with the greatest crisis that we have ever witnessed in our whole history—that which accompanied the outbreak of the war with Germany. That emergency was boldly grappled with, and in military terminology " held." Success in the struggle was all the more vital to the safety of the economic fabric because the crisis came at the end of another quarter century of economic development—namely, that which had witnessed the adolescence of the small investor under the fostering guardianship of centralised financial control and responsibility. It is not often that history, particularly the history of such a period as the nineteenth century, falls into watertight compartments in this fashion.

" DEPERSONALISED " RELATIONSHIPS

In the period extending from about the advent of the nineteenth century down to Waterloo and onwards to the era of the Reform Bill no definite movement towards economic amelioration had begun. In truth, conditions had worsened. Brougham declared that tradesmen's books were covered with debts on which not 1 per cent. could be collected. The shifting value of the currency made matters worse. The man who has contracted on the basis of depreciated paper is embarrassed when the paper moves towards par ; yet this was the case with the depreciated Bank of England note in 1814 and 1815. The pressure was greater than in 1810 and 1812.[1] Machinery was everywhere replacing the human unit. Weavers, who in 1797 had earned 26s. or 27s. a week, were glad to work for a penny an hour in 1832. As the hand-looms were replaced by the power-looms domestic industry vanished and the factory took its place. In 1833, in one district in Lancashire, 41,000 persons were subsisting on 2d. a day. In the rural districts men driven off the land by the enclosure of the common fields were eager to earn the miserable pittance that accrued to them as the reward of being yoked to the cart or the plough, like the beasts of the field. After Waterloo many interruptions to the running of the new financial machine—and they came with the tenacious periodicity of sun-spots—tended to worsen the transitional conditions. Further, that phenomenon so characteristic of a financial—as distinct from a feudal—environment, the impersonal nexus, replaced the intimacy and mutual knowledge which had existed under the older régime. The relations of labour and capital, as Professor Ashley says, were " depersonalised." As a factor in the cosmopolitan financial machinery the impersonal relationship and obligation have a vital and beneficial part to play ; but in weakening the personal tie between employer and employed they have raised up a multitude of fresh problems. The more expensive the machinery the more limited the class which can afford to provide it, and the wider the gulf which yawns between them and the actual workers. Ultimately, as we can now see, there was destined to come a time when finance must find the means of activity for capital, just as capital had provided work for labour. But that time was not within sight even in the " hungry 'forties." The new finance was to be unable, for decades to come, to subdue the erratic

[1] Smart, *Economic Annals*, p. 462.

economic tendencies arising from the fact—palpable as long ago as Xenophon's time—that " man is the hardest of all animals to govern."

A STATE OF ECONOMIC DISORGANISATION

It has been argued that even experienced men were taken by surprise when so great a load of national misery followed in the train of peace after Waterloo. The war expenditure, suddenly checked, demonstrated that the apparently expanding national prosperity was a mere shell. The burden of the debt was 30s. per annum on every inhabitant of Great Britain, and Cobbett roused working-class audiences to enthusiasm by his advocacy of repudiation. The gigantic task of retrenchment and amelioration was crippled by the survival of an obsolete relic of the mediæval anti-usury sentiment which we have seen to have been gradually dissipated but not wholly destroyed. As the law stood, the borrowing of money on mortgage was forbidden where the rate of interest exceeded 5 per cent. Mortgage is essentially a business for insurance companies ; but these organisations would not handle it. They lent on annuities, at 8 per cent., with the stipulation —not unusual in our own day—that the borrower should insure his life at 2 per cent. so that money which he might have got at 6½ per cent. was made to cost him 10 per cent., and even 12 per cent., because of the existence of utterly obsolete legislation. These obstacles did not entirely vanish (*ante*, p. 139) until the reign of Queen Victoria had begun. Wage-earners were forbidden to combine, and out of the very prohibition itself arose a determination to acquire the political power which should enable its victims to abrogate such a hindrance to the progress of the industrial classes. Political and social nostrums of every species were thrust upon a people too ignorant to discriminate. Political parties found themselves in a revolutionised environment, and under the necessity of dealing with difficulties which had never existed before, since the economic circumstances out of which they arose were wholly novel. Banking was mainly

BIRTH OF MODERN FINANCE 247

local, unorganised, undisciplined, incoherent, rough and ready. The Stock Exchange was still under the suspicion of the majority of those who knew of its existence. Practically all the vast and far-flung system of joint-stock enterprise with limited liability was as yet unborn and in fact undreamt-of : investment, of the multitudinous modern types, a thing unknown. A disorderly scramble for wealth, checked and governed here and there by such elementary rules as even a scramble necessitates, represented what is to-day the most highly organised, delicate, and susceptible factor in the fabric of civilisation. In the light of these considerations we need hardly be astonished that Mr. Hirst has characterised the contemporary financial conditions at the birth of the modern Money Market in such severe terms. " At this present time [1911]," he says,[1] " there is hardly an important country, except China . . . which would not be ashamed to own such a law and system of currency and banking as England boasted a century ago." Very remarkable is the fact that Mr. Hirst's retrospect almost touches the year (1810) of the Bullion Committee—the first really serious and (up to the existing economic limits) exhaustive endeavour to analyse and grapple with the laws by which a Money Power is conditioned. The change since then has been more than revolutionary. It is easier in 1915 for a resident in Saskatchewan to make an investment in New Zealand than it would have been in 1814 for a capitalist in Scotland to find safe employment for money south of the border. To-day it is simpler to operate in a market 3000 miles away than it was in 1815 to buy a pound of tea in the nearest country town. " To-day the half-dozen chief capitals of Christendom are in closer contact financially, and are more dependent one upon the other, than were the chief cities of great Britain less than a hundred years ago ; and this has produced, and is producing more and more, an international and economic solidarity which is having a most powerful influence in lessening the animosity of rival nationalities."[2] In 1815 disorganisation was every-

[1] *Stock Exchange,* p. 19.
[2] Lord Mayor of Liverpool : *Liverpool Daily Post,* April 21, 1914.

where; in 1915 organisation and discipline have become ubiquitous. In 1815 the time had come for a great liberation of human energy, and finance was to be the liberator and organiser. Its policy was destined to change the whole basis of society.

THE MEANING OF "FINANCE"

But what is finance, and wherein does it differ from the capitalism of the capitalist-entrepreneur? The frontier that divides them is not easy to define, especially as the two terms are still frequently employed as if they were synonymous and interchangeable. Yet it is essential, in a scientific inquiry to distinguish between them. It is probably correct to say that as long as we speak of the internal resources of an enterprise we allude to capitalism. Finance intervenes from the outside, by the organised and conditioned supply of capital and supervision from external sources, upon terms which are in accordance with the dominant financial sentiment of the moment. Capital is the food, but finance organises its supply. Finance is the organising force, but capital the nutriment which it administers. Capitalism stimulates abstention and saving in order that capital may be created out of the resulting fund. Finance introduces the scientific method and relies upon organisation rather than upon parsimony. Capital, in the *post*-Waterloo era, had a single eye to production, whereas modern finance is doubly concerned in consumption. Leadership *by* moneyed men is capitalism. When the moneyed men themselves are led and disciplined we have finance. As processes increased in complexity and materials became more expensive, the scope of capital was widened, and that of the individual undertaker narrowed. Capital took command of labour, the while that finance was organising to take control of capital. The capitalist ceased to be a mere middleman, and became an organiser and controller of production. The producer accepted the guidance of the capitalist. So, by an analogous process, the banker ceases to be a mere money dealer, and becomes the supervisor and controller of capital. The capitalist

BIRTH OF MODERN FINANCE 249

(i.e. the capitalist-entrepreneur) accepts the guidance of finance. The factory system, under capitalism, was the disciplined aggregation of labour in one place. Finance is the disciplined aggregation of capital under one central control.

Therefore one is the organisation of physical, the other of financial, force. Capital is the blood, finance the brain. Capital is the mechanic, finance the craftsman. Finance is the architect, capital only the builder. If politics be defined as the attempted concentration and administration of power, then finance is the attempted concentration and administration of the *source* of power. Language—that earliest, and for a time supreme, instrument of social consolidation and advance—is the storage of ideas. Finance is the disciplined storage of the means to realise them. Capital is inorganic, or at least non-organic. Finance is organic. Money is the common carrier of capital and finance is its master. Current financial opinion is an unmistakable reality and a potent force, though it may differ widely from the purely capitalistic view which exists contemporaneously with it. The stream of new issues, checked by the refusal of bankers and underwriters to accept further responsibilities, stands for finance. A lock-out in one of the great textile trades represents capitalism. The capitalist works with his own money : it is the business of finance to aggregate that of other people and place it to the best advantage alike from the point of view of the owner and of society at large. " The banker " [as part of the organisation of finance] " has one hand on the pulse of commerce, with the other he feels the heart-beats of finance." The aphorism is that of Mr. F. E. Steele of Parr's Bank. " Take £100 payable on demand," said Bagehot, " and pay it back in cheques of £5 each, and that is our English banking." Take a body of men engaged in such transactions, subject them to scientific discipline and control, energise them in the interest of the whole economic mechanism, and that is our modern finance. Capitalism is the individual species, finance the biocœnosis which contains it, and largely governs the conditions of every other biocœnosis throughout the world. If life consists in the metabolism of the biogens, it is equally true that finance consists in the metabolism of capital. Stop the metabolism, and the structure, be it physical or financial, perishes. Every scheme must satisfy the economic test or die. It must procreate or perish.

Upon capitalism lies the responsibility of immediate maintenance, and upon finance the organisation of capitalism for the perpetuation of its capacity to discharge that function. Capitalism can produce immense quantities of average goods, but only finance can regulate their production so as to bring them into consistency not with immediate demand but with ultimate need. Exchange of surplus commodities brings each party to the bargain into contact with new utilities and gratifications. But exchange, in its most facile and advantageous form, must be backed by confidence and security ; and their provision and regularisation are the rôle of finance. Say defines the capitalist as " the person who makes the advances." Then the financier is he who dissipates the capitalist's timidity, receives and aggregates the advances, and adjusts the mechanism so as to secure their most efficient distribution and protection. Capital provides for to-morrow ; finance for next year and the next decade. Capital takes the short, finance the long route to the goal. This choice of the extended path is the biological analogue of the postponement of birth, reaching its highest development in uterine or quasi-uterine gestation, which is so important a step in the organisation of life and the curtailment of the struggle for existence. Capital seizes and exploits the present opportunity, riding triumphantly on the crest of the booms as they come. Finance discerns the cloud of coming menace, no bigger than a man's hand. It sees the advancing stringency afar off, and braces the economic fabric to resist the shock. Finance tends more and more to employ the touchstone of abiding social utility, while capitalism is satisfied if the scheme answers to the test of present monetary profit. Scientific finance involves the aggregation, organisation, coordination and distribution of credit, under an integrated control, for the consolidation of the social structure. The teleological explanation of finance is social evolution. Even its most accomplished exponents, practical or theoretical, have not yet completely grasped the conditions of finance as a social force. Probably they never will grasp them, any more than they will attain finality in their conception of civilisation and in their attempt to realise it. But they move steadily (sometimes, indeed, rapidly, in contrast with the pace of geological evolution) towards the goal; and, best of all, they now possess very definite ideas what the goal is and where it is to be found.

It is a paradox that in a financial age men are ranked for what they are, rather than for what they possess, whereas the reverse is the case under a landed or capitalistic régime. Mr. Morgan, not his millions, was the great power in Wall Street. It was his personality at the helm, not his millions in the hold, which made for the safety of the ship in one of those tremendous financial cyclones which, in his days, broke periodically over the American financial world.[1] Force and status, generating rigidity, as the bases of social organisation, give place, in an era when finance is dominant, to negotiation, dexterity, and intellectual energy. Such a state of things tends to produce and perpetuate acute economic contrast, in spite of all that religion and social panaceas like Socialism attempt to do in the direction of equalisation. Money transforms the civilisation whose spirit is fixity into that whose spirit is progress. In other words, the financial influence tends to create and encourage that Difference which is, and has been since time began, the great well-spring of natural selection. The exploitation of the natural products of the earth, once

---

[1] "If J. Pierpont Morgan should make a bond issue from the Desert of Sahara and put his name on it it would be subscribed probably, not because he is connected with these institutions [i.e. the institutions which were alleged to constitute the American Money Trust], but because he has lived an earnest and tremendously strenuous life in the study of these questions for half a century, and the people have bought and bought and bought securities that his name has been put to, and have believed that they came out right." (Mr. G. W. Perkins, before the Money Trust Committee (Washington), January, 1913).

extensive over whatever maximum of space a wandering and conquering horde could range, tends now to become more and more intensive over a minimum area, whose teeming population (at the stage which we have reached) is largely fed by a financial tribute willingly paid by a multitude of foreign debtors.

Organised finance, as we shall shortly see, is more closely related to the biological sciences than with and to the mathematico-physical group. Mathematics and physics are concerned with laws and quantities that are immutable. Pure capitalism is their economic analogue, while the work of the capitalist-entrepreneur represents a rather higher level of achievement. But finance rises into an atmosphere infinitely more subtle and refined. Finance is a dynamic and not a static force—a plastic, as distinct from a rigid, entity. Religion and government, custom and law, language and art, are static, or nearly static, forces. Adventure, invention, trade, discovery—all those processes which finance is concerned to organise, foster, and develop, and upon the prosperity of which it depends for its return—are dynamic. Every advance in its cosmopolitanism weakens the static factors of the social fabric. The economic frontier no longer corresponds with the political. Save that they are adjusted and readjusted from time to time after some great international upheaval, the political frontiers remain the same from age to age. But the economic frontier changes from day to day and from year to year, expanding in one direction, contracting in another, and tending all the time by its ceaseless attrition of political barriers to wear down the artificial frontiers which political expediency or jealousy erects. The dynamics of financial energy, precipitated into the sphere of Latin-American statics, have revolutionised the whole economic structure of Brazil and the Argentine. Every element of the financial mechanism which we have studied —the bank, the principle of negotiability, the company, and the Stock Exchange—helps to maintain social fluidity and to prevent any return to the rigidity of feudalism. The stability of class-existence which is fostered by a purely feudal régime, and dissolved by a money-economy, is itself a negation of the Law of Variation upon which evolution depends. The square man may be in a round hole: but he must stop there or die. Every man under a feudal régime was born to his place, and fixed there for life. Custom held him where he stood, like a ninepin nailed to the floor. In an industrial, and all the more in a financial, epoch he can move. A man in motion looking out for a better economic opportunity makes a far more valuable and productive item in the aggregate of social wealth than the same individual shackled to a given plot of manorial lands under a rigid feudal economy. Freedom of movement sets up what has been aptly called the "cross-fecundation of ideas," which would have been excluded in a society divided into arbitrary and impassable frontiers. This breeds cross-cultures, and engenders new types. Liberty does not mean merely the freedom of the intellect to follow the light of reason, but the deliverance of the body from all that prevents its pursuance of the pathway towards the amelioration of its physical habitat and environment. The moving man is wealth, while the fixed man is illth. This is the reason why feudalism killed, while finance makes alive again. Doubtless rigidity was originally essential to hold the society together against the aggression of its rivals. But rigidity must have excluded variation and produced static immobility. It tended to stifle the working of the propensity to variation. In such conditions, unless relief is afforded by the advent of some new solvent, the society will be strangled by its own yoke, destroyed by the unrelenting rigour of its own discipline. That solvent is money, as organised by finance. Man's mastery of his environment is founded in consciousness, caution, and analysis; and those essentials are nowhere endowed with so keen an edge as when they are tempered in a financial atmosphere. The crucial and supreme financial test for any proposition is—can it earn adequate profits upon the invested capital? But that is only another way of inquiring whether the scheme is adapted to its environment, so as to be capable of flourishing therein.

S

Even as we scan it, the financial test shades off into the biological.

THE PREDOMINANCE OF LONDON

For the task to be achieved Britain had immense advantages joined to an unchallengeable predominance in the elementary finance of the age. London had ousted Amsterdam, as the Dutch capital, in earlier days, had ousted Italian cities, from the supremacy of the existing financial régime. Nations began to borrow mainly in England, as they had once done mainly in Holland. Napoleon had " regarded the remarkable credit development in England as the prime source of its military power ; but he was equally satisfied that . . . it would be quite possible to bring about its collapse."[1] Amsterdam still took an occasional share. Barings and Hopes, of Amsterdam, for instance, handled a French 5 per cent. issue at 57 in 1817. Next year it was quoted at 85, and it saw 109 before the revolution of 1830. But when it was issued no Paris firm was strong enough to take a hand in it. Not till 1848 was there any encroachment on the exclusive territory of the London houses and the international Jewish groups. Moreover, twenty years of war had concentrated the world's trade in the British Empire, and had made Britain the one country in the world where capital might be invested with the maximum of contemporary safety. How huge—relatively to the age—were the available supplies may be demonstrated by one vivid example. In May of 1818 the Bank of England opened a subscription list for £7,000,000, for the purpose of funding Treasury bills. The list was to be open for three days ; but, as a matter of fact, there were already impatient subscribers waiting outside the Bank at two o'clock in the morning of the first day. When, at length, the doors were opened into the chief cashier's office, the rush was so great that one door was lifted completely off its hinges. Inasmuch as the whole £7,000,000 was subscribed by the first ten persons who were successful in reaching the counter, all

[1] Foxwell, Preface to Andreades, *History of the Bank of England*, p. xviii

BIRTH OF MODERN FINANCE 255

the rest of the assembly had to go away disappointed.[1] Britain was not only the banker of the world, but carried her financing into arenas where, at all events after the Napoleonic wars, it assumed a quixotic aspect—as, for instance, in taking over, jointly with the Netherlands, the annual payment of 1,000,000 florins, being half the yearly charges on a loan of 25,000,000 florins granted to Russia, during the Great War, by a Dutch house at Amsterdam.

CAPITALISM V. FINANCE

Early *post*-Waterloo enterprise was capitalistic rather than financial. The capitalist-entrepreneur class, largely composed of self-made men (felicitously described[2] as a " broad-bottomed oligarchy "), rose rapidly into a position of great influence in Parliament—a position which, to a large extent, especially as regards Lancashire and Yorkshire, they still maintain. Not a few of the manufacturers were reinforced from the yeomen classes. These could no longer combine agriculture with domestic manufacture, by the spinning-wheel and the hand-loom. The competition of the specialised capitalist manufacturer was too strong for them, and, where they hesitated to remain specialist farmers, they became specialist manufacturers themselves, providing the capital by the sale of their holdings. But they were mainly capitalist employers, as distinguished from financial organisers. Nathan Meyer Rothschild had been a Manchester cotton capitalist before he became a financier. Most of his contemporaries remained capitalists to the end, possessing no ability which was capable of transporting them into the more subtle atmosphere of finance. The influence of the early capitalist employers, unorganised and groping, was utilised to promote the interests of capital alone. They could not take the broader view of finance, for they did not know what finance was. " Finance," said Huskisson, in 1822, " of all political subjects is that which requires the least comprehension or capacity; it is that which, in its own

---

[1] Turner, *Chronicles of the Bank of England*, p. 108.
[2] By the late Professor Sidgwick : *European Polity*, p. 318.

nature, is most on a level with the reach even of ordinary half-educated minds." These were the views of the man who next year became President of the Board of Trade ! Mr. Gisborne, in 1836, pleaded in the House of Commons[1] that some allowance must be made, in the case of the new joint-stock banks, " for the freakish dispositions incident to youth." As if there were any room for freakishness in so serious and vital a thing as finance ! Such men as Grenfell and Baring had to form financial and economic opinion at the most critical stage in modern British history. They stood almost alone in the possession of expert knowledge. " Surprising as it may appear," says a writer in the *Westminster Review*,[2] " it is no less notorious, that up to the year 1818 the science of Political Economy was scarcely known or talked of beyond a small circle of philosophers, and that legislation, so far from being in conformity with its principles, was daily receding from them more and more." The consequence of this ignorance of the existence and capacities of financial science was to tinge all early nineteenth-century sentiment with the capitalist ideal. So it is that the virtues of capitalism become the darling protégés of early nineteenth-century sentiment. As social control " takes the tinge of the source from which it springs," Professor Ross has urged that " when the moneyed man holds the baton we hear much of industriousness, thrift, sobriety, probity, and civility."[3] If social ascendancy be transferred to some other quarter, the social ideals will undergo a corresponding modification—that is to say, " the character of social requirement changes with every shifting of social power." A capitalistic age enforces a capitalistic moral code, and elevates it to the niche which, in a monastic era, would be adorned by faith and asceticism.

A NEW AUTHORITY ESSENTIAL

But the code of capitalistic virtues, the ideals of capitalistic achievement, must have been impotent to conform to

[1] *Annual Register*, 1837, p. 178.
[2] Quoted by Toynbee, *Industrial Revolution*, p. 4.
[3] *Social Control*, p. 85.

BIRTH OF MODERN FINANCE

the canons of modern society, had they not been disciplined from a new source of authority. " The scope of the human intellect," says Brooks Adams in his *Theory of Social Revolutions*,

" is necessarily limited, and modern capitalists appear to have been evolved under the stress of an environment which demanded excessive specialisation in the direction of a genius adapted to money-making under highly complex industrial conditions. To this money-making attribute all else has been sacrificed, and the modern capitalist not only thinks in terms of money, but he thinks in terms of money more exclusively than the French aristocrat or lawyer ever thought in terms of caste. . . . As the capitalist is more highly specialised than the soldier ever was, he is more helpless when his single weapon fails him. . . . It would seem to be almost mathematically demonstrable that the capitalist will in the near future be subjected to the pressure under which he must develop flexibility or be eliminated. . . . Meditating upon these matters, it is hard to resist the persuasion that unless capital can, in the immediate future, generate an intellectual energy, beyond the sphere of its specialised calling, very much in excess of any intellectual energy of which it has hitherto given promise, and unless it can besides rise to an appreciation of diverse social conditions, as well as to a level of political sagacity, far higher than it has attained within recent years, its relative power in the community must decline."

The doctrines might well have been enunciated of the early nineteenth-century capitalist, at a time when finance was not strong enough to take control. For in the age of the Reform Bill, and for thirty years onwards, the political aspirations of the capitalist order were mainly characterised by a desire to bring the " upper class " down to its own level, while the " lower classes " were simultaneously to be kept to their old place. Humanity, with all its resources and aspirations, had no interest for it except as sources of income. This is the reason why early nineteenth-century capitalism did so little, while late nineteenth-century finance attempted and achieved so much, for the æsthetic and intellectual interests of humanity. Perhaps it was also the reason why the great Sir Robert

Peel said that he respected the aristocracy of birth and of intellect, but not the " aristocracy of wealth." Such men as Peel had in his mind's eye were awake to the end, but blind to the means. The central article of their creed was the necessity of giving absolute freedom of operation to the industrial entrepreneur. Early nineteenth-century capitalism was employed in determining, by means of internecine rivalry, *who* should supply goods to the customer. Nineteenth-century finance is less concerned with that question than with a problem of much more profound social interest, namely, *what* goods shall be supplied, and whether their supply cannot be encouraged by extensive loans of money—of course, on approved security. Competition, as Arnold Toynbee told us, " is neither good nor bad in itself ; it is a force which has to be studied and controlled." Early capitalism neither studied nor controlled ; modern finance does both. The early nineteenth-century capitalists had not even glimpsed the system under which, in our day, there is an incessant accumulation of capitalist profits to feed finance, combined with a system of beneficial enterprise upon which finance exercises itself. They did not understand that unorganised and undisciplined capitalism is simply an illegitimate drain on the moral and physical forces of the nation, a species of enterprise which will wait long, perhaps, before it presents the bill ; but when it comes will inexorably insist on a terrible payment.

THE PHYSIOLOGICAL ANALOGY

What, then, were the essentials of financial organisation, for the purpose of energising and disciplining capitalist enterprise ? What, in a word, are the postulates of a Money Market ? If we are correct in believing that finance is an undying corporate organism, which has evolved around the original nucleus represented by the Bank of England, then the question of the requisites for its continued orthogenic evolution will best be answered by seeking for some analogy among the biological sciences. We shall find it in that science—physiology—which is concerned with the description and explanation of the phenomena manifested by living beings. But is it argued, the critical reader may ask, that the Money Market *lives*? An organism, in a certain figurative sense, it may be: but surely the reasoning is not going to be pushed as far as the contention that it possesses life? It certainly is not the intention of the present essay to suggest that the Money Market lives in the sense of being a subsisting physical and individual entity. That it lives as a deathless corporate organism, however, is reasonably arguable. It has already been urged that the Bank of England has a conscious self, capable of accumulating and transmitting experience by means of a corporate identity which was, and is, the same from age to age. If we desired to adventure further we might almost be tempted by the terms of such definitions of life as are given, e.g. by Spencer. His favourite definition of life was " a co-ordination of actions."[1] He added that " an arrest of co-ordination is death, and imperfect co-ordination is disease." This is equally true of the Money Market, and could be predicated of it without the alteration of a syllable—so close and intimate is the parallel between corporate and individual existence. Elsewhere [2] the great philosopher formulates another definition. Life, he declares, is " the continuous adjustment of internal relations to external relations." But this, again, could be predicated of the Money Market. The parallel is the more striking if we remember that the Money Market grows, by absorption, transformation, assimilation, and incorporation, towards increasing complexity of structure and enhanced capacity of self-protection, self-adaptation, and self-repair, just like living matter, and not by mere superficial deposition, like the crystal.

Thus encouraged, we pursue the physiological analogy. The whole of the variety of vital manifestations may be divided into three species of process: to wit, changes in substance, in energy, and in form. It follows that the general elementary vital phenomena fall into three groups—metabolism, the mechanism of energy, and the assumption

[1] *Principles of Biology*, p. 60.   [2] *Principles of Biology*, p. 80.

of form.[1] Every living cell is continually occupied in taking in certain substances from its environment, subjecting them to chemical transformation in its interior, and giving out other substances. This metabolism is operative in nutrition and digestion, in respiration and circulation, in secretion and excretion. Out of the ingested matter living substance is continually being again formed by the living substance which already exists, though it is itself continually undergoing decomposition. The analogous process in the economic sphere is the incessant collection, aggregation, and utilisation of huge masses of credit material. To maintain these aggregates at their proper and expedient maximum for the time being is the business of the great banks; but there is an immense subordinate contribution by the savings banks, co-operative societies, building and land societies, joint-stock companies (including the insurance and investment trust species), and all organisations which create accumulations of money. On the one hand, money is kept out of hoards or even temporary sterile storage, and on the other, it is thrust into fruitful activities again as fast as it returns from each successive journey. If the supplies are too freely furnished, we have inflation—a word singularly applicable to both the body physical and the body financial. The normal metabolism is either interrupted by crisis or diverted into the wrong channel by unreasoning speculation. If the supplies are insufficient, we have malnutrition, decline, and weakness. If, though sufficient in quantity, they are unskilfully administered—a plethora at one time, a modicum at another—we get, physiologically speaking, malaise, rapidly passing into distress (and probably marked by significant variations in temperature, capable of clinical measurement) if there be not a more precise adjustment of nourishment to necessity. Therefore—to resume the financial train of thought—the distribution must be skilfully managed so that the economic

---

[1] The physiological framework of the argument is largely based upon Max Verworn's Art. "Physiology," in the Supplement to the last edition of the *Encyclopædia Britannica*.

structure may, in the matter of its banking facilities, be approximated to a market area, with a resulting equalisation of supply to demand and of the price (interest) at which the supplies are furnished. In the clinics of the physical frame, the test is that of the thermometer. In the clinics of finance, it is the price of Consols and the ruling bank rate—together a " crisisometer " of the most acute sensitiveness. And both in iatro-physic and iatro-finance we do not hesitate to change the conditions so as to get the vital phenomena into accord with what we know to be the essentials of health and activity. That is to say, we endeavour to create a means of rapidly transporting a surplus of capital from the point of superfluity to the locus of demand or stringency. The mobility of money is just as important as the mobility of men, and just as fruitful of benefit to mankind at large.

THE NECESSITY OF METABOLISM

We saw that the mere aggregation and administration of nourishment would not suffice, since mal-distribution might interrupt the metabolism. The reason is that the substances taken in by the cell are stores of potential energy, which it is capable of transforming, under conditions of health, into kinetic energy. This, in turn, distributed in accordance with local and functional needs, maintains the manifold activities of the organism—its motion, heat, and perhaps electricity. So in the economic organism there is an incessant supply of energy arising from the transformation of the credit-material into capital, and from the distribution of this vital force, by means of the Money Market organisation, in accordance with local and functional needs. The units of this currency possess a reciprocally procreative power. Such credit-material includes cheques, notes, bills of exchange, securities, bills of lading, dock warrants, delivery notes and a few other varieties of assignable, negotiable, or quasi-negotiable instruments. These, to fulfil their function, must possess facility of valid transfer and stability of value up to the utmost limits of contemporary possibility, and be sufficient in quantity to meet all the needs of an immensely expanded trade and to finance a widely extended social and imperial programme both at home and abroad. If the currency be partially paper, whether notes or securities, there must be the machinery for its conversion with the maximum of celerity and certainty into a form—gold—capable of easiest assimilation even when the organism is disturbed and diseased. Yet, paradoxically speaking, in the case of a note and cheque currency (as distinguished from a security currency) the capacity of convertibility should be enhanced in an inverse ratio to the desire to convert. That is to say, the knowledge that convertibility is uninterruptedly assured should steadily diminish the desire to take advantage of it. The process must be capable of sustaining itself and the community in a time of stress, and not only in the normal conditions of business. With the credit-material we require a credit-mechanism highly co-ordinated and correlated, freed from the shackles of mediævalism and prejudice, and capable of co-operating with the currency in fostering, by means of distributed and redistributed credit facilities, under an adequately centralised control, a maximum of legitimate financial, commercial, and industrial activity, proceeding evenly and not spasmodically. Reverting to the physiological analogy, the distribution may be described as *local* where, for instance, a great joint-stock bank shifts money from a locus of superfluity to an arena of stringency, or where a Stock Exchange, by the high prices of a certain class of security, attracts capital to the industries they represent, until an advance in quotations indicates that the local need is satisfied and the power of absorption satiated. The process may be characterised as economically *functional* where some vital portion of the organism is threatened with disaster, and extensive stores of kinetic energy have to be employed for its protection and revival into healthy activity. This is exactly what was done in the Baring crisis, where the diagnosis was favourable : and left undone in the Overend-Gurney fever, where it was plainly indicated that contemporary iatro-financial resources and skill were unequal to the disease, and could only be employed with the gravest peril to others beside the patient.

THE ASSUMPTION OF FORM

But, further, the chemical transformations in living substance manifest themselves in changes of form—as in the case of growth, reproduction, and development. This last includes the constant struggle of the organism into closer adaptation with its environment. Specialised functions will come to be discharged by specialised organs. The development will, in the higher organisms, proceed as far as consciously directing and co-ordinating functions, ultimately evolving into mind, by means of which the organism becomes aware of itself, and, standing as it were outside its own personality, contemplates itself, and essays to protect itself and to guide and control its own destiny. It realises its oneness—grasps the pregnant fact that its different elements are not isolated and self-dependent factors, but inseparable parts of an interdependent whole :—

" The living structure is evidently organised : that is to say every part of it bears a definite relation to every other part. As, however, the structure is the outcome of metabolic activity, it follows that the metabolic activity of the living body is also organised, every aspect of it bearing a definite relation to every other aspect. That this is actually so has become more and more clear with the advance of physiology, particularly in recent times. The fundamental mistake of the physiologists of the middle of last century was that they completely failed to realise this. Such processes as secretion, absorption, growth, nervous excitation, muscular contraction, were treated as if each was an isolable physical or chemical process, instead of being what it is, one side of a many-sided metabolic activity, of which the different sides are indissolubly associated."[1]

Mutatis mutandis, every word of this may be predicated of organised finance. The gradual growth of this self-knowledge, this capacity for self-protection, this deliberate selection of an aim, this considered concentration and co-ordination of the whole of the resources of the organism

[1] Haldane, *Mechanism, Life and Personality*, p. 78.

to attain the selected end (and even to deflect the cosmic processes where necessary in the effort to master them)—all these manifestations are as palpable in the financial organism as in the physical. For instance, we can hardly miss the analogy between the disciplinary control which is wielded by the financial hierarchy and the intelligent directive supremacy of the brain over practically all the thoughts, the movements and functions of the organism. Nor can we overlook the remarkable parallel between the cerebellum as the organ of co-ordinative movement in the higher animals and the similar co-ordinating functions discharged by the great banks and the leading Stock Exchanges. If it be removed, intelligence remains, but the power of co-ordination is gone.[1] The same results would follow the removal of the financial factor from the modern social complex.

The further we go the more striking is the comparison. The nerve current set up by contact with an external object is carried by afferent or sensory nerves to the nearest ganglion, whence it may—or may not—be hurried to the higher and more remote nerve centres. These, if they are made cognisant of it, may, by means of efferent or motor nerves, despatch a mandate to the affected part. The case of a man touching a hot stove is directly in point. In man every new sensation goes to the co-ordinating brain. Every nerve centre, like every branch bank and every Stock Exchange, has an individuality of its own. Sensation being produced, the nature of the object must be discerned by means of perception. Now perception is simply the comparison of a given sensation with others among the previous sensations of the organism. Continually repeated comparisons are accumulated into experience. When, finally, this is employed in " the intellectual establishment of new and original relations "[2] reason is at work. The lower mental state which gives us the compound reflex action called instinct, and passes into automatism and habit, is represented by the act of hoarding, and

---

[1] Huxley, *Lessons in Elementary Physiology*, p. 517.
[2] *Dynamic Sociology*, p. 159.

BIRTH OF MODERN FINANCE

dissipated as the higher faculties of judgment are brought into play. The truth is that as we contemplate the separate markets of the Stock Exchange and the myriad branches of the great banks, all in the most intimate relationship with the co-ordinating centre, and with the hierarchy at the head, it is impossible to doubt that here we have the financial analogy with the ganglia, those nuclei of nervous intelligence which instantly report from every point of the physical frame any danger or disorganisation following upon " irritation of any part of the branches."[1] Huxley completes the sentence by saying " branches of the nerve " ; but if we ourselves complete it by " branches of the bank " we shall be brought face to face with the fact that language designedly used in a physiological treatise drops naturally into its place as a characterisation of an economic phenomenon. Even so, conversely, does the economist fall back upon physiology for his illustration. " The nervous system of the human frame is not more delicate and sensitive through all its ramifications to any injury inflicted upon any one part, than is that mysterious network, commercial credit."[2] As finance becomes more and more composite and complex the means of supplying its needs and controlling its movements must acquire an exceeding delicacy of adjustment. And just as the living animal organism can only do its best when it is free from the attacks of enemies and disease, so the economic organism must aim to facilitate social progress by an evolution so steady, so peaceful, so even in its movement, as to attain the maximum of protection and the minimum of interruption for its own activities. These are the ideals. The story of the struggle —conscious or unconscious—for their realisation is the history of financial evolution between Waterloo and the present time.

AN EXTRAORDINARY PARALLEL

Close as is the parallelism thus far between the physical and financial organisms we shall find that it is possible

[1] Huxley, *Lessons in Elementary Physiology*, p. 467.
[2] Lord Overstone, *Tracts*, p. 153.

266 EVOLUTION OF THE MONEY MARKET

to discover and analyse parallelisms that are more intimate still. We have already noticed (*ante*, p. 243) that the history of the Money Market since Waterloo falls into three periods or compartments, practically watertight. If we endeavour to characterise these periods, and if we then take a wholly independent characterisation of the three stages in the development of organic life, we shall find ourselves confronted with a truly amazing affinity. Below, to the right, are the three " distinguishable sets of conditions " in organic development, as interpreted by Hobhouse,[1] and to the left a summary of the three " sets of conditions," all equally distinguishable, which mark the evolution of the financial organism in the nineteenth century.

(i.) [1815–1866]. Reluctant synthesis of the separate banking elements. Jealousy between the Bank of England and the joint-stock and private banks. Legal proceedings by the Bank of England against the London and Westminster. Successful efforts by the private bankers to keep the latter out of the Clearing House. Mechanical banking, only organised, co-ordinated, and correlated to a slight extent, and that in the dire extremity of crisis, because of the lack of the predominant force which can attract harmony. Disappearance of the less-adaptable factors by lethal selection or absorption.

(i.) In the formation of any new organic type there is a synthesis of elements previously separate, and in their separateness either held ineffective by counteracting forces, or if acting, acting mechanically for simple lack of that with which they can harmonise.

(ii.) [1866–1890]. Gradual dying away of this hostility,

(ii.) In the individual or the type so formed these

---

[1] *Development and Purpose*, p. 359.

begun by an acknowledgment from the Bank of England, after the Overend - Gurney crisis of 1866, that the joint-stock banks had contributed very materially to the salvation of the City from disaster. Growing and universal recognition of identity of interest, and continuous, though not always well-devised, efforts towards intimate correlation, ultimately culminating (1890) in a call upon the banks and finance houses, by the Bank of England, to unite in the famous Baring guarantee fund. One or two early and slight relapses, in the 'seventies, towards the earlier jealousies and antagonisms. Development of a corporate individuality of aim and sentiment among the leaders of finance.

(iii.) [1890–1915]. Incessant advance of the processes of amalgamation and absorption, ultimately transforming a local into a national banking system. Definite advent of the financial hierarchy. At the Bankers' Dinner on July 1, 1911, the Governor of the Bank of England announces that certain steps had been taken to provide more regular means of communication between the Bank of England and the outside institutions than had existed hitherto. In plain English, the hierarchy acknowledges its own existence.

elements, acting in a determinate relation, have a certain scope of operation, the filling up of which constitutes the development of the individual.

(iii.) Both as a condition and result of this development elements of energy originally foreign to the organism are absorbed and arranged so as to subserve the organic movement.

At the second stage there will become observable the reversal of the antique cosmic tactics, as the organism—physical or financial, as the case may be—grapples with the elementary selective process, and of set purpose transforms doliogenic into orthogenic, and ultimately into aristogenic evolution. We must not imagine, however, that throughout its history the movement has been continuously progressive. There have been indiscretions, mistakes, misjudgments, and reverses—a trial here, an endeavour there—a perpetual zigzag, but on the whole advance. " Looking down," say Thomson and Geddes,[1] " from the summit of a pass which it has taken us all day to reach, we see the village in the valley from which we started at daybreak, and it seems like a great stone's throw off. The dips and ascents, turns and twists, of our path are all lost to sight; only those who have walked over it know what the climb has really been. So it is with a retrospect on evolution." But with increasingly vivid consciousness of the real nature of the movement the aberrations diminish in frequency and seriousness. " The structure of the eye, wing, beak, and claw that make perfect the swoop and pounce of the falcon are the result of countless ancestral experiences in the course of which the structure which made some slight approach to this point of perfection prevailed over others, and *prevailed more surely the more nearly it reached its goal.*"[2]

[1] *Evolution*, p. 69. [2] Hobhouse, *Mind in Evolution*, p. 9.

CHAPTER IX

THE AGGREGATION OF CAPITAL—THE ABSENCE OF BANKING PRINCIPLES

THE aggregation of money (cash), even the money of the industrial workers, into potentially productive masses, had already made some progress when the modern Money Market came into being. The landowner and the capitalist-entrepreneur no longer had a monopoly of such banking facilities as were available. The primeval instinct of hoarding survives longest in the class which is, for the time being, lowest in the social scale, and mistrustful of those higher up. When instinct gives place to reason, under the stimulus of a better social environment, money (cash) is transformed from a barren store of value into a phalanx of fecundity, because hoarding is superseded by the deposit account. The change, at the lower extremity of the social scale, is clearly discernible before the end of the eighteenth century. The crowd around Forbes's Bank in 1797[1] consisted of "Fishwomen, carmen, street porters, and butchers' men" clamorously demanding payment of their interest receipts. The process of transformation from hoard to deposit—not always an interest-bearing deposit[2]—went on (though not without interruption)

---

[1] Forbes, *Memoirs of a Banking House*, p. 84.

[2] NOTE ON INTEREST ON DEPOSITS
This is a necessary qualification. It is impossible to bring into the scope of any definite generalisation the practice of the banks in the matter of interest, or no interest, on deposits. There was no fixed rule. The safety of the money was often considered an ample return to the depositor. "In peaceable Times," said a speaker in the House of Commons in 1738, "we know that no private Man will keep his Money by him, but will rather lodge in some Bank or Banker's Hands without any interest: because in such hands it is secured against Pilferers, Thieves, and Robbers, which it cannot be in his own Habitation." (*Historical Register*, 1738, p. 33). Probably the introduction of the joint-stock banks in 1833 was the beginning of deposit business on a really extensive scale and in the sense of

through all the Napoleonic turmoil. " What class of the community is it that makes the smallest deposits ? " said the Select Committee on Promissory Notes in Scotland and Ireland (1826) to a Scottish witness. " They are generally the labouring classes in towns like Glasgow," said he. " In country places like Perth and Aberdeen it

"money left at interest either at call or for a longer period." (Seebohm, 1875 Committee, Q. 4671.) The older issuing banks, with their small capitals, would not have been justified in accepting deposits to any large extent. Some of the private banks in the provinces had paid interest on deposits, and were apparently very " keen " to get them, but the London bankers distrusted the system. The country bankers have always been in a better position in this matter, because their deposits were made for longer periods, and were less subject to sudden demands for repayment than those of their London confrères. Probably, as Bagehot argued (*Lombard Street*, p. 88) the operation of a successful note issue advertised the credit of a banker and set in motion a flow of deposits towards him.

To some extent, no doubt, the public itself helped to maintain an indefinite policy with regard to interest on deposits. There is an old story of a man, with a considerable sum of money, who came to London, in the earlier part of the nineteenth century, to look for a banker. He called at several houses and inquired the terms offered for the deposit of his money. One offered 2 per cent., another 3, another 3½, while yet another made tentative offers, but could not be drawn into a definite arrangement. Ultimately, the moneyed man went to Child's Bank, where, in reply to his inquiry what interest they would allow on the money at his disposal, he was told that they would accept the custody of it, but would give him no interest whatever upon it. Thereupon the inquirer exclaimed, " This is the place for me ! " and immediately opened the account. The innovation of interest on deposits as a general rule, is generally believed to have been made by the London and Westminster in its early struggling days. It offered to keep the accounts of tradesmen who could not afford to maintain large unemployed balances, and to charge only a commission. At the same time it offered 2½ per cent. on deposits from £10 upwards at call.

The Bank of England refused—and still refuses—to follow this example. The reason why some, at all events, of the new Bank of England branches, opened about 1830, did not pay their expenses was probably their refusal of interest on deposits. (See below.) This diverted money to the more compliant institutions—to wit, the joint-stock banks. Weguelin told the 1857 Committee that the reason why the Bank refused interest on deposits was that it would have to invest the money at a higher rate, and keep it " closely " employed—in other words, it would have to practise " banking up to the hilt," and this was very undesirable. It was said, in 1866, that the Bank of England had for many years refused deposits at interest, out of consideration for the numerous joint-stock banks which were its customers. The Governor, moreover, declared that allowing interest on deposits was "not pure banking, but a dealing in money." They must not trade like joint-stock companies. He denounced in the strongest terms the practice of allowing interest on deposits at call. The downfall of Overend and Gurney and of many other houses, he said, was traceable to the policy of receiving money at call and investing it " in speculations in Ireland, or in America, or at the bottom of the sea, where it was not available when a moment of pressure arrived." Apparently

AGGREGATION OF CAPITAL

is from servants and fishermen, and just that class of the community who save from their earnings in mere trifles."[1] When the money was finally withdrawn it was to purchase a house or engage in business. Shyly, but surely, it was issuing from the retreats whither fear had driven it for centuries past, and where millions, doubtless, still lie hid,

[1] It has been argued that this was not the case in England. "The personnel of those who put their money in the savings banks are mainly household servants and tradesmen. Not much of the deposits of the savings banks really belonged to the artisan and labouring classes." (Leone Levi, Gilbart Lectures, 1875.) Perhaps this was the reason why Mr. Gladstone never liked the Trustee Savings Banks. They "smelt of class," he said. Whatever may have been the case with the Trustee Savings Banks, the analysis of the status and occupations of the Post Office depositors in 1865 shows that over 25 per cent. were mechanics and artisans, domestic and farm servants, porters, policemen, labourers, boatmen, fishermen and seamen. (Bowie, *Romance of Savings Banks*, p. 58.)

---

the Governor was apprehensive of the pressure of the large depositor, which has driven many a banker into dangerous paths. Down to 1839, for instance, the banks in Australia had been accustomed to allow the Government 4 per cent. on money on deposit. Then Sir George Gipps (the Governor) insisted upon 7 or $7\frac{1}{2}$ per cent. interest, and the banks, who had no mutual arrangement with regard to keeping down the deposit rate, were compelled to submit. But in their endeavour to utilise the money at a profit, while at the same time paying $7\frac{1}{2}$ per cent. upon it, they were driven into advancing it upon all kinds of illegitimate security, with the result of disaster and, as one critic says, "almost universal bankruptcy." This danger is all the more pressing because it is the large depositor who looks first to the rate of interest as a source of profit. The small depositor is more concerned with the safety of his money than with the return upon it.

To return to the Bank of England—when a critic of the Bank management, whose remarks had led to this pronouncement, went on to say that he did not mean deposits at call, the Governor of the Bank declared that the difference between deposits at call and deposits at notice was a mere matter of detail, and that he must "repeat his entire disapproval of the practice of paying interest upon any deposits whatsoever." This refusal by the Bank of England to allow interest was stated by Messrs. Hodgson, M.P., and Palmer, before the 1875 Committee (Q. 7697), to be the reason why it was beaten, in the provinces, by the branches of the joint-stock banks. "The facilities which private and joint-stock banks give to their customers are more attractive, I suppose, to the public," said Palmer. Herein is the reason why the deposits of the Bank are not themselves any source of power, for the Bank has always refrained from attracting them as other banks do. Where its duty and its power conflicted it chose the path of duty. It might have attracted an immeasurable mass of deposits if it had chosen to do so. Even its country branches, so conservative, as we shall see, in their methods, attracted deposits to them without interest, in competition with the country bankers who paid interest on their deposits. The effect of this policy was that in the original form of its suzerainty the Bank was actually in the position of protector of its own rivals. It discharged the "function of supporting

never to be discovered till they are melted for the last great assay.

SOME REVIVAL OF HOARDING

The hoarding instinct, thus cautiously yielding to the attractions of safe custody and occasional interest on deposits, was revived to some extent by the Napoleonic bugbear. The historian, Knight, says that during the early years of the nineteenth century " a guinea, a half-guinea, or a seven-shilling piece had become a rare sight in Great Britain." If the money went abroad, it was either melted down and recoined, at a considerable resulting profit, or was instantly imprisoned in a hoard. Mr. Merle (of the house of Cox and Merle), giving evidence before the Bullion Committee in 1810,[1] said that he saw

[1] Minutes, p. 30.

---

its competitors in times of trouble only to be underbidden by them in ordinary times." (Ellis, *Rationale of Market Fluctuations*, p. 48.) The recent acceptance by the Bank of England of " special deposits " is really not a breach of its ancient tradition. These special deposits, the first of which was money belonging to the Hampshire County Council, are accepted by the Bank and lent in the market. The Bank supervises the transaction and takes a commission for its trouble, but the money is not a bank deposit in the true sense of the word. (See the statement of the Governor at the Bank of England meeting, March 19, 1890.)

Bound up with the question of deposits was the importance of the note issue to the early banks. If deposits were meagre, they had only their capital and their note issue to rely upon. There must have been many cases where little or no public money was entrusted to the banker by clients, in the modern sense of the term, so that the whole amount available for use in his business consisted of his capital and his note issue. Mr. C. H. Boase has instanced the Dundee Banking Co. as a business which from 1764 to 1791 possessed hardly anything but its note circulation and its capital. There was a kind of unwritten law—now long since abrogated—that the liabilities of a bank must not be more than three times its capital. When deposits at last came freely and in bulk, the savings banks and building societies were also competing for the money. Of course, the banks' clienteles, at all events for deposits, were not of the same calibre as the units of the building society. These latter were of the active type, eager to turn their money to good account and to watch the transformation. The former were more of the passive type, frequently with mixed incomes, putting money on deposit (which they would formerly have hoarded) merely as a provision against emergencies, which the more active class was confident of financing as they arose, without provision previously prepared.

The allowance of interest on the minimum monthly balance of current accounts as distinguished from deposit accounts has been discontinued by the great London banks since 1877, though it is still occasionally offered by upstart little " banks " as a means of attracting the unwary City clerk to risk his slender and temporary surplus funds.

AGGREGATION OF CAPITAL

no gold nowadays. His clerks, who were out collecting every day, did not, perhaps, bring in more than a seven-shilling piece. He instanced the receipt of five hundred guineas from Dorchester as a very exceptional occurrence. In fact, he knew that they had been in a hoard. In Ireland, a more backward country, the facts were worse. Mr. Edward Wakefield told the Committee that a fine of 1000 guineas for the letting of an estate in Queen's County had been paid in tarnished gold, though the rent itself was invariably paid in paper. A girl had been tried at Trim Assizes in 1808 for robbing her father of a hoard of 800 guineas. Still more extraordinary, a tenant had borrowed bank-notes at 12 per cent. with which to pay his rent, although he had abundant gold for that purpose in the house. As late as 1841 the Bank of Ireland was steadily receiving 30,000 guineas a year. They were " full and perfect, having the appearance of having been hoarded."[1] But this phenomenon simply meant that financial evolution was still at an earlier stage in the Emerald Isle than in England, where this kind of thing gave way before the steady magnetism and growing reputation of the banks. By the time of the 1841 Banks of Issue Committee hoarding had become very rare in England and Scotland.[2]

THE NEED FOR AGGREGATION

There was certainly the most urgent need for the systematic aggregation and organisation of savings. For the investor of small or moderate means there existed very few of those opportunities, whose name in our day is legion, of turning accumulated money into safe and remunerative channels. The word " investment " itself, in a financial sense, was unknown to the greatest of English lexicographers. " That so few are found to make any savings," said Whitbread to the House of Commons in 1807, " may in a great degree be accounted for by the difficulty of putting out the little they can

---

[1] T. Wilson, Governor of the Bank of Ireland, 1841 Committee, Q. 2624.
[2] Evidence, Q. 2375, 2386, 2388, 3030–3036.

raise at a time."[1] Brougham, speaking in the House of Commons on April 9, 1816, described the mania for haphazard speculative export which had characterised the period immediately succeeding Napoleon's retreat from Moscow :—

" Not only clerks and labourers, but menial servants, engaged the little sums they had been laying up for a provision against old age and sickness. Persons were found tempting them to trade with Holland, Germany, and the Baltic ; they risked their mite in the hope of boundless profits, it went with the millions of the more regular traders. The bubble soon burst, like its predecessors of the South Sea, the Mississippi, and Buenos Ayres ; English goods were selling for much less in Holland and the North of Europe than in London and Manchester ; in most places they were lying a dead weight, without any sale at all ; and either no returns whatever were received, or pounds came back for thousands that had gone forth. The great speculators broke ; the middling ones lingered out a precarious existence, deprived of all means of continuing their dealings, either at home or abroad ; the poorer dupes of the delusion had lost their little hoards, and went upon the parish the next mishap that befell them."[2]

It was a case of Adventure—that perpetual stimulus of human endeavour which made Elizabethan England great—failing for lack of efficient organisation.

THE BANKING MAGNET AT WORK

The importance of the banking influence, as a loadstone drawing cash out of hoards, for the stimulation and furtherance of the power of production, was soon appreciated. " The effective currency of the country," said the Bullion Committee, in an interesting passage,[3]

" depends upon the quickness of circulation and the number of exchanges performed in a given time, as well as upon its

[1] Bowie, *Romance of the Savings Banks*, p. 11.
[2] Mr. Slater believes that the forced sales at knock-out prices of all this flood of exported goods created an idea that Britain was determined to ruin the continental manufacturer by the process which, in our day, is denominated " dumping." This suspicion " paved the way for the subsequent building up of hostile tariffs against England on the Continent of Europe." (*Making of Modern England*, p. 14.)   [3] Report, p. 63.

AGGREGATION OF CAPITAL

numerical amount, and all the circumstances, which have a tendency to quicken or to retard the rate of circulation, render the same amount of currency more or less adequate to the wants of trade. A much smaller amount is required in a high state of public credit than when alarms make individuals call in their advances and provide against accidents by hoarding, and in a period of commercial security and private confidence than when mutual distrust discourages pecuniary arrangements for any distant time. But, above all, the same amount of currency will be more or less adequate in proportion to the skill which the great money-dealers possess in managing and economising the use of the circulating medium. Your Committee are of opinion that the improvements which have taken place of late years in this country, and particularly in the district of London, with regard to the use and economy of money among bankers, and in the mode of adjusting commercial payments, must have had a much greater effect than has hitherto been ascribed to a much greater amount of trade and payments than formerly."

Mr. Tritton told the Bullion Committee that the number of traders in London who employed bankers had much increased during the last few years ; while, at the same time, the greater economy of method on the part of the bankers themselves had enabled them to reduce the quantity of notes kept in their possession by about one-eighth, as compared with the aggregate eight years before.[1] This latter evidence was that of Mr. Thomas Richardson, who confirmed previous witnesses in their opinion that it was a more general custom for tradesmen and individuals " to keep bankers now than some few years ago." It was the passing of the Bank Restriction Act which had been the signal for the formation of many establishments for banking in the country. In 1809, the first year when bankers were required to take out a licence, the number issued was 702, which gradually rose to 940 in 1814. In 1813–1814 the number of licences taken out by country bankers for issuing notes was 733, and the number of partners in these banks was 2234.[2] At the beginning of the nineteenth century there were 68 banks in London.

[1] Minutes, p. 228.   [2] *Political Encyclopædia* (1848), Art. " Bank."

The steady process of financial democratisation is further evidenced and emphasised in the smaller values of the notes issued by the Bank. Down to 1749 the smallest Bank of England note was £20. After that year £10 and £15 notes were issued, and in 1793 the first £5 note made its appearance. The £15 note then became an anomaly, and disappeared, though the £1 and £2 notes, which began to be issued in 1797,[1] did not remain a permanent feature of the Bank's practice. An examination of the figures given in the Bullion Committee's report in 1810 shows that the ratio of small notes as against large notes had been steadily increasing from the year 1798 to the year 1809. In 1798 the notes of £5 and upwards, including Bank Post Bills, amounted to £11,527,250, whereas the notes under £5 only aggregated £1,807,502 ; but in 1809, while the notes of £5 and upwards amounted to £14,133,615, those under £5 had advanced to £4,868,275.[2] The large notes were extensively issued in stock transactions, both on account of the trouble of counting coin and to avoid disputes as to its weight and goodness. The Committee did not think it fair to require from the Bank a similarly detailed statement with regard to the volume of mercantile discount, so that comparative figures are not available ; but the directors had said, in general terms, that the amount of these transactions had been progressively increasing since 1796, and that their total

[1] When the Bank endeavoured to meet the competition of its provincial rivals by issuing £2 and £1 notes, in 1797, their liability to forgery, combined with the terrible penalty which was at that time attached to the offence, rendered the notes unpopular, and they were discontinued after about twenty years of currency. The ignorant public at large could not understand why it was right for the Bank of England and wrong for the man in the street to make bank-notes. It was mainly the bankers themselves, inspired by Cruikshank's famous drawing, who ultimately succeeded in abolishing the capital penalty for forgery. As Francis says, " Men were being hung in strings " for this crime, and there were numerous refusals to prosecute on the part of those who, while they resented the forgeries, declined to shed the blood of the wretched forgers. Over 900 country bankers signed one of the petitions against capital punishment, and of the three City signatures, the first was that of the head of a firm which has always been in the forefront of the humanities—namely, that of Mr. N. M. Rothschild (as he was then).

[2] These are the average figures. For detailed statistics, see the Appendix of the Report, p. 45 *et seq.*

AGGREGATION OF CAPITAL

in the year 1809 bore a very high proportion to the largest aggregate in any year preceding 1797. The Committee added that the largest amount of mercantile discount standing by itself could never, in their judgment, be regarded as any other than a great public benefit; but that the resulting excess of paper currency issued, and kept out in circulation, must be regarded as an evil. What was really wanted (though the Committee did not say so) was the enormous credit-currency, in the shape of cheques, as well as of securities of various types, and largely cosmopolitan in vogue, which the modern Money Power has created.

THE SAVINGS BANK MOVEMENT

Before the joint-stock banks—the "automatic and costless" collectors and distributors of the nation's floating capital—could begin their gigantic task of aggregating the cash resources of the community, even those of its most unpretentious members, there came into being another agency, destined to carry on a powerful rivalry, in the lower ranges of banking, with the joint-stock institutions. In 1807 Mr. Whitbread brought a Bill before Parliament in which it was provided that the Postmaster-General was to instruct postmasters to receive deposits from the poorer classes; but nothing came of the scheme. The year 1816, however, witnessed an impetus to the establishment of savings banks, then just beginning to be known. They were largely on a philanthropic basis. As Jevons said, " The savings banks were designed to act as eleemosynary institutions, as, in fact, public schools of thrift." The interest, sometimes as much as 33 per cent., was paid by public subscription. A Bill for the regulation of the new institutions failed to pass, but the sympathy of the Legislature was obvious, and the movement steadily gained ground. Facilities promote saving. The successful establishment of these institutions aided the cohesion, centralisation, and utilisation of even the humblest and remotest financial items—so humble that in Ireland the deposits were left in separate bags, so that the suspicious depositors might verify the respective amounts at each transaction ! [1] Savings moneys, owing to their peculiar limitations, are rather investment capital than working capital. But at least they aggregate what must otherwise be scattered, and they train the depositor in the way which leads him to the current account, the Stock Exchange investment, the insurance of his life, and the building of his own house. The savings banks and the regular banks might almost be described, in Cairnes's phrase, as " non-competing groups," each group " discharging special functions of its own and scarcely trenching at all upon the legitimate sphere of the other." [2] This difference between the two clienteles was the main point in Sir William Harcourt's reply to a deputation of country bankers, who, on April 26, 1893, laid before him their objections to the extension of Post Office Savings Bank business. He remarked that " there is a lacuna, a gap which is not filled up "—by the joint-stock banks ; that is to say, the distinction between our savings banks and those of Germany lies in this—that the English savings bank stands in a class by itself. It is a semi-philanthropic institution which does not, strictly speaking, conduct a banking business at all. All its funds are invested in securities and none are employed commercially. But the German savings banks on the Schulze-Delitzsch model make small advances to tradesmen and others to assist them in their business. They consequently conduct a form of banking with which savings banks in this country are almost entirely unacquainted. The Savings Bank, therefore, does not tend to further the productive interests of the area whence the savings are drawn to the same extent or in the same way as the ordinary joint-stock institution. Modern joint-stock enterprise quite recently set itself to bridge the gap. In 1904, the Lancashire and Yorkshire Bank announced the establishment of a special savings department. At the same time it pointed out that savings put into the Post Office or Trustees' Savings Banks could not be used to promote trade, whereas if they were

---

[1] Bowie, *Romance of the Savings Banks*, p. 22.
[2] F. E. Steele, *Economic Journal*, Vol. III. p. 638.

AGGREGATION OF CAPITAL

deposited in its own savings department, the money could be employed in the furtherance of the trading interests of the district where it was accumulated.

Certainly the small depositor was a much more significant economic phenomenon than the large. After the movement had progressed for twenty years, it was said of the Brighton Savings Bank in 1837 that out of the sums placed there by 567 depositors, nearly one-half of the individual deposits did not exceed £5. The average of the deposits, with compound interest added, did not exceed £5 13s. 10¾d. At the time of the Reform Bill (1831) the total number of depositors in friendly and charitable societies was 367,812, of whom 187,770 had less than £20, their average deposit being £7. Only 4237 had over £200 on deposit. But however modest the amounts, the main economic consideration is that in an earlier age the money would have lain dead in hoards. In all probability, the liberation of these hoards did much to neutralise the effect of the sudden check in the supply of gold and silver from the Spanish-American lands, at a time when they were in the throes of revolution. The reduction of the gold supply was one of the operative causes of the fall in prices which followed the peace. The fall would probably have been worse but for the simultaneous liberation of hoarded bullion, largely under the stimulus of banking magnetism.

THE TRUSTEE SAVINGS BANKS

In 1828 came another, if not, for a time, very important, stage in the aggregation of savings, in the shape of the first Act of Parliament granting permission to the Trustee Savings Banks to receive deposits for investment by the trustees themselves, according to the rules of the bank. This enactment (9 George IV. c. 92, section 12) provides that

" Nothing in this Act contained shall extend to prevent the Trustees of any Savings Bank, already established or to be established, receiving any sum or sums of money from any depositor for any purpose except to be paid into the Bank (of England) to the Account of the Commissioners of Redemption of the National Debt; and it shall be lawful for such Trustees to apply any such sum or sums of money in any other manner for the benefit of the several depositors, according to the rules and regulations of such Savings Banks respectively : anything in this Act contained to the contrary notwithstanding."

When the various witnesses before the Select Committees of 1858, 1888, 1889, and 1902 were asked why this provision was inserted, none of them could give any very intelligent answer, beyond the surmise that it was probably done in order that the trustees might receive more than the statutory total maximum of £150 from a single depositor, if he were disposed to trust the investment of the excess to the trustees themselves. There was no attempt, as will be seen from the wording of the clause, to limit the investments to any particular class of purchase. As a matter of fact, down to the end of 1876, the total holdings of the investments departments of the 10 trustee banks which possessed them only amounted to £1,020,919.[1] It is, however, an assumption not unreasonable that the Government had noticed the widening area of investments, and thought that possibly the trustees of savings banks might encourage the thrifty proclivities of their clients by turning some of their surplus funds into these new channels. Certainly, even if the investment departments were not a success for the next fifty years, the proprietors of these modest accumulations began to be cognisant of the power which they conferred. One of the questions posed by Dr. Fletcher at the great Chartist meeting on Kersal Moor in 1839 was whether the demonstrators would be prepared, at the request of the Convention, to withdraw all the sums that they had in the savings banks, and to convert all their paper money into silver and gold.

[1] This was not wholly regrettable, at that stage of the financial education of democracy. The investment of money in securities through a savings bank may ultimately awaken distrust in the case of a clientele which is imperfectly acquainted with the meaning of investment. At a time when Consols were steadily falling from the height which they attained in 1897, keen resentment was frequently awakened among savings bank depositors who sold their holdings by their discovery that they got considerably less than they had paid for them. Their inference, based upon imperfect knowledge of the real nature of the transaction, was that they had been cheated.

AGGREGATION OF CAPITAL

Year after year the Savings Banks movement went steadily forward. The Birmingham Penny Bank, established in 1851 (it ultimately failed in 1865), occasionally opened over 300 accounts in a day, making 1000 repayments and receiving 1000 deposits during the same period. During the Stock-Exchange panic of 1859, attention was called to the fact that the investments by the Government broker at the rate of £10,000 a day on behalf of the Savings Banks had not been suspended.[1] The Yorkshire Penny Bank, started in 1859, became so huge that after fifty years of existence the solicitude of the great banks for its welfare led to united action of the highest possible significance (*post*, p. 661). It should be added that the Post Office Savings Bank did not come into existence till 1861. For the greater part of the century, therefore, it contributed nothing to the aggregation of the unconsidered trifles of potential capital.[2] The 1902 Committee estimated that by 1921 Savings Banks deposits would have swelled to £270,000,000. As against this vast sum practically no provision has been made, in the case of the Post Office Savings Banks, for depreciation, and in the event of an extensive run the Government would certainly have to pay in paper, since even the assistance of the joint-stock banks would not suffice to meet such a huge demand.

THE PRIVATE BANKERS

Thus far of the commencement of the minor components to feel the centripetal attraction of the bank. In the higher

---

[1] Morier Evans, *Commercial Crisis of 1857-1858*, p. 167.

[2] The initiation of the Post Office Savings Bank of course extended the scope of the machinery for attracting into efficient aggregates stores of money which had otherwise been too timid or too insignificant to take their place in the financial array. But in establishing the Post Office Savings Banks Mr. Gladstone himself admitted that he was aiming at another object besides the promotion of thrift. He desired to provide the Chancellor of the Exchequer with " a strong financial arm, and to secure his independence of the City by giving him a large and certain command of money." (Morley, *Gladstone*, Vol. II. p. 52.) When an attempt was made to further this policy and extend the limit of deposits in Post Office Savings Banks, George Rae, the author of the *Country Banker*, circularised every bank in the kingdom in opposition to the scheme, and created such a hostile aggregate of banking opinion that the Bill was withdrawn.

social stages, the movement assumed an immensely wider scope and a far more imposing magnitude. There was a rapid extension of banking facilities concurrently with the growth—slow, but sure—of a banking science, and with the more thorough preparation, thus rendered possible, for the creation of a central financial control. The older type of private banker was as conservative by tradition and by habit of mind as he was frequently Tory in his politics. He was enmeshed in unquestioning allegiance to tradition and custom, held fast in an unvarying professional orbit. He had not the pluck, or the intellectual independence to put himself in opposition to the Government. Lord Cockburn[1] said the old private bankers were " the conspicuous sycophants of existing power. All the Whig business of the country would not have kept them going for a week, and Government dealt out its patronage in the reception and transmission of the public money only to its friends, so they all combined banking with politics. Not that they would discount a bad bill for a Tory, or refuse to discount a good one for a Whig ; but their favours and their graciousness were all reserved for the right side." That was before Waterloo. In the *post-*Waterloo age, private bankers who are anything but sycophants, and joint-stock bankers of the same independent type, have brought the leaven of a better spirit into the business.[2] They have stored up the dearly bought experience of the earlier difficulties and crises and engendered that sense of strength and responsibility which

---

[1] *Memorials,* p. 252. Cockburn was referring especially to Edinburgh bankers.

[2] Cockburn's scathing criticisms could certainly, for instance, have had no application to Thomas Coutts. When George III. heard that Coutts had advanced £100,000 to Sir Francis Burdett (his son-in-law), in order to enable him to fight the Middlesex election, he sent for Coutts and challenged him on the subject. Coutts admitted that the facts were true, whereupon the King drew out the whole of his private balance and placed it in the hands of a Windsor banker. As this individual shortly afterwards closed his doors, the King had every reason to regret his lack of confidence in Coutts, and Coutts himself was the last to laugh over the incident. Queen Charlotte had written at the same time, threatening to withdraw her slender credit balance in three days from date. Coutts replied that if her balance had been half a million, he would only have required *three hours'* notice of its withdrawal.

AGGREGATION OF CAPITAL 283

has given the financial hierarchy the capacity and opportunity to talk on terms of equality with the political powers of the world.

But while we acknowledge so much, there remains the fact that the first half-century of the modern Money Market, between Waterloo and the Overend-Gurney crisis, was a troublous time in the history of banking. The bankers were learning the trade of financing an Empire, and they made many mistakes. The Bank of England itself, down to 1857, had not learned how to protect its own reserve, or to manage a foreign drain. Banking depends for its success—and for its existence—upon continuous allegiance to scientific standards, many of them known and formulated, but others even now (after nearly a century of extensive banking experience) outside the range of precise definition and comprehension. " The principles of banking are deductions from facts ; the science of banking is a collection of these principles ; it is of importance to have a correct notion of the nature of this science. In the physical sciences, as in chemistry and electricity, we often discover a principle, and then apply it to a practical end. But in banking and in political economy generally, we first collect our facts, and then ascend from facts to principles."[1] Again, " Science," said Herbert Spencer, " is organised knowledge, and before knowledge can be organised some of it must be possessed." No such organised knowledge is possible, or even conceivable, when every bank is an isolated institution, managed in accordance with no scientific or professional principles, by any person who chooses to establish it. Modern banking, as regards the breadth of equipment necessary to the practitioner, and the difficulty and intricacy of the work he does, is quite on a par with any of the so-called learned professions. It could not have existed as a mere congeries of isolated institutions. It is only after the joint-stock principle creates *groups* of banks, welded together as branches of a single strong institution, and under one skilful central control, that we can trace

[1] Gilbart, Preface to *Practical Treatise on Banking.*

the beginnings of a change for the better. With increased knowledge comes increased mastery over the phenomena of which knowledge is the record, with a resulting enormous accession both of strength and flexibility, as we shall see in due course.

LACK OF SCIENTIFIC CIRCUMSPECTION

Unfortunately, the trust deeds of these early banks clearly showed that contemporary banking knowledge, even when an attempt was made to employ it in legally defining a scheme of operations, was of the most hazy character. The 1836 Committee on Joint-Stock Banks was astonished to find that in the deeds of settlement of the existing banks advances on real property were in no instance forbidden. " The deeds of three companies are silent on the subject : the rest expressly allow it."[1] The practice of the great private banks (which, owing to the peculiar character of their clienteles, avoided commercial bills, and lent mainly on mortgage) may have opened the way for this most insidious of perils. " Messrs. Drummond are calling in their mortgages," said Lord George Bentinck in 1847,[2] as crisis loomed before the City. Further, most of the deeds of the new banks were also silent as to the *purchase* of land : one company expressly allowed it, two expressly forbade it. Many deeds expressly forbade the advance of money on mining shares. Some deeds sanctioned and others expressly prohibited, while the rest ignored, advances on " public foreign Government stock." One bank, in 1836, possessed an absolutely unlimited power of issuing shares to any extent. There was no restriction as to the amount of capital to be paid up before the commencement of business. " This," said the Committee naïvely, " will be found to vary from £105 to £5."[3] As the Chancellor of the Exchequer said, in the debate on the Address in 1826, the banks which sprang up in the country districts were " conducted on views widely remote from solid principles of banking." Mr. Smith, in defending

[1] Report, p. vi.   [2] Disraeli, *Life*, p. 451.
[3] 1836 Committee's Report, p. viii.

AGGREGATION OF CAPITAL

his fellow-bankers in the country, declared that they were men of "prudence, honour, and integrity"—as was undoubtedly the case—and denied that they had ever encouraged "a rash spirit of speculation." But to encourage speculation is one thing, and to have an imperfect knowledge of the best methods of financing and fostering trade, while maintaining an array of sound and liquid assets, is quite another.[1] The crisis of 1825 was partly precipitated by the dangerous facility with which the country banks, competing for business, advanced money

---

[1] An example of the methods of a careful private banker—as exemplified in his assets,—may be useful. James Wood, the mercer and banker of Gloucester, whose estate was the subject of litigation in 1841, had his assets and interests in the annexed form :—

	£	s.	d.
New Annuities	66,221	11	0
East India Stock	3,000	0	0
Three per Cent. Consols	57,500	0	0
New Three-and-a-Half per Cents.	333,098	13	8
Bank Long Annuities	9	5	0
Three per Cents. Reduced	9,380	19	10
Reduced Three-and-a-Half per Cents.	181,000	0	0
Bank Stock	52,000	0	0
Rents due from his freehold and copyhold property at the time of his death	4,677	15	0
Rents of leaseholds due at the time of his death	710	10	9
Mortgages	15,639	6	1
Interest on ditto, due at his death	1,391	12	9
Bonds, bills, and notes of hand	5,408	5	10
Interest on ditto at his death	395	19	11
Banking Accounts due to his estate at the same time	11,325	1	4
Debts owing to him for shop goods	138	7	9
Balance of cash in the hands of Sir John Lubbock & Co.	9,756	12	6
Cash found in his house	2,416	10	0
Silver	49	1	0
Copper	0	0	11
Bank-notes	5,237	0	0
Check	9	0	0
Old Gold—six five-guinea pieces, five two-guinea ditto, nine one-guinea ditto, and two foreign pieces, all of which were sold for	51	16	6
Old Silver—69 pieces produced	5	4	0
One old gold piece	0	2	6
	£759,422	16	4

These holdings are solid enough to satisfy the most exacting critic. Their solitary weakness, from a banking point of view, lies in the smallness of the aggregate of bills and notes of hand—£5,408 only. So small an amount was quite inadequate to produce, by means of an incessant sequence of maturities, that uninterrupted flow of cash into the coffers which is one of the most urgent desiderata of a modern banker.

on anything and everything. The old private bank, or (until a sound and scientific supervision was established) the branch of a larger institution, under the pressure of local and personal influence, was only too liable to be driven into the financing of building or property schemes, or into the advance of money upon such hopeless assets as a canal scheme or a working brickyard.[1] It might fill its portfolio with paper quite incapable of negotiation outside the locality. This was one of the troubles of the Northumberland and Durham Bank as recently as 1857. It held about £250,000 of small bills on Newcastle shopkeepers—" bills which were probably good in themselves, but which were not available out of Newcastle." The banker had not then, at all events to anything like the same extent, the powerful auxiliary which he now possesses, in the shape of immense accumulations of capital invested in the joint-stock form. In an age of rapid industrial progress, the pressure upon him was severe. Adequacy of capital was not studied.[2] In 1836 there was one bank whose total capital was only £600,000, though it had nearly forty branches in Bristol, Birmingham, Liverpool, Leeds, Manchester, Nottingham, and other places. In 1837, it was possible to cite the case of a bank which took no account, in its balance-sheet, of bad debts running to £20,000 or £30,000 (a much more important sum in those days than now), which paid large dividends, and the shares of which were quoted at 10 per cent. prem.[3] But this was a mild state of affairs in comparison with the existence of numerous concerns carrying on an extensive business upon a

---

[1] Brickyards have survived as a banker's bogey down to within the last year or two. At the meeting of the Stamford, Spalding and Boston Banking Co. in 1911 the chairman, in announcing the provisional agreement for its acquisition by Barclay's, said that the company had got money locked up in advances to brickmakers at Peterborough against securities which were of ample value when the advances were made, but could not at the moment be realised for their full amount.

[2] Odd opinions on the subject were not confined to irresponsible people. Thomson Hankey was once told by Lord Overstone in his own counting-house that all the capital of Jones Loyd's Bank consisted of the desks, ink, pens, and books. "That is all my capital," said Lord Overstone, "the rest belongs to me. It has nothing to do with my banking business." (Speech at the Institute of Bankers, *Bankers' Magazine*, 1879, p. 477.) [3] *Annual Register*, 1837, p. 181.

AGGREGATION OF CAPITAL

capital of which no particulars whatsoever were the subject of public knowledge, each being managed upon principles of its own, with no idea of, or attempt at, uniformity.

SOME LURID INSTANCES

After critically reviewing an imaginary banking portfolio, where the contents included the lease of a coal mine, fifty shares of £50 each (£5 paid) in a commercial company, a second mortgage, and a block of building land, Rae declared[1] that such securities had, to his own knowledge, at one time or another (probably before 1850) been held by banks against advances. The Bank of Otago started by locking up more than a third of its capital in a loan to a provincial Government—that of Southland, N.Z. —whose debentures were absolutely unsaleable. It was alleged that in consequence of the eagerness of the joint-stock banks for business, many a needy tradesman, whose utmost credit ought to have been £3000, had been able to " adventure himself among the merchants " to the extent of £80,000 or £100,000, with the resulting huge loss of all who confided in him. The truth is that to review the banking troubles of the first half-century of the money market, with an analysis of their causes, is to catalogue the offences which are anathema to banking in the twentieth century. Banks crashed in apparently endless succession.[2] Permanent mortgages ruined one and chaotic book-keeping another. It was reported to a House of Commons Committee in 1837 that the books of the

[1] *Country Banker*, p. 124.
[2] In 1810, about 100 private banks stopped payment. In 1812, a great number failed, in 1814 and 1816 ninety-two commissions in bankruptcy were issued against banks estimated at 360 in number. Altogether, it would be a moderate statement to aver that between 1791 and 1818, many hundreds of banks stopped payment. These figures are those given by Mr., now Sir, J. R. Paget in Gilbart Lectures, 1888. In each of the years 1825 and 1826, there were about 800 annual licences issued, but their numbers were again reduced by 80 bankruptcies, and in 1832 only 636 licences were demanded. From 1839 to 1843 inclusive, the number of bankers gazetted as bankrupts was 82 ; and the number of banks of issue which failed during the same period was 29. (*Political Encyclopædia* [1848], Art. "Bank."). For a vivid account of a " run " on one of the old country banks (early in the century), see *John Halifax, Gentleman*, chapter xxxi. The scene is generally understood to be laid in Tewkesbury.

Agricultural and Commercial Bank of Ireland were "in a perfect chaos." Attwoods, Spooner and Co. collapsed through financing its partners by huge overdrafts. The Western Bank of Scotland fell in consequence of advancing on non-existent stocks, supposedly hypothecated to it. The depletion of its resources to pay huge promotion profits—£5000 to £20,000—crippled many a bank at its most critical age. Strahan's was brought down by financing foreign railways, besides being " up to the eyes " in advances on the security of British mines. Overend, Gurney's themselves had £94,000 locked up in " land in France and Sweden "—pretty assets for bill brokers! " Their losses were made in a manner so reckless and foolish that one would think a child who had lent money would have lent it better."[1] Hallett, Ommanney and Co. had guaranteed 10 or 12 per cent. dividends on the shares of two coffee companies for three years. Here and there very doubtful customers were accommodated at the rate of 50 and 60 per cent., and this by banks of reputable position, in defiance of the eternal distinction between a bank and a 60-per-cent. shop. Huge speculations in railway stocks by the manager, in defiance of his board's instructions, brought the East of England Bank to the ground. When it fell it was interested in no less than seventy railway undertakings, although sound banking principles would have prohibited the acquisition of a permanent interest even in one. The Consolidated took over the business of the Bank of London when that institution collapsed in 1866, and was pulled down by its weight. It revived in a fortnight, but with irreparable damage done to its reputation. Puget Bainbridges and Co. prepared no balance-sheet after 1855, but went on till 1866, and then paid the penalty of confusing the business of a banker with that of a money-lender by advancing on inconvertible security. Sir C. R. Price, Marryat and Co. took over certain ironworks for a debt and worked them at a continuous loss, paying the penalty in the shape of suspension. Gilbart[2] alludes to a

[1] Bagehot, *Lombard Street*, p. 19.
[2] *Banking*, edited by Sykes, Vol. I. p. 418.

AGGREGATION OF CAPITAL

story that in 1847 even the Bank of England was drawn into this class of business to the extent of financing an iron concern in Wales. Certainly the Bank of England itself lent money on permanent mortgages.[1] Roskel, Arrowsmith and Kendal had a cotton mill on their hands. The London and Eastern financed brickyards and wharves, these enterprises being the private speculations of its own officials.[2] Henry Fauntleroy's huge forgeries were undertaken—so he said—in an effort to extricate the firm of Marsh and Co. from the embarrassments arising from immense building speculations.

EARLY EXPERIMENTS IN BRANCH BANKING

At the meeting of the shareholders of the English Joint-Stock Bank in 1866, the late Mr. Peter Broad submitted the statement of the position of affairs at the various branches of that institution during the half-year preceding its stoppage. He said that at Aldershot last year " the loss was £630, and in consequence of the fraudulent conduct of an employee, they lost £6000 more. At Brighton they had bad debts amounting to £1500, while their trading at Bristol had resulted in a loss of £15,000. The Bournemouth branch caused them a loss of £2560. The loss at Bideford was estimated at £5000, and at Chatham £5600. The Bournemouth branch caused them a loss of £2560.

[1] " The Bank of England have raised the interest on ——'s mortgage one-third per cent, making an additional annual charge of £1500 a year to him. . . . I know nothing so likely to rouse the landed aristocracy from their apathy and to weaken their idolatry of Peel so much as this warning note of the joint operation of his free trade and restrictive currency laws." (Lord George Bentinck, to a friend, Disraeli, *Life*, p. 448.)

[2] Minute of directors' meeting of the London and Eastern Bank, March 30, 1855 : " The manager brought before the Board the wish of Colonel Waugh, of Branksea Castle, to become one of the bank's connections, and stated that his account would be a very large and profitable one for the bank, as he intended to embark in large transactions as a clay and brick manufacturer.—Resolved that Colonel Waugh's wishes with regard to opening an account and receiving business accommodation from the bank be duly met." It is no part of a bank's business to supply a trader with working capital. Its function is to tide him over a tight time. If he is short of capital, the bank is not the proper source of permanent accommodation or relief. In the case of the London and Eastern, when the crash came, two years later, Waugh was indebted to the bank to the tune of £244,000, or within £6000 of the entire subscribed capital of the concern.

The loss at Croydon was £3350 and at Dorking £176. At Eastbourne the loss was £100 and they had about £6000 locked up as a loan to a building society for a number of years." The speaker added a few instances of profitable branches, and proceeded: "The loss at Hastings was £1300; at Northampton £4000; at Nottingham £3000; at Rochester £3000; and in the City £6500." Doubtless the comparative absence of modern facility of communication may have had something to do with the disastrous results of early branch banking. Even when something like a scientific method obtained at headquarters, the branches of the early banks were chaotic in method and action. Mr. Robert Paul told the Parliamentary Committee on the Small Note Currency in 1826 that bank branches "were accompanied with so much hazard, require such constant watching and inspection, and involve us altogether in such a degree of superintendence, that, upon the whole, my general impression is that the branches are not the most advantageous part of our business." Money could not fly on the wings of the wind from the head office to the branches, nor could the branch manager (especially if he was only a local tradesman, guarding his till with a blunderbuss) be kept under the supervision of the head office to anything like the extent which is possible nowadays. Indeed, the 1841 Committee seems to have imagined that there was some ratio between efficiency of control from the head office and the mileage distance of the branches. The quaintness of the Committee's ideas, in the light of modern achievement, is brought out in their warning, that "the Law does not limit the number of branches *or the distance of such branches from the central bank.*"[1] Sir Robert Peel seems to have had misgivings on this subject. In the course of a speech on the Bank Act of 1844 he said: "I doubt the policy which some banks have pursued of establishing very numerous branches. I doubt whether banks having fifty or sixty branches, some in very small towns, renting

---

[1] In an appendix to the report, the mileage distances of all the branches are measured. The Wilts and Dorset (now Lloyds) had branches as far as fifty-four miles from headquarters.

AGGREGATION OF CAPITAL 291

expensive houses and appointing agents with considerable salaries, can derive profit from such a course." Bell, in 1855, ridiculed the prevalent apprehensions on this subject. He was " amused " by the idea that all branches should be " within the distance of an easy day's ride [presumably on horseback] to and from the parent bank."[1] His views, however, did not find immediate acceptance. The chairman of the Imperial Bank told his shareholders in 1865 that he " was not in favour of branch banks, especially when they were at a great distance." Great stress was laid on this question of distance, as involving inefficiency of supervision, even as late as the time of the 1875 Committee.[2]

Still, distance and difficulty of supervision did not account for all the laxity. There was enough and to spare at the head offices. When the Bank of England sent Mr. Hodgson to Newcastle at so recent a date as November, 1857, to report upon the exact position of the Northumberland and Durham Bank (which had applied to Threadneedle Street for assistance) that gentleman found a state of affairs which could not be accounted for by the facts palpable to his observation. " He inquired whether there was not some old sore of which nothing had as yet been said. He was told there was one "—the Derwent Iron Co., which the Bank had financed to the tune of £947,000. There were debentures and a mortgage, both of doubtful value, to secure £330,000. The rest was totally unsecured. Threadneedle Street declined to assist and the bank stopped payment. The Birmingham Banking Co. closed its doors

[1] *Philosophy of Joint Stock Banking*, p. 25.
[2] See, for instance, the evidence of Jervoise Smith (Smith, Payne & Co.) QQ. 7005 *et seq*. Rae (*Country Banker*, p. 135) has an allusion to the days when branches might be distant several days, even by post, from the head office. The Birmingham Joint-Stock Bank laid it down as a principle that " the bank should devote itself to the interests of the town and neighbourhood, instead of investing part of its capital in branches in remote towns." (Chairman at meeting, February 3, 1868.) There was the same—and in this case more reasonable—horror of remote discounts. " Your managers," said the Sheffield and Hallamshire Chairman in 1865, " would never have thought of discounting distant paper." This craze about distance was probably the real source of the legislative provision of 1853, which imposed a stamp duty of one penny upon all cheques dated more than fifteen miles from the bank on which they were drawn.

with an amount due to it from its own manager of £76,000. Another institution had lent £14,000 to its own clerks. No doubt the pressure on the banks to enter into these illegitimate transactions was all the greater because of the lack of the huge aggregations of capital destined for joint-stock enterprise which provide so great a proportion of the requirements of modern industry. Doubtless, also, the pressure was accentuated by the lack of trust, finance, and investment companies, which alone can undertake business of a type that involves a prolonged lock-up, with no possibility of intermediate realisation. Under the weight of incessant demands on the part of an expanding national trade the banks failed to understand the axiom laid down by one of Thomson Hankey's relatives, that "Nothing is easier to conduct than the business of a banker, if he will only learn the difference between a mortgage and a bill of exchange." "When it appeared," asks Morier Evans,[1] "that a house which offered two shillings in the £ was a debtor to the Liverpool Borough Bank for £30,000 unsecured, who could say which was the more culpable party?" The effect of such incidents must not be measured in terms of gold, or with reference only to the immediate and traceable damage. As P. W. Kennedy (manager of the Ayrshire Bank) urged in 1841,[2] the stoppage of a bank produced injury far in excess of that represented merely by any deficit upon the realisation of the assets. At the same time we must remember that, down to 1850 at all events, and probably to a later date, the supply of managers was not equal to the demand. There was no Institute of Bankers and no systematic and scientific training as there is now. The difficulty was not entirely obviated for many years. Even in 1877 it was declared "almost impossible to keep up the sufficient supply of well-fitting and properly qualified bank managers."[3] The trustee savings banks did not escape the maelstrom of incompetence and malversation. The cleric-" actuary " of a Hertford institution defrauded it

[1] *History of the Commercial Crisis*, 1857–1858, p. 37.
[2] 1841 Committee, QQ. 2243, 2244.
[3] Crump, *English Manual of Banking*, p. 122.

of £24,000, and the sexton-" actuary " of a Dublin savings bank made away with £40,000. The establishment of the Post Office Savings Bank was partly at all events a result of recurring losses, falling upon the poorest sections of the community, arising from the incompetent management of some of the Trustee Savings Banks. Abortive attempts had been made in 1848, 1850, 1853, and 1857 to impose a greater responsibility upon the trustees and managers of the Trustee Banks, but the efforts were successfully resisted, although in several cases the incompetence was admitted, and although half of the banks in existence in 1861 were only open for one day a week.

MISCHIEF OF UNLIMITED LIABILITY

The persistence of unlimited liability—the inheritance from an older régime—facilitated banking abuses, though it may seem a paradox to suggest it. The (then) principle of partnership law rendered ineffective, in the case of debts contracted between a partnership and one of its partners, the common law remedy for the recovery of debts between party and party. This made it difficult, except by cumbrous equity proceedings, to enforce demands upon the partner shareholders. In the case of the Northern and Central Bank about £400,000 was thus rendered irrecoverable. Gilbart—himself the head of a bank whose shares then, and for long years afterwards, carried unlimited liability—said, in 1853, that the unlimited liability on bank shares had led to the provision of further accommodation for such institutions long after their serious condition was obvious, but in reliance upon the assets of shareholders liable to " the last shilling and the last acre." They should have been stopped, but there was no power capable of stopping them as long as there was unlimited liability to rely upon. Weguelin, when Governor of the Bank of England, located the weakness in the same place. He thought the main difficulty of unlimited liability was this, that in the event of mismanagement, the shareholders who become cognisant of it would not expose it for fear of precipitating unlimited liability on themselves, whereas if the liability were limited, they would act. The *Economist* (December 12, 1857), took the view, " that the principle of limited liability would ensure a better class of shareholders and a better class of directors—that it would necessarily tend to greater caution on the part of the public in dealing with banks, and thus enforce a more circumspect management." The subject is more fully and appropriately treated at a later stage, when we are considering the joint-stock banks.

BEAR ATTACKS ON BANK SHARES

The difficulties of the period were enhanced by the possibility of the short-selling of bank shares. Inflation was the opportunity of the bears, and their sales (not then prevented by Leeman's Act)[1] produced heavy falls, and " runs." In the dark year 1866 some of the sales of shares were made on behalf of high officials on the staffs of the companies whose shares were sold, and helped to accentuate the panic. The bear raid on the shares of the London and County Bank included such expedients as the initiation of conversation in omnibuses and visits to publichouses and similar places of resort, in order to spread rumours adverse to its solvency. Anonymous circulars were sent to country shareholders advising an immediate sale of the shares, and signed " A True Friend." It need hardly be pointed out that this class of thing would not only, in our time, be most emphatically condemned by financial opinion, but that the operators, if detected, would probably be successfully indicted for conspiracy. The directors of the English Joint-Stock Bank had gone into the market and spent £13,000 in order to counteract bear operations in its shares.[2] Common action, now becoming recognised as an *occasional* financial resource, was again

---

[1] 30 and 31 Vict. c. 29. Introduced March, 1867.
[2] It is now an accepted financial axiom, at the board tables of all responsible companies, that directors have nothing to do with speculative operations in a company's shares, and that, save in exceptional circumstances, they take no cognisance of them. But in many cases the older joint-stock banking companies were expressly authorised, in their deeds of settlement, to buy their own shares, " and that to any amount " (1838 Committee on Joint-Stock Banks, vi.).

AGGREGATION OF CAPITAL

invoked with regard to this abuse. It was suggested, at the Union Bank of London meeting in 1866, that the boards of the principal joint-stock banks in London should unite in making representations to the Stock Exchange with regard to the dealings in bank shares, and the suggestion brought forth the reply that, as a matter of fact, there was already a committee sitting to deal with the subject. These untoward incidents, however, were effectively checked by Leeman's Act, which, by insisting on the statement, by the seller, of the distinguishing numbers of any bank shares sold by him, renders bear sales of such securities practically impossible.[1] It has been said, however, that the Act operates to prevent the prices of bank shares from being so finely adjusted as is the case with other securities, because the acute "professional" interest is precluded from influencing quotations by such speculative sales as are feasible in other departments of the market. But bank shares are excluded from the list of the permissible counters at the disposal of market operators for the same reason as banks themselves from the scope of public hostility against Trusts—because the institutions stand in a place by them-

---

[1] Some of the joint-stock banks even go so far, at the present time as to prohibit the holding of their shares by any member of their staff. The idea is that the sale of his holding by a member of the staff of the bank, whose identity was known to the market, might set the tongues of the gossips wagging, although, as a matter of fact, the transaction had nothing whatever extraordinary about it. The Stock Exchange, relying upon its own disciplinary powers rather than upon statutory regulation, has not strictly enforced Leeman's Act. In Perry v. Barnett (15 Q.B.D., p. 388) a defendant in 1885 successfully pleaded the Act against plaintiffs' brokers, who had not inserted in the contract note, sent to defendant, the distinguishing numbers of certain bank shares sold to him. The Court of Appeal held that the usage of the Stock Exchange, to disregard the Act, was unreasonable as against strangers who were unacquainted with it. In Neilson v. James (9 Q.B.D., 546) A sold bank shares, through a broker, to B. The jobber, relying on Stock Exchange usage, omitted compliance with Leeman's Act. The Bank failed before the settlement, and the buyer B repudiated the transaction on the ground of the jobber's non-compliance with the Act. In this he was successful. A then sued the broker for omitting to make a valid contract, and recovered, as damages, the price at which the shares had been sold.

The conditions imposed by the Government, when the Stock Exchange was reopened on January 4, 1915, included terms which were, in effect, the temporary extension of the restrictions of Leeman's Act to *all* sales of securities, so as to eliminate the bear altogether for the time being.

selves, and are under unique responsibilities which justify an equally unique policy. The Act has had the effect, at all events, of shutting out, to a very considerable extent, this species of mischievous and selfish attack upon institutions liable to be vitally affected by the very shadow of a suspicion, such as might be created in a moment by heavy sales of their shares.

OBSOLETE SURVIVALS

Operating the most delicate of businesses in such an unsystematic and undisciplined fashion as we have examined—a species of " fair-weather banking " calculated to make a modern banker's blood run cold—it is no wonder that of the twenty or thirty new banks established in the early sixties *The Times* should allege in 1866 that ten or twelve had got into such a position that their directors dared not face the shareholders. The story almost tempts the reflection that perhaps widespread banking facilities were invented too soon, sharing the premature existence which has been attributed to the steam engine. The truth was that the whole economic organisation, in the period in which joint-stock banking took its rise, was passing through a transitional stage, of a radically critical character. The transformation which was to rear the new fabric could not be effected until the last of the older structure had tottered to its fall. " Economic history is not catastrophic," said F. W. Maitland. The economic eighteenth century lasted from 1688 to about 1866. It was the projection of the old conditions into the new era (so that, in the economic sense, the eighteenth and nineteenth centuries were for more than five decades concurrent) that caused much of the financial disquietude of the mid-Victorian age.[1] They survived,

[1] This projection or persistence, of antique and obsolete conditions and infirmities into a new era was strikingly illustrated in the almost cataclysmic suddenness with which the German War crisis of 1914 burst upon the Continent. It was argued at the time that the continental financial organisation, although it was making great advances, was as yet only in the transition stage from the older conditions which have ruled for the last seventy or eighty years. Continental finance, it was said, stands at the present time in a position analogous to that occupied by the British financial

AGGREGATION OF CAPITAL

like the cæcum in the human frame, into an era which had no use for them. They menaced its well-being just in the same way as that obsolete organ which is the cause of the most popular of surgical operations. But the financial organism, more fortunate than its biological analogue, can ruthlessly destroy vestigial structures which may threaten its welfare. Financial appendicitis is susceptible of much more general and drastic treatment than the analogous human trouble known to surgical science. The same influences which swelled the central aggregates of money coincidently destroyed, as we shall see, the older and weaker institutions, which were incapable of adaptation to the changed environment. Their incapacity was the subject of contemporary criticism. Gilbart declared in 1858 that two of the non-clearing banks whose failures

---

organisation previous to the Overend-Gurney crisis. In such circumstances, as we have seen, there is always a projection of the older conditions into the new era, with the result that until the transition stage is completed an element of weakness and instability exists in the rising fabric. There is certainly great force in the argument that the eighteenth-century conditions on the Continent may have extended down to 1914, and that their presence in a fabric subjected to a sudden and colossal strain may account, in some degree, for the catastrophic conditions which eventuated during the last few days of July, 1914—in contrast with the calmness prevailing in Great Britain, which had passed through the corresponding stage of convalescence half a century earlier.

This theory was strengthened by the consideration of the admitted difference between the conditions of England and the Continent respectively with regard to the circulation of coin on the threatened outbreak of trouble. We have noticed that the instinct of hoarding is one of the most ancient of all human tendencies. It has, however, been almost entirely destroyed in this country by the counter-attraction offered by the convenience of a current account and the payment of interests on deposits. Moreover, the fact that this country has not for many centuries been invaded has almost utterly eradicated from the mind of its population the idea of hiding coin on the threatened outbreak of any political or military complications. Very few people at the time of the declaration of war even thought of drawing their money out of the bank and hiding it in the house or in a tree. But withdrawal and hoarding would be one of the first instincts of the ordinary continental bank depositor as soon as trouble made its appearance in a distinct form. He would realise that his money, if left in the bank, might be commandeered by the Government or by the invader, and he would rush to get it out so as to hide it away. That process on the Continent would soon go so far as to reduce the actual available coin to a minimum, and in that way might cause the greatest possible hampering of all commercial and financial transactions. Money on the Continent, as a matter of fact, flew to its retreat like a mouse to its hole. Continental bankers knew it, and were compelled to make drastic preparations, which accentuated the trouble in the stock markets and (on the Continent) turned crisis into something like cataclysm

had been the most prominent in recent history were " in a state of insolvency long before joint-stock banks were established in London." Two members of the firm of Messrs. Quilter and Ball pointed out to the Bank Committee of 1858 that " many of the houses which fell in 1847 had once been wealthy, but had long ceased to be so. Those of 1857 had, with few exceptions, never possessed adequate capital, but carried on extensive transactions by fictitious credit.[1] That was one species of menace arising from obsolete survivals. There was, however, a much larger class, the nature and destiny of which will demand exhaustive analysis in a separate chapter on bank amalgamation and absorption.

[1] See p. 379

CHAPTER X

THE RISE OF THE JOINT-STOCK BANKS

DURING the whole period characterised by the errors and misfortunes which formed the main subject of the previous chapter, the two classes of bankers—private and joint-stock—had existed side by side. But the one was steadily disappearing before the other, even as the red man vanishes before the white. The huge entities represented by the new joint-stock banks either established competing branches which supplanted the private institutions, or else absorbed them out and out. It will be necessary to retrace our steps in order to review the process, and in a later chapter we shall consider its significance. The survey of the weaknesses of the English banking, in priority to the description of the advent of the most effective of remedial agents, is a sequence of treatment which has been deliberately adopted as likely to be more vivid than the reverse order.

At an earlier stage we saw that the Act of 1708, amending the charter of the Bank of England, prohibited the formation, by any number of persons exceeding six, of any institution in the nature of a bank. It was imagined that private firms of six persons, or less, working with *unlimited* liability, could not imperil the supremacy of the gigantic new enterprise, armed and defended by its *limited* liability. Further, we saw that the Act 15 Geo. II. c. 13, s. 5, prohibited the issue of bills or notes, payable on demand, by "any *body politic or corporate* whatsoever, erected or to be erected, or . . . for any partnership exceeding the number of six persons." As notes were supposed to be the life-blood of a bank, this enactment created the erroneous belief that a prohibition of note issue was, in effect, an insuperable obstacle to rival banks. Yet even before Gilbart discovered the fatal secret, that a note issue was not essential to banking, and started the London and Westminster Bank, Joplin[1] had pointed out, in 1823, that the Bank's charter did not, in fact, " prevent public banks for the deposit of capital from being established." The Government, in the same year as Joplin's discovery, proposed to the Bank that it should consent to the creation of joint-stock banks of (note) issue not less than sixty-five miles from London, in return for a ten-year extension of the charter. The Bank refused ; but in the light of the panic of 1825, and with the date for the renewal of the charter (1833) rapidly approaching, the Bank directors, after a fortnight of negotiation, agreed to the Act of 1826. This broke their monopoly of *corporate* note issue by permitting the establishment of joint-stock banks outside a circle with a radius of sixty-five miles from London, provided they had no establishment in London or within sixty-five miles thereof. The exception kept the National Provincial Bank of England out of London (compelling it to do all its London business through the London and Westminster) down to the time when it had 120 Midland branches and a subscribed capital of £2,100,000 with £1,080,000 paid up.[2] The Act (7 Geo. IV. c. 46) also empowered the Bank of England itself to open country branches.[3] In 1833, when the charter was renewed, the Act (3 and 4 William IV. c. 98) definitely enacted (sec. 3) that " any body politic or corporate, or

[1] Joplin was the founder of the *Economist*.
[2] It opened in London in 1866.
[3] The Bank of England itself was enabled by the Act 7 George IV. c. 7, to advance money on deposit and pledges on goods in Manchester, Glasgow, Sheffield, and other towns, to the extent of £366,000. The Bank established branches, between 1826 and 1829, in Gloucester, Manchester, Swansea, Birmingham, Liverpool, Bristol, Leeds, Exeter, Newcastle, Hull, and Norwich, and later at Leicester and Portsmouth. The directors offered to open a much greater number of branches rather than have permission given for the establishment of the new-fangled joint-stock banks. But the Government held the view that it was beyond the power of the Bank to open a sufficient number of branches to meet the growing financial needs of the country. The country bankers strongly objected to the new branches. Their memorial, dated May 9, 1828, regretted that the Treasury had taken no steps to compel the withdrawal of the country branches of the Bank of England. The bankers asked that they be regarded

RISE OF THE JOINT-STOCK BANKS

society, or company, or partnership, although consisting of more than six persons, may carry on the trade or business of banking in London, or within 65 miles thereof, provided that such body, etc. . . . do not borrow, owe, or take up in England any sum or sums of money on their bills or notes payable on demand, or at any less time than six months from the borrowing thereof, during the continuance of the privileges granted by this Act to the Bank of England."[1]

" NATURAL SELECTION " AMONG BANKS

In addition to Joplin and Gilbart the idea of the modern joint-stock bank had also shaped itself in the brain of a

---

[1] This was the brief explanatory section designed to set all doubts at rest. The Act itself was explanatory of 7 Geo. IV. c. 46, and provided in specific terms that during the continuance of the privilege of the Bank of England no body politic or corporate, and no society, company, or partnership exceeding six persons, should make or issue in London, or within 65 miles thereof, any bill of exchange or promissory note or engagement for the payment of money on demand ; provided always that nothing in the Act is to be construed to prevent (1) any body politic, society, company, or partnership from carrying on banking business at a greater distance than 65 miles from London, so long as they have no house of business or establishment as bankers in London, or within 65 miles thereof ; or (2) to prevent such persons from making their bills or notes payable in London, or from having an agent or agents in London ; but no such bill or note shall be of less amount than £5, or be re-issued in London or within 65 miles thereof.

---

as parties in the intended application for the renewal of the Bank charter (1833), and that "no special privilege or monopoly be granted to the Bank directors which would place them in a position other than that of perfect equality with country bankers in the competition which, by means of their branches, they are now carrying on with your memorialists." But see *post*, p. 343, for more complete details.

W. Reid, in a coarse history of the *Life and Adventures of the Old Lady of Threadneedle Street*, compared the Bank to Sarah, and the new branches to the child that she bore in her old age (1832). Mr. Kirkman D. Hodgson, in his evidence before the Select Committee of the House of Commons in 1875, stated " that the branches of the Bank of England were not extending. On the contrary, the branches at Exeter, Norwich, Gloucester, Swansea, and Leicester had been closed, as they did not pay their expenses. With regard to that, I should say that the branch at Exeter was closed and a branch at Plymouth was opened in lieu of it for the Government convenience." Mr. Hodgson continued, " I do not suppose that Plymouth does now pay its expenses. I know that the branch is kept up more for the Government convenience than for any profit which accrues from it to the Bank of England." The Portsmouth branch was transferred in April, 1914, to the London Joint-Stock Bank. The Bank is restrained in the matter of branch office ambitions by the fact that it is the holder of the national reserve. Its position must be materially weakened if, like the Imperial Bank of Germany, it counted branches by the score and the hundred.

w

Baring. At all events, it was in the course of the debate on the Address in 1826 that Baring said he " would recommend them to establish banks, either by joint-stock companies or on the common principles on which they at present stood, but so as to induce persons of capital to become bankers." Adam Smith had already said that " the constitution of joint-stock companies renders them in general more tenacious of established rules than any private co-partnery; such companies, therefore, seem extremely well fitted for " the trade of banking.[1] Arguing in favour of the grant of liberty for their establishment, and against the " chartered privileges of the Bank of England," Lord Liverpool dropped into unconscious Darwinism. He cited the case of Massachusetts, where only twelve chartered banks were allowed. In contrast to this, said he, was a system " of unlimited liberty, which was thought to be less objectionable in itself, and to gain equally the same end; because, when all restriction was removed, the solid and more extensive banks would not fail, in time, to expel the smaller and weaker."[2] This is simply the theory of natural selection applied in the financial sphere. Since " other banks we must have," said another speaker, " wherein lies the magic of the number six, as applied to the members of these necessary establishments ? "

JOINT STOCK, BUT UNLIMITED LIABILITY

The expression " joint-stock " has now come to be so closely associated with limited liability that it is necessary to impress the point that these early joint-stock undertakings were only large co-partnerships with unlimited liability.[3] It was not until the Act of 1826 that joint-stock

[1] *Wealth of Nations*, Ed. Cannan, Vol. II. p. 246.
[2] *Annual Register* 1826, p. 32.

[3] BANKING WITH UNLIMITED LIABILITY
The evolution of limited liability has already been discussed in detail in Chapter VI. At this point it may suffice to say that in 1826 the limited liability of the shareholders of a joint-stock company could only be secured by royal charter. There were only five joint-stock banks with limited liability in 1826. When the Treasury was in correspondence with the three senior Scotch banks in 1881, they pointed out that the question of the limitation of the liability of their proprietors to the amount

RISE OF THE JOINT-STOCK BANKS 303

banks, for instance, were enabled to sue and to be sued in the name of their principal officer. At that time the Commercial Bank of Scotland, for example, had 540 " partners " (not shareholders) and the National Bank of Scotland 1238. In prosecuting an action as recently as 1871 the Union Bank of Australia was compelled

of the subscribed capital could never have been the subject of any authoritative decision. The point could only arise, they said, through the insolvency of one of these five common law banking corporations of the United Kingdom, namely, the Bank of England, the Bank of Ireland, the Bank of Scotland, the Royal Bank of Scotland, and the British Linen Company Bank.

Apart from these five institutions, holding the privilege of age and prestige, the bank with limited liability would in 1826 have been a phenomenon, and a very unwelcome one at that. Yet when, fifty years later, the great joint-stock banks adopted limited liability, George Rae (North and South Wales Bank meeting. January 27, 1880) pointed out that the three foremost banks of the United Kingdom, namely the Banks of England, Scotland, and Ireland, were all limited banks. The limitation of their liability had never resulted in a single breath of discredit resting upon them. Therefore, said Rae, " the principle of limited liability is not a new-fangled notion at all . . . it is the principle of *unlimited* liability that is by far the newer of the two." Limited liability as a privilege granted, for the asking, to *companies* generally (other than assurance) was created by the Act of 1855 (18 and 19 Vict. c. 133) ; but banking companies were excluded from the operations of the Act as regards the limitation of liability, as they were also from the Act of 1857. The Act of 1858 (21 and 22 Vict. c. 91) offered a permissive limitation of liability so far as regards the general obligations (but not the notes) of banks, subject to thirty days' notice being given to each customer, and to the display, in the offices of the limited bank, of half-yearly (February 1 and August 1) statements of its assets and liabilities. The great Companies Act of 1862 left existing banks limited or unlimited, according to their then constitution ; but no new joint-stock bank could be formed in such a manner as to preclude the unlimited liability of its shareholders in respect of its notes, if any. Finally, limited liability was conferred on banks generally by the Act of 1879 (42 and 43 Vict. c. 76).

A meeting was held on October 23, 1879, with a view to the simultaneous adoption of limited liability. Fifty-eight banks were invited and thirty-seven were represented. Of these, the London and County, National Provincial, Capital and Counties, and Bury Banking announced their intention of becoming limited whatever the others might do. As most of the representatives of the other banks had no definite instructions, a circular letter was addressed to the whole fifty-eight, with the result (as stated by the Chairman of the Manchester and Liverpool District Banking Co. at the meeting on January 28, 1880) that " of the seven unlimited English joint-stock banks carrying on business in London, five, viz. the London and Westminster, London and County, National Provincial, City, and Capital and Counties, have taken preliminary steps to become limited ; and two, viz. the Union and the London Joint-Stock, at present decline to make the change. Of the fifty-eight unlimited English provincial banks twenty have expressed their intention to become limited. Twelve of the twenty, viz. (1) London and County, (2) National Provincial, (3) Capital and Counties (which are also London banks), (4) Bury,

to set out the whole of the names of its 1700 plaintiff-partners.[1]

The harbinger of the great modern joint-stock banks (other than the Bank of England) was the London and Westminster Bank, which opened its doors, at 38 Throgmorton Street, under the management of J. W. Gilbart,

[1] Stated at meeting, July 10, 1871.

(5) Pares's Leicestershire, (6) Leicestershire, (7) Yorkshire, (8) Carlisle City and District, (9) Carlisle and Cumberland, (10) Birmingham and Midland, (11) North and South Wales, (12) Sheffield, have taken the necessary action preliminary to making the change. Thirteen are willing, but waiting for others. Four are known to be unwilling; and the remaining twenty-one have not responded to the inquiry, so are assumed to be waiting or to be indifferent or hostile to limitation."

Reluctance did not last long. George Rae told his shareholders in 1884 that at the time of the passing of the Act, there were eighty-five unlimited banks in the three kingdoms. Of these, said he, seventy-four had registered under the Act with united capitals amounting to £163,000,000, leaving only eleven unlimited banks with a total capital of £4,000,000 or $2\frac{1}{2}$ per cent. of the whole.

There can be no doubt that (as the *Economist* had urged in 1857—*ante*, p. 294) the limitation of liability has tended to induce a better class of investor to become the holder of bank shares. " Since it has been known to the public that we are about to take this step (that is to say, to limit the liability) I know of wealthy men who have bought shares in the concern. They would not look at the shares before, because of the unknown liability which they might of possibility be subject to." (Chairman at London and County meeting, December 31, 1879). Barclay's have effected a species of compromise between limitation and non-limitation. Half their shares carry a limited liability and enjoy unlimited dividends, while the other half are fully paid with a maximum dividend of 10 per cent.

As long as the unlimited liability existed, the executor of the testator who held a single share in an unlimited bank was bound to wait for three years after the sale of such share or shares before he could distribute one shilling of the property. It had to remain in hand until all potential legal responsibility had come to an end. Occasionally the demands made in the case of banks with unlimited liability were appalling. The first estimate of the liquidators' requirements in the City of Glasgow Bank was £2750 for every £100 stock. Unlimited liability kept open the accounts of Douglas Heron and Co., and the prolonged demands upon its shareholders and their families, from its failure in 1772 until after the passing of the Reform Act. The present law on the subject is sec. 6 of the Companies Act of 1879 (42 and 43 Vict. c. 76), which provides that a bank *of issue* registered as a limited company shall not be entitled to limited liability in respect of its notes. In the event of a winding up, and an insufficiency of assets both for the noteholders and the general creditors, the noteholders have priority, and after their demands are satisfied the members of the company shall contribute towards payment of the general creditors a sum equal to that received by the noteholders out of the general assets.

An earlier and more curious source of trouble was found in the fact that spiritual persons could not legally engage themselves in trading

in March, 1834, with a paid-up capital of £50,000. The London bankers had made common cause against the scheme, so successfully as to compel the raising of the capital in the provinces rather than in the metropolis. The directors were refused admission to the Clearing-house[1] (sharing this exclusion with the Bank of England) and the

---

[1] NOTE ON THE CLEARING-HOUSE.

The system of clearing—a species of highly concentrated representative barter—(now modified and adapted to the needs of many factors of the industrial organisation besides the banks) was originally operated through a goldsmith-banker like Blackwell, about the middle of the seventeenth century, and evolved into a street-corner transaction between clerks who met for that purpose. Mr. Lawson says that the business was done " on the top of a post." Then a large recessed window in one of the banking-houses became the rendezvous, until the resulting hubbub compelled the banker to turn his visitors summarily into the street. About 1773 the Clearing-room was definitely established at Martin's, who received 19s. 6d. a quarter for the use of it. It was probably in allusion to this that Gilbart told the 1841 Committee (Q. 1368) that the Clearing-house had existed for sixty years. Then, apparently, a room at Smith, Payne and Smith's was utilised. (*City Men and City Manners*, p. 18.) The Union of London and Smiths' Bank (as successors to Smith, Payne and Smith) have in their possession the bank's clearing-book of March 3, 1777. Slightly later, apparently, a neighbouring public-house offered greater comfort and facility, and became the Clearing-house until the familiar premises in Post Office Court, Lombard Street, were taken, in 1810, as a result of agreement among the principal City bankers. The report of the Bullion Committee (1810) had referred in approving terms to the " contrivance " of bringing all " drafts daily to a common receptacle, where they are balanced against each other." Clearing-house business had exhibited a very considerable increase during the recent years before 1810. (Evidence of the Inspector of the Clearing-house before the Bullion Committee, Minutes, p. 236.) At this time there were forty-six bankers using the Clearing-house, as against forty-two ten years before. (Bullion Committee, Minutes, p. 236.) The clearing averaged about £4,700,000 daily, and the differences were paid in bank-notes. About £220,000 in notes sufficed to effect all the daily balances. On settling days on the Stock Exchange the whole amount of the drafts paid in was about £14,000,000. (The figure is nowadays nearer £100,000,000.) The Continent did not follow this example of banking organisation. Outside Great Britain, the cheque and the Clearing-house were not adopted for many years to come, and

---

companies. As numbers of such spiritual persons, namely clergymen, had become shareholders in the joint-stock banks it was suddenly discovered that all these concerns were illegal and all their contracts void. The Act of 1814 was passed to obviate the difficulty.

In the case of the earlier Colonial banks formed by Crown charter, the extent of the liability was defined by the charter itself. For instance, " And we hereby further will and declare, that these presents are upon this express condition, that on the winding-up of the affairs of the said company, all and every the proprietors for the time being of any share in the capital thereof shall be liable to contribute to the payment of the debts and liabilities of the said company to the extent of twice the amount of their subscribed shares, that is for the amount subscribed, or so much thereafter as shall not have been previously paid up, and for an additional amount equal to the amount so subscribed."

EVOLUTION OF THE MONEY MARKET

Bank of England itself refused to open a drawing account on their behalf. At a later date, the Bank of England offered to open an account if the new institution renewed its application, but the condition was imposed that the London and Westminster should not remit money to and from its branches. Gilbart declined to accept these terms,[1]

[1] Gilbart, 1841 Committee, Q. 1307.

the regular use of banking accounts was very rare beyond the greater commercial centres. Buyings and sellings were for cash, and the simplest forms of credit remained unknown.

The adoption of the practice of writing the name of the bank across the cheques which it sent to the Clearing-house was the origin of the crossed cheque, now so indispensable a factor of the financial machinery that its absence is unthinkable. This, at least, is the accepted explanation. In 1856, however, Mr. Pellatt, the member for Southwark, in introducing the second reading of the Bill, to legalise the crossing of cheques, gave a different account. He said that " a gang of swindlers paid into a bank some bills due on a certain day at a certain house. When the banker's clerk presented himself, they seized him, tied him up, took away all his bills, went round with them to the different bankers, and then left the town with their booty. The system of crossed cheques was adopted in order to prevent the repetition of such wholesale robbery."

The earliest crossed cheque, on the " Grasshopper " (Martin's) is dated 1806. Nowadays the transfer tickets issued for the final adjustment of clearing transactions are, of course, settled at the Bank of England, which is the bankers' bank. But down to the year 1864 the Bank (which was for many years excluded from the Clearing-house by the private bankers) maintained the practice of cashing the drafts in the old-fashioned way, by sending clerks to the other banks for the money. In 1844, only twenty-six of the private banks were members of the Clearing-house, and no joint-stock bank had so far crossed its threshold. The private bankers, to whom the Clearing-house itself belonged, admitted the joint-stock banks to the clearing on June 8, 1854. The list of " clearers," as displayed in Post Office Court about 1842, before the joint-stock banks were admitted, contained these names (*Political Cyclopædia*, Vol. I. p. 273):

Barclay	Denison	Jones	Robarts	Stone
Barnard	Dorrien	Lubbock	Rogers	Veres
Barnetts	Fuller	Masterman	Smith	Weston
Bosanquet	Glyn	Prescott	Spooner	Williams
Brown	Hanbury	Price	Stevenson	Willis
Curries	Hankey			

The policy of exclusion in force down to 1854 had originally been directed against the Bank of England and the London and Westminster Bank. It was to this that Gilbart alluded when he told the 1841 Committee (Q. 1368) that the Clearing-house was practically a public institution like a market, and it was unjust that the bankers who controlled it should keep the joint-stock banks out of it. An association of omnibus proprietors, he added, could be tried for conspiracy if they attempted to run a rival omnibus off the road, " and yet a body of bankers may conspire for a similar object without any interference by the Legislature at all." About the time when the Bank of England was finally admitted to the clearing it had offered to perform the entire collection for all the bankers free of charge ; but, for some reason or other, this proposition

RISE OF THE JOINT-STOCK BANKS 307

and no account was opened. The older institution, moreover, opposed by counsel the petition of the younger bank to the House of Commons, for power to sue and be sued otherwise than through an officer. Threadneedle Street also attacked the new bank on the ground of its accepting bills of exchange drawn at a shorter period than six

was declined. The circulation of the large notes (£200 to £1000) formerly employed in adjusting bankers' accounts fell from £5,856,000 in 1852 to £3,241,000 in 1857. The Clearing-house, as Bagehot used to say, enables the bankers to get on with less till-money in proportion to the amount of their transactions, and therefore sets more cash free for active use. It " is [1844] the means in ordinary times of saving the use of notes to the extent daily of about £3,000,000." (Bosanquet, Letter to Sir R. Peel, Parker, *Life of Peel*, Vol. III. p. 141.)

It has been stated that the Clearing-house was originally the property of the private banks. As attraction or absorption reduced their numbers, the shares passed, by a species of survivorship, to the remaining members. By 1895 only four were left—Barclay's, Brown-Janson's, Robarts-Lubbock, and Smith-Payne. The Clearing-house was then acquired by a company, and the shares distributed among all the banks who were members of the institution. The last admission was in April, 1914, when it was unanimously decided by the Committee of London Clearing Bankers to admit the London and Provincial Bank as a member. By this addition the number of town clearing banks was raised to seventeen, exclusive of the Bank of England, which clears on the charge side only. The admission meant much more than the provision of additional facility for the admitted bank. There is a growing preference in the bill market for " clearers," and a turn in the rate can be secured, as a rule, for this fine variety of acceptances. Among these the London and Provincial bills will, of course, be found in future, and, having regard to the growth of acceptance business in English banking, the point is not a negligible one. The Metropolitan clearing, established in 1907, brought the nearer suburban branches of the clearing banks, in addition to those of the London and Provincial Bank (not at that time in the Clearing-house) and Coutts's, into the regular clearing, and superseded to a large extent the antiquated system of " walks."

The idea of the Country Clearing is said to have originated with Mr. W. Gillett in the spring of 1858, but it was developed by the late Lord Avebury. Before his time London bankers sent their cheques daily by post to the country banker on whom the cheques were drawn, and the amount was then paid over, less commission, to the London agent of the remitting banker. The country bankers settled among themselves in the same way. Nowadays all the cheques payable in the country are passed through the Country Clearing, and each country banker remits to his London agent, the difference being settled in the same way as the Town Clearing. The saving in expense, time, and labour is so enormous as to be incalculable. Non-clearing banks (town and country) keep an account with a clearing banker, and pay other banks by drafts thereon. Forty years ago the proposal was also made for a clearing discount establishment, which should register all bills discounted or advanced upon by bankers or bill-brokers, so as to enable them to ascertain at any time the total amount of paper then " out " from any given firm ; but the scheme was not realised.

In 1873 the beginnings of a similar clearing method were applied to Stock Exchange transactions, and, after surmounting many difficulties,

months, which was alleged to be a contravention of section 3 and 4 William IV. c. 98. In this case the Bank of England won the day; but, of course, the law has long ago been altered. It was not until after a lapse of more than twenty years—namely in 1854—that the seat in the Clearing-house was obtained.

PREJUDICE AGAINST JOINT-STOCK BANKS

Such rivalries and jealousies sound almost incredible in these days of banking solidarity. Yet they were

---

the system has become a most valuable instrument for the rapid adjustment of a maximum of transactions in a minimum of time. The first Stock Exchange clearing was carried out at the end-February account, 1874. Thus we reach what has been called the third stage in the evolution of trade—first barter, then money, and then the mere clearing of balances. The banking transactions cleared in London in the year 1913 amounted to £16,436,000,000. This immense sum represents the multitudinous adjustments necessary to ensure the smooth running of the vast business mechanism. It is necessary, however, to point out that in considering the figures, " the increase in the price of commodities is reflected both in the Board of Trade returns, and also in the Clearing-house figures " (*Clearing-house Report*, 1911). The effect of the system is to settle the whole business transactions of the world through bank ledgers. The ultimate significance of the Bankers' Clearing-house lies in the overwhelming evidence which it affords of the increasing scope and popularity of a cheque currency. Inasmuch as the immense volume of modern business can undoubtedly be more efficiently and more easily conducted upon a quasi-subjective than upon an objective basis every increase in the volume of Clearing-house transactions is a matter of the utmost moment to the welfare of the whole economic fabric. The clearing system has now spread so far, and become so universal, that it is the merest financial truism to say that London is the Clearing-house of the whole world.

The Clearing-house system has developed rather differently in the United States. The functions of an American Clearing-house are very much wider than those of the analogous institutions in Great Britain. The primary purpose of a Clearing-house is the rapid and facile adjustment of the banking transactions of each day, and this fact has never been lost sight of by the organisation on this side of the Atlantic. But in the United States the members of a given Clearing-house assume the duty, as such, of protecting any bank (being a member of the organisation) which is in a position of temporary embarrassment. Further, agreements with regard to uniform rates of interest on deposits are common among the members of American Clearing-houses. There was an instance at Buffalo as early as 1881. These agreements sometimes go to the length of stipulating the minimum balance (say $2000) upon which any interest shall be paid, and also of defining the charges on the collection of banking items. Analogous restrictive arrangements are in force all over the United States among members of the various Clearing-houses. Such arrangements are familiar enough in Europe; but they do not, with us, form part of the functions of a Clearing-house, but rather of the various associations of bankers, which do not necessarily coincide as regards membership with the personnel of the Clearing-house.

RISE OF THE JOINT-STOCK BANKS   309

typical of the general sentiment of dislike for the joint-stock banks. A London private banker, in the early thirties, dishonouring a cheque which overdrew the balance of a small client, remarked that the customer would probably go to the London and Westminster, the " only receptacle for such accounts."[1] The Union Bank of London (now the Union of London and Smiths' Bank) held its first meeting in 1830, on a first floor in Coleman Street, with hardly enough proprietors to move and second the resolutions.[2] The present site of the bank was acquired when the head office was still located in a little shop in Moorgate Street. It was bought by two of the directors on their own account; the Board had not sufficient enterprise to make the venture.[3] During the railway boom of the thirties the Bank of England issued a notice that all bills bearing the endorsement of a joint-stock bank would be refused discount, whatever other endorsements they might carry. J. Horsley Palmer (who had been Governor earlier) doubted whether the joint-stock banks in their then form (1837) and the Bank of England were capable of co-existence[4] Samuel Jones Loyd (Lord Overstone) told the House of Commons Committee in 1832 that the joint-stock banks were deficient in everything requisite for the conduct of banking business, except extended responsibility. At a later date, he regretted that the Treasury letter of 1857 suspending the Bank Charter Act, was not delayed another twenty-four hours. If it had been, said he in the House of Lords, all the London joint-stock banks would have " tumbled to pieces." As late as 1862 the critics of the newly-established London and South Western Bank stigmatised it as being " only a twopenny-ha'penny company."[5] This kind of bitterness among institutions which should be riveted to the rock of common cause and mutual interest,

[1] Ewings, general manager, London and Westminster, meeting, January 19, 1870.
[2] Chairman, at meeting, July 14, 1869.
[3] G. H. Milford at Jubilee Dinner of the Union Bank, February 4, 1889.
[4] Overstone, *Tracts and other Publications*, p. 7.
[5] So stated at meeting, August 3, 1904.

made a tradition which may well have survived to our own day, as a kind of ineradicable fear. If added to the terrible memories of unlimited liability it would go far to explain the investor's gingerly handling of bank shares, even at the present time.

SPREAD OF JOINT-STOCK BANKING

The success of Gilbart's experiment and of other large institutions established under the influence of his example, caused the number of joint-stock banks (as distinguished from private banks) to increase at an amazing pace. Prejudice could not stop them. One fervid exponent of their advantages persuaded himself that it was "utterly impossible" for a joint-stock bank to fail.[1] Time and events have falsified this "glorious optimism." While it prevailed, however, it did its work. An official return gives 34 as the number of the joint-stock banks—mainly provincial—established between their first legalisation in 1826 and July, 1833. By the end of 1835 the total was 60. Mr. Turner[2] says that more than 40 were started in the spring of 1836. Mr. Easton's figures,[3] with reference to the number of joint-stock banks formed, are :—

1826–30	 10	1851–55	..	.. 1
1831–35	 28	1856–60	..	.. 0
1836–40	 34	1861–65	..	.. 26
1841–45	 3	1866–70	..	.. 5
1845–50	 0	1871–74	..	.. 11

According to some valuable tables in the *Bankers' Magazine* for August, 1844, the number of joint-stock banks in the United Kingdom at that date was : England and Wales, 106 ; Scotland, 20 ; Ireland, 10 ; and there were besides 10 joint-stock Colonial banks in London. In 1851, according to Mr. Easton's estimate,[4] there were in England and Wales 962 bank branches. In 1858 the total number of bank offices in the United Kingdom was

---

[1] *A Few Words on Joint Stock Banking*, 1836.
[2] *Chronicles of the Bank of England*, p. 145.
[3] *Banks and Banking*, p. 60.
[4] *Banks and Banking*, p. 60.

RISE OF THE JOINT-STOCK BANKS 311

over 2000.[1] In 1870 the number of branches in England and Wales had increased to 1651, in 1875 to a total of 1885, in 1878 to 2195, and in 1883 to 2381. This last figure almost exactly coincides with the results attained by Mr. Jas. Dick, who in papers read before the Institute of Bankers,[2] calculated that in 1883 there were 317 banks, with 2382 offices, in England and Wales—one office to every 11,315 of the population. In 1891 the number of banks had decreased to 261, but the branches had advanced to 3231—one for every 8915 inhabitants. In 1901 the figures were 172, 4872, and 6676 respectively —less banks, more branches, and a larger supply relatively to population. Mr. Newmarch's figures of bank offices in the United Kingdom from 1858 to 1878, supplemented by later details from the *Bankers' Magazine*, stand thus :—

	Number.		Number.		Number.
1858	2008	1886	4460	1899	6367
1866	2588	1896	5627	1900	6521
1872	2924	1897	5811	1914	9316[3]
1878	3554	1898	6119		

The working of the remorseless process of absorption is evidenced by the fact that in 1844 there were 106 joint-stock banks with 498 branches. In 1894 the total of the separate banks was less—99—though the branches had swelled to 2577. In 1902 the respective figures had again diverged, to 67 and 4230. In the twenty-three years to December 31, 1913, the number of joint-stock banks in England and Wales decreased from 104 to 43, while simultaneously the number of branches rose from 2203 to 5802. Private banks, in the same period, were reduced in number from 38 to 8. During the seventeen years to the end of 1913 no fewer than 114 separate banks passed out of existence, and in some cases their capital disappeared from the aggregate banking capital of the kingdom. The Right Hon. F. Huth Jackson, addressing the Liverpool and District Bankers' Institute in November, 1913, gave the reduction of the " individual banks " since 1887 as

[1] Hartley Withers, *English Banking System*, p. 34.
[2] *Journal*, Vol. XIII. p. 320.
[3] Includes foreign and colonial bank offices in England.

having been from 366 to 133. He added that 209 had disappeared through purchase or amalgamation. It is, in fact, a financial paradox that the augmentation of banking facilities, especially during the last quarter of a century, actually synchronises with large diminutions of banking capital in the United Kingdom, as a result of these amalgamations and absorptions. In 1878 the total banking capital of the United Kingdom was diminished by £946,783, in 1897 by £625,717, and in 1907 by £458,120.

COLONIAL BANKING

Simultaneously with these developments at home, the process of bank establishment and extension began in Canada. In 1817 and 1818 the first banks were created in Lower Canada (now Quebec), and the Royal Assent to a similar incorporation in Upper Canada (now Ontario) was given in 1821. The bank soon opened branches and agencies, and began to discharge the widest functions of banking for the benefit of the community. Of the banks thus created (three in Lower Canada, one in Upper Canada, one in New Brunswick, and two in Nova Scotia), all but one, in Quebec, have become leading institutions, and all are either in operation at the present time, or have become amalgamated with other banks—with the exception of the one in Upper Canada, which became entangled in political intrigue, and failed in 1866, after a career of nearly half a century. In 1855 there were nine joint-stock banks with offices in London, " which may with propriety be called colonial banks "—the Bank of Australasia, Bank of British North America, Colonial Bank, English, Scottish, and Australian Bank, Ionian Bank, London Chartered Bank of Australia, Oriental Bank, South Australian Banking Company, and the Union Bank of Australia.[1]

INCREASE OF CHEQUE CURRENCY

This spread of banking facilities, and their eager utilisation, in the period between Waterloo and 1858, and especially between 1826 and 1858, attracted the attention

[1] Bell, *Philosophy of Joint Stock Banking*, p. 73.

RISE OF THE JOINT-STOCK BANKS

of parliamentary committees. " Banks are rapidly extending in all directions," said the 1836 Committee " New companies are daily forming, and an increased number of branches and agencies are spreading throughout England, even in small towns and villages." The Select Committee of 1858 pointed out that a large part of the funds in bankers' hands " has been derived from sources not heretofore made available for this purpose . . . the practice of opening accounts and depositing money with bankers has extended to numerous classes who did not formerly employ their capital in that way." Mr. Rodwell (the chairman of the Association of Private Country Bankers) told the Committee that the practice of keeping a bank account had lately increased fourfold among the farmers and shopkeepers of the Ipswich district. Even farmers[1] who only paid £50 a year rent now kept deposits with bankers. " The practice of opening accounts and depositing money with bankers, having extended to numerous persons who never before thought of such an employment of their capital, was considered to show an advance of the middle classes in prosperity and habits of economy."[2] Many classes, remarks Gilbart, whose accounts would not have been taken by the old London bankers are now (1859) received with courtesy and even thankfulness. The process went steadily on right through the century. Banking was democratised and popularised " The beginning of banking in the little villages is by some shopkeeper—perhaps the chief shopkeeper in the village—exchanging almost anything that comes into the village, whether cheques on our banks or bank-notes, for whatever cash he has in his till ; he does it without charge, knowing that he can take all those cheques to the issuing bank in the next town and have them exchanged there for local notes, with which local notes he makes his purchases."[3] Mr. (now Sir) Inglis

---

[1] The chairman of the London and County Bank, in 1861, selected the English yeoman as the recipient of a special encomium upon his punctuality and straightforwardness as a banker's client.
[2] Morier Evans, *Commercial Crisis* 1857–1858, p. 32.
[3] F. Seebohm, of Sharples and Co., Hitchin, 1875 Committee, Q. 4595.

Palgrave told the 1875 Committee that the diminution of the local note issues in the agricultural districts was due to the falling off of population, or, at least, to its stationary character, and also to the fact that " cheques to a very great extent supersede the use of notes,"[1] and this among a class peculiarly prone to hoard, because of its suspicious nature. " We deal largely with the small farmers and the small shopkeepers . . . our bank has fostered the trade of the country in regard to what we may call the smaller classes of the community to a very great extent indeed."[2]

The bankers, even in the forties and fifties, laid themselves out to secure this most desirable species of client. The London and South Western was established with the deliberate object of catering for this new class. As the Chairman once said (meeting, August 3, 1904), it was intended to be a " popular bank, a great middle-class bank, and a shopkeepers' bank." It even came to be believed by bankers—and their views were endorsed by the *Economist*—that a great number of small accounts is a much more valuable acquisition to a bank than a small number of great accounts. By 1914 the banker has made it an article of faith. A few pounds realised upon each of a multitude of small accounts is much better than financing Alexander Collie and his " drawing posts," with the result of seeing " half the reserve fund " disappear at a single whiff. So it is that there is now no town in Great Britain which lacks a branch of at least one of the great joint-stock banks. Even in good-sized villages there is a sub-branch open once or twice a week. Conditions are much the same in other industrial countries. Over $5,000,000,000 of commercial paper is estimated by Mr. Babson[3] to be discounted in the United States by the National banks alone. The Bank of France will discount paper in as small a denomination as 5f. Forty per cent. of its loans do not exceed 50f. in

---

[1] Q. 5494.
[2] Wade, National Provincial Bank of England, 1875 Committee Q. 1963.
[3] *Commercial Paper*, p. 80.

RISE OF THE JOINT-STOCK BANKS 315

amount.[1] The number of these bills, of 8f. and under, averages about 250,000 a year, and in 1910 reached 334,373. In the same year the trade bills under 100f. reached 4,452,300, and the amount of Stock Exchange business conducted for clients of the Banque de France is now over £25,000,000 a year. The Reichsbank is equally accommodating where the bill is for 10m. This means not only facilities, but supervision, for the class which avails itself of such opportunities. The bill payable at a bank is itself a presumptive testimonial to the existence of a knowledge as well as a supervision of the drawer's affairs as evidenced by his keeping an account there. It carries to that extent the *cachet* of the institution, while at the same time it enforces a moral responsibility, a sense of being trusted, upon the man who has to provide for it. The discounting bank will require the maintenance of a satisfactory balance, and will make itself (*post* p. 435) the invigilator of the customer's methods. Self-confidence, self-reliance, self-appreciation, are all enhanced and emphasised by these facilities. After all, the extension of the practice of keeping a bank account is only, so to speak, the outward and visible sign of an inward and personal force. Every bank account brings into play, in the personality of its possessor, all the instincts of economy, thrift, industry, and ambition which tend to elevate the whole intellectual level of the race, and, as has been well said, endow the possession of a bank account with something like moral dignity. " Bankers for their own interest," said Gilbart in 1859, " always have a regard to the moral character of the party with whom they deal ; they inquire whether he be honest or tricky, industrious or idle, prudent or speculative, thrifty or prodigal ; and they will more readily make advances to a man of moderate property and good morals, than to a man of large property but of inferior reputation." The aggregation of the money and its utilisation as a cosmopolitan driving power is one thing ; the spirit that prompts and

[1] So stated by Van Tuyl, New York State Superintendent of Banks. *New York Times*, August 3, 1913.

fosters the aggregation is quite another. If it were possible to measure their respective influences, the latter would be found the more powerful of the two.

THE UTILITY OF CHEQUE CURRENCY

This question of the cheque currency is so indissolubly bound up with the extension of joint-stock banks that the present stage will be an opportune point for its discussion. In spite of the new increase of the gold supplies arising from the Australian discoveries of 1851, there was a huge and unintermitted strain upon the yellow metal, due mainly to the enormous increase in the commercial requirements of the world, but also partly to an augmented taste for luxury, which caused a greater absorption of gold in the arts. Even the huge supplies of gold poured into the world's lap from American, Australian, and South African sources would not have availed to finance the volume of modern industrial enterprise. The world's production of gold which was £72,800,000 in the decade 1841–1850, rose to £266,600,000 during the ten years 1851–1860. Yet, as Lord Overstone said (1857):—

"The aggregate amount of money in the world must have been largely augmented by the increased production of gold during the last ten years, yet the rate of interest throughout the world is unusually high. The operations of trade have expanded with excessive rapidity, the demand for capital has proportionately increased, and a high price, that is, a high rate of interest, is paid for it. More capital is required than can be immediately supplied."

Even in 1866, it was possible to say that the trade of the world was expanding to the full measure of the increased supplies of the precious metals—which was only another way of pointing to the urgent necessity of expanding and utilising a more extended and facile credit currency, if social progress was to be maintained. This has been done by the creation, at the hands of the Money Power (in a very special sense, for the banks have been the sole creators) of a cheque currency almost inconceivable both in its magnitude and in the beauty and delicacy of the mechanism by which it is operated. Down to 1847 the great crises were largely caused, or at all events, greatly accentuated, by the excessive note issues of a multitude of banks, many of which had little or no capital resources beyond that evanescent species created by the note issues themselves. The Bank of England subsisted on its note issue, and the private banks, like Drummonds and Coutts's, relied upon permanent mortgages and investment in securities rather than upon the fostering of commercial activity. Considering that 80 per cent. of their deposits were sometimes invested in permanent securities (as distinguished from short-dated obligations) it is obvious that the credit system, in the sense in which we understand it, could only have been in a very immature stage. But for the advent of this cheque currency[1] the operation of the Bank Charter Act must have further restricted the gold supply. As the Bank of England note is, under the Act, a mere bullion certificate, " the subsequent enormous development of English trade, if it had been possible at all, must have been accompanied by the heaping up of a vast mass of gold in the Bank's vaults "[2]—save in so far as the option to hold silver bullion (under sec. 3 of the Act) was exercised. But as the note issues declined, and the cheque system grew, the paper currency almost automatically came to be its own guarantee, since, save in exceptional and abnormal cases, a man does not draw a cheque unless he knows it will be met. Bank of England notes have become a matter of secondary, or even tertiary, importance as a factor of the national currency—and this all the more since the issue of the new Treasury notes. Every new client of a bank is *ipso facto*, from the moment of opening an account, a user of the cheque—a thing so distinctively British as to be called

[1] Before 1853, all cheques were unstamped, and were illegal if dated more than fifteen miles from the bank on which they were drawn. Cheques of this character, however, were legalised after 1853, provided they bore the impressed or adhesive penny stamp. But the duty was evaded by the simple expedient of dating the cheque from the town on which it was drawn, and in 1858, all cheques without exception were subjected to a penny stamp.
[2] Withers, *Meaning of Money*, p. 30.

by the late Lord Avebury the "Union Jack of Commerce." The client employs a cheque currency where previously he employed a coin and note currency. As coin takes the place of barter, so at a later stage, bank-notes, bills, and securities take the place of coin. Finally, cheques invade the domain of the bank-note, the bill, and the security so as to transform commercial transactions into a continuous series of book readjustments rather than the exchange of currency against commodities. "The cheque has hurled the note down from its pinnacle of power."[1] Mr. Pownall calculated[2] that modern payments assumed the following proportions :—

```
Coin .......................  0·728
Notes ......................  2·039
Cheques and bills ..........  97·223
```

Other authorities have arrived at conclusions which are substantially identical.[3]

AUTOMATICALLY REGULATED CURRENCY

The cheque currency is much more adaptable than the note currency, because it passes for exact amounts instead

[1] D. Drummond Fraser (London City and Midland Bank), paper read before the British Association, August 3, 1906.

[2] *Economic Journal*, Vol. II. p. 535.

[3] "The same phenomenon is observable in the United States. A glance over the totals of the items for all National banks from 1866 to the present day shows that the increased business of the country has been met, not by any significant increase of the note issues, but by an extraordinary increase of the deposit-currency—i.e. checks drawn on bank deposits. While notes have arisen from about $300,000,000 to $700,000,000, deposits have risen from $600,000,000 to $4,400,000,000, and the figures for banks outside the National system strengthen this showing, for they issue no notes, providing only deposit-currency.

"But this is not the real comparison ; with the notes should be compared, not actual deposits, but the amount of checks drawn on these deposits. The real extent of the use of the deposit-currency as a medium of exchange can be approximately seen in the amount of clearings. These figures disclose the fact that transactions to the amount of over $150,000,000,000 are performed annually in the United States by the deposit-currency as a medium of exchange. In other words, modern business has created methods of exchanging goods by first expressing their worth in dollars ; borrowing on their value thus expressed, which, accordingly, appears in a deposit account to the credit of the borrower, and on which checks are drawn to be used in paying maturing obligations. Thus, goods on the way from the producer to the consumer are coined into means of payment." (Professor Laughlin (of the University of Chicago), *New York Times*, December 8, 1913.)

of round figures. A well-controlled cheque currency is the most elastic thing of its kind. Yet the question of excessive issue, so menacing in the case of notes, is controlled almost automatically as to cheques, by the necessity of the drawer having the balance at his command before he issues the cheque. If, however, through fraud or error, an issue of cheques be attempted otherwise than against gold, an automatic and irresistible restraint would be in operation within twenty-four hours. The cheque makes for safety, shutting out disaster and enhancing our factor of steadiness. Not only has this currency itself been brought into use, but it has been rendered available even to the humblest members of the commercial community by the evolution of the branch-bank system. The aggregation and diffusion of the vivifying force are simultaneous. Every branch bank irrigates the otherwise arid area of society. The cheque—the bill of exchange *drawn on a banker and payable on demand*—is an emblem by means of which there is carried out a ceaseless process of adjustment and readjustment in bankers' books. We move towards Herbert Spencer's ideal " nation of perfectly honest men, where all trade is carried on by memoranda of debts and claims, eventually written off against one another in the books of bankers."[1] There is the minimum wear and tear of the metallic basis, and a coincident tendency to regard it as being only theoretically present. As in the case of loans made to, or bills discounted for, bill-brokers, so also in the case of cheques generally and the dividends on leading public securities, the money never leaves the bank. The transactions are almost wholly book entries, and a " wonderful economy," as Mr. Burn terms it.[2] In fact the best credit, like the best securities, is of the subjective rather than the objective type. "There seems no reason," says Mr. Lavington,[3] "why there should not develop a common control over the cheque currency, which, on the one hand, should avoid those financial conditions which directly promote speculative activity, and on the other operate directly to

---

[1] *Essays*, Vol. III. p. 326. [2] *Stock Exchange Investments*, p. 65.
[3] *Economic Journal*, 1911, p. 60.

reduce the inflation which such activity fosters. To these ends the *permanence* of our banking institutions and their increasing concentration seem peculiarly adapted."

Since the spread of banking facilities, and their extensive utilisation by a new class of client—phenomena noted both by the 1836 and 1858 Committees—cheques have steadily increased in number, and decreased in amount. The tendency is all in the direction of a continuance of this movement, at all events, so far as number is concerned. London cheques are, indeed, becoming an international currency. Cheques on London banks given to hotel keepers on the Continent often " remain out " for months, and when finally cleared are covered with the endorsements of the persons and firms through whose hands they have passed.[1] As the country becomes more densely inhabited and credit institutions are perfected, it hardly admits of question that this custom of using cheques, drafts, and similar currency will become even more general, and that credit will serve as the medium for almost the entirety of exchange transactions.[2] If this cheque currency were not provided by the banks, it would have to be provided by the State, or society would have to do without it. Its value to society, less the bank dividends, is the measure of social advantage which it produces. As soon as the cheque replaces the note, the necessity for keeping vast hoards of gold becomes less urgent. The inevitable result is to minimise the strain on the gold and notes, which once more " gravitate " towards London and there find employment. The characteristic business activity of a given locality may be slackened and the demand for money quiet, but in the metropolitan centre of the world's financial system money is always wanted somewhere.

NATURAL SELECTION AMONG BANKS

At an earlier stage of the argument (*ante*, p. 302) we noticed the working of Natural Selection among the banks,

[1] Palgrave, *Dictionary of Political Economy*, Art. " Credit " (Cheque).
[2] Seager, *Introduction to Economics*, p. 327.

RISE OF THE JOINT-STOCK BANKS 321

weeding out those—mainly private institutions—which were least capable of adaptation to their new environment. It will be necessary to consider both the process, and its results upon the evolution of banking and the Money Market generally, in somewhat extended detail. But inasmuch as the movement is not confined to any single one of the three periods of the organic development of the Money Market, it will be desirable to defer its examination until we have reviewed (with the panics as a background) the general Money Market conditions subsisting between Waterloo and the Overend-Gurney crisis. When we have reached that epoch—the turning point of nineteenth-century Money Market history—we shall be better equipped for the analysis and comprehension of the real significance of Natural Selection, and the Survival of the Fittest, in their operation as relentless lethal factors of financial evolution.

CHAPTER XI

THE PANIC OF 1825 AND THE " PRESSURE " OF 1836–1839

WHEN the modern Money Market, with some approximation to its present form, presents itself after Waterloo, the glamour of age, experience, and financial predominance had already gathered around the Bank of England. It had grappled with more than one crisis. It had been the rallying point of the money-interests in many a storm. Even its quasi-disciplinary position—earlier evidenced rather in the form of resentment—(p. 232) is demonstrated by Mr. Whitmore's evidence before the Bullion Committee in 1810. Mr. Whitmore, who was Governor of the Bank at the time, told the Committee[1] that he well remembered the Bank limiting a certain sum of discount to be made to each commercial house applying for it. Dorrien was asked by the 1819 Committee if an unusual demand for discount, from a given house, at a time when the exchanges were unfavourable to this country, would be considered in the light of the last-named factor of the problem. He said it would :—

" Is that because such a state of exchange might affect the credit of the house ? "

" No, with reference to the good of the country at large."

As banker to the Government, but in no sense as a Government-bank, Threadneedle Street had been an inexhaustible source of financial aid throughout the Napoleonic wars. During that period, said Harman to the 1832 Committee, " the Bank was the right hand of the State." Its reserve had come to be considered practically as the National

[1] Minutes, p. 93.

Reserve. Moreover—and this is far more important—it had accumulated no small portion of the famous " psychological reserve " which was destined to be of such infinite value to Bank and country in a greater crisis than any that the Napoleonic nightmare ever precipitated. In a word, the Bank enjoyed the fame of solidity, antiquity, and success. When a country bank has conducted a note circulation through the storms of fifty years the fact, said Stuckey, has a moral effect upon its standing.[1] The Bank of England at the date of Waterloo, had conducted a note circulation through the storms of over a hundred years. There was no man living who could remember England without the Bank. " To the discretion, experience, and integrity of the Directors of the Bank," said the Bullion Committee, five years before Waterloo,

" your Committee believe that Parliament may safely intrust the charge of effecting that which Parliament may in its wisdom determine upon as necessary to be effected : and that the directors of that great institution, far from making themselves a party with those who have a temporary interest in spreading alarm, will take a much longer view of the permanent interests of the Bank, as indissolubly blended with those of the public."[2]

Although the synthesis of the money market factors was as yet in its primal stage, that with which they were destined to harmonise was already secure in public estimation. Contemporary appreciation of the unique standing of the Bank was apparent everywhere. The foundations of the " monarchical form " of the Money Market were already laid. Grenfell's observation that no Chancellor of the Exchequer was, or could be, a match for the Bank of England in financial negotiations, affords us a glimpse at current opinion of the business capacity of the Bank management. Vansittart, the Governor of the Bank (1818), is " one of the most intelligent men " in financial matters that Lord Liverpool has ever known.[3] Of course, these sentiments were not universal, as the Parliamentary debates amply

[1] Stuckey, 1841 Committee, Q. 556.
[2] Bullion Committee, Report, p. 75.
[3] Yonge, *Life of Lord Liverpool*, II. 333.

attested. Ricardo, again, harboured extreme hostility to the Bank of England. In a letter to Malthus in 1815, he says, " I always enjoy an attack upon the Bank, and if I had sufficient courage, I would be a party to it." Critics of the Waterloo period argued that the " Ministery " would not effectively deal with existing abuses because " the monopoly [of finance] facilitate the raising of whatever loans they want." When Stanhope introduced his Bill to make bank-notes legal tender, Tierney declared that " its advocates were two of the most suspicious characters in the world—a Chancellor of the Exchequer and a Bank director " (Baring).[1] When, in the interval between Waterloo and the first Reform Bill, the tightening grip of the Bank made itself felt in all directions (in spite of increasing competition) downright antagonism appeared, and the Bank's rivals, as we shall see, made common cause against it. There is probably something to be said for the view that the Bank of England occupied, in the period between Waterloo and Reform, a position which was afterwards menaced to some slight extent by the advent and the jealousy against stock banks, but steadily consolidated between 1857 and the Baring crisis.

THE PANIC OF 1825

The need of a synthesis was not long in making itself felt. The minor crisis[2] of 1822 was not, indeed, very wide

[1] Spencer Walpole, *Life of Perceval*, II. 211.

[2] " CRISIS " AND " PANIC "

Although the words " crisis " and " panic " are freely used as synonyms —Gilbart has a third term, "pressure"—they really allude to two entirely different things. A crisis is the penalty which is paid for a general error in prediction, or, at least, in expectation. It is a state of things which tends to produce a panic, but the latter is not the invariable and inevitable consequence of the former. Panic is the acute stage of crisis. Every panic involves the existence of a crisis, but the converse proposition that every crisis produces a panic would certainly not be true in our time, whatever may have been the case in 1825, 1847, 1857, and 1866. Since 1866 we have had five periods of crisis—1873, 1878, 1890, 1907, and 1914—but not one of them has developed into panic. " Panic is an ebb in credit, and in proportion as the admixture of credit in currency is large, is the disaster great." (Davenport, *Economics of Enterprise*, p. 283). Probably the best distinction ever drawn between panic and crisis was that of Mr. Hammond Chubb, who said that " a crisis is caused by an insufficiency of capital for carrying on the undertakings which have been set

in its range. Down to that year country bank-notes under £5 were prohibited after the resumption of cash payments by the Bank of England. In 1822, however, Parliament passed an Act permitting country banks to issue these notes until the expiration of the Bank Charter in 1833. The almost immediate result was that many country banks were tempted into over-issue, and brought catastrophe upon themselves. The author of the *Bank of England* (1865) insists that this caused a gold panic, involving losses of £30,000,000. The Bank of England protested strongly against the action of Parliament, because it had defeated the Bank's own purpose of furnishing the gold for paying off small country notes, and had, in effect, postponed that consummation apparently until 1833, though in fact only till 1829. The conversion and reduction of the Navy 5 per cents. (into 4 per cents., and the old 4 per cents. into $3\frac{1}{2}$ per cents.) in 1822 curtailed incomes and tempted investors, as the Governor of the Bank of England said at the time, " to entertain any proposition, however absurd, any project, however wild and abortive," and produced the panic of 1826. By the beginning of 1825 the public was as

---

on foot ; a panic is the unreasoning fear of those who find themselves likely to be affected by such a condition of things."

"A panic," said Professor Sumner, " is properly psychological. It is a wave of emotion, apprehension, alarm. It is more or less irrational. It is superinduced upon the crisis, which is real and inevitable, but it exaggerates, conjures up possibilities, takes away courage and energy. It is not possible to preach down a crisis ; it is a fact, and is there ; it must run its course, and be accounted for with all there is in it. The soberest man appreciates the facts the best. It is useless to preach confidence to him in the face of the facts which infuse suspicion and warning. A panic can be partly overcome by judicious reflection, by realisation of the truth, and by measurement of facts." The condition of *mental* disturbance which is part of every panic cannot be regulated by the will, nor kept within bounds by the statute law. (Van Antwerp, *Stock Exchange from Within*, p. 214.) The panic marks a lack of confidence quite as much as a lack of money. " Panics do not destroy capital," said Mill, in 1867. " They merely reveal the extent to which it has been previously destroyed by its betrayal into hopelessly unproductive works." (Address to Manchester Statistical Society, December 11, 1867.) The description in the present essay of the crises and panics of the nineteenth century makes no pretence to be exhaustive. It is believed, however, that the unceasing growth of the prestige and predominance of the Bank of England, and the ultimate evolution of a completely centralised financial power, can be better described with the panics and crises as a background than by their treatment as a separate department of the subject.

mad as in the Bubble days. *The Times* and *Morning Chronicle* of January 23 and 24, 1825, contained the prospectuses of thirty-five new companies.¹ In other directions there were evidences of fast-increasing optimism. Money was plentiful. It was admitted that the bankers " had been induced . . . to lay out their funds in discounting bills of unusually long dates."² Bills of twelve and eighteen months were not uncommon. It " seemed mathematically demonstrable that wealth was easily attainable when money could be borrowed from one set of persons at 4 per cent. and invested with another set of persons at 10 or even 20 per cent. interest."³ By the end of 1825 there had been promoted 624 companies, with a total capitalisation of £372,173,100.⁴ It was believed that there were fortunes everywhere to be had for the mere trouble of picking them up. " Whether or not warming-pans and skates were actually exported to the Tropics, it is certain that Scotch dairy-women emigrated to Buenos Ayres for the purpose of milking wild cows and churning butter for people who preferred oil."⁵ These bubbles, said one of the members for the City, " had been the creation of a few scheming attorneys, and idle and needy speculators, not of the real merchants of London."

THE ADVENT OF THE NEW NATIONALITIES

Simultaneously with these untoward manifestations, new nationalities—like new companies—were arising in all directions. The borrowers in London included Naples (5 per cent. bonds at 92½), Prussia (5 per cent. at 72), Greece (5 per cent. at 56½; Ricardo handled the issue), Spain (5 per cent. at 56, followed by another 5 per cent.

---

¹ Very few of these prospectuses, however, occupied more than six to eight inches single column of *The Times*. The double column and the half-page prospectuses were then unknown. Moreover, the advertisements appeared for a week at a " stretch "—which shows that the investor's mind ninety years ago moved rather more sluggishly than it does in modern " booms."

² *Annual Register*, 1825, p. 123.

³ Spencer Walpole, *History of England*, Vol. II. p. 123.

⁴ Henry English, *Complete View of Joint-Stock Companies formed During the Years* 1824 *and* 1825.

⁵ *Political History of England*, Vol. XI. p. 205.

issue at 30¼), a "malarial swamp," known as Poyais, and Buenos Ayres (6 per cent. at 85 issued by Barings). A Peruvian 6 per cent. loan was so attractive that the bonds were sold by auction, as high as 90, from the benches of the Royal Exchange.[1] In the period which separated 1818 from 1832, about £40,000,000 in foreign loans was issued on the London market. Of the twenty-six Foreign Government loans aggregating about £52,394,000 issued 1823 and 1826, no less than sixteen were in default within a few years. The Stock Exchange had not begun to use its power as a correctional tribunal in matters of international financial ethics. The absence of adequate means of analysing claims to credit on the part of foreign borrowers led directly to disaster.

When at last the inevitable trouble eventuated Nathan Meyer Rothschild (who had insisted upon fixed rates of interest in pounds sterling, not subject to the waywardness of the Exchanges[2]) employed his immense resources in the support of the slumping market, and placed his unique experience at the disposal of the Government. But there were but few of those strong holders whom a developed and disciplined finance has brought into being. The insurance companies did not wield a tithe of their present power, the investment trust companies had yet to be born, the banks were easily terrified, and the cool-headed private investor who nowadays will " sit tight " constituted but a very small proportion of a moneyed public not yet fully educated. Originally even the Bank of England itself had undoubtedly encouraged the speculative fever, by increasing its issues and by undue liberality in advances. In May, 1825 it suddenly reversed its policy, and endeavoured to contract its issues and advances. By itself, however, the Bank was not strong enough. In spite of a certain improvement in financial organisation, there was no such check, as there is now, in the shape of a *permanent* and firmly consolidated community of opinion and action among the banks and

---

[1] *City Men and City Manners*, p. 24.
[2] He was following the example of the mediæval lenders who stipulated for repayment in coin of a certain fineness.

328 EVOLUTION OF THE MONEY MARKET

issuing houses themselves. Instead of the coolness of judgment and deliberation there was an extremity of nervous tension. It was optimistic in one direction, where the note issues of the Bank of England and the country banks were increased by nearly £8,000,000 between 1823 and 1825, only to be suddenly contracted afterwards. It was pessimistic in the other, so that the sight of a sick woman sitting on the steps of a bank brought a crowd together, and its whispered conjectures about the ailing female precipitated an immediate run upon the institution whose portals were her temporary refuge.[1] Multitudes thronged Lombard Street, clamouring for their money. It was the unusual demand for gold exports and the difficulties of Sir Peter Pole and Co. which ultimately brought panic and compelled half-reluctant community of action by the otherwise incoherent, unorganised and disunited financial forces.

TENTATIVE AND TEMPORARY COHESION

The isolated factors rushed together when the storm burst; but they would not be warned before, and they soon fell a-wrangling after. When Mr. Richards (the Deputy-Governor of the Bank of England) was before the Committee of the House of Commons, he recalled how two members of that committee and the City bankers had consulted him at his own house with regard to the difficulties of " a certain banking institution." He said that arrangements had been made to take care of the clearing on that particular evening (Saturday, November 26) so that a panic should not be precipitated. He assured his visitors that " upon anything like a fair statement the Bank would not let this concern fall through." On the Sunday morning there was another meeting, to which certain eminent merchants—friends of the house—were invited. After hearing all the facts, the Bank directors authorised the statement that assistance would not be wanting. It was agreed that £300,000 should be provided the next morning, for which the Bank was to receive, and

[1] Morier Evans's *History of the Commercial Crisis*, 2 n.

did receive, a number of bills of exchange and notes of hand, as well as an overriding mortgage on the property of the chief partner in the threatened institution—Sir Peter Pole and Co. Simultaneously, there was a run upon the country bankers, especially in Devon and Cornwall. At Exeter it was the consequence of a placard posted in the streets calling on people to realise their " dirty paper " and stick to gold. On Sunday, while friends of the threatened London institution were in consultation, the partners in the London banking houses were being fetched out of church to answer appeals from the country. All day long gold was leaving London in post-chaises of four horses to help the country bankers.

" WITHIN TWENTY-FOUR HOURS OF BARTER "

Sir Peter Pole and Co. suspended on December 5. When it became known that the accounts of forty-four country banks were domiciled with them the concussion was tremendous. Williams, Burgess and Co. went down at the same time, though it was confidently stated that their assets were equal to 20s. in the £ of their liabilities. The height of the crisis extended from Monday, December 12, to Saturday, December 17. The Usury Laws, by limiting the rate of interest outside the Bank of England to 5 per cent., shut out the possibility of assistance by private capital, which would probably have adventured itself at rates from 7 to 10 per cent. But one expedient, destined to be again and again reverted to, and ultimately to become classic, was the seeking of assistance to the extent of £2,000,000 from the Bank of France. The policy of restriction, pursued until Wednesday night, did incalculable injury. The Bank had been warned, years before, of its danger. " The restoration of peace," said the Bullion Committee (Report, p. 77) " by opening new fields of commercial enterprise, would multiply instead of abridging the demands upon the Bank for discount, and would render it peculiarly distressing to the commercial world if the Bank were suddenly and materially to restrict their issues." Recurring and disastrous experience has long taught us the fatuity of restriction. " Immediately that no one can get credit to pay with, there is a frightened scramble to enforce payment in money, to get money to pay with, to hoard money against possible necessities. The attempt of the banks to hold fast to their reserves is the very force which is prompting the taking of them away."[1] The Bank's adoption of the policy of expansion, and the resultant issue of £5,000,000 of notes, snatched the country from the brink of the cataclysm which it already overhung. A small parcel of £1 notes (less than £500,000) discovered by the Bank of England, and added to the other supplies, was rapidly distributed among the country bankers and materially assisted in allaying the panic. By December 24 the trouble was at an end. Altogether seventy-nine banks suspended payment, though many of them paid 20s. in the £ and ultimately resumed business. Constable was unable to raise money even upon the MSS. of the Waverley Novels. Scott himself was one of the victims—perhaps one of the hardest hit of all—who suffered in the collapse of 1825. " Skene, this is the hand of a beggar," said he, as he greeted a friend. Francis says the directors of the Bank of England were unable at one time to cash a batch of notes to the value of £16,000 presented by a City banker. Bagehot described the panic as so tremendous that its results were well remembered after nearly fifty years. " We were within twenty-four hours of barter," said Lord G. Bentinck in the House of Commons.[2] Undoubtedly the panic was terrible, both in scope and intensity. The author of the *Bank of England*[3] puts the loss at £45,000,000. Exchequer Bills and Bank Stock were at one time unsaleable.[4] " Persons of undoubted wealth and capital were walking about the streets of London not knowing whether they should be able to meet their engagements for the next day."[5] Mr. Richards (the Deputy-Governor of the Bank) said, with, perhaps, unconscious pathos, that after the storm was over " those who had been busied in that terrible

[1] Davenport, *Economies of Enterprise*, p. 285
[2] *Annual Register*, 1847, p. 101. [3] p. 52.
[4] Huskisson, House of Commons Debate, December 12 and 13.
[5] Macleod, *Dictionary of Political Economy*, Art. "Crisis."

scene could recollect that they had families who had some claim upon their attention. It happened to me," he added, " not to see my children for that week."

THE RÔLE OF THE BANK

Certainly when the Bank of England at length abandoned its restrictive policy it flung itself into the breach with characteristic intrepidity. " At the time of this panic," said Nathan Meyer Rothschild, " I think there was a great deal of credit due to the Governor of the Bank." The Governor said that during the crisis " we lent by every possible means and in modes we had never adopted before. We took in stock as security, we purchased Exchequer bills, we made advances on Exchequer bills, we not only discounted[1] outright, but we made advances on deposit of bills of exchange[2] to an immense amount—in short, by every possible means consistent with the safety of the Bank, and we were not, upon some occasions, over nice ; seeing the dreadful state in which the public were, we rendered every assistance in our power." The Deputy-Governor declared that " the Bank had taken a firm and deliberate resolution to make common cause with the country " ; and the country clearly realised the necessity of reciprocity by making common cause with the Bank. The meetings " in most of the trading towns " and the resolutions passed " for the support of commercial credit "[3] evidence a state of affairs very different from the selfish isolation of the mediæval trade bodies. At Bradford the banking firm of Charles, Henry, and Alfred Harris and Co. (which ultimately became the Bradford Old Bank) received

[1] All through the war and during the panic of 1825, the London bankers discounted largely with the Bank of England. Since then, they have ceased to do so, and their endorsements are unknown in the Money Market.

[2] Gurney used to say he had seen the day when he could not get money on Exchequer bills, but he never yet saw the day when he could not get it on bills of exchange. (Committee on Banks of Issue, 1841, Q. 2157.) Vincent Stuckey took the other view, alleging that except on two days of his life, he could always get money more easily on Government securities than on bills of exchange. Comparisons similarly " odious," but rather more to the disadvantage of a Government security, were made after the Overend-Gurney crash. Since then the disastrous fall in Consols has not helped to increase their popularity as a bankers' holding.

[3] *Annual Register*, 1825, p. 124

as fine a compliment as was ever bestowed upon a banking institution. The principal inhabitants issued a placard in which they not only expressed their confidence in the Bank but offered to guarantee its solvency. " We, the undersigned, are desirous to express our entire confidence in the perfect stability of the Bank of C., H., and A. Harris, of this town, and are not only ready to accept in payment any of their notes, but offer our united guarantee for the safety and respectability of the firm." At the Mansion House meeting in London it was unanimously resolved that those present would " refrain from any interference with the measures of the directors of the Bank, who, the meeting was satisfied, will do their duty towards the public."

A BOARD OF " STAID OLD MERCHANTS "

The country certainly could have had no more experienced coadjutors than the Bank board. They possessed a unique knowledge of the " inside " of contemporary finance. The twenty-four directors of the Bank of England are, and always have been, selected from the mercantile community of London, virtually at the choice of the existing board, whose recommendations are, practically without exception, adopted by the proprietors. Down to a period long after the 1825 crisis it was possible to say with truth that the Bank Board was composed of " staid old merchants," whose ranks, in accordance with long-established custom, could never be recruited from bankers. This mercantile element was largely made up of a special class, the representatives of the great accepting houses. The London merchant, at a time when the word " merchant " retained its ancient primary significance, lent his credit, in the shape of his " acceptance," in return for an agreed commission, to importers less able to bear the scrutiny of the market. In that way not only did he make handsome profits, but he aided and stimulated the tendency of London to become the world's financial centre. He was in all the better position to assist in clustering cosmopolitan finance around London and to consolidate the position of London itself, when he, himself, sat at the board table of the world's greatest bank. Conversely, knowing all the secrets of European finance, he could serve the Bank well, and help to keep it out of danger.

RENEWAL OF JEALOUSIES

Unhappily, the synthesis which had manifested itself in the presence of the common peril was only temporary. The counteracting forces pulled it apart again as soon as the peril died away. The bankers became envious of Threadneedle Street. We have already seen that the Act of 1826 (7 Geo. IV. c. 46) broke the Bank of England's monopoly of *corporate* note issue by permitting the establishment of other joint-stock banks, provided (*a*) they were outside a sixty-five-mile radius with London as the centre, and (*b*) had no establishment in London. By the same statute the Bank of England was empowered to establish country branches (*ante*, p. 300 and note). These branches revived the jealousy of the other bankers as soon as the peril of the 1825 crisis was beginning to be forgotten, or its terrors at all events lenified by time. The new branches gave great dissatisfaction to the country bankers. These branches refused to take the notes of any other bank, unless it had opened an account and lodged a sum to meet them. The Bank declined to discount any bill drawn or endorsed by a bank of issue, either joint-stock or private.[1] It doubtless pressed the remains of its monopoly for all they were worth. Perhaps it is not surprising, therefore, to find common cause made against it by the other banks. Their proprietors certainly had not the least idea of the real meaning and tendency of the phenomena which excited their jealousy and apprehension. On December 7, 1826, the private bankers met at the London Tavern in Bishopsgate Street, and passed several resolutions, among which were these :—

" That the late measures of the Bank of England in the establishment of branch banks have the evident tendency to

[1] Gilbart, evidence before 1841 Committee on Banks of Issue, Q. 1309.

subvert the general banking system that has so long existed throughout the country, and which has grown up with, and been adapted to, the wants and conveniences of the public."

" That it can be distinctly proved that the prosperity of trade, the support of agriculture, the increase of general improvement, and the productiveness of the national revenue are intimately connected with the existing system of banking."

" That the country bankers would not complain of rival establishments founded upon equal terms ; but they do complain of being required to compete with a great company, possessing a monopoly and exclusive privileges."

" That should this great corporation, conducted by directors who are not personally responsible, succeed, by means of these exclusive advantages, in their apparent object of supplanting the existing banking establishments, they will thereby be rendered masters of the circulation of the country, which they will be able to contract or expand according to their own will, and thus be armed with a tremendous power and influence dangerous to the stability of property and independence of the country."

NO " SYSTEM " AT ALL

The " general banking system " that had " so long existed " was not a system at all. The banks were a mere loose agglomeration of isolated institutions, united only against an inexorable synthesising movement. In Chapter IX the almost total absence of banking principles has already been demonstrated and discussed. Bankers' jealousy of the approach of standardisation and centralisation, if it had been successful, would have destroyed all chance of the financial world-supremacy of London. They did not know—how could they ?—that waste diminishes as correlation increases and improves—that strength to resist disaster is enhanced by community of action, and that the financial predominance of London, in an immeasurably busier world, must come to depend upon the intimate co-ordination of the financial functions. To them, the Bank was a monster of monopoly, capable of any excesses in its greed for profit. These are strong expressions. But it is a fact that some of the country bankers, at all events, believed the Bank to be bent upon its own aggrandisement

PANIC OF 1825—" PRESSURE " OF 1836

at any cost and by any means. In the memorial presented to Earl Grey and Lord Althorp in 1833 (with reference to the pending legislation, the result of which has been stated, *ante*, p. 300) by the country bankers there was a lurid suggestion of the possibility of Bank of England directors speculating in indigo, stimulating the market in London by financing the dealings from Threadneedle Street, while at the same time depressing business in cottons by contracting discounts at the Manchester branch—and making a big profit out of the double operation! Contemporary political pamphleteers declared that the Bank was already imperium in imperio. According to one apprehensive critic (in 1834) the Bank of England and the East India Co. " were intended to be at all times trading corporations, but . . . may be now more properly viewed as petty States, acknowledging a feudatory dependence to the supreme power."[1] The critic would have been still more perturbed if he had known that the financial power was not only to become a " petty state," but was actually destined in coming years to receive its own financial ambassadors from British Dominions and from foreign governments. Bank and Ministry, he argued, were conspirators, each anxious to further the other's evil designs, in return for reciprocal respect of its own interests :—

" There has ever existed a reciprocal understanding, on the score of mutual interest, between the Bank Parlour and the Treasury, that for certain advances, or other important obligations on the part of the establishment, they should be permitted to retain a power ever most disastrously exercised. The Government and the Bank have become partners, as it were, and each peculiarly alive and sensitive to the wants and embarrassments of the other."[2]

Doubtless the spread of these sentiments, before they found such ornate expression, may have inspired the cry " To stop the Duke, go for gold ! " which was raised when the Reform Bill was rejected by the Lords in May, 1832, and there was a momentary prospect that the Duke

---

[1] *Legitimate Consequences of Reform,* p. 71.   [2] *Ibid.,* p. 75.

of Wellington might form a government in place of Lord Grey's ministry which had resigned. The Bank's stock of specie was reduced to £4,919,000 in consequence of the advice contained in the inflammatory placards posted throughout the metropolis.

AN " ADUMBRATION " OF BETTER THINGS

Yet the predominance of the Bank was the single factor of the situation which had in it the potentialities of financial salvation. Here and there, in spite of many misunderstandings, the dim beginnings of sustained intimacy and confidence can be discerned. Ever and anon (even when the loom of crisis is absent from the environment) there is a momentary recognition of the existence of a common cause. When Remington and Co. were the subject of rumours in December, 1828, five of the principal bankers in London investigated the position. They were so well satisfied that each of them advanced £20,000 on such securities as they found the bank to possess. In addition, they made a declaration of their entire conviction of the solvency of the house. Such a pronouncement had the effect of inducing the return to the firm of many accounts which had been withdrawn. Unhappily, the perfunctory character of the investigation has to be inferred from the fact that when, within a few weeks, the collapse took place, it appeared that the investigators had been content with the production of sealed packets of securities endorsed with the names of the stocks which they were alleged to contain. It had never occurred to them to see if the contents were actually there ! Again, in 1831 a Government proposal for a 10s. per cent. tax on all transfers of funded property had to be abandoned because of the united opposition of the money interest. Once more, in an endeavour to lessen the shock of the terrible " slump "—in foreign stocks— of 1835, the principal holders of foreign securities formed themselves into a committee to purchase all stock which stood at a lower price than 40 per cent. Although this scheme was found inadequate to meet the necessities of the case, it is a valuable evidence of the drift of opinion

PANIC OF 1825—"PRESSURE" OF 1836

in the direction of concentrated self-protective action. Censorious as they were, the Bank of England's rivals gave it occasional words of praise. In 1832 George Carr Glyn told the Bank Committee that the London bankers were in almost hourly intercourse with the Bank of England manipulating their balances, and that they received every facility from the central institution in doing so. These balances were small enough in all conscience, in comparison with what they were destined to become. At that time, and onwards to the year 1877 (*post*, p. 505) the bankers' balances always appeared as a separate item in the Bank statement. For instance, here is the statement of the liabilities and assets of the Bank of England on March 6, 1832 :—

	£	£		£	£
Circulation:—			*Public Securities:*—		
London	15,224,000		Advances on Exchequer Bills: Deficiency	2,808,000	
Country	2,784,000		Other Exchequer Bills	744,000	
		18,008,000	Exchequer Bills purchased	2,700,000	
Deposits, Public, viz.:—			Stock and Annuities	11,672,000	
Exchequer account	110,000				17,924,000
For payment of Dividends	497,000		*Private Securities:*—		
Savings Banks	74,000		Bills discounted:		
West India Compensation	—		London	1,303,000	
Other public accounts	1,791,000		Country	1,634,000	
		2,472,000			2,937,000
Deposits, Private, viz.:—			East India Bonds	—	
London Bankers	883,000		City Bonds	727,000	
East India Company	876,000		Mortgage	1,452,000	
Loans from ditto	—		*Advances:*—		
Bank of Ireland and Royal Bank of Scotland	48,000		Bills of Exchequer	24,000	
Other deposits	3,083,000		Exchequer Bills, Stock, etc.	9,000	
Deposits at branches	591,000				2,212,000
		5,481,000			23,073,000
			Bullion		5,317,000
		£25,961,000			£28,390,000

The fact of the appearance of these bankers' balances is extremely important, as we shall ultimately discover when we come to scrutinise the last flicker of internecine rivalry among the banks (*post*, p. 503 ff.).

THE "PRESSURE" OF 1836–1837–1839

Before long, however, the shadow of another crisis was falling across the pathway of the unorganised banking community. The Act of 1833 led to an enormous increase in the number of provincial joint-stock banks. Most of them issued notes (it was before the passing of the Bank Charter Act) and all of them (including those in London) added to the volume of outstanding paper currency, in the shape of bills. In 1834, Lord Wharncliffe warned the Ministry against the " prodigious " extension of joint-stock banks, and the insufficiency of their capital. Speculation was again getting out of hand, particularly with regard to the latest new market toy—railways. Hosts of new companies were floated. They sprang up in Liverpool and Manchester like mushrooms. Speculation was stimulated to an unwholesome extent, until the exchanges became depressed, and the resultant drain of gold from the Bank of England set in. Huge blocks of American bills and securities were sold on this side, and the proceeds remitted in specie across the Atlantic for the purpose of forming the metallic basis of the New National Bank of the United States. The Bank of England contracted its note circulation and paid away gold. The early menace of disaster had been grappled by the Bank. The Government was " pressing the Bank to support the commercial interests."[1] When the manager of the Northern and Central Bank, which had 1200 partners, on November 28, 1836, helped to precipitate a run by leaving £108,000 in his cab, an application to the Bank of England for assistance was made, and there was an immediate advance of £100,000 with the promise of a further £400,000 at a later date. But assistance in the first instance was given only on the condition that all the branches except that of Liverpool should be wound up. Further support was granted subject to the stipulation that the bank should discontinue business after February 18, 1837. Investigation showed an appalling state of affairs ; but the Bank of England persisted in its task, having first secured itself by entering judgment for £1,000,000, so as to be able to enforce its claims upon the shareholders. Threadneedle Street ultimately provided a total of £1,370,000. Esdailes, the London bankers, received timely aid on similar terms, and in January, 1837, a London banking house was

[1] *Journal of Thomas Raikes*, Vol. III. p. 157.

PANIC OF 1825—" PRESSURE " OF 1836

assisted on the strength of a guarantee given to the Bank by the other London bankers—a transaction which dimly foreshadows the famous Baring episode some fifty-three years later. All the advances to banking interests were repaid with one trifling exception. But the country banks, as yet unschooled in the principle that the banking fabric is one and indivisible, went on inflating the currency for their own profit, and in that way invited disaster. They justified McCulloch's declaration that " the vicious part of our currency is, that it is not supplied by one but by hundreds of issuers, all actuated by conflicting views and interests."[1] On March 26, 1836, their issues were £3,094,025. By the end of December they had swollen to £4,258,197. On the top of all this came the report of the 1836 Secret Committee on joint-stock banks, " marked by a decided hostility of tone."[2] It " ascribed to them scarcely a single excellence."

In the presence of so many disquieting factors, the Bank finally resolved upon sterner measures with a much more extended scope. Its secret hint to its Liverpool agent, cautioning him against handling the paper of certain American houses strongly suspected of dealing heavily in accommodation bills, somehow became a matter of general knowledge. The three houses in question—Wildes, Wiggins, and Wilson, colloquially known as the " three W's," had £5,500,000 of acceptances in circulation at the beginning of the year 1837.[3] By " some unaccountable indiscretion " the Bank's hint to its Liverpool agent became the subject of public gossip, and the " three W's " suspended payment in March as a consequence of the withdrawal of accommodation and the public knowledge of the fact. These houses, when wound up, paid good dividends. Macleod declares that the Bank of England at this time advanced £6,000,000 in the north of England to check the development of trouble. Still, the Bank's discrimination and its policy of refusing to discount any bill drawn or endorsed by a bank of issue (whether joint-stock or private)

---
[1] Quoted by Lord Overstone, *Tracts*, p. 148.
[2] Gilbart, *Logic of Banking*, p. 100.
[3] *Annual Register*, 1837, p. 183.

hit the joint-stock banks which had bought American paper, and sent it out again with their own endorsements.[1] The complications were threatening and extensive. " Even the House of Baring are in a frightful dilemma: Lord Ashburton has been obliged to support them with £800,000 and the Bank is called upon by them for fresh advances. They are still under acceptance for a million and a half of American paper."[2] The sequelæ of this trouble did not finally pass away, however, until the end of 1839. Apparently there was, indeed, some recrudescence of peril, for Samuel Jones Loyd, in 1847, alluded to the " threatened insolvency " of a bank in 1839.[3]

BORROWING FROM THE BANK OF FRANCE

When the stock of bullion had declined to £2,522,000, the Bank had been compelled to adopt an expedient which was destined to become historic in the case of the Baring crisis—namely, that of borrowing £2,500,000 from the Bank of France, and £900,000 from Hamburg. The " deal " was done through Barings, who, in spite of their heavy commitments already mentioned, were apparently quite equal to this gigantic undertaking. " There are in Europe," said the Duc de Richelieu in 1819, " six Great Powers—England, France, Russia, Austria, Prussia and Baring Brothers." In 1839 fifteen of the principal banking houses in Paris agreed to accept bills drawn by Baring Brothers, for the account of the Bank of England, to the extent of the loan, in return for a commission of ½ per cent. The bills were to be discounted by the Bank of France, while the Bank of England was to deposit English securities in the hands of the French institution. The transaction excited considerable contemporary comment, as tending —so it was said—" to lower the character of the important institution with which it had originated." More to the point, however, was the criticism that such a transaction

[1] Macleod, *Dictionary of Political Economy*, Art. "Banking in England."
[2] *Journal of Thomas Raikes*, Vol. III. p. 157.
[3] Reply to the petition of merchants against the Bank Charter Act, *Tracts*, p. 287.

pointed to the dying down of international rivalry, and favoured the continuance of peace. The interdependence of the financial system was indeed beginning to be obvious. The compiler of the *Annual Register* for 1837 could see even cosmopolitan finance plainly enough. He said (p. 181) that " the least derangement in the commercial affairs of the one nation [the U.S A.] is immediately and seriously felt by the other " (Great Britain). The ideas about lowering the dignity of the Bank seem, however, to have proved, for a time at least, the stronger, as became clearly obvious not so long afterwards.

The transaction evidently rankled in the minds of some of those who had been concerned in it. They seem to have supposed that there was something premature or undesirable about it. So it was that when, in 1846, the positions of the two great central banks were reversed, and the suggestion was made that the Bank of England should help the Bank of France, an explanation, obviously inspired from influential sources, was inserted in the City article of *The Times* (December 5). It was argued that, as a matter of fact, the Bank of France had had very little to do with the transaction. At best, the Bank of France was only in the ultimate background, and but a very small proportion of the bills " found their way into that establishment." It was very broadly hinted, therefore, that any requests from the Bank of France for assistance would cause a decided increase in discount rates, " and thus another is added to the numerous reasons which already exist to call for the exercise of caution." The expression of these views has been repeated in various City circles since the Bank borrowed money from the Bank of France at the time of the Baring crisis. It has been said that the bankers have no business ever to avail themselves of foreign support. How, it is asked, can our banking system maintain itself if, in difficult times, it has to go abroad for aid ? The answer is that while sixty years ago that argument might have held good, it is no longer valid in our own time, because there is now a cosmopolitan financial fraternity such as did not exist in 1840. The internal, or national, interests of the great banks are being unceasingly extended on a cosmopolitan basis.

Summing up the history of the " pressure " of 1837–1839, when writing, twenty years after, the solitary volume ever published of his *Dictionary of Political Economy*, Macleod stated that in 1838 the Bank " followed for a second time the principles laid down by the Bullion Report, and there can be no doubt averted a calamity only second in magnitude to the catastrophe of 1825." Macleod did not number the 1836–1837 and 1839 episodes among the great crises. They were not, he said, " important from a scientific point of view." If Macleod could scrutinise them once more, as part of a sequence whereof the later crises form a part, he might express a different judgment. Certainly he would see, as we shall, how the violence of the recurring crises was steadily diminished as cohesion and co-ordination took the place of isolation and selfishness ; and how at last the tendency to recurrence was itself mastered, and the decades rolled on with none of the sinister financial phenomena that marked their path in the days of disunion and indiscipline.

CHAPTER XII

THE BANK CHARTER ACT AND THE 1847 PANIC

ROUSED into reflection by the recent menace of a common peril, the joint-stock banks took a step towards unity. An Association of Joint-Stock Banks was formed in 1838, and all such establishments in England, Wales, and Ireland were invited to be represented at a meeting in London. The meeting appointed a committee to " communicate with the Government and to promote the passing of such laws as would be beneficial to joint-stock banks." Meanwhile the Bank of England steadily pursued its policy of disciplinary discrimination and supervisory co-ordination up to the limits of its power. Its *financial* predominance was for a time beyond challenge, however much its erstwhile monopoly might be encroached upon. Even the encroachment upon its monopoly was to be money in its pocket. It is a financial paradox that while the Act of 1833 brought into existence a small army of capable rivals of the Bank of England, it was destined also to make every one of them into a useful client of the Bank. It would have seemed inconceivable in 1833 that banks which had been established in practical defiance of Threadneedle Street, should in days to come provide the Old Lady with no small part of her resources. There were always the envious voices. " The power of the currency is vested," said a hostile critic—the President of the Manchester Chamber of Commerce—" in twenty-six irresponsible individuals, for the exclusive benefit of a body of Bank proprietors." But whatever jealousy might allege, it is a fact that in the period during which this *financial* supremacy lasted, the prestige of the Bank was so firmly consolidated that when (in the 'seventies) the Bank ceased to retain the premier position as a holder of deposits, its moral predominance—as we shall see—became more pronounced than ever. In the 'forties, it had assumed a quasi-parental attitude. It had begun to welcome co-operation and to reciprocate by granting advantages. A number of the country bankers worked with Bank of England notes exclusively, having fixed amounts of credit assigned them at 3 per cent.[1] The banks in Liverpool which were established before 1844 made an arrangement with the Bank of England under which they restricted their issues to its notes, and in return the Bank gave them the privilege of always having bills under discount with it, to an agreed maximum amount, at ¾ per cent. below the minimum of the day.[2] But already the practice of the Bank of England was much stricter than that of the joint-stock banks. The 1841 Committee was told that the branches never allowed an account to be overdrawn. The inflexible refusal of interest on deposits, again, was a costly factor of the Bank's policy, deliberately adopted in its determination to "make common cause with the country." The idea put to the Committee was that if the Bank took steps to attract more money it would have to mitigate its conservative methods or it would drain funds out of circulation. Glimpses behind the scenes show an equally resolute private procedure. Largely as a consequence of their conservative policy—and also, naturally, of their kinship with Threadneedle Street—the Bank's provincial branches have always maintained a kind of suzerainty over those of the joint-stock banks. Whenever a joint-stock bank applied to the Liverpool branch of the Bank of England, Turner (the manager) always insisted[3] on having a copy of the deed of settlement and a list of the shareholders. "I myself correspond," said he, "with the Bank [of England, head office] as to whether the great mass of the shareholders are respectable parties: whether they are

---

[1] See statistics, 1841 *Report on Banks of Issue*, p. 259.
[2] Rae, 1875 Committee, Q. 5190. [3] 1838 Secret Committee, Q. 342.

THE BANK CHARTER ACT—1847 PANIC

parties who are personally known to me to be of wealth and consequence, or whether (as in some instances) they are persons of very little calibre and are very second-rate people : I give my opinion whether the account ought or ought not to be granted." The Bank's hint to Turner in the matter of the "three W's" has already been recounted. Paul Moon James, himself a private banker, acknowledged the salutary results of the Bank's policy. "The Bank of England's rules are very sound, though they are not altogether adapted to the general trade of the country, but they are always corrective, and the influence is beneficial ; there is no doubt of it."[1] Of course the Bank enjoyed many advantages. It could buy securities with its own notes, which country bankers could not do. Hence Hobhouse argued that the Bank could create capital by buying securities, though the country bankers could not.[2]

THE BANK CHARTER ACT

Between the 1837–1838–1839 "pressure" and the 1847 panic the Bank Charter Act was passed, in 1844. The later crises and panics cannot be adequately analysed without some preliminary survey of this statute. The principal points of the Bank Charter Act (7 and 8 Vict. c. 32), for our purpose, are :—

(1) The separation of the note-issue department from the rest of the machinery of the Bank. It has been truly observed that the issue department might be in Whitehall and the rest of the Bank in Threadneedle Street, so complete is the separation.

(2) The provision that, save in the case of notes under the sum of £14,000,000 (being £11,000,000 on the security of the debt due from the public and £3,000,000 on Exchequer bills and other securities), the Bank must possess bullion[3] in the

---

[1] 1841 Committee, Q. 1518.   [2] 1841 Committee, Q. 166.

[3] The provision that one-fifth of the metallic basis of the note issue may consist of *silver* bullion, is now more honoured in the breach than in the observance. The weekly account published by the Bank regularly contains a space for the particulars of "silver coin and bullion," but the space is as regularly empty. In 1897, there was a suggestion, said to have been inspired from bi-metallic sources, for taking advantage of this provision by the storage of silver bullion, but as soon as the suggestion became known, there was a perfect hurricane of opposition and it was instantly dropped.

Issue Department to the value of the notes issued. Peel selected £14,000,000 as the maximum, after ascertaining that £16,000,000 had been about the lowest note circulation in recent years.

(3) The stipulation that all persons may demand notes in exchange for gold bullion at the price of £3 17s. 9d. per ounce of standard gold.

(4) A reduction of the sum paid by the Government to the Bank for managing the National Debt to £340 per million on £600,000,000 and £300 per million beyond.

It was further provided (section 5) that if any banker who on May 6, 1844, was issuing his own notes should cease such issue,[1] Her Majesty in Council might authorise the Bank of England to increase the amount of securities in the Issue Department to a sum not exceeding two-thirds of the aggregate of notes which the banker so ceasing to issue might have been authorised to issue. The Act fixed the maximum circulation of the country banks in England and Wales at £5,153,417 for 207 private banks and £3,478,230 for 72 joint-stock banks. The present figures of 7 private banks and 4 joint-stock banks are about £307,294 and £94,425 respectively. As a result of this enormous reduction, itself the consequence of a succession of lapses and amalgamations, the Bank's potential aggregate of notes has risen to £18,450,000.

ARE THE SECURITIES EAR-MARKED ?

It is an interesting academic question whether the securities in the Issue Department are hypothecated for the benefit of the note holders. An authority of the first rank—Mr. Freshfield, solicitor to the Bank—in 1856 offered the opinion that the provisions of the Bank Charter Act are not for the benefit of the note holders, but for ascertaining the limit of issue. That is to say, in his judgment, the gold and securities are not held against the note circulation only, but against the liabilities generally. The dominant belief is, however, that the directors of the

---

[1] The licence of £30 a year was, moreover, a very effectual deterrent to the issue of notes by any new office, opened after 1844, of a provincial bank.

THE BANK CHARTER ACT—1847 PANIC

Bank, both then and now, have been, and are, of a different opinion, and that they consider the securities to be earmarked against the notes. In the words of a distinguished American authority, it has been " the common understanding, from the first, that the devotion of the resources of the Issue Department to the payment of its notes was indefeasible."[1]

PEEL WANTED A STATE BANK

Peel, it is fairly certain, " intended to pave the way for a power of issue restricted to a State Bank of the State itself."[2] He would have preferred a central bank of issue under the auspices of the Government. But he was before all things practical, and when he saw a great Bank already in existence, with a century and a half of experience and prestige, he sought no further :—

" The true policy of this country is to work, as far as it be possible, with the instruments you have ready to your hand— to avail yourself of that advantage which they possess from having been in use, from being familiar, from constituting a part of the habits and usages of society. They will probably work more smoothly than perfectly novel instruments of greater theoretical perfection . . . we think it the wisest course to select the Bank of England as the controlling and central body."[3]

Peel bore emphatic testimony to the unselfish public spirit of the Bank directors throughout the whole of the arrangements :—

" I must, in justice to the gentlemen who conducted the negotiations on the part of the Bank, declare that I never saw men influenced by more disinterested or by more public-spirited motives than they have evinced throughout our communications with them. They have reconciled their duties as managers of a great institution, bound to consult the interests of the proprietors, with an enlightened and comprehensive view of the public interest."

Peel may or may not have been right in his preference, but he was on safe ground when he laid stress on the evils of uncontrolled competition among banks of issue, which

[1] Dunbar, *Theory and History of Banking*, p. 204 n.
[2] The late John Dun, 1875 Committee, Q. 6240.   [3] Peel, *Speeches*, 357-8.

had produced crisis more than once. Certainly the centralisation of the note issues—which had become practically a monopoly up to the time of the issue of the Treasury notes in 1914—has had many critics. Sir G. C. Lewis (who was Chancellor of the Exchequer in 1857) used to say that " Peel's Act did great good except for a week once in ten years, but in that week it did so much evil as almost to counterbalance the good which it had effected before." Again and again, as the country note issues fell in, it was urged that the issue of notes was the prerogative of the State, that it should either be reserved to the State or allowed to all the banks without distinction, and that no private institution, such as the Bank of England, ought to be permitted the practical monopoly of it. It was argued by George Rae[1] that the destruction of the country issues must extend the ravages of money panics to the provinces, which had been hitherto largely free from them. The country notes rested on their own reserves of gold. Abolish them and put Bank of England notes in their place, and these latter " would be subject to the same law of fluctuation as those in circulation in the capital and elsewhere, and every movement in the bullion in the Issue Department would be as quickly felt at Leicester as at Liverpool, at Saffron Walden as in the City of London." John Dun, of the Alliance Bank, drew attention, before the 1875 Committee, to another aspect of the problem. He argued that if his bank and others had a power of issue they could extend their branches to many places where it would not pay to carry on a branch at which the cash balance would have to be held in legal tender, with resulting loss of interest.[2] He added that " over-issue is a physical

[1] 1875 Committee, Q. 5054.
[2] The Country Banks of Issue Bill, 1865, proposed to remove the restriction of six in the number of partners, instead of leaving the Act of 1844 to work out the gradual extinction of the insecure issues of private establishments. It also projected the removal of the restrictions upon banks with more than six partners issuing their notes within sixty-five miles of London. This would have struck a blow at numerous banks established within the sixty-five-mile radius, and only issuing the notes of the Bank of England. In the course of the debate upon the Bill it came out that there had been a meeting of bankers, at which it was resolved, by forty-one to twelve, that the Chancellor of the Exchequer be requested to withdraw the Bill. This, as a matter of fact, he did.

THE BANK CHARTER ACT—1847 PANIC 349

impossibility where you have the issues in the hands of respectable and solvent banks, and where the convertibility of the note is a condition of issue."[1] Current banking opinion largely confirms John Dun's view.[2] It is really the gospel of note issue and the basis of the new £1 notes.

So long as a note issue is always convertible at the will of the holder, and cannot, consequently, become a forced paper currency, it is difficult to see how any of the ancient perils and abuses could revive, even if it were made by the banks, as distinct from the Treasury. In the United States and Canada, silver and nickel coins are abundant; but gold is so seldom seen that there are many Canadians whose life experience has never included the sight of a yellow coin. After all, it comes to this—that in the earlier stages of social development man demanded a coin which was actually and intrinsically equal in value to the amount which it nominally represented. All the old currency troubles arose from attempts to override this instinct by force of law and arms, and from its instant and overwhelming revival in the presence of the slightest financial trouble. But nowadays, habituated as we are to a *non-standardised* paper currency—that is to say, cheques—there is no reason why we should not accustom ourselves to a *standardised* paper currency—to wit, notes. The argument is all the stronger if we remember that behind a cheque there is only the credit of the drawer, whereas behind the note would be the credit of a bank—one of a group of giant institutions which grows stronger every day. But after the Treasury note experiment of 1914 the extension of a *banking* note issue, outside the Bank of England, is probably a remote contingency in spite of its undoubted utility to relieve the strain on gold.

DISCRETIONARY NOTE ISSUE BY THE BANK?

Certainly the Bank Charter Act " absolutely cut off the creation of banks of issue, except by the union of existing banks, and made the future elasticity of English currency

[1] 1875 Committee, QQ. 6279, 6280.
[2] See, for instance, *Bankers' Magazine*, 1911, p. 840.

dependent upon deposits of coin or bullion with the Bank of England."[1] The Act destroyed the bank-note as an instrument of credit, making it a mere bullion certificate. It left to the bill of exchange (especially in its most important form, the cheque), to other forms of commercial paper, and to securities, the functions hitherto discharged, in part at least, by the bank-note. The bank-note currency was, in effect, solidified, while all the other factors, having vastly more important functions cast upon them, assumed a wider rôle, and therefore stood in the more peremptory necessity of regulation by scientific control. So far as England is concerned, the note issue is now, to all intents and purposes, centred in the hands of the Bank of England. Bank-notes other than those issued by the central institution are rapidly becoming mere survivals—for the 1914 Treasury notes are not a liability of the Bank of England and are not, in fact, bank-notes at all. That state of things which the Bank originally sought to establish by stratagem and conflict has come into existence as a concession to the generally-admitted necessities of the case. It is now emphatically true that a Bank of England note " is part of the currency of the country."[2] Bank-notes are indispensable, since the currency, of which they form a part, is none too large—even when they are included—for modern purposes. But their standardisation as the emission of one predominant institution or of the National Treasury itself, is in complete accord not only with the financial necessities of the age, but with the constant tendency towards centralisation.

In the light of the three suspensions of the Act (in 1847, 1857, and 1866), it has again and again been suggested that the directors might be entrusted with a discretionary power in the matter of a limited issue beyond the authorised total when, in their opinion, the market position is such as to necessitate that policy. This proposal was in 1873 embodied in a Bill of which the text is printed in the *Bankers' Magazine* for November, 1914, p. 588. Mr. Joseph Ackland

[1] Conant, *Banks of Issue*, p. 120.
[2] Jessel, M.R., in Suffell *v.* Bank of England, 1882. 9 Q.B.D., p. 563.

thought that this power might be exercisable to the extent of £2,000,000 whenever the Bank rate reached 7 per cent.[1] In our own time the general recognition by bankers that the standardised note currency, as distinct from the unstandardised cheque currency, was inadequate to sustain the strain arising from any serious disturbance, such as the outbreak of war, led in 1914 to the appointment of a Bankers' Committee. It considered the iron-bound provisions of the Bank Charter Act, and made certain recommendations. These, as stated by Sir Edward Holden, and the reason why they were not adopted, will be found set out in full among the references to the German war crisis (*post*, p. 672). As the Bank Charter Act was never in terms suspended during the crisis, the Bank steadfastly observed the provisions of the Act by holding bullion against every note issued in excess of the legal limit. As late as the report for the week ended February 3, 1915, the notes issued were £84,965,815, against which gold coin and bullion was held to no less an aggregate than £66,515,815. At a very early stage in the war crisis, however, the emergency machinery irregularly employed in 1847, 1857, and 1866, for the suspension of the Bank Charter Act was put upon a statutory basis. Instead of the Treasury being left to the exercise of the power of suspension in reliance upon a subsequent Parliamentary indemnity, an authority to suspend, if necessary, was deliberately conferred upon it by section 3 of the Currency and Bank Notes Act, August 6, 1914 (*post*, p. 679).

BANK CHARTER ACT AND WAR LOAN, 1914

It has been contended that the arrangement under which the Bank of England undertook to make advances on the War Loan of 1914 up to the full limit of the issue price, is constructively a breach of the principle, if not of the letter, of the Bank Charter Act. The full amount of the War Loan was £350,000,000. Obviously, the Bank is not in a position to advance even a third of this amount on the security of the stock unless it can tap resources

[1] *Bankers' Magazine*, 1896, Vol. II. p. 107.

which have not hitherto been utilised. Now, those resources are obviously not its own note issue. The full amount of the statutory issue at the present time is £18,450,000. The Bank can only go beyond that figure against bullion in its vaults or else by a breach of the provisions of the Bank Charter Act. Suppose it, then, to be called upon to lend very large amounts on War Loan. Whence are the funds coming? Presumably, they would be provided by the issue of further Treasury notes, which can, of course, be put in circulation to any extent consistent with sound economic principles. As these notes are not an obligation of the Bank but of the Treasury, their issue in such circumstances would not be a direct breach of the Bank Charter Act. But inasmuch as Peel's object was to prevent the issue of any notes which had not gold at the back of them, the principle of the Bank Charter Act would be abrogated, though its strict letter no doubt would still be observed.[1] Moreover, it has been argued that heavy advances against War Loan would, in effect, be reduced to mere book entries, owing to the intimate relationship between the Bank of England and the rest of the banks, including, of course, the institution which numbered among its clients the persons, or companies, seeking the advances in question.

THE ACT STILL CRITICISED

The Bank Charter Act is, even in 1914, the subject of critical attack. Allusion has already been made to the Bankers' Committee which sat in 1914 to consider its shortcomings. Among laymen, as distinguished from bankers, criticism of the Act is largely based on the assumption that it was passed to insure public immunity from the

---

[1] The intention of the statute of 1844 was in fact partially defeated by the Cheque Bank, which issued guaranteed cheques, and secured for them a wide circulation. This was practically an evasion of the Bank Charter Act, but did not become sufficiently important to attract much attention to a really interesting experiment. The cheques were, in effect, bank-notes for non-standardised amounts. As the Chairman of the Bank of England said (Bank Court, September 11, 1873), the tendency of the Cheque Bank was to establish a sort of currency of notes of less than £5. The Government took the opinions of its law officers and was advised that there was nothing illegal in what the institution was proposing to do.

THE BANK CHARTER ACT—1847 PANIC

painful consequences of financial misconduct, whereas its central purpose was to establish the unfailing convertibility of Bank of England notes. Lord Avebury could never agree with the view that the Bank Charter Act had failed because its operation had had to be suspended in 1847, 1857, and 1866. As he used to observe : " No one would say that a reservoir of water was useless because it was tapped in a season of drought." It is better, Peel had argued, " to prevent the paroxysm than to excite it." German critics have alluded to the recurring suspensions of the Bank Charter Act as amounting, in effect, to the breaking of the Bank. They were, in truth, nothing more than the actual or potential issue of emergency currency ; and the history of every crisis in the nineteenth century demonstrates the complete adequacy of the remedy to assuage the ravages of the disease. Certainly, the glamour of long-standing is gathering around the statute. " Time has . . . raised the empirical measure passed in 1844 into an institution which shares in the veneration enjoyed by every national institution in England."[1] And whatever may be the ultimate verdict upon the Bank Charter Act, it is certain that this reiterated discussion of the predominance of the central institution could not, and did not, fail to enhance the prestige of the Bank by picturing it as an institution which exercised sovereignty in financial powers —the " assumption that the issue of money is a prerogative of Sovereignty," Peel called it, in his Cabinet Memorandum.[2]

BANKING LEGISLATION SUMMARISED

The upshot of all the banking legislation from 1697 to the Bank Charter Act was, according to Sir Henry Thring :[3]

(1) That no country bank of issue consisting of more than six persons could have a branch bank in London.[4]

[1] Andreades, *History of the Bank of England*, p. 373 n.
[2] Parker, *Peel*, Vol. III. p. 135.
[3] App. 1 to Report of 1875 Committee.

[4] THE POSITION OF THE SCOTTISH BANKS
In providing that no bank could come to London, or within sixty-five miles thereof, without losing its right of note issue, the draughtsman of the Bank Charter Act overlooked the Scottish banks. The original Charter of the Bank of England omitted all allusion to them because

354 EVOLUTION OF THE MONEY MARKET

(2) That no country bank could increase its partners beyond six without forfeiting its issue.

(3) That no country bank of issue could issue any amount of notes beyond the average amount it issued at the time of the passing of the Act of 1844.

Scotland, at the time, was an independent kingdom. The Hon. Alexander Melville, who was a banker in London at the time of the passing of the Bank Charter Act, told the 1875 Committee (Q. 4970) that Peel, in 1844, never intended to allow the Scottish banks to come to London. " It might seem odd," the late Lord Avebury once remarked, " that Sir Robert Peel did not anticipate that the Scotch banks *would* open branches in England, since geologists told us that even the fossil footsteps of their extinct animals point southwards." Anyhow, Roundell Palmer gave a definite opinion (November 27, 1855) that the Clydesdale Bank was not debarred by 7 and 8 Victoria, c. 113, from establishing an agency in London. Such a state of things aroused keen jealousy among the English bankers. It was pointed out in the sixties that—for instance—the National Provincial Bank of England was unable to issue notes payable to bearer within sixty-five miles of London, and was prohibited from acting as town agent to its own branches, though these privileges were enjoyed by competing Scottish and Irish banks. The draughtman's " slip " seems to have been by far the principal topic of inquiry before the 1875 Committee. The grievance against the Scottish banks in 1875 was, however, less their note issue than the alleged fact that they cut rates, although the objection was the stronger because they were in effect subsidised by Parliament in that they were allowed to combine a London office with an extra-London note issue. When E. H. Palmer was asked (1875 Committee, Q. 7761) if the Bank of England objected to the Scotch banks coming to London he declined, " as representing the Bank of England," to give any answer. His colleague, K. D. Hodgson, M.P., said that " the mind of the Bank of England upon that point may be said to be a sheet of blank paper." Another criticism of the practice of the Scottish banks was directed to the matter of foreign acceptances. It was described as an " objectionable practice " which was not legitimate banking business. The Bank of England was stated to decline all acceptances except Bank Post Bills. As for the London and Westminster, " many accounts of great value were refused, simply on the ground that they would involve foreign acceptances." (Evidence of W. H. Crake, 1875 Committee, Q. 7318.)

The Scottish banks had entered into an agreement not to open branches in the English provinces. They argued that as they did not, and the English note-issuing banks did, come into competition with the Bank of England as the main issuing body, there was no ground for the opposition to their London offices. Mr. Goschen's Bill of 1875 was intended to limit the English banks of issue to banking in the provinces of England only : to limit the Scottish banks of issue to banking in Scotland, and the Irish banks of issue to banking in Ireland. A deputation which included practically every English banker of standing was received by the Chancellor of the Exchequer (Stafford Northcote) on May 30, 1876, to ask him to suggest to the Scottish banks that the arrangements made with them postponing their further extension in England might be further prolonged until such time as Mr. Goschen's measure might be reintroduced. The Chancellor said the Government were " not in a position to adopt the principle of Mr. Goschen's Bill," and he therefore felt a " delicacy " in going to the Scotch banks. In fact, he declined to go.

The Scottish banks have always maintained their ground, and their note

THE BANK CHARTER ACT—1847 PANIC

(4) That no country bank could issue notes within the City of London or sixty-five miles thereof.

(5) That notes could not be issued of a less value than £5.

1844 AND 1914 COMPARED

Below, for purposes of comparison, is the first account published by the Bank of England under the requirements of the Bank Charter Act, and a typical account in 1914, selected so as to ante-date the German war crisis and the consequent distorting influence upon the figures :—

ACCOUNT OF THE LIABILITIES AND ASSETS OF THE BANK OF ENGLAND

Dr.			Issue Department		Cr.
	Sept. 7, 1844 £	June 17, 1914 £		Sept. 7, 1844 £	June 17, 1914 £
Notes issued	28,351,295	55,487,475	Government debt	11,015,100	11,015,100
			Other securities	2,984,900	7,434,900
			Gold coin and bullion	12,657,208	37,037,475
			Silver bullion	1,694,087	—
	28,351,295	55,487,475		28,351,295	55,487,475

Dr.			Banking Department		Cr.
	Sept. 7, 1844 £	June 17, 1914 £		Sept. 7, 1844 £	June 17, 1914 £
Proprietors' capital	14,553,000	14,553,000	Government securities	14,554,834	11,046,570
Rest	3,564,729	3,153,752	Other securities	7,835,616	37,462,213
Public deposits	3,360,809	17,637,031	Notes	8,175,025	27,069,490
Other deposits	8,644,348	41,869,267	Gold and silver coin	875,765	1,644,121
Seven-day and other bills	1,030,354	9,344			
	31,423,240	77,222,394		31,423,240	77,222,394

THE PANIC OF 1847

Only a brief period elapsed before there came an overwhelming demonstration of the futility of the idea that

issues bear the highest name. In Scotland and in Ireland, of course, the note issue has not been diminished as a result of the Act of 1844. Still, in spit of the exceptional position of the Scottish banks, the modern tendency towards centralisation has become manifest in their direction also. They must have gold, and when they want it they have to go to the Bank of England for it. Thus the movement towards the contralisation of the periodical demand for specie has been accentuated in two ways. In the

legislation, *by itself*, could avert financial upheavals. Within three years of the Bank Charter Act, as Herbert Spencer scornfully said, " arose one of those crises which were to have been prevented. Within another ten years," he added, " has arisen a second " (that of 1857). Something infinitely more subtle and pervasive than statutory regulation was required. Another twenty years were to elapse before there was full appreciation of the nature of the real remedy, and of the fact that the Bank Charter Act did not, and could not, meet all the necessities of the case.

The 1847 crisis was mainly the consequence of the railway mania. During the three preceding years about £185,000,000 had been required to finance the railway schemes sanctioned by Parliament. Deficient harvests and the reduction of the duty on corn stimulated speculation, and sent gold out of the country to pay for grain imports at the very time when the railway madness was transforming circulating into fixed capital to the extent of tens of millions at a time. The public was wild to try its new joint-stock toy upon railway enterprise, which was regarded as quite a national speciality. The investor's bitter experiences in the earlier boom, when he financed ambitious but new and irresponsible nationalities in all parts of the world, had inclined him to turn a more sympathetic eye upon domestic investments. " My impression," said Cotton, the Governor of the Bank, " is that there never was a time when so many parties engaged in operations so much beyond what they ought to have done, with reference to their capital, as in the year 1847, and when there was so great a transfer of capital from floating to fixed." Money was withdrawn from ordinary uses, in order that it might be employed in railway speculation.

---

first place, the disappearance of the country note issues and their replacement by Bank of England notes has thrown the strain of the demand for gold upon the central institution at all times of stress. In the second place, the periodic demand for specie arising from the maintenance of the Irish and Scotch note circulation reacts instantly upon the Bank of England whenever it becomes palpable. There consequently arose, in the period subsequent to the Bank Charter Act, an increasing reliance upon the central institution, which was bound to develop into a great accession of authority for Threadneedle Street.

THE BANK CHARTER ACT—1847 PANIC

This reduced the amount of capital available for commercial purposes : and this in an age of rapid advance. Between March and September, 1845, the railway schemes alone would have involved a capital expenditure of £340,000,000—according to some authorities even £400,000,000. No doubt many of these schemes were of vast importance and utility to the nation at large, in glaring contrast with the wild, futile, and ludicrous projects of the earlier days—such, for instance, as those of the South Sea excitement and the 1825 frenzy. The peremptory requirement of the age was quicker and cheaper transport, and the increasing aggregations of capital (now to some extent bereft of their shyness) offered ample facilities for its provision. Moreover, the progress of the country in its great manufacturing industries had been actually arrested by the difficulty and slowness of distributing the produce. The power loom brought into being more goods than the horse and the canal could convey to the points of effective demand. But there was no attempted discrimination between the sound and the unsound, between the prudent and the flighty. That most elementary guarantee of serious intention—the deposit of a stipulated percentage with the application—was not insisted upon. Requests for allotments were accepted from anybody or everybody, without the least inquiry about his ability to pay the amount necessary to complete the transaction.

The inevitable consequence was that the City swarmed with " stags," all of the most irresponsible type. Mr. Edward Callow, writing in our own time from almost ancient memory, has told us that " a solicitor or two, a civil engineer, a Parliamentary agent, possibly a contractor, a map of England, a pair of compasses, a pencil, and a ruler were all that were requisite to commence the formation of a railway company in those halcyon days—at any rate, so far as drawing up the prospectus was concerned." There was little restraint until the Bank of England imposed it. George Hudson—though his very name is nowadays unfamiliar—was the protagonist of the boom. Every scheme that he fathered seemed to succeed and every commodity that he touched—even advance acquisitions of iron—appeared to turn to gold in his hands. " The Government, having originally encouraged the movement, took no active steps to avert its consequences."[1] The utmost that it did was to let things take their course in a direction where discouragement was likely to be encountered. The necessity of lodging with the Accountant-General 10 per cent. of the capital of the proposed lines seems, in 1846, to have imposed some check upon the craze. Efforts to induce the Accountant-General to waive the deposit of this percentage were unsuccessful, in spite of the argument that, inasmuch as the sum to be paid must be at least £10,000,000, it would not be withdrawn from the market without creating " the greatest and most diffuse inconvenience and pressure." As a matter of fact, it did not do so, although the total aggregated well over the original estimate of £10,000,000. Trouble was saved by what a contemporary critic described as the self-adjusting power of the Money Market.[2] When the danger was realised, a drastic policy was adopted. In January, 1845, the Bank fixed its rate for three months to come at $2\frac{1}{2}$ per cent. In March of the same year the Bank announced for the first time that its published rate was also its minimum rate. On April 15 it was intimated that the minimum rate would apply to all bills, whatever their term. Further, when the applications for discount exceeded the sum available on a given day, a *pro rata* proportion of the bills was to be returned. That stipulation, unknown for at least fifty years, stopped the drain of bullion, strengthened the position of the Bank, and at least deferred, if it did

[1] *City Men and City Manners*, p. 78.
[2] " Everybody wondered beforehand how so large a sum could be paid out of the amount of notes then in circulation. But the Bank acted with the railway deposits as she had been accustomed to act with the public deposits previous to the payment of dividends. As fast as the money came in, it was lent out, and thus a transaction of large magnitude was effected without much difficulty. This shows the importance of a Government bank. Had the deposits been required to be lodged in the Exchequer, and there to remain until reclaimed by the railway companies, the operation could not have been effected." (Gilbart, *Logic of Banking*, p. 240.)

THE BANK CHARTER ACT—1847 PANIC

not prevent, the advent of acute crisis. It was temporarily ameliorative, and no more.

A RECKLESS GAMBLE

For it did not stop the gamble. In March, 1845, the £50 shares (£2 10s. paid) of the Leeds and Thirsk railway were at $3\frac{1}{2}$, in September at $23\frac{3}{4}$, and in November at $4\frac{3}{4}$. The York and North Midland's capital issue was £1,500,000, but the stock stood at one time at a premium of £7,500,000.[1] Shares once vainly offered at a farthing apiece had come to be those of a promising undertaking,[2] but in other instances the advance was mere inflation, either in London or the provinces, where the provincial Stock Exchanges had sprung into vigorous life within the last fifteen years.[3] But on November 6, almost in the midst of the excitement, the Bank deliberately advanced its $2\frac{1}{2}$ per cent. rate to $3\frac{1}{2}$ per cent., so as to check the gamble by forcing the realities of the position upon the notice of the nation. Thus we get in plain operation the most elementary of disciplinary methods—the mere directing of attention to the danger. The second mode is witnessed at the time of the Overend-Gurney crisis. It consists in cautionary action, combined with a refusal to assist those whose reprehensible methods have produced the trouble. The third, or Baring, mode consists in cautionary measures, combined with determined efforts to *prevent* catastrophe, In forcing a consideration of their real position upon the victims of this madness, however, a very useful curb upon the whole movement was brought into operation, with the result that it was possible to say, before long, that probably there was not a single new railway company in which the majority of the shareholders would not vote for the abandonment of the scheme. Unfortunately reflection came too late. Fostered by these unwholesome conditions there were scandals, multitudinous and huge, resulting in the infusion of " water " which has clogged the development of the great railways ever since, and is the main

---

[1] Morier Evans, *Facts, Failures, and Frauds*, p. 37. [2] *The City*, p. 66.
[3] See p. 538, where their establishment is discussed.

indirect cause of all the unrest among modern railway servants. Absence of supervision and control led to the spending, as Lord Clanricarde once said, of £450,000,000 upon railways which could have been built for £200,000,000 less.[1]

FIRST SUSPENSION OF THE BANK CHARTER ACT

Crisis, in fact, was only deferred, not altogether averted. In the spring of 1847 failures began to occur in a steady stream. There were many in April and May. Forced sales of corn, on account of the French Government, with the resulting reduction of prices from 96s. to 56s. a quarter brought down many houses connected with the corn trade, and augmented the trouble, already worsened by the potato famine in Ireland. When the continuous drain of bullion had reduced the whole resources of the Bank to £2,558,000 (on April 10) the realities of the position became painfully and conspicuously manifest. The 4 per cent. rate was raised to 5, with such instant effect that £100,000 in sovereigns, actually shipped for America, was re-landed—a very significant fact, destined to be emphasised as the Bank learned, during the next fifteen years, how easily gold could be attracted, or its exit stopped, by the manipulation of its own rate. Discounts became practically impossible. Even the best were done at 9, 10, and even 12 per cent. After the first week in May the pressure ceased for a time. But on August 19 there came a bombshell in the shape of the suspension of Sanderson's, the great discount house. During the month of September, "fifteen of the most considerable houses in the City of London stopped payment." On October 1, the Bank announced a $5\frac{1}{2}$ per cent. rate, and intimated at the same time that no advances would be made on public securities. Liverpool bills of the finest character with three days to run, and carrying the endorsement of the Bank of France, were refused by the Bank of England. On October 18 the Royal Bank of Liverpool collapsed. Other failures

[1] House of Lords, May 14, 1866.

THE BANK CHARTER ACT—1847 PANIC

during October were Reid, Irving and Co., with liabilities of £1,500,000; Cockerell and Co., £600,000; Gower Nephews, £450,000; Barton, Irlam and Higginson, £1,000,000; the North and South Wales Bank, destined to recovery and prosperous distinction under the brilliant pilotage of George Rae; the Newcastle Joint-Stock Bank, and smaller private institutions at Abingdon, Manchester, Salisbury, and Shaftesbury. The resulting crisis was only one degree less severe than that of 1825. Consols, which had averaged $98\frac{3}{4}$ in 1846, were $78\frac{3}{4}$ in October, 1847. The stringency is well illustrated by the fact that the national security stood at $84\frac{1}{2}$ for the mid-October account, nine days before the settlement, and $83\frac{1}{2}$ for cash. This works out at about 50 per cent. per annum. A seller of Consols for cash was paying that rate for the accommodation. The Bank of England, said Sir Charles Wood, " was pressed directly for assistance from all parts of the country . . . the whole demand for discount was thrown upon the hands of the Bank of England." The Bank itself was said to be borrowing at 7 and $7\frac{1}{2}$ per cent. The depreciation in securities and property was contemporaneously appraised[1] at £400,000,000, while the loss from the failures of banks and mercantile houses was estimated at £80,000,000.

THE BANK'S INTREPID POLICY

The evidence given before the House of Commons shows that between September 15 and November 15, 1847, the Bank assisted a very large firm in London, with liabilities of several millions sterling, and thereby prevented them from stopping payment. It was understood that the operation was for that purpose. A sum of £50,000 was advanced to one country banker and £100,000 to another, on the security of real property, and £300,000 to the Royal Bank of Liverpool on bills of exchange. This advance, however, proved inadequate, and, as the bank had no more security to give, it suspended payment. Another bank was assisted with £100,000 on bills of

---

[1] *Bank of England*, p. 54.

exchange, in addition to its usual discounts, and still another received £50,000 on the same class of security, on condition of withdrawing its issues ; but the bank stopped before the arrangements could be completed. Still another large joint-stock bank was assisted to the extent of £800,000, another with £200,000 on local bills and £60,000 on London bills, while yet another was assisted to the extent of £100,000 on local and London bills. Only the assistance given to bankers has been recounted, without regard to concurrent aid given to various companies and mercantile undertakings, either to save them from disaster or to enable them to resume payment. The stringency was felt most severely in England. The Chancellor of the Exchequer got himself into trouble by saying that " the Scotch banks " applied for assistance to the Bank of England. He had to explain (House of Commons, December 9) that he meant " some banks in Scotland," the Bank of Scotland *not* being one of them. Looking at England alone, however, we can see that the firm stand made so ungrudgingly in the national interest was something of a demonstration of the baselessness of Lord George Bentinck's sneer at " the moneyed interest—the money-changers and usurers—Jones Loyd, Peel and Co."[1]

A RELUCTANT SUSPENSION

The Government held out for three weeks against any removal of the restraints of the Bank Charter Act. But on October 22 or 23, owing to the refusal of the Chancellor of the Exchequer, Sir Charles Wood, to relax the stipulation of the Bank Charter Act, a deputation of the leading City bankers interviewed the Prime Minister (Lord John Russell) who, it is understood, coerced his Chancellor into action, at a midnight interview. The Act was in effect suspended on the Saturday, October 23, subject to an 8 per cent. rate—though the Government letter was not despatched till the Monday. Free discounting at 9 per cent. at once began. When the Government letter was published on the Monday, the panic was over. The Bank,

[1] Disraeli, *Life of Lord George Bentinck*, p. 459.

argued its partisans, did not ask for the suspension. It was the City bankers who had pressed for it. After the crisis was over the Bank itself declared that it could have continued payment, and that the suspension had been unnecessary; but this view is not generally accepted, though, in fact, the Act was never infringed. The potentiality of its suspension calmed all fears within an hour—or within ten minutes, as Gurney said—of the Government's decision becoming known. The old hoarding propensities had, however, reappeared and even extended themselves to bank-notes. At least £4,000,000 in *notes* was being hoarded, from a fear that no more notes would be obtainable. Many of them were in halves, in order to defeat thefts. But with the suspension of the Bank Charter Act all this money came pouring out of its hiding-places, and the bullion and banking reserve of the Bank of England rapidly assumed their pristine proportions. The mere consciousness that loans could be had, itself prevented them from being required. The relief arising from a suspension of the Bank Charter Act is moral rather than financial, as Professor Dunbar declares. What the bankers said to Sir Charles Wood was " Let us have notes. We don't mean, indeed, to take the notes, because we shall not want them; only tell us that we can get them, and this will at once restore confidence." Under the stimulus of such an intimation, Consols rose five points in three days. But the day of scientific finance had yet to come. Some of the banks which were saved in 1847 were only preserved for a later collapse. There was no change in management or method, and consequently the final catastrophe, which was to give them their place in the limbo of the extinct, was merely postponed. Two more crises were to sweep across the City before this age of evanescent concord, and otherwise permanent disunion and isolation, finally passed away, and finance emerged into the bracing atmosphere of deliberate and sustained co-operation.

CHAPTER XIII

THE 1857 PANIC—THE WIDENING ARENA AND THE "NEW SPIRIT" IN FINANCE

THE close of the Crimean War gave a great impetus to trade and encouraged inflation. Credit freely bestowed, and speculation stimulated by an abundant harvest, left the market open to cold shivers. The outbreak of the Indian Mutiny was one, and the collapse of the railway mania in America, accompanied by the failure of New York banks, furnished another. There was an organised bear syndicate at work in the United States, holding meetings, circulating false reports, challenging the validity of securities, and generally spreading mistrust with a view to the precipitation of panic. In England the liability to swift disquietude had been magnified by a series of episodes characteristic of the time and of the comparative looseness with which financial affairs were conducted in an era when so much was fresh and experimental. Walter Watts, in 1850, had been tried for robbing the Globe Assurance office of the sum of £70,000. He had done it by manipulating the bankers' pass-book. Those who saw the book stated that it presented a mass of erasures and alterations which ought at least to have excited suspicion if it had not at once led to detection. November, 1855, brought the revelation of the Dock Warrant frauds by Joseph Windle Cole and the still more unpleasant revelation that Overend, Gurney and Co., after they had discovered (in 1853) the fraudulent nature of the documents upon which Cole was raising money, had concealed the facts.[1] The episode, and con-

[1] Report of Messrs. Quilter, Ball and Co., *Facts, Failures, and Frauds*, p. 194. See also *Times*, January 7, 1859.

temporary discussion of it, went far to damage the prestige of the firm and to pave the way for the tragedy of 1866. But to return to the enumeration of the scandals of the "fifties." In 1856 the body of John Sadleir, M.P., a former Junior Lord of the Treasury, was discovered on Hampstead Heath.[1] Sadleir had poisoned himself. After his death it appeared that by a series of ingenious frauds he had robbed the Tipperary Bank of £200,000. It had to suspend payment. Sadleir had also issued forged shares to the extent of £150,000 in the Swedish Railway Company, as well as bogus title deeds, acceptances, and securities in all directions. As Sadleir had been Chairman of the London and County Bank these revelations created a huge sensation. Later in the year came the news of the manipulation of the share transfers of the Crystal Palace Company by which W. J. Robson had succeeded in adding £10,793 to the outstanding Preference shares and £17,230 to the issued Ordinary capital. The total frauds amounted to over £28,000. As it was impossible to cancel the transactions, these amounts had necessarily to be added to the outstanding capital of the company. Practically simultaneously with this affair an examination of the Great Northern share registers, at King's Cross, disclosed the fact that during several years one of the clerks, Leopold Redpath, had succeeded in issuing forged stock to the amount of £220,000. The Attorney-General, who was consulted on the subject, gave his opinion that as the stock thus fraudulently created had become so blended with the rest of the company's issues as to be indistinguishable, there was no possibility of apportioning the dividend to the genuine stock only. Consequently until the forged stock had been, so to speak, legitimised, no dividends could be paid. The whole of this forged stock had therefore to be added to the existing capital of the company[2]

---

[1] In recent years it has been alleged that Sadleir escaped to America, and that the body was not his.
[2] The Forged Transfers Act of 1891 is, of course, only intended to guard against single forgeries and does not contemplate gigantic frauds of this type, which would be almost impossible of achievement under the strict conditions of a modern office.

of which it still, therefore, in 1915, forms a considerable part.

ADVENT OF THE CRISIS

The crisis of 1857 actually " arrived some months before it was due, having regard to the prevailing belief that ten years was the period required to obliterate the memory of one financial cataclysm and induce the speculation which provokes another."[1] Early in the year, when some of the greatest City names were being freely bandied about, it was understood that Rothschilds had seen one firm through its difficulties and Overend, Gurney and Co. another. The Bank of England had lowered its rate in June (to 6 p.c.) and July (to $5\frac{1}{2}$ p.c.) though it only held inadequate stocks of bullion—£10,909,000 on June 18. The Ohio Life and Trust Co. with deposits of £1,200,000, stopped payment on August 25, and the discount rate in the United States rose as high as 24 per cent. On October 12 the Bank of England issued a " guarded caution " to its agents. This was followed on the 17th by the arrival of the news of the failure of 150 banks in Pennsylvania, Maryland, Virginia, and Rhode Island.[2] On October 8 the Bank had already raised its rate to 6 per cent. On the 12th it was advanced to 7 per cent., and on the 19th to 8 per cent. The Western Bank of Scotland applied for assistance, but the directors of the Bank of England were, frankly, afraid to face so huge a responsibility. Meanwhile, the " principal discount house " had asked for assurances that it might rely upon the Bank if the need arose. Another discount firm applied to the Bank for £400,000, and simultaneously an English bank was assisted. To aid in allaying the panic produced in Scotland by the failure of the City of Glasgow Bank, over a million sovereigns were despatched. On October 27 the Liverpool Borough Bank collapsed before assistance

[1] Spencer Walpole, *History of England*, p. 106.
[2] The United States has no expedient precisely corresponding to the suspension of the Bank Charter Act. But during the crisis of 1857, although it was notorious that the Constitution of the State of New York forbade suspension of specie payments, directly or indirectly, yet the Judges of the Supreme Court met and agreed not to grant any injunction unless the bank appeared to be insolvent or guilty of fraud. (Sumner, *History of American Currency*, p. 184.)

1857 PANIC—THE WIDENING ARENA

could be rendered to it. The Bank of England announced, however, that it would not reject any otherwise good Bill merely because it bore a Liverpool Borough Bank endorsement.

THE BANK IN THE BATTLE LINE

Discounts almost entirely ceased in London, except at the Bank of England, said the Governor. The Bank had, in fact, become the only source whence aid could be expected. At the height of the crisis, the Bank directors declared, " nearly the whole of the requirements of commerce were thrown on the Bank." As for Consols, observed K. D. Hodgson, " they were, to my positive knowledge, unsaleable for notes, and it was notes that you wanted." In this emergency, said the 1858 Committee,[1] " everything depended on the Bank of England, and it appears to your Committee that the proceedings of that establishment were not characterised by any want of foresight or of vigour." On November 4 the Bank rate went to 9 per cent. On the 7th Dennistoun and Co. stopped, with liabilities of over £2,000,000, and on the 9th the Western Bank of Scotland (which had previously applied for assistance) collapsed. On November 11, when the bullion in the Bank was £7,171,000, against liabilities of £60,000,000, Sanderson, Sandeman and Co., a large firm of bill brokers, stopped with deposits of £3,500,000, and total liabilities of £5,298,997. On the same day the City of Glasgow Bank closed its doors.[2] At this stage it became known that the wealthy house of Messrs. George Peabody and Co., the American bankers and merchants, had been compelled to apply to the Bank of England for assistance, and it was not until considerable negotiation had taken place that the arrangements were concluded. These were effected on the security of Mr. George Peabody's private property, and the capital of the firm, backed by the guarantees of several of the metropolitan joint-stock banks. The amount

---

[1] Report, section 18.
[2] It subsequently resumed, only to collapse again, under still more tragic circumstances, in 1878. The magnitude of the Sanderson failure was greatly reduced by subsequent payments as bills ran off.

advanced was speedily repaid, and eventually it was stated that the total sacrifice sustained was only equal to about one year's profit.[1] The total list of important failures during October, and up to November 19, occupies more than a page in Morier Evans' *Commercial Crisis, 1857–1858*.

BANK CHARTER ACT SUSPENDED

The Bank Charter Act was suspended on the 12th—a day on which the discounts at the Bank totalled £2,373,000. Parliament ultimately passed a special enactment suspending the Act till February 1, 1858, provided the directors did not reduce their rate below 10 per cent. As they reduced it to 8 per cent. on December 24, the Bank Charter Act was automatically revived. McCulloch says that on the morning of November 13 the total reserve (as shown on the previous evening) was £384,144, while the bankers' balances alone aggregated £5,458,000. On this occasion, again, the Bank insisted that it would have weathered the storm without the suspension of the Bank Charter Act; but this optimistic opinion found only limited acceptance outside the Bank itself, having regard to the small amount of the Bank's own reserve and the possibility of the bankers' balances being withdrawn. Anyhow, there was in 1857, as distinct from 1847 and 1866, an actual, and not merely a potential, infringement of the Act in the shape of the issue of notes unsecured by bullion. This took place to the nominal extent of £2,000,000, but there was never more than £928,000 (November 20) actually in the hands of the public. By the end of next year the Bank rate was $2\frac{1}{2}$ per cent., and the stock of bullion no less than £18,921,000. The 1857 episode has, indeed, been described as the most unjustifiable panic of the century. Many of the houses which suspended under the sudden stress of crisis were able to resume. For example, a Sheffield and Liverpool firm which suspended in November, 1857, resumed in May, 1858, paying every claim in full, with 5 per cent. interest, and offering to discount such of its long-dated acceptances as had not then matured. As for

[1] Morier Evans, *Commercial Crisis*, 1857–1858, p. 49 n.

1857 PANIC—THE WIDENING ARENA

the violence of the panic, there was again a diminution, in comparison with earlier catastrophes. The Governor of the Bank of England said the panic was not so severe as that of 1847, though the real commercial pressure was more intense.[1] At all events it had one beneficial result—a further extirpation of the obsolete and rickety survivals of an earlier economic age.

THE STOCK EXCHANGE CRISIS OF 1859

Although the crisis in its banking and commercial aspects subsided rapidly there was a recrudescence elsewhere at Easter of 1859. The inauguration of the conflict between France, Sardinia, and Austria destroyed the equilibrium of the Stock Exchange. The decision to close the " House " on the Saturday before Easter Sunday was in effect revoked, and the " House " was opened on Saturday. From that date forward the condition was practically one of panic. Turkish fell 10 to 12 points in a day, and even Consols, then a more stable security than now, fell $1\frac{1}{2}$ points in the same period. Stock Exchange business began to be prolonged to a very late hour in the evening. The danger of the position became very palpable when it was known that extensive assistance had had to be provided in certain quarters. The scene in the " House " at the commencement of business on April 27 was said to recall the most distressing memories of the Spanish panic. On May 5 the Bank of England put up its rate to $4\frac{1}{2}$ per cent., and from that time onwards the panic began to abate. Morier Evans gives an almost pathetic touch to the story of the panic of 1859 when he says :—

" It was a common thing at this period to meet brokers and to ask them respecting their position. The general reply was, ' Well, I hope to pull through ; but I fear it will be a difficult affair.' Another, ' I am safe, but regularly skinned ; everything I hold is down some ten, twenty or thirty per cent., and many of my kind friends will not be able to pay their differences. Another, ' Very dreadful, everything gone but my credit.' Another, ' I have fortunately obtained assistance and shall escape the hammer this time.' "

[1] McCulloch, *Dictionary of Political Economy*, Art. " Crisis," p. 640.

As usual, the Bank of England bore the brunt of the shock. The discount brokers did not employ their funds to any great extent, especially as they were themselves restricted by the curtailment of facilities. Remembering what occurred within the next seven years there is something very remarkable in the fact, well known in 1859, that the Overend-Gurney firm were then, as in 1857, among those who rendered the necessary aid in cases where it could be shown that the securities were of an appreciable character, and that operations had been carried out on a sound and legitimate basis.

EVIDENCES OF VITAL CHANGE

It is at this stage that we begin to encounter, in many directions, the signs of the solidification of British banking around London. For seventy years, as we have seen, London had been the financial centre of the world ; but it is not until the period between the 1847 and 1866 crisis that we discover unmistakable indications that British banking itself was being gripped from the metropolis and was coming to look Londonwards for its inspiration, even as the Moslem looks towards Mecca. When once we are alive to the tendency a multitude of scattered incidents assume an aspect of coherence as being among its causes or effects. One great international episode—the Franco-German war—was destined to destroy whatever chance of continental rivalry might be left ; so that by 1875 London was supreme alike in the cosmopolitan and domestic Money Markets.

When the 1858 Committee called attention to the vast increase in the practice of opening bank accounts [1] the Committee added that the aggregate of these various deposits " finds its way to the employments of trade, and especially *gravitates* [observe the word] to London, the centre of commercial activity, where it is employed first in the discount of bills or in other advances to the customers of the London bankers." The tendency, of course, was not new. The " capital, cash, and the bills of more than

[1] See *ante*, p. 313.

an hundred country bankers," said Sir J. Wrottesley, in
1826, " had been placed in the hands of London bankers."
The movement was the more facile and comprehensible
because country issues, limited as they were, took the place
of the gold, and left it free for London. Thus they exerted
a steadying influence on the rate of discount, which would
have been higher in their absence.[1] In the thirties and
forties of the last century the gold constantly found its
way back to London, in spite of the Bank's efforts, in its
own interest, to keep the metal in circulation. When the
Bank of England was most anxious to supply the country
with gold, the sovereigns sent down by one mail coach
returned with the next. The country bankers raked in
the gold and sent it to London, relying on their own notes
for currency. Of course a fair amount of gold in circulation
not only mitigates the pressure on the Bank of England
that might otherwise immediately result from a national
contingency like a bad harvest, but also obviates the
necessity of large exchanges of notes for gold when there
happens to be a drain of the yellow metal out of the country
as in the case of large foreign loans.[2] This tendency of
gold towards London was in any case the reverse of hoarding. That antiquated vice was practically at an end,
though the period between the crisis of 1857 and the crash
of 1866 seems to have been characterised by some slight
recrudescence of the habit. In the words of the chairman
of the Imperial Bank (meeting, July 21, 1864), there were
a number of men who were not banking, but who kept
their money in old " chests, boxes, and saucepans." As
late as the seventies the bucolic mind was still suspicious
of Bank of England notes ; its misgivings could only be
said to be " dying out."[3] Upon these striking facts with

[1] See the views of George Rae and John Dun on this point in the survey
of the Bank Charter Act, p. 348.
[2] 1875 Committee, QQ. 6899, 6914.
[3] The discouragement of hoarding, in these later periods at all events,
extends far beyond that species of it which is attracted only to the secret
accumulation of savings. There is constantly an interval between the
moment when services are rendered to society for payment made, and the
point when a part of this payment will be required from the recipient in
discharge of some debt or obligation. During that period the money may

regard to the "gravitation" of money the Select Committee of 1859 reported as a significant circumstance manifest in the decade between 1847 and 1857—" a most remarkable development of the economy afforded by the practice of banking for the use and distribution of capital."

The expression "gravitates" is singularly felicitous, though it is possible that the Committee did not realise how rapidly the mechanism of the Money Market was being modelled on the lines of the Solar System, or how supremely important, if not vital, to modern social consolidation the process actually was. We may recall that it was the bill broker—the money scrivener—who in the eighteenth and earlier nineteenth centuries connected the various banks in the country with the Bank of England, and in that manner materially accelerated and facilitated the advent of the supremacy of Threadneedle Street. The tendency has persisted to the present hour. The vital requisite of the bill is negotiability—ready convertibility into money in case of need ; " and to render bills of exchange thus convertible they must be payable in London, the discount centre of England. Bills not payable in London are simply unmarketable. . . . They are only a shade more eligible as banking assets than overdrafts would be." London is a " common centre of liquidation, towards which the bills from all parts of the kingdom gravitate as they become

---

be made active and fruitful. There are thousands of persons of comparatively small means who are compelled to accumulate sums of money to meet recurring claims, such as rent, insurance, and the like. That is to say, in the absence of a banking system these sums would swell gradually into hoards in the interval between one pay-day and another, and the system would be adopted on a large scale, even by persons who were not actuated by nervousness or furtiveness. In the absence of banking facilities these persons would be tempted, if not compelled, to hoard the money during the comparatively brief periods between each recurring call. Even this class of hoarding, however, tends to disappear under the operation of the facilities offered by the far-flung network of branch banks. Instead of being hoarded, these small sums are paid into a bank account, and are in that way at once set free as moving factors of the currency, adding to its volume and velocity. If it be borne in mind that this principle is active with a large proportion of the customers of every branch bank in the country, it will be seen that its aggregate influence on the volume and velocity of the circulation is something enormous. These considerations have a special interest in view of the fact that the primeval tendency to hoard was here and there reawakened by the war crisis of 1914.

1857 PANIC—THE WIDENING ARENA

due."[1] How keenly the importance of the Londonwards tendency appealed to the bankers of that period may be inferred from the fact that the National Provincial Bank of England forfeited a note circulation of nearly £450,000 in order to be able to open a London office. Again, every absorption of a country bank, by increasing the metropolitan reserves, emphasised the centralisation of national financial resources in London. Further, the repression of " banking up to the hilt " has strengthened the gravitational force. Down to the 1857 crisis the provincial banks rediscounted to an immense extent in London. In a City colloquialism, they incessantly bit off more discounts than they could chew, and had to come to London to obtain relief. This practice has been steadily reduced, and at the present time, so far from rediscounting and borrowing in London, the great provincial banks have large deposits in the City.

SCOTLAND FEELS THE " PULL "

Under the stress of these conditions Scotland, with its admirable banking system, began to feel the magnetism of London. " Thirty years ago," said J. S. Fleming, manager of the Royal Bank of Scotland,[2] " I daresay it was quite an exception for a Scotch merchant to accept bills payable in London, or to think of having a London bank account ; but nowadays it is quite an exception with large mercantile houses in Glasgow and Dundee, and other Scotch towns, to accept a bill payable in Scotland ; they are all domiciled in London. Their remittances from abroad come home in the shape of bills drawn on London and payable there." These circumstances and considerations ultimately brought the Scottish banks to London about ten years before the date when Fleming spoke.[3] Once more, there is the indirect dependence on the Bank of England as an incessant stimulus to the gravitational tendency. " If a country bank wants notes, it probably sends to London something that can be converted into notes.

---

[1] Rae, *Country Banker*, p. 86 *et seq.*   [2] 1875 Committee, Q. 28.
[3] See note on the Scottish banks, p. 353.

But those notes must be got from some place or other, and ultimately somebody gets them from the Bank of England through the instrumentality of the banking account that he has with the banking department."[1] Even the stockholdings held by the banks gravitated, for the same reason, to London. The Provincial Bank of Ireland, for instance, held the bulk of its Government stock in London, and not in Dublin, because there was only a limited market in the Irish capital as compared with that available in the British metropolis. The dominance of the London Stock Exchange was plain.[2] The factors of the Money Market were becoming more powerful as they were drawn into closer cohesion.

THE VOGUE OF THE DRAFT ON LONDON

This gravitational force, however, succoured by the acceptance system, has had an operation far wider than the United Kingdom. It has, for more than a century, been the practice of leading London mercantile houses to sell the use of their credit, in return for a commission, to people whose paper, in the absence of such an acceptance, would only take a relatively low rank. The acceptors lend their credit but not their cash. Lending by acceptance was, and is, in fact, lending a good name, lending something which is essentially psychological, though far more intimately the property of the lender, and far less liable to the attacks of panic than actual cash deposits. In plain English the man with second-class credit paid a commission to the possessor of first-class credit and thereby secured an improvement in the discount terms which was equal to an amount far in excess of the small commission paid for the accommodation. But in carrying on this very high-class credit business the accepting houses obviously rely, and must rely, upon an uninterrupted stream of remittances to meet the various obligations as they mature. In a word, they undertake, for a commission, to assume a responsibility which, in fact, seldom or never falls upon them; and, by a paradox familiar to all students of English

[1] T. Cooke, 1875 Committee, Q. 6679.
[2] Marshall, Secretary of the Provincial Bank of Ireland, 1836 Committee.

banking, their responsibility in this respect is frequently, if not always, far in excess of their capacity to discharge it, if, as a matter of fact, they are actually called upon to do so. The effect of this system, from the point of view of our national economy, is that we are able to take toll of a vast aggregate of foreign trade in which we have no direct concern whatever, by lending our acceptances to finance it. A draft on New York or Berlin may be imagined as negotiable in Canton against shipments of silk to New York itself ; but if the silk exporter is to get the best rate for his drafts, he will see that they are drawn on London. The inter-action of the great economic forces is again illustrated herein : England's trade is fostered and facilitated by the fact of London's supreme position as the financial centre of the world ; and the magnitude of her trade, in turn, by creating a demand for drafts on London [1] in every place where trade is carried on, tends to emphasise and perpetuate the financial centralisation. "A study of the bills which are lodged by the London discount houses as security for short loans is a lesson in commercial geography. They are drawn from all parts of the world and are based upon every conceivable kind of produce. It is the lending on these bills which practically constitutes the operations of the Money Market."[2] And over all these seething movements of the foreign exchanges (the consequence of the multitudinous transactions which are necessary to the adjustment of the world's vast trade) there is incessantly bent the unfaltering gaze of that faithful, but often unregarded, sentinel, the Bank of England. Naturally, the unique solidity and responsibility of the great English accepting firms and banks is a potent factor of the process. There is no reason, on the face of things, why American private financial firms should not do a large acceptance business. (The American national banks are forbidden by law to give acceptances.) But the fact is that they do not attempt it because the endeavour would bring

[1] The expression "draft on London," as employed by bankers, means a *foreign* draft on London.
[2] J. Russell French, General Manager Bank of New South Wales, address to Australian Institute of Bankers, 1907.

their credit, excellent as it is, into disadvantageous contrast with that of the London houses—houses which, paradoxical as it seems to say so, have been largely the creation of strangers who have (especially since the Franco-German war of 1871) come within our gates from abroad. The existing vogue of the bill on London has never been more vividly described than by Sir Felix Schuster :—

" A bill of exchange on London is the recognised medium of settling international transactions. The dealing in such bills is of constant occurrence. *London names are universally known.* True a certain number of bills are drawn on Germany, or France, or Belgium, for goods shipped there from transatlantic countries, but the number of such bills is comparatively small, and they are only used in connection with trade between those respective countries, and not as international mediums of exchange. As regards shipments of goods to the United Kingdom, the shipper almost invariably obtains payment for those goods by selling his bill on London to the local bank; but not only that, in most cases he would prefer, when he sends goods to any part of the continent of Europe, or to the United States, to draw a bill on London against them, leaving the purchaser to settle with the London banker. In using the term banker, I include, of course, the large number of so-called merchant bankers who make a speciality of this kind of business. Thus the China merchant who sells tea to Russia or Germany, or silks to the United States, will probably obtain payment through the medium of the London Money Market. There is an absolutely free market because there is always a supply, and there is always a demand, and that really in every part of the world. This illustrates Lord Goschen's statement that the source of English banking supremacy is in her stupendous exports, but it also explains the difficulty which confronts English bankers when they attempt to build up a foreign bill case."

American observers have been equally emphatic. For instance, Mr. Stickney tells his countrymen that " the wares of commerce follow the drafts of commerce. I venture to suggest," he says,

"that you may subsidize ships to sail the seas, and your armies and navies may carry the flag to all the islands of the

1857 PANIC—THE WIDENING ARENA

seas, but you will never control the commerce of the world, nor the wealth of the world, nor the world itself, until you have a banking system which can manage the exchanges of the world during commercial crises, and maintain at all times a fairly uniform rate of interest." [1]

THE BILL BROKERS AND THEIR WORK

Herein lies the reason for the increase of bill business simultaneously with the huge progress of British trade in the first half of the last century. In 1845 the Rothschild firm alone was doing £100,000 a week in the foreign exchanges.[2] " The City bankers prefer placing their money with the bill brokers to investing it in exchequer bills."[3] But the West-End bankers, dealing with a different clientele, selling longer credit, and still lending on mortgage, retained their old fancy for the exchequer bill. Under the stimulus of conditions in which trade fostered the bill and the bill fostered trade, the bill brokers themselves, whose " intermediate agency " had been the subject of allusion by the Bullion Committee, have gradually specialised, and now include several sub-species. The bill broker was originally, no doubt, as he is now, a middleman between the banker and the holder of bills. He necessarily became a specialist in the credit of individual borrowers. He possessed in that capacity a more profound knowledge than the banker could possibly attain of the resources, commitments, and character of an extended clientele, and upon his discretion depended the safety of the banker in lending soundly. " It is by reason of the existence [of the bill brokers] in the complex machinery of the London Money Market," said Mr. A. F. Wallace, Governor of the Bank of England,[4] " that holders of bills of approved credit on this country are never in any sort of doubt that they can get cash for them at a price ; and it is with their help that the bankers, on

---
[1] Quoted by Withers, *Meaning of Money*, p. 99.
[2] *The City*, p. 101. This book is the original form of *City Men and City Manners*, which was published in 1852.
[3] Gilbart, *Logic of Banking*, p. 198.
[4] Anniversary Dinner of the National Discount Co., July 11, 1906.

the other hand—the custodians of the deposits of the country—can employ for the benefit of their shareholders a large portion of cash which must otherwise remain idle."

When one of the greatest of modern bill-broking firms—Overend, Gurney and Co.—went down, the public realised for the first time how huge a factor in the mechanism of modern finance the " money scrivener " had become. Among the sub-species now discernible, one is only concerned to sell bills on commission, practically by canvassing. He is a true broker, for he lives on his brokerage. This type approximately represents the ancient money scrivener, and held, down to Bagehot's time, the predominance as far as mere number was concerned. Another buys the bills to sell again at a favourable opportunity. He is financed by the banks, their profit being represented by the interest they charge him, and by another benefit of scarcely less importance, namely, the use of his unique knowledge and experience of " Paper," and the personalities who create it and back it. His speciality is bill dealing, or bill jobbing, a business which has increased largely since the Overend-Gurney crisis, and especially during the last thirty years. In the third and highest position comes the discount house, with large capital resources of its own, and frequently with extensive public deposits. This type of bill broker is strong enough to hold on its own account under practically any circumstances than can arise. The National Discount Co., Ltd., the Union Discount Co., Ltd., and Alexanders and Co., Ltd. are the main components of this class.

" OPEN CREDITS," ALIAS FINANCE BILLS

But to revert to the 1857 period. This was the time when the " open credit," otherwise the finance bill, acquired a certain sinister prominence. The bill of exchange, which was originally objective, as being almost invariably drawn against the sale (or transformation to a higher commercial value) of commodities, becomes subjective when it takes the purely " finance " form, and can be employed (frequently, but not necessarily, with securities in the background)

1857 PANIC—THE WIDENING ARENA

for the raising of large sums wherewith to finance a market operation in which no commodities change hands or are ever intended to do so. Expanding financial ambition was bound ultimately to discover that although, in austere theory, a bill should " pay itself " by means of the sale of the commodities which originally brought it into existence, yet there was no absolute necessity for adherence to this rule. If the creation of a bill is a convenience to its creators, why should they only undertake it when there is an actual commercial transaction at its base ? The answer to that question was the wide extension of the vogue of the finance bill. By 1857 the system of " open credits " had achieved a wide vogue :—

" There was no real basis to the transaction, but the whole affair was a means of raising a temporary command of capital for the convenience of the individuals concerned, merely a bare commission hanging upon it. . . . It is stated that the chief business of a particular firm, which at the time of its suspension [in 1857] owed £900,000 upon a capital of £10,000, consisted in permitting itself to be drawn upon by foreign houses without any remittance previously or contemporaneously made, but with an engagement that it should be made before the acceptance arrived at maturity."[1]

Contemporary distrust of this species of kite-flying is curiously illustrated in the fact that Gilbart uses the following as one of the illustrative syllogisms in his *Logic of Banking* (p. 293) :—

" RULE III.—Whenever the whole of a class possess a certain attribute, whatever does not possess that attribute does not belong to the class.

" All legitimate bills are *drawn against value received;*

" No kite or accommodation bill is *drawn against value received;*

" Therefore, no kite or accommodation bill is a legitimate bill."

The purely finance bill has no commodities behind it. Its creation is the result of an arrangement between two eminent houses, in different countries, that the one shall

[1] Morier Evans, *Commercial Crisis,* 1857–1858, p. 73.

draw and the other accept at three months' sight. Since both houses are of first-class standing, their confederation can at any moment call into existence a gilt-edged bill capable of being sold anywhere at the best rate ruling. The buyer finds the money : neither of the original parties to the transaction is under the necessity of providing a shilling or a cent until the bill matures. There may, or may not, be collateral. Frequently the whole affair is a case of blank credit, from inception to completion. Kept within due limits, and managed by responsible people for legitimate ends, the system has much in its favour. An American banker, at a time when bills on London are scarce, may legitimately create bills, not against goods but against collateral, in anticipation of the time, for instance, when shipments of cotton increase the supply of bills and they can be acquired at greater advantage. Nor is such business limited to private firms. Foreign Governments frequently resort to this species of " kite-flying," in anticipation of resources to be created by an intended loan issue. Its celerity and facility of operation, where the parties to the transaction are of first-class standing, make it one of the most effective of financial expedients. At the same time it would be idle to deny that every year sees the market more censorious in the matter of finance bills. Its vigilance in that respect has been redoubled since the American crisis of 1907.

THE BANK IN THE DISCOUNT MARKET

The fact of this redoubled vigilance in modern times may aid in emphasising the vast importance of the rôle of invigilator which the Bank has played ever since it became necessary to keep a stern eye upon the creation and circulation of paper. Neither then, nor now, did (or does) the Bank aim at unintermitted dominance in the discount market. Like a schoolmaster, it will occasionally leave its pupils to themselves ; but if ever there is a transgression, or an attempted transgression, of certain limits, the preceptor promptly resumes disciplinary functions. The resumption of control is less directed to the profit of the Bank shareholders than to the protection of the public welfare. " The interests of the proprietors or shareholders have invariably to give way when national or more important issues are at stake."[1] If the shareholders seek consolation for their compulsory allocation to this Quixotic task, they must find it in the " superlative safety of their investment."[1] The Bank re-entered the discount market about the time of the Bank Charter Act. For five years onwards from the " pressure " of 1839 the directors kept the Bank rate between 4 and 5 per cent. They consequently lost control of the discount market, where the ruling rate was not above 2 per cent. In September, 1844—the year of the Bank Charter Act—their total discounts were £113,000. From the 7th of that month—the date of their first " account " under the new Act—their policy was modified by the reduction of the rate to $2\frac{1}{2}$ per cent., followed by a sustained effort to maintain it at a level consistent with market conditions. The joint stock and private banks began to " feel a draught." In 1847 a meeting was held at which it was suggested that the London clearing banks should unite and keep their own cash reserves and settle the rate of discount among themselves, without reference to Threadneedle Street. Cattly, of the London and Westminster Bank, moved, and Sir Andrew Lusk seconded, a resolution that the joint-stock banks fix a rate for themselves. This was carried, but at the next meeting the resolution was rescinded and the practice of following the Bank of England was reverted to. By 1848 the Bank was an acknowledged and powerful competitor in the discount market and half the London discounts was in its hands. " The Bank rate," said Samuel Jones Loyd,[2] " formerly was 4 or 5 per cent. ; if the market rate of interest was below 4 per cent., the Bank ceased to discount till it got up again to that point. But in point of fact, latterly the discount department has become a very active department of the Bank." Gradually, but surely, the Old

[1] Governor of the Bank (A. F. Wallace) at dinner to Mr. Asquith, June 20, 1906.
[2] Before the Select (Secret) Committee on Commercial Distress, 1848.

Lady gathered up the threads. Sir David Salomons told the 1858 Committee that sometimes the Bank led, and sometimes followed, the current market rate. " Generally they are supposed to follow, but I think that sometimes they have led." It happened occasionally that the Bank of England was out of the market altogether for weeks and even months at a time, because the joint-stock banks were doing business below the public rate of Threadneedle Street. The bill brokers were being supplied by the joint-stock banks with ample funds for all the business obtainable at rates which were kept far below the Bank of England minimum. But the Old Lady could press the " rigour of the game," if she chose, even better than the late Sarah Battle. Threadneedle Street always held the Ace of Trumps ; for while the bill brokers were competing in this fashion with the Bank of England by means of funds supplied by its rivals, they invariably relied on the Bank to come to their assistance if they were driven into a corner. They lent right up to the hilt, with the result that if they were suddenly called upon by the banks for a large sum of money placed in their hands, their only way of getting it was to apply to the Bank of England. The Bank got the rough and the others got the smooth. At the time of the 1857 crisis " one broker had £5,000,000 and we were led to believe that another had between £8,000,000 and £10,000,000 ; there was one with £4,000,000, another with £3,500,000, and a third above £8,000,000. I speak of deposits with the brokers."[1]

In 1858 the Bank gave a turn to the screw, and again tightened its grip. It was intimated that in future advances to the bill brokers would only be made as a regular thing at a time when the Bank commanded unusually large supplies of public money, that is to say, during the six weeks immediately before the payment of dividends on the public funds. At any other time, applications from bill brokers for assistance would be treated as exceptional incidents. One consequence of the enactment was that in the Stock Exchange crisis of 1859 the discount brokers

[1] Neave, Governor of the Bank of England, 1857 Committee.

1857 PANIC—THE WIDENING ARENA

had practically no funds to employ. Gradually, as the years went on, and the resources of the joint-stock banks became far greater than those of the central institution, the regulation began to be more honoured in the breach than in the observance. It was subjected to that process of attrition which never fails to wear away the rigidity of a rule, unless there is a stern authority able to insist upon its observance. Courcelle-Seneuil[1] had indicated the essential defect of the position in 1864, almost simultaneously with the first manifestation of the advent of the real remedy for any money market aberrations. " The Bank of England," said he (with regard to one species of aberration), " cannot regulate the circulation : it could only do so if it had a monopoly of the business of discounting, and could stop any tendency to speculation in trade by the refusal of credit. But it is precisely at these times that trade has no need of the Bank of England. People only apply to the Bank when the ordinary sources of credit begin to be exhausted." In reliance on the Bank's intervention, bankers and bill brokers habitually overlent themselves in tranquil times, and then, by suddenly withdrawing or " pinching " facilities at the first approach of crisis, helped to accentuate the very trouble that they feared. But about 1883 the Bank intimated that in future the regulation of 1858 would be strictly observed. In that way stern discouragement was opposed to the practice of lending money down to the last shilling of the available balance in reliance on the aid of the Bank in the last extremity. The new policy had at least two very valuable results. In the first place it tended to consolidate the resources of the Bank in a time of stress by relieving it from the necessity of assisting speculators who had got out of their depth. On the other hand, it acted as a valuable admonition to the speculators themselves and thereby aided in the suppression of various undesirable forms of activity.

It has been said (*supra*) that about 1864 the advent of the *real* remedy for every species of market aberration

[1] Quoted by Andreades, *History of the Bank of England*, p. 381.

became observable. That panacea was obviously the firm establishment of the *moral* primacy of the Bank, as something distinct from, and entirely independent of, its *financial* predominance. In 1864 the financial supremacy still remained, though it was nearing its termination. Bankers, as a class, remarked a writer in 1863,[1] "merely look to the Bank of England returns, and tacitly follow in the wake of that mammoth establishment." The Governor of the Bank could boast in 1864 that its paid-up capital was so great that it might take in all the other banks with their paid-up capital and "rest," and leave them far behind. When this predominance in deposits ceased to be a fact the moral primacy was potent enough to take its place. In that way a supremacy no longer maintainable upon one basis is firmly founded upon another. But before we proceed, in connection with the advancing Overend-Gurney crisis, to investigate this pregnant development, it is desirable to look at the Bank's concurrent modifications of its policy with regard to the manipulation of the bank rate as a check upon the effect of the foreign exchanges.

CHECKING THE OUTFLOW OF GOLD

The old eighteenth-century device for stopping a foreign drain was to contract the paper currency so as to attract gold from abroad to fill the gap. In 1860 Mr. Goschen suggested the raising of the Bank of England rate of discount by 1 per cent. at a time, without intermediate changes, whenever gold began to leave the country. He saw that fractions of 1 per cent. divided by fractions of a year were ineffective in the cosmopolitan Money Market, especially in the presence of rapid and facile transport and communication, capable of use by astute bullion brokers well acquainted with the nature and utility of accommodation bills. Money has no nationality. It follows the best yield. The whole floating supply of cash will make its way to the locus of the highest bank rate (provided it be backed by an unassailable credit and the minimum of incertitude as regards other conditions) as surely as water

[1] *Bankers' Magazine*, p. 323.

finds its level. If the movement is merely a change of locus within the United Kingdom, it is a domestic drain and can be met with Bank of England notes ; but a foreign drain must be satisfied with gold and nothing else. Not only may it be necessary to stop it, but to set in motion a flow in the opposite direction. This the Bank can always do. The device suggested by Mr. Goschen attracted £4,000,000 gold from France and £10,000,000 from America, even in the panic year 1866. Money was literally swept up in order to be sent to London to fertilise under the high rate ruling there. The soundness of the principle was again demonstrated during the time when France was paying to Germany the war indemnity after the conflict of 1870. France had to get the money from all parts of the world. She would have obtained a disproportionate amount of it from England if the Bank had not protected itself by maintaining the rate at a high figure during the whole period when France was engaged in collecting the money.

In 1907, again, there was a kind of international conspiracy to throw upon the Bank of England the whole strain of meeting the American demands (arising from the panic—*post*, p. 644). By the manipulation of their rate, however, the directors ultimately compelled the Bank of France to assist by sending three millions to London. When the bank raised its rate in October, 1907, beginning at $5\frac{1}{2}$ per cent. and advancing to 7 per cent. on November 7, it received gold from twenty-four countries as a result of the increase.[1] But there was no attempt at aggrandisement—merely the protection of London. When the position was ameliorated, in the spring of 1908, the Bank rapidly reduced its rate from 7 to $2\frac{1}{2}$ per cent., so as to permit the replenishing of foreign resources out of the South African and other supplies.

Of course, it would be foolish to exaggerate the scope and importance of the rôle played by Threadneedle Street. The Bank rather defines than regulates the rate. It " raises the rate when its own accounts show that it is

---

[1] U.S. Monetary Commission, *Interviews on Banking*, p. 27.

386 EVOLUTION OF THE MONEY MARKET

necessary, but it cannot make money dear or cheap of its own free will."[1] To hold the fluctuations within limits and keep the flow of gold Londonwards, in a Money Market which is the clearing-house of the world, is at once the most difficult and the most beneficent of tasks. Its successful performance is materially aided by the ever-firmer consolidation of our position as a great creditor nation, which compels the foreign co-operation as a matter of self-interest. The mere knowledge that the Bank of England can summon gold from foreign sources creates an anxiety, among the foreigners themselves, to save us from the necessity of summoning it. The sentiment is not the fruit of any altruistic inspiration, but it exerts a very beneficial influence all the same.

TRANSFORMATION OF THE EXCHANGE HOUSES

Certain other modifications were (roughly) contemporaneous with the crisis of 1857. Extensive trading commitments, besides consolidating the financial supremacy of London, making it the world's gold storehouse, and transforming the bill on London into a cosmopolitan currency, brought the transition from the trading house to the exchange, the accepting, and then the issuing house. It was quite a natural evolution. The London trading firm became known in a given country as the possessors of considerable wealth. They became virtually the dictators in the sphere of the financial relationship between London and the country with which they traded. As their financial strength was enhanced, their influence widened. Down to a period almost within living memory the heads of the larger firms met twice a week on the Royal Exchange, and decided among themselves the rates which ruled exchange and credit between the various monetary centres. At this time the foreign exchange business was practically a monopoly in the hands of great private banking houses like the Rothschilds', Barings', Ambroses', Huths', Doxats', Bates's, Salomon's, Curries',

[1] **Jervoise Smith,** 1875 Committee, Q. 7297.

Wilsons', and Raphael's. There were then no foreign bank branches in London, but after the Franco-German war, the foreign banking element in London increased enormously, as we shall see in due course (see *post*, p. 493). But as the names of these houses became so familiar in the arenas of exchange and trade, the Governments of the countries with which they trafficked came to them for temporary accommodation, and their status was improved by providing it. When larger financial operations were contemplated the Governments naturally applied in the same quarter. In due course the inexorable evolutionary tendency led the former trading firm to drop its strictly mercantile connections and devote itself entirely, or almost entirely, to accepting, and to public loan issues. Loans were domiciled with the firms that issued them, and there came to be a traditional association, as regards sponsorship and guardianship, of house with country—as, for instance, the Rothschilds with Brazil and Chili—though modern financial rivalry has tended to prevent anything like exclusive dealing. As the years went on, this foreign loan business and the larger species of transactions of that type attracted the greater houses away from the foreign exchange business, so that Lord Rothschild and Lord Revelstoke, for instance, gave up attending the meetings held at the Royal Exchange, and thereby created an opening for new firms specialising in this particular class of operation, such as Samuel Montagu and Sons. The foreign exchange business of the older houses still survived, but as it was now a subordinate and not a primary activity, it was open to the inroads of rivalry by the foreign banks. Their advent, immediately subsequent to the Franco-German war, brought them on the scene at the precise moment when conditions were most advantageous. The older practitioners were subordinating the exchange business to loan issues, while the new joint-stock banks were rather timid about tackling a business so complex, and so forbidding of aspect, as foreign exchange. So it happened that in course of years the foreign banks, by opening offices in London, practically monopolised exchange operations. At last the time came, during the last Boer war, when the London offices of foreign institutions, like the Deutsche Bank and the Crédit Lyonnais, were able to introduce large amounts of foreign capital into this country and to use it with profit to themselves and to our trade. With its unfailing liberality of sentiment and breadth of vision, London has always realised—with occasional and exceptional outbursts of jealousy, perhaps—that these changes meant benefit for itself and the enhancement of its predominance. Mr. W. F. Spalding, in an essay contributed to the Institute of Bankers in 1911, said :—

" We are sure that in the banking and commercial development of our country the results will amply demonstrate that wisdom of our free banking policy, and that ultimately we shall come to see that these foreign branch banks render us an important service in the preservation of our Empire. It is certain that the more they open here the greater will be the advantages to the trade and finance of the country, internal as well as external. Still more will they serve to promote that friendly and harmonious understanding amongst other nations which follows more intimate commercial intercourse, and always fosters the spirit of peace necessary to the prosperity and wealth of the world."

The powerful competition of the foreign banks, however, only handicapped by their non-membership of the Clearing-house, at last compelled the attention of the English banks. About 1905 the London, City and Midland broke away from the preconceived notions of purely English banking by embarking determinedly upon Foreign Exchange business. Within a couple of years it had become necessary to open a special Foreign Exchange office in Finch Lane, and there were forty to fifty clerks already engaged in the work of the new department. A couple of years later the London and County Bank purchased premises in Cornhill for the purposes of their rapidly growing Foreign Exchange business. So well has

1857 PANIC—THE WIDENING ARENA

the new departure prospered that the legend "Foreign Exchange" now adorns the window of practically every branch bank, and the English bankers are rapidly recovering the ground which they need never have lost.

The whole process by which the trading firm evolved into the accepting house, and the latter again into the issuing house, was another of those specialisations which mean so much, whether we are concerned with the history of the vertebrates or the working of the Money Market, with Mammal or with Mammon. The particular instance which we are considering has aided finance in the discharge of a double and difficult duty. In floating colonial and foreign loans it has had to collect the money and at the same time to allay the apprehensions of the lenders with regard to its apparent departure to the distant and unknown destination. The investor in foreign bonds trusts the banker rather than the borrower. He looks to the issuing house in the case of a Dominion loan also, though his Imperial fervour has in recent years helped to dispel his suspicions of this type of security. Yet even a colonial municipality, borrowing in its own name, and without the intervention of some great banking institution, might perhaps secure only a modicum of its requirements in the absence of the quasi-guarantee which attaches to the name of the banker. The lender to a New Zealand Harbour Board does not know (in the sense of capacity to give legal evidence of the fact) that the harbour even exists. The undertaking, and the authorities which control it, are to him mere names. But the prospectus bears the imprimatur of an Australasian bank, whose multitude of branches include one in the city which possesses the harbour. In the presence of the assurance thus conveyed, the investor's dubiety changes into determination. Another example is available in the irrigation enterprises of the Western States of America. It is estimated that there has been expended in this species of development not less than $200,000,000. "How far," said Messrs. J. P. Morgan and Co., addressing themselves to the Money Trust Committee (March, 1913), "would such development have gone, how far would those regions have been opened to agriculture, had dependence for obtaining that great sum been placed upon the near-by communities, or even (by means of public auction) upon investors in New York or Chicago, who know little of the safety of such investments ? " Still more forcibly do these considerations apply in the case of a foreign industrial enterprise. Under the new conditions the investor who is nervous of his own judgment, while he dislikes the restriction of dividends in the majority of Investment Trust stocks, will be offered securities of various types, the proceeds of which are designed to aid the evolution of rising communities. They are authoritatively backed, so as to offer him, as it were, the guarantee of a fair run for his money. He will invest under the cover of obvious and unchallengeable responsibility—that of the issuing house. It follows from these premises that even upon the evolution of democratic communities (of which it is fatuously supposed to be the enemy) finance bestows a fostering care. Its solicitude is an inalienable necessity of the situation ; for the two impossibilities which confront social reformers, who love to believe themselves omnipotent, are the transformation of a woman into a man and of financial suspicion and mistrust into the confidence which will advance money on a long-dated bond.

THE PROTESTS OF THE VISIONARIES

As the last relics of the older economic era tottered to their fall, and the new conditions essential to financial integration began to be palpable in many directions, the alarmist sentiments of the older school found voice in the criticisms and complaints of Carlyle, Ruskin, and Tennyson. They all " thought scorn of that pleasant land—the Utopia of the economists' imagining."[1] Carlyle denounced the trading ambitions of the Cobdenists. They were mere " pig philosophy." Tennyson entertained, and did not scruple to express, an aristocratic contempt for the trading classes. He thought that war was a cure for commercial

---

[1] Spencer Walpole, *History of Twenty-five Years*, p. 47.

dishonesty.[1] With far more accurate insight the City was forming for itself a different view about war. "Tom Baring told me yesterday [1853] that the notion of war was anything but popular in the City, and that men of intelligence and property would require a wonderfully good case to be made for it before such a nuisance would be tolerated."[2] Ruskin, however, was far more inflamed than his fellow-visionaries by the conditions he saw around him. He despaired of remedy " until this disgusting nineteenth century has—I cannot say breathed, but steamed, its last." Ruskin ventured to formulate his theories in " Unto this Last," regarded by himself as " the truest, rightest-worded, and most serviceable things " he had ever written. Yet the ideal men whom he contemplated were only the fancies of his own romantic intellect, having no existence outside his own pages, and therefore impossible of control by an economic science which has to deal with mankind as it is, and not as the Ruskins nobly try to make it. If Ruskin's dislike of machinery, and his passionate reprobation of trade competition, and profit, had not been thrust aside by the financial pioneers of the nation, we should long ago have been on the verge of an economic Niagara. Happily for mankind, the curtains which had for millions of years concealed the cosmic mystery were beginning to be lifted by the fearless hands of science. The time was at hand when man would control, rather than quarrel with, his environment, when reconstruction rather than futile criticism would engage his energies. For while these querulous voices were raised in worthy but mistaken protest and exposition, there was being elaborated a theory which was to solve the problems that perplexed Carlyle and Ruskin, and then to receive its not least convincing illustrations in that very arena

[1] "The niggard throats of Manchester may bawl
　　What England was, shall her true sons forget ?
　We are not cotton-spinners all
　　But some love England and her honour yet.
　And these in our Thermopylæ shall stand
　And hold against the world the honour of this land."
　　　　　　　The " Third of February," 1852.
[2] Lord Clarendon, *Memories of Henry Reeve*, Vol. I. p. 306.

of human enterprise which to them was nothing but concrete greed and selfishness. On July 1, 1858, there were read before the Linnean Society the two papers, by Darwin and A. R. Wallace respectively, which formed the basis of the *Origin of Species* and the foundation of the whole Darwinian hypothesis. Remembering, as we must, how many elusive tokens of this tremendous principle had been fitfully glimpsed in the years that were past, and how much its definite enunciation and acceptance were to mean for mankind, it was as if—

> " The sentinels, whose tread we heard
> Through long hours when we could not see,
> Paused now, exchanged with cheer the word,
> The unchanging watchword, Liberty.[1]

HIGHER IDEALS OF PERSONAL CONDUCT

One last topic, rather psychological—or perhaps hygienic—than financial, may well engage passing allusion before we turn to the onset of the Overend-Gurney crisis and the complete transformation of the entire spirit of English finance which follows it. In the presence of the more strenuous conditions, arising from expanding responsibilities of all kinds, both the nation and its components began to consider questions of hygiene and health. The people which is in the thick of a great financial and industrial battle can no longer afford to indulge in such habits of self-indulgence as characterised it in an easier age. The first general Public Health Act (11 and 12 Vict. c. 63) had been passed in 1848. It was optional, and empowered a local inquiry into sanitary conditions on the petition of one-tenth of the ratepayers. The Act was widened in scope in 1858 (by 21 and 22 Vict. c. 98) and again in 1861 (by 24 and 25 Vict. c. 61). Further, the Act of 1872 (35 and 36 Vict. c. 79) split up the whole country into sanitary districts, under a special authority, instead of leaving the initiative to the ratepayers in each district. This legislation coincided with a change in personal habits from the dissipation of the eighteenth century towards the restraint

[1] Samuel Longfellow.

1857 PANIC—THE WIDENING ARENA

which is so conspicuous a characteristic of the business community—and especially of the City—in our time. Pitt thought little of drinking two or three bottles of port at a time,[1] and save for an occasional resulting delusion that there were two Speakers instead of one in the Chair, he seems to have been little the worse for it. It is recorded with obvious satisfaction and admiration by Sir William Forbes that only *once* in the course of the long career of John Coutts, the banker, was he found in his counting-house so " disguised with liquor " as to be incapable of transacting any business.[2] That kind of thing had to be got rid of in the presence of the new conditions. So it was that just at the time when the nation itself was waking up to the importance of public health, the protagonists of finance, on the Stock Exchange as well as in the bank parlours, were also becoming aware that if a man is to retain a cool and dispassionate judgment, discipline and self-restraint must rule his conduct. Gilbart, who did not miss much of what was going on around him, clearly discerned the change :—

" It is peculiarly necessary that a banker should pay regard to the state of his own health, and to the discipline of his own mind, so as to guard against any morbid or gloomy apprehensions with regard to the future. He should attempt to form a cool and dispassionate judgment as to the result of passing events ; endeavouring so to arrange his own affairs as to be prepared for whatever may occur, but taking care not to increase the present evil by predicting greater calamities. If he suffer a feeling of despondency to get the mastery of his mind, he will be less able to cope with the difficulties of his position. He will then, probably, refuse reasonable assistance to even first-rate customers, realise securities unnecessarily at a heavy sacrifice, and keep in his till an amount of unemployed treasure excessively disproportionate to the extent of his liabilities. This will increase the pressure. Fear, too, is always contagious. A banker of this melancholy temperament will impart his apprehensions to others, and thus the panic will become more widely extended."[3]

[1] Rosebery, *Pitt*, p. 267.
[2] *Memoirs of a Banking House*, p. 10.
[3] Gilbart, *Logic of Banking*, p. 79.

The biologist needs not to be told of the paradox exhibited by the exhilaration of self-sacrificing effort, nor of the probability that " among the pleasures on which experience lights should be some connected not with the maintenance of the race at its then level, but with the further expansion of its powers."[1] We shall soon be in the presence of a flood of generous strivings, almost as lofty and unselfish in their inspiration as those which characterised the passionate fervour of a Benedict or a Dominic. The Dominicans were not more truly the watch-dogs of the Lord (Domini canes) than are the heads of the financial hierarchy the sentinels of civilisation.

[1] Hobhouse, *Mind in Evolution*, p. 390.

CHAPTER XIV

THE OVEREND-GURNEY CRISIS AND THE END OF ISOLATION AND DISUNION

As we leave the 1857 crisis behind us, and witness the gradual shaping of the events that accompanied the Overend-Gurney cataclysm, we are approaching the end of an age. Not vainly did the leader of nineteenth-century scientists hand to man the key of the great enigma. Not vainly, two years later, did the authors of *Essays and Reviews* confront the thunders of ecclesiastical censure as " atheists and Socinians." The decade which saw the publication of *Essays and Reviews,* as well as the Overend-Gurney crash, was the half-unconscious spectator of the definite change in financial method and purpose from passivity to resolution, from obscure and disunited meandering to the deliberate and united selection of a goal, from timorous hesitancy in the battle with the cosmic environment to an unflinching determination that the mastership of fate should be achieved. When we have traced the events that led to the crisis of 1866, and examined the catastrophe itself, we shall become aware of the presence of " confederacy in a flood," sweeping away the last relics of the older instability to make room for the adamantine bastions of the financial fabric that was destined to be raised in its place.

AFTER THE COMPANIES ACT OF 1862

The Joint-Stock Companies Act of 1862 brought in its train a rush of new issues, with total capitals of £100,053,000 in 1863, £155,887,500 in 1864, and £106,995,000 in 1865. From 1863 to 1866 no fewer than 3480 companies were born. The recklessness was pronounced enough to wring from the Master of the Rolls the declaration that "no doubt many companies were started for the purpose of being wound up." The novel verb "to finance" was interpreted in a sinister sense by a multitude of new banks as well as certain finance companies which advanced long money to the new undertakings (many of them home and foreign railways), though they had only short money in their coffers. There was an increase in the ratio of promissory payments to actual payments, raising what Herbert Spencer called "irrational expectations." It is significant that at the critical turn of events the figures of company registration fell rapidly away to £68,569,903 in 1866 and to £28,861,390 in 1867. It did not again pass the £100,000,000 mark till 1872; for the total of £138,726,301 in 1869 includes a company registered with a nominal capital of £100,000,000, though its paid-up capital never exceeded £200.

As the banking business became more popular and more trusted, more money flowed in, not only from customers, but from shareholders. The Joint-Stock Companies Act, 1857,[1] fixed £100 as the minimum denomination of a bank share, but this was, in effect, repealed by the Companies Act of 1862. New banking companies were a special "fancy" of the period. In the language of a sardonic contemporary observer, "if there be one financial fable more likely than another to be believed in by the British public, it is that of a bank." The writer adds the reason: "every man with any claim to monetary respectability employs a banker, and therefore thinks himself thoroughly conversant with banking in all its various branches."[2] With such conditions to encourage their advent, twenty-eight new banks came into existence in 1863. They obtained subscriptions from the public to the extent of £34,150,000. It is significant—and withal satisfactory—that £4,850,000 of this was destined for colonial banking enterprise. More remarkable still, however, were the

[1] 20 and 21 Vict., c. 49, s. 13.
[2] *Bubbles of Finance*, p. 217.

figures revealed on analysis of the positions of the great established banks. Even at the time of the actual crisis, in 1866, the capital and reserve of the London and Westminster Bank only amounted to about £6 10s. against each £100 of deposits and other liabilities. There were, of course, some institutions which exhibited larger proportions. The figures in the case of the Metropolitan and Provincial Bank were £74 to each £100 of deposits. But the fact that the London and Westminster had already attained so high a position, while the proportion of its capital and reserves to its total liabilities remained so low, is an ample demonstration of the changing aspect of banking science and the diminishing importance of the shareholders' capital as a factor in the support and success of these great institutions. The principle that a small capital and large deposits formed the elements of successful and profitable banking was already well understood. Banking science was steadily improving also. How well the ebb and flow of the till-money and the short-loan funds had become regulated in the 'sixties was evidenced by the statement of the manager of the London and Westminster Bank, in 1866, that for ten years they had never had occasion to turn Government Stock into money. Nevertheless, the very magnitude to which banking had grown rendered it peculiarly susceptible to attack, in a period which had seen scandal after scandal, and crisis after crisis. Moreover, although there was skill and nerve at the centre, the vast mass of the public was as yet only at the amateur stage in finance, and therefore easily alarmed. Never had there been so promising an opportunity for the unscrupulous bears, who did not hesitate to use it. Their scandalous attacks upon bank shares, at length frustrated, in 1867, by Leeman's Act, have been discussed in another connection (*ante*, p. 295). Yet the signs of incipient courage in the investor were becoming discernible here and there (*post*, p. 466) as the scope of enterprise broadened and capital accumulated. In spite of the nervousness about bank shares (largely a consequence of the terrible memories of unlimited liability) Sir John Lubbock was able to state

CC

in 1875 that there were more than 50,000 shareholders in joint-stock banks.[1]

OVEREND, GURNEY AND CO.

Overend, Gurney and Co., who were to give their name to the next (and last) of the great financial convulsions of the nineteenth century, called themselves "Money-lenders."[2] They were in fact bill brokers, handling £60,000,000 to £70,000,000 of commercial bills per annum. The private firm had been transformed into a joint-stock company in 1865. Its capital was fixed at £5,000,000 in 100,000 shares of £50 each, the paid-up capital being £1,500,000. The private firm was stated to have made profits of £250,000 per annum. During the last nine months of their business Overend, Gurney and Co., Limited, discounted bills to the extent of £56,000,000, and helped to spread the "fatal facility of credit" which brought collapse in its train.

In view of the magnitude of their transactions, the old standing of the firm, and the well-known fact that it had more than once rendered assistance to other houses in time of stringency (as we saw earlier), it is perhaps hardly surprising, as we look at the contemporary records, to discover how little attention was paid to the premonitory symptoms of the approaching trouble. At the time of George Rae's death—and English banking never produced a keener intellect than his—it came out in the *Liverpool Daily Post* that even his shrewdness had not detected the menace of the Overend-Gurney position until the very eve of the disaster. Rae's bank, the North and South Wales, had a considerable sum deposited with Overend, Gurney and Co. for employment, by them, as bill brokers. Rae, in the ordinary course of business, happened to have a conversation with one of the partners in London a short time before the failure of the firm :—

"As you are here, Mr. Rae," said the partner in Overend's, showing him some Liverpool bills, "I should like to know what you think of these people."

---

[1] Speech on Bankers Act Amendment Bill, March 17.
[2] So Chapman, a partner, in giving evidence as to the dock warrant frauds. (*Great City Frauds*, p. 118.)

THE OVEREND-GURNEY CRISIS

Rae shook his head ominously at some large acceptances by a man he knew to be very weak. The partner then showed him another acceptance, which Rae said was worse than the first, and a third, which was worse than either. Without the slightest hesitation, but yet in quite a casual manner, Rae, on leaving, said, " By the way, if you have no particular use for that deposit of ours, I think it would be convenient for us to have it."

The money was transferred to the North and South Wales Bank, and Overend and Gurney failed a few days afterwards. Such an incident does not stand alone. It seems to be frequently the case that the imminence of crisis is characterised by a firm conviction that all is well. Moreover, a spring crisis was unprecedented. The crises of 1837, 1847, and 1857 had all been in November—and the Baring episode again stamped the brand of " dangerous " on that unlucky month.

SIGNS OF THE COMING STORM

The mutterings of the coming storm became plainly audible in April, 1866. In that month the Joint-Stock Discount Co. failed, and Barned's Bank at Liverpool followed, with liabilities of £3,500,000. In the Barned's Banking Company case, the Bank of England only presented the bankruptcy petition because the directors desired their own solicitor to see the accounts. The Bank of England itself was well secured, but in contemporary language " it was the interest of the Bank to support people," and a scrutiny of the affairs of Barned's Banking Company from the inside was one of the expedients adopted to that end. Simultaneously with this episode the contractors for the London, Chatham, and Dover Railway had had to raise money by issuing stock at $27\frac{1}{2}$; yet Mr. Gladstone, moving the Budget on May 3—the day on which the Bank rate went from 6 to 7 per cent.—merely expressed his disquietude about the exhaustion of our coal-fields in the twentieth century. He uttered no word concerning the crisis then actually incumbent over the City. Events steadily developed towards the crash. The failure of Pinto, Percy, Ashby and Co. involved Overend, Gurney and Co. in heavy losses, and undoubtedly precipitated considerable distrust. Vague reports got into circulation that the firm was trading vastly beyond its capital, and helped to stimulate the existing disquietude. The profound anxiety which had arisen in the City was again accentuated by the delivery, on May 9, of a judgment to the effect that certain bills accepted by the Mid-Wales Railway Co., and held by Overend, Gurney's and two other firms, were of no validity. By this time the heads of the threatened company were fully alive to their danger. But when application was made to the Bank of England for assistance the directors took the view that it would be vain to offer aid to one single establishment, unless they were prepared to render similar assistance in other directions. They declined, for instance, to advance more than £30,000 to the English Joint-Stock Bank, against £47,000 worth of country bills, all of them payable in London. In order, however, to be quite sure of their ground, the Bank directors had the Overend-Gurney position closely scrutinised. George Grenfell Glyn, of Glyn-Mills (who afterwards became Lord Wolverton), was requested, in collaboration with R. C. Bevan and R. J. K. Hodgson, to examine the Overend-Gurney assets and report whether they were such as to justify assistance from the Bank of England or from Lombard Street. They met at Glyn's, and after very careful consideration, found themselves unable to advise the giving of help.[1] Aid was refused— so it was said at the time—with "sincere regret" and with a full knowledge of all that the refusal would involve.

"BLACK FRIDAY"

On the Thursday morning (May 10) Overend-Gurney shares opened at 3 discount, fell to $4\frac{1}{2}$ discount, and closed at $10\frac{1}{2}$ to $9\frac{1}{2}$ discount. At half-past three o'clock on that day the secretary of the great firm issued an official notice of suspension :—

"We regret to announce that a severe run on our deposits and resources has compelled us to suspend payment, this course

---

[1] So stated in *Bankers' Magazine*, 1887, p. 232.

THE OVEREND-GURNEY CRISIS 401

being considered, under advice, the best calculated to protect the interest of all parties."[1]

The liabilities amounted to about £10,000,000, of which £6,000,000 was due to depositors who held bills as security and £3,500,000 to unsecured depositors. Naturally and inevitably the announcement of such a suspension precipitated the panic. In psychological terminology, which has a peculiar fitness n application to crises, it brought mob-suggestibility into play. The panic—really of the mercantile rather than of the banking type—was tremendous in aspect—more so, perhaps, than in reality. All the issuing banks poured in their bills and Consols at the Bank of England, saying : " We must have this, and we must take the Bank of England notes down with us to-night, because we expect we shall have a run upon us to-morrow."[2] There was a wild rush to sell. In fact, everything was pressed for sale without the slightest regard to its intrinsic value. The following day was Black Friday, of tragic memory, even at the distance of half a century. Failure after failure added impetus and volume to the cataclysm. Many stocks went to negative prices. People were willing to pay those who would take them off their hands. The English Joint-Stock Bank "temporarily" suspended with liabilities of £800,000, Peto and Betts, contractors, for £4,000,000, and Shrimpton, railway contractor, for £200,000. The Imperial Mercantile Credit Association and the Consolidated Discount Co. followed in rapid succession. There were yet others, but the mere names would have no meaning to the present generation. Not only were the actual failures so disastrous, but the menace of further calamity was hanging over the city like a cloud. The shares of the Agra and Masterman's Bank, which had been quoted at 33 prem. when the year opened, finished at 1 discount on Black Friday. The bank ulti-

---

[1] The final meeting to conclude the liquidation of Overend, Gurney and Co., Ltd., was not held until November 16, 1893, by which time London had passed through the Baring crisis !
[2] Hodgson, M.P., 1875 Committee, Q. 7847.

mately failed on June 6, having paid out over £3,000,000 across the counter.[1]

WERE CONSOLS UNSALEABLE ?

Bagehot, dealing[2] with the attitude of the Bank of England at this time of financial cataclysm, says :—

" There was nevertheless an instant when it was believed the Bank would not advance on Consols, or at least hesitated to advance on them. The moment this was reported in the City, and telegraphed to the country, it made the panic infinitely worse. In fact, to make large advances in this faltering way is to incur the evil of making them without obtaining the advantage. What is wanted and what is necessary to stop a panic is to diffuse the impression that though money may be dear, still money is to be had. If people could be really convinced that they could have money if they wait a day or two, and that utter ruin is not coming, most likely they would cease to run in such a mad way for money."

But the late Luke Hansard, of Martin's Bank, who had been through the panic, denied that the Bank ever refused to lend on Consols, though borrowers might, he admitted, have had to pay very high rates for accommodation. Addressing the Manchester and District Bankers' Institute, January 18, 1901, he said :—

" I have recently consulted with a well-known bill broker, who was engaged in active business at the time, and he confirms me in the statement that loans on Consols or other securities could easily be obtained. But it was essential that the borrower had in his hand securities undeniably first-class, such as Consols, or good bills of exchange, and not the various forms of redundant finance paper existent at that period, and largely held by Overend, Gurney's. I venture to think that, from the distance of time, a kind of enchantment is given by some modern writers and critics to this and other exciting periods of our financial history, the actual incidents of which they are apt to over-colour."

---

[1] It should be added that the actual failure was precipitated by a run on the Indian branches, caused by false telegrams from London that the head office had suspended payment.
[2] *Lombard Street*, p. 64.

THE OVEREND-GURNEY CRISIS

The actual prices of Consols during the latter part of the week of which the Friday, May 11, was Black Friday, exhibit no traces of such serious disturbance in the Consol Market as would indicate the impossibility of selling. On the corresponding day a year earlier (May 12, 1865) Consols were $90\frac{1}{2}$. In 1866 the quotations were :—

Money	Account
Wed., May 9.—86, $86\frac{1}{4}$, $86\frac{3}{8}$, $86\frac{1}{2}$,	Wed., May 9.—$85\frac{1}{4}$, $85\frac{1}{8}$, 85, $84\frac{7}{8}$, (ex d.)
Thur., ,, 10.—$85\frac{3}{4}$, $85\frac{7}{8}$, $85\frac{5}{8}$, $85\frac{1}{2}$, $86\frac{1}{4}$, $85\frac{3}{4}$	Thur., ,, 10.—$84\frac{3}{4}$, $84\frac{7}{8}$, $84\frac{5}{8}$, 85, $84\frac{3}{4}$
Fri., ,, 11.—$85\frac{1}{2}$, 85, $85\frac{1}{2}$, $84\frac{3}{4}$, $85\frac{1}{2}$, $84\frac{5}{8}$, $85\frac{1}{4}$, 85, $85\frac{1}{2}$	Fri., ,, 11.—$84\frac{3}{4}$, 84, $84\frac{1}{4}$, $85\frac{1}{4}$, $84\frac{1}{4}$, $85\frac{1}{4}$, 85
Sat., ,, 12.—$86\frac{1}{4}$, $86\frac{1}{2}$, $85\frac{3}{4}$, $86\frac{3}{4}$, $86\frac{1}{2}$, $86\frac{3}{4}$	Sat., ,, 12.—$85\frac{5}{8}$, $85\frac{1}{2}$, $85\frac{3}{4}$, $85\frac{3}{4}$

A year later, on May 10, 1867, the price was 91.

We saw that aid was refused to Overend, Gurney and Co. But in other quarters, where assistance could be justifiably given, there was no refusal. Every borrower who came with adequate security was liberally dealt with, and, even if accommodation could not be afforded to the full extent, relief was given to the utmost margin justified by the circumstances. The Bank excelled itself. "I do not believe," said the Governor, subsequently reviewing the circumstances, "that anyone would have thought of predicting, even at the shortest period beforehand, the greatest of these advances," made during the episode which he described as a tornado.

THE LETTER TO THE GOVERNMENT

The historic importance of this, the last, suspension of the Bank Charter Act[1] justifies the inclusion of the full correspondence between the Bank and the Government. The letter to the Chancellor of the Exchequer was in these terms :—

"BANK OF ENGLAND,
"*May* 11, 1866.

"SIR,—We consider it our duty to lay before the Government the facts relating to the extraordinary demands for assistance which have been made upon the Bank of England to-day, in consequence of the failure of Messrs. Overend, Gurney and Co.

---

[1] For the ultimate legislative "regularisation" of this power of suspension, during the German war crisis of 1914, see *post*, p. 679.

"We have advanced to the bankers, bill brokers, and merchants in London, during the day, upwards of £4,000,000 sterling, upon the security of Government Stock and bills of exchange—an unprecedented sum to lend in one day, and which, therefore, we suppose would be sufficient to meet all their requirements, although the proportion of this sum which may have been sent to the country must materially affect the question.

" We commenced this morning with a reserve of £5,727,000, which has been drawn upon so largely that we cannot calculate upon having so much as £3,000,000 this evening, making a fair allowance for what may be remaining at the branches.

" We have not refused any legitimate application for assistance, and, unless the money taken from the Bank is entirely withdrawn from circulation, there is no reason to suppose that the reserve is insufficient.

" We have the honour to be, Sir,
" Your obedient servants,
(Signed) " H. L. HOLLAND, Governor,
" THOS. NEWMAN HUNT, Deputy-Governor."

Below is the text of the reply sent to the Governor and Deputy-Governor of the Bank :—

" To the Governor and Deputy-Governor of the
Bank of England.

" GENTLEMEN,—We have the honour to acknowledge the receipt of your letter of this day to the Chancellor of the Exchequer, in which you state the course of action at the Bank of England, under the circumstances of sudden anxiety which have arisen since the stoppage of Messrs. Overend, Gurney and Co., Ltd., yesterday.

" We learn with regret that the Bank reserve, which stood so recently as last night at a sum of about £5,750,000, has been reduced in a single day by the liberal answer of the Bank to the demands of commerce during the hours of business, and by its great anxiety to avert disaster, to little more than half that amount, or a sum (actual for London and estimated for the branches) not greatly exceeding £3,000,000. The accounts and representations which have reached Her Majesty's Government during the day exhibit the state of things in the City as one of extraordinary distress and apprehension. Indeed, deputations composed of persons of the greatest weight and influence, and representing the private and joint-stock banks of London, have presented themselves in Downing Street, and have urged, with unanimity and earnestness, the necessity of some intervention on the part of the State to allay the anxiety which prevails, and which appears to have amounted, through great part of the day, to absolute panic.

" There are some important points in which the present crisis differs from those of 1847 and 1857. Those periods were of mercantile distress, but the vital consideration of banking credit does not appear to have been involved in them, as it is in the present crisis.

" Again, the course of affairs was comparatively slow and measured, whereas the shock has in this instance arrived with an intense rapidity, and the opportunity for deliberation is narrowed in proportion. Lastly, the reserve of the Bank of England has suffered a diminution without precedent relatively to the time in which it has been brought about, and in view, especially, of this circumstance, Her Majesty's Government cannot doubt that it is their duty to adopt, without delay, measures which seem to them best calculated to compose the public mind and to arrest the calamities which may threaten trade and industry.

" If, then, the directors of the Bank of England, proceeding upon the prudent rules of action by which their administration is usually governed, shall find that, in order to meet the wants of legitimate commerce, it be requisite to extend their discounts and advances upon approved securities, so as to require issues of notes beyond the limits fixed by law, Her Majesty's Government recommends that this necessity should be met immediately upon its occurrence, and in that event they will not fail to make application to Parliament for its sanction.

" No such discount or advance, however, should be granted at a rate of interest less than 10 per cent., and Her Majesty's Government reserve it to themselves to recommend, if they should see fit, the imposition of a higher rate. After deduction by the Bank of whatever it may consider to be a fair charge for its risk, expense, and trouble, the profits of these advances will accrue to the public.

" We have the honour to be, gentlemen,
" Your obedient servants,
" (Signed) RUSSELL,
" (Signed) W. E. GLADSTONE."

" Downing Street, May 11, 1866."

The resolutions of the Bank directors were conveyed to Earl Russell and W. E. Gladstone in this letter :—

"BANK OF ENGLAND,
"May 12.

"MY LORD AND SIR,—Having laid before the court of directors the letter received from you yesterday with respect to a further issue of notes, if necessary, beyond the limit affixed by the Act of 1844, we have now the honour to enclose a copy of the resolution of the court thereupon.

"We have the honour to be, my Lord and Sir,
"Your most obedient servants,
"H. L. HOLLAND, Governor,
"THOS. N. HUNT, Deputy-Governor."

(Copy of resolutions enclosed.)

"At a court of directors of the Bank, on Saturday, the 12th of May, 1866.

"RESOLVED—That the Governors be requested to inform the First Lord of the Treasury and the Chancellor of the Exchequer that the Court is prepared to act in conformity with the letter addressed them yesterday.

"RESOLVED—That the minimum rate of discount on bills not having more than ninety-five days to run be raised from 9 to 10 per cent.

"HAMMOND CHUBB, Secretary."

It has been said that the Bank of England was not represented in the deputation from the banks which saw the Chancellor of the Exchequer in 1866, and to which allusion is made in the letter from Lord Russell and Mr. Gladstone. Critics have declared that this was mere bravado on the part of the Bank, because the other banks could have shut it up at once by withdrawing their reserves. In any case, however, there was no actual breach of the Bank Charter Act, though it had been authorised. In fact, the reserve did not reach its lowest point (£859,980 cash, against £27,199,322 deposits, or 3·2 per cent.) until nearly three weeks after suspension had been authorised. It is true, however, that during the crisis the bankers, in response to an appeal from the Bank Court, paid into the Bank of England every night the notes which would under ordinary circumstances have remained in their own tills.[1] But so prompt was the effect of the suspension of the Act, that on the Saturday it looked as if the crisis were at an end—although, unhappily, at the next account day thirty Stock Exchange houses announced their inability to meet their obligations. The first sign of recovery from the crisis was the willingness of the bill brokers to negotiate short-dated bills, while at the same time they declined to touch the long-dated variety:—

" I have consulted with one or two foreign bill brokers who were on 'Change in 1866, and they all say that though there was some difficulty in selling bills on May 10 [before the Overend-Gurney suspension], most of the bills then refused were readily sold on the following 'Change day, May 15. To use the expressive phrase of one broker, the bills that could not be sold on the 10th went like ' hot cakes ' on May 15."[2]

During five days the Bank made a total of advances and discounts of £12,225,000 and during three months about £45,000,000. This " expansive " policy based on the " expansive theory " has been too often tested, during the past half-century, against the " restrictive " method to leave any doubt as to the wisdom of the former.[3] The issue of Treasury notes, during the German war crisis of 1914, is the most recent instance of its adoption. Restriction, if its application could be limited to insolvent houses, might be an acceptable policy. But there is only a limited possibility of discrimination between the solvent and the insolvent. Moreover, a thoroughly solvent house —competent, if given time, to pay even 40s. in the £— may find itself utterly unable to liquidate its assets when everybody else is trying to do the same. That is partly Mill's view—that the extension of credit is mischievous when it can only retard and aggravate an inevitable collapse, itself already generated by inflated credit. Credit should be extended, in Mill's opinion, when the collapse

---

[1] *Bankers' Magazine*, 1867, p. 359.
[2] Luke Hansard, Address to the Manchester and District Institute of Bankers, January 18, 1901.
[3] Conant, *Banks of Issue*, p. 459.

has actually occurred.[1] Bagehot urged that the only preventive of panic was the possession of such an abundant reserve as would enable the Bank of England to act upon the expansive theory at time of need, and lend abundantly. Ellis argues that the real preventive is "not so much lending little as lending well."[2] But the fact is that scientifically elaborated and disciplined banking enables us to combine both expedients, and to lend the maximum of credit with the minimum of risk.

NO REAL BREACH OF THE ACT

The Bank of England note issue was increased from £22,345,000 on May 9 to £26,121,000 on May 16. This was an increase of £3,776,000, of which £1,231,000 was in £5 and £10 notes and £2,545,000 in notes of £20 to £1000—there being 309 of the latter denomination. There was, as we saw, no actual breach of the Bank Charter Act. The demand for the large notes was accepted at the time as an indication that the banks were preparing themselves for all eventualities. Yet it is a striking fact, as indicating the growth of public confidence in the stability of banking institutions, that money came in faster than it went out. John Dun, of the Alliance Bank (now Parr's) declared, before the 1875 Committee, that deposits actually increased in times of panic "because prices are so disarranged and people are so frightened that they do not know what to buy with their money, and they put it for safe custody into the bank until better times come." In 1863, Dun added, the deposits of his bank were £7,253,000 ; in 1864, £7,343,000 ; in 1865, £7,951,000 ; in 1866 (the Overend-Gurney year), £8,400,000 ; in 1867 (when the shadow of the Overend-Gurney affair still overhung the City), £9,083,000 ; but in 1868 they fell back to £8,832,000. "About this time people began to get courage, and to take the money that had been lodged in the banks, and to invest it. In 1869, when confidence had returned, deposits fell to £8,234,000." (Q. 6766.) It is

[1] *Principles*, Book III, chap. XXIV, sec. 4.
[2] *Rationale of Market Fluctuations*, p. 92.

THE OVEREND-GURNEY CRISIS

worth noting that the same tendency shows itself among the banks themselves. So far as the figures can be followed, bankers' balances at the Bank of England have always been larger at a time of crisis than in periods of normal quietude. This is a demonstrable fact with regard to every crisis down to 1866, but it is not demonstrable since because the Bank no longer gives the necessary data. For instance, the annual averages of the bankers' balances in 1845 were £1,200,000; in 1846, £1,500,000; and in 1847, £1,400,000. But the balances rose to £2,000,000 on October 30, 1847, in the presence of crisis, and advanced to £2,100,000 on November 6. From that point onwards to the end of the year they were never below the average figure, and on January 8, 1848, they were up to £3,800,000. So again in 1857, the average of the balances for that year was £3,300,000, but during the height of the crisis in November they rose to £5,500,000 on November 25, and had actually advanced to £6,200,000 on December 16. Turning to another source of information the phenomenon becomes observable once more by inference at the time of the Overend-Gurney crisis. During the month of April, 1866, the " Other Deposits " (which include bankers' balances) never exceeded £14,956,004. On May 3 they had fallen to £13,587,965, and on May 10 to £13,515,537, but on May 17 they had suddenly risen to £18,620,672, on May 24 to £18,790,917, and on May 30 to £20,467,080.

THE END OF AN ERA

With the Overend-Gurney cataclysm there closed the era of isolated, incoherent, and disunited finance. The elements of the developing organism had, in the words of Hobhouse, been " held ineffective in their separateness by counteracting forces." But from the close of this period onwards we shall see that the elements begin to act in a determinate relation, which becomes more intimate and—shall we say ? —cordial, with every year that passes. There was even in 1866 a loyalty of co-operation so conspicuous as to draw a tribute from the Governor of the Bank of England, at the Bank Court in September of that year. We shall see the " new spirit " extend the frontiers of its influence year by year, until at last the correlation, co-ordination, and integration are so complete that the organism emerges unscathed from the terrific ordeal of the German war crisis of 1914. But before we proceed to scan the manifestations which ushered in the new financial age we must devote some scrutiny to a new factor, and the strengthening of an old force, in the Money Market. The new factor consists of the Investment Trust companies. They made their first appearance in the decade which saw the great Joint-Stock Companies Act of 1862 and the Overend-Gurney collapse. The old force is the process of natural selection at work among the banks, exhibiting itself in a persistent amalgamation and absorption which has now, in our day, concentrated 75 per cent. of the banking deposits of the country under the control of less than a dozen immense institutions. This process, and its significance in the Evolution of the Money Market, require detailed examination. The point which we have now attained is the most apt for the undertaking. We can look backward at the obsolescence of the older modes, and forward to the advent of the conditions amid which we live. The convenience of the standpoint will be the justification of such apparent anachronism as its selection may here and there seem to involve.

CHAPTER XV

NATURAL SELECTION AMONG THE BANKS—ABSORPTION AND AMALGAMATION

WE proceed forthwith to consider in detail that process of absorption and amalgamation which, by extinguishing the private banks, and the less powerful joint-stock institutions, prepared the way for banking centralisation as a factor of the modern Money Power. Bank absorption had its origin in rivalry, not in scientific aspiration for more effective control. Like other movements, it was simply doliogenic, and not orthogenic. The fact that centralised scientific control has been one of the *results* of the movement need not blind us to the truth that this was not one of its initial purposes. In their anxiety to extend their clienteles the new joint-stock banks began to buy up everything and anything that was on offer in the way of old banking businesses. Darwin had not then propounded his immortal hypothesis, but its principles were vaguely enunciated with reference to banking evolution. Lord Liverpool declared in 1826 that "the solid and more extensive banks would not fail, in time, to expel the smaller and weaker." The 1836 Committee, like other contemporary observers, saw natural selection at work, and remarked upon it, without grasping its meaning. Contemporaries are not likely to see any economic process in its true perspective. "A principle of competition exists," said the Committee, "which leads to the extinction of all private banks, and to their conversion into banking companies." These observations are strangely prescient, especially as Catastrophism

412   EVOLUTION OF THE MONEY MARKET

still held the scientific field. One of the modes of operation was the transfer of the services of the experienced private bank manager or cashier to the new joint-stock institutions, which offered him a better salary and far brighter prospects of professional advancement.[1] In 1832 there were 62 private banks in the metropolis. Taking the wider survey of England as a whole, Mr. Easton estimates[2] that there were 600 private banks in 1808 and 721 in 1810. In England, down to the year 1837, during the opening years of the movement, a total of 113 private banks had been merged in the joint-stock banks.[3] In 1844 their number had been reduced to 335 with 93 branch offices. In 1894 it was 101 and 464 branch offices. In 1903 only 42 private banks remained. In the 23 years to December 31, 1913, private banks were reduced in number from 38 to 8. The "principle of the issue of transferable shares acts at once in private banks," the 1836 Committee had said. Between the years 1830 and 1869, not a single new private bank was established in London.[4] No fewer than 24 private banks failed in 1840, 17 without paying any dividend. The annexed figures, from a Parliamentary return of the number of private banks and joint-stock banks from 1826 to 1842, display in juxtaposition the record of declining private banks and the increasing joint-stock institutions :—

	Private Banks.	Joint-Stock Banks.		Private Banks.	Joint-Stock Banks.
1826	554	—	1835	411	55
1827	465	6	1836	407	100
1828	456	7	1837	351	107
1829	460	11	1838	341	104
1830	439	15	1839	332	108
1831	436	19	1840	332	113
1832	424	25	1841	321	115
1833	416	35	1842	311	118
1834	416	47			

[1] *Manchester Banks and Bankers*, p. 238.
[2] *Banks and Banking*, p. 67.
[3] J. W. Gilbart, Committee on Banks of Issue, 1841, Q. 936.
[4] Union Bank of London, Chairman at meeting July 14, 1869.

NATURAL SELECTION AMONG THE BANKS

At the time of the Jubilee in 1897, the *Bankers' Magazine* printed the annexed informative survey with reference to English banks :—

In 1837 .. 128 joint-stock banks, say 800 branches.
                400 private bankers,
,, 1897 .. 358 head offices,   5627   ,,
        Say 200 private banks.

The average quarterly circulation of the private banks and joint-stock banks from September, 1834, to July, 1844, is scarcely less instructive and suggestive :—

Quarter ending Sept.	Private Banks. £	Joint-Stock Banks. £
1834	8,370,423	1,783,689
1835	7,912,587	2,508,036
1836	7,764,824	3,969,121
1837	6,701,996	3,440,053
1838	7,083,811	4,281,151
1839	6,917,606	4,167,313
1840	6,350,801	3,630,285
1841	5,768,136	3,311,941
1842	5,098,259	2,819,749
1843	4,288,180	2,763,302
20 July, 1844	4,624,179	3,340,326

The record of the change is rendered more vivid still if we endeavour to bring population into relation with banking facilities. In the year 1800 there were in London, exclusive of the Bank of England, 68 banks, and in the rest of England 388 ; or 456 in all, representing one bank to about every 19,500 of the population :—

" These, it must be remembered, were entirely in the hands of private bankers. In one hundred years [to 1900], the number of banks—head offices and banks with branches—had by failure and amalgamation decreased to 303, but the number of bank offices had increased nearly ten-fold—namely, to over 4300—and there was now a bank to about every 6900 of the population. Some of these bank offices, however, were not open every day. Again, there were in 1800 probably 46 bankers in London who might have been called clearing bankers, all of them, of course, private bankers, whereas there are now but three private banks in the Clearing-house—namely, Messrs. Smith, Payne and Smiths, Messrs. Robarts, Lubbock and Co., and Glyn, Mills, though, indeed, the latter was technically registered under the Companies Acts."[1]

Precisely the same trend, arising from the cognate causes, was early observable in Scotland. In 1819 there were 36 Scottish banks; in 1844, only 24; in 1873, 11; and in 1890 the number had again fallen to 10, at which it now stands. In 1913 Mr. Frederick Huth Jackson stated that in the whole of England and Wales the number of individual banks had declined since 1887 from 366 to 133. Of these no less than 209 had disappeared, he added, through purchase or amalgamation, and there were only 40 country banks left.[2] At the end of the year 1914 this number had been further reduced to 36.

By the time that the modern series of amalgamations was consciously entered upon in the early 'sixties, the tendency was at once recognised, admitted, and obeyed. The private discount firms were going the same way. "Finding," said the proprietors of the West Surrey Bank to their customers in 1864, "that public opinion has taken a strong bias in favour of joint-stock banks, we have resolved to accept the advantageous offer"—to be absorbed by the South Eastern Banking Co. Two years later, in 1866, Arthur Crump declared that "private banks may be looked upon now as institutions of the past."[3] The generalisation was perhaps premature. But in 1915 we may fairly say that amalgamation has replaced local banking by national banking. There still remain with us a few private banks which will never be amalgamated or extinguished, though the absorption of Robarts-Lubbock by Coutts's in 1914 was a dramatic surprise from a quarter where the traditions were regarded as ultra-conservative. At the end of 1914 there were only two of the London clearing banks—Glyn's and the London and South Western —which had never absorbed another institution. In March,

[1] Lord Hillingdon, Institute of Bankers, November 7, 1900, *Bankers' Magazine*, 1900, p. 744.
[2] *Bankers' Magazine*, December, 1913, p. 717.
[3] Arthur Crump, *Banking, Currency, and the Exchanges*, p. 45.

1915, the latter of these two banks entered into a partnership with Cox's in the business of Cox and Co. (France) Ltd.

ABSORPTION IN THE COLONIES

By the time of the Overend-Gurney crisis the working of the absorption principle was plainly discernible in the colonies (now the Dominions). In 1836 the Cape of Good Hope Bank was established, in 1854 the Cape Commercial Bank, and in 1859 the Queenstown Bank. These banks were governed by local directorates, had an unrestricted note issue, and were under no obligations to publish statements of their position. They gradually became more or less "family parties," making advances only to the directors, their relatives, and friends. The result was that as the trade of the colony grew external capital had to be introduced, first, in 1861, by the London and South African Bank—the pioneer of the Imperial banks—and then, in 1862, by the Standard Bank of South Africa. By about the year 1864 there were twenty-eight small Cape banks in existence, with an aggregate capital of less than £1,000,000; but as soon as the Imperial banks began to be active the local banks began to feel the pressure. Sixteen of them failed, and about 1864 the inexorable process of absorption and amalgamation set in. The Imperial banks played, as one observer said, the part of Aaron's rod. The capital of the Standard Bank was increased in 1863 from £1,500,000 to £2,000,000, for the purpose of taking over the Commercial Bank, the Colesburg Bank, and the British Caffrarian Bank. In describing these negotiations the chairman hinted that banks at King William's Town, Cradock, Somerset, Burghersdorp, and Bloemfontein were all anxious to amalgamate with the big institution. In these pre-cable days, however, the development of the colonial banks was checked by the lack of efficient central control. They wanted, for their firm establishment, precisely the scientific supervision which was being extended over the home institutions. No sooner did the cable supply the means of supervision, and at the same time facilitate and quicken the transmission of intelligence generally, than the stronger colonial banks began to advance rapidly. One by one the old colonial institutions failed or were absorbed (except a single concern, which was liquidated without loss), until at last, on September 20, 1890, the oldest of all the original institutions—the Cape of Good Hope Bank—closed its doors. In South Africa itself the process of consolidation has now reached a point at which there are three large institutions —the National Bank of South Africa, the Standard Bank, and the African Banking Corporation, as well as the Netherlands Bank of South Africa—a small institution, with its head office in Amsterdam.

If we turn to Canada the same phenomenon presents itself, just at the period when the older economic age gave place to the new. The Bank of Upper Canada, which collapsed in September, 1866, had been lending money on "wild lands" and other analogous "securities." It seems perfectly clear from the contemporary record that the Bank of Montreal materially assisted in bringing about the collapse of the Bank of Upper Canada by refusing to take its notes wherever that could be done, and by insisting upon their immediate transformation into cash where it could not. The policy of the Bank of Montreal was severely criticised at the time. But a careful examination of the records indicates clearly enough that it was actuated by a recognition of the principle that a weak institution must be weeded out, so that it may not threaten the stability of the financial fabric as a whole. That events should move in this way in distant colonies, under social and political conditions entirely different from those prevailing at home, shows that the economic influence which extinguishes small banks in the presence of larger institutions is not a local manifestation peculiar to conditions in Great Britain, but is as widely applicable as Gresham's law itself. It is the financial operation of an eternal biological principle. Nor has it been confined to the banks. In the insurance world, for instance, where truly stupendous financial aggregations are involved, the selective process is just as palpable as it is among the banks. Its exponents

NATURAL SELECTION AMONG THE BANKS 417

buy, absorb, amalgamate ; and the larger masses of capital, thus continually reinforced, are all within the financial sphere of influence.

THE PHENOMENON IN GERMANY AND FRANCE

The same incessant, inevitable, and ineluctable tendency towards the absorption and extinction of the smaller banker, is manifest in Germany, where Loeb says that the number of private bankers in Berlin fell from 538 in 1892 to 370 in 1899.[1] All the great German banks have been absorbing the smaller institutions. The " process of concentration and agglomeration which has been going on for a considerable time made rapid progress in the last decade ; the big banks absorb smaller ones, take up private firms, chiefly in the provinces, and continue them as branches or agencies."[2] A typical instance of this evolution was the arrangement whereby the Disconto-Gesellschaft will practically control the A. Schaffhausenscher Bankverein. The arrangement brought into being an alliance with more than £50,000,000 of deposits—figures only exceeded (at the time—May, 1914) by those of the Deutsche Bank. In the course of the last few years the Disconto-Gesellschaft has acquired the Norddeutsche Bank in Hamburg and the old Rothschild connection at Frankfort. It has opened branches at Bremen, Mainz, Essen, and Saarbrüken, and secured a voice in the affairs of the Bayerische Disconto-und-Wechsel Bank and the Bank für Thuringen. The analogous evolution is visible in France. " . . . Societies such as the Société Générale, the Credit Lyonnais and the Comptoir d'Escompte founded agencies of branch offices in the provinces. Gradually the number of these agencies has increased and covered France with a close network. In this way they gather capital everywhere : everywhere they try to compete in certain transactions with the local banks, which produces something of a crisis, and brings about a slow transformation of some of the local banks and the disappearance of

---

[1] Quoted in Riesser, *German Great Banks*, U.S. Monetary Commission, p. 626.   [2] Joseph, *Evolution of German Banking*, p. 33

others. The local or provincial banks in France are then in a transition state."[1]

Taken for all in all, bank absorption, with the consequent centralisation of control, has been the most persistent, significant, and prolific of the processes which have formed the Money Market. For the correlation between the Money Market and its social environment is never absolutely complete. Each tends to change, and thus to change the other, by the working of the law of equilibration. Direct equilibration takes place when a congeries of isolated banks is gradually amalgamated, absorbed, and co-ordinated under the control of a central group. Indirect equilibration—the Survival of the Fittest as Spencer called it, or Natural Selection in the Darwinian phrase—produces the gradual disappearance from the new economic environment of those organisms which were incapable of adapting themselves to its stern necessities :—

" We know, also, that organisms may develop which, in one way or another, are so misshapen or defective that they cannot survive, though they have all the essential characteristics of organisms. They maintain their existences as organisms for a short time, blindly struggling, as it were, to preserve the defects which make them incapable of surviving."[2]

They cannot vary into correlation, much less transmit the variation to a new generation, and they are " weeded out." The record of the process is the history of an advance from weakness to strength, from looseness to solidity, from isolation to welded union. It has now reached a stage at which about four or five banks do half the banking business of the country. So Sir Felix Schuster told his American interlocutors.[3] The net result of these processes of amalgamation and absorption is that to-day it is a fact that 75 per cent. of the total banking deposits of the United Kingdom are controlled by an organised group which consists of less than 30 banks. This is the financial hierarchy. Such a consolidation is bound to

[1] Liesse, *Evolution of Credit and Banks in France*, U.S. Monetary Commission, pp. 199, 223.
[2] Haldane, *Mechanism, Life, and Personality*, p. 102.
[3] U.S. Monetary Commission, *Interviews on Banking*, p. 46.

NATURAL SELECTION AMONG THE BANKS 419

impose its will upon the comparatively unorganised proportion—25 per cent.—which remains outside.[1] But the movement has, throughout the last eighty years, been the subject of such unceasing controversy, and is still so largely misunderstood, that it will be desirable to review its real " drift," meaning, and consequences, in some detail. We shall then be better prepared to consider its relationship, as a process of steady consolidation, to the contemporaneous and unceasing enhancement of the prestige of the Bank of England, and then to survey the combined operation of these two movements upon the later evolution of the Money Market.

BANKING EVOLUTION BY ABSORPTION

Nearly every objection to the development of the bank into the super-bank, by the elimination of the private banker, will be found ultimately to be based upon the theory that the private banker was much more accommodating in his business methods than the manager of a

---

[1] THE ABSORPTION PROCESS ILLUSTRATED
A single example of an actual scheme of amalgamation, extending over some fifty years, may be usefully illustrative. Parr and Co. were established at Warrington and St. Helens about 1788. In 1865 they became Parr's Banking Co. In 1878 they absorbed Dixon and Co. of Chester (established 1813), in 1883 the National Bank of Liverpool (established 1863), and in 1891 Fuller, Banbury and Co., and in 1892 the Alliance Bank. The concern then became known as Parr's Banking Company and the Alliance Bank. In 1894 it absorbed Croxon, Jones and Co. of Oswestry (established 1792), Sir Samuel Scott and Co., and Shrubsole and Co. of Kingston-on-Thames. In 1896 the title was changed to Parr's Bank, Ltd., and in the same year the institution absorbed the consolidated Bank (originally established as the Bank of Manchester in 1829) which had itself acquired Denison, Heywood and Co. (late Heywood, Kennard and Co.), Hankeys and Co., and the Bank of London. In 1898 the Derby and Derbyshire Banking Co. (established 1833), in 1900 the Ashton, Stalybridge, Hyde, and Glossop Bank (established 1836), in 1902 Pare's Leicestershire Banking Co. (established 1856), in 1908 Robin Brothers of Jersey and the Whitehaven Joint-Stock Banking Co. (established 1829), and in 1909 Stuckey's Banking Co. (established 1806) were successively absorbed. But Stuckeys themselves represented the result of a process of absorption which had operated upon Walters, Waldron, Timbrel and Barton, Frome ; Phelps and Co., Crewkerne ; John, Edmund and H. B. Batten, Yeovil ; Woodland and Co., Bridgwater ; Whitmash and White, Yeovil ; Ricketts, Thorne Wait and Courtenay, The Castle Bank, Bristol ; Sparks and Co., Crewkerne ; Reeves and Porch, Wells, Glastonbury, and Shepton Mallet ; Kingslake and Co., Taunton ; Tufnell, Falkner and Falkner, Bath ; Badcock and Co., Taunton ; Dunsford and Co., Tiverton. See the details in pedigree form *Bankers' Magazine*, March, 1910.

joint-stock bank. The latter, it is said, is a machine, while the former was a sympathiser. To put it in technical language, the loan and advance policy of the modern bank manager is objective, whereas that of the old private banker was largely subjective. The modern joint-stock bank manager will only concern himself, as regards security, with something palpable to the touch, whether it be a bond, a share certificate, a guarantee, the deeds of a house as a short equitable mortgage, or what not. But the old private banker was in numerous instances quite content to " sense " his customer—to psychometrise him in the light of personal knowledge of his family and business antecedents. " In the old days the private banker was the friend of all his customers. There was a real affection between the banker and his customer. They tried to understand and to help each other as friends."[1] When Brassey, the railway contractor, in his early days was beginning in a very small way, he was " encouraged " by his private country bankers, and in turn he " encouraged " them by keeping his huge accounts with them to the end of his business career.[2] Barings' and Rothschilds' originally " made themselves " by their solicitude for their younger customers.[3] Bagehot has pictured the position of the private banker in terms so felicitous[4] that it would be sacrilege to attempt a paraphrase :—

" I can imagine nothing better in theory, or more successful in practice, than private banks as they were in the beginning.

---

[1] Chairman, Lloyds Bank meeting, February 8, 1897. The speaker continued : " I am very glad when, under our joint-stock system, our managers cultivate some of that warmth of feeling and anxiety to please and help their customers ; not, of course, running any undue banking risks, but trying to make their customers feel that their banker is their best friend to go for advice." Mr. Pownall has a story which illustrates the value of this personal intimacy : " I remember a remark made to a banker about a farmer who rode remarkably good horses. Said his friend, in the tone of one giving a friendly warning, ' So-and-So has a very expensive mount.'

" ' Yes,' said the banker, ' that's his business. He breeds 'em, and he sells 'em at the meet.' " (*English Banking*, p. 29.)

[2] Haig Miller, *On the Bank's Threshold*, p. 69.
[3] Chairman at Alliance Bank meeting, January 24, 1865.
[4] *Lombard Street*, 9th Edition, p. 267.

A man of known wealth, known integrity and known ability, is largely entrusted with the money of his neighbours. The confidence is strictly personal. His neighbours know him, and trust him because they know him. They see daily his manner of life, and judge from it that their confidence is deserved. In rural districts and in former times, it was difficult for a man to ruin himself except at the place in which he lived ; for the most part he spent his money there, and speculated there if he speculated at all. Those who lived there also would soon see if he were acting in a manner to shake their confidence. Even in large cities as cities then were, it was possible for most persons to ascertain the fair certainty, the real position of conspicuous persons, and to learn all which was material in fixing their credit. Accordingly, the bankers who for a long series of years passed successfully this strict and continual investigation, became very wealthy and very powerful."

This is a picture of almost idyllic conditions. By way of contrast we may recall Gilbart's sardonic declaration[1] that "the apostles of the principles of joint-stock banking found the mass of the population bowed down in superstitious homage to those idols of gold, of silver, of wood, and of brass, which were raised before their eyes in the persons of the private bankers."

A union of pecuniary sagacity with social and intellectual refinement represents the beau-ideal of a banker, and was realised over and over again in the personality of the proprietor of the old private banks. Yet who can doubt that these benefits are to a great extent perpetuated by means of local directorates, such as those of Barclay's ? Probably it is a fact that the modern joint-stock bank manager is not so accommodating as his predecessor, at the private bank. But the other aspect must not be neglected. The manager of the branch of the joint-stock bank is governed by the principles of banking science as he has learned them behind the counter, and as they are administered by his board. The proprietor of a private bank is simply a despot who may quite possibly be guided far more by personal fancy than by scientific principles. If these fancies lead him in the right direction, well and

[1] *Logic of Banking*, p. 170.

good. If not, he becomes a mere arbitrary financial tyrant, capable of doing a vast amount of damage to a very delicate fabric. It is undeniable that there may occasionally be an undue rigidity in the rules of an amalgamating joint-stock bank, involving it in disregard of local customs long prevalent in the parlour of the local institution which it has absorbed. Still this is a question of management which will adjust itself as time goes on. In any case, it involves a levelling up, rather than a levelling down, of method. It has been suggested that this policy is likely to press hardest upon the agricultural district, because a local manager sent down from London will not possess such knowledge as would alone enable him to do safe business among an agricultural clientele. Mr. Wolff, in his book on *People's Banks*, has spoken of the " host of unsatisfied seekers of credit—farmers, tradesmen, builders, manufacturers ; some of them very substantial —men that used to borrow from their local bankers, who gave them credit readily." But it may be doubted if, as a matter of fact, any of these are left unsatisfied if they can produce proper claims upon the consideration of the bank manager ; and if they cannot, the denial of financial accommodation is a good, rather than an evil. " The movement for the ' organisation of credit,' which is so remarkable a feature of our time, tends to provide everybody with the credit he is worth."[1] What the client gets is strictly fair treatment, but he will not obtain the exceptional accommodation that the old firm might have given him—and perhaps paid dearly for its misplaced generosity. No doubt a large metropolitan and provincial bank which has an extensive Stock Exchange connection is tempted in a time of market activity to feed the Stock Exchange and starve the provincial client. But country banking is not, and cannot be, quite as free and liquid as the London type. Overdraft, for instance, is characteristic of country practice. The London banker would call for collateral and put the transaction in the shape of an advance. The joint-stock bankers appreciate the

[1] Cassel, *Nature and Necessity of Interest*, p. 116.

NATURAL SELECTION AMONG THE BANKS

circumstances, and do their best to adjust supplies to needs. As the chairman of Parr's Bank rightly said, at the time of the amalgamation of that institution with Stuckey's Bank: " Very natural regrets are sometimes expressed when a country bank is absorbed by a large central institution. But we, ourselves, began as a country bank. We know country banking thoroughly. We are still a country bank, and we both can and do sympathise with country and local needs." The contrary view is largely the offspring of the resentment of that large class of borrowers who insist that bankers are merely rapacious dividend hunters, rivalling Shylock both in the terms upon which they grant accommodation, and in their insistence and grip upon the security they exact for it.

THE DEEPER SIGNIFICANCE

It is only when we analyse the problem more deeply that we discover the presence of elements far more serious and important than the alleged lack of personal sympathy on the part of the joint-stock banker. The whole environment of banking has changed, and the banker has been compelled to change with it. In many instances, the old private client of the private banker has been transformed into a joint-stock company with a large issue of debentures. In former days, a banker who accommodated a client without security, or upon a psychological security, had the whole of the borrower's assets to fall back upon. Nowadays, if he were to take the same risk, and it matured, he might find himself postponed to a huge mass of debentures. Joint-stock banking is not a giant financial entity, bent upon absorbing, amalgamating and expanding merely in order that its tentacles may have a wider sweep and its aggrandisement a larger opportunity. The expansion of joint-stock banking and the concurrent elimination of the private banker have been, and are, essential processes for the adaptation of the financial mechanism to its nineteenth and twentieth century surroundings. If these processes had not manifested themselves and won their way to success, modern commerce as financed by the old private bankers would offer a remarkable analogy to an attempt to drain the valley of the Thames and supersede the river by means of a four-inch pipe. Absorption and centralisation are as peremptorily essential to the conditions of modern commerce and industry as they are inexorable in their movement. Since commerce and industry are aggregated into masses which grow larger every year, banks must of necessity adjust themselves to the altered circumstances by placing themselves in command of such resources as will enable them to accommodate the larger commercial entities. In fact, it has been candidly admitted[1] that the consolidation of German banking received a great impetus from the foundation of the United States Steel Corporation in 1901, and from the profound realisation that Germany could only fight the concentrated industrial enterprise of her competitors by means of concentrated capital of her own. In the struggle against the pressure of such an environment—a pressure that has grown heavier with the extended area of human enterprise and with the advancing years—the private banks and the smaller joint-stock banks have always been forced into subjection to the law that every group strives to utilise all weaker groups within its reach. And this is, after all, only a special case of Spencer's " truth that each species of organism tends ever to expand its sphere of existence—to intrude on other areas, other modes of life, other media : and, through these perpetually recurring attempts to thrust itself into every accessible habitat, spreads until it reaches limits that are, for the time, insurmountable."[2]

During the last century of banking history the pressure has exerted itself by various modes and in different degrees. In the majority of instances it has been gentle, but insistent. There have been negotiation and purchase, frequently with a retention of some of the old directorate and managers as parts of the personnel directing the larger entity. Where the pressure was stronger it has

[1] By Riesser, *German Great Banks*, U.S. Monetary Commission, p. 641.
[2] *Principles of Biology*, Vol. I. p. 320.

been suggested that the obligations of local private banks to their London agents had increased to such magnitude as to leave them no alternative but agreement to a proposal for amalgamation. In other instances the collapse of a private bank was deliberately waited for—where the position was desperate, owing perhaps to practically compulsory entanglement in the financing of purely local undertakings, and where the purchase of the goodwill and the taking over of the open position would have been unprofitable and dangerous. When the collapse came the great joint-stock bank " scooped " the connection of the defunct concern.[1] And even where the private institution " pulled itself through," there would remain a vague malaise that opened the way to absorption. A weak bank which is able to survive a crisis may thereby be rendered so conscious of its infirmity that it seeks alliance and absorption lest another assault sweep it away. It may preserve its solvency, but its prestige has been damaged. Conversely, a bank which confronts a crisis with assured confidence and solidity and possibly helps weaker institutions, is a tonic to its own enterprise. It is shown the way to new conquests by the very events in which it has participated. This relationship of strength and comparative weakness may bring other and still more remorseless forces into play. In various instances, the severity of the rivalry of powerful competitors has compelled consent to absorption. In the case of the Bank of Africa, in 1912, it was quite frankly admitted that the institution was affected by the severe

[1] For an instance see National Provincial Bank meeting, May 11, 1870. It must not be supposed, however, that all the great banks have been continuously hunting for chances of amalgamation. The late Mr. J. Spencer Phillips once told the shareholders of Lloyds Bank (January 29, 1904), that with the exception of one private bank, no institution had ever been asked to amalgamate with Lloyds. The overtures had always come from the other side, and for every one bank that had been taken they had refused three. Mr. Phillips added that the most important of the suggested amalgamations of recent years—namely that of the Manchester and Liverpool District Bank with Lloyds, had been proposed by the former institution. They approached Lloyds. Lloyds would no more have thought of approaching them than they would have thought of approaching a bank in the planet Mars. After five months of difficult and delicate negotiation, however, the Lancashire public got wind of the proposal, and so strong an opposition developed that the whole scheme had to be dropped.

competition among the various banks, and had been largely forced into proposals for amalgamation by the leverage of these conditions.

Other forces may be discovered. The keener competition among bankers has undoubtedly tended to diminish the rate of profit on a given capital. Apart altogether from any " squeezing out," there was bound to come a time when the reduced return rendered it no longer worth the while of a private banker to employ his money and energy in the banking business, since he could, by investing it, obtain at least an equivalent return without the labour of supervision and the concomitant risk. The voice of the joint-stock charmer would under such circumstances naturally reach more willing ears. Again, the private bank is necessarily of slow growth. It can only safely expand proportionately with the capital at its proprietor's command. It cannot keep pace, for instance, with the rapid rise into commercial importance of some manufacture specialised to a particular locality, or, if it can, there is the converse peril of over-commitment in a single industry. The capital of the joint-stock bank is permanent, not liable to be withdrawn or tampered with to meet all circumstances arising on the death or bankruptcy of a partner. Conversely, it can be argued that while the liability of the joint-stock bank shareholder is limited, that of the private banker is unlimited. His position is that the whole of his resources are at the disposal of his creditors.[1] Yet if he did not close his doors till all his capital was gone, the recourse against the private fortune would be of doubtful value. Further, a network of branches can work more economically from the point of view of the minimum of till-money, since they can command gold at a few hours' notice, where the isolated private bank must either keep it lying idle in the safe, or run the risk of delay in meeting a sudden demand for the metal.

[1] As late as 1895, the proprietors of the Reading Bank, a private concern, reminded their customers of this fact by adding at the foot of their balance-sheet : " N.B.—The responsibility of the partners to the full extent of their property is in no way altered by the publication of an annual balance-sheet."

NATURAL SELECTION AMONG THE BANKS

Subject to the avoidance of "banking up to the hilt," the reduction of the till-money to a minimum is at once the privilege and the obligation of the great banks. The larger the total available resources, the more colossal the waste if they are not utilised up to the utmost attainable and legitimate limit of their potential energy.

NECESSITY FOR HUGE RESOURCES

A private banker with limited means could not safely accept a very large account—at all events, if it exposed him to demands for correspondingly extensive accommodation. Yet the influence of the banker over the material destiny of a given industry may be enormous. The joint-stock banker commands resources undreamed of by his private predecessor. He is guided by a volume of experience which the private banker could never have accumulated. The importance of the distinction lies in this—that the financial impotence of the private banker might cripple an industry which was capable of being prudently fostered, or render inevitable some trouble which, in the presence of effective aid, might have been prevented. Thus, the continued existence of these small local institutions might, in fact, have been an obstacle to social progress. As long as they were in occupation of the ground, the entrance of the more powerful London bankers would only have precipitated an era of financial throat-cutting in the shape of the fiercest competition for local business, or else the larger institutions might have been compelled to hold up the smaller entities against disaster.[1] That being the case, the larger institutions might have hesitated to enter the field, and as long as they were absent local industry would have been checked by the limited resources available in the coffers of the private banks for financing. The branch bank is a part of an integral whole commanding, up to the limit of necessity, the entirety of its resources. The private bank

[1] The District Bank of Newcastle was saved, in 1847, by advances made, on his sole responsibility, by Mr. Grote (the manager of the local branch of the Bank of England). Such a responsibility is too great to be thrust on one pair of shoulders.

is an isolated unit with no reserve outside itself. It is the practice of a London bank taking over a country rival to level up its liquid assets to that proportion of its liabilities which is customary with the London institutions. For that reason the process of amalgamation makes for additional strength, both financial and psychological. The private bank can only employ its own capital, however great the needs of the district which it serves : the branch bank introduces the fruits of a distant superfluity to relieve a local stringency. An independent private bank is almost bound to be wasteful because it needs a much larger capital than will suffice for a branch bank. The private bank must maintain itself against all contingencies, while the branch bank has reserves in the background. The knowledge on the part of the client that the whole resources of a great institution are, at need, behind the branch bank is part of the pyschological reserve which helps to maintain public confidence in times of disturbance. Mr. (now Sir) B. E. Walker has argued[1] that " the probability of loss to the depositors in one or more of twenty small banks is greater than the probability of loss to any of the depositors in one large bank." A few strong banks with numerous ramifications mean confidence. A multitude of scattered, separate and isolated concerns may easily spell apprehension and disaster. Banking opinion, reinforced by public sentiment, is constantly requiring larger general reserves and larger bullion reserves. Old standing is of less attractiveness than an audited balance-sheet showing a substantial and adequate array of liquid assets. These can only be provided where there exist correspondingly large resources. Deposits attract deposits, because confidence is infectious.

HUGE ADVANCES NECESSITATE HUGE FUNDS

Obviously, the gigantic advances and overdrafts which a modern banker is called upon to provide could not have been furnished out of the resources of one, or even three or four, of the component institutions which go to make

[1] *Economic Journal*, 1894, p. 245.

up such immense credit-shops as Lloyds and the London City and Midland. The standing and financial resources of the banker are of supreme importance to enterprises of the size and scope which modern joint-stock undertakings frequently assume. The demand for accommodation, moreover, becomes wider with every year that passes. The bankers of the mid-Victorian era did not encounter anything like the competition for the use of money which now confronts their successors. As far as the conservative investor is concerned, we have Dominion and Provincial Governments, in addition to municipal and other public authorities, all seeking to use money which might otherwise be at a banker's disposal. In the case of the more speculatively-inclined proprietor of funds, there are the attractions of all the other classes of investments tending to draw the money from the banker's till into securities. The ordinary commercial demand for money, together with its employment in investment, once made up practically the totality of the call upon available supplies. But in recent years there has arisen a species of intermediate demand in the shape of the short-term loan. This gains a wider vogue because it is only in a minor degree liable to the canker of depreciation, and its popularity again adds to the strain upon the supplies of capital at a given moment. These forces were only to a minor extent in operation in the fifties and the sixties. A modern banker is therefore in the position of having to face much more extensive demands for financial accommodation, coming from a far-flung national enterprise of immensely greater magnitude than existed in the middle of the last century, while at the same time, he is surrounded by powerful competitors fighting for the use of the funds of which, in other circumstances, he might have had the almost exclusive disposal. Of course, the resulting huge commitments have their temptations and their drawbacks. There are temptations, because a small loan involves as much labour as a large, so that the former tends to be discouraged under the tendency to minimise labour and maximise profits. There are drawbacks, realised as long ago as 1875, when seven of the largest London banks, as well as two discount companies, had to reduce their dividends and their reserve funds to the extent of £981,500 in order to cover the losses incurred by the Collie frauds ; and again in 1878, when the City of Glasgow Bank collapse revealed the loan of *six* millions to *four* firms. These untoward incidents were all the more galling because the chairman of a great joint-stock bank had stated a few years before, that a £20 note would cover all their loss upon £7,400,000 of bills discounted in a year.[1] But the danger of these huge commitments is keenly realised by the modern banker. The manager knows that he must not involve the bank so deeply in association with a particular industry as to make its decline or paralysis a menace to the institution itself. Bankers quickly adopt defensive tactics. " They say ' I have enough of that kind of accommodation. I have 100 shipbuilders or shipowners ; I am not going to give out more than a proportion of my money to that particular trade.' "[2] The large joint-stock bank is independent enough to take a decided stand against a request for accommodation, or the renewal of advances already granted, while a similar decision on the part of a private bank might mean ruin. It can afford to fix and enforce a limit beyond which accommodation to a given individual or firm shall not be allowed to pass, no matter how good the security may be. But a private banker may find himself so far committed that he cannot draw the line, or if he does, he may be compelled to erase it by the knowledge that if he remains obdurate, the client may go down, carrying his banker with him. Within a few hours of one of the latest absorptions by the London City and Midland, it became known that certain accommodation granted in connection with the financing of a going concern would not be continued. A private local banker would scarcely have dared to take such a step, and to let the facts become public property. That is the difference between the authoritative and

---

[1] London and County meeting, August 3, 1871.
[2] Charles Gow, London Joint-Stock Bank, U.S. Monetary Commission, *Interviews on Banking*, p. 82.

deliberate policy of a huge financial aggregation and the hesitancy and inconsistency of a myriad isolated units, each playing for its own hand.

MULTIPLICITY OF BRANCHES

In another direction is the need for multiplicity, rather than for magnitude of banking facility. For instance, when the London and South Western began opening branches in the sixties, the London suburbs had as yet received no attention from banking caterers. It has been asserted that there was no branch bank in existence between the City and Croydon in one direction and between the City and Watford in another. In the early seventies, there was no branch bank further south than the Elephant, further north than Park Street, Camden Town, or Stratford on the east or Notting Hill on the west.[1] The multiple shop and a larger middle-class have brought the urgent need of change. In the early days of the movement there was apprehension. Cooke (chairman of the Manchester and Liverpool District Bank) was certain in 1875 that London was " overbanked."[2] But in our time many modern commercial organisations have scores, if not hundreds, of shops in different parts of the country. The financial relations between these various establishments can be simply and easily adjusted by means of the branch-bank system which exists alongside of them, though in its absence (or its replacement by isolated private banks), endless complexity and trouble would be experienced. The adjustments are facilitated by the grouping together of certain allied banks, so that money for the credit of any office within the group can be paid in at any other office which is included in the alliance. These arrangements themselves accelerate the movement towards absorptions and amalgamations. A local south of England bank may easily be handicapped by having no office, and no direct representation, in Liverpool. The opening of a

[1] Bank Inspector's Retrospect, *Bankers' Magazine*, July, 1912, p. 72.
[2] 1875 Committee, Q. 6604.

branch is an expensive experiment, but a working arrangement with a northern bank goes far to solve the problem. Ultimately amalgamation with the northern institution effects a complete solution. Conversely, the country bank which has got a good footing in London has entered the cosmopolitan arena. In either case, commerce and industry benefit, and through them, the whole community. Yet again, the smaller joint-stock bank when it becomes amalgamated with the larger acquires better credit among investors, and consequently attracts a stronger class of shareholder to its register. This is a very important consideration indeed. Of course, it would be uncandid and unscientific to ignore the fact that the numerous branches which are feeders in prosperity, may become suckers in adversity. They swell the resources of the institution during periods of quietude, while they might conceivably be bleeding it at hundreds of points if a " run " supervenes. But a " run " is now so extremely rare a phenomenon, and is likely to become so much more uncommon, that this consideration becomes of less moment every year.

BANKING IS NOT PARTNERSHIP

The existence of this power of independent discrimination against transactions of an undesirable type perpetuates and strengthens a financial censorship which is of the utmost utility to the entire economic fabric. Where huge advances are desired, there is almost universally a tacit understanding that the client shall not only give the banker all his business, but all his confidence. A client who is discounting with two banks is a danger to both. In excluding his duplicity the banker assures his own precise knowledge of his client's position, and the client himself is furnished with expert financial restraint and guidance; sympathetic but firm, advisory and yet authoritative. If he is reasonable, he is kept out of difficulties; and if, as a result of some unforeseen contingency, trouble nevertheless overtake him, the banker, fortified with precise knowledge of the position, is likely to see him through. As Riesser says, with the growth of the power and capital of the

NATURAL SELECTION AMONG THE BANKS

banks, " cases have become increasingly rare where a complete prostration of business or a crisis has resulted in the discharge of employes." Yet all the time the banker is an external expert auxiliary and adviser, not a joint adventurer. He is an expert, because, unlike his predecessor, who was involved in all kinds of commercial and industrial undertakings concurrently with banking (see *ante*, page 287), this modern practitioner devotes himself entirely to his profession. Since 1844, " banking has been almost entirely restricted to banking *alone*."[1] He is an *external* auxiliary, because in no circumstances will the canons of modern banking, rigidly enforced by a central primacy, tolerate the banker as partner. They prohibit his provision of working capital, or his advance of large amounts to clients with only small capital resources of their own. That is the difference between English and German practice.[2] It has been acknowledged by German authorities as " a division of labour between the pure deposit banks, and the banks engaged in promotions and flotations." It has been admitted that this distinction " necessarily affords greater security to depositors than does the German system."[3] The fact is undoubted, in spite of the contrary opinion frequently and fervidly urged by disappointed

---

[1] Seebohm, 1875 Committee, Q. 4850.
[2] This difference in the methods of the banking systems of the two countries had excited some disquietude in Germany before the war. The *Frankfurter Zeitung* in an article quoted in the *Bankers' Magazine* for October, 1912, page 515, said, " Credits given to industrial companies by banks are fully justified in all cases when this money fills the gaps in the amounts required for actual industrial purposes. When work is abundant, considerable stocks of raw material and half-manufactured articles must be held, although payment for the wholly manufactured production is not made for some time. In such cases it is perfectly legitimate for companies to apply for help to the banks and for the banks to grant these credits. It is quite a different matter, however, when bank capital, which should always be regarded as a temporary loan, begins to be regarded as a permanent investment. . . . It would be easy to give numerous examples to show the danger credit granters and credit receivers run when a company is under heavy obligations to a bank. Still, it must be emphatically recognised that industrial companies could not expand without bank credits, and it is because of the willingness of the banks to help that the German industry has become great. But a strict line of demarcation must be drawn between temporary credit and the help received from a bank which in time becomes to all intents and purposes a permanent investment."
[3] Riesser, *German Bank Enquiry*, 1908–9, Vol. II. p. 812.

clients of the English banks. The German banker becomes a large shareholder in the industrial enterprises of the Fatherland.[1] Riesser thinks that during the next decades great progress will undoubtedly be made among the credit banks " in the direction of the organic development of long term industrial credit[2]—the very thing that an English banker would not look at. The latter declines closer association than that of a temporary co-operator. He will " finance " in a legitimate way, but only in circumstances which engage him for such brief intervals as provide him, by means of a sequence of maturing paper, with constantly recurring opportunities of extricating himself from any threatened trouble. Further, the conversion of established businesses and their promotion as companies and the placing of their securities have been, and are, an integral part of the business of German banks. Riesser insists[3] that the German system of the participation of banks in promotion has a particular advantage in that it leads the banks to watch permanently over the development of the companies they have promoted. He declares that English banks lend their money for flotation business, though they will not themselves be concerned in it. That is precisely where their strength lies. That is one of the secrets of their influence, which is that of the unbiassed and skilled observer, rather than of the interested participant. In England the banker is only the professional agent who lends his specialised skill and resources to facilitate the issue operation. The rest he leaves to those other factors of the Money Market, the joint-stock companies and the great investment trusts. He himself is never a promoter, never a partner, nor will he, under any circumstances, allow himself to be transformed into one. The traditions that have come down to him from mid-Victorian disaster tell him why, and the argument is conclusive and all-compelling. But his policy

[1] For instance, in the report of the Dresdner Bank for 1897 there is a statement that " in conjunction with Messrs. Siemens and Halske, of Berlin, we have formed the Mexican Electric Works, Limited, for the purpose of lighting the City of Mexico with electricity."
[2] *German Great Banks*, U.S. Monetary Commission, p 248.
[3] *German Bank Enquiry*, Vol. II. p. 813

stands on a surer foundation with a united banking sentiment behind it, than if it were merely the rule of one institution among a multitude.

THE BANKER AS SUPERVISOR

To revert to the single banker of the discounting client—the old-fashioned rule of country (and indeed, of town) banking was " to require that a man shall have only one [discount] banker, and to close his account if it is discovered that he has two." So said Rae,[1] and added the cogent question : " How can you know, with any approach to exactitude, what a man is doing, or how his affairs stand, if he is transacting a portion of his business elsewhere ? " Gilbart held the same views. " The object of a party keeping two bankers is usually to get as much accommodation as he can from each," said he.[2] The rule is adopted and enforced in Canada. " In their insistence on the rule that a man shall borrow from only one bank, the (Canadian) banks have done more than appears on the surface to make their system a unit."[3] The reason of the rule is plain. A banker who is discounting for a customer is taking a certain risk for the purpose of facilitating his client's business operations. He has a right to know, up to the utmost limits of possibility, what that risk is, and how far it extends. If all his customer's discount business is concentrated on a single account, he can form a very accurate judgment. But if, as a matter of fact, the client has two or three discount accounts open with different bankers, not one of them is in a position to calculate the amount of paper which is afloat, or to form any adequate judgment about its backing. Three separate data are required with respect to Character, Capacity, and Capital in the formation of a judgment as to the credit of a given client. When the character is known, the reliability of the man and the moral risk of the transaction can be weighed. When his capacity has been tested, his modes of operation and the

[1] *Country Banker*, p. 252.   [2] *Logic of Banking*, p. 192.
[3] J. F. Johnson, *Banking Problems* (American Academy), p. 551.

allied business risk can be adjudicated upon. When knowledge of the capital possessed by the client is added to the other data, it becomes possible to measure the resources and thus to assess the value of the ultimate protection upon which the banker must fall back in the last resource. But the data are imperfect where the discount business is done with two or more banks. As long as a customer asks his banker for no accommodation, he may, if he chooses, run a dozen accounts ; as soon as he wants discount accommodation the banker will cease to stand at ease and come sharply to attention. He enforces a wholesome rule which commands the allegiance of the whole banking community. We shall, as we proceed, discover the beginnings of an equally fruitful invigilation on the Stock Exchange.

If we extend our scrutiny we shall discern in operation over the whole commercial field a kind of banking censorship controlled by an independent compactly-centralised authority. This has an immense protective value. We know from the testimony of Lord Aldenham[1] that the Bank of England exercises an unfailing vigilance with regard to the balances of its principal customers, the great clearing banks. If a bank is not in the clearing it must of necessity keep an account with an institution which enjoys that privilege. The latter institution can bestow upon the balances of its customer the same unfailing surveillance as Threadneedle Street devotes to the balances of the clearing banks. Thus the network of supervision spreads downwards from the Bank of England to the humblest bank account kept in the most modest branch in some remote town in the provinces. The banking customer's outgoings, incomings, bills, notes, cheques, are all subjected to an unceasing scrutiny. The regular payment on the life assurance policy, the recurring dividends and coupons, the occasional remittances to investment brokers, all mark the progressive client, just as the converse phenomena evidence lack of judgment and financial deterioration. Scanning a multitude of accounts, bankers have all the materials for a skilled diagnosis. An increase in the number of bills, a

[1] Quoted, p. 507, in another connection.

struggle to transform short credit into long, are all signs of a sinister rise in the financial temperature, harbingers of approaching malaise, trouble, stringency, or crisis. " Every cheque and bill carries a meaning, not always discoverable or worth discovering, but often very much so."[1] The scrutiny is not only that of the manager where the transaction is within his powers or of the Board if it is beyond them. It is a business of a bank director continuously to examine the particulars of the bank's investments and advances, whether they take the form of discounts, loans, or overdrafts, and to use the information thus obtained in guaging the bank's position. The director may from time to time be on the rota as a member of the discount committee, and it will be his business to use the best of his knowledge in his character of a private supervisor. So the foreign banker has his " Opinion Lists " in which he records the financial history of his clients. A good classification in the list means that the banker will pay more for the bills ; a bad one, less. This interest in customers' private affairs used to take curious shapes among an earlier generation of bankers. Old Fuller once reproved the extravagance of one of his best clients in ordering a second pint of beer ! What was then the occasional eccentricity of an individual banker has been elaborated into the systematised policy of the banking hegemony. Under its regulation the client is forced to consider what the manager, or the inspectors, or the directors on their round of visits, may think of his proposals, his methods, and his financial resources ; and the power of the censorship, be it remembered, is considerably enhanced by the weighty " banker's opinion," which means so much, as one of the unseen buttresses of the financial fabric. Further, this supervision is adapted to a subtle psychological necessity, itself the offspring of the banking system, arising from the tendency of a certain type of banking client to enact for himself, in the matter of his obligations to the bank, a less elevated ethical code than he would obey in his dealings with others. Every branch manager knows

[1] J. Spencer Phillips, Institute of Bankers, November 1, 1905.

this failing and dreads its manifestations. It represents an inchoate or intermediate stage of financial ethics, which may in time give place to sounder principles, but must for the present be the subject of incessant vigilance. When it is remorselessly excluded the scope of operation open to the sinister elements is more and more circumscribed. To raise the rate, or more strictly regularise the terms, against an individual or a group may have a wholesome deterrent effect, while at the same time, no occasion is given for general alarm or anticipation of stringency. Those who are disciplined have no object in prating about it. As Gilbart pithily says : " There is many a man who would be deterred from dishonesty by the frown of a banker, though he might care but little for the admonitions of a bishop."[1] As cosmopolitan relationships ramify, we shall see that it becomes possible, and even necessary, to extend this supervision over the whole civilised world.

" SECURITY, SECURITY "—AND WHY ?

After all, speculative mania is only a feverish desire to trade beyond one's capital. Liquidity of resources and accessibility of assets, both of them so essential to modern banking policy, involve a vast advance upon the banking conditions which were the rule in the eighteenth century, and a simultaneous necessity for the utmost circumspection. Yet bankers are reproached for meeting every request for accommodation with the parrot cry of " security, security." But the banker's demand for security is not directed so much to the protection of his own position as to the diplomatic, and if necessary the decided and definite, discouragement of a customer who is obviously trading beyond his capital and is, therefore, as large a danger to the commercial community as to himself. Reckless speculation, excessive over-trading, commercial " running to seed " have now to reckon with a censor, and with one whose behests cannot be disobeyed. " The influence which bankers can generally exert over the business of

[1] *Logic of Banking*, p. 117.

NATURAL SELECTION AMONG THE BANKS

the country is very great, and considering the extreme delicacy of our Money Market, the more needful it is that the influence should be continually exerted on the side of prudence."[1] In banking, as in all true social science, the radical question is not what a given individual thinks his needs to be, but what an organised and competent authority, looking at the social rather than the individual aspect, assesses them at. The banker who has a very good idea what the client's capital amounts to, is the best judge of the amount of business which it will finance, and of the moment when the limit has been reached. Beyond that limit any paper becomes "as chaff before the wind in the winnowing of the first monetary tempest."[2] That is the reason why a bank may not have a single unsound account in its books, and yet itself be unable to meet its obligations in the full banking sense of the word. The consolidation of banking aids the winnowing work. There is supervision in the mass, as well as by the individual bank. The client who doubts it has only to change his account from one bank to another in order to discover its existence and its influence with all those who are interested in his solvency. Nor is that scrutiny utilised only with regard to the safety and profit of the transaction, but also in the light of its relations to the well-being of the financial fabric as a whole. "There were other and higher motives that prompted the directors to exert their utmost on behalf of the bank, beyond the mere question of a stake in the property."[3] A certain advance may be secured beyond all challenge, and be as profitable as the bank could wish, and yet it may not "suit" as George Rae would have said, because there are contemporary circumstances, and public considerations, that demand severer tests than these.

THE CUSTOMER AS SHAREHOLDER

Finally, the establishment of this friendly, though critical supervision—impossible in the case of a "crowd"

---
[1] Palgrave, *Bank Rate and the Money Market*, p. 104.
[2] Rae, *Country Banker*, p. 80.
[3] Chairman, National Provincial Bank meeting, May 14, 1868.

of isolated private banks—has been materially assisted by the diminution of the identity of interest between shareholder and customer which was so conspicuous a feature in the early days of joint-stock banking. As regards private " influence " the customer is more at arm's length. The head office of a great London institution, supervising the affairs of a local branch, is not susceptible to the class of pressure under which these abuses arise. Consequently it does not stumble into the pitfalls which beset the feet of the older private bankers and so often involved them in disaster. Many of the early nineteenth-century banks were actually founded by those who became immediately the largest shareholders. For instance, the Commercial Bank of Scotland originated in the return of a batch of bills to a wealthy client of the Bank of Scotland, with the intimation that it was not " convenient " to discount them, and that, moreover, the customer was " doing too much business." The customer consulted a few wealthy friends and they resolved upon creating a more accommodating bank for themselves. But, obviously, there are dangerous elements present when the same people play the double rôle of proprietors and customers. The lapse of time and the consequent distribution of interests have almost entirely dissolved this intimacy of relationship, with the result that a modern manager or a modern board is much less susceptible to the pressure of private influence than used to be the case. In the absence of a common standard, and a power capable of enforcing its maintenance, there would be still another species of illegitimate pressure upon the banks—to wit, that of the shareholder complaining that some other institution than the one in which he is interested lends its money to better advantage. Pressure of that kind, if it be effective, leads to the taking of illegitimate risks in the effort to increase dividends, and is utterly opposed to all the canons of sound banking.

MORE EFFECTIVE DISTRIBUTION OF CAPITAL

We pass from the disciplinary and censorial aspects to the problem of the distribution of capital, as affected by the

NATURAL SELECTION AMONG THE BANKS

process of bank absorption and amalgamation. The private and isolated bank faced a financial hurricane alone. The modern centralised institution, reinforced by the mobility of modern capital (a mobility which is largely its own creation) is able to shift money into a disturbed area, and thus to check the onset of crisis, while at the same time regulating its disposal by means of the control exercised over its local branches. Money is more fluid than ever before. Yet the country bankers in early days actually dreaded this fluidity of money. A " banker (belonging to a very great and respectable firm in Norfolk) " told H. W. Hobhouse that if all the local note issues were suppressed and one uniform issue established, he would not be able to keep money in his own district and lend it to the farmers at 5 per cent. It would all go to the " large marts, Liverpool, Manchester, and so on," where there was a demand for it at 6, 7, or 8 per cent. interest.[1] It really did go, for Vincent Stuckey told the Committee that deposits went from country bankers' coffers to London wherever interest ruled high[2] and Manchester bills were being discounted with Norfolk money, thanks to the London bill broker as intermediary.[3] Stuckey objected to these developments. He said it was impossible for any person in the world—at least, any person sitting in London—to determine, either by himself or by deputy, what amount of money is adequate for the needs of Somersetshire or Lincolnshire. He would hardly consider any individual serious who proposed such a thing.[4] The answer is, of course, that the unfailing allegiance to scientific standards must be combined with lissom adaptability to local conditions, and these, in turn, must not crystallise into rigidity.[5] If we were starting a banking system *de novo*,

[1] 1841 Committee, Q. 302.   [2] 1841 Committee, Q. 633.
[3] 1841 Committee, Q. 1527.   [4] Q. 270.
[5] A good example of mistaken rigidity can be found in the history of the amalgamations out of which the Standard Bank of South Africa has been built up. In January, 1871, the Directors of the London and South African Bank, " determined to prohibit advances on diamonds, and a month later, owing apparently to fresh representations on the subject having reached them, they issued instructions that ' no advances are to be made on diamonds or consignments thereof accepted,' and that ' this decision is to be accepted as final.' The Directors added the request that

said Bagehot to the 1875 Committee, uniformity might be possible; but under the existing state of things it is not.[1] Centralisation stands for the tendency to persist, while localisation encourages the tendency to diverge. The one means continuity of experience, the other a wholesome variation in the direction of more precise adaptability. Concentrated corporate inheritance and tradition are sources of strength, whereas the old hereditary *personal* control was bound, sooner or later, to put the square man in the round hole. The banking system of the provinces must be *sui generis*; yet centralisation prevents over-specialisation, such as that which destroyed Triceratops by the weight of his own protective frontal armour. That is our twentieth-century advantage over the older localised financial mechanism. The fluidity which was once an object of dread is to-day a valuable auxiliary of the banker. At the meeting of the London and Provincial Bank in 1910, Sir Joseph Savory said that the branches of that institution fell into three groups : (1) The metropolitan and suburban ; (2) the branches in the eastern counties ; and (3) the branches in the principality of Wales. These three groups represented three entirely different interests—namely, the trading, professional, and domestic clients of the metropolitan branches, the agricultural customers in the eastern counties, and the coal, iron, and tin-plate industries in Wales. Slackness of agricultural demand in such a case as this would, of course, suggest that the surplus funds should seek a more profitable outlet in South Wales or the Metropolis. The bank which does not possess branches

[1] 1875 Committee, Q. 7966.

' the question be not again referred home for reconsideration.' This policy not only shut the London and South African Bank out of what at that time and for years afterwards was a lucrative source of income, but was calculated to estrange some of their best customers, inasmuch as many of the most respected firms in the Colony were directly or indirectly interested in the diamond business." (Amphlett, *History of the Standard Bank of South Africa*, p. 74.) Meanwhile the Standard Bank, in contradistinction to this ironclad method, was doing a large business in the shape of advances on diamonds, with the result that in 1877 the London and South African Bank dropped like a ripe plum into the Standard Bank's mouth.

operating under all these different conditions, is necessarily at a disadvantage in comparison with an institution whose offices are of wide geographical distribution. In recent years, indeed—the cheap money era from 1892 to 1897— amalgamation with country banks was powerfully stimulated by the necessity of obtaining some outlet for money which was unlendable in London at 2 per cent. Thus the London and County before its amalgamation with the London and Westminster was hampered because its branches were mainly scattered over agricultural districts, and " we have no large manufacturing towns like Manchester, Bradford, or Newcastle, which absorb enormous sums of money."[1] With the onus of employing large balances thrown on a London office, and a London connection, while the Bank rate was at a low figure, a difficult situation was created. The converse case was offered by Parr's Bank which, as its chairman said, " had channels in our northern banking system for the lucrative employment of money which London bankers have not."[2] Money, like goods, is cheapened by rapid and facile transport from point to point. Distribution is as important a function of capital as of commodities. Further, the transport of capital from the point of superfluity to the locus of stringency is a function that is discharged not only in the geographical sense, but with regard to the varying needs of different industries. Where signs of depression in one coincide with inchoate activity in another, the flow of banking facilities can be instantly diverted, in a much more effective and economical fashion than would be possible in the case of groups of traders operating with their own capital, and liable to all the delays and difficulties of extricating it from one commitment before it was available for entry upon another. The private banker had no such expedient open to him as the removal of money away from a scene of depression to a centre of demand. Thanks to extended correlation and co-ordination, the distribution is now so completely under scientific control that occasional local superfluity only manifests

[1] Chairman at meeting, February 1, 1877.
[2] Chairman at meeting, January 26, 1877.

itself spasmodically in such a comparatively trivial matter as silver coin, of which there is now and then a surplus in one part of the country as against a deficiency in another. The change means widely enhanced economy and efficiency. In banking as in biology, the greatest gap and the greatest step in organic nature is that between single-celled and many-celled organisms.[1]

SEASONAL DISTRIBUTION OF CAPITAL

Quite apart from spatial distribution is the question of distribution from the point of view of time. The accommodation required at one season of the year in a given district may vary considerably from that required at another. "At harvest time," for instance, "the entire product of the year's industry changes hands, often within a period of two or three weeks."[2] Conditions may be quite the reverse in another part of the country. A bank which has a branch in both places can take advantage of these time variations so as to keep its money fully employed all the year. But the private bank, restricted to the single area, had no such opportunities. The elaborate Clearing-house arrangements inside the organisation of every great bank are also in themselves a most valuable auxiliary of business efficiency, though the system could not be worked by a scattered multitude of disconnected private institutions. By all these varying modes the co-operative activity enhances the volume of productive economic energy to an extent far beyond that which would be possible without it.[3]

ILLUSTRATIONS FROM DOMINION BANKING

These important principles are very actively operative in Dominion banking. "At one moment," said Sir Edmund Walker,[4]

[1] Geddes and Thomson, *Evolution*, p. 86.
[2] Seager, Introduction to *Economics*, p. 337.
[3] This differentiation, specialisation, and consequent adaptation can be seen at work within a joint-stock bank directorate itself. As Gilbart argued in his *Logic of Banking*, it is desirable that a board should possess a variety of talents. One director may be wealthy, another may have special business experience, a third an extensive acquaintance among commercial men, a fourth a specialised knowledge of finance, a fifth great discrimination of character, a sixth the administrative and forensic capacities that make a good chairman.   [4] Address to the Institute of Bankers, 1911.

NATURAL SELECTION AMONG THE BANKS

"they might be considering the conditions of a particular manufacturing industry, as would be the case in Great Britain; at the next those of one of the five widely separated timber areas, each having its own particular characteristics; the fishing interests of the Atlantic or of the Pacific, placer gold mining in the Yukon, copper smelting in British Columbia, silver mining at Cobalt, or the prospects of the new Porcupine country; the great agricultural, pastoral, dairying, and fruit industries; or immigration and settlement and their effect upon town and railway building."

These varying demands and tendencies operate reciprocally one upon another. The new branches opened in the Canadian west exhibit a preponderance of loans and discounts over the deposits. There becomes necessary a complementary movement to balance this state of affairs by creating in the east a preponderance of deposits over loans and discounts. In the effort to attain this end, new branches are opened. Thus the adjustment of supply to needs is incessantly proceeding with unfailing benefit to the business of the Dominion. The deposits, which exceed the loans and discounts in Quebec and Ontario, are marshalled to adjust the contrary state of affairs in Alberta and British Columbia. The Bank of Montreal borrows at Halifax to lend at Calgary. Deposits, said the chairman of the Union Bank of Canada at the meeting in 1912, "come in from all over the Dominion; they are totalled in the head office, and a safe proportion of them is loaned out wherever conditions demand and warrant it." From these head offices, "as from a higher altitude," it is "easiest to survey the extent of the general needs, to calculate the proper mode of distribution of the available resources, and to direct them more readily and quickly into the various channels below."[1] The working of the system has never been better described than in the pamphlet published by Mr. (now Sir) B. E. Walker of the Canadian Bank of Commerce, some twenty-five years ago. "My own bank," said Sir E. Walker,

"gathers deposits in the quiet unenterprising parts of Ontario, and lends the money in the enterprising localities, the whole

[1] Riesser, *German Great Banks*, U.S. Monetary Commission, p. 606.

result being that thirty-eight business centres, in no case having an exact equilibrium of deposits and loans, are able to balance the excess of deficiency of capital, economising every dollar, the depositor obtaining a large rate of interest, and the borrower obtaining money at a lower rate than borrowers in any of the colonies of Great Britain, and a lower rate than in the United States, except in the very great cities in the east."

Even more important than the distribution is the fact that the cool supervision of the east can check any undue inflation in the rising west. The western microbe of inflated credit languishes when it comes into contact with the serene atmosphere of Montreal. So perfectly is the distribution of capital made, that as between the highest class borrower in Montreal or Toronto and the ordinary merchant in the north-west, the difference in interest paid is not more than 1 or 2 per cent.

COSMOPOLITAN DISTRIBUTION

Thus a bank is analogous to a market. The essentials of a market are the unfailing presence of a seller when a buyer arrives, and of a buyer when a seller comes. The essentials of a bank are the inward flow which balances the outward drain, and leaves the maximum of deposits at the disposal of the banker for employment in advances, loans, and discounts. The Bank compounds the risk of their non-coincidence in point of time, space, and species, and in that way reduces the reserve which must otherwise be held against its occurrence. If the outward drain largely exceeds the inward flow, we have a "run." If vice versa, money becomes unlendable, and unless it can be drawn off to some area where it is not redundant, there must be a readjustment to meet the new conditions. The absence of opportunity to adopt this policy was, until the New Bank Act, the weakness of the banking system in the United States. The banks had no branches. Consequently there were banks in New York refusing interest on deposits because they did not want them, while other banks in the west and south were far in arrear of the financial needs of the districts which they tried to serve, because they had no access to other sources of supply than those of their immediate district, and these were insufficient. The banks of Massachusetts might have hard work to find satisfactory investments at 4 per cent., while Colorado banks were offered more good discounts at 10 per cent. than they could take.[1] Cosmopolitan finance is the same process of continuous redistribution operative over larger areas and in disregard of artificial frontiers. It can be discerned in the frequent shifting of surplus funds to London by foreign banks doing business here when there is a shortness of money on this side. These supplies relieve the pressure on the English market and at the same time put money in the pockets of the foreign bankers who have the disposal of them. The practice of holding large amounts in bills payable at various business centres is now, indeed, being generally adopted by all the great banks as a species of geographical insurance against the overwhelming pressure of crisis at one particular point. The Bank of Montreal, for instance, exhibits huge totals due to it from foreign centres, and forming a secondary reserve, rapidly available in New York or London for use against contingencies. Bullion would take time to arrive and drafts might not be honoured : but the ready cash reserve is instantly available. These expedients tend to create a cosmopolitan banking censorship, at the hands of a hundred skilled invigilators. The harvests, the budgets, the proposed new loans, the latest financial experiments of all the countries, the failures (too few, as Mr. Babson says, foretell disaster), gold movements, foreign trade, labour conditions, stock exchange tone and movements, commodity prices, social conditions, political factors—all are held under scrutiny, as well as the position of the various leading financial institutions. Such a censorship is practically extended to the prices of securities when there is a multitude of bankers watching a myriad margins. The wider the range of joint-stock enterprise becomes, the greater the scope of the censorship as the securities of the various companies take their place—higher or lower, as

[1] Breckenridge, *Canadian Banking System*, p. 377.

the case may be—among collateral. Nor is the censorship only available against a probable fall. Inflation would attract an equal reprobation. In safeguarding its own interests and those of its clients the Money Power establishes a censorship of the world, and is, in fact, the financial sentinel of all civilisation. Malaise at the extremities reports itself at the centre as promptly as the nerves of a burnt finger bring a mandate from the brain, ordering the instant withdrawal of the injured member from contact with the source of harm. In the cosmopolitan relationship, the foreign banks, unless they open London offices of their own, desire the alliance of an English institution which can reciprocate on a generous scale, and the larger the bank—the greater the number of its branches—the more valuable does the reciprocity become. This relationship itself consolidates the banking fabric ; for the clients of the English bank may stipulate for foreign banking facilities which could not be given if the alliance did not exist, however desirable they might be in the interests of international trade. In fact, the modern bank is now so many-sided, both in its resources and its activities, as to give redoubled force to the truism that " nothing can hurt a bank without doing it some good at the same time."

THE QUESTION OF COMPETITION

Supremely important above all other considerations touching the present problem is probably this—that the centralised control and the co-operation of the banks for self-protection, as trustees of the nation's finances, under the headship (as we shall see) of the Bank of England, have not ended the rivalry of the banks and finance houses *inter se*. The best individual achievement can only come through aggregate regulation. Remorseless competition among individuals brought the corporations, in the shape of the guild and the regulated company, into existence. The necessity for the regulation of competition among corporations gives us the banking hierarchy. In its sinister form—as in the case of oil—the killing of

NATURAL SELECTION AMONG THE BANKS 449

competition might result in a trust. But there is no such banking " trust " as City censors love to denounce. The rivalry has not even been mitigated—save in the sense that all modern financial and commercial strife is tinctured by a greater courtesy and restraint, by an exclusion of aimless and mischievous strife, by a more thorough recognition and acceptance of the rules of the game, and by a more profound recognition of the banks' fiduciary relationship to society at large. Balance-sheets[1] are

[1] PUBLICITY FOR BANK ACCOUNTS
Such a system of publicity as that which now keeps every bank in the limelight was not thought of in early banking days. Professional auditors were not asked to assist or examine. Up to 1832 even the directors of the Bank of England never had accounts before them (Leone Levi, Gilbart Lectures, 1878). The proprietors had always decided, by large majorities, against publication. Nathan Meyer Rothschild said that the Bank maintained its credit because its concerns were not made public. When statements began to be published, Lord Overstone said they were " imperfect and delusive." There had been some tentative (and almost humorous) suggestions about the desirability of publicity. The Lords' Committee of 1826 had reported that the constant exchange of notes between the different banks made them checks upon each other, so that " any over-issue is subject to immediate observation and correction." In contrast to this mild form of supervision, it is almost inconceivable that the Bank of Manchester should once have claimed the patronage of the public on the ground that only two of the directors had access to the accounts, and that none of the others were allowed to inspect them. This, it was argued, combined " all the secrecy of a private bank with the advantages of a public institution." The chairman of the City Bank in 1865 said it was " not desirable or for the interests of the company to appoint a paid accountant to investigate the affairs of the bank. . . . The Bank of England and several of the chief banks of London, including the London and Westminster, the Union, and other joint-stock banks, had no auditors at all, and yet were most flourishing institutions." The secrecy was deliberate. " The London and Westminster and other banks . . . *took care* to keep every abstract of their reports out of the papers till such time as they were publicly read at the meeting." (Chairman of the Bank of Wales meeting, May 17, 1864.)
Peel gave the original cue. " It has been frequently proposed," said he, in his speech on the Bank Charter Act (May 6, 1844), " to require from each bank a periodical publication of its liabilities, its assets, and the state of its transactions generally ; but I have seen no form of account which would be at all satisfactory." But it was exactly fifty years before the hint was generally accepted. Before the 1875 Committee, in the transition stage of public opinion on this subject, Mr. Frederick Seebohm objected to the compulsory publication of a private banker's accounts, on the curious ground that he might be deterred, in circumstances of emergency, from taking such precautionary and protective steps as might alter the aspect of his accounts, and might possibly increase the strain upon him. (Q. 4948.) Mr. (now Sir) Inglis Palgrave thought the objection lay in the hardship of a statutory compulsion after the private banks had been left alone, as regards the publication of their accounts, for a hundred

scanned by rivals who are keenly conscious of one another's infirmities. Competition and combination subsist side by side, and both play their respective rôles. Branches are still occasionally opened merely for " protective " purposes, and with small prospect of their paying their way. But these are comparatively rare manifestations. In the

years. (Q. 6006.) " For the first time in our existence," he added, " during a period of one hundred years, we have made a statement to anyone outside our business—I mean to the right hon. gentleman in the chair—of the state of our deposits "—referring, of course, to his own bank (Gurney's). To the same Committee Mr. K. D. Hodgson, M.P. (appearing with the deputy-governor of the Bank of England), stated that in his opinion the published accounts of the Bank not only gave the whole of the information which could be useful to the public, but a good deal more. As for publishing the individual deposits of bankers, said he, " you might as well ask what deposits are held by merchants, brokers, and especially money-brokers."

George Rae agreed that joint-stock banks should be compelled to publish accounts, but he thought private bankers should not be placed under the same obligation, though he added : " I do not know exactly where you are to draw the line." (1875 Committee, Q. 5291.) Private bankers in a given district were frequently a clan. They were all acquaintances and friends, and consequently indisposed to display any insistent curiosity into the state of each other's assets. That may be the reason why the increase in the habit of publishing bank balance-sheets has accelerated the movement towards amalgamation. It enabled A to obtain an insight into B's position, which he could not otherwise have done, and in that way provided him with data for the formation of a judgment whether or not amalgamation would be desirable or profitable. " In addition to its other advantages," said John Dun (*British Banking Statistics*, p. 61), " the publication of a balance-sheet is calculated to exercise an appreciable effect in preventing the management from straying far from the recognised lines of sound banking. The knowledge that the balance-sheet must run the gauntlet of adverse criticism may, without discredit, be admitted by directors and managers as an incentive to keeping advances within due limits, and maintaining ample reserves readily available for any emergency. I have never heard any valid argument against the publication of balance-sheets."

Glyn Mills began to publish their accounts (but not to disclose their profits) after the conversion of the private firm into a joint-stock company (with unlimited liability) in 1885. A few years later the Baring crisis made it clear that public opinion required the publication of accounts, and that if the figures were big and solid, the publicity would attract business to the bank. It was not, however, until 1894 (exactly half a century after Peel's original hint) that the publication of detailed statements of assets and liabilities began to be the regular practice, thanks largely to the efforts of the late Lord Goschen. Finally, we have the necessity for publicity made into a postulate of banking. " The public should have ample means to know where confidence can be safely reposed through the published half-yearly reports properly audited by accountants." (Sir Felix Schuster, Bankers' Dinner, May 8, 1912.) Beyond the secret reserve, there is no secrecy about the position of a modern bank.

Illustrations, from banking history, of the urgent necessity of balance-sheet preparation and scrutiny will be found *ante*, page 288.

main there is a conscious acceptance of the postulate that "the highest organism is that which, while maintaining its unity, allows the fullest development of individuality in its parts. The controlling factor necessary to replace the rude efficacy of the struggle is the intelligent apprehension of the organisation possible for [financial function[1]] and the subjection of current standards of value to that principle." It is not a case of co-operation or amalgamation replacing conflict, but of being superimposed upon it. The synthesis is higher and more intimate; but analysis will always reveal the same conflicting factors. This is essential to the efficient working of the Money Power itself. Only by the keenness of rivalry can its factors be maintained at their highest pitch of efficiency for the time being. The reason is that a group—so long as it is concerned with the discharge of one species of function, and guided by one dominant interest—is only the aggregate of its units. A failure of efficiency in the components must menace the authority and capacity of the mass. Efficiency involves co-ordination and correlation, but not subjection. Therein lies the reason why banking co-operation, as unofficially governed from the Bank of England, implies nothing in the nature of a trust. The law of mind fosters an economy of energy, and in banking, as in so many other directions, intelligent combination lowers the price paid by the consumer for the commodities or facilities supplied. The disciplinary process is simply carried up to, but not beyond, the point where it can bind the components together without killing the tendency to variability and the eternal propensity to progress by change. So efficient and cohesive is the co-operation in Canada that the Canadian chartered banks have been described by an American critic[2] as in effect one single institution. Yet

[1] "Human life" in the original passage, Hobhouse, *Mind in Evolution*, p. 393.
[2] J. F. Johnson, *Banking Problems* (American Academy), p. 550. One of the most brilliant of modern financial critics alleges that in Scotland the process has been carried too far. Unity has become practically union. "In Scotland . . . coherence and co-operation among the banks are carried to an extreme of which the mercantile community frequently complains. The banks are few and stand together like a close corporation;

there is active and competitive independence. "As lenders of money they are independent units. For that matter the branch of each bank has a great deal of independence. All are independently seeking for deposits. . . . Nevertheless, from a national point of view, despite the competition among the banks and their branches, there is considerable reason for regarding the chartered banks of Canada as one institution." Over fifty per cent. of the banking business of Canada is done by six banks. These conditions seem to be the inevitable concomitants of modern economic progress. In an early stage of human development rigidity and continuity—such as that of feudalism—are the peremptory necessities. Then comes an age when variability must be given its scope, or society will be crushed within its own coat of mail. Finally, there arises the need for the combination of both continuity and variability, in order to keep humanity upon the upward path ; and organised finance is ready with the means to that end, in the shape of the present centralised supervision and control of the whole banking machinery of the country. Ultimately, no doubt, world-banking will be operated under a centralised control.

THE MEANING OF RIVALRY

At one time it was supposed that the country might, in the course of years, be roughly marked out into spheres of influence respectively predominated by the great banks. Mr. John B. Martin thought that territorial banking groups represented the ultimate goal. The dream has not been realised. The number eight has even been mentioned as that of the minimum of groups which should be consistent with the public interest. But so far enterprise has been too eager and combative for these visions to be actualised. As recent events demonstrate, it is likely to remain so. Within twenty-four hours of the announcement in April, 1914, of the absorption of the Wilts and

---

they agree absolutely and arbitrarily among themselves as to the rates they will allow to depositors, the rates at which they will advance or discount and the terms and commissions for which they will do business for customers." (Hartley Withers, *English Banking System*, p. 49.)

Dorset Bank by Lloyds, the London City and Midland arranged to open 17 new branches in the territory thus constructively vacated by the Wilts and Dorset. Within a couple of months there followed the news of another absorption by the London City and Midland itself. The rivalry thus becomes keener; but it is more free and more fair, though it is certainly none the less strenuous for that.[1] It ceases to be an aimless competition with no moral or intellectual elements. It moves, like all modern trade competition, away from undisciplined and wasteful strife. It is a competition in augmented efficiency, not in extra production; the rivalry to evoke a better method, not to swamp a market and precipitate a mere contest in staying power, utterly without any economic value. Competition, as Seager says, " prevents the banks from retaining for themselves the profit which results from the use of their credit."[2] They share it with their customers, and through these customers the whole business community is benefited.

The combination of the central discipline with local flexibility is Riesser's justification for describing the result as a " concentration of capital and power." He objects to the word " concentration," or even " concentration of capital," alone, because, as he argues, there is a decentralisation of operation through the branches. A uniform policy, without hard and fast rules, becomes a potentiality, and the general economic interest can be better surveyed and more effectively safeguarded than if only a limited capital, or widely scattered resources, were available. Hard and fast rules of universal application are in fact

[1] Even the position of the door of the bank is a factor of its " pulling " power where clients are concerned. A modern bank has a specialised department engaged in selecting the best position for the branches. As the difference between the popular and the unpopular side of a road may exert a considerable effect upon the business done at a branch bank, even this obscure psychological factor has to be taken into consideration when the choice of a site is made. As a bank chairman said thirty years ago, the finest locality is the market place. As the banks themselves are representative concentrated markets, their ideal place is in that arena which has witnessed the higgling of generations. It has been suggested that the increase of branch offices, like other forms of rivalry among the banks, should now be the subject of some species of restrictive agreement.

[2] Introduction to *Economics*, p. 336.

impossible, except in so far as they are basic principles of banking itself—such as the avoidance of second mortgages. But even the variability itself is the subject of ruthless supervision. No bank can benefit by any banking novelty, if it be such as to meet with the disapproval of the rest of the banking fraternity. As Mr. Chisholm says,[1] " The fact of so much of the country's finance being summed up in a dozen huge balance-sheets has made criticism so keen that bankers are put on their mettle to show the utmost preparedness for any conceivable emergency." Banking of this disciplined type, with its substitution of the higher control for the lower, is free from what Mr. Lavington has called[2] " the fundamental defect of free enterprise— that individuals maximise their returns over the short period of one or two generations " without regard to the present or ultimate social consequences of their efforts. Keen and regulated competition, moreover, is itself a corrective of loose banking principles. The narrower the margin of profit, the greater the necessity to guard against its attenuation by bad debts, and consequently the closer and more critical the scrutiny bestowed upon every proposal which the banker receives. The branch manager of the A bank is not deterred by modern canons from fighting with the B bank for new accounts ; but there would be short shrift for him if he attempted to effect his purpose, as in the old unregenerate days, by the circulation of rumours that the B bank was in difficulties, or if he should attempt to seduce the customers of other bankers by offering accommodation on security or upon terms refused by them. He may fight, but he must fight fair. He may struggle to enhance the profit of the component, but woe betide him if he menace the well-being of the mass.

THE LIMITS OF COMPETITION

It is the simple truth to say that banking is the one business of all businesses in which there exist special reasons for the creation of some disciplinary and regulating

---

[1] *Bankers' Magazine*, September, 1910.
[2] *Economic Journal*, 1911, p. 53.

NATURAL SELECTION AMONG THE BANKS

organisation capable of defining and standardising professional practice. The reason is easy to discern. With regard to rivals in any other business the cynical public may possibly say with Iago :—

> " Now whether he kill Cassio
> Or Cassio him, or each do kill the other,
> Every way makes my gain,"[1]

But in banking the public goes down with the unlucky combatant, and therefore cannot afford to tolerate his misplaced pugnacity. The modern banker, if he is to keep within legitimate limits, must not afford accommodation to a customer against security which is below the accepted standard. He must not raise his deposit rates above the figure which he can safely pay from the profits of legitimate transactions. " Deposits are not safely placed where people show great anxiety to get them, and one of the most obvious evidences of people wishing to have them is that they will pay more for them than their neighbours."[2] If the rate on deposits be made too high an undue amount of money finds its way into the banker's hands, and he is tempted to take risks which he ought to avoid. " The more you pay for your money the more risk you must run in its employment."[3] Ten per cent. for money means bad debts.[4] Ruinous rivalry, produced by competing deposit rates, compelled the entertainment of illegitimate business and precipitated the last Australian banking crisis (1892–93) upon us. Moreover, money is kept out of investment if the banker pays too attractive a rate for it. But when we have reached a state of things in which there is one banking office for about every 5000 inhabitants of these islands, it is obvious that unless banking competition is disciplined it will be forced into a lowering of the standard. Unregulated competition encourages " banking up to the hilt," which is too great a menace to national solvency for a serious business

---

[1] *Othello*, Act V. Sc. 1.
[2] T. Cooke, chairman, Manchester and Liverpool District Bank, 1875 Committee, Q. 6807.   [3] Cooke, Q. 6540.
[4] Chairman, North and South Wales Bank meeting, July 20, 1866.

community to tolerate. A president of the Institute of Bankers,[1] chairman of the largest joint-stock bank in England, once said :—

"A joint-stock bank which came into our fold some years ago, whose reputation and position were second to none in the kingdom, and justly so, too, and [which] was a model of good management in other respects, employed every farthing they possessed, save and except what they required for, till-money, up to the hilt every day ; feeling sure that by means of other investments, which were gilt-edged though not consols, they would always be helped over the stile if pressure came. And that, I may say, is not an exceptional case."

This is not only unfair but dangerous temerity, of the precise type which amalgamation should put an end to. Again, a customer who cannot be accommodated by one bank will threaten to transfer his account to another. The cadging client is as dangerous as the manager who hawks his money among customers of other banks. Fortunately the cadger has but small chance nowadays. " There have been cases of firms—even firms of magnitude —which have wrathfully declared that they would never submit to the conditions their banker has thought it wise to propose to them, and after a vain offering of their account to several competing establishments, have found that they could not improve matters by a change of bankers."[2] But if this species of menace were once allowed

---

[1] Quoted by Hartley Withers, *English Banking System*, p. 92.

[2] Pownall, *English Banking*, p. 40. At the time of the German war crisis of 1914 there was an understanding among the banks that they would not take accounts from each other. This prevented the playing off of one bank against another by clients whose proposals were of the utterly unacceptable type. It was also, as we shall see, a chivalrous renunciation, by the larger concerns, of the opportunity to profit at the expense of the smaller.

There are, of course, occasional instances of two managers of the same bank competing for business against each other, but these are rare, and in time, no doubt, will disappear. " A man, locally well known and wealthy, went into the first bank and asked for a small loan on very first-rate security. He was told—it was the autumn of 1899 before the rate for money rose that year—that he might have the advance at 4 per cent. He thought this too high, and went into the second bank, saying what rate he could have the loan for at the first bank, and was offered it there at $3\frac{1}{2}$ per cent. He then went on to the third bank, told his story, and was offered what he wanted at 3 per cent. We can only hope that such a way of doing business will not be continued. It is certainly contrary

NATURAL SELECTION AMONG THE BANKS

to become effective, in the creation of cut-throat competition, the security of the whole banking fabric would be imperilled, and we might be standing on the perilous edge of financial chaos before we knew where we were.[1]

THE BIOLOGICAL ANALOGY

The vitally important consideration is that this rivalry of the great banks *inter se* conforms to the biological law of unceasing competition, and the resulting selection of

[1] From this point of view the practice of tempting banks to tender for accounts—e.g. those of municipal bodies—is mischievous. This system is all the more open to objection because it frequently involves the hypothecation by the banker of certain of his holdings as security for the account. In other words, he is compelled surreptitiously to tie up and earmark assets which ought to be free.

---

to all sound principles of banking. (*Bankers' Magazine*, 1901, Vol. I. p. 163). American bankers have striven to defend the system of touting for accounts. "The comforting influence of success consoles the hustler for the supposed loss of his dignity, and this loss is further compensated by the thought that he is really serving a public which other banks do not reach." (*Bankers' Magazine*, 1903, Vol. II. p. 451.)

Since the change of feeling which synchronised with the Overend-Gurney crisis there has been a general disposition among the banks to eliminate rate-cutting, by mutual arrangement. "The banks agree upon a tariff, as it were, of rates, and upon the basis of that tariff a very keen competition is maintained." (Chas. Gairdner, manager, Union Bank of Scotland, 1875 Committee, Q. 928.) The Northern Bank of Ireland, the Belfast Bank, and the Ulster Bank had minimum agreed charges and agreed modes of business when J. T. Bristow gave evidence before the 1875 Committee. (Q. 3432.) Appendix No. 3 to the Report of the Committee gives the full agreed tariff (two pages) of the Scottish banks, with regard to interest, discount, and commission on bills, charges for negotiating documents payable on demand, for drafts, transfers, and for other services. Seebohm said, however, that the principle was not applicable to England. "Anything like uniformity of charge in a manufacturing or an agricultural district would become an absurdity." (Q. 4735.) The Swiss banks in 1876 entered into an elaborate agreement "to insure, reciprocally free of charge, the receiving in payment and reimbursement of bank-notes, the collection of Bills of Exchange, and the payment of drafts." (See text in *Bankers' Magazine*, 1878, p. 101.) In June, 1914, the Swiss banks entered into a further convention for the maintenance of a standard rate of interest on deposits, and for the abolition of ruinous competition in the cheapening of banking facilities. The Union of Berlin Bankers and analogous organisations in many other German cities fixed minimum interest and commission charges for the purpose of stopping the "cutting of rates." In 1907 forty-six of the principal Norwegian banks agreed upon a scale of minimum commission charges for the collection of bills. The Union of Swedish Banks, with forty-seven members, was a similar agreement. Most of the great banks in the British colonies have analogous understandings, especially with regard to the rates at which they will transmit funds to and from this country. Unrestrained competition would spell unremunerative rates.

type, as the price paid for progress. The banks *must* submit to it. They can no more escape its pressure than a bank manager can withdraw his physical frame from the eternal jurisdiction of gravitation, or by taking thought add a cubit to his stature. Yet at the same time the recognition of a community of interest and responsibility, above and beyond the rivalry, is an entirely novel factor of the evolutionary process. There is, in a word, as a direct result of absorption and amalgamation, an initiative springing from a multitude of points, dominated by a central scientific control which every day adds to its stores of tradition and experience, and consequently becomes more capable not only of doing effectively all the business of the moment, but of handling any contingencies that may arise. " The psychologic law tends to reverse the biologic law."[1] We get the survival of the plastic instead of the survival of the fittest. Hitherto, through countless ages, the struggle for existence has proceeded with sole regard to the individual or racial interests of the combatants themselves. They have not been concerned to minimise, or modify, or suspend it, because its continuance might be antagonistic to interests other than their own. The strife has been absolutely self-regarding. But now, in the internal discipline of the Money Power, is a recognition that while the rivalry goes on the self-regardant factor must be modified, the rivalry be regulated : and it can only be regulated from the inside, not from without. The aggregate of banking resources is managed and protected with the profoundest sense of fiduciary responsibility to society at large. The biological propulsive force is left in operation, but it is mellowed and elevated by the acknowledgment of a higher allegiance than self-interest. There were many cases during and after the Baring crisis where the offer of a lucrative account, to be transferred from another bank, was strongly discouraged by assurances that there were no grounds whatever for the apprehensions of the would-be transferrer. One result of the agreement, among the banks, at the time of the

[1] Ward, *Psychic Factors of Civilisation*, p. 259.

NATURAL SELECTION AMONG THE BANKS 459

German war crisis in 1914, not to take accounts from one another, was a renunciation on the part of the larger constitutions of the opportunity presented by the crisis to " scoop " accounts from the smaller concerns. Such conduct represents the summit level of chivalrous financial rivalry. " Absolute strength and absolute safety," said the late Mr. J. Spencer Phillips,[1] " are the first considerations in conducting a bank. Profit, though a very important item, comes second, and a very long way second behind the others. . . . We have let certain old accounts leave us, simply because we were determined that under no circumstances whatever would we lock up any of our money where we could not recover it again." The principle is frankly recognised on the Continent. " It is clear," remarks Riesser,[2] " that powerful banks and groups of banks . . . under centralised control, can serve the German Empire as one of its most potent agencies in both its economic and world policies. This is true, at least so long as the leaders of the banks continue, as they have done, to regard their duty to the state as one of their important obligations." *Mutatis mutandis*, how truly these words can now be predicated of the *British* Empire also ! For " the evolution of a comparatively small number of powerful banks leads to the attainment of that decisive and concerted action in times of emergency and grave financial peril, which the delicacy of our mechanism of credit renders a necessity to the national well-being, and of which the events of the Baring crisis in 1890 are an excellent example."[3] When Mr. Sykes wrote, the Baring crisis was at once the classic and conclusive instance. The German war crisis of 1914 provided us with an infinitely more cogent demonstration.

SOLIDITY AND THE WAR CRISIS

When the crisis came, it was necessary to act quickly and unitedly—in other words, to enforce the adoption of a common policy upon the whole of the banking interests

[1] Lloyds Bank meeting, February 11, 1895.
[2] *German Great Banks*, U.S. Monetary Commission, p. 755.
[3] Sykes, *Banking and Currency*, p. 105.

of the country. The task was comparatively simple because the control was in the hands of the few great institutions. But if the conditions had been those of seventy years or eighty years ago, and it had been necessary to deal with the multitude of small, isolated, and independent banks, a united, coherent, and co-ordinated policy would have been all but impossible. Some, at all events of these banks, would have collapsed at the very outset. In falling, they would have pulled others down, and crisis might easily have evolved into panic, before we had known where we were. The mass of conflicting desires and expedients, merely neutralising one another, which would have been manifest among a random cluster of detached institutions, was rendered impotent in the firm grip of a beneficent autocracy. As it was, the banks acted as one, and not as many.[1] This is not a mere theory. Instructions were actually issued to bank managers that they were to exercise the utmost limit of generosity in the grant of advances during the period of crisis. They were not to restrict accommodation unless the proposition was of such a speculative character that it was quite impossible for a banker to entertain it. More than that, if the proposition stood on the border line between the legitimate and the illegitimate, they were not to " turn it down " without

[1] In contrast with British conditions of linked solidity were those subsisting in the United States until the banking system was reorganised. " Allowing for a few instances of group control," the " 20,000 or more commercial banks are all separate and distinct concerns, and institutions in the smaller communities must either provide wholly for their own needs or seek accommodations in the larger cities." (*Re-discount and the New Federal Reserve Act*, issued by the First National Bank of Boston, Mass.)

Germany had learnt the same lesson before the war. " One great advantage of having the banking power in Germany strongly consolidated showed itself in recent years, when the problem of meeting a difficult political and financial situation had to be solved. The Reichsbank and the leading private banks were able to agree readily upon a joint national policy of contraction at home and of avoiding foreign loans that might weaken the German markets. Thus within two years Germany not only made herself independent of foreign credits, but accumulated ready funds to such an extent that the Reichsbank's gold reserve increased by more than 100,000,000 marks. At the same time the discount rate in Germany dropped below that of England. The results during those two years were a strong proof of the soundness of the German banking system." (Riesser, address to New York State Bankers' Association, *New York Times*, January 25, 1914.)

NATURAL SELECTION AMONG THE BANKS

reference to the head office, although in normal times they might have considered that banking caution required the giving of a negative answer. Instructions like this, sent to thousands of bank managers from a mere handful of radiant points, represent something very different from the state of things which may be imagined as existing when there is no central grip at all and consequently no jurisdiction which can make itself felt at practically an hour's notice over the whole arena of British banking enterprise. The charges of restriction and niggardliness brought against certain banks in the early weeks after the actual crisis had their basis—such as it was—in the very few cases where over-cautious branch managers were unable instantaneously to comprehend the nature and importance of the new policy which they were required to administer. Taken as a whole, the successful passage of such an emergency, unprecedented in menace and magnitude, was a triumph of co-operation and co-ordination. The evolutionary movement which rendered possible the solid and successful resistance to the crisis of 1914 would perhaps be better described as the " promotion of the capable " than the survival of the fittest. It means that the greatest (except love) of all the cosmic forces has been ineluctably harnessed to the chariot of human progress. It is no longer free to run wild, in the fields of blunder, misconduct, and crisis, where seventy or eighty years ago it roamed unchallenged, leaving disaster and ruin behind it. The older banking was only a species of concentrated capitalism. The banking of the twentieth century is finance in one of its most advanced and most highly organised contemporary forms.

OPPOSITION HERE AND THERE

Hostility to bank amalgamation has found concrete expression in endeavours to discover a more excellent way. The federation system, out of which the National Provincial Bank of England was developed, was intermediate between the independent local banking régime and the control of a huge London institution. In the federation system, each bank had its own board, but all were controlled by a central directorate in London. The system was a fruitful source of contention, and was early abandoned. The Gurneys of Norwich were at one time the head of a group known as the Associated Gurney Banks at Ipswich, Lynn, Wisbech, Yarmouth, and other places ; but Gurneys themselves have now been absorbed by Barclay's. London banks with numerous and scattered provincial branches like Barclay's and Parr's, represent a species of modern modification of the federation plan, since they have numerous local directorates whose members are all specialists in the economic conditions of their own district. In recent years there have been efforts at the " resumption of the offensive " by country banks, in the shape of efforts to protect and consolidate their position against London incursions, by the absorption of joint-stock and private neighbours, where such alliances were practicable. But the only serious menace to concentration has been declared to be, at all events in Germany, its challenge by another power—industrial cartels and syndicates. Certainly, in England downright opposition has rarely achieved its aim, though in a very few cases successful efforts have been made by influential customers of a bank to prevent the loss of its identity by amalgamation with another institution. This happened, for instance, in 1903, when the clientele of the Manchester and Liverpool District Bank compelled the abandonment of a scheme for amalgamation with Lloyds, and again in 1910, when proposals for the absorption of the Lancashire and Yorkshire Bank by a London institution were rendered abortive by the strong opposition of the customers of the bank before the shareholders had even been consulted on the matter. Riesser could at one time have been effectively quoted as a cordial sympathiser with these tactics. He declares[1] that while the decline of [German] private banking (due largely to adverse legislation) is "only one phase of the modern struggle for existence," it nevertheless represents

[1] *German Great Banks*, U.S. Monetary Commission, p. 759. But see his present views, p. 656.

" one of the dark sides of the progress of concentration."
Yet his only definite reason for this view is that concentration has wrought injury to " the sound and vigorous elements among the class of smaller private bankers " : and that these small bankers might operate with social advantage if they adopted "specialisation and adaptation to local conditions and needs." However applicable such arguments may be to German conditions, enough has been said to show that in English banking, the gain would be overwhelmingly counterbalanced by the disadvantages. Riesser's point that the small banker can fulfil a useful function by dealing in, and advising upon unlisted securities, is obviously inapplicable to British conditions, since our bankers are not share-dealers or share-" pushers." Still, Riesser's views with regard to absorption appear to command sympathy among German bankers. At the Bankers' Congress in Berlin in 1912, there was adopted a declaration that private bankers constitute an indispensable link in the organisation of banking, stock exchanges and credit. This resolution was intended as a protest against the domination of practically the whole of the German banking world by groups under the control of a mere handful of great joint-stock banks—the so-called four D's.[1]

[1] The four big D's of German banking at this time were the Deutsche, Dresdner, Darmstädter, and Disconto institutions. They were alleged to form a Central European Money Trust. As in the case of the American Money Trust, the charges were : (a) the control of immense resources (about £200,000,000), by means of a common policy, for a monopolistic purpose ; (b) the employment of the interlocking system, so that the financial or commercial proposition which was " turned down " at the Deutsche Bank would find the other three roads locked against it ; (c) the acquisition, by various means, of the controlling interest in smaller, and possibly rival, concerns with a view to their subordination to the main scheme of absolute predominance.

CHAPTER XVI

THE FINANCIAL TRUSTS—"INVESTMENT BY PROXY" AND ITS EXTENSION

IN spite of the large sums lavished in financing the " new " nationalities, and in equipping the ephemeral joint-stock ventures of 1826, as well as the innumerable railway projects which followed them, it remains true that down to the accession of Queen Victoria a huge proportion of investment was on mortgage. The reason, as Sergeant Onslow told Parliament in 1825, was that land was " the best and readiest security[1] which could be offered for money." The Solicitor-General said at the same time, that nine out of every ten estates in the kingdom were loaded with mortgages—one of the results of the terrific taxation necessitated by the Napoleonic wars. A multitude of small investors clung to the Funds. Baring said in 1830 that out of the holders of the 274,823 stock accounts then on the books of the Bank of England, 250,000 did not receive a greater half-yearly dividend than £100, and the number of half-yearly dividends of £500 did not exceed 2000. Of course, when the early Victorian public completely lost its head, as it did in the railway mania, the investing class was temporarily recruited from all sections of the community. The Government return of railway shareholders, issued in 1846, shows that there were upwards of 20,000 subscribers to the lines and branches

[1] In its primary legal significance the word " security " still refers only to money *secured* on property, and not to investments in the stocks or shares of a company or the issues of a public authority. This limited antique meaning it will be taken to have in a will, unless the context clearly indicates that the testator used it as synonymous with " investments." So said Lord Justice Romer as recently as 1904. (Re Rayner, 1904, 1 Ch. at p. 189.)

seeking authorisation in one session alone. These recruits included attorneys' clerks, college scouts, butchers, coachmen, dairymen, beer sellers, butlers, footmen, and mail guards. But, broadly, the proposition remains true that these classes did not enter the arena of investment for many years after the railway craze. When the mortgage began to go out of favour investment in stocks and shares of the industrial type, as well as in the best class of foreign bond, was still a privilege restricted to the wealthy. A typical list of shareholders of the mid-Victorian period will be found to include practically only representatives of the wealthy, landed, and professional classes. Their holdings, moreover, were all in large blocks.[1]

Middle-class respectable people, especially, believed that all money invested outside the pale of Government securities was embarked in speculation. They had yet to learn the meaning and solidity of a first-class industrial debenture, with a huge margin behind it. The best that

[1] In my *Mechanism of the City* I illustrated this point by contrasting the personalities in the list (dated April 21, 1864) of the shareholders of the Alamillos Co., with the last return on the Selfridge file. In the case of the Alamillos shares, the first 25 names on the list represent the occupations annexed, together with the number of shares inserted in brackets : a wharfinger (300), a solicitor (60), a brass manufacturer (107), a vice-admiral (825), a firm of merchants (55), a professor of chemistry (10), a broker (285), a gentleman (550), another gentleman (350), a copper smelter (350), a doctor of medicine (52), a civil engineer (75), a Treasury official (26), a spinster (136), a banker (50), a lady of title (3), a clergyman (10), a gentleman (1000), a member of the Stock Exchange (16), a clergyman (100), a solicitor (321), a member of Parliament (207), an architect and surveyor (50), a decorator (30), and a banker's clerk (21). In contrast with the comparatively elevated social status of these investors, we get in the Selfridge list such shareholders as a cabinet maker (25), a commercial traveller (50), a gas collector (10), a clerk (30), a hospital nurse (10), a domestic servant (5), an outfitter's assistant (5), a farmer (100), a dressmaker (5), a housekeeper (5), a schoolmistress (10), a lady's maid (10), a grocer (5), an ironmonger (10), a valet (40), a printer (10), a caretaker (2), a governess (30), and a bespoke tailor (3).

There was originally an idea that shares of small amount—especially bank shares—would attract an inferior class of holder. So thought the 1836 committee. But as Gilbert pointed out in 1859 (*Logic of Banking*, p. 222), the only effect of reducing the size of the share—originally, at all events—was to increase the number held by the average shareholder, and not to attract small capitalists. "In the banks of £100 shares," said Gilbart, " each proprietor has taken upon an average 28 shares, on which he has paid the sum of £444. In the banks of £20 shares, each proprietor has taken 43 shares, and paid £359. In the banks of £10 shares, each proprietor has taken 52 shares, and paid £400, while in the only bank of £5 shares, each proprietor has taken 117 shares, and paid £585."

could be said of the nervous middle-class in the 'sixties was that it was *beginning* to lose its nervousness. "It is unnecessary," observed Arthur Crump in 1866,[1] "to remark that the number of persons who *do* remove their money for better investment is certainly increasing." These were the timid pioneers who had hitherto ranked railway stocks among purely speculative purchases, quite unfit for the investor. But after the Overend-Gurney crisis they began in a gingerly fashion to study traffics and to watch yearly reports. The small capitalist, however, still clung to the funds and the savings banks. With the latter we have already dealt (*ante*, p. 277): and with regard to the former it may suffice to say that in 1869 there were 5065 Government stock accounts of less than £30 in the books of the Bank of England, and no less than 481 of them were under £5 in amount.[2] In 1870 came the Elementary Education Act, and from that period to the present time there have been working the influences which have now created the modern investing public, its personnel numbered by hundreds of thousands, and representing every class of society except the absolutely destitute.

A "FELT WANT" IN INVESTMENT

There was good reason for mid-Victorian nervousness in the matter of investment. The traditions of the railway mania were yet comparatively fresh, and the tragedies of unlimited liability loomed large in the public eye. Inexperienced credulity had been the prey of roguery and imprudence in all directions. "There is no doubt that within the last twenty or thirty years enormous sums of money, representing the savings and accumulation of the individual interest of this country, have been dissipated and lost in the attraction of new but unsound investments." [3] Discouraged by these unwelcome episodes the aspiring possessors of surplus funds thought they knew that good investments were to be had, yet distrusted their own

[1] *Banking, Currency and the Exchanges*, p. 244.
[2] Letter of the Governor (Crawford) to the Chancellor of the Exchequer (Lowe), January 25, 1870.
[3] Stock Exchange Commission, 1877–1878, Report, p. 10.

THE INVESTMENT TRUSTS

judgment in the selection of them. To would-be investors, in that frame of mind, the proposition of investment by proxy under good auspices was not unattractive. On the other hand, the opportunity of dealing with large aggregates of money by means of distributed risks certainly possessed a charm for the early exponents of investment trust finance, though it may be doubted if they realised whereunto this would grow. For the moment their business was to aggregate the money of a large number of proprietors into the capital of an investment trust company, and then to employ the fund thus created to the best advantage suggested by the knowledge, experience, and skill of the various groups of City men who had placed themselves at the head of these new undertakings. So it is that in the establishment of the investment trusts we have really a distinct factor of the Money Market,[1] a species of the genus company which is as worthy as insurance to rank as an independent force, fulfilling a definite (and now indispensable) function.

THE TRUSTS A LATE DEVELOPMENT

Investment trusts[2] were practically unknown to the early Money Market. The long list of enterprises floated in the boom year 1825 includes many enterprises which look like financial trusts, but on examination prove to be something different. A so-called Investment Bank[3] with a capital of 4000 shares of £50 each proposed to deal with

[1] The Money Market is generally said to comprise four factors : (1) the Bank of England, (2) the "cheque-paying banks," as Mr. Withers calls them, in order to distinguish public banks from private mercantile houses, who, although they do an acceptance and quasi-banking business, have no customers who are entitled to draw cheques upon them ; (3) the bill brokers and the mercantile and discount houses and (4) the Stock Exchange. In the present survey, however, the joint-stock companies and certain specialist forms of joint-stock enterprise like insurance, and the trust, finance and investment companies have been treated as distinguishably separate factors of the Money Market.

[2] The word "trust," as here employed, signifies an organisation totally different from a "trust" in the American sense of a monopoly-control of some commodity or facility. This distinction is very important. The English investment trusts are not monopolies, and have no monopolistic ambitions.

[3] *Times,* January 7, 1825. The advertisement appeared for several days.

"Life Interests, Policies of Insurance, Contingent and Reversionary Interests, Ground Rents, Improved Rents, Rent Charges, and other property." "The objections to speculative theories," said the prospectus, " cannot apply to the present proposed institution, which possesses nothing adventurous in its character." A United British and Foreign Loan Co. capitalised at £2,500,000 offered[1] 4 per cent., and intended to " facilitate " transactions in foreign securities, and to make advances on public works in progress in the United Kingdom. An Irish Investment and Equitable Loan Bank (capital 10,000 shares of £50 each) adopted[2] the same programme so as to " cause British wealth to flow in Irish channels." The Equitable Investment Society and the Metropolitan Investment Society[3] were merely schemes for buying " Landed Property," especially near the metropolis. The first of the investment trusts, in the modern sense of the term, appear to have been the International Financial Society and the London Financial Association, both established in 1863. The business of the London Financial Association was defined as the lending of money on railway securities, provided the lines were finished. But criticism was offered of any loans on unfinished lines, because if the contractor failed the company must either lose what it had advanced or become more deeply involved by putting up money to complete the work. An undertaking of this type was an attempted compromise between the distrust of the investor and the necessity for carrying on railway enterprise. The railway could not wait for the public temper to change, or for its securities to filter slowly into the hands of investors. Therefore it deposited its securities with a finance company, and the latter agreed to accept the railway's debts for a specified sum. The finance companies were able to sell their shares at high prices to investors, who imagined that they had placed a buffer between themselves and the industrial risk. It was only when the unrealisable character of the securities had begun to be apparent that

---

[1] *Times*, January 17, 1825.   [2] *Times*, January 19, 1825.
[3] *Ibid.*

THE INVESTMENT TRUSTS

the weakness of the system stood out in glaring conspicuousness.

PRINCIPLES OF TRUST OPERATION

The best early enunciation of the principle involved in the investment trust company is contained in the prospectus of the Foreign and Colonial Government Trust, issued in 1868 :—

" The object of this Trust is to give the investor of moderate means the same advantages as the large capitalist in diminishing the risk of investing in Foreign and Colonial Government stocks, by spreading the investment over a number of different stocks and reserving a portion of the extra interest as a sinking fund to pay off the original capital.

" A capitalist who at any time within the last twenty or thirty years had invested, say, £1,000,000 in 10 or 12 such stocks selected with ordinary prudence, would, on the above plan, not only have received a high rate of interest, but by this time have received back his original capital by the action of the drawings and sinking fund, and held the greater part of his stocks for nothing.

" Some parties, believing that it would be a convenience to the public if such a mode of investment were made generally accessible, have made arrangements by which well-selected Government stocks, to the value of £1,000,000 sterling, will be placed in the names of the following trustees, viz. :—

" The Right Honourable Lord Westbury,
" The Lord Eustace Cecil, M.P.,
" G. M. W. Sandford, Esq., M.P.,
" George Wodehouse Currie, Esq., M.P.,
" Philip Rose, Esq."

The trustees had decided that a certain group of dividend-paying Foreign and Colonial stocks should be selected for purchase with the funds of the Trust — namely, Austrian, Australian, Argentine, Brazilian, Canadian, Chilian, Danubian, Egyptian, Italian, Nova-Scotian, Peruvian, Portuguese, Russian, Spanish, Turkish, and United States bonds—not more than £100,000 being invested in the stock of any one Government. The average rate of interest on the investment in these stocks was given as 8 per cent., while profits were expected from the repayment at par of a large number of them, purchased considerably below that figure. The certificates of £100 each were to bear 6 per cent. interest, and to be issued at 85. This, as a matter of fact, was an investment trust in the modern sense of the term. Designed for the benefit of the middle-class investor in the later 'sixties, it was destined, as we shall see, to be the model of another trust, issued under practically the same auspices, nearly fifty years later, for the purpose of attracting a democratic clientele by a direct appeal to the " people."

THE DISTRIBUTION OF THE RISKS

On the part of all the investment trusts of this period there was the clearest recognition of the protection afforded by the geographical distribution of the risks, itself a specialised application of one of the principles of insurance. " Our great safety," said the chairman of the Governments Stock Investment Co., " is having a wide area in which we trade instead of depending upon one municipal capital or one country. We have forty or forty-two different investments, that is, investments secured by different Governments."[1] The insurance element was specifically mentioned in the prospectus of the Submarine Cables Trust, issued in 1871, which called attention to the advantage of standardised investment " by distributing the risk over a number of kindred undertakings and making one insure the other." One risk was to be offset by another, so that the investments might almost be described as a group of co-operative insurers. The prospectus of the Gas, Water, and General Investment Trust urged that " the capital of the company will be spread over a large number of securities in such a manner that, by the principle of average, the investor will obtain a good rate of interest, without being subject to violent fluctuations in dividends or exposed to the necessarily precarious nature of an investment in any one concern, however sound." Yet another specialised form of this financial trust was the

[1] Meeting, January 2, 1873.

THE INVESTMENT TRUSTS 471

mortgage company, whose business, as ultimately elaborated, might be described as long-dated banking. For instance, in Australia the settler sometimes experienced difficulty in obtaining an advance for a term of years. The banks were disinclined to accommodate him except by means of short-dated promissory notes and accommodation bills. At this period they would not, as a rule, advance their money on mortgage, though their practice became less rigid later. Their discount of promissory notes and bills was generally subject to the condition that there should be a second name to them. This necessitated the settler obtaining the acceptance or endorsement of the merchant to whom he was consigning his wool or other produce, and for this accommodation, of course, he had to pay. The result was that the commission, added to a bank charge of probably 9 or 10 per cent., was a very real obstacle to the progress and settlement of the colonies. The problem to be solved was the provision of the means of lending money for a term of years at a reasonable rate, and the solution was the formation of such companies as the Trust and Agency Co. of Australia, which directly cultivated that class of business with considerable success.

THREE DISTINCT TYPES OF " CREDIT SHOP "

By this time, then, the rise of the trust and investment companies enables us to discern in activity the three classes of "credit shop"[1] each selling the same commodity, but each specialising in a particular species of it, clearly differentiated from that sold by the other two. The bank sells short credit only. The finance company caters for a class of business which requires a much longer credit than a banker can give, consistently with his duty of maintaining his assets in liquid form. The investment

---

[1] This word "shop" is immemorially attached to banking and credit business. In the very early days of Martin's there is a charge paid to a useful functionary for "killing the bugges in the shop," and as late as 1814 we find the Craven Bank inserting in its balance sheet, "By Banking Shop and outbuildings now purchased, formerly rented only, £488." The reason for the survival of the word is, of course, the fact that the banker's business was originally only a subordinate function actually carried on in a shop devoted to other purposes.

trust company, again, enters a given transaction for a much longer period than a finance company, if, indeed, it does not purchase the investment for permanent holding. It was the attempt to combine these three functions in one enterprise which led to the collapse of the Birkbeck Bank. The capital had been obtained on a building society basis, while the deposits were sought as if the institution receiving them was a bank in the strict sense of the word. Finally, when the capital and the deposits were aggregated, the funds were employed as if the company was an investment trust, not liable to be called upon to repay any part of the money which was employed. The same fate would probably have waited on the scheme proposed in the 'sixties by the town clerk of Liverpool, for empowering municipalities to establish savings banks, and to employ a third of the deposits in municipal undertakings such as waterworks. At all events, the Australian banking crisis of the early 'nineties was an example of the consequences which followed an abandonment of sound banking principles in the attempt to combine long-term loans with the liability to pay specie on demand.

BOLD EXTENSIONS OF THE TRUST PRINCIPLE

From 1884, when the Mercantile Investment and General Trust was founded, to 1890 there was quite an epidemic of trusts. Attempts to form bank share trusts were indeed unsuccessful, owing to the refusal of the great banking companies to accept the trusts as shareholders. But as regards other trust enterprises, no less than twelve were established in 1889, under the stimulus of Mr. Goschen's conversion of Consols. The reduction of the interest created a demand for investments which were in effect a mixture of stocks, in the belief that an average of second-rate—or even third-rate—holdings would give a return greatly superior to that obtainable on Consols without the introduction of any really abnormal risk. The sponsors of the Nitrate and General Investment Trust Co., early in 1889, urged that the average yield of the holdings of a trust company could be materially raised by including in

THE INVESTMENT TRUSTS 473

its holdings the stocks even of very speculative enterprises. It was proposed, therefore, to invest some part of the funds of this trust " in the best of the nitrate companies which have been introduced to the London market." Nor did nitrate represent the most speculative of the industries which the growing boldness of the investment trusts tempted their directors to touch. The African Gold Share Investment Co. did not actually propose to form companies or to purchase properties, but it was prepared to guarantee and provide capital for gold-mining enterprises on favourable terms, and in this way it was believed that the high yield obtainable on the shares of these undertakings would raise the average return on the capital invested. Finally we have a reversion to mortgages. The Union Mortgage Banking and Trust Co. initiated, with a capital of £2,000,000, a scheme for lending on the first mortgage of improved agricultural property in the United States, so as to combine the advantages of that species of security with the higher yield obtainable in a " newer " country than Great Britain. The proposal was that the company should receive money from investors at a fair rate of interest in exchange for its debentures. These were, in turn, to form a charge on all its mortgage investments, reserve fund, uncalled capital, and other assets. The money was then to be invested—and here once more is the crucial point of the whole argument— " at a higher rate of interest in small amounts, thus acquiring the guarantee for safety afforded by the law of average." The prospectus of the River Plate and General Investment Trust Co. (capital £1,000,000) defined the maximum single risk to be taken. The business of the company, the directors said, was that " of distributing its capital over a number of different securities on the principle of averages, no investment being made exceeding £10,000 in any one undertaking without the unanimous resolution of a meeting of the trustees." Candour requires the admission that some of the investment trust enterprises of the Baring crisis year were not so much genuine finance and investment trusts as gigantic relief funds, designed to take huge blocks of securities from various parties who found it inconvenient to go on "nursing" them. Further, under the stimulus of a popular craze of the familiar type which gives us mining and rubber booms, these undertakings launched out into insurance, executorship, trusteeship, safe deposit, loan and commission business of every sort and kind, the sale and purchase of land on commission, agency, and company promotion, with results that became only too familiar to the investor in the early 'nineties. The existence of these abuses of the principle, however, need not blind us to its undeniable utility when operated under skilful and honest administration.

THE TRUSTS AND THE "PEOPLE"

The theory that the trust companies represent, at all events in one of their aspects, an endeavour to provide investment by proxy on behalf of a class insufficiently experienced to act on its own account was strikingly confirmed when, on March 20, 1914,[1] there appeared the prospectus of the People's Trust Co., Ltd. This venture was obviously modelled on the Foreign and Colonial Investment Trust which had been established forty-six years before (*ante*, p. 469). Messrs. Glyn, Mills, Currie and Co. were the bankers of the later enterprise, and a member of their firm had been a trustee of the earlier undertaking. One of the trustees of the Foreign and Colonial Trust was Mr. Philip Rose, of Baxter, Rose, and Norton, whose successors, the firm of Norton, Rose, Barrington and Co., were solicitors nearly half a century later to the People's Trust. But the most striking and suggestive analogy is found in the fact that while the earlier trust was formed, as we have seen, "to give the investor of moderate means the same advantages as the large capitalist," the later undertaking was "established to extend *to the working and industrial classes*" a form of investment much appreciated by a richer clientele. The prospectus proceeded to say that the new company would "enable even the smallest capitalists to acquire an interest in English and Foreign

[1] See the *Financial News* of that date for the prospectus.

railways, Colonial and Foreign loans and great commercial undertakings, and to share in large financial operations. The company will adopt the principle that has been found to work so well with existing trust and investment companies of distributing its capital over a wide area and in a large number of undertakings, and it has been proved that by so doing a satisfactory return can be obtained without taking undue risks." Thus, in 1868 it is the man of moderate means who is invited to invest by proxy, but in 1914 the gradual devolution of capitalistic capacity has made it desirable to provide investment by proxy for the " working and industrial classes." As there is no class, at a more modest level than this, from which investors may be recruited, we may correctly say that the opportunity of advantageously investing money has been now brought within the reach of everybody who has money to invest.

TRUST FUNCTIONS HAVE BEEN MODIFIED

About the general success and the pronounced importance of these companies as factors of the modern Money Power there of course can be no two opinions. One has only to look around at the vast aggregation of influence represented by the Lord St. David's group, or by other powerful trust companies, to see how well the principle works, and how thoroughly it has adapted itself to the needs of the period during which it has been elaborated. Whether, however, the system is destined to remain permanently necessary, in the form in which it first functioned, is another matter altogether. Originally the investment trusts represented the standardised investor. They sought to aggregate the funds of people who were too nervous or too inexperienced to invest their own money. In that way they enabled this class of moneyed individual to secure financial benefits which had otherwise been out of his reach. The aggregation professed to take all the precautions, with regard to the distribution of the risks and the mixture of the types, which a prudent investor of the shrewdest stamp would have adopted for the protection of his own money. Its directors seldom changed investments once made. They awaited redemption and collected interest meanwhile. Nowadays, at the point in the evolution of the trust company which has so far been reached, this ideal still survives and new trust companies are still created. But while the trust company still functions, for the present, in its original form, it is becoming less a means of vicarious investment than a recognised and necessary factor of the modern Money Power, taking its share in the guidance of the policy of the great financial hierarchy which now controls the economic destinies of the world.

WIDELY EXPANDED FUNCTIONS

It watches the market, changes its investments, gets out of this and into that as the economic or political ebb and flow suggest. It competes for underwriting, and in that way not only makes money when the issue goes well, but acquires new holdings on bed-rock terms where it is "stuck" with part of the stock or shares which it has underwritten. Further, a very important and characteristic function of the modern trust company is its work in City salvage. An enterprise which has a valuable property and good prospects finds itself at the end of its capital resources. The time is not congenial for a public issue; how, then, is the company to be maintained in existence and saved from the loss of all the capital already expended on its property? The answer is that the trust company will be prepared, on terms, to elaborate a reconstruction scheme and to guarantee its success—that is to say, to guarantee that if the shareholders do not come forward with sufficient funds, it will itself put up the money. In this way, companies which have reached the end of their tether are frequently snatched from disaster and almost as frequently transformed into prosperous enterprises. Of course, the position of their affairs must stand the scrutiny of expert examination. But that is rather a gain than a loss from the point of view of the financial fabric as a whole. These activities, almost entirely characteristic of the *post*-Baring period, constitute quite a different programme from that which was originally undertaken in the 'eighties. There are two reasons for the change. The one is that the existence of a centralised Money Power did not fully dawn upon the world until the Baring crisis had demonstrated its immeasurable potency for good; the other is that the modern middle-class investor is now, on the whole, sufficiently educated to do his investment work for himself, selecting his own securities and keeping them in his own strong-box or at his own bank. In the earlier decades he was delighted to discover that responsible persons would accept the charge of his money, and invest it in such a manner that he could get a safe 4 per cent. upon it. Nowadays he takes the responsibility himself; and he is all the more inclined to do so because he can get 5 per cent. with perfect safety, without the intervention of a trust at all. The finance, investment, and mortgage trusts, however, remain as standardised corporate investors, in that it is their constant and very successful endeavour to raise the rate of return on their money without infringing the canons of financial prudence. Their invocation of the law of average makes them self-insurers : so that inasmuch as they possess a specialised skill, the risk is taken by those who are capable of measuring it. " To confine speculation to those who have aptitude and training for it, and to discourage stock and commodity gambling, is one of the economic problems of the day."[1] There is only a minor element of gambling to be considered in the case of the trust companies : but there is an undeniable assumption of a legitimate (and socially beneficial) financial risk on the part of those who have aptitude and training for it. The great trust and investment companies, again, are a class of strong holders, performing a fruitful function at all times, but most of all in days of market stress. A trained investor (whether an individual or a corporation) is a " good " holder, whereas his untrained nervous confrère is a " bad " one. The difference between the accumulation of stock in " good " hands or " bad " may be of great moment to market conditions, and consequently

[1] H. R. Seager, *Introduction to Economics*, p 176.

to the prices of securities, in the hour of stringency. It may mean the difference between stress and crisis, or between crisis and panic. The cool heads of the managers of a great trust company are not turned by crisis or by the threat of panic. They do not rush to fling everything on the market. They are more likely to steady it by timely purchases. As they are in constant communication with the other controlling influences of the Money Market, their trained and fearless co-operation is one of the bulwarks of the financial fabric itself. It will possess an augmented and invigorated potency when the movement towards a completely centralised control of the allied insurance function, vast in influence and resources, shall at length be crowned with realisation.

In Germany the rôle of the trust company is to some extent filled by the subsidiary banks (Tochtergesellschaften) which carry on industrial finance by means of capital supplied by the parent company. Occasionally they are regarded as branch banks, but they are not truly such in the English sense.

PART IV

THE STRUGGLE TOWARDS CONSOLIDATION

CHAPTER XVII

FINANCIAL CONFEDERACY " IN A FLOOD "

AT this advanced stage of the investigation of the Evolution of the Money Market, a brief retrospect will be salutary and invigorating. We began about the year 1385 with the embryology of finance, scrutinising the early beginnings of the various factors and functions which make up the financial organism as we know it to-day. We noted the gradual increase of specialisation and differentiation of the functions, resulting in the steadily enhanced complexity essential to ultimate advanced development, under the control of a central co-ordinating force. We watched the first vague awakening of the self-consciousness of finance when the establishment of the Bank of England brought into being the possibility of a continuity of tradition, and an unbroken accumulation of experience, simultaneously surrounding itself with prestige and ultimately gaining some measure of predominance. But before this could be established the sinister interposition of incoherence, isolation, and lack of discipline manifested itself in the establishment, practically at random, of innumerable so-called " banks," working without system and drifting by the score into the maelstrom of insolvency.

Then came the revolutionised conditions whose onset we can trace in the years that follow Waterloo. The Bank of England, in spite of the advent of enterprising rivals, grew stronger than ever. Its prestige became plain and palpable. The joint-stock banks sprang into being and began to realise their responsibility as trustees of the working capital of the nation. The last traces of obsolete anti-usury sentiment vanished into oblivion. The joint-stock trading companies, freed from the mediæval shackles which had prevented the facile transfer of their shares and the limitation of their liability, commenced, in spite of many initial blunders and scandals, to be among the financial energies. Specialised forms of joint-stock activity—such as those represented by the insurance companies and the great investment trusts—added further factors of complexity to the organism. Yet all these components of finance, now transcending insular limits and becoming cosmopolitan in their vogue, were incessantly and inexorably subjected to a centripetal force which concentrated them more and more around the Bank of England and the group of giant financial interests which consciously or unconsciously, willing or unwillingly, was beginning to acknowledge the sway of Threadneedle Street. In the presence of these conditions we reach the point where we need no longer speak with a certain vagueness and hesitancy about the co-ordination of finance, but where we can rather begin to analyse it as an insistent economic phenomenon palpable to, if not always comprehensible by, contemporary observers of the mid-Victorian era. We can discern the elements entering into a determinate relation as we enter the second post-Waterloo period of development in the financial organism,—the years from 1866 to 1890, between the Overend-Gurney collapse and the Baring episode. For more and more as the organism comes to rely upon its own circumspection and experience for guidance does it become essential for the different activities and experiences to be more intimately correlated. Unification is the peremptory necessity of intelligent advance.

THE COSMIC PROCESS DEFLECTED

The Overend-Gurney crisis marks the decisive determination of the evolution of the Money Market as aristogenic rather than doliogenic. It is evolution upwards under the guidance of Mind, as distinguished from the fostering of qualities and faculties that assist survival, without regard to their moral aspect. There is a deliberate and resolute

FINANCIAL CONFEDERACY "IN A FLOOD" 483

selection of the pathway of " conscious voluntary progress, according to a free law, a conscious striving after a higher goal, for the individual and for the race."[1] " Within the scope of perhaps little more than a generation," said Sir Michael Hicks Beach in 1899,[2] " the relations between the great banks and the Bank of England and the Money Market have materially changed." A generation reckoned retrogressively from 1899, brings us exactly to 1866. From that date onwards financial consolidation struggles towards its destiny with a new and solemn resolve—*Mihi res, non me rebus, subjungere conor.* The changed direction of the evolutionary movement confronts us with other principles than the biological. The analogy to material organisms becomes at many points imperfect. Equilibration—a wider law than Natural Selection—becomes the dominant impulse. It marks the tendency of the organism (*a*) to adapt itself, by means of morphological and physiological modifications, to the changes going on in the environment, rather than to be destroyed by its *lack of the capacity of adjustment*, and then (*b*) to subdue the environment to its own purposeful activity. Natural Selection begins to be limited to the animal world, though still affirmed to be active in the nobler sphere, as in the contemporary comment that the strong banks became stronger and the weak weaker, as a result of the Overend-Gurney panic. Elsewhere the biologic law, or law of nature, is repealed by the psychologic law, or law of mind, disciplining and controlling a creature whose whims and waywardness are among the elemental cosmic forces that are ever struggling to resume their sway and to direct the world upon a pathway of their own choosing. Under the novel impulse the evolution of the Money Market "is at war with the conditions which maintain and yet limit it, and its triumph is the submission of the conditions to its perfected nature."[3] The reason is that the most stringent disciplinary selection will perpetuate the best types in the largest proportion, and so strengthen the aristogenic tendency of the whole

[1] Le Conte, *Relation of Biology to Sociology*, p. 7.
[2] Lord Mayor's Dinner, June 28.
[3] Hobhouse, *Mind in Evolution*, p. 406.

process. Just as the astonishing results of social evolution (the entire industrial organisation in all its marvellous complexity) could never have arisen if men's egoistic activities had been absent, so in the absence of their altruistic activities there could never have supervened certain higher effects of their labours. As a consequence of the deflection of aim there begins to be visible a partial reversal of the fundamental biologic law enunciated by Spencer. The economic structure of society, which for centuries has been passing from the homogeneous to the heterogeneous, begins to manifest among its financial organs a simultaneous movement towards heterogeneity of function and homogeneity of policy and purpose, a transformation from less to greater coherence. The tendency towards a greater differentiation and complexity of movement is simultaneous with a realised unity of interest, a dawning consciousness of capacity, an exclusion of excessive, superfluous, wantonly-competitive and consequently mischievous heterogeneity. By the new organic unity, the cosmic tendency will be contested, rather than obeyed. The physical development of the human individual is " based on a determinate interaction of structure and environment," and therefore is only to a very limited extent within human control. But the development of human society, and of the functions necessary to its existence and prosperity, *is* within human control, because this development is only the continual adjustment of variable relations, and for that task human intelligence is competent, and steadily becomes more so. The recoil need not be evidenced from finance alone. One of the most luminous intellects of the nineteenth century—the late F. W. H. Myers—averred that the period " about 1873 " was coeval with " the crest, as we may say, of perhaps the highest wave of materialism that has ever swept over these shores."[1] It was also coeval with the awakening of a resolve that materialism should for the rest of the world's history be yoked to the car of human progress. Such a change marks a veritable economic convulsion. Biology

[1] *Human Personality*, Vol. I. p. 7.

pure and simple would wage war upon it, as being a functionally noxious variation, or relaxation, tending to bring the whole evolutionary process first to standstill and then to ultimate retrogression. But it is the supremacy of mind which at once necessitates and justifies the revolution. The environment may indeed transform the animal, but it is the business and the privilege of man to transform the environment.[1] " The course shaped by the ethical man— the member of society or citizen—necessarily runs counter to that which the non-ethical man—the primitive savage, or man as a mere member of the animal kingdom—tends to adopt. The latter fights out the struggle for existence to the bitter end, like any other animal; the former devotes his best energies to the object of setting limits to the struggle."[2] The goal of the movement is " the mastery by the human mind of the conditions, internal as well as external, of its life and growth."[3] Human progress remains anthropocentric, but its ideals are elevated with every scientific relaxation of the pressure of the *status quo*. In fact, the organic conception will soon become inadequate and we shall be driven to look for a corporate *personality* living and moving behind the phenomena palpable to the senses. The nature and significance of the change cannot be adequately examined or characterised by studying the events of a single year, even if it be a year so pregnant with destiny as 1866. The revolution did not come in a moment. It spread itself over the whole period between 1866 and 1890.

ICONOCLASM AND CONFEDERACY

In every direction, as we study contemporary sentiment and policy, we can discern a larger measure of independent opinion and self-reliance in the financial sphere, combined with a more vivid appreciation of the value of permanent co-operation, and a persistent aspiration for closer unity of action and cordiality of relationship. The rationalising

---

[1] Ward, *Psychic Factors of Civilisation*, p. 257.
[2] Huxley, *Struggle for Existence in Human Society*, p. 203. The argument is that of the Romanes Lectures.
[3] Hobhouse, *Mind in Evolution*, p. 402.

tendency which had led to a challenge of the primacy of Consols as a bankers' security (*ante*, p. 331) began to take the form of revolutionary declarations against them. The banks' large holdings of national securities became the subject of much vehement criticism. Paul Moon James used to tell the story of a loss of £14,000 on selling Exchequer Bills in order to raise funds to meet a run.[1] Bills of Exchange, said the National Discount chairman,[2] were quite as good as Government securities. This was financial iconoclasm, and no mistake. Yet far more remarkable are the accumulating evidences of rapprochement, fraternity, confederacy. There is, to begin with, a striking contemporary testimonial from Morier Evans,[3] to the conduct of the members of the Stock Exchange during the Stock Exchange crisis of 1559. He declares that

" the honourable conduct of the majority of the members deserves the highest commendation ; few instances were mentioned of irregular dealing, and though some individuals were found to have engagements open, in a variety of securities, not in due proportion with their capital or connections, no barefaced attempts at fraud or misappropriation were discovered. It was also greatly to the credit of the more fortunate brokers and jobbers, notwithstanding all more or less suffered from the collapse, that they aided, as far as possible, their more needy brethren ; and many cases could be cited in which substantial relief was afforded, even at the risk of individual involvement, during the worst phases of the panic."

In 1864 there was a series of commercial failures. The banks, both private and joint-stock, drew together, both for self-protective purposes and in the interests of the community :—

" Throughout the length and breadth of Lombard Street, this is freely acknowledged by individuals who have been continually behind the scenes, and who must allow that never before has there been the like disposition to assuage the commercial suffering witnessed. It is encouraging thus to speak

[1] *Bankers' Magazine*, 1870, p. 755.
[2] Meeting, July 21, 1869.
[3] *History of the Commercial Crisis*, 1857–1858, p. 153.

FINANCIAL CONFEDERACY "IN A FLOOD" 487

of the banking and financial community, because in other periods their predecessors have not always exhibited similar willingness to accommodate mercantile distress when temporary aid would have afforded relief."[1]

These manifestations, albeit only straws upon a mighty current, showed clearly whither its stream was tending.

DEFINITE PLANS OF CO-OPERATION

It is, however, when we reach the Overend-Gurney crisis that the "new spirit" begins to be overwhelmingly apparent, both *in esse* and *in posse*, in action and in ambition for greater achievements. After the storm, at the meeting of the Bank of England, on September 13, 1866, the Governor of the Bank (Mr. Lancelot Holland) thought he was entitled to say that not only the Bank of England, but the entire banking body, had acquitted themselves most honourably and creditably throughout the very trying period of the crisis. There seems, indeed, to have been a single exception to the general cordiality. On Black Friday itself one of the representatives of a joint-stock bank is reported to have said to the Bank of England: "I can draw a couple of cheques to-morrow morning which will shut you up at once."[2] Such relics of antagonism created for a moment a species of anti-climax when the suggestion was made that the large reserves maintained by the joint-stock banks in Threadneedle Street would give the public an exaggerated idea of the power of these institutions, and might even put them in a position "to command, perhaps, the stoppage of the Bank of England." The prominence early given to the size of these balances caused the misgiving to revive spasmodically during the seventies. "But I am not afraid," said Bagehot,[3] "that the bankers would ever ruin the Bank of England, because they depend upon it."

The revolution in Lombard Street and Threadneedle Street sentiment was indeed almost panoramic in comparison with the efforts, made only a few years previously, to prevent

[1] *Bankers' Magazine*, 1864, p. 996.   [2] Gilbart, Vol. II. p. 354.
[3] 1875 Committee, Q. 8216.

the joint-stock banks from coming into existence. There was lively appreciation of the Governor's allusions to the co-operation of joint-stock banks, and the banking interest generally, in harmony with the Bank of England. Arthur Crump (who subsequently became City Editor of *The Times*) proposed to translate the abstract into the concrete by the formation of a council on which the Board of every bank having a certain status should be entitled to be represented.[1] At the approach of disturbances the council's powers were to be invoked, while at the same time the knowledge of its existence would help to assuage the antagonistic feelings so hurtful to sound banking progress. Crump went on to suggest that the " banks as a body might, through the medium of this tribunal, receive a warning of any important change that was expected that might seriously embarrass certain houses." The prestige of the members would give the high tone to the tribunal, and its edicts " might carry sufficient weight to influence the whole profession in following their advice." What was wanted in times of trouble, said Crump, was a power composed of the most efficient and experienced persons, to judge whether those who seek assistance had really come into their difficulties by natural causes, not capable of being anticipated by ordinary human foresight. The formulation of these ideals does the greatest credit to Crump's insight and prescience, though nearly another half-century was destined to elapse before they completely materialised. But the subject was not allowed to rest. " We lack united action," said a contemporary authority :—[2]

" Hence on many points we are weak. Take monetary panic. Could this anomaly of the richest country in the world exist were it confronted by a united banking system ? It is strong, because the English banks are a fortuitous concourse of atoms : because they fight singly, a moneyed mob, without organisation, without order, without plan. Look at the banks as the great shoulders of panic press steadily against the solid form of the Bank of England. . . . How powerless

---

[1] *Banking, Currency, and the Exchanges*, p. 62 *et seq.*
[2] In the *Bankers' Magazine*, 1871, p. 651.

FINANCIAL CONFEDERACY "IN A FLOOD"

would panic become when met at the central point by the confederated reserves of the English bankers."

Financial admonition could not be expressed in plainer terms, or—for that period—with more absolute justification.

THE BANK IN CONTEMPORARY METAPHOR

The imagery of the " great shoulders of panic pressing steadily against the solid form of the Bank of England " makes a picturesque and forcible simile. It shows us how the conditions presented themselves to the eyes of critical observers who had come through the dark days of 1866. Banking co-operation coalesced from the first around the Bank of England as naturally and inevitably as the " chaotic world-stuff " condenses into star-clusters, suns, planets, and satellites. At this stage, at all events, the coalescence and the ultimate allegiance were not a consequence of the Bank's connection with the State, though the earliest development of prestige had undoubtedly been aided by it. McCulloch, in 1858, had declared that " the Bank of England has become—unfortunately in our opinion—an engine of the State."[1] But it was not as an " engine of the State " that the Bank assumed its sovereign sway. Where a certain social force is being inexorably subjected[2] to a scientific control, and where, side by side

[1] McCulloch, *Dictionary of Political Economy*, p. 647.
[2] This subjection was going on at every level of the social structure. Labour, quickened by the sharpening of intellect upon intellect among the new industrial communities, began to use the financial weapon on its own account, for the furtherance of that which T. H. Green called " freedom in the higher sense—the power of men to make the best of themselves." Twenty-eight Rochdale weavers had started the new co-operative movement in the year of the Bank Charter Act—1844. In 1863 the English Co-operative Society came into being, followed by the Scottish Wholesale in 1868 and the Co-operative Union in 1869. The capital of these societies has been drawn from the members' own savings, and the profits of the enterprises themselves have largely provided the sums necessary for their further extension. Among themselves the co-operative societies now " carry on every kind of business (excepting only the provision of alcoholic drinks), from agriculture and manufacture to transport and banking. They have their own arable, pasture, and fruit farms, and their own creameries, butter and bacon and biscuit works, cocoa and jam and sauce and pickle factories . . . their own tea estates in Ceylon ; their own buyers in foreign countries and their own ships on the sea ; their own thousands of distributive stores ; their own arrangements for insurance ; their own banks, and even their own common libraries." (See

with this subjection, there is arising a supereminent power in the same field of activity, the two movements are bound ultimately to coalesce. The men who had been through the Overend-Gurney hurricane saw clearly enough that, although the joint-stock banks might become very vast and solid institutions, there was something behind the Bank of England which did not depend on the bullion in its vaults or the magnitude of its operations. That which Sir Felix Schuster, at the Bankers' Dinner in 1914, called the " wholly exceptional position which the Bank of England holds as the centre of our system " was in 1866 dawning more and more clearly upon the financial world. A host of metaphors was being employed to enforce the lesson of the obvious fact. Nowadays, when naval symbolism strikes the right note everywhere, it has been picturesquely said that the Bank of England is the " Flagship of the Banking Dreadnoughts." In the later sixties people talked of the " primacy " of the Bank of England. It had concentrated the reserves and was the " bank of bankers," declared the chairman at the National Bank meeting on January 28, 1868. It was the " pivot upon which the Empire turns." It set the standard of banking polity. " All joint-stock banks, so far as I know, take their model after the Bank of England. They endeavour to follow the same line of conduct," said Sir David Salomons, M.P., at the Bank of England Court, March 17, 1870. And the " guiding principle " of the Bank, as defined by the Governor at the Court on the following September 15, was " to employ their moneys in some readily-convertible security "—so as to be ready, in all emergencies,

---

Sidney Webb, *Cambridge Modern History*, XII. p. 739.) Undertakings of this class are in effect great capitalist enterprises, differing only from the normal type in procuring their capital from the " small " rather than from the " big " man. The largest of these organisations, the Co-operative Wholesale Society, is managed by a committee of 32 ex-workmen, elected annually by the 2,000,000 members, and their training in the niceties of financial and business administration is perhaps a greater national asset than the actual pecuniary benefit arising from the operations which they direct. The co-operative movement gains confidence as it advances. In the United States a comparatively modest group of financial co-operators will embark upon the purchase of a town. Turnerville, Conn., was so purchased in October, 1913. (*Journal of Commerce*, New York, October 26.)

FINANCIAL CONFEDERACY "IN A FLOOD" 491

for the effective discharge of their high functions. So it was that there came an official forecast that the Bank would never lose its capacity of taking its proper part in times when the community looked to it for advice, counsel, or assistance.[1] Acting in this lofty capacity, the Bank itself came soon to be called the supreme bankers' tribunal, the High Court of Finance, the " moderator of commercial and financial operations,"[2] while its semi-annual Courts were described as the " Senate of Commerce." Moreover, as the experiences of three periods of acute trouble had plainly demonstrated, the Bank of England was the only bank of any importance in the country from whom in a time of crisis or panic any *fresh* ready money could be obtained.

PRESTIGE EVEN BECOMES EMBARRASSING

A prestige which had become cosmopolitan and transatlantic was now and then a source of slight embarrassment. When Gledstanes' failed in 1872 it was urged by a bank chairman, in extenuation of losses arising from the collapse, that he and his colleagues had " relied, rightly or wrongly, on the fact that a partner of the insolvent firm " was on the Bank of England board.[3] At the Bank Court on September 12 the Governor made allusion to this Gledstanes' episode. He said that although there were thirty-four City merchants in the Bank directorate, yet " during a quarter of a century I do not think there has been one single failure till the other day." His quarter-century reminiscence evidently retraced its steps to the crisis year of 1847, when, " in the month of September, fifteen of the most considerable houses in the City of London stopped payment. . . . The Governor of the Bank of England was himself a partner in one of those firms (Robinson and Co.); a gentleman who had lately filled that office was another victim; two other bank directors were included in the list."[4] The very fact that such an incident

[1] Bank Court, March 16, 1871.
[2] *Bankers' Magazine*, 1872, p. 555.
[3] Chartered Mercantile Bank of India meeting, October 15, 1872.
[4] Disraeli, *Life of Lord George Bentinck*, p. 443.

as the presence of a partner in Gledstanes' at the Board of the Bank of England should be seized upon is eloquent of the aspect which the Bank presented to the men who had seen Black Friday. The boast of Sir David Salomons,[1] that the London and Westminster Bank directorate could " challenge comparison with the ' Old *Woman* in Threadneedle Street,' " involves an acknowledgment that there was something to be challenged. Foreign observers were keenly alive to the pre-eminence of the Bank. Baron James de Rothschild observed, in 1875, that the Bank of England was " une véritable Banque, c'est la Banque d'Angleterre. C'est de là qu'émanent, peut ainsi dire, toutes les autres petites banques." Even then it was pointed out that the supremacy of Threadneedle Street was quite as much the result of former renown as of present financial position. In the wise words of the *Economist*, " Age as well as honesty helps the prosperity of a bank." Bagehot's classic—which may perhaps be described as a remonstrance against the tremendous responsibilities of the Bank, as well as a recognition of their immensity—had appeared in 1873. Leone Levi said that the Bank of England was " a *banque de luxe* in ordinary times, and of *dernier ressort* in times of crisis."[2] " At this distance," said a writer in the *New York Bankers' Magazine*,[3] " English banking seems to me to be merely one great Bank, which keeps a reserve on hand at all times." The advantages offered by the Bank of England " are peculiar to the Bank of England from the nature of its credit "—so said K. D. Hodgson to the 1875 Committee. The Royal Bank of Scotland, in one of its official circulars, described the situation of the Bank of England as " entirely exceptional."[4] As a kind of contrast to these panygyrics, it may be added that in 1878 the irrepressible John Jones[5] declared that the Bank had become " a mere

---

[1] London and Westminster Bank meeting, January 15, 1873.
[2] Gilbart Lectures, 1878.
[3] 1878, p. 880.
[4] November 17, 1880.
[5] A jovial but eccentric City character who amused the Bank Courts for about forty years. He died on September 6, 1909, aged ninety-five.

FINANCIAL CONFEDERACY "IN A FLOOD" 493

pawnbroking establishment for the members of the Stock Exchange."[1]

POTENTIAL RIVALRY WEAKENED

The prevailing tendency towards a London centralisation of financial authority was reinforced, just at the psychological moment, by the removal from the cosmopolitan financial arena of the only possible rival to London. The City was, for the time, supreme : but Paris might, if history had been written otherwise, have challenged its dominion. So vivid was the realisation of England's predominant position, with London as its financial nucleus, that the Overend-Gurney trouble in 1866 has been described as a " run on England." For that reason, no doubt, the Foreign Office, after the crisis, issued a circular explaining the difference between a mere shortage of money and a state of insolvency. Even London gold had achieved an international name. Sir John Herschel in 1869 had called the sovereign " a cosmopolitan coin, really containing what it purports to contain, a fixed quantity of gold." The British sovereign—" with its many virtues and privileges, its stability, its unfailing supply, its universal currency, and the absolute confidence it commands all over the globe "—has played a marvellous part. In our time, of course, the American eagle, the French napoleon, and the Russian gold rouble are becoming as cosmopolitan and almost as favourably known. But in the years

[1] The Hon. A. L. Melville, Chairman of the Association of Country Bankers, told the 1875 Committee (Q. 4982), the story how he had once invoked the authority of the Bank of England against one of its own branches :—

" On one occasion we sent their branch bank at Leeds a cheque, and they paid us the £50, or whatever it was, less 1s. I wrote and asked why the cheque was not paid in full, and the answer was that the 1s. was their charge for paying the money over in London. I said to my head clerk : ' Now, be on the look-out, and as soon as the Leeds branch of the Bank of England send us a cheque let me know." He told me, and I said : ' Pay it, less 1s. ' ; so we sent the amount, less 1s. They wrote very indignantly, and asked : ' Why is the cheque not paid in full ? ' I said : ' If you refer to such a date and such a cheque, you will find that you charged me 1s., and if you charge me 1s. I shall charge you 1s.' They were very angry at this, and they wrote me a huffy letter and said they should refer it to the Bank of England (*the Bank of England, as you know, is a great authority with all of us*). I said : ' It is the very thing that I want you to do,' and they referred it to the Bank of England, and I have never had it charged since."

that immediately followed the Overend-Gurney crisis, the sovereign was as striking a phenomenon as the city whence it came. And now to all the advantages which had accumulated in the hands of London there was suddenly added no small proportion of the financial business hitherto conducted by Paris. Since 1848 the French capital had assumed a more important rôle in international finance. But the Franco-German war, and the large efflux of gold from France in consequence of the outbreak of Communism, caused the suspension of specie payments by the Bank of France. That contingency, in turn, crowned the predominance of London, by rendering Paris unable to fulfil her former function of a clearing-house for international commercial debts. Already, in 1870, the position of Paris was reluctantly admitted to be menaced. A French orator declared that Paris was dethroned from her place as queen of financial centres, and that London had taken front rank.[1] After the war Paris bankers removed to London, or established branches there.[2] " Since the termination of the Franco-German war a great number of powerful establishments, connected with all the principal foreign countries, have formed their headquarters in London."[3] The wealthy classes of the Continent also began to send their money more plentifully to this country for investment. It could be well employed, for France paid away all her available metal to Germany, and thus had to throw upon London the brunt of supplying the world's demand for coin. British firms endorsed the French bills for millions of the war indemnity in return for a commission of 1 per cent. At the same time it was hinted that illustrious personages in Germany were

[1] *Bankers' Magazine*, 1870, p. 777.
[2] The converse case to the establishment of foreign bank branches in London is that of the English banks which open branches (technically, separate companies) on the Continent. This experiment has been made in quite recent years, for instance, by Lloyds and the London County and Westminster Banks, both of which have a branch in Paris. The new departure is, of course, a totally different thing from the establishment of numerous banks in the Colonies, India, South America, and elsewhere, by English companies formed for that express purpose.
[3] Chairman of the London and Westminster Bank at the meeting on January 20, 1875.

influencing and financing the establishment of German banking and bill-broking institutions in England. Therefore international balances ceased to be kept in Paris. Exchange transactions, calculated, as Bagehot says, "to such an extremity of fineness that the change of a decimal may be fatal, and may turn a profit into a loss," require the maximum attainable stability for their successful conduct. The imposition of stamp duties on foreign bill transactions in France was consequently another factor operation in the diversion of business to London, by causing a stampede of money-dealers across the Channel. To the disquietude produced by the Franco-German war and its aftermath, there must be added the artificial attraction of gold constantly produced by manipulating the English bank rate—a policy which has never been allowed to cease. (See *ante*, p. 384.) As a result London, Bagehot adds, "has become the great settling-house of exchange transactions in Europe, instead of being, as formerly, one of two." London, in the language of a contemporary critic, became "the monarch of all the financial nations." Circumstances, "commercial and political, tended gradually but surely to make London the centre of the commerce of the world, and, consequently, of banking."[1] The movement was incessantly recorded by those sensitive instruments which unfailingly and unerringly indicate any change in city circumstances. Attention was called on August 1, 1872, to the record figures of the Bankers' Clearing-house for the previous week. They amounted to £147,553,000. It was a colossal aggregate to the men who saw it.[2] Yet the last return before the outbreak of

[1] Chairman at the City Bank meeting on July 16, 1872.
[2] Another good illustration of the indirect results of the extension of London's financial responsibilities was furnished in 1877 when a house in Lombard Street, a property of the Drapers' Company, originally let in 1678 for £25 a year, came into the market. The mere site was re-let for £2600 a year ground rent, while the expenditure of £10,000 by the lessee on a new building enabled him to realise an immediate return of £7000 a year in rent. Four years later—in 1881—to look in another direction, the *Bankers' Magazine* estimated British investments at home and abroad at £3,465,000,000, producing an annual return of about £157,000,000. To-day it is believed that the *foreign* investments alone produce £200,000,000 yearly.

the German war of 1914 showed a total of no less than £337,450,000!

PARIS, LONDON, AND BERLIN

The Franco-German war and the resulting changes, however, had their compensating advantages for France. The issue of the great war loan[1] on national security rendered investment familiar to a multitude of French people who had hitherto hoarded their money, with the consequence that French capital, to a much larger extent than ever before, was added to the cosmopolitan currency of the world. As far as financial resources are concerned, there can be no doubt that France was infinitely richer, relatively to her population, in 1914 (before the war of that year), than she was before the Franco-German campaign of 1871. The widely extended knowledge of investment facilities has been one of the chief operative factors: " Patriotism makes it a duty for us to acknowledge the fact that the Bourse represents one of the live forces of France," wrote Anatole Leroy-Beaulieu in one of the finest tributes ever paid to a Stock Exchange—

" It has been for France an instrument of regeneration after defeat, and it remains for us a powerful tool in war and in peace. Let us recall the already remote years of our convalescence, after the invasion, years at once sorrowful and comforting, when with the gloom of defeat and the suffering of dismemberment, mingled the joy of feeling the revival of France. Whence came our first consolation, our first vindication before the world ? Whether glorious or not, it orginated on the Bourse."[2]

Another potent influence was the increasing control of the proceeds of French thrift by the more cautious types.

---

[1] The subscription lists of the indemnity loan were open only one day (June 27, 1871), and applications reached the astounding—specially astounding in view of the condition of the country—total of £196,000,000. When the succeeding issue of £130,960,000 was offered, in July, 1872, it was subscribed to the extent of £1,751,360,000, or more than twelve times over, by 934,276 applicants. The issue of French Rentes made in 1901, to the amount of £10,640,000, was subscribed twenty-four times over. The fortyfold or fiftyfold subscription of the French loan in July, 1914, was to some extent, no doubt, artificial; but the real " taker " was present in sufficient force and numbers to offer a remarkable demonstration of the enormous reserve power that lies in the small investor.

[2] Quoted by Van Antwerp, *Stock Exchange from Within*, p. 383.

FINANCIAL CONFEDERACY "IN A FLOOD" 497

This made for gigantic aggregation on conservative lines, rather than for speculative aggrandisement of that volatile species which soon dissipates the most extensive resources. It is probably true that but for the change in her financial outlook and habits, engendered by the German war of 1871, France would not have survived the second struggle, the war of 1914. Because of this reinvigoration, it could hardly have been disputed that up to the commencement of the war which began in 1914 Paris was once more gaining ground as a financial centre. It practically monopolised Russian bonds and Russian industrials until, during the last six or seven years, before the war of 1914, the dexterous tactics of Mr. Crisp succeeded in diverting a large proportion of this business to London. But Paris remained practically the only market for numerous international specialities. Its attractions were enhanced, in the eyes of English finance, by the fact that the French investor buys to hold, and does not watch the market for a trifling increase in capital value, and a consequent opportunity to sell. It is not suggested that Paris was in a position to challenge the supremacy of London, but it certainly was establishing a financial reputation of its own. If London was the clearing-house, Paris was becoming the bargain centre of the world. Important financial negotiations tended more and more to be carried on there. Possibly the reason was that Paris offered (and will doubtless continue to offer) greater facilities than London for combining business with pleasure. But, whatever the explanation, the fact is undoubted that London and Paris, each in its own special sphere, controlled, up to the outbreak of the war of 1914, the financial destinies of the world. They might have been, to some slight extent, menaced by the advance of Berlin: but Berlin suffered by the passing of the German Exchange Act of 1896, which in attempting to prohibit speculative operations in grain and certain classes of securities, set still another influence at work to enhance the international importance of London. German capital, both for investment and speculation, came to London in increasing volume. The repeal of the Bourse Law in 1908 only slightly checked the tendency. Not only did German capital before the outbreak of the war of 1914 seek investment in purely British enterprises, but there existed hundreds of businesses in this country which were "run" entirely by German capital. Many of them were in the form of companies where only an infinitesimal proportion, if, indeed, any at all, of the shares were in British hands. The war, and the consequent economic damage to Germany, must inevitably react upon Berlin. As events are moving, therefore, there seems no reason to doubt that Paris is destined to play an even more important part as a financial centre than that which has fallen to her lot during the last ten years. But London will remain supreme at the centre provided that she commands cheap money; and cheap money is only a possibility, in the presence of insistent modern demands for it, if the supply is maintained at its maximum by the efficient drainage of every possible source of replenishment. And that is the business of centralised finance.

LESSENING VIOLENCE OF CRISES

Resuming the study of the "new spirit," we may say that in this increasingly intimate and cordial co-operation lay the explanation of the fact that the Overend-Gurney crisis, in comparison with its predecessors, was characterised by a diminished violence. "Although this crisis was important enough in itself, and was full of big events, on account of the vast size to which the Money Market itself had grown, it cannot be said, I think, to have been, in proportion, so disturbing as previous crises were."[1] Each crisis, from 1826 downwards, has been less catastrophic than its predecessors. Mr. Robert Wigram[2] mentioned Sir George Cornewall Lewis, Mr. Gladstone, Sir Stafford Northcote, the late Lord Goschen, and Lord St. Aldwyn as having all of them recognised that each succeeding crisis has been of lessening intensity. There

[1] Giffen, in Ward's *Reign of Queen Victoria*, Vol. II. p. 5.
[2] National Provincial Bank of England meeting, January 30, 1908.

FINANCIAL CONFEDERACY "IN A FLOOD"

has been no London panic since the Overend-Gurney cataclysm. "I have," said the late Luke Hansard, "witnessed no real general panic since 1866." The crises of 1873 and 1878 dashed themselves in vain against the iron bastions of a confederacy that was growing stronger every year.

THE MINOR CRISIS OF 1873

The year 1873 saw a minor crisis, the offshoot of a panic in New York. Transatlantic disaster was ultimately precipitated by the failure of Jay, Cooke and Co., and caused the closing of the New York Stock Exchange. But its origin was fervid overtrading and speculation—not confined to the Stock Exchange—and the rapid conversion of circulating into fixed capital—the same sinister elements which made the London crisis of 1847. International difficulties on the Continent, and particularly a crisis on the Vienna Stock Exchange, as well as the settlement of the immense war indemnity between Germany and France, helped to accentuate the strain. In London, however, the emergency never developed into anything worse than mild crisis. The reserve in the banking department went down in seven weeks from £13,347,000 to £8,071,000; but a prompt and rapid raising of the rate from 3 per cent. on August 20 to 9 per cent. on November 7 had results of an almost magical type, and demonstrated how thoroughly efficient a weapon the Bank possessed in the manipulation of its rate. London would probably have felt the effect of the American crisis even less but for the fact that its nerves had been shaken in 1872 by the failure (August 22) of Gledstanes and Co., one of whose partners was a director of the Bank of England. Gledstanes' were carrying on transactions to the amount of over £1,500,000; but when they failed their bank balance was a few hundreds, and their only other assets certain Eastern property which no banker would look at. Still, even this shake-up proved entirely ephemeral. At all events, by the end of November the rate had returned to 5 per cent., and all danger was past. The British financial public was astonished at its own calmness. Beyond slight feverishness on the Stock Exchange there was nothing approaching alarm and disturbance. As a contemporary critic said : " Perhaps never in our recent financial history was a period so fraught with perils as easily passed through." American observers noted the phenomenon, and acted upon their inferences from it. In 1874 the New York banks formed an association for the regulation of their own affairs, and for the mitigation (and, if possible, the prevention) of panics.

But the most remarkable manifestation was the contemporary frank acknowledgment that in the administration of the Bank of England was to be found the reason why so difficult a period had passed with so little trouble. It was pointed out that the directors of the Bank, whatever may have been their ideas as to their responsibility in previous periods, had undoubtedly acknowledged them on this occasion. Moreover—and this is the most significant of contemporary inferences—" the public seemed to have a kind of intuitive perception of this, and the policy pursued in the Bank parlour inspired confidence."[1]

THE " PRESSURE " OF 1875

The troubles of 1875, arising from the failure of J. C. Im Thurn and Co., the Collie frauds, and other financial incidents, never reached the stage of crisis, much less of panic. The Bank from the first had the whole situation well in hand, and, save where the losses specifically fell, no harm was done. Unfortunately, another source of ultimate malaise was insidiously sprouting. The widespread apprehension aroused by unlimited liability had a very dangerous reaction, even after limitation had come. The investor began to look eagerly for some security which, even in the worst circumstances, could not be a source of unlimited demands upon him. He found it in the fully-paid foreign bond. The result was the mania for the purchase of doubtful foreign securities, which, during the fifteen years from 1860 to 1875, involved the loss of untold millions, and was the primary, though distant, origin of

[1] *Bankers' Magazine*, 1874, p. 289.

FINANCIAL CONFEDERACY "IN A FLOOD" 501

the Baring crisis. The amount of loans wholly or partially in default in 1873 was stated by Leone Levi to be £332,399,800 of principal only. That was the year which witnessed the first meeting of the Corporation of Foreign Bondholders.[1]

CYCLIC SEQUENCE OF CRISES

By this time the apparently cyclic sequence of crises, at intervals of roughly ten years, had attracted the attention of one of the most brilliant scientific minds of the nineteenth century. A study of certain diagrammatic statistics, dealing with the prices of corn, the state of the funds, rates of discount, and number of bankruptcies from 1731 to 1862, produced upon the mind of Professor Jevons " a deep conviction that the events of 1815, 1825, 1836–1839, 1847, and 1857 exhibited a true but mysterious periodicity."[2] The investigator came to the conclusion that these crises had some causal connection with the recurrence of the sun-spots. Writing in 1875, Jevons added: " The principal commercial crises have happened in the years 1825, 1836–1839, 1847, 1857, 1866, and, I was almost adding, 1879, so convinced do I feel that there will, within the next few years, be another great crisis." In connecting these crises with the sun-spot cycle Jevons took its length as 11·1 years. Had he employed Mr. J. A. Broun's revised figure of 10·45 years, he would have hit the exact year of the next crisis—to wit, 1878. His theories have by no means secured general acceptance ; but as there can, at this time of day, be little doubt of the existence of psycho-magnetic influences upon the world and its inhabitants, future research will probably show that Jevons was on the right track, even if he could not reach the goal.

MISGIVINGS ABOUT CENTRALISATION

It comes to this, then,—that London was supreme in the financial world : and the Bank of England was supreme

---

[1] See Chapter XIX on The Stock Exchange for further details of the foreign bond scandals and the surrounding circumstances.

[2] *Investigations in Currency and Finance*, p. 224. The apparent periodicity of crises which had been noticed as early as 1857. See earlier allusions enumerated in Palgrave, *Dictionary of Political Economy*, note at end of art. " Crises." But it was Jevons who devoted to the subject that laborious and indefatigable research which characterised all his work.

in London. Supremacy emphasised the dependence of the other institutions upon the Bank. What Bagehot said was that " all our credit system depends on the Bank of England for its security. On the wisdom of the directors of that joint-stock company it depends whether England shall be solvent or insolvent."[1] But the evolution of these conditions, though they were destined ultimately to prevail, did not go altogether unchallenged. Thomson Hankey (a director of the Bank) saw the drift towards a Financial Suzerainty, and vehemently protested. " The *Economist* newspaper,"[2] said Hankey,

" has put forward what, in my opinion, is the most mischievous doctrine ever broached in the monetary or banking world in this country—viz. that it is the proper function of the Bank of England to keep money available at all times to supply the demands of bankers who had rendered their assets unavailable. Until such a doctrine is repudiated by the banking interest the difficulty of pursuing any sound principle of banking in London will be always very great. But I do not believe that such a doctrine as that bankers are justified in relying on the Bank of England to assist them in time of need is generally held by the bankers in London."

Hankey had the keenest objections to the huge load of responsibility which was accumulating on the Bank's shoulders. He wanted a bank, not a Financial Suzerainty. Bagehot, in *Lombard Street*, was rather concerned to criticise the expediency of the exclusive dependence of the whole fabric of English banking upon the wisdom of a single Bank, than the co-incident emergence of a Financial Seigniory from conditions so likely to produce it. Hankey's objections were to the responsibility thus thrown on the Bank of England. It was, he urged, " quite impossible for the Bank, however prudently its own business may have been managed, to make others, with whose conduct it has nothing whatever to do, equally circumspect."[3] Let the Bank mind its own business, *as a bank*, and let others mind theirs. " The more the conduct of the

---

[1] *Lombard Street*, p. 35.   [2] September 22, 1866.
[3] *Principles of Banking*, p. 110.

FINANCIAL CONFEDERACY "IN A FLOOD"

affairs of the Bank is made to assimilate to the conduct of every other well-managed bank in the United Kingdom the better for the Bank and the better for the community at large."[1]

Apparently Hankey might have spared his criticism of the *Economist*, for by 1874 that newspaper was veering towards his opinions. On December 5 of that year the *Economist* declared that the Bank of England is " now *only* primus inter pares, though it had once distanced every competitor. It is felt on all sides that the old system of paternal Government is passing away." This outburst seems to have been inspired by a slight relapse towards the old invidious rivalries, in the shape of a scheme arising from jealousy of the moral ascendancy of Threadneedle Street. The great joint-stock banks had become bigger than the Bank of England, so far as the mere magnitude of their deposits was concerned. It was acknowledged that the moral primacy, being more dependent upon former renown than upon financial resources, could not itself be challenged. But the question was whether the great joint-stock banks should continue, in effect, to provide the Bank of England with a reserve. Between 1844 and 1877 there were sixty-one occasions when the Bank reserve was " not sufficient to meet the London bankers' balances." Palgrave tabulates the excesses :—

	Excess		Excess
Years 1844–1853	1	Years 1862–1869	21
Years 1855–1861	11	Years 1870–1877	28

In October, 1873, the banking reserve—notes and coin—at Threadneedle Street was £9,954,000, while the balances of the London bankers at the Bank of England were £10,500,000. On October 21 of the next year the banking reserve stood at £9,425,000, while the balances of the London bankers were no less than £11,169,000. In addition to the citation of facts like these, it was argued that the Bank rate differed from that obtaining in the open

---

[1] *Principles of Banking*, 2nd ed. p. 31. These views had originally been expressed in the first edition (1867), but they were deliberately reaffirmed in the second (1873).

market, with resulting annoyance and inconvenience. The old 1847 plan of a separate rate (to be enacted by the banks other than the Bank of England), was revived. The detailed scheme suggested that the clearing bankers derived no profit from their balances at the Bank of England, and that if these balances were kept as part of a separate reserve, organised by the clearing banks, they might easily be raised to £8,000,000.[1] The fund could then be employed for mutual support and assistance among bankers in times of difficulty. The idea was that this separate reserve should be at the Bank of England, though it should not appear among the liabilities in the weekly Return. The obvious answer was that the possession of these fresh deposits would only strengthen the Bank as a competitor of its joint-stock rivals. Another argument, which seems to have closed the controversy, was that if the clearing banks created their own reserves and enacted their own rate they would be in an awkward position if, in the middle of a financial crisis, they were ultimately forced to make an appeal for aid to the great institution which, in times of prosperity, they had flouted. Contemporaneously with these suggestions came a hint from an "influential source" that the Bank of England "does for its customers just what all banks do for theirs—it transacts their business and *accommodates them at times*." This mordant "tip" caused a great deal of vapouring at the moment, because the unmistakable inference was that if the clearing banks established an independent reserve the accommodation might not be forthcoming again.

AN IMPORTANT CHANGE OF POLICY

Anyhow, the controversy brought about an important change in the practice of the Bank. Down to May 11, 1876, the yearly return of the Bank of England to the House of Commons invariably included "the balances

---

[1] When in 1915 Sir Edward Holden began the publication of the gold reserve of the London City and Midland Bank, it is a curious coincidence that the first published figure was £8,000,000. But this was the reserve of an *individual institution*, not of an aggregate of banks.

FINANCIAL CONFEDERACY "IN A FLOOD" 505

held on account of the London bankers on the last day of each week." With this information there was given the total amount of bills discounted as well as that of the temporary advances. In 1877, however, the Bank objected to supply these latter items, but it included the balances of the London bankers in the return for that year. When, however, Mr. Edmund Backhouse, the member for Darlington, applied in 1879 for the return to be made for the year 1878, Thomson Hankey, who was a member of the House of Commons, as well as a director of the Bank (and who was no doubt acting under the inspiration of his co-directors at Threadneedle Street), went up to the table of the House and deliberately struck out from the return the column designed to contain the information as to the balances of the London bankers. This had the effect of reducing the annual return to a mere recapitulation of the weekly published statements, and consequently there was no advantage in moving for it.[1] The omissions, says Palgrave, are to be regretted " quite as much in the interest of the Bank of England itself as of the public at large."[2] The London bankers' balances would reflect, more quickly than anything else, the presence of any disturbing factor in the Money Market. They would be as valuable for the diagnosis of the ills of the body financial as is the temperature for the same critical examination of the ills of the body physical. At the same time it is quite true that nervousness might arise if it were seen, especially in a time of emergency, that the reserve was below the total of the bankers' balances. The Bank of England, knowing of the existence of apprehension, would itself be the less inclined to grapple with the difficulty. It has been urged that this consideration is the reason why the Bank does not supply the details. It may consider—so ran the reasoning—that a censorship of financial intelligence is as necessary as the analogous tribunal in war time, and that it exerts just as valuable a soothing influence on the

---

[1] The story is told in the *Bankers' Magazine* for 1898, Vol. LXV. p. 352.
[2] *Bank Rate and Money Market*, p. 6.

public mind. In support of this view there is the weighty opinion of Sir Edward Holden,[1] who has said :—

" When the joint-stock bankers had lent up to their recognised ratio of reserves to liabilities, they could stop lending. But the Bank of England was not quite in the same position, for when no additional funds could be had from the joint-stock banks, borrowers went, as a rule, to the Bank of England. If the Bank of England stopped lending, then difficulties would ensue. They therefore were compelled, in order to meet the demands of trade, to allow their reserves to run down below their recognised ratio. Under circumstances of great demand, it might happen that the reserve of the Bank of England would fall even below the balances of the joint-stock banks. To publish such a condition of affairs to the whole world might injuriously affect not only the position of the Bank of England, but also our whole financial position as the centre of international finance."

But the public, nowadays, can face unpleasant facts without starting a run on the banks. The experiences of August, 1914, proved that the " bald-headed man in the motor-bus " has a much cooler cranium than his critics have supposed.

THE BANK'S OFFICIAL VIEW

The Bank's own view was defined before the Institute of Bankers on February 17, 1904, by Mr. A. C. Cole, then a director of the Bank (and Governor in 1910). Mr. Cole said with reference to the publication of the bankers' balances : —

" there was no objection to it provided the bankers agreed to it. But it was not necessary, nor as a matter of principle desirable, for the Bank of England to make the publication. The attitude of the Bank of England in this matter had been a simple and reasonable one, namely, that they would not be justified in giving the information respecting their customers' affairs unless ordered to do so by Parliament, especially as these customers had always opposed such information being given. If this opposition could be got over, all that was necessary to arrange for was that each of the clearing bankers shall on

[1] Bankers' Institute meeting, January 15, 1907.

FINANCIAL CONFEDERACY "IN A FLOOD" 507

every Wednesday state their balance at the Bank of Enlgand to an official of the Clearing-house, who could then add the balances together and publish the total weekly."

The speaker added that the Bank of England looks at the bankers' balances as a whole. "When one bank pays away by cheque," said Mr. Cole, "it must come back on the account of some other bank, and the total of the clearings by cheque does not affect the total of the bankers' balances."

In the absence of the separate statement, after 1877, definite inference as to the size of the bankers' balances becomes impossible—save at exceptional times. For instance, the advance of the "other" deposits from £30,300,000 on November 12, 1890, to £36,400,000 on November 19 of the same year, shows an increase of over £6,000,000 during the week of the Baring crisis. This was almost certainly due to the augmentation of the bankers' balances. Such figures indicate, on the one hand, a determined consolidation of resources in the hands of the central institution, and, on the other, a vivid realisation of the unity of interest between the Bank and the joint-stock and private satellites which circle around it. The Bank, watching the balances of the joint-stock banks, gains insight, and insight means power. Lord Aldenham (himself a director of the Bank) put the Bank's point of view very vividly in some letters at the end of Professor Bonamy Price's *Chapters on Political Economy*. He said :—

"Next to the Government account, the account of the collective bankers is the most certain and the most intelligible. . . . We know of the bankers' better than of any account in our books, what is the minimum balance wherewith they can live. They must have X" [their normal balance] "in their account (a quantity unknown to all but us), and $X-Y$, therefore, never appears. But if $X+Y$ is seen then we know that Y" [their abnormal balance] "must remain untouched and uninvested—must, in fact, form an addition to our reserve; X is ours for profit *if we like to use it*, but Y is ours only for safe custody. Where is the danger? On the one hand, the possession of that account is of the greatest importance to us, as affording the most perfect and accurate measure of how far the public can at all act independently of us."

The Bank uses, in the market, 40 per cent. of its competitors' balances left in its hands, and thus fights them with their own funds. So, at least, Sir Felix Schuster has declared.[1] The public deposits are generally believed to average from 20 to 25 per cent. of the total at a given time. They are, however, worth more from a banker's point of view than the deposits of a private firm or commercial enterprise, because their movements are largely calculable in advance, and consequently the Bank can make the most of them. But with all this it never forgets its duty of maintaining its own position as an impregnable financial stronghold. Mr. Withers has said[2] that " the Bank's cash reserve is relatively about twice as big as those of the other banks which are strongest in this respect, and perhaps twenty times as big as those of the weakest."

MODERN PLAN FORESHADOWED

As the plan of an independent bankers' reserve had failed to commend itself, owing to its tendency to disturb " the primacy so long maintained by the Bank of England," it was modified into a scheme for creating a combination of the leading bankers under the presidency of the Bank. Some understanding between the Bank of England and its principal competitors, said the advocates of this view,[3] would certainly contribute to the general interest both of bankers and the public. But this scheme was met with the objection that in a time of monetary stringency the interests of the Bank of England—the predominant custodian of the gold reserve—might conflict with those of the bankers, who would desire to see the rate kept down. Thus responsibility would come into conflict with interest, and the situation would be still further complicated by the fact that some, at all events, of the causes which tend to force the raising of the Bank rate are beyond the control of the Bank itself or any of its competitors. For the

---

[1] U.S. Monetary Commission, *Interviews on Banking*, p. 49.
[2] *Meaning of Money*, p. 212. [3] *Economist*, January 7, 1876.

FINANCIAL CONFEDERACY "IN A FLOOD" 509

banks are really only intermediaries—financial conduit pipes. They can only define, without being able entirely to control, the terms of a bargain between their principals. In the words of Professor Bonamy Price, " a banker is the interpreter of the forces at work, and he makes a trial of the rate which those forces prescribe "—just as a jobber does of the price which market conditions suggest.

OLD HOSTILITIES VANISHING EVERYWHERE

But although all these schemes proved impracticable or unsuccessful, and although their enunciation produced a momentary flashing of the old jealousies, it was clear from evidence on all sides that the age of isolated banking had closed. A sense of the common cause was manifest everywhere. Mr. Gladstone's attempt in 1869 to increase the permissible limit of savings bank deposits to £100 in one year, and to £300 in the total, was defeated by the united action of the banks, led by the North and South Wales (Rae's Bank), the London and County, and the National Provincial. In 1872 there was the suggestion of a kind of financial council, " from which bankers should not be excluded." When the question of unlimited liability became urgent in the early seventies, the larger joint-stock banks in London again collaborated and jointly took legal advice on the subject.[1] There was a Committee appointed by the London and Provincial bankers, private and joint-stock, issuing and non-issuing, to watch the progress of Mr. Goschen's Banks of Issue Bill in 1875. That Committee " consisted practically of the banking interest in England."[2] Mr. Billinghurst, of the London and Westminster, suggested that agreements approved by the heads of the great banking establishments on questions of practice, might be " made universal in the banking world, and . . . almost override the law by establishing a unanimous custom."[3] The Scottish banks

---

[1] Chairman at the London and County Bank meeting, August 7, 1873.
[2] Jervoise Smith, 1875 Committee, Q. 6863.
[3] Speech at meeting to consider establishment of the Institute of Bankers, May 29, 1878. *Bankers' Magazine*, p. 569.

KK

had set the example. "The Scotch banks," said a critic in 1876,[1]

" possessed the advantage over the English banks in that they are a homogeneous body—few in number, all joint-stock, with large capitals and numerous branches, and with almost equal privileges. What, therefore, affects one, affects all; and as their head offices are, as a rule, concentrated principally in the capital, they can speedily meet to discuss any matter affecting their interests, and decide on a common course of action. Such homogeneity is difficult, if not impossible, with English bankers."

When the City of Glasgow Bank crash eventuated in 1878, the other Scotch banks at once came to the rescue of its clients with an offer of 10s. in the pound on the amount of their deposits. When a trivial incident started a " run " upon one of the great banks in 1879 offers of assistance were immediately made by the other institutions. They were not required, for the run subsided in a few hours. For all that, the statement of the Chairman,[2] that " banks should stand by each other," demonstrates how the " new spirit " was permeating the entire financial atmosphere, and making its presence felt in quarters once regarded as the headquarters of conservatism. Reproach, indeed, began to be pointed at those who failed to recognise the " new spirit," and to evince the sense of comradeship. In 1879 Arthur Ellis criticised[3] the policy of isolation and secrecy, the refusal on the part of lenders to " fortify " one another with money and information in the mutual interest of the whole body. There was " free competition untempered by restraints which might be organised in the interests of the whole market." Rae doubted if reform were possible. To give effect to the general principle of " no advance without security " would require, said he,[4] " a greater degree of concert and a livelier sense of a common danger, on the part of English banks, than exist at present." But assuredly the banks were adversely affected by this policy of secrecy, since it left them entirely

[1] C. W. Croft, *Bankers' Magazine*, p. 551.
[2] London and County Bank meeting, February 6, 1879.
[3] *Rationale of Market Fluctuations*, p. 36.   [4] *Country Banker*, p. 40.

FINANCIAL CONFEDERACY "IN A FLOOD" 511

at the mercy of the bill brokers. Such reticence was expensive, said Ellis, as the immense Collie frauds of 1875 only too clearly proved. Certainly the power of the bill broker was enhanced—mischievously enhanced—by any failure of candour and co-operation. The bill broker is "almost too important a factor," said Sir Felix Schuster, "because his liability is one which can only be met in ordinary times, and in troubled times he is at the mercy of the banks and of circumstances."[1] But there was at least this to be said—that when a bill broker was "forced into the Bank" in order to put himself in funds to repay call money, and when the existence and activity of this last resource were common knowledge, prestige was one inevitable outcome, and an opportunity of disciplinary regulation another.

" NEW BLOOD " AT THE BANK

New conditions in the banking world (and especially the vast load of responsibility which was accumulating on the shoulders of the Atlas of Threadneedle Street) brought the necessity for younger blood at the Bank of England. Some of the weaknesses which began to manifest themselves had been glimpsed thirty years earlier. The Lords' Committee of 1848 had urged that

" the objections which have so often been urged against the Bank . . . are a want of permanence and of consistency, derived from its system of periodical elections of governors and deputy-governors . . . the evil consequences of filling these high and important offices by a mere rotation of seniority, and the intimate connection subsisting between the directors and the commercial world of London, which may cast on them a degree of pressure difficult at times to be resisted. It appears, further, to be apparent from the evidence that the immediate pecuniary interest of the proprietors may at times supersede or control larger and higher considerations. This ought not to be."

McCulloch urged the same point. In allusion to the directors of the Bank he said that " their *interests* as merchants were opposed to their *duty* as bankers : and

[1] U.S. Monetary Commission, *Interviews on Banking*, p. 42.

formerly—we do not say corruptly—but yet undoubtedly, the latter gave way to the former." An attempt was made to provide a larger measure of continuity by allowing a greater proportion of the directorate to remain unchanged. The original Act[1] provided that " in all future Elections of Directors there shall not be chosen above Two-thirds of those who were Directors the preceding Yeare." By 35 and 36 Vict. c. 34, " seven-eighths " is to be substituted for " two-thirds." Finally under the supplemental charter of 1896 the proportion of directors eligible to re-election is brought within the control of the proprietors themselves by the grant to them of power to make a bye-law on the subject. The gradual modification in the composition and characteristics of the Board did not go unnoticed in the mid-Victorian age of change. A speaker, in 1865 (one of the Cave family), declared that " whenever the Bank of England board wanted a new Governor they looked about for a man of ability, who had made a large fortune for himself, as the proper person to be employed in making a large fortune for others."[2] In the seventies the infusion of the younger blood was quite a City phenomenon. " I remember," wrote Walter Bagehot,[3]

" seeing a very fresh and nice-looking young gentleman and being struck with astonishment at being told that he was a director of the Bank of England. I had always imagined such directors to be men of tried sagacity and long experience, and I was amazed that a cheerful young man should be one of them. I believe I thought it a little dangerous."

These innovations could not proceed without a resulting infusion of physical vigour into the functions of the Governorship, which generally fell to the recruits in about twenty years from their appointment to the Board. Bankers in the strict sense of the word—lenders of money on short-term commercial paper—have never been admitted to the Bank board, partly because they are to some extent competitors with the Bank, and partly because

[1] 8 and 9 Will. III. (1694), c. 20.
[2] Crédit Foncier and Mobilier of England meeting, April 20, 1865.
[3] *Lombard Street*, p. 210.

FINANCIAL CONFEDERACY "IN A FLOOD" 513

they would, if appointed, combine the opposing rôles of banker and client in one personality, and thus bring their duty into conflict with their interest—which McCulloch, as we have seen, alleged to have already occurred. For analogous reasons a seat at the Board is not available to brokers, bill discounters, or directors of other banks operating in the United Kingdom. It has been argued that the exclusion of bankers unduly narrows the field of selection. Certainly the rule works capriciously. It would enable the head of the great Rothschild house to be a director of the Bank, as it did actually admit Lord Revelstoke to a seat at the board table. At the same time, it would have excluded Lord Avebury, or George Rae, or John Dun, or any other of the great bankers of the last century, simply because they *were* bankers. In accordance with the austerity of procedure—a certain dignified and almost majestic aloofness—which characterises the Bank in relation to its *own* affairs,[1] however,

---

[1] From the beginning "the Bank of England set its face against gratifying idle curiosity, and denied the right of anyone to pry into its operations." (Leone Levi, Gilbert Lectures, 1878.) As a writer in 1847 said : " The directors of the Bank of England have always declared and acted upon the opinion that secrecy in regard to its condition is important to its prosperity. To such an extent has this feeling been carried that year after year large and increasing dividends were declared and paid without the exhibition to the proprietors of a single figure by which such a course could be justified, the simple recommendation of the directors having always satisfied the proprietors as to the policy of preserving this mystery. The printing of the report of the Committee of Secrecy in 1832 revealed the true condition of the corporation, and it is not likely that the directors will ever again be allowed to involve its proceedings in the same degree of concealment." (*Political Encyclopædia*, 1847, p. 268.) As a matter of fact, the Bank has never abandoned its sphinx-like policy. Since 1857 no details of the Bank's investments have been published. We can, however, get occasional negative glimpses. The Bank practically ostracised foreign securities. (See discussion at Bank Court, March 16, 1871.) In 1876 the Governor, after having undergone the usual tickling by the irrepressible John Jones, boasted that the Bank dividend " had been earned without the aid of Turkish bonds or investment in any other foreign Government securities." (Bank Court, September 14, 1876.) Down to 1875 the Bank gave information as to the amount of bills discounted. Since then it has ceased to do so. Since 1877, as we have seen, it has been impossible to discover the amount of the London bankers' balances at Threadneedle Street. In 1881 the Bank ceased to give particulars as to the amount of its note circulation in London and the provinces respectively. " It is not the practice of the Bank to lend at all on produce." (Mr. A. C. Cole, *Institute of Bankers*, February 17, 1904.) The Bank discounts no bill which has more than ninety-five days to run. It never lends call money.

these subjects are seldom discussed. At the Bank of England meeting, March 18, 1893, while the memory of the Baring crisis was still comparatively fresh, the question was raised whether any of the then directors of the Bank were interested in great financial houses negotiating foreign and other loans. The Governor (David Powell) did not deny it, but expressed his own hope that the most distinguished houses in London would not be unrepresented on the Bank board. At the same time, he said that care had always been taken that the court of directors should not be *mainly* composed of gentlemen thus interested.

A PERMANENT SUB-GOVERNOR

More nearly in accordance with the suggestions of the Lords Committee of 1848 (*supra*) has been the frequent (though not very recent) proposal that a larger measure of continuity in the personnel of the Bank should be provided by the appointment of a permanent sub-governor —a man of the highest type and calibre of mind, able to hold his own in a field of achievement where the general level is so high. He should, it has been said, retain office for a long term (say, seven or fourteen years), with the stipulation that his whole time should be devoted to the Bank, in return for an adequate salary. One point made against this proposal was, however, the fear that a permanent sub-governor might become too strong to be controlled by the Board. Moreover, there is the undoubted fact that, so far, the system of election to the Governorship has worked well. In the case of the Baring crisis, it threw up the one man who could ride the storm, and this with an uncanny precision almost equal to that with which the American presidential system produced Abraham Lincoln on the eve of a gigantic national emergency requiring to be handled with consummate pertinacity and skill. But it does not follow that every Baring crisis will throw up a Lidderdale—though the 1914 emergency produced a Cunliffe. We might possibly witness a financial crisis of the most profound gravity confronted by a Bank Governor whose infirmity of purpose had only been revealed by the contingency in which it was to be a fatal factor. As against this defect, some slight degree of continuity does, in fact, exist in this respect, for by custom the Governor and Deputy-Governor are elected for a second year of office. But all these objections have been met and all the proposals superseded (as we shall see in due course) by the establishment of a banking council at the Bank, to which the heads of all the great clearing institutions are now invited. (*Post*, p. 662.)

THE CRISIS OF 1878

In the midst of the rapid and pregnant developments of the 'seventies came the crisis of 1878. It was primarily due to the collapse of the City of Glasgow Bank, which showed a loss of about *six* millions on *four* accounts. In December, when the West of England Bank failed, the drain upon certain banks averaged 16 per cent. of their deposits, and in one instance reached 26 per cent. But there was never panic; from the first the situation was thoroughly in hand. Lord Rothschild is said to have characterised the 1878 crisis as the most important time " ever known in the history of English banking "; but this, of course, was before the Baring affair and before 1914. The events of 1878, and the rapid progress of banking confederacy, did not go unregarded by a circle of observers which grew wider and more numerous every year. At first the confederacy was misunderstood. Its existence, even in the mediate form which it had assumed in 1878, soon generated the idea on the part of the public that there was a kind of duty incumbent upon the great banks to protect weaker institutions in all circumstances. When the Munster Bank stopped, in 1883, there was considerable resentment at the Bank of Ireland's refusal to find money to prevent the failure. The bank had, indeed, advanced certain funds, but did not feel justified in advancing as much as would have been necessary to obviate the stoppage. The *Freeman's Journal* and *United Ireland* accused the Bank of Ireland of " strangling " the Munster Bank, threatening that if assistance were not given " Irish public opinion would demand the stripping of the Bank of Ireland of its indefensible and ill-used monopoly of public money." The resentment started a run on the Bank of Ireland itself with the result that the Bank of England came forward with about £1,000,000 in gold to help its confrère. The money withdrawn from the Bank of Ireland in this way was merely transferred to other institutions and not hoarded! Disabused of the rather mistaken view about the universally altruistic obligations of the confederacy, the public became suspicious of banking centralisation. But at the critical moment, as we shall see, these suspicions were almost entirely dissipated by an overwhelming demonstration of their baselessness. At no point in the 'seventies and 'eighties, therefore, was there any serious check to the centripetal tendency.

THE DISCOUNT POLICY OF THE BANK

The Bank of England, after 1878, was the undisputed master of the situation, wielding an irresistible power in defence of the economic fabric as a whole, and often discharging its self-imposed task to the loss of its own shareholders. In the Gilbert Lectures of 1878 Leone Levi painted a glowing, but not unduly vivid, picture of its predominance :—

" With consummate skill and wisdom the Bank of England has always advanced *pari passu* with the age in which it lives. In all the appliances for the economy of the currencies, all the inner working of the Stock Exchange and Clearing-houses, the Bank of England has always taken a leading part ; and if the Rothschilds and the Barings, the London and Westminster and the London and County Bank, can compete successfully with the Bank of England in seizing large enterprises, in supporting large operations of trade, and in contracting loans for foreign Governments, they are, nevertheless, largely indebted to the Bank of England for the guidance of their operations and the concentration of their forces. . . . the Bank represents at present nearly the greatest accumulation of riches existing in the world ; that its influence is felt in all the markets of Europe, and that there are no enterprises in the most remote countries where it is not, to some extent, present through its intervention and its capital. And since, nowadays, all the monetary transactions of the country are reduced to a book-credit transaction at the Bank of England, the Bank can at any moment measure, by the state of that book, the exact position of capital all over the country, and so exercise upon it a prompt and salutary control. In former days, when the usury laws were in operation, that control was exercised by capriciously fixing the amount of bank notes in circulation. Now it is exercised simply by the rate of interest, or by the conditions, more or less onerous, on which the Bank would grant accommodation. . . ."

These discount conditions attained plain definition at the time when Leone Levi spoke. In 1878 the Bank had caused it to be known that in future it would, at its discretion, discount for its own customers at the market rate, without considering itself bound by the minimum rate which it had advertised for the time being. Thus the ostensible minimum is not the actual minimum — a state of things described by Mr. F. E. Steele as one of the anomalies of the Money Market. The Bank is practically always in the position of being an important holder, some of whose stock is indispensable to the market, and, therefore, it wields the prerogative of defining the rate at which it is willing to make its stocks available. From the time of the 1878 crisis down to 1890 the directors maintained an incessant struggle to protect their bullion. Especially in the years 1884 to 1890, when there was comparative market quietude and a scarcity of good bills, the market rate tended to underbid the Bank, and the directors again and again borrowed money on their Consols (though they were not in need of it) in order to stiffen the rate and protect the bullion. The policy of the directors during the year or so immediately preceding the Baring crisis might almost create the impression that they envisaged the coming menace, and went deliberately to work upon entrenchments. In the April before the crisis, the "other deposits" were £25,844,000 and the Government securities £15,771,000. In the April after the Baring crisis the "other deposits" had risen to £28,694,000, while the Government securities had moved in the reverse direction, to as low a figure as £8,932,000. The natural conjecture was that the Bank was securing more loan and discount business, and reducing its holding of Consols, in order to provide itself with adequate resources. As for business generally, history repeated itself. The crisis[1] brought stagnation in its train. After the crisis was over, in 1891, the Bank began practically to discount any approved bill, not having more than fifteen days to run, and since 1895 any bill which has not more than sixty-three days to run may be sent in by a bill broker. The whole policy of the Bank in the matter of its discount business has been summed up by Mr. N. E. Weill[2] as consisting of the following measures :—

" 1. As was the intention of the Bank Act of 1844, to take up bills as long as the cash held by the bank allows of doing so; if the reserves are exhausted, any offering of bills is refused.

" 2. To reject, as the Prussian Bank did in 1872, all bills originating from speculative quarters (accommodation bills).

" 3. To purchase, as is the practice exercised by the Bank of France in periods of tight money, exclusively bills with comparatively short periods to run.

" 4. The policy sometimes adopted by the Bank of England, of borrowing money from the market in order artificially to create a tightness of money, thus imparting the necessity of diverting the whole demand for money from the open market to its own counters.

" 5. The measure most frequently adopted during the last decades—that of raising the rate of discount. This operates in two directions : (*a*) Industrial and commercial activity is restrained ; the level of prices is reduced. All demand for money, so far as it can be so, is delayed ; all hoarded money is attracted, and all indispensable money is invested in order to enjoy the high yield. Industry is moved to consider whether or not it has been over-stimulated. (*b*) Rates of exchange rise ; gold is attracted from abroad ; its exportation is stopped; the maturity of money due to foreign countries is postponed, and new liabilities of foreign countries to the home country are created by the increasing export of commodities."

---

[1] The Baring crisis forms the separate subject of the next chapter.
[2] *Bankers' Magazine*, 1901, Vol. II. p. 355.

The discount history of the last thirty years may be briefly recapitulated in the statement that the market has frequently asserted its independence, sometimes by anticipating the action of the Bank and occasionally by lagging behind it to the extent of days or even weeks. When there are more bills about than the other banks can handle, their owners have to seek the aid of the Bank of England, which in that way gets control of the market. This is what Mr. Withers calls a "natural" control. But if low discount rates combine with the foreign exchanges to imperil the gold reserve, or to exert an unfavourable influence upon its proportion to the Bank's liabilities, the Bank itself can (if it choose) borrow until it has succeeded in creating an artificial scarcity of money and in bringing the market rate[1] into consistency with its own views. This is characterised by Mr. Withers as an "artificial" control, in contrast to the "natural" control arising from the ordinary course of events. The knowledge that the Bank of England could adopt this "artificial" expedient, had undoubtedly helped to regulate the discount market, to keep the number of finance bills within safe limits, and to prevent the creation of too extensive foreign claims upon a centre where (in contradistinction to the state of things in France and Germany) gold is always to be had. But some of these methods have in recent years been described as unbecoming and clumsy. Mr. Burn was told in 1909 that the device of selling Consols for cash, and buying them back for the account, as a means

[1] Of course, it is the market rate which governs the flow of gold into this country. The Bank of England can only control the flow of gold if it can raise the market rate to that figure at which it will become effective. Nobody is going to borrow from the Bank of England at 5 per cent. if he can get money in the outside market at 4 per cent. But the discharge of this duty occasionally involves the Bank in the adoption of what is practically a Quixotic policy. A case in point is furnished by Sir Inglis Palgrave: "Thus, for instance, in the autumn of 1870 the Bank put its rate up to 5 per cent. and kept it there for a period of 119 days, though the market rate did not stand at anything like so high a figure during that time. In this case the Bank was carrying out strictly and honestly one of the most difficult of the important duties with which it is charged, and that is the duty imposed on it as custodian of the bullion reserve of the country. In pursuance of this duty the Bank put its rate up, though there was no corresponding disposition to a rise in the outer market, and this action on its part attracted, in time, sufficient gold to its treasury."

of draining surplus money from the market, had not been adopted by the Bank of England for several years.¹ But whatever the tactics of the directors, it is clear, as soon as the discount houses are forced to borrow at the Bank, that the creation of credit on the part of the bankers has reached what they regard as its limit. The Bank of England is then in control of the market. It could, if it chose, charge 10 per cent., 15 per cent., or 20 per cent., but its practice is only to charge such a rate as the circumstances demand. And it must not be forgotten that it intervenes, not only to prevent the inflation of credit, but to allay undue nervousness on the part of the bankers—that is to say, where there is baseless discrimination against a given accepting-house on the ground that its paper is too plentiful. With the banks themselves doing a large acceptance business, they are compelled, both in their character of acceptors and as invigilators of the acceptance business generally, to keep the most critical eye upon the paper in circulation. But Threadneedle Street dislikes the over-critical as much as it distrusts the over-optimistic. And, after all, what duty can require more exquisitely delicate discretion than the necessity for discriminating against the paper of a given accepting-house which is considered to be getting a trifle out of its depth ? Where the merest breath of suspicion can work unbounded and irremediable havoc, the disciplinary jurisdiction must be invoked against unjustifiable contraction as well as for the prevention of inflation.

[1] *Stock Exchange Investments*, p. 39.

CHAPTER XVIII

THE BARING CRISIS, 1890

IN the quarter-century between the Overend-Gurney collapse and the Baring crisis the world had begun to turn a critical, and at times censorious, eye upon the centripetal tendencies of finance. The absence of panic made the opportunity for contemplation. Beyond the "pressures" of 1873 and 1878 there were no untoward incidents on the scale once decennially familiar. The unwonted experience even compelled us to find a new word, which should describe a heavy fall in prices, unaccompanied, as of yore, by crisis or panic. The term was found in "slump," which makes its recognised appearance in City parlance about 1888.[1] Unoccupied with any immediate perils of recurring crises the economists produced a flood of literature. They issued 1768 publications on the monetary question between 1871 and 1891. Simultaneously the importance of the banking function became yearly more conspicuous. Banking, said Mr. H. G. Turner, of the Commercial Bank of Australia,[2] voicing truths to which the age was rapidly awakening, " is an occupation that will ever play a prominent part in the welfare or otherwise of the community. Its importance is as yet but dimly apprehended, its latent possibilities are scarcely dreamed of; and to you, the rising generation, will be entrusted the solution of financial problems which will only be achieved by diligent study and wise conference and co-operation." The "latent possibilities" had, indeed, just received dramatic illustration. In 1885, Egypt was drawing nigh to bankruptcy.

[1] By 1895 even the *Tablet* was using it!
[2] *Bankers' Magazine*, 1886, p. 874.

This calamity was averted by monthly advances from the House of Rothschild with no legal security, but merely on the strength of a private note from the then Secretary of State for Foreign Affairs (Lord Granville). Later, the firm obtained its reward when a loan for £9,000,000 was negotiated and issued. Yet the profit derived from the latter transaction was nothing more than the merited compensation to the firm which, with unfailing public spirit, had accepted the risks then attendant upon international politics affecting Egypt. The great coup whereby the British Government became possessed of 176,602 shares in the Suez Canal had occurred in 1875, four years before the death of Baron Lionel. Then the Government authorised Messrs. Rothschild to purchase those shares from the Khedive at a price of £4,080,000, the money being voted by Parliament in the following year. The Bank of England itself would have advanced the £4,000,000 for the purchase of these shares, but for the statutory prohibition of the advance of money to the Government without the authority of Parliament, which had disquieted the directors in the days of Pitt.[1]

These were remarkable manifestations. Together with the steady process of bank absorption, as well as cash aggregations of hitherto unprecedented magnitude, they generated a certain uneasiness with regard to the " increased centralisation of capital." Giffen pointed to what was, even then, the obvious existence of " a banking hierarchy, which dominates not only the banks of the United Kingdom, but has many foreign connections." At its head and centre was, and is, the Bank of England. But at the psychological moment, when the public became alive to what was going on, the harvest of the process was reaped in the salvation of England from another crisis which, if it had been suffered to develop, would have left its mark on financial history for the next fifty years. Confederated finance intervened to snatch a great financial house from imminent disaster. In doing so much it offered the world such an object-lesson as had

[1] Governor of the Bank at the Bank Court, March 16, 1876.

never confronted it before. The existence of the hierarchy was discerned, challenged, and justified almost simultaneously.

TROUBLE LOOMS AHEAD

The firm of Barings' occupied a position almost as commanding as when the Duc de Richelieu ranked them among the Great Powers of Europe. When Bagehot invented Treasury Bills, late in the 'seventies, the finest encomium he could bestow upon them was the forecast that they " would rank before a Bill of Barings'." Towards the end of the year 1890 the large increase in the volume of acceptances assumed by the Barings created great uneasiness. It has been suggested that general over-confidence was created by the great accumulation of capital in the hands of the new investment trusts (*ante*, Chapter XVI), which were " not always so much alive as are individuals to the danger of great mistakes."[1] The proximate cause of the crisis was, however, over-sanguine lending to foreign borrowers—mainly South American—not yet fully schooled in the principles of national prudence in the region of finance. During the seven years previous to the crisis Barings' placed upon the market a volume of securities to the value of more than £100,000,000. Argentine specialities " went to pieces " in the summer of 1890, and Barings' involved themselves to the extent of a further £6,000,000 in the endeavour to mitigate the collapse. There was not the remotest chance of relieving the pressure by the issue of an Argentine loan. The full extent of the trouble was not known until November 8, when Mr. Lidderdale (the Governor of the Bank of England) became aware that Barings' were on the eve of suspending payment, and that the liabilities were £21,000,000. An eminent banker and a member of the Treasury Committee of the Bank of England (Mr. Bertram Wodehouse Currie and Mr. Benjamin Buck Greene) were instructed, partly on account of their friendship with Lord Revelstoke, to inquire into the position of affairs. The rest of the story is best told by the protagonist in this tremendous episode.

[1] Palgrave, *Dictionary of Political Economy*, Art. " Crises."

At the Bank of England meeting on March 11, 1891, Mr. Lidderdale said :—

" You must all have learned from the press that in the second week in November it became known to the Bank that the great house of Baring was in difficulties. For an announcement that the firm were embarrassed by their operations in South America the Governors would to some extent have been prepared ; but they were not prepared for the actual facts. The situation was at once recognised as very grave, and as one which demanded prompt and decided action on the part of the directors. We had a reserve ample for ordinary requirements, but not sufficient to meet the demands certain to come upon the Bank the moment Messrs. Barings' difficulties became known. The old and well-approved remedy of raising the rate would not have met the urgency of the case, as the condition of financial affairs in several countries of Europe, as well as in the United States, made it certain that gold to the required extent could not be attracted here except slowly, and then only by rates so high as to involve much suffering to our trading commercial community.

" It was therefore decided to adopt exceptional measures, even at a considerable sacrifice to the Bank. In the course of a couple of days we secured, by the sale of Exchequer bonds to the State Bank of Russia, the sum of £1,500,000 in gold, and obtained from Paris, as a loan, by the prompt and liberal action of the Bank of France, a further sum of £3,000,000, as an addition to other resources. Four days of that week were occupied in the preparation of a statement of Messrs. Barings' position, and on November 14 I was enabled to assure the heads of Her Majesty's Government that there was good reason to believe, without committing myself to definite figures, that the assets would yield a substantial surplus over the liabilities, if sufficient time were allowed for the liquidation. Without this belief in their full eventual solvency nothing could have been done to save the firm.

" When I tell you that the liabilities of Messrs. Baring Brothers were over £21,000,000 sterling you will recognise that the burden of carrying them over their difficulty was not to be lightly undertaken, even by the Bank of England, and that the risk of doing so was more than the Bank was called upon to undertake alone. It was necessary, therefore, to invoke the aid and support of the financial community in forming a guarantee fund to justify the Bank in providing the money required. I am glad to be able to recognise the promptitude of the response made. It was nearly five o'clock on the afternoon of Friday when the guarantee list was opened, and headed with £1,000,000 sterling by the Bank of England. In half an hour the amount reached £3,250,000; by eleven o'clock the next morning (Saturday) it was £6,500,000; at twelve o'clock I was able to announce that the liabilities of the firm would be duly met.[1] This, however, did not prevent large further additions to the guarantee fund, which eventually reached £17,250,000, rendering it certain that, even if the liquidation proved disappointing, the loss to any individual guarantor could hardly be serious."

WHO WERE THE GUARANTORS?

The names of the guarantors were not published. Some idea of their identities, and the extent of their respective responsibilities, can, however, be collected from contemporary documents and statements. Illustrative instances are:—

London and Westminster Bank } now amalgamated	{ £750,000
London and County Bank	{ £750,000
Union Bank of London (now the Union of London and Smith's Bank)	£500,000
Union Discount	£250,000
London Joint-Stock Bank	£500,000
Consolidated (since absorbed by Parr's) . . .	£200,000
City (since absorbed in London City and Midland) .	£250,000
Parr's Bank	£150,000
Union Bank of Australia	£100,000

[1] The text of this historic guarantee should be added, for the sake of completeness :—
"GUARANTEE FUND,
"Bank of England, *November*, 1890.
"In consideration of advances which the Bank of England have agreed to make to Messrs. Baring Brothers and Co., to enable them to discharge at maturity their liabilities existing on the night of the 15th of November, 1890, or arising out of business initiated on or prior to the 15th of November, 1890,
"We the undersigned, hereby agree, each individual, firm, or company, for himself or themselves alone, and to the amount only set opposite to his or their names respectively, to make good to the Bank of England any loss which may appear whenever the Bank of England shall determine that the final liquidation of the liabilities of Messrs. Baring Brothers and Co. has been completed so far as in the opinion of the Governors is practicable.
"All the guarantors shall contribute rateably, and no one individual firm, or company, shall be called on for his or their contribution without the like call being made on the others.
"The maximum period over which the liquidation may extend is three years, commencing the 15th of November, 1890."

It will be seen that even in the comparatively brief period since the Baring episode, the resistless process of absorption has been busy among these great institutions. Of the nine banks mentioned in the list, no less than five have undergone changes in constitution—and this in less than a quarter-century.

THE CRISIS THAT PASSED IN SILENCE

The Baring episode demonstrated anew the fact of the lessening intensity of crisis in the presence of a potent financial confederacy. Therein lay its profound significance. In earlier crises alarm was general. The Baring affair was rigidly localised. It was purely a London crisis. Only the centre knew what was going on. The outposts were hardly aware that there was anything exceptional in the situation. There was no suspension, either of the Baring firm itself or of any other great house; for Murrietas' did not collapse till March, 1892. In 1866 there was a 10 per cent. rate for three months; in 1890 the rate was never for a moment over 6 per cent., and only over 5 per cent. for three weeks. Mr. Lidderdale declined to precipitate alarm by forcing up the rate. He maintained it at 6 per cent., and insisted that the great joint-stock banks should continue discounting as usual. The traditional and classic remedy of the suspension of the Bank Act was offered by the Chancellor of the Exchequer, but declined by the intrepid Governor. Mr. Lidderdale's great anxiety was to prevent the calling by the banks of the loans to bill brokers. In the event of any such policy of contraction being adopted the bill brokers must inevitably have been driven to the Bank itself for assistance. If it were granted, the position of the Bank itself would have been weakened. If it were refused, panic must assuredly have been precipitated. There is a City tradition that one of the joint-stock banks—it would not be fair to give any hint of the alleged identity[1]—endeavoured to evade its share in the agreement to refrain from calling in its loans. It reverted to the old and discredited policy

---

[1] Moreover, it is now merged in another institution.

THE BARING CRISIS, 1890

of isolated self-defence. The matter was brought to the attention of Mr. Lidderdale, who, with characteristic decision, sent for the manager and informed him that if the bank did not loyally adhere to the agreement he would close its account at the Bank of England and announce the fact in the evening newspapers. He is said to have given the manager an hour to make up his mind. It would be superfluous to add what the manager's decision was.

So skilfully was the whole episode handled that, as far as the public was concerned, it was history before it was actuality :—

" In former times alarm was diffused over the whole kingdom, London was drained of its reserves to fill up the wants of the country, and the imprudences of banks having caused or aggravated alarms, there was a general uneasiness in the banking world, and a consequent . . . indisposition to grant assistance to the trading world. But on this last occasion there was no general alarm in the country. Banks outside London were hardly sensible of the crisis, and even in London there was no panic except in Capel Court. No bank failed in town or country, and no suspicion of danger to banks seems to have existed among their customers. Some great issuing houses lost their position, and narrowly escaped suspension. . . . It was not a panic causing general alarm among the public, but a crisis of a special kind, which might easily have been extended so as to have caused such a panic as never yet has occurred in any country. The danger was prodigious ; but it was averted. In previous crises the danger was not averted, and things were allowed to drift, so that great houses and banks failed and general alarm ensued." In 1890 " it may fairly be said that, for all practical purposes, nothing was known of the crisis in the country at large until it was all over."[1]

AN EPOCH-MARKING CHANGE

In plain English there were crisis and caution, never panic ; but if the firm had been allowed to go down the panic would have been appalling and unprecedented in scope and magnitude. The truth is that the whole character of the later crises has altered. They have lacked

[1] Palgrave, *Dictionary of Political Economy.*

the factors of unreason and rottenness which distinguished all panics down to 1847. In these earlier calamities it might have been said, with literal accuracy, that people lost their heads, and consequently were unable to measure or comprehend the real character of the circumstances in which they found themselves; and further, that if they had been, they might not have wrung much comfort from a consideration of the ramshackle conditions observable in many directions. But from the later panics and crises the element of dismay, despair, and almost of stampede, have been conspicuously absent. In brief, while the prestige of Threadneedle Street is plain to the seeing eye in both the eighteenth and nineteenth centuries, the latter is marked by the unceasing tightening of the bonds which bind the banking community together, while the former has nothing better to afford than a spasmodic defensive rally, laudable enough in its way, but of trifling utility as a merely temporary expedient, adopted whenever danger appears on the horizon and forgotten when the menace subsides.

The real significance of the Baring Guarantee Fund is revealed by the reference to the invocation of "the aid and support of the financial community." In the earlier crisis of 1836 the Bank acted by itself in saving the Northern and Central Bank. In the Overend-Gurney affair the Bank—if the expression be permissible—stood aside by itself, and let disaster come. Its Governor had words of cordial praise for the joint-stock banks; but no effort was made to unite them into a financial phalanx in common cause against the foe. But in this last instance—that of the threatened Baring collapse—there is a financial hierarchy in the background. The Bank is not the single combatant who must fight or retire, but the leader of the most colossal agglomeration of financial power which the world has so far witnessed. The defensive measures of an isolated protagonist are replaced by the recognition of the common cause, the invocation of the corporate experience, and the assumption of the corporate responsibility. One of the other factors of the Money Market—to wit, the

Stock Exchange—sent an official letter to Mr. Lidderdale expressing its appreciation of his conduct. This carried all the greater weight because the Stock Exchange was not only well acquainted " with the unexampled character of the crisis," but fully able to estimate the magnitude of the menace behind it.

THE CRITICS OF THE BARING GUARANTEE

Criticism, as might have been expected, was rife; nor have the echoes entirely died away even in 1915. Among a few of the older bankers, whose 'prentice memories antedated Black Friday, there were those who thought that the crash should have been allowed to come. They did not like the " propping " process nor the subsequent prolonged nursing of assets. With regard to the latter point, remembering the magnitude of the interests involved, and the difficult and depressing City circumstances amid which the liquidation had to be conducted, it was a marvellously rapid performance.[1] Yet it must be admitted that for five years after the Baring episode " the Stock Exchange lay fallow, with business and credit worn to a shadow."[2] The last official pronouncement from the Bank of England on the subject was on March 16, 1893, when the Governor, at the Bank Court, observed :—

" It will be remembered that the period of three years for which the guarantees were originally given will expire in November next, and looking to the question how far the

[1] Some comparative figures may add to the completeness of the survey :—

	Liabilities at time of failure.	Assets including private estates.	Liabilities and Assets nine months after failure (O.-G.) and seven months after failure (B. B.)	
	£	£	£	£
Overend, Gurney and Co. Actual	9,837,784	11,058,487	4,451,710	3,535,947*
Contingent	8,890,231	8,890,231	—	—
Baring Brothers	20,963,300	24,770,032	8,336,973	11,863,377

* Large part very doubtful.

[2] Landell, *Quarterly Review*, July, 1912.

liquidation could be carried out without material loss before that date, it was felt desirable, in the interests of the guarantors, that the time should be extended ; and I am happy to be able to say that practically the whole body of guarantors have consented to continue their guarantee for one-fourth of the original amount—which is all that is required—for one year certain from November next, and for a further period of one year if deemed expedient in the interests of the guarantors."

No claim was ever made on the guarantors. Letters were issued by the Bank of England on January 10, 1895, announcing the close of the liquidation, and a formal release of the guarantors from all claims. As the Overend-Gurney liquidation did not finally close until 1893, it was, in the concluding phases, concurrent with the Baring adjustments—and offered an instructive contrast in the matter of the speed at which the respective processes had been conducted. It has been well said that there could be no greater testimony to the abilities, tact, and personality of Lord Revelstoke than is to be found in the simple fact that the Baring liquidation was so successfully accomplished, every debt discharged, and the prestige and fame —if not the pre-eminence—of Barings' themselves left absolutely unimpaired.

In other directions criticism was less concerned with the length of the liquidation than with the expediency of the policy itself. If a house was rickety, said the censors, it had better be allowed to come down. When the dust had cleared, we should know where we stood. In fact—so ran the argument—nothing but the otherwise inevitable onset of a great public calamity could justify the adoption of such an expedient as that which the Bank of England chose as the remedy for the Baring disease. Moreover, it was urged that the Bank and its allies were so far committed in their Baring guarantees, that they would have been helpless to tackle, much less to defeat, the menace of another catastrophe. This may have been true, to some extent. But Professor Dunbar certainly goes too far when he declares that

"it was the *general opinion* at the time that the directors deliberately set at risk a substantial part [£1,000,000] of the property of their stockholders in a manner required neither by any legal obligation nor by a calculation of probable advantage, and their right to deal in this manner with the interests entrusted to their care was questioned by some writers. By a natural, though illogical, process the success of the operation disarmed criticism, objection died away, and thus a precedent was established which, in any future case of the same kind, the Bank would find it hard to set aside." (Dunbar, p. 226.)

The author of the present essay was through the crisis himself, and recalls no such " general opinion " as Professor Dunbar purports to record. It is, indeed, true that some of the guarantors did not like the business. Loyalty, not conviction, brought them in. Yet leading participants, who described the guarantee, for instance, as the " most unbusiness-like transaction I ever undertook," were soon avowing that if it had to be done again they would not hesitate to co-operate. After all, the taking over of an open position was no new device, though never before attempted on such a scale. It had been adopted, e.g. by Lloyds Bank at the time of the failure of the Birmingham Bank, with regard to the branches of the latter institution at Coventry, Dudley, and Walsall.[1] Again, in 1870, when Harvey's and Hudson's suspended payment, Henry Birkbeck, senior partner of Gurney and Co., organised local arrangements in the Norfolk district which minimised the resulting financial difficulties and localised the disturbance. Arthur Crump[2] argued that the crisis was a lesson in the menace of " unfettered one-man power," and that the hand of Nemesis was visible in the blow which had struck down Bismarck and Baring almost simultaneously.

It would be saying too much to suggest that the City is never likely again to witness the building up of a firm enjoying the financial pre-eminence which once attached to the Baring house. But, at any rate, the advent of a firm enjoying the super-eminent glamour of the Barings is in the highest degree unlikely, not only on account of the enormous magnitude of resources which must be

---

[1] Chairman's speech, Lloyds Bank meeting, February 6, 1868.
[2] *Economic Journal*, Vol. I. p. 389.

possessed before the premier position could be achieved, but also because of the rivalry which must be defeated and the perils which must be passed before success could be attained. "The supply of financiers," said Mr. Lehfeldt,[1] " cannot be effectively increased, for it is rarely possible for a new competitor to raise himself to the level of the existing financial firms."

A FINAL SURVEY OF THE STOCK EXCHANGE

At this point, the end of the second period in the history of the modern Money Market, the Stock Exchange factor looms so large as to demand detailed consideration. Such it will receive in the next chapter, before we enter upon the study of the final stages of the developing financial organism, as they have been observable in the years that divide the Baring crisis from the present day. An analysis of the activities of the Stock Exchange will, moreover, bring joint-stock enterprise once again within the survey, since practically every important company is "known" in Capel Court. The present late term has been selected for the introduction of this final investigation of the functions of the Stock Exchange because we are enabled, in that way, to complete the study by a view of every factor of the Money Market, in the form in which they presented themselves when the German war crisis of 1914 burst like a thunderclap upon the City.

[1] *Economic Journal,* 1910, p. 558.

CHAPTER XIX

THE STOCK EXCHANGE AS A FUNCTION OF THE MODERN MONEY MARKET

[The succeeding analysis of the functions of the Stock Exchange will doubtless gain in clarity and coherence if we make a preliminary attempt at a succinct summary of it, in sections corresponding to those into which the subsequent treatment will fall. We commence with—

(1) HISTORY. A brief summary of the nineteenth-century history of the Stock Exchange, including the rise of the provincial Stock Exchanges. We proceed to

(2) THE INTERNAL DISCIPLINE of the Stock Exchange.

(3) THE TYPES OF SECURITY, standardised (a) QUALITATIVELY, to suit all temperaments, and (b) QUANTITATIVELY, for celerity of handling and definition of interests; leading to

(4) THE PUBLIC STANDARDISATION OF PRICES at a given moment, the means by which it is achieved, and the purpose which it serves in attracting the maximum of capital for investment purposes, and in preventing the taking of unfair advantage of a seller's urgent necessity or a buyer's eagerness. This, in its turn, brings us to

    (5) (a) THE COGNOSCIBILITY AND LIQUIDITY of securities, especially in relation to their use as credit instruments; and

    (b) THE CONTINUOUS REDISTRIBUTION of securities—that is to say, freedom of dealings, creating the utmost facility of exchange, because money which is leaving the market is continually replaced by fresh supplies; and

    (c) THE EXTREME SENSITIVENESS of the market (largely the result of an unprecedented celerity and adequacy of public and private news-service), itself the harvest of an incessant stream of influences, impinging upon the arena and interpreted by the shrewd intellects there concentrated. This fullness of knowledge and keenness of judgment exclude (to a considerable extent) the mischief arising from imperfect information as to the nature and scope of the conditions which determine prices. But this freedom and sensitiveness in co-operation create unique opportunities for

    (d) SPECULATION, and confer upon the Stock Exchange

534 EVOLUTION OF THE MONEY MARKET

(6) A POWER OF INTERNATIONAL FINANCIAL CENSORSHIP, because it can refuse recognition to any class of security whose sponsors have failed, or refused, to act up to the standard of financial ethics which money market sentiment for the time being approves and enunciates.

It is not suggested that these sections are entirely disconnected and respectively watertight. On the contrary, the treatment must of necessity be characterised by a certain amount of overlapping and dovetailing. But the sections have their clarifying and mnemonic utility, nevertheless.]

SECTION I

BRIEF HISTORICAL SKETCH, 1815–1915.[1]

THE history of the Stock Exchange (as distinct from the analysis of its functions) in the period between Waterloo and the present time, needs no extended treatment, at all events as a mere record of events, for our present purpose. The main facts are the enlargement of the building, the enormous expansion in the number of securities known to the market, the increasingly closer intimacy with the other stock markets of the world, and the establishment of the various provincial Stock Exchanges. The development of Stock Exchange functions, however, as well as the growing intimacy of the institution with other factors of the Money Market, and its exertion of a correspondingly enhanced stimulus upon economic progress as a whole, by the aggregation and incessant redistribution of the driving-power—capital—are subjects which it will be necessary to analyse at some length. They may advantageously be preceded with such a brief summary of Stock Exchange history as shall suffice to place them in their proper focus.

FINAL CENTRALISATION OF LONDON SHARE BUSINESS

Before the middle of the nineteenth century all London stock and share business was centred in the Stock Exchange. From its erection in 1764 down to 1837 the Rotunda of the Bank of England was the Consol market. The public was advised by critics of the Stock Exchange

[1] The earlier history has been treated at some length in Chapter V

to "go personally into the Rotunda, and there (avoiding the Jobbers, as they would any other beasts of prey) meet each other and re-establish a fair and open market."[1] But the bewildering confusion and uproar ultimately became so great a nuisance that in 1837 Sir Timothy Curtis, the then Governor of the Bank (with a clause in an Act of Parliament to support him), drove the vociferous intruders from the building in the same way as the proprietor of Garraway's seventy years before had expelled the brokers and jobbers from his Coffee House. This was the final step in the centralisation of London transactions in stocks and shares. The truth of this proposition is not affected by the recent establishment of small subordinate markets, such as that for rubber shares in "the Lane" (i.e. Mark Lane).

It was the railway boom, however, which caused the greatest expansion of Stock Exchange membership. Down to about 1843 the share market was in the hands of four or five brokers and a comparatively small number of jobbers. By 1845 it had become the focus of speculation, the centre of the wild gamble in English and foreign railway scrip. Men who had a few months ago been only clerks were now carrying on a huge business in the popular counters, to the envy of older individuals who had not been so alert to seize the opportunity. In another year or two the membership was within sight of four figures. Nearly all the members were dependent for their livelihood on commissions and "turns" derived from time-bargains. "When," said a writer as late as 1851,[2] there exists a body of nearly 1000 members, the actual 'money' or bona-fide, business would be utterly inadequate to provide employment for them all." These words have remained true down to the present hour, except that the investment business is probably a much larger proportion of the whole in 1915 than it was in 1815. Still, "if only genuine investment business were transacted, in Capel Court, the membership would have to be very considerably

---

[1] *Art of Stock Jobbing*, Pref., p. vii.
[2] *City Men and City Manners*, p. 30.

reduced."[1] Absolutely, of course, the volume of speculation is larger (in active periods such as 1910, that is to say), and consequently the number of members has much increased again. The augmented caution of the public, and its growing fondness for speculative investment (as distinguished from mere speculation), is one of the factors which tends to augment the volume of investment buying. If we seek to discover evidence of this modification there is a test available—at all events since 1868—in the ratio of London bankers' clearings on Stock Exchange settling days to the total for the entire month. If this ratio be high, it will, prima facie, indicate extensive public activity on the Stock Exchange, and if it be low, the reverse. Of course, the speculative element cannot be separated from that which represents investment. The figure was 15·3 in 1868. Since then its highest point has been 21·7 (in 1881) and the lowest 12·6 (in 1913). The curve since the advent of the present century has been decidedly downwards, though the same graph, drawn with regard to the clearings on Consols settling days—the index of the conservative investment tendency—shows no substantial irregularity since 1845. This suggests the steadiness of the proportion of the public's money which goes into investment, and therefore, prima facie, indicates a relative decline in the volume of speculation.

The old suspicions about the Stock Exchange have revived, from time to time, under the stimulus of occasional " revelations." Now and then they have appeared where they would not have been expected. At the first meeting of the Overend-Gurney shareholders, on May 23, 1866, it was resolved " that no member of the Stock Exchange be on the Committee." Nowadays the presence of a member of the Stock Exchange on such a committee would, provided he were capable and responsible, be welcomed; if, indeed, his presence were not regarded as essential. Modern distrust of the Stock Exchange is largely that of the less educated type of Labour Leader, who regards it as

[1] J. F. Wheeler, *Stock Exchange*, p. 92. The allusion is to normal circumstances, not to those subsisting when, as in the early days of 1915, stringent regulations exclude all speculative business.

THE STOCK EXCHANGE (1815–1915)

an institution which in some mysterious way is able to exploit the workers, and to make large sums of money by merely altering certain figures from one day to another.

ENLARGEMENT OF THE BUILDING

Extensive enlargements of the Stock Exchange, over the site occupied by about fifteen houses in Throgmorton Street and Old Broad Street, were completed in 1885. The new space was largely devoted to the Foreign Market—a proof of the steadily widening cosmopolitanism of finance. "Even as the architecture of a nation is an index of its character," remarks Mr. Duguid,[1] "that of the Stock Exchange is intimately related to its history of never-ceasing growth. Structural extension has always been going on in all directions; it is going on now (1901) at its centenary, and, presumably, always will be going on." That is only another way of saying that the Stock Exchange conforms to the eternal and immutable biological law of incessant adaptation to its environment. It must adapt and advance, or else it must degenerate and decline. The number of securities known to the market would almost of itself indicate the peremptory necessity for structural extension. The prototype of the familiar (daily) *Official List* was first published in August, 1697, under the title of the *Course of the Exchange*. It then contained six securities. In 1747 the quoted securities had increased to twenty in number, but even so late as 1825 only thirty-four stocks were "known to the market" in the sense of being quoted in the *List*. It must not be supposed, however, that dealings were confined to these securities. The shares of about 152 companies, with a paid-up capital of about £34,000,000, were familiar to the market in 1824, before the "boom" of 1825 so hugely increased the number. The *List* was a single-page publication up to 1867, four pages then to 1889, eight pages for the next eleven years to 1900, twelve pages from 1900 to 1902, and sixteen pages since.

"A cursory glance over this really formidable *Official List* brings forcibly to mind London's supreme position as banker,

[1] *Story of the Stock Exchange*, p. 308.

538 EVOLUTION OF THE MONEY MARKET

broker, and clearing-house to the wide world, while it emphasises the constantly increasing overflow of British capital into channels that make for enterprise and development even in the most remote quarters of the globe. Soda and newspapers, theatres and saw-mills, hotels and clothiers, sponges and molasses, soaps and cereals, these are some of the items that catch the eye as one glances over the *List*. What would be found there if all the securities admitted to the ' House ' were published in the *List* may be left to conjecture ; and what will this eloquent array of enterprise in figures look like a century hence, if the *List* continues its present rate of growth ? "[1]

The total nominal value of the quoted securities was £5,480,000,000 in 1885 and £10,200,000,000 in 1909. At the end of 1913 it was £11,262,457,883. The first issue of the almost equally well-known *Stock Exchange Year-Book*, in 1875, dealt with 1027 securities known to the London market. The 1915 issue gave particulars of 9662 states, provinces, municipalities, public authorities, and enterprises, whose issues are known to the market. As a single issuer is frequently responsible for three or more species of security the total cannot be far short of 30,000.

CLOSING OF THE STOCK EXCHANGE

The London Stock Exchange (as well as the provincial institutions) remained closed from July 31, 1914, to January 4, 1915, in consequence of the German war crisis. The closure is discussed in Section V (*b*) of this chapter.

THE PROVINCIAL STOCK EXCHANGES

The middle of the nineteenth century, from 1830 onwards, was the period of the establishment of the provincial Stock Exchanges. They, like their earlier analogues, the provincial banks, have now attained a large importance and done much to encourage classes of enterprise which, in their nature, are of purely local attractiveness, and must be fed with capital through conduit-pipes supplied from local sources. Nothing short of a study of the local share lists will convince the observer how great has been

[1] Van Antwerp, *The Stock Exchange from Within*, p. 362.

THE STOCK EXCHANGE (1815–1915)

the contribution of these local exchanges to the most remote and minute irrigation of national prosperity and the ubiquitous fostering of productive enterprise. The growth of the provincial Stock Exchanges has brought joint-stock facilities within the reach of many prosperous enterprises which were too small for the attention of the London market. In that way it has maintained the activity of numerous local industries which might otherwise have vanished. The investor in a local joint-stock undertaking, with quite a modest capital, is frequently in a very advantageous position. He has the operations under his own eye—a privilege denied to the buyer of interests in the mighty concerns which have their share dealings domiciled in Throgmorton Street. There is still a large class of investor who will not let his money out of his sight—who will help to finance a local undertaking which he can *see* (as he once saw the house or the chapel that was mortgaged to him), though nothing would induce him to lend money to the London County Council. If the aggregate of invested capital—and therefore of potential productivity—is to be maintained at its maximum, this class must be catered for, and the provincial Stock Exchanges do the work. These provincial Stock Exchanges are, of course, voluntary associations, though their long standing and responsibility have conferred upon them the character of quasi-public institutions.

A TYPICAL INSTANCE—MANCHESTER

As an early example of the provincial Stock Exchange, Manchester had notable features. Its daily list, as early as 1845, quoted 148 British railway companies and 23 foreign railway securities, the majority of them French propositions. Apart from railway interests, the only remaining quotations were comprised in a " miscellaneous " section of fifteen companies, of which six were canals. Of banks there were three, all in £20 shares £10 paid—Manchester and Liverpool District 13; Union Bank of Manchester 12¼; and Manchester and Salford 14½. The two former retain to-day an honoured place under their original titles, though the capital is changed and the market value far more greatly appreciated. The third was in recent years amalgamated with another institution. There was also a place in the list for Manchester Exchange Buildings (becoming "Royal" later), the £100 shares being quoted at £135; and for two cemetery enterprises. In spite of the inclusion of these last-named securities, it was a very "live" market that existed in Manchester in those days. This small list recorded no fewer than seventy transactions on the day—a number by no means despised in these later times, while the membership of the Exchange, at 84, was only slightly below the present total. The Manchester Stock Exchange list of to-day gives quotations for over 1000 securities, and the nominal value of the interests represented is stated to be over £3,000,000,000.

PROVINCIAL BROKERS ORGANISED

Since 1890 the provincial Stock Exchanges have consolidated their interests. They have created their own central organisation—the Council of Associated Stock Exchanges. It meets annually, or oftener if necessity arises. The various Stock Exchanges are generally represented by their chairman and deputy chairman. The indefeasible title to securities, created by the Forged Transfers Acts, was mainly the work of the provincial Stock Exchanges (principally Liverpool).[1]

Outside the large provincial Stock Exchanges, there has in our time gradually grown up another refinement of adaptive specialisation—a body of brokers carrying on business in separate towns, none of them large enough to support a Stock Exchange, yet offering to a single local broker, or accountant, the chance of doing many a "deal" in local securities. In June, 1914, the first general meeting of the Association of Provincial Stock and Share Brokers signalised the rise of a protective and disciplinary body designed to organise these solitary units for corporate

---

[1] These Acts enable the creation of an insurance fund as a means of compensation against losses arising from forged transfers, out of a trifling charge (not more than 1s. per cent) added to the transfer fee.

THE STOCK EXCHANGE (1815–1915)

purposes. This is what Spencer would have called segregation, ending in organisation and an enhanced capacity to resist the forces of disintegration. Thus the same inexorable process of subjection to concentrated authority in essentials, with free play for variability in non-essentials, which we saw operative all over the field of banking, is observable at work in the allied factor of the money market. The provincial Stock Exchanges represent the differentiation and specialisation of function which, inside the London Stock Exchange itself, take the form (a) of the division of the members into brokers [agents for clients outside] and jobbers [independent non-fiduciary dealers] and (b) of the separation of the business into definite markets—the Consol, mining and foreign, for example—each concerned in its own class of securities. The analogous process of extension and differentiation is going on in the United States :—

" While the membership (1100) [of the New York Stock Exchange] has not increased, and will not be permitted to increase, of the 590 odd firms identified with it 104 have their offices in other cities—from Boston to New Orleans and from Richmond to Los Angeles. The number of branch offices has grown to 505, situated not only in all the principal cities in America, but also in Berlin, London, Paris, Frankfort, Montreal, Toronto and Ottawa. The business of the Exchange thus comes from every part of the country, and from the principal markets of Europe. It has been roughly estimated that 60,000 persons are directly interested in the New York Stock Market all the time, while the number of those less directly affected may be computed at 2,000,000 in America alone, this being the approximate number of shareholders in American securities."[1]

Of the total exports of American manufactured goods seventy per cent. is supplied by industrial combinations whose shares are listed on the New York Stock Exchange and owned by nearly 1,000,000 investors. In New York the small man, who buys and sells odd lots, has special firms who cater for him. Writing the official apologia

[1] Mr. W. C. Van Antwerp in *The Financial News*, February 6, 1914.

of the New York Stock Exchange, Mr. J. G. Milburn says: "Another large class of transactions consists of the buying and selling of stocks by or for the dealers in lots less than the unit of 100 shares, or, as they are called, odd lots. There are many houses engaged in the same kind of business, which constitutes about 20 per cent. of each day's business of the Exchange in normal times, and the bulk of it is investment business." Bond issues of the minor municipalities which are too small to be recognised by the Stock Exchanges of Canada or Europe are peddled out by a special class of brokers in the larger Canadian cities—another illustration of the democratisation of investment as well as of the ineluctable tendency to specialisation. The class that buys these bonds has only a few dollars at a time for investment, but their utilisation in the creation of a reserve fund of this kind serves the double purpose of consolidating the proprietors' financial position and furnishing the embryo municipalities, on fairly easy terms, with funds otherwise unavailable. There is a vast investing class " tapped " by these brokers, though it is as yet out of reach of the Stock Exchanges. Baltimore offered a loan of $5,500,000 and had no takers: tightness of the Money Market, it was explained. The city cut the price to 90 without materially stimulating the demand. Then the publisher of the *Sun* offered to sell $10,000 worth of the bonds at the newspaper office, and people poured in and bought that block and other blocks until the *Sun* had sold almost $1,000,000 worth.

STOCK EXCHANGE PANICS

The panics and crises from 1825 to the present time have already been comparatively treated. The effects of these crises on the Stock Exchange were briefly included in that survey, so far as was necessary for its adequacy.

Section II

THE DISCIPLINE OF THE STOCK EXCHANGE

At the basis of the internal discipline of the Stock Exchange (itself a vital factor in the concentric control of the social driving-power at the hands of the financial hierarchy) there lies the fact that a member of the London Stock Exchange, as such, has no rights which are enforceable at law. He is annually elected to membership for one year. Upon his recurring re-election, each year, depend the whole of the privileges and facilities which he enjoys as a member of the " House." If the Committee decide not to re-elect him his membership comes to an end. If they expel him at some intermediate point of the year (unless their decision is contrary to natural justice, or is itself a violation of their own rules—see below) the sentence is final :—

" The Stock Exchange is a voluntary society. It has upwards of 2000 members. It exists for the purposes of buying and selling, to which all its other functions are subordinate. There is no reason to doubt that as between its own members it administers substantial justice. The power it wields extends to expulsion—that is, the taking away from the person expelled his occupation in life. Such a body can hardly be interfered with by Parliament without losing that freedom of self-government which is the very life and soul of the institution."[1]

The member who is expelled, or who fails to secure re-election, cannot go to the Law Courts and obtain from them any remedy for the consequences of the expulsion or the failure to re-elect him. If the Committee, in expelling him, could be shown to have acted *mala fide*, or in defiance or disregard of its own rules, the case might be otherwise.[2]

[1] Report of Select Committee of the House of Commons on Loans to Foreign States, 1875.
[2] See the whole law on the subject reviewed in Brown and Others *v.* the Committee of the Stock Exchange—a case of expelling members for alleged disgraceful and dishonourable conduct. (*Times*, August 27, 1892, p. 3.) Gainsford Bruce, J., said : " This Court is not a Court of Appeal from the Stock Exchange Committee on matters of discipline, whether they are right or no. It is not contended that there is either a want of good faith

But from a failure to re-elect there is *no* external appeal. No Court would assume the responsibility of requiring a Committee, discharging important and responsible quasi-public functions, to re-elect a member against its own judgment. For his subsequent misconduct and its possible serious consequences, the Court and not the Committee would in that case be responsible. This right of private judgment (as contrasted with judicial or statutory regulation) is among the fundamental necessities of a Money Market system, as we shall see when we come to examine the subject in detail. The Stock Exchange Committee, then, is an autocratic body of a character very similar to the Benchers of an Inn of Court. It enforces, and cannot be prevented from enforcing, a moral code of its own. " So long as the Stock Exchange has the power of expelling one of its members without appeal or redress, it can be bound by no law which it does not choose to obey. When it loses that power, its means of self-government are gone, and the Society as at present constituted is at an end."[1]

THE QUESTION OF INCORPORATION

Objections to incorporation, and to any statutory regulation of the governance of the institution, spring from considerations like these. Legislation is not lissom and plastic enough to be adaptable to the conditions. The 1877–1878 Commission gave a qualified approval of the transformation of the Stock Exchange into a corporate body either by means of a Royal Charter or an Act of Parliament. But at the same time they expressed their " conviction that any external control which might be introduced by such a change should be exercised with a sparing hand." " Any attempt to reduce these [Stock

---

[1] Report of Select Committee of the House of Commons on Loans to Foreign States, 1875.

or a breach of the rules." These observations affirm the principles laid down, as regards expulsion from clubs in Fisher *v.* Keane (11 Ch. D. 353) and Dawkins *v.* Antrobus (17 Ch. D. 615). Harker and Another *v.* Edwards (57 L.J.Q.B. 147) shows that the rules are final even as against an outsider, unless he can show that decisions based upon them are unreasonable or contrary to natural justice. (Esher, M.R., at p. 148.)

THE STOCK EXCHANGE (1815–1915)   545

Exchange] rules to the limits of the ordinary law of the land, or to abolish all checks and safeguards not to be found in that law, would, in our opinion, be detrimental to the honest and efficient conduct of business." Similar views have been expressed with regard to New York. " In its present form," said the *Wall Street Journal*, " the [New York] Stock Exchange is a private organisation. It can inspect any member's books at any moment. If it suspects him of wrongdoing it can tap his telephone wire, and has done so in the past. It can terminate his membership for conduct which no legislation could possibly touch." That is to say, in the words of the New York Stock Exchange itself (*post*, p. 548 n.), the better course is to prevent abuses by measures from within, rather than to arbitrarily and impetuously impose the regulations from without. Incorporation has since then been roundly condemned by the Committee appointed by Governor Hughes, of the State of New York, in 1908 to report on any legislative changes which might seem desirable for the protection of investors :—

" We have been strongly urged to recommend that the Exchange be incorporated, in order to bring it more completely under the authority and supervision of the State and the process of the courts. Under existing conditions, being a voluntary organisation, it has almost unlimited power over the conduct of its members, and it can subject them to instant discipline for wrongdoing, which it could not exercise in a summary manner if it were an incorporated body. We think that such power residing in a properly chosen Committee is distinctly advantageous. The submission of such questions to the courts would involve delays and technical obstacles which would impair discipline without securing any greater measure of substantial justice. While this Committee is not entirely in accord on this point, no member is yet prepared to advocate the incorporation of the Exchange, and a majority of us advise against it, upon the ground that the advantages to be gained by incorporation may be accomplished by rules of the Exchange and by statutes aimed directly at the evils which need correction.

" The Stock Exchange in the past, although frequently punishing infractions of its rules with great severity, has, in our opinion, at times failed to take proper measures to prevent wrongdoing. This has been probably due not only to a conservative unwillingness to interfere in the business of others, but also to a spirit of comradeship which is very marked among brokers, and frequently leads them to overlook misconduct on the part of fellow-members, although, at the same time, it is a matter of cynical gossip and comment in the street. The public has a right to expect something more than this from the Exchange and its members. This Committee, in refraining from advising the incorporation of the Exchange, does so in the expectation that the Exchange will in the future take full advantage of the powers conferred upon it by its voluntary organisation, and will be active in preventing wrongdoing such as has occurred in the past. Then we believe that there will be no serious criticism of the fact that it is not incorporated. If, however, wrongdoing recurs, and it should appear to the public at large that the Exchange has been derelict in exerting its powers and authority to prevent it, we believe that the public will insist upon the incorporation of the Exchange and its subjection to State authority and supervision."

These striking words might be predicated, almost verbatim, of any scheme to incorporate the London Stock Exchange. The general soundness of the principles enunciated is not affected by the intervention of the British Government in the affairs of the Stock Exchange in the period following the outbreak of the war of 1914. That was a colossal emergency, arising from circumstances over which the Stock Exchange had no control whatever. It had been partly caused by the courageous and energetic action of the Government itself, in dealing with a crisis of unprecedented magnitude. The Government intervened by means of the exercise of powers which are not, and could not be, possessed by the Committee of any private institution. But its intervention, in circumstances of appalling gravity, is quite a different thing from an attempt to stereotype, by means of legislation, a series of activities which depend for their utility and success upon unfailing adaptability to every change in the environment amid which they function. The possession of adaptability is vital to the Stock Exchange for the very nature of the things in which it deals. If it were to be deprived of that characteristic power, degeneracy and atrohpy would rapidly supervene.

UNFETTERED CONTRACT AND UNSHRINKING DISCIPLINE

If, for instance, the disciplinary powers were weakened, not only would the " society as at present constituted " be at an end, but no free market for choses in action and negotiable securities could continue. If there exist an assemblage of men dealing in negotiable documents of title to valuable commodities, there must be created and maintained a stringent personal responsibility on the part of the dealers, and a corporate authority able not only to control the modes of dealing, but also, up to a point, to exert a discreet supervision over the character of the commodities dealt in. Partial organisation cannot enforce discipline. The whole of the class must be within the compulsion of the enactment which it is proposed to apply. Unfettered contract necessitates unshrinking discipline, if it is not to degenerate into the chaos of optional repudiation. Stringent regulations keep down the sinister element which has been described as the crowd of minnows following every speculative Triton. This is the curse of a market like Paris. It is antagonistic to the maintenance of the maximum attainable degree of steadiness, for the crowd of irresponsible operators " adds to the oscillation of prices, just as loose ballast will add to the roll of a vessel."[1] In this principle lies the reason for the emphatic approval, by the Stock Exchange Commission of 1877, of the strict disciplinary powers of the Committee, and of the maintenance of the practice of members treating each other as principals in the matter of bargains made. " In the main, the existence of such an association and the coercive action of the rules which it enforces upon the transaction of business and upon the conduct of its members has been salutary to the interests

---

[1] Ellis, *Rationale of Market Fluctuations*, p. 113. Ellis was editor of the *Bankers' Magazine*, and for a short time City editor of *The Times*.

of the public."[1] In applying the principle to the suggestion of an open Stock Exchange the Committee did not see the facts quite so clearly. The main argument against the admission of the public to the " House " is not based upon the limited floor space, nor yet upon the desirability of " removing a certain amount of jealousy and suspicion " from the public mind.[2] It arises from the necessity of maintaining a high standard of discipline and responsibility among persons doing the business of the species which is carried on by the Stock Exchange. Large speculative commitments, on the part of such crowds of irresponsibles as would frequent an open Stock Market, would precipitate disaster upon the City in less than a week. " We are assured on all hands that a man who desires to speculate or gamble, and employs a broker to buy or sell for him, makes through his broker precisely the same bargain on

---

[1] Report of the Select Committee on the Stock Exchange, 1878: In reply to certain allegations by the Money Trust Committee the New York Stock Exchange said of the broker's responsibility: "How may be punished for reckless and unbusiness-like conduct, and even for errors of judgment. In all his transactions he has to conform to a standard which the law does not undertake to prescribe. Whether he violates these rules is determined, not by an outside layman, but by a select body of members of the Exchange, chosen to uphold just and fair dealing, who ascertain the facts with business-like directness, and who are empowered to expel, which is the ruin of a man's career as a broker, or to suspend, which is a deep humiliation." It was set forth that the rules of the Exchange require that all transactions on the floor and every contract to purchase or sell contemplate actual delivery, and trading in differences is not countenanced. The region beyond the present rules was described as " the region of the motives of men," and the remark was made : " How far regulation can extend in that region at all without obstructing legitimate business is one of the serious problems." These arguments are almost as equally applicable to the London Stock Exchange as to the New York institution.

It was added, by way of meeting other critical attacks upon the method and organisation of the New York Stock Exchange, that " there is no justification for the claim that its government is, or has been, blind, sordid, or unintelligent. The history of the Exchange, as a whole, is conclusive evidence to the contrary. It would not stand at the head of the exchanges of the world if those had been its characteristics. It is of the nature of things that there should have been sporadic evils, but an institution is not to be judged by its normal condition, and not by abnormal incidents. Due allowance is to be made, so far as the abnormal is concerned, for the patent difficulty of framing regulations that avoid, on the one hand, being too oppressive, and, on the other hand, defy evasion and circumvention, and the better course is to trust to measures being finally worked out to *prevent them from within, rather than to arbitrarily and impetuously impose them from without*."

[2] Commission Report, p. 9.

the market that the genuine investor does; and that he is as much bound to accept and pay for, or to deliver, the stock which he has bought or sold as the man who is dealing for investment or parting with securities which he wishes to sell."[1] But how long would that measure of responsibility be sustainable in an open Stock Market?[2] So it is that the strict supervision of the personalities engaged in the dealing leads inevitably to a standardisation of method, as well as to efforts in the direction of the establishment of a corresponding standardisation in the character of the securities dealt in. The dealing body will tend to become a definitely regulated association, doing business in a specified place and in accordance with strict rules.[3] In plain English, it will become a portion of a centralised machinery, performing an essential economic function. Inasmuch as it deals in choses in action and not in actual commodities for use or consumption, it will move towards a higher degree of centralisation and standardisation than a commodity market. Dealings in securities can be centralised in London long before the same degree of concentration by representative barter is applicable to mercantile transactions, where the transport of the goods is a factor of the problem.

THE FUNDAMENTAL PRINCIPLE OF ACTION

The fundamental and unfailing principle of the Committee's action, and " that to which most of its regulations are directed, is the inviolability of contracts."[4] On the

[1] Report, p. 20.
[2] For example, imagine an open Stock Exchange and the sale therein (whether as a " bear " or for actual delivery) of 1000 Chartered at (say) 1. Within the next few hours, sensational news sends the shares to $1\frac{1}{2}$, and the seller has lost £500. Would he not be most insidiously tempted to absent himself from the market, so as to avoid, if possible, the completion of his unlucky bargain?
[3] The " Curb Market " in New York is an open-air market where anybody may buy and sell securities not listed on any organised market. But few of the disciplinary measures available in the organised market can be invoked on the " curb."
[4] Hirst, *Stock Exchange*, p. 50. The Stock Exchange Commission of 1877 noted that " out of the millions of contracts made on the Stock Exchange such a thing is hardly known as a dispute as to the existence of a contract or its terms."

record plate, laid among the foundations of the Stock Exchange itself in 1801, there had been set forth the then amount of the funded debt (£522,730,924), with an allusion to the "inviolate faith of the British nation." That principle was destined to underlie every operation of the rising Money-Power. Its effort to impress the same rigidity of good faith upon all who seek the favour of the Money Market, and its sternness in the imposition of financial ostracism where there is a lapse, form the mainspring of all the services it renders to mankind. If it were once weakened or abandoned, the entire fabric of finance must come tottering to the ground, bringing civilisation —at all events in the form in which we are familiar with it— into simultaneous ruin.[1] The Chairman of the Stock Exchange told the Select Committee on Foreign Loans in 1875 that even if all contracts before allotment were rendered illegal by statutory enactment, the Committee would expel every member who refused, on the ground of illegality, to perform a contract of that character.[2] Thus the existence of the autocratic disciplinary power enables the Stock Exchange to maintain its policy and practice at a higher ethical level than that which, at a given period, is defined by current political opinion or by statute. Even so the international Money Power enforces a higher ethical code than any which could be imposed by merely political authority. The Stock Exchange would, for instance, decline to allow a plea of the Gaming Act[3] by one

---

[1] See *post*, p. 613, for a more detailed analysis of this most important function of international financial discipline.

[2] "It was suggested by some witnesses that the evils which your Committee have described would be met by legislation rendering illegal all contracts before allotment. But your Committee were distinctly told by the Chairman of the Stock Exchange Committee that if such a law were framed that Committee would expel a member who, having dealt in a loan before allotment, refused to fulfil his contract on the ground of its illegality. In all cases when a contract is made illegal for some reason which does not carry with it a moral taint, a legal debt is changed into a debt of honour, and thus the payment, instead of being prevented, is made more certain. (Report of Foreign Loans Committee.)

[3] 8 and 9 Vict. c. 109, s. 18. Stock Exchange transactions are not specifically mentioned, but in 1851 Grizewood *v.* Blane (11 C.B. 526) decided that gambling for differences is within the Statute. This Act is the Magna Charta of the swindling touts and cover snatchers. See *post*, p. 610.

THE STOCK EXCHANGE (1815-1915)

of its members. Mr. Scott, among certain reservations, added after the Report which was issued by this Select Committee, offered proof that " the internal legislation and administration of the Stock Exchange enforce a higher standard of morality than the law can reach." He cited a case in which a member, who was expelled on a charge of dishonourable conduct, had sued the Stock Exchange Committee, on the ground that their action was not legally justifiable. The trial, which lasted seven days, proved abortive, because the distinction between the ordinary law and the standard of morality enforced by the Committee could not be appreciated by the jury, although quite intelligible to the Judge.

INTERNAL COMPETITION REGULATED

There is now an official scale of commissions (dating from May 22, 1912) designed to oust cut-throat competition between one member and another.

SECTION III.

THE TYPES OF SECURITY

We saw, at an earlier stage (p. 142) that the Stock Exchange was a market for choses in action. It is concerned with choses in action of a very special type. The combination of interest-bearing power with the faculty of being handled like gold or cotton " makes a Stock Exchange article a thing *sui generis*." A cotton warrant is a barren thing. It bears no interest. A Stock Exchange security—at all events of the type which a banker would look at—is fertile ; and hence is a much more gratifying and sedative security than the unproductive species. It is a procreative chose in action. Now it is evident that choses in action, being *titles* to things as distinct from the *possession* of the things themselves, being memoranda of claims as distinct from actual *occupatio* of the thing claimed, will necessarily group themselves into classes, according to the strength of the respective claims and the prospect of ultimate reduction to possession, as judged by the person who is for the time being interested in them, as seller or potential buyer. The actual possession of a substantive object puts an end to the risk of not being able to obtain it. The possessor holds the object itself, and is, humanly speaking, assured of receiving its produce, whatever that may be. There will in such an instance be no grading of the security,[1] no differentiation in the safety of possession—that is to say, where we are speaking of an organised and civilised society. But it is otherwise with the chose in action. There will be degrees in the probability of the benefits conferred by the title being fully and uninterruptedly reducible to possession, or as to their exact character and amount when so reduced. The choses in action will therefore, in a highly organised market, be graded *qualitatively*. But for the achievement of their most complete efficiency in the process of capital re-distribution, there must be another gradation also. Stocks, bonds, shares, liens, mortgages, are all rights " carved out " of property, parcelled out in small fractions, and thus rendered capable of utilisation as productive stores of value, and as dealable entities, by a myriad holders. This is the *quantitative* classification of securities. The qualitative and quantitative classifications respectively require detailed analysis.

(a) *Standardisation of Quality*

For these choses in action, themselves requiring some intellectual subtlety for a clear comprehension of their nature, admit of a still more delicate distinction, according to their character as subjective or objective securities, and again according to their respective priorities *inter se*. They are subjective if the ultimate basis of the claim be a trust or a confidence reposed by the purchaser in the ability and willingness of the seller to fulfil a promise, although, if the fulfilment be refused, there may be no

---

[1] Other than such distinctions as those between occupatio, detentio, possessio, and dominium, which need not detain us here, since they do not touch the point of the distinction between a thing and the right to a thing.

effective recourse against the defaulter. This is the case of British Consols or United States bonds. All the security obtained by the buyer is the credit, arising from the traditional honesty of his debtors. If they decline to pay interest, or to reimburse the principal, he has no remedy whatever. There is no legal means of enforcing his claim. Nothing tangible is in his hands, or within his reach. No legal tribunal possesses a jurisdiction competent to assist him. The Stock Exchange alone, wielding a weapon peculiarly and inalienably its own, may aid him. But its method is of the negative rather than the positive type.[1] " Public loans are contracted by acts of a legislative nature, and when their terms are afterwards modified to the disadvantage of the bondholders this is done by other acts of a legislative nature which are not questionable by any proceeding in the country."[2] Money lent under such conditions is advanced " upon the faith of an engagement of honour because a Prince cannot be compelled like other men in an adverse way by a court of justice."[3]

[1] See section 6 for a full exposition of this *modus operandi*.

[2] Westlake, *Chapters on the Principles of International Law*, quoted in his *International Law*, Vol. I. p. 318.

[3] Hall, *International Law*, 6th edition, 1909, p. 431. This lack of effective remedy most frequently becomes prominent when there is a default, or a funding scheme, the result of genuine inability to pay, or worse still, when there is a brazen refusal, having its inspiration in downright dishonesty, to honour outstanding obligations, as in the prolonged default by Honduras. It may also arise during hostilities, when one of the belligerents is called upon to determine whether it will pay interest on so much of its debt as is demonstrably in the hands of enemy-holders. The practice of Great Britain, ever since there was any solid financial opinion, has been to pay (but not necessarily at the due date, if it coincide with the existence of hostilities) even to enemy-holders. Thus Mortimer, writing in 1785 :—

" Many of our fellow-subjects in America, as individuals, and many of the Revolted Provinces, as bodies corporate, have monies vested in our funds, and, though they openly revolted from their Sovereign and the Parent State, yet their capitals were as secure, and their interest as regularly paid, during the late fatal and dishonourable civil war against them, as if no such unhappy event had taken place. The Dutch likewise, though they violated the faith of treaties, and forced Great Britain into a war with them, found their immense property in our Funds perfectly secure, and were left at full liberty to withdraw it by sale at market, the same as any other of the public creditors. The confiscation of this property—money being the sinews of war—would, in other countries, have been considered as sound policy." (*Every Man His Own Broker*, p. 44.) By

So in the case of many investments (such, for instance, as railways) " the investor's security is not the property, but the earnings of the property." If there were a default on the debentures of one of the Heavies, the holders could not, with any resulting benefit to themselves, seize the line and hold it. In contrast with this state of affairs, the objective security is tangible. The buyer of the claim is endowed with recourse against a material entity. If he be the holder of a first mortgage debenture his trustees hold realisable property. They do not rely merely upon the good faith of the borrower. Yet in some cases this species of security approximates the subjective type.[1]

---

[1] OBJECTIVE AND SUBJECTIVE
The distinction is worth some emphasis. By " objective security " I mean security such that its existence is independent of any opinion that may be formed about it : by " subjective security " that whose acceptance and allocation in the scale of market estimation depend entirely on opinion, since its soundness is guaranteed by nothing that is tangible, nothing that can be made physically cognisable by the senses. The objective security is backed by an entity : the subjective rests upon confidence and belief. It might almost be permissible to say that the subjective is judged by a standard that is wholly within the mind, and the objective with the aid of criteria that are largely without the mind. Subjective value thus depends upon opinion as to present and future conditions. The physical security, palpable to the creditor's grasp, in the

way of contrast, we may note that in 1782 there was a threat by the King of France to make reprisals on the Dutch for an act of piracy by " stopping the interest on the money placed by the Dutch in the French Funds." (*Annual Register*, 1762, Chronicle 9, 67.) See also the case of Frederick the Great, quoted in Westlake, *infra*.

" A State contracting a loan is understood ' to contract that it will hold itself indebted to the lender, and will pay interest on the sum borrowed under all circumstances.' No attempt to the contrary of this implied undertaking has been made either in the case of war or in that of reprisals since Frederick the Great withheld the payment to British subjects of the interest on the Silesian loan by way of reprisal for the capture of Prussian vessels under rules of maritime law which he disputed. The affair was compromised, but that did not prevent an adverse opinion on Frederick's conduct from being so generally declared both at the time and since that it is universally taken to have settled the question. The reason commonly given is that the debts of a State are debts of honour, to which it may be added as cause, rather than as reason, that if the rule were otherwise States would have to contract their loans at much more onerous rates of interest." (Westlake, *International Law*, 2nd edition, 1913, Vol. II. p. 41.)

These enunciations do not, however, alter the fact that securities issued by a sovereign power are of the subjective order, since, as recent events (the German War of 1914) have shown, there is no tribunal capable of enforcing the principles of International Law if they should be disregarded.

THE STOCK EXCHANGE (1815–1915)

Half-way between the two classes comes the hypothecation of revenue to the service of a given loan, where there does indeed appear to be objective security. But in such instances, inasmuch as the attempted enforcement of the claim must generally take place before a judiciary and in tribunals controlled by the defaulter, the security is in effect subjective, though in appearance it belongs to the other species. Securities of the subjective type are likely to be benefited by the subtle force of public appreciation based on the fact that their possession confers a status (Giffen instances Bank Stock), or is fashionable among the

---

case of the objective type, does not (and generally cannot) enter into the estimate of the subjective species.

Maple's debentures are of the objective type, since they are defined and standardised claims to interest-payments arising from an entity—to wit, physically palpable assets and activities—actually owned by a corporation of which the holder is a creditor and existing in total independence of any opinions that may be formed about them. But Russian bonds are of the subjective type, because their security depends on the national credit—a purely psychological asset weighed within the observer's mind —of the Czar's Empire, and not upon any group of assets and activities that can be seen and held by bondholders possessing a proprietary right therein. The buyer buys on his *opinion* of Russian credit, not upon the strength of visible or tangible assets.

It may be said that here, as in the case of Maple's debentures, the ultimate reliance of the investor is upon Russia and her possessions as a going national concern. But this is not the case, because Maple's assets can be seized by its creditors and, in certain well-defined contingencies liquidated. But the Russian Empire, as a sovereign power, cannot be liquidated. If the Russian Government refused to pay the interest on its debt, or to reimburse the principal, the bondholders would be perfectly helpless in the legal sense. It is at this point that the Stock Exchange intervenes with a protective expedient open to no law court and available to no Government (*post*, p. 613). But the expedient is itself subjective, for it amounts to the setting of financial opinion against the borrower who has aroused resentment. Subjective weapons are employed against a subjective offence. No amount of adverse *opinion* can destroy the objectivity of Maple's assets (except the good-will, which is a subjective item); but the adverse opinion of the financial hierarchy could work havoc upon Russian credit. Shakespeare has shown us the distinction in terms at once felicitous and precise :

> " Who steals my purse steals trash ; 'tis something, nothing ;
> 'Twas mine, 'tis his, and has been slave to thousands ;
> But he that filches from me my good name,
> Robs me of that which not enriches him,
> And makes me poor indeed " (*Othello*, Act III. sc. 3).

That is to say, my purse is a tangible and transferable entity, independent of any opinion about it : but my credit is a non-transferable, intangible, impalpable, subjective asset. Objectivity is rooted in mere *per*ception : subjectivity in *con*ception and judgment.

people whose opinions colour financial sentiment.[1] The extension of the Trustee List, which is almost entirely composed of subjective securities, has done much to rectify the over-valuation of the limited number of stocks which it formerly contained. The former smallness of the list was a source of real mischief. Where a demand which is continuous and insistent remains concentrated upon a small group of securities, inflation is inevitable, however unchallengeable the intrinsic value of the stocks may be. But the important point is that the best securities in the world are all of the subjective type. In other words, the maximum substantiality of security coincides with the minimum objectivity of recourse. The supposedly natural law, which would lead us to associate gage with grip, a palpable pledge with a protected investment, is repealed by that infinitely more subtle psychologic principle, the law of mind, just as the biological process itself is being reversed as organised society becomes strong enough to deflect its movement.

THE PRINCIPLES OF GRADATION

The buyer of a security, then, buys a *claim* to benefits. Where the existing degree of probability is very high, or where it is, in fact, humanly speaking, a certainty that the benefits will be reducible to possession safely and regularly, their amount will be only slightly in excess of the reward of his patient waiting for their receipt. In Money Market terms, it will approximate to the lowest rate of interest—pure interest—at which, for the time being, money is procurable. There will only be the minimum charge for risk, in addition to the interest. This is the position of loan issues by the British Government or by the Dominion

---

[1] In our more critical age, with its inquisitive temperament and its impatience of traditional valuations, this factor will diminish in force. As long ago as 1899 it was possible for Giffen himself to say (*Economic Journal*, 1899, p. 360) that "the number of capitalists constituting the Consol market and able to engage in large business, had conspicuously diminished in the last twenty years, till now it is quite obvious that the market is insignificant, to a degree, compared with other markets on the Stock Exchange " . . . "the market is so small that there is no free dealing in them." Yet in Gilbart's time it was boasted that the market in Consols was so free as to permit easy dealings on Sunday.

THE STOCK EXCHANGE (1815-1915)

of Canada. They are securities which, paradoxical though it may seem to say so, are entirely of the subjective type. Their solidity is unimpeachable. The absence of a public response to the prospectus would not imply the presence of any really definable financial risk, but only that the rate of interest offered has not been made precisely coincident with that at which capital is available at the moment. The case is otherwise with such a chose in action as is represented by a share in a company formed to undertake some new and hitherto untried form of industrial enterprise. The quantum receivable by the purchaser is, in this instance, a claim which may possibly never materialise into the possession of any profits whatever. Such claim will, in any case, involve him in the exercise of considerable patience, restraint, and possible anxiety while the benefits are maturing. It will be necessary to tempt him with the prospect of larger ultimate benefits than would have sufficed to attract his capital into the British Government or the Dominion loan. He will expect interest and remuneration for the risk he runs. In special circumstances the temptation may have to take the form of an offer of cent. per cent. before he can be induced to allow his money to change its state from the passive to the active rôle. But he has an objective recourse against the assets of the company, such as they are, precisely as in the case of a higher type of objective security trustees for the debenture-holders have control of the property upon which the debentures are charged. These varying degrees of risk attaching to the respective choses in action are differentiated and standardised in the case of companies (in a manner analogous to the fine adjustment of a microscope) by the division of their issues into debentures of all priorities as well as into guaranteed, preference, ordinary, deferred and convertible[1] shares. The debenture-holder and the preference shareholder take the prior charge, while the ordinary shareholder assumes the ultimate risk

---

[1] A convertible stock or share is designed to give its holder (seldom the company) the option of exchange into a junior security, offering a higher yield, or saleable at a better price, if he choose to exercise it.

as a quasi-insurer of the fixed income of his financial seniors. The debenture-holder gets the larger proportion of " interest " in his income, while the shareholder's return is mainly of the " profit " type—unless, indeed, we accept Savigny's view that the ordinary share stands for a part of ownership, and produces true *dividends*, while the senior securities receive what is strictly *interest*, and not dividends. Anyhow, in addition to these prior stocks there has lately been created another class of differentiation, viz. that existing between the two halves of a split bank share, one half being fully paid and the other half carrying the reserve liability. Thus every type of temperament— all the way from the most timid and conservative to the most sanguine and adventurous—is catered for in these graded risks. This is essentially a modern scheme of adjustment. The psychological adaptation is a process of the utmost nicety, practised upon one of the most nervous and whimsical of creatures. Few people, outside the ranks of those who closely study the investor, know how wayward and capricious he (and nowadays she also) can sometimes be. The late J. W. Birch (who was Governor of the Bank in 1880–1881), once told Sir Inglis Palgrave that a security on which the interest included a half per cent. (such as a $2\frac{1}{2}$ per cent. or a $3\frac{1}{2}$ per cent. stock) never enjoyed the same standing as one yielding a rate expressed in integers, such, for instance, as a 3 or 4 per cent. security.[1] Yet upon the successful interpretation of the investor's " fancy " for the time being depends in no small degree the adequacy of the supplies of capital to the needs of society. A market which was restricted to gilt-edged and mainly subjective securities, or another which knew nothing save the deferred shares of industrial companies, would each of them fail to tap more than a small proportion of the contemporaneously available capital supplies of the community. Adapt to the temperament of the purchaser the risk (if any) attachable to each chose in action that is offered, and capital is concurrently attracted to each class at the lowest rate. That is to say, the driving

[1] *Bankers' Magazine*, 1907, Vol. II. p. 451.

THE STOCK EXCHANGE (1815–1915) 559

power of enterprise is supplied at the lowest possible price per unit. The cheaper the capital supply, the larger the social dividend available upon it.

(b) *Standardisation of Quantity*

Thus far of the *qualitative* classification. We turn to the quantitative definition of stock-market commodities. The buyer must know both the extent (quantity) and the relative priority (quality) of the claim which he purchases. The essential characteristic of a Stock Exchange security is a " combination of interest-bearing power, either actual, probable, or only potential and contingent, with the division of the article into equal [interchangeable] parts, so as to be capable of exact definition and of being submitted to the speculative manipulation of a great market."[1] The original fixation of a par value is a convenience ; but since the market price will adjust itself to the actual return in dividends or privileges, as well as to the prospects, its existence is by no means essential. Many American companies have shares of no par value. The London market has experience of penny and even farthing shares, where the purpose of issue was definition of interests, and not the raising of capital. The reason is obvious. A corporation has been described by Professor Irving Fisher as " simply a dummy set up to hold wealth owned in fractions, a sort of clearing house for the entry of the debts and credits of real persons."[2] As long as the "fractions" are mathematically correct, relatively uniform, and adequately and validly cognoscible, their absolute magnitude is a secondary consideration. The aggregation of the " fractions," however, becomes in time a matter of importance. Any extension of dealings in securities must have brought an appreciation of the necessity of cutting them up into blocks of some standard size. If registered shares, only transferable with formality, are an obstacle to rapid dealing, the objection applies with almost equal force to bearer securities which are in blocks of varying

[1] Giffen, *Stock Exchange Securities*, p. 3.
[2] *Economic Journal*, 1897, p. 207.

magnitude, here ten shares and there a hundred, here sixteen and there seventy-nine. They must be standardised; and the standardisation leads inevitably to the bearer bond, issued in denominations of £20, £100 (" stock "), £500, and £1000, to suit the financial ambition and capacity of its various classes of purchaser. This quantitative standardisation is certainly visible early in the seventeenth century. In 1622–1624 there was founded, in the Republic of Siena, the Monte dei Paschi non Vacabile, a bank empowered to grant loans at a reasonable rate for the rehabilitation of Sienese industry and agriculture after the wars of the sixteenth century. Certain Grand Ducal dues, valued at 10,000 scudi per annum, were hypothecated as security for a nominal capital of 200,000 scudi, divided into 2000 luoghi or five per cent. bonds of a standardised denomination of 100 scudi each. How far the movement towards a wide range of marketability had already gone, even in the seventeenth century, we can judge from the observations of a Jewish writer[1] who contrasts the facility of the bearer bond with the sluggishness of the merely transferable security. " It is true," says he,

" that Rabbenu Asher and his school expressed no view concerning Shetarot (instruments) of all kinds, which the Rabbis introduced in order to extend commerce. That is because dealings in such instruments were not very common, owing to the difficulty of transfer. But the authorities were thinking only of personal bonds. In the case of *bearer bonds*, the circulation of which at the present time is greater far than that of commodities, all ordinances laid down by the Rabbis for the extension of commerce are to be observed."

An Austrian loan of 1761 is the first instance of a bond to bearer with coupons attached[2]—another factor of

---

[1] R. Sabbatai Cohen, quoted by Sombart (*Jews and Modern Capitalism*, p. 78).

[2] The earlier and more extended vogue of the bearer security on the Continent, as compared with the registered or inscribed stock in England, has been simply a necessary consequence of the unstable political conditions. These, and the unceasing continental wars, for a long time placed a premium on the impersonal obligation, as being capable of more rapid, secret, and effective transport from holder to holder. Employed in this way the bearer bond is a self-protective expedient of the same

international credit currency added to the bill of exchange. The bill of exchange itself, indeed, is only a short-dated negotiable security — in effect, say, a 4 per cent. bond (presumably secured by commodities) maturing in 3 months from date of issue. The bearer bond (itself the product of the principle of negotiability[1]) or, in the alternative, the rapid and facile transfer[2] of the chose in action, is essential to a wide and free market and to the attraction of small capitalists thither. In this quantitative standardisation, moreover, lies the extraordinary adaptability of the bearer security to employment in speculation, and as an international currency.

Very significant is the fact that when the standardised denomination has been too high for the clientele or market, there have been dealings in actual " fractions " in order to accommodate those who could not afford the integer. The majority of the early English railway securities were in share denominations ranging from £20 to £100 per

[1] For the principle of negotiability, see *ante*, p. 19.
[2] *Ante*, p. 177.

---

type as the protective coloration of insects and animals in order to preserve them by rendering them inconspicuous. Some insects, for instance, are coloured green, like a leaf, while the grasshopper is green-brown, in order to harmonise with the ground upon which he sits. There is a moth (Xylina Vetusta) which has by ages of modification come to look just like a broken piece of wood, so that not one person in a thousand would notice it. The Alpine hare becomes white among the snow and the swallow migrates as the winter storms begin to approach. Examples like these might be multiplied in myriads if the topic were pursued. The effort is simply to preserve the creature from being hunted down and destroyed by its enemies, and this is one of the main objects for which the bearer security was originally utilised. The negotiable security in a cosmopolitan money market enables capital to escape from a point which it regards as one of danger to another where the menace is non-existent, or at all events, is less severe. The bearer bond or share-certificate might almost be described as the offspring of a " sport " or " saltatory variation," important enough in its original protective purpose, but developing, in consequence of a variation in the organism itself, into a far greater prominence as regards the cosmopolitan currency of finance. Darwin quotes, with approval (*Origin of Species*, p. 23), the observation of Youatt, a well-known agriculturist, who spoke of the principle of Selection as " that which enables the agriculturist not only to modify the character of his flock, but to change it altogether." The breeder fosters and endeavours to perpetuate the serviceable " sport " ; and finance does the same. That negotiable securities *are* currency is shown by the fact that they are completely within Spencer's description of bank-notes, cheques, and bills of exchange as " memoranda of claims."

share. To meet the needs of small investors, these were in the days of the railway boom divided into halves, quarters, fifths, and eighths. In the case of the Manchester and Leeds, the £100 shares were divided even down to a sixteenth of a share (£6 5s.). In the twentieth century the £20 bearer bond and the 2s. rubber share are among the ordinary phenomena of a democratic market :—

". . . there is no longer a plutocracy, but a veritable financial democracy. When these thousands of millions of certificates are minutely segregated, there are only found atoms of certificates of stocks and bonds, and atoms of income —so great is the number of capitalists and independent individuals who divide these securities and these incomes among themselves."[1]

So it is that, by a kind of economic paradox, the species of security originally elaborated by professional capitalists to facilitate their own operations among themselves has set in motion the mighty current of democratisation in finance, abolished the " Court Jew," compelled the borrower to appeal more and more to a popular clientele, and bulwarked the honest modern State with inexhaustible stores of credit. The internationalisation of the negotiable (and to a less extent of the assignable) security brings us to that state of affairs which, in the early nineteenth century, was regarded as a kind of economic portent, when " every holder of Government stock can receive his dividends at various places at his convenience without difficulty. The Rothschilds in Frankfort pay interest for many Governments ; the Paris House pay the dividends on the Austria Metalliques, the Neapolitan Rentes, and the Anglo-Neapolitan Loan, either in London, Naples, or Paris."

WANTED, AN INTERNATIONAL CODE

Inevitably there follows the aspiration for an authoritative international code applicable to all internationally negotiable securities. Mr. H. D. Jencken, hon. secretary

[1] M. Alfred Neymarck, at the International Congress of Securities, 1900, quoted by Van Antwerp, *Stock Exchange from Within*, p. 412.

THE STOCK EXCHANGE (1815–1915)

of the Association for the Reform and Codification of the Law of Nations, addressing the Institute of Bankers as long ago as 1880, said :—

" Of the importance of the question of establishing international rules regulating the rights and liabilities of the holders of negotiable securities, no doubt can be entertained. These negotiable instruments are the carriers of the accumulated capital of civilised races ; the enormous total they represent is divided among men of every grade, of every class of social life ; by the millionaire bankers, the artizan or the peasants, wherever we travel we find these securities treasured up as the ultimate resources of families, the reserve to fall back upon in the hour of need. Proportionately, as international intercourse and commerce increase, the need becomes more urgent, that these securities should be based upon a uniform system of law and practice, universally recognised in Europe, and in the transoceanic continents inhabited by Europeans."

If mediæval intellects could evolve and apply the Law Merchant (*ante*, p. 28), why should we hesitate at international financial regulation, enacted and enforced by a cosmopolitan Money Power ? In that direction Money Market ambition ever more vehemently turns. Mr. Zangwill was right when he said that " in the security necessary for international investments lies the prime hope of the world's peace. . . . The Jews, the original missionary people, in whom all the families of the earth were to be blest, have made the millennium possible by the creation of the Bourse."

SOME IDEALS OF STANDARDISATION

If the standardised security could be made to represent an unwavering measure of value across the period that divides its creation from its maturity, then indeed we should have a new economic implement, of utterly immeasurable utility to the world. But although coin itself is standardised as to its fineness by the elimination of the obsolete and disreputable expedient of debasing, we are not yet able to standardise its purchasing power across the gulf of the years.[1] Till we can achieve so much, the standardised and unwavering commodity value of the security at (a) issue and (b) maturity respectively (but not in the intervening period, of course) is reserved for the finance of the future. The lender must continue to advance the money or credit equivalent of a given quantity of commodities, and to take the risk of receiving, at the maturity of the loan, a money repayment which may be considerably less in commodity value. In 1873 Mr. Anderson moved for a commission to inquire whether the Bank Charter Act " might not be so remodelled as to fix the Bank rate of interest without regard to the inevitable and incessant variations in the value of money " ; but nothing came of so quixotic a proposal. Its adoption, if we can conceive it as possible, must mean rigidity ; and that is the one quality which a money market does not want, and could not possess without the serious deterioration not only of its power of self-adaptation to circumstances of kaleidoscopic mutability, but of its sensitiveness as the clinical thermometer of the world. In fact, the more absolute the safety of the security, the more sensitive is the price likely to be, since there is the minimum chance

[1] Professor Irving Fisher, of Yale University, has suggested that this can be done by means (in the U.S.A.) of a compensated dollar. Professor Fisher's proposal is the creation of what he calls a ".virtual gold dollar," represented by paper certificates transformable into a varying (not a fixed) *quantum* of the gold bullion in which each dollar of the certificate will be redeemed at the request of the holder. At present the American Treasury pays out 25·8 grains of gold nine-tenths fine per dollar. That figure will represent, at a given moment, a certain amount of purchasable commodities. Professor Fisher desires that the relationship between the gold dollar and the commodities which it will purchase should first be standardised by means of an official Index Number of prices. That will make a starting-point. The Professor then proposes that, month by month, a new redemption figure should be substituted for the original 25·8 grains, so that the *quantum* of gold bullion represented by each dollar in the gold certificates would always buy the same amount of commodities. It follows that any depreciation in the value of gold, with a consequent rise in commodity prices, would be compensated for by the creation of a heavier " virtual gold dollar." Conversely, if gold appreciated, and the prices consequently fell, the " virtual gold dollar " would be made lighter. Professor Fisher contends that if this were done the purchasing power of the dollar would remain practically unchanged from year to year. The general adoption of the scheme throughout the world would, its author argues, abolish much, if not all, of the economic disturbance resulting from fluctuations in the value of gold.

of any such oscillation in the measure of safety or the yield as might provide automatic compensation for the variations created by the incessant changes in the value of money-credit. There have been suggestions for neutralising these fluctuations by the standardisation of the rate of interest on such types of security. It is quite true that the standard type of the British Funds for many years was a $2\frac{1}{2}$ per cent. issue. But it is equally certain that the British Government could not now (1915) issue a $2\frac{1}{2}$ per cent. security save at a discount which would bring the price to a very humiliating level. When the $2\frac{1}{2}$ per cent. type was conspicuous there arose an idea that the Dominion issues might be standardised on a $2\frac{1}{2}$ per cent. basis. Since then we have had an era of dear money, which would have brought the quotation of these $2\frac{1}{2}$ per cent. stocks, had they existed, down to about 65, if not to 60, with the result of giving an altogether false appearance of deterioration to Dominion credit.[1]

[1] Standardisation has, however, been applied in many other directions. As early as 1841 there was established at Liverpool the Cotton Brokers' Association (whose formation marked the advent of a specialised *commercial* mechanism modelled on the London Stock Exchange), designed to organise, regulate and standardise wholesale dealings. The new method was destined to carry regulation and standardisation into fields—e.g. the wool business—where it might well have been deemed, a few years earlier, to be impossible of application. The result is that transactions in commodities standardised as regards their quality take place with the same celerity as those in stocks and shares standardised as regards the quantity of capital and the respective seniority and species of claim represented by each unit. In banking certain standardised forms (that is to say, application forms, allotment letters, call letters, offers of new shares and so forth) were drafted by a committee appointed by the Institute of Bankers, and accompanied a report on the subject adopted by the Council of the Institute on June 24, 1912. But the greatest need of all, perhaps, is the standardised balance sheet which would enable effective comparisons to be made of the respective positions of the various banks. "No reform is more desirable than a uniform balance-sheet, drawn up on identical lines for all banks—and this I should like to see arrived at by common agreement amongst the banks." (J. Spencer Phillips, Chairman of Lloyds Bank, at annual meeting, February 5, 1909). The schedule to the Government Banking Bill of 1879 in fact contained a model balance sheet (reproduced in the *Bankers' Magazine*, 1879, p. 457).

Section IV
STANDARDISATION OF PRICE

Standardisation of quality and quantity lead us inevitably to standardisation of price, at a given moment. We turn to Stock Exchange quotations—a phenomenon of extraordinary economic significance, whose very familiarity blinds us to its real character as a stupendous advance in the humanities. "The Stock Exchange has come into existence because of a demand for trade facilities that will adjust differences of opinion in reference to future values of corporation securities and give the purchaser some idea of values."[1] The idea is conveyed by means of price, for price is really a special case of value. It is, with us, value expressed in terms of gold. If all our economic ideals could be realised, price and value would invariably coincide. That they frequently fail to equalise is a consequence of:—

(1) The buyer's or seller's urgent necessity;
(2) Imperfect information as to the conditions which should determine value; or
(3) The absence of effective machinery for facilitating the process of exchange.

In its efforts to provide what Mr. Van Antwerp calls "a perfectly-constructed price-making machinery that will enable people to invest their savings or sell their holdings," the Stock Exchange does not entirely exclude these factors of disturbance. Where a market is "all one way" (especially if some sudden craze sends quotations up, or a panic thrusts them down) the price may easily cease to be a reflex of the value. There may be a huge difference in the degrees of information possessed by the two parties to a bargain. One may be a specialist observer, with unique sources of knowledge: the other the man in the "street." But even if so much be admitted, the fact remains that in a quasi-public market, where current prices at a given moment are notorious in their

[1] McVey, *Modern Industrialism*.

THE STOCK EXCHANGE (1815-1915)

wide dissemination, the factors of unfairness, to say nothing of victimisation, are reduced to the minimum that is attainable in an environment where many of the commodities are themselves of a highly speculative nature. The Stock Exchanges of the world come very near (and it is their constant effort to attain still closer proximity) to the ideal. The dealings in international securities, in fact, constitute the finest existing instance of a nearly perfect market, and will in no short time, if the existing processes go on, approximate still more nearly to it.

INTERNATIONAL SECURITIES—ARBITRAGE

The international security has its vogue in a group of markets that are practically one, physical separation notwithstanding. The same bill, or the same bond, may be the means of adjusting a payment in many different sections of this market. In the case of a cosmopolitan bond or share, the sale in one market centre takes place all but simultaneously with the purchase in another: and the telegraph announces the exact result to both parties:—

"The existence of a mass of Stock Exchange securities which are the object of extended dealings among capitalists in every great city . . . constitutes a new sort of money available for international use, facilitating all kinds of transactions between different countries, and economising a vast quantity of unproductive metal, for holding which the banking and trading community would otherwise have to pay."[1]

By means of arbitrage, the prices of securities are maintained at nearly a common level in all the markets of the world[2]—which really means that these widely-separated

[1] Quoted in Ellis, *Rationale of Market Fluctuations*, 27.
[2] A., in New York, sells the security X by cable in London, at the same time buying it in New York. The London purchase price of X is now, in effect, a remittance to New York, saleable as such to a person who, in buying it, provides A. with the money to pay for his New York purchase. Prompt and accurate knowledge of the slight shade of variation between the prices of X. in New York and London respectively, will enable A. to carry out this arbitrage transaction with considerable advantage to himself, while at the same time he renders valuable services to the money market at large. Subsequent skilful dealing will probably enable these transactions to be adjusted without the necessity of sending the securities across the Atlantic.

568 EVOLUTION OF THE MONEY MARKET

markets are in fact one, and not several. Arbitrage may be called *place*-speculation, in contrast with the ordinary type of *time*-speculation. Where the factors are fully known, there is no risk. Arbitrage ceases to be speculation and becomes trade. The weak point in arbitrage is the question of transporting the subject-matter of the bargain, if the necessity should arise. The cable is instantaneous, but the mail-steamer is not. Giffen thinks that the very fact of their being used for arbitrage purposes tends to increase the public estimation of these international stocks.[1]

THE CRUCIBLE WHENCE PRICES EMERGE

In all real stock markets, be they international or merely local, prices at a given moment are now practically standardised.[2] They are no longer formed " by the higgling of two or more traders talking over their transactions, but rather by a mechanical process, representing the average of a thousand and one units."[3] The buyer or seller can ascertain, from the records of the tape or the " Official List," or the " Business Done," what was the actual quotation at any hour of the business day. No advantage can possibly be taken of his ignorance, or his necessities. If, in fact, some unscrupulous broker should attempt so perilous an enterprise, the obligation to give the name of the jobber, and to be answerable to the Committee, affords ample and ready remedy. That ideal of the trade unions, a recognised quotable standard price for

---

[1] *Stock Exchange Securities*, p. 94.

[2] The various more or less intimate alliances of farmers and agriculturists, rural co-operative movements, and similar organisations are in effect efforts to regulate markets and obtain something like a standard price for the eggs, cheese, butter, and potatoes. The modern consumer is well aware that, without any formal agreement, his local tradesmen maintain a general level of prices, so that all the greengrocers, for instance, will quote a given quality of asparagus at the same price on the same day. This is a movement towards the standardisation which characterises the Stock Exchanges of the world. Far different are the conditions where the farmer, remote from complete knowledge of the position of the butter trade, parts with his produce to a middleman at an utterly unfair price, or where the fisherman, faced with the possibility of the rapid deterioration of his catch, is compelled to let it go at a figure which affords him no adequate remuneration for his labour and peril.

[3] Sombart, *Jews and Modern Capitalism*, 83.

THE STOCK EXCHANGE (1815–1915)

labour, is but an adaptation of Stock Exchange method. "Every transaction," says Mr. J. E. Milburn,[1] "is recorded, and the quotations that go out are the result of all these manifold operations. They are the product of the judgments, temperaments, hopes, fears, and doubts of the vast multitude that participate in them:—

"It is a scene of competition; the conservatism of investment face to face with the enterprise of speculation; speculation in the expectation of a rise in prices, with speculation in the expectation of a fall; optimism with pessimism; and the resultant of this play of forces is the market price of the securities dealt in moment by moment, hour by hour. The Exchange is the crucible in which all these various elements are, as it were, chemically combined and concentrated to produce what we call market values. All these elements are indispensable as supplements and correctives of each other. Eliminate speculation and the conservatism of investment would arrest the development of the country. Eliminate speculation in the expectation of a fall in prices and the danger of inflation of prices would be constant. Without the free interplay of all these forces a market would not perform its function of fixing values for the purposes of trade and commerce. To say that the swift, ceaseless stream of transactions in such a market as the Exchange is, or can be, polluted in its main body is to our minds absurd."

HOW PRICES ARE FIXED

The steady and unrelenting contest between the judgment of the bull and the bear is essential to a sane and accurate level of prices. "No other means," said the Hughes Committee, "of restraining unwarranted marking up and down of prices has been suggested to us."[2] Thus, the self-interest of the buyers and sellers makes the price. It can be made in no other way, and the process yields the truest approximation to accuracy and adequacy that the wit of man can devise. The market price at a particular moment will tend to be fixed at the point on a scale of

---

[1] Official Apologia for New York Stock Exchange, April, 1914.
[2] Quoted by Huebner, *Scope and Functions of the Stock Market*, American Academy, Vol. XXXV. p. 16.

quotations at which the most urgent (or marginal) seller meets the most indifferent (or marginal) buyer, or conversely, where the most urgent buyer meets the most indifferent seller, according to the relations of supply and demand in the market.[1] The jobbers, watching all the multitudinous factors, read the collective scale in the light of their specialised knowledge as accurately as they can, and announce the result to the broker who desires to do a bargain in the given security. "The Exchanges," said Judge Grosscup, of the United States Circuit Court, "balance like the governor of an engine the otherwise erratic course of prices. They focus intelligence from all lands, and the prospects for the whole year, by bringing together minds trained to weigh such intelligence and to forecast the prospects. They tend to steady the markets more nearly to their right level than if left to chance or unhindered manipulation."[2] As for the jobber, the "conduit-pipe" of the market, his "turn" should in theory represent the minimum profit which is necessary to induce him to accept the labour and risk of a market intermediary. He is the bridge from the time at which sales outweigh purchases, to the time at which purchases exceed sales: and vice versa. He either possesses, knows where to purchase, or how to borrow, a stock of the articles "known" to that section of the market in which he specialises. Thus he watches, with the eye of a lynx, all the influences which may augment, or cause to deteriorate, the value, or the price, of the stocks in which he specialises. He is the "nucleus of a perpetual fair."[3] But since the human intellect, even at its best, is incapable of adequate knowledge of all the multitudinous influences which affect the myriads of quoted securities, the jobber specialises in a selected group. He knows all that is to be known about their capital, dividends, prospects, and perils; he is acquainted with the state of the market in them—whether it is oversold or not, and whether the holdings of a big

---

[1] Mavor, *Applied Economics*, p. 129.
[2] Chicago Board of Trade Case, May 8, 1905.
[3] Palgrave, *Dictionary of Political Economy*, Art. Dealer.

"deceased account" are awaiting an opportunity of realisation. His fullness of information is reflected in the price which he is willing to " make." His information and judgment are employed, like the sword of a mediæval soldier, as all that he can interpose between himself and fatality. They are added to the common stock of knowledge, illuminating the field of supply and demand : and every potential buyer or seller has " an equal and fair opportunity to profit by the resultant effect on the market of all these various agencies." Changes in the earning power, or in the prospects, of enterprises, or in the political or economic aspect of their surroundings, are incessantly reflected, sometimes sooner, sometimes later, by adjustments in the quotations of their securities. Wealth being a flow, and not a fund, the quotation of a security is the price of the right to the flow, calculated with reference to the prospect of its unbroken maintenance (in the case of a municipal bond), its possible increase in volume (as in the instance of an industrial ordinary share with good prospects), or sudden cessation at any moment (as in the case of a mining share). Low prices in all the shares of companies engaged in a given industry will keep capital out of it. High prices (the factor of manipulation and inflation excluded) will have the reverse effect. Attraction will go on to a point where the sensitiveness of the market indicates that up to the limit of reasonable prudence, as fixed by market shrewdness, the industry is adequately financed. Too high a price diverts a stream of capital which might otherwise flow into a particular stock, and even leads to realisations for investment elsewhere.

These incessant, close, and accurate professional calculations of the value of securities, based upon the consideration of their earning capacity and upon profound analysis of their political and social surroundings—the strength of the foes of that particular class of enterprise, the resources available for the consolidation of its position, and so forth —are modern additions to the Stock Exchange armoury. They were scarcely wielded at all in the early days of wild and illogical speculation, based more upon craze than prudence, and more upon price than value. But their utility, as a reinforcement of the banker's interest in ready liquidity and in stable and commensurate values, stands in need of no emphasis. Without an organised and regulated market the holder of stocks must be naked to every blast of rumour :—

"Suppose for a moment that the stock markets of the world were closed, that it was no longer possible to learn what railways were paying dividends, what their stocks were worth, how industrial enterprises were faring—whether they were loaded up with surplus goods or had orders ahead. Suppose that the information afforded by public quotations on the stock and produce exchanges were wiped from the slate of human knowledge. How would the average man, how even would a man with the intelligence and foresight of a Pierpont Morgan, determine how new capital should be invested ? He would have no guides except the most isolated facts gathered here and there at great trouble and expense. A greater misdirection of capital and energy would result than has been possible since the organisation of modern economic machinery."[1]

In conditions such as these the holder would not have the means of appraising the accuracy, or the significance, of what he heard. He might be tempted to let his holdings go at any price which a " smart " buyer offered. As it is, the price-movements are largely, and ever more largely, guided by reason, knowledge, and experience, They only rarely come under the influence of unreason or panic. So it is that price determinations and quotations represent, in Riesser's words, " the fullest and truest possible reflex of existing supply and demand, as well as ' other economic factors which nowhere else are subject to such comprehensive perception and accurate measurement.' "[2] The accuracy of the reflex has not been impaired in Great Britain as in Germany, by the intrusion of the bank upon the domain of the Bourse. Here the two functions are kept dis-

[1] Conant, *Wall Street and the Country*, pp. 92–93.
[2] Riesser, *German Great Banks*, p. 772.

THE STOCK EXCHANGE (1815–1915)

tinct, with a resulting enhancement of the sensitiveness and efficiency of both.

THE LIMELIGHT OF PUBLICITY

A market of this type is the observed of all observers. Its business is not and cannot be done in a corner, to suit the convenience and the interests of a clique. Syndicates, cliques, and pools there are, of course. But at one time the market was wholly dominated by them.[1] When securities were lodged in comparatively few hands the rich men who owned them could look after themselves and protect their own interests. The Stock Exchange was of little use to them, save as an arena for creating a market for their holdings. This led to manipulation and flagrantly artificial markets. But to-day there is (the quoted writer is speaking of New York, but his words have a universal application) such a wide distribution of securities that

" holders look to the Exchange to protect their interests by eliminating artificial influences and by the establishment, in their place, of natural and stable markets, free from crookedness. This the Exchange has sought to do, as never before, by a rigid supervision of applications for listing and by preventing all forms of manipulation and other artificial devices. The result is that the New York market to-day is a real market, in which natural forces find freer expression than they have ever found before in America. That this is healthy progress, in line with New York's increasing prudence and conservatism, is obvious; and that it is a necessary outgrowth of the public demand is demonstrated by the fact that where there were 300,000 holders of securities three decades ago, there are now 2,000,000."[2]

Herein lies the reason why the internal discipline of the Stock Exchange, rather than the external dictates of the Legislature, must be relied upon to exclude undesirable factors and methods.

---

[1] See, for instance, as to the railway fever, p. 356 ff., and as to Foreign Bond Scandals, p. 620 ff.

[2] W. C. Van Antwerp, *Financial News*, February, 1914.

Section V

(a) THE COGNOSCIBILITY AND LIQUIDITY OF SECURITIES AS CREDIT INSTRUMENTS

Credit, not coined money, is the basis of finance. As Lord Farrer says that credit, in comparison with gold, is a " substitute not only of infinitely greater power than the instrument which it displaces, but of infinitely greater expansibility," how distinct must be the public utility of that influence which is rapidly transforming the bulk of the social possessions into the available implements of credit-creation ! It follows that the larger the proportion of the world's wealth that is available for employment in the creation of sound credit facilities, the more ample and more readily available must be the supply of that peremptory need. The present Lord Goschen has said that the capital available for investment is " all the wealth of the world devoted to reproductive purposes, to the creation of more wealth." But the prime necessity of credit-material is liquidity. It is hardly too much to say that our whole system of credit rests upon the negotiability and liquidity of Stock Exchange securities. Bankers would not lend at normal rates if there were no market in the background. A well-margined loan of £100,000, against a security which can be realised at an hour's notice, can be made at a much lower rate than that which must be charged if the facility of realisation were not there. As between a freehold property, admittedly worth £10,000, and a parcel of Grand Trunk bonds, quoted in the *Official List* at prices aggregating £10,000, no banker will hesitate a moment if it be a question of holding one or other as the security for an advance. The Trunk bonds can be liquidated in ten minutes ; the land cannot be transformed in ten days. " The best collateral," remarks Mr. Babson,[1] " is that listed on some large stock exchange, because it can be more readily quoted there than in the private market ; and, to be satisfactory, collateral must not only

---
[1] *Commercial Paper*, p. 19.

THE STOCK EXCHANGE (1815–1915)

be listed, but quoted, and quoted regularly through bona fide sales and purchases, at least several a day." The reason is that the stocks of a given undertaking will be the more sought after as investments and the more valuable as credit instruments if they form part of a large issue, well known to the market. A higher level of quotations is attainable when the stock can be widely held, and when dealers are not afraid of it, than when its limited quantity creates the dread of a " corner." The wider the market, the more certain is the advent of selling as prices rise and of buying as quotations fall—or, in other words, the more incessant is the tendency towards an equilibrium unattainable save by the working of a market mechanism. Therefore the stocks of a first-class undertaking capitalised at £2,000,000 are in a more advantageous market position than those of a modest enterprise with a capital of £100,000, even though the latter's dividend-earning capacity is no whit inferior to that of its far more ambitious rival. Stocks, of which only a limited quantity exists, will respond more quickly and extensively to manipulation, and that is not a quality which recommends them to investors, much less to bankers.

The Stock Exchange, as Bagehot declares,[1] " is the simplest of markets. There is no question in it of the physical quality of commodities : one Turkish bond of 1858 is as good or bad as another : one ordinary share in a railway exactly the same as any other ordinary share : but in other markets, each sample differs in quality, and it is a learning in each market to judge of qualities, so many are they and so fine their gradations." Securities of the type of Grand Trunk bonds are (like a sovereign) cognoscible at sight, pass their full title by mere manual delivery, and can be liquidated at a price which can be estimated within the limits of a fraction. Therein lies their inestimable superiority as credit instruments over documents of title to land. There is no organised market in mortgages. If there were, there must of necessity be a glaring contrast between its inevitable and prolonged delays

[1] *Economic Studies*, p. 11.

and the potentiality of sale for cash down, which is one of the characteristics (in normal times) of the majority, at all events, of Stock Exchange securities. The land will have to be examined by the intending buyer, and surveyed on his behalf. The title will have to be perused, requisitions will probably be made upon it, other documents of title may have to be produced to elucidate critical legal problems, the increment " duty " and other claims will have to be satisfied, and a hundred obstacles overcome. The Trunk bonds, like the whole class of securities which they represent, are (of course within the limits of their value, seniority, and other allied considerations) a model basis for a credit operation. The land is an imperfect and unsatisfactory implement when applied to the attainment of a similar end—though in our day, thanks to the joint-stock company, even the ownership of land can be mobilised by means of negotiable securities.

MOBILISATION OF THE ASSETS OF CIVILISATION

The process is, in fact, going on in a thousand different directions. Every conversion of a commercial undertaking from the private to the joint-stock form operates to render its assets much more susceptible of employment as the basis of credit. Some of the assets, such as goodwill, may be of the subjective type, merely psychological. Goodwill may be only a presumption that the old customers will resort to the old shop. Yet where it exists and has a solid basis, it may take its place among the assets of the company, form part of the " backing " of the shares, and in that way become a banker's security and the seed of additional wealth. Even the *organisation* of a group has a capital value : even the personal reputation of some great entrepreneur can be made the basis of large credit operations. The shares of the joint-stock enterprise (of course assuming them to be acceptable to the banker) can be employed as sole or collateral security, practically at a moment's notice, where an endless tangle of legal complications would have had to be unravelled before similar facilities could be obtained by means of the aggregate of disjointed assets owned by a private partnership. The Money Market, by the operation of the principles of assignability and negotiability, is rapidly turning every social asset into a new reproductive centre. Every atom of the social possessions is endowed with fecundity, and swells the forces which subdue man's environment to his service. Reserve financial power, once in the form of flocks and then in the shape of goods, is now in the form of claims. An emergency is met by the sale of claims—or by a loan upon them—and not, as of yore, by the difficult and possibly disadvantageous realisation of commodities. "Anyone with fixed capital can command circulating capital at any moment—he can either borrow upon it from his bankers or sell it on the Stock Exchange to a dealer, who will borrow on it from a banker if there is no immediate purchaser. In turn, those who have circulating capital can either invest directly in fixed capital by purchasing on the Stock Exchange, or indirectly by depositing with a banker."[1] The net effect is to increase the strength and elasticity of the modern industrial system up to a point which would be totally unattainable in the absence of these facilities, though the actually available cash is all the while a " mere bagatelle."

The system opens the way to credit operations of immense scope and potency on the part of municipalities and other public authorities. The rateable value, the municipal property, and the corporate responsibility of a given city are excellent security for a loan by its bankers. But large advances, made merely in a few instances, would strain the resources of the most powerful banking institution if there were available no method by which the obligation might be distributed over a wider area than the bank itself. In fact, a bank would hesitate to advance £250,000, for thirty years, to a municipality, if the transaction were intended to remain, for the whole of that period, within the limits of its own ledgers. The creation of a municipal bond (or a registered or inscribed stock, according to the contemporary taste of the investing public) obviates this difficulty. At the first favourable

[1] Giffen, *Essays*, Vol. II. p. 42.

opportunity the obligations are distributed over a wide area—but among a class, be it remembered, whose willingness to buy them is conditioned by their possession of the characteristic of marketability. Nor is this all. No sooner are the bonds placed than they become, in the hands of their new proprietors, credit instruments for their own use. As one of the shrewdest of American observers —J. J. Hill—said : " The issue of a state, city or county bond affects credit volume more powerfully and produces more directly the effects of an increase in money volume because it is acceptable as collateral for nearly or quite its face value in credit issues."[1] A parcel of £1000 of $4\frac{1}{2}$ per cent. bonds of the City of Winnipeg is an instrument which will, at a moment's notice, attract £700 or £750 of credit from the stock at the shop where that most fruitful of commodities is sold—to wit, the bank. The idea of the private citizen borrowing on the security of the town hall appears to be, on the face of it, an outrage upon civic dignity. But the Money Power does, in effect, bring such a transaction into being. The municipality, in its corporate capacity, borrows upon security whereof the town hall is a part ; and the private citizen, armed with a portion of the obligations thus created, borrows upon *them*, in his turn, for the financing of his business. Thus, to carry the chain of causation no further, an aggregate of bricks and mortar becomes the source of a lively fund, by which the social wealth is augmented and developed. The few hundred shares, quoted on the Stock Exchange, and employed by a tradesman as the occasional basis of an overdraft, add to his confidence, his consciousness of mastery over his environment and his capacity for enterprise.[2] Multiplied by thousands, the

[1] The ideal " quite " is reached in the case of the British War Loan of 1914, on which the Bank of England agreed to advance to its full issue price for three years from the date of issue. But see note on the Bank Charter Act, *ante*, p. 351.

[2] He is, for instance, in a much better position than Christian, the Taverner, who, on August 16, 1281, acknowledged having received six casks of wine, value £13, from William Varache, for sale, together with four silver cups, which he would account for when he had sold the wine ; and, for so doing, he pledged *himself* and his chattels. (*History of the Wine Trade in England*, Vol. I. p. 304.)

aggregate moral force represents a procreative economic factor of mighty range and efficiency. The man who can go to his banker with security which justifies his request for an advance, almost as of right, is an individual of very different moral calibre, of greatly augmented and energised value as an economic unit, in comparison with the suppliant who enters the bank parlour with bated breath and whispering humbleness, in dread of all that may eventuate if he be told that his proposal is " not good enough." Moreover, the rate he will pay is very different from what it was in bygone ages. The evolution of the money market has wrought a beneficent change. Herein, perhaps, lies the reason why some of the sternest censors of our social organisation have borne involuntary testimony to the utility of the Stock Exchange. Governor Sulzer of New York (a severe critic of finance) in a message to the State Legislature,[1] said that "these Stock Exchanges are an inevitable necessity. They cannot be destroyed without doing irreparable injury to business. When properly conducted they constitute an efficient agent for promoting industrial and commercial prosperity." Again, " the Stock Exchange itself," said Mr. J. Ramsay Macdonald,[2] " is a necessary institution, and will continue to be so for a long time to come."

SECTION V

(b) *THE CONTINUOUS RE-DISTRIBUTION OF SECURITIES*

The Stock Exchange, then, is a market devoted exclusively to dealings in public, standardised, and assignable (or negotiable) choses in action. Its function is to supply the various factors of social progress (governments and other public authorities, as well as commerce and industry), by means of an incessant process of redistribution, with the maximum of capital at the minimum rate for the time being. The Stock Exchange attracts

[1] *New York Times,* January 28, 1912. [2] *Socialist Movement,* p. 63.

possessors of money or credit capital to purchase these various choses in action. It adapts their multitudinous degrees of risk to the fancy of each purchaser (see section 3[*a*]), so as to draw from myriad hiding-places the maximum increment of the working capital of contemporary enterprise. The banks aggregate the otherwise loose and impotent supplies of money, and the Stock Exchange is one of the most effective means of drawing it from them so as to be at the service of production. The banks are the anabolic force and the Stock Exchange the katabolic function. The Stock Exchange is an organisation for the transport of capital to the point of maximum utility at the minimum of cost. It strives thereby to effect " the continuous redistribution among capitalists of the disutilities involved in the supply of capital outstanding in the hands of entrepreneurs."[1] The *Official List* will indicate, at any given moment, the locus and manner of the distribution and the terms upon which it is being effected. By means of this organisation—far-flung in its scope, yet sensitive as a clinical thermometer—" the surplus wealth of the country which has more than it needs for its own requirements," as Lord Milner said, " is easily transferred to the countries which have less. The whole world tends more and more to become a single market, in which all productive industry is competing for all the capital which is available to keep industry going."[2] Studying the functions from this point of view, it is obvious that the jobber, and in the same sense, though not in the same degree, the underwriter and the speculative purchaser (other than the manipulator, whose case is on a different footing) render social service equal in efficiency and value to that of the great transport systems. There is, however, one striking distinction between the two species of service.

That of the railway, for instance, is a conveyance of commodities over an interval of *space,* away from a locus where they are not required, in order to place them within the sphere of an effective demand. The other (that of

---

[1] Lavington, *Economic Journal,* March, 1913, p. 38.
[2] *Journal of the Institute of Bankers,* 1913.

the jobber) is a transport of choses in action over an interval of *time*; and the object sought to be attained is to have them in readiness when the lapse of a longer or shorter period shall have brought the effective demand into being. In both instances the act of transport is a legitimate object of reward, by means of the profit arising from the service rendered. If there is any balance of merit, between the railway and the jobber, it lies with the latter. The railway carrying goods from London to Birmingham, is assured of remuneration, and incurs no appreciable risk. It does not purchase the goods, though it enjoys a lien upon them. They are, in the vast majority of cases, capable of being sold for a sum far in excess of the cost of transport. But the jobber with a heavy " book " (or, indeed, the underwriter) accepting the liability to carry £100,000 of New South Wales Four per Cents. over the interval of time which may separate the date of purchase (or, in the case of the underwriter, of issue) from the advent of willing buyers, places himself under the double responsibility of (1) purchasing outright the choses in action which he has undertaken to transport over the longer or shorter period of waiting, and (2) bearing the loss arising from depreciation meanwhile. These are risks which he would certainly not be willing to incur—at all events, at the slender remuneration which he usually receives—were it not that behind him is an organisation. It consists of the banks and discount companies, and the Stock Exchange, as well as other interests, like the great insurance enterprises, more remote from the centre of financial gravity, but none the less essential factors of the Money Market. The selling investor, the issuing authority, or other seeker of liquid capital, is the gainer by the existence of these facilities. He or it may, broadly speaking, choose his or its own time for the transaction, insuring against the risk of the non-advent of buyers by the payment of a commission for its transfer to other shoulders. The ultimate buyer is also a gainer, for the security is held at his disposal till he has the enterprise and the money necessary for its acquisition. Further, there is a continuous benefit arising from the generally uninterrupted potentiality of dealing in the stock. The jobbers' capital makes the market cheaper in operating cost, by lowering the expense of dealing, while at the same time it steadies prices. Giffen even thinks that the existence of the Stock Exchange, and its disposition of a considerable capital and credit, " tends to keep up the level of the prices of securities above what would otherwise be maintained."[1] He agrees that it is difficult to estimate the effect of the fund; but if its withdrawal be supposed, we can infer that there must be a resulting all-round fall in prices. As the market becomes more and more international, this utility is enhanced. A stock with two or three markets is a choicer thing from a banker's point of view than a stock which has only one. Sombart even declares that " a security which does not circulate is no security at all." Clearly, this bridging of the gap between the social necessities of the present and the resources, responsibilities, and obligations of the future is analogous to the " cosmic forces of light and gravitation and electricity acting over the abysses of space."[2] Seeing that an issue is almost invariably the signal of some social need, just as a sale of stock marks the readjustment of an investor's interests, the absence of this mechanism would frequently involve a period of waiting. There might be loss far more than commensurate with the remuneration that is paid for the use of the facilities. That is to say, there is a balance of social service to the credit of the Money Market above and beyond the actual profit which it receives.

THE ORGANISATION OF CAPITAL REDISTRIBUTION

Giffen's argument enforces the consideration that this process of continuous redistribution, so vital to the maintenance of the social supply of capital, is only carried on by means of an incessant expenditure upon the machinery. The imagination boggles at the amount employed to maintain the work of a modern Stock Exchange like that of

---
[1] *Stock Exchange Securities*, p. 39.
[2] Marvin, *The Living Past*, p. 18.

London or New York. This is apart altogether from the amount invested in the securities with which the market is concerned. The jobber and broker (the latter always a principal, in relation to his fellow-members) employ, in the aggregate, vast sums of personal and money capital. The argument is not vitiated by reason of the fact that a large proportion of the money is borrowed on the security of the stocks in which the dealer specialises. Clearly, but for the specialisation, it would not find employment in that way. For this service the dealer must be remunerated. The "turn" will vary in accordance with the risk, as measured by the jobber himself, of the purchased security remaining on his hands. It will widen if the danger be enhanced, while it will shrink if a rapid market convert the dealer into a mere duct, swiftly conveying a rapid flow of stock from one holder to another. The result is—at all events to an extremely large extent—an abolition of the insecurity arising from the investor not being able to get out. The existence of the facility is a factor of the machinery of insurance, though it is but seldom regarded in that light. The risks and inconveniences of fluctuating values are minimised by the existence of a class which is always ready to take or deliver at the market price. It thereby provides a channel practically always open, through which capital may flow in search of its most advantageous use. "This practice," said Chief Baron Kelly in 1869,[1]

" affords to the public the very great advantage of being enabled by means of a stockbroker and a jobber to buy or sell at any moment any quantity of stock, or any number of any description of shares, at the market price of the day, and concluding the transaction at the latest on the selling day, whereas, without such practice, everyone having any given amount of stock, English, foreign, or colonial, or of debentures or shares in railways or other joint-stock companies to buy or to sell must wait until a seller or a buyer could be found to sell or to buy the exact quantity of stock or shares which is to be parted with—a state of things which in this country, where some hundreds of these purchases and sales are effected every day, would be found intolerable."

[1] In Grissell v. Bristowe, Law Rep. 4 C.P. at p. 53.

Save that the language is a little too sweeping (and the sentence a trifle too breathless), this is an admirable characterisation.

AN IMMENSE "CONSUMER'S SURPLUS"

The jobber and the broker are, of course, only parts of the mechanism ; beyond them is the investing and speculating public, without which the jobber and the broker would be impotent and superfluous. But it is clear that when, by means of the jobber's presence in the market, a facility of rapid transfer is made available to persons who would not, in its absence, have purchased the securities which they hold, the service rendered to social development is not that of the jobber only. It is that of the jobber plus the organisation which places the new purchaser within the jobber's reach. He is but one factor of a great transport system. The jobber is the outward and visible agent of an organisation immensely mightier than himself, without which he would not dare to deal. Thus it is mathematically demonstrable that there is a social gain arising from the organisation itself, beyond the mere professional service which is remunerated by the jobber's turn and the broker's commission. Society is the richer by a utility for which it does not pay. The existence of any number of A's, nearly always prepared, on terms, to buy out any number of B's, is a stupendous phenomenon. It demonstrates the endowment of capital with the maximum of mobility. In the technical language of modern economics, it stands for an immense "consumer's surplus." There is a balance of advantage, entirely above and beyond the mere mechanical process of transferring the chose in action, conferred upon both parties to the bargain which passes through the jobber's hands. It takes the shape of the rapid transport of capital from one point of time to another. These facilities enable the investor to secure the repayment of his money at any moment. He will not get it from the City of Toronto, from Lipton, Ltd., or any other of the original borrowers. Their obligation in the matter has not yet matured. It may not mature for half a century. Between that remote date and the present the gap¹ is bridged by some other lender who is willing to step into the shoes of the original possessor of the money, taking over his privileges at an agreed price. The Stock Exchange mechanism discovers the substitute. Nor are we concerned only with the gap of time. It is no small innovation when the capital can be in one *place* and the proprietor thereof in another—when he may transfer it from New Zealand to Russia and from banking to railway building without leaving his chair. This involves two postulates : (*a*) the mobility of the capital, and (*b*) its security and capacity of being controlled in the physical absence of its proprietor—both of which are a huge advance upon that state of things in which capital is immobile, and only safe when the sword of its owner is unsheathed to protect it. So it is that the negotiable or assignable security adds to the utility of money and the Stock Exchange enhances the utility of both. Why is it that thousands of small capitalists all over England have

[1] The " gap " may occasionally become a gulf. The story of human progress, at every stage and in every field, is stamped with the sinister brand of the spasmodic. Enthusiasm is followed by stagnation, enterprise by reaction, energy by apathy. The spirit of enterprise inspires the initiation of some great undertaking—a railway, harbour, tunnel, a line of shipping, or a vast distributing agency—and the public, fired by the vision of a good profit, joined with another conquest over Nature, offers eager financial co-operation. The work is commenced ; and then, as gradually and imperceptibly as the boats swing round with the ebbing tide, there comes the subtle reaction. Many of those who willingly made themselves responsible for a portion of the required capital are now anxious to withdraw, if they can. Other assistance is difficult to obtain, owing to the onset of nervousness and apprehension. So far as original co-operators are concerned, their financial obligations are in most cases enforceable ; but fresh co-operation is unobtainable, at any possible commercial figure, during the interregnum of apathy and distrust. If it were not for the existence and public spirit of the Money Market, providing a financial and commercial leadership and community of purpose, the constant recurrence of these contingencies must continually place enterprise in the humiliating position of the man who began to build, and, being unable to finish, became the scorn and mockery of his neighbours. The intervention of the Money Market obviates the disaster and bridges the gulf of hesitation. As a rule a strong syndicate of bankers and financiers, will " see the business through," relying upon the reawakening of public spirit for the reaping of the reward of its own courage by the placing of the securities which represent its own financing of the undertaking. Some of the early finance companies (*ante*, p. 468) were formed for this business exclusively. But it is better done as a part, than as the whole, of a financial function.

cheerfully put their money into public loans and private undertakings, although they realise that a need for the invested money on their own part might arise at any moment? The answer is that they know of the existence of a market machinery which in the case of all recognised securities and in all normal circumstances would enable them to go out and others to come in at practically a few minutes' notice. When it is averred that "there is no place in the world where good stocks are more easily realisable at a minimum of loss, or purchasable so near the market price, as on the London Stock Exchange," this social service—this consumer's surplus—is emphasised, though the critic—Mr. Hirst—is not at the moment concerned with that aspect of the mechanism.

CHEAPER CAPITAL SUPPLIES

The harvest of this sowing is a huge cheapening of the cost of capital supplies, by the consequent augmentation in the general economic well-being, and by the attraction, to the investment arena, of savings resulting from the operation of those conditions. These interacting forces generate a possibility of undertaking vast social utilities which would have been impossible, or only imperfectly effective, if the necessary capital had had to be procured at such figures as 12 per cent., or anything like it. The cost of the services must have been enhanced to meet the high interest charges, with the result of placing them out of the reach of large sections of the population which are at present able to enjoy them. Railway capital, raised at 12 per cent., would be fatal to workmen's tickets, at anything like the current rates, on such lines as the Great Eastern. And when, as in certain of the turbulent central American republics, the rate of interest rises to 12 per cent. *per month*, practically all the beneficent social enterprise must be crushed out of existence under such a tremendous pressure. "Few people realise," said Sir George Paish,[1]

"that in the period in which improvements in the methods of production and distribution have been so rapid the return

[1] *Statist*, January 18, 1913.

THE STOCK EXCHANGE (1815–1915)

upon capital has steadily fallen. It has done so largely because the creation of joint-stock enterprises has enabled the small investor to participate in trade and industry, and because the return upon the capital placed in public enterprises whose securities enjoy a free market is much lower than the return sought for and obtained upon capital embarked in private ventures. . . . If any one stops a moment to think of the difficulty of obtaining capital in the past and of the high rates of interest paid upon it, one will realise the immense advantage enjoyed to-day by every one—first from the production and distribution in a wholesale manner by means of great corporations, whose capital is supplied by investors of all kinds, and, second, from the steadily declining return upon capital which has resulted from the replacement of private enterprises by the great corporations whose capital is provided by the multitude."

WHERE THE MACHINE STOPS

We are by this time in a position to understand the closing of the Stock Exchange in 1914. Clearly, this " conduit-pipe " equipment for the transfer and absorption of securities can only be effective up to a point. It depends for its efficiency upon the simultaneous existence of both buyers and sellers. But, although it is capable of adjusting itself, by means of price variations, to a temporary predominance of either class, it cannot sustain itself against the total disappearance of all buyers, contemporaneously with the rush of immense aggregates of real, speculative, and hostile[1] sales. In circumstances such as

[1] " Hostile " sales are a new type. They must be added as a separate class because there is not the slightest doubt that many of the sales sent from the Continent to the Stock Exchange for the End-July Account, and more especially between that account and the closing of the Stock Exchange, were deliberately designed to smash the market and create a panic for the furtherance of German interests. Professor Keynes in the *Economic Review* for September, 1914, contends that it was rather previous *purchases* by foreigners than sales on their account which caused the closing of the Stock Exchange. He argues that these purchases, made at an earlier date and carried over either in that account or from previous accounts, created large liabilities which the continental, and mainly German, clients did not meet. For that reason he urges that it was the liabilities of foreigners *to* the Stock Exchange, and not the liabilities to foreigners *from* the Stock Exchange, which precipitated its close. But even if these facts be true (and that there were huge " hostile " purchases admits of no doubt) it still remains a fact that the enormous pressure of sales after the account of July 29th, and after the closing of the continental Bourses, formed the main operative influence. Moreover, if large

these the market necessarily ceases to be a mechanism for the *transport* of capital from place to place. If it remained open the jobbers, in the event of a preponderance of sales, must themselves become the buyers of stock, instead of the agents for its transport. In other words, there is a limit to the financial capacity of *the mechanism itself* as an absorbent, and when it has been reached the closure of the Stock Exchange is the only expedient which will save the situation. Its adoption does not signify that the machinery has broken down. It means only that a mechanism designed for one purpose cannot be suddenly adapted to another. A Stock Exchange cannot, any more than a railway company, be suddenly called upon to *purchase*, to an illimitable extent, commodities which it has only undertaken to *transport* from one holder to another. This is equally true whether the desire to sell arises from a "panicky" feeling on the part of the holder, or is the consequence of pressure by a banker who is calling in his loans. The concurrent fixation of minimum prices for a large group of gilt-edged securities was an auxiliary expedient, designed to the same end as the closing of the Stock Exchange.

THE TIME LOAN AS CALL MONEY?

This principle admits of a still more subtle application. A very large proportion of the investment securities known to the Stock Exchanges have a fixed term to run. That is to say, they represent, in effect, time loans. There is precisely the same contract between borrower and lender as there is between a banker and a depositor who has placed money on deposit for three months, or six months certain, in consideration of receiving a higher rate than would be paid on call money. Now, the Stock

---

"hostile" purchases from the Continent had in fact been made for the End-July Account and the continental purchasers failed either to take up the stock or to arrange for it being carried over, the acting brokers would all have been turned into sellers and these "hostile" purchases must have increased the volume of sales at the critical moment. That actually occurred. One firm was "left" with £170,000 worth of stock purchased on continental account.

Exchange, being merely a means of transporting capital from one point to another, can have no cognisance of these arrangements, save in so far as they affect the value of the security. But when, in the presence of panic, the lender loses his head and rushes to the Stock Exchange to sell out, he is constructively endeavouring to transform a *time* loan into a *call* loan at the expense and risk of the Stock Exchange. It is no part of the business of the Stock Exchange to afford him facilities for that purpose. A man who has lent money on a five per cent. debenture with fifteen years to run has no possible claim upon the Stock Exchange for the immediate redemption of this loan. Yet that is, in truth, what he seeks when he expects the Stock Exchange to take it off his hands in a time of crisis or panic, whether there are buyers about or not. The Stock Exchange is not in this respect a universal insurance organisation, guaranteeing the immediate return of invested capital at a moment's notice to all who choose to ask for it, no matter what the circumstances may be.

SECTION V

(c) *THE SENSITIVENESS OF THE MARKET*

The incessant interaction of a multitude of forces, such as we surveyed in the previous section, creates that state of sensitiveness which has led to the Stock Exchange being described as " the nerve centre of the politics and finances of nations, because in this market all that makes history is focussed and finds instantaneous expression."[1] It has been called the " barometer of future business conditions." Giffen declares[2] that it is " sensitive to every breath that blows." More and more, as the sensitiveness of the mechanism increases, are all coming events discounted [3]

[1] Duguid, *Stock Exchange*, p. 2. The tendency to employ physiological metaphor because the physiological analogy is so exact, has been illustrated at an earlier stage (p. 265).
[2] *Stock Exchange Securities*, p. 78.
[3] Osborne (*Speculation on the New York Stock Exchange*, 1904–1907) is sceptical about the " discounting " faculty—the " superhuman quality of speculative foreknowledge," as he calls it (p. 147). But his arguments are far from conclusive.

in the tone of the market and the figures of the Official List. The efforts of dealers constantly tend toward the evenness of movement—Spencer's ideal of *steadiness*— which enables the Stock Exchange to minimise violent shocks to the price-list by discounting the result of coming events. Approaching crises are almost invariably indicated, and their force mitigated by the liquidation of securities, if that suffice to break the approaching wave. If not, the market discounts them by a succession of markings down. Thus (save under wholly exceptional circumstances of panic) the movement exhausts itself in a series of wavelets frequently distributed over all the markets of the world by means of the cable, rather than in the shock of one huge tidal onrush directed against a single market breakwater. The actual announcement of the expected occurrence will often produce no market effect whatever, so successfully has it been anticipated and measured :—

" In addition to other influences which promote an earlier rise and fall, there must be mentioned the more careful study and attention to the financial situation which is given by dealers in the stock markets and in great financial centres. They often forecast the grounds for a rise or fall in prices before the general public is awake to the situation."[1]

Prices fell steadily in New York before the panic of March, 1907. But even with panic at its worst, quotations began to rise as thousands of the most acute brains diagnosed the passing of the trouble. Both fall and rise discounted coming conditions rather than offered a reflection of existing circumstances. Just as the thermometer provides us with the means of measuring, and therefore of equalising, temperature (within certain physical limits), even so do the Stock Exchanges enable us to secure a greater evenness of economic movement than would otherwise be possible. Crisis, panic, and collapse are fatal factors when they enter the arena of human progress and happiness. They upset all calculations, dissipate energy in a thousand unprofitable directions, rear a crop of disaster where once

[1] Burton, *Financial Crises and Periods of Industrial and Commercial Depression*, p. 234.

was a happy and prosperous population, overwhelm the embankments which stand between humanity and the menacing waves of its physical surroundings, and put back the hands upon the dial plate of the world's enlightenment by decades at a time. Prevention is said to be better than cure. To see the crisis coming, to mark the distant onset of the danger, and to be thus effectively warned into the adoption of precautionary, protective, and ameliorative measures, is surely a social advantage. If there exist a sensitive instrument (a crisisometer, or financial pressure gauge, shall we call it ?) which will manifest disturbance at the first onset of the peril, it must of necessity be an invaluable factor in the clinical outfit of society at large. How different might have been the story of many a nation, our own included, if our ancestry had possessed such a guide to the accurate prognosis of political and social malaise !

THE FABRIC OF INTER-RELATIONSHIP

Close inter-relationship among themselves and with all the other elements of the financial and commercial fabric has made the Stock Exchanges of the world into the most sensitive indicators of the force and direction of any abnormal pressure. The whole fine-spun fabric responds instantly to the lightest breath of alarm, the merest threat of disturbance. It is an almost automatic caution, as inevitable in its action and almost as unerring in its indication as the temperature of the body in modern pathology. If, occasionally, in spite of early warning from the Stock Exchanges of the coming danger, catastrophe actually burst upon the business world, the fault is more frequently to be found in the factors which are controlled by the Governments than in those which are controlled by the Stock Exchanges. This argument was strongly emphasised by the Committee of the New York Stock Exchange in its reply to certain allegations made before the Money Trust Commission :—

" Because the Exchange is a great market for active securities, the first symptoms of business distrust and disturbances become apparent upon its floor. It is a fact that a large volume of securities is carried on call loans obtained from the banks, and that the first symptom of a stringency in the Money Market is a rise in the rate of call money. The responsibility for the conditions that bring about a recurrent stringency in the Money Market does not rest upon the traders in securities or upon the Exchange. They are due to the non-elasticity of the currency system and the fact that its volume continues substantially the same, irrespective of the demands of business."

Because the " first symptoms of distrust become apparent upon its floor," a short-sighted public, unfamiliar with the technique of finance, imagines that this is the locus of the trouble. The clinical thermometer might as logically be blamed for the dangerous temperature of the patent. The more discriminating observer is learning to watch the trend of Stock Exchange opinion and incident as a most valuable guide to the accurate appreciation of contemporary economic conditions and prospects :—

"A shrewd man, one of the old school of New York City wholesale merchants, who was nothing whatever to do with Wall Street or the Stock Exchange, yet whose trade arteries extend to many parts of the country, has long governed his business by the published reports of Stock Exchange transactions. If he sees there revealed a wholesome, normal, and conservative expansion in all lines of business and a money market that betrays no uneasiness as to the future, he presses on into new lines of endeavour, confident that the immediate future is serene. If he finds an urgent liquidation on 'Change, with the coincident phenomena of impaired credit instruments, he draws in his lines and waits. It makes no difference to him who is rocking the boat, nor why ; experience has taught him that if it rocks, the time has arrived to go ashore."[1]

" DISCOUNTING " WAS ONCE MISUNDERSTOOD

This market habit, or faculty, of discounting the coming event was in earlier days totally misunderstood and severely criticised. The venomous writer of the *Art of Stock Jobbing Explained* argued[2] that " the Funds were

[1] Van Antwerp, *Stock Exchange from Within*, p. 204.
[2] Introduction, p. iii.

higher before the taking of Paris than they were immediately after, although the Battle of Waterloo decided the fate of France and the enemy of England. Had the Funds been the barometer of public credit, as they are supposed to be, they ought to have risen 10 or 15 per cent. on that occasion ; but, on the contrary, Omnium, which was at the taking of Paris 12½ per cent. premium, fell to 6½." Such market paradoxes are of frequent occurrence in our own day. The coming event has been fully discounted. Its advent has been descried while it was yet afar off. The necessary market arrangements for its arrival have been made. The market is the buffer between the credit mechanism and the shock that might otherwise derange it. The resulting manifestation of steadiness is not sinister, but salutary. In our own day the fear of a certain contingency has been known to send prices down, and its actual occurrence to put them up ! The market is invariably timid in the presence of the impalpable and the uncertain, but grows bolder when the peril becomes visible, and consequently susceptible of critical appraisement.

INTRICACY OF RELATIONSHIP

The extreme sensitiveness of the Stock Exchanges is, of course, not entirely due to their own native perceptivity. It is rendered more acute by the mutuality of sensibility which exists between the Stock Exchange and the other factors of the money market. At every point the Stock Exchange is in the most intervolved and indissoluble contact with the banks, insurance companies, trust and finance groups, industrial enterprises, issuing houses, promoters and private capitalists, and through them with commerce and industry throughout the world :—

" In the commercial market goods pass from hand to hand, and alongside of this process of exchange in the commercial market there is going on in the money market an exchange of credit instruments based upon these very products of industry which are in circulation. This reciprocal action of the commercial market and the money market is a continuous one."[1]

[1] Dr. Heiligenstadt, *German Bank Enquiry of* 1908, Vol. I. p. 112.

The relationship is of the utmost intricacy. There is, for example, a constant interaction between the deposits in banks and the price of Stock Exchange securities. Bankers habitually finance the Stock Exchange : and they can do it more effectively with large deposits than with small.[1] That is to say, the general level of prices, in the presence of large deposits, and under normal circumstances, will be higher, and the general aggregate of activity more extensive, than where only meagre resources are in the bankers' hands. And here again, if some abnormality diminish the deposits, prices are *ipso facto* weakened. With their fall, margins run off, and more deposits are withdrawn to repay bankers ; or else the banker himself sells the pawned stock on the market. Stock Exchange activity subsides, and public confidence, which is unfailingly reflected in Stock Exchange conditions, dwindles in proportion to the change. The flow of enterprise is checked, and the whole economic fabric, as it were, shrinks in upon itself. Moreover, a market which is largely financed by borrowed money will be more susceptible than would be the case if the funds were proprietary. A dealer —or an outside speculator, for the matter of that—who is financed by short loans on a narrow margin will keep his ears closer to the ground than the man whose stock-in-trade is held by means of his own funds. One has his banker, like a shadow, behind him. The other has no censor but himself. The necessity of adjusting these bargains at every settlement is also a wholesome deterrent, as it is a source of additional impressibility in the market mechanism. There is no opportunity to forget, for the alarum will inevitably sound, even though it be at the end of so abnormally extended a period as the much-dreaded nineteen-day account. It has been argued that shorter settlements would tend to curb irresponsible speculation, or rather gambling. The New York system of daily

---

[1] This is one reason why a rise in the Bank rate frequently causes a fall in speculative securities on the Stock Exchange. Operations in these stocks are being carried on with borrowed money, and with the rate above a certain figure they cease to be profitable. Therefore the transactions have to be closed.

settlements, it is said, is even more peremptory in its pressure[1] than the London fortnightly method. The New York broker trusts his client only for a day, whereas the London broker takes the risk for a fortnight or even more. The fact that there are ten failures in London to one in New York gives some plausibility to this view. But even in London, the fortnightly settlement itself, by revealing the actual condition of the market in the matter of its open engagements, has the effect of producing immediate, and occasionally extensive, readjustments in current quotations and existing commitments. Even the outsider benefits from these public opinions on the change in values, and may often derive caution and admonition from them. Bargains outside the market are done on the basis of prices *inside* it. In most cases they would be impossible, or at least difficult, if the price-basis and the auxiliary facilities did not exist. The analogy of Horace White[2] is a very happy one : " The twain [the Stock Exchange and the rest of the Money Market] are gigantic bodies which act and react upon each other like planets revolving around a common centre "—or, better still, like Sirius and his inseparable companion. Therefore it may be a problem of great complexity to find the causes of the conditions prevailing at any time—a problem, shall we say, as delicate as that which confronted Adams and Le Verrier, when the apparent aberrations of the planet Uranus guided them to the then unknown source of disturbance, and revealed Neptune on the far-distant confines of our planetary system ?

Thus Stock Market and Money Market incessantly and reciprocally reinforce each other's perceptivity. We noted the jobber's unfailing professional vigilance in the Stock Market. Among the personnel of the allied factor of the Money Market, the average bill broker has a very keen nose for the realities of the financial position. He detects an excess of kite-flying in the realm of the finance bill,

[1] But these short settlements would be impossible in an international market like London.
[2] "The Stock Exchange and the Money Market," in American Academy Volume on *Banking Problems*, p. 570.

and is instant to mark what is done amiss in the matter of superfluous commercial paper. Of course, as regards finance bills, a fear that the Bank of England—that unfailing friend of the bill broker—might discriminate against them in times of stringency, has always exerted a restraining influence on their creation. But apart from this apprehension, there is a keenness, a vigilance, a rapidity of inference, among the " money-men " which instantly discovers and appraises the slightest indication of the presence of untoward influences. The first thing that spread suspicion with regard to the City of Glasgow Bank was the demand of the bill brokers for an extra ¼ per cent. over the market rate on its acceptances. This set people talking. When, at the onset of the Australian banking crisis of 1893, the London office of one of the threatened institutions offered by cable to send out gold to the assistance of the head office, the fact was instantly known in Lombard Street, and became the subject of ominous remark :—

" Such is the rapidity with which rumour flies about in these times that the weakness of a firm hardly makes itself felt in South America or even in remote eastern cities, but the news flashes from one European centre to another, and the commercial paper bearing the name or names whispered about passes from one bank or discount house to another without finding anyone willing to take it."[1]

This sensitiveness of the market would, perhaps, reach its maximum usefulness in indicating the approach of any attack upon the central gold reserve, by means of large withdrawals engineered by gigantic foreign interests, such as were attempted (with no great success) on the eve of the war with Germany in 1914. If the money thus withdrawn had originally been merely hoarded in London, its movement could make no difference to the market, though the loss on the hoarding would have been immense, even in days of cheap money. But if it were utilised in the market, or invested in securities, the initial attempts at withdrawal and realisation would be " smelt " by the

[1] Arthur Crump, *Economic Journal*, Vol. I. p. 390.

THE STOCK EXCHANGE (1815–1915)

bill-brokers and instantly reflected in the prevailing " tone." For is not really, perhaps, the liability to the onset and the pressure of sales at the first scent of crisis, but the certainty of getting gold which has " made " the London Money Market, and at the same time endowed it with the delicacy of a mathematical instrument. The absence of that certainty has exerted the reverse influence upon London's rivals, notably Paris and Berlin. Mr. Pownall has said that " our money market is sensitive because we choose that it shall be so." The more sensitive the instrument, the more precise the degree of vigilance attainable by its aid.

AN APPARENT INCONSISTENCY

But is there not, the critical reader may interpose, some inconsistency between this appreciation of the acute sensitiveness of the market, on the one hand, and the stress laid elsewhere upon the Spencerian doctrine of the necessity that social evolution, in all its varying functions, should be a *steady* progress ? No such inconsistency exists. The essential of a steady movement is the existence of some indicator which will instantly announce the slightest deflection from the normal course and either remedy the trouble automatically or attract palliative measures from some external source. This is the purpose of the automatic steam governor on an engine, just as it is also that of the use of the clinical thermometer by the nurse. In the one case the steam pressure, and in the other the temperature of the patient must be the subject of an incessant observation. But this can only be effected if there exists some admonitory instrument capable of detecting and recording any abnormality. The clinical thermometer which was incapable of registering any change of temperature less than five degrees would be perfectly useless in the hands of the most skilful practitioner. The more sensitive it is, the more acute and more decisive is the diagnosis made upon the faith of its readings. Applying the arguments in the financial sphere, we are irresistibly driven to the conclusion that the more sensitive the market (within reasonable limits, that is to say), the greater its value as an indicator of economic disturbance and the more rapid and precise the potentiality of sanative measures. Observe, however, that sensitiveness, like other serviceable characteristics of a complicated machine, may be overdone. It should not degenerate—as it occasionally does—into "nerves." A "panicky feeling"— rare in our day—is as great a menace to the well-being of the market as would be a sluggish incapacity to respond to the various impulses and stimuli that impinged upon it. Viscount Goschen told the Institute of Bankers, in November, 1913,[1] that . . . the Money Market was just as subject to nerves as the individual. "The pace at which the world had been living, and was living, increased, and swifter cable and telephonic communication with all parts of the world had given the Money Market a fit of 'nerves' for which it needed a 'rest cure.' It was quite sound organically, but its digestion was weak, and it was constantly subjected to sudden fits of depression."[2]

[1] *Financial News*, November 6.
[2] THE SUPPLY OF FINANCIAL INTELLIGENCE.

As soon as international monetary relationships arise, there is a rudimentary news service to reinforce them. The transmission of bills of exchange seems to have been originally accompanied by news-letters "covering" them. When once the English monarchs began to borrow abroad it became necessary to have skilful agents in the various commercial centres. They must be capable not only of raising money, but of reporting intelligently upon the movement of events. They must be able to interpret the "tone" of international politics, as nowadays a financial house deduces, from a multitude of minute indications, the probable movement of money rates, or a jobber exercises, with a dexterity equal to that of a mediæval swordsman, the financial foresight which is the price he pays for survival. An inspection of Gresham's correspondence will demonstrate, as Burgon points out (*Gresham*, Vol. I. p. 261), that in conducting the policy of England towards Flanders (a State which formerly occupied a far prouder rank among European Powers than it does at the present day), Cecil depended almost entirely on Gresham, and placed implicit confidence in his "advertisements."

Before its functions were divided into those of the banks and those of the Stock Exchange respectively, the daily assembly, the sixteenth-century Money Market, was largely and necessarily interested in the current commercial, political, and social, gossip of the day. In the seventeenth century, even in the earliest days of 'Change Alley, it was admitted that the dealers enjoyed the advantage of a better service of news, both home and foreign, than was available to the Government itself. The Jews were specially skilled in the organisation of news services. There is in existence a report by the French Ambassador at The Hague, written in 1648 (quoted by Sombart, *Jews and Modern Capitalism*, p. 173), which

Section V

(d) *SPECULATION*

In its essential English significance, the word "speculation," as Mr. McCulloch said, is "only another name for foresight." It means merely intelligent scrutiny, sight reinforced by mind, *per*ception joined to *con*ception.

(albeit rather highly coloured, perhaps) shows this cosmopolitanism in its early stages. "They carry on a correspondence on both these subjects [news and commerce] with those they call their brotherhoods (congregues). Of these Venice is considered to be the most important (although neither the richest nor the most populous), because it is the link, by way of the brotherhood of Salonica, between the East and the West, as well as the South. Salonica is the governing centre for their nation in these two parts of the world, and is responsible for them to Venice, which, together with Amsterdam, rules the northern countries (including the merely tolerated community of London and the secret brotherhoods of France). The result of this association is that on the two topics of news and commerce they receive, one might almost say, the best information of all that goes on in the world, and on this they build up their system every week in their assemblies, wisely choosing for this purpose the day after Saturday —i.e., the Sunday—when the Christians of all denominations are engaged in their religious exercises.

" These systems, which contain the minutest details of news received during the week, are, after having been carefully sifted by their rabbis and the heads of their congregations, Jewish stockbrokers and agents, handed over on the Sunday afternoon to their men of great cleverness, who, after having arranged a preconcerted plan among themsélves, go out separately to spread news which should prove the most useful to their own ends ; ready to start manipulations on the morrow, the Monday morning, according to each individual's disposition, either selling, buying, or exchanging shares. As they always hold a large reserve of these commodities, they can always judge of the most propitious moment, taking advantage of the rise or fall of the securities, or even sometimes of both, in order to carry out their plans."

The same phenomenon had attracted the attention of Addison, who says (*Spectator*, September 27, 1712), that the Jews are " so disseminated through all the trading parts of the world that they are become the instruments by which the most distant nations converse with one another, and by which mankind are knit together in a general correspondence. They are like the pegs and nails in a great building, which, though they are but little valued in themselves, are absolutely necessary to keep the whole frame together." Sombart says that Medina, Marlborough's banker, paid him £6000 a year for the first news of what was happening at the wars. Sir Henry Furnese, early in the eighteenth century, maintained " throughout Holland, Flanders, France, and Germany . . . a complete and perfect train of intelligence . . . the fall of Namur added to his profits, owing to his early intelligence." These, however, were semi-*private* news services. There is nothing like a *public* financial intelligence supply (save in the shape of lists of prices) until the post-Waterloo Era. Consequently eighteenth-century enterprise lacked one of the most efficient of its admonitory and protective expedients. The best that could

That is precisely what Shakespeare indicates when he makes Macbeth say to Banquo's ghost :—

"Thou hast no *speculation* in those eyes
Which thou dost glare with."
(*Macbeth*, Act iii. Sc. 4.)

Practically every form of intelligent enterprise is speculation—even the acceptance by a tailor of an order for a

---

be said was that the speculator was kept ahead of the market by early copies of a few French newspapers, by carrier-pigeon service, or by fast fishing boats, which "sneaked" his expresses across the Channel. When Croker, writing from the Admiralty in 1813, said that the Plymouth "telegraph" had announced a new victory, he was referring to a series of signals which were not, strictly speaking, telegraphs at all, and which certainly would have been useless as an auxiliary to the complex business of a modern Stock Exchange. "The arms of Russia and Persia," said a writer in 1827, "were encountering each other on the banks of the Araxes, but the sound was too distant to disturb the repose of Europe." Nowadays the whole market would be affected by it—long before the actual clash occurred. The shareholders of a New Zealand company, though they were informed in 1840 that a profit of £27,000 had been made upon the land sales for the first year of the company's existence, had to wait for the news of the arrival of the emigrant ships before the dividend based upon these profits could be declared. (*Annual Register*, 1840, Chron. p. 85.) In 1840 and 1841 tea prices fluctuated to the extent of 6d. and 8d. a pound on the arrival of every mail. The cable has ended all such manifestations.

The City article, a very important factor of the news service, is untraceable, as such, earlier than the boom of 1824–1825. Before that time such City information as was available to the public in general was to be found only in scattered paragraphs. A list of prices, supplied by a stockbroker in return for the advertisement obtained by appending his name, was really the only information of a quasi-official character. When the need for a better news equipment became peremptory, and the regular City column began to supply it, the innovation was at first keenly disliked. It put the public on a par with the "insiders," and the latter resented the equalisation. The *Post* and the *Herald* made such a determined fight for the rights of the Peninsular bond-holders as to antagonise the Stock Exchange. Under the stimulus of the stern criticism in the City columns of these newspapers, the public declined to touch any foreign stock which was not known to pay punctual dividends. At that time the City editor was known as the "City correspondent" of the newspaper with which he was connected. In the early days of the City article during the boom of 1825–1826, the writers simply jotted down their notes on small slips of paper, sitting in the North and South American Coffee House. A few years later, however, it was noted as a remarkable thing that "two or three of the City article writers have separate offices, paid for by the proprietors of the journals with which they were connected." (*The City*, p. 128.) The evening newspapers must have been severely handicapped, seeing that down to 1848 the last "copy" from the City had to be delivered by 2 p.m. at the latest. (*The City*, p. 136.) The City article of 1825, like its modern enlargement, the financial daily newspaper, occasionally ventured to analyse the pretensions of rotten companies, to the dismay of their promoters. But from the first it had been keenly supported by the public at

THE STOCK EXCHANGE (1815–1915)   601

suit of clothes, since he may not actually possess the material and has no absolute assurance that he can obtain either material or labour. In an earlier age, when each man produced for himself, he took the risks in every instance. He was speculator, producer, and consumer in one individuality. Nowadays he specialises in a particular class of risks, which his experience enables him to measure :

---

large. In 1864, moreover, warm appreciation was expressed of the self-restraint and public spirit manifested by the writers of the various City articles. In fact, it was plainly said that the dexterous policy of the daily press had done very much to prevent the advent of a panic, which, if it had taken place, " would only have been equalled by the frightful period of 1826–1827."

The Overend-Gurney crash of 1866 practically coincided with the opening of the regular exchange of quotations by cable between the London and New York Exchanges. This was an enormous expansion of facilities both for news collection and rapid business. " In 1866 cable transfers from the United States did not exist ; the first American Cable Company commenced business in 1867, or the latter part of 1866, but the machinery for arbitrage in the value of money with that country, which has since been developed by all the houses engaged in that class of business, was hardly in existence. Indeed, cable transfers were not an important factor until some ten years later. Prior to that time, rapid business was practically impossible ; so far as the United States was concerned, it took nearly fourteen days for a mail out, and nearly fourteen days for a mail home, making a month's interval with any *certainty* as to the result of the operation. Now, you can control any transfer of capital or credit by a cable immediately, and the result of that operation immediately affects this market, while the credit, capital or cash itself is brought here at the expiration of seven days." (Luke Hansard, Address to the Manchester and District Institute of Bankers, January 18, 1901.) The same facilities are now available, of course, for business, not only between London and the United States, but with the remotest parts of the earth.

To-day, the City article has expanded into a newspaper all by itself. Daily financial newspapers like the *Financial News*, the *Financial Times*, and the *Financier* are simply expanded City articles printed as separate newspapers. The single City article, in its original form, has long ceased to be capable of dealing, in the available space, with all the multitudinous phenomena which are of interest to the new investing public. Therefore each separate paragraph of the old City article becomes a separate " market " and often a separate page, in the modern financial newspaper. A corresponding expansion has taken place in the City articles of the great political newspapers, which now frequently devote a page or more to a subject which they once regarded as adequately accounted for within the limits of a single column. Nowadays there are even different " schools " of financial journalism—the " old " and the " new "—the former distinguished by a conservative and severe reserve, the latter by a sprightliness which occasionally condescends to humour ! Modern financial journalism demands intellectual attainments of the highest order— and the requirement does not go unsatisfied. So well is the public supplied with news that the present-day speculator who desires to conduct large operations on advance intelligence must employ methods of the

and his fellow-creatures are content to remunerate him for his enterprise in fields with which they are not familiar. So, the tailor takes the risk either of having the clothes ready-made, to meet an expected demand, or of undertaking to produce them to order. In the former case he is a bull: in the latter, a bear. He does not possess the

most exceptional type such as the employment of agents among the miners on a given property, who cable the latest aspect of the mine.

The mere supply of the quotations themselves has now become an immense business in London. This is done largely by the Exchange Telegraph Company over the familiar " tape " though the City editors have their own auxiliary organisation, while the financial dailies employ a small army in the collection of the latest prices in every market. In New York the Stock Exchange itself owns the entire stock of the New York Quotation Company, which, for a specified rental supplies members' offices south of Chambers Street, New York City, with a "ticker" service. For $100,000 a year, under contract terminable upon one day's notice, it sells the quotations to a subsidiary of the Western Union, the Gold and Stock Telegraph Company, which also maintains a "ticker" service. The latter, however, can supply persons only as the Exchange approves. It has been well said that even the "ticker," by the wide publicity which it gives to prices, extends the protection which it is the business of the Stock Exchanges to provide.

There is no doubt that the huge expansion of foreign investment has been largely the result of the excellence and the far-flung scope of the news service, which has brought the various fields of economic activity closer and closer together, and consequently more and more within the immediate cognisance of the investor. It has quickened and facilitated communication, so that not only has the *machinery* of investment been specialised and accelerated, but the investor's dislike of the distant and the obscure has been overcome by abundant information. There are no means of ascertaining how much money, in other circumstances left on deposit with bankers or placed on mortgage, has been tempted into the arena of foreign investment by this closing in of the frontiers of the world. Statistics on the subject are utterly outside the range of potentiality. But if we recall how, forty years ago, the mortgage and the bank deposit were the popular forms of investment with whole classes whose money is now in Argentine railways, or in the municipal undertakings of Australasian cities, we shall be convinced that this factor of accurate and immediate information is one of the most remarkable achievements of the financial organisation, though it is only in a slight degree officially connected with it. When the keenest business intellects of the world are engaged in obtaining the best information with regard to the objects of market traffic, there must, even when obvious and undeniable abuses are allowed for, be a balance of public benefit.

At the same time, it would be unscientific to ignore the converse impulse. If the supply of financial intelligence stimulated foreign investment, the latter also increased the demand for news, and, in the shape of advertised prospectuses, provides the newspaper proprietor with the means of supplying it. Among nations, as among individuals, the creditor is stimulated into curiosity about the debtor's circumstances, and in the case of the creditor-nation a widened and more sympathetic intellectual grasp of world politics is the inevitable result. Nor is that all. The sensory powers are compelled to a higher development when the materials

material out of which he has undertaken to make the bespoke garments. But he believes he knows where he can get it : and this is the position of the speculator on the Stock Exchange.[1] Even the most cautious buyer of Dominion Government securities hopes for " an increase in capital value," and is to that extent a speculator. His investment is only speculation for the long shot instead of the short.

DEFINITELY ORGANISED SPECULATION

Organised speculation has now become a clearly differentiated function as distinct from a merely spasmodic outburst.[2] Just as trader and consumer became differentiated in a town-economy, so speculator and trader become differentiated in a world-economy, because the risks become too large, and the labour of watching and measuring them too severe, for any but a specialised class :—

" Both the writer and the reformer must reckon more than they have yet done with the fact that speculation in the last half-century has developed as a natural economic institution

---

[1] Many years ago there was a law on the French Statute books, subsequently repealed, prohibiting short sales. M. Boscarry de Villeplaine, a deputy chairman of the Association of Stockbrokers, was conversing with Napoleon regarding a pending discussion in the Council of State looking to the repeal of the law. " Your Majesty," said de Villeplaine, " when my water carrier is at the door, would he be guilty of selling property he did not own if he sold me two casks of water instead of only one, which he has ? " " Certainly not," replied Napoleon, " because he is always sure of finding in the river what he lacks." " Well, your Majesty, there is on the Bourse a river of Rentes." (Quoted by Van Antwerp, p. 87.)

[2] It was, of course, temporarily suppressed when the Stock Exchange was re-opened, on January 4, 1915, by the application of the principle of Leeman's Act to *all* bargains.

---

of food, clothing and shelter come from an almost infinite variety of sources, and have to be adapted for use by multitudinous devices and processes. The most extensive knowledge of the world's material resources, their location, nature, value, qualities, and capacities, is needed by a race which is evolving, under financial inspiration, along these lines. Its requisites for adaptation to its environment, its consequent capacity for survival in the midst of the struggle for existence, will be entirely different from the corresponding qualities in a race which inhabits a self-contained area, lives on its own produce, fights with weapons cut from its own trees, and carries on its primitive transport by means of its own cattle. Every foreign investment is a new advance towards the federation of humanity. The financial press and the city article are the standard bearers of the campaign.

in response to the new conditions of industry and commerce. It is the result of steam transportation and the telegraph on the one hand, and of vast industrial undertakings on the other. The attitude of those who would try to crush it out by legislation, without disturbing any other economic conditions, is entirely unreasonable."[1]

Stock Exchange conditions, essential as they are to the discharge of its distributive functions, encourage speculation. The jobber is a professional risk-taker. The very existence of the market, so facile, so accessible, so instant in operation, and with all its commodities standardised, tends of itself to stimulate speculative activity and to maintain (as we have seen) a condition of extreme sensitiveness. Under normal circumstances, and with regard to all securities in which there is a free market, the buyer can always protect himself by a sale, and the seller by a purchase. In technical language, he can always cover himself by a counter operation—or by an original " put " or " call "—and this at the first scent of danger. Such facility, accessibility, and promptitude of action, and such a restricted arena, do not characterise commodity markets to anything like the same degree : and the real estate market not at all. Therefore we get the supremacy of the sanguine, which makes a real estate " boom " in a new country ; or else the supremacy of the sceptical, which turns the boom into a slump, with no bears to mitigate it. The nearest approach to the Stock Exchange is the standardised commodity market of the Mark Lane and Metal Market species, reinforced by the produce warrant system, which dates from 1733, when it was adopted by the East India Company. Outside these great " both-ways " markets, the seller must look about, perhaps vainly, for his buyer or the buyer for his seller : and while he is finding him, the opportunity (or the inclination to take the risk) may have passed away. Thus, sensitiveness encourages speculation and thus breeds a still keener sensitiveness, and the enhanced volume of business gives

---

[1] Emery, *Speculation on the Stock and Produce Exchanges of the United States*, p. 9.

an ever-finer quotation—the sixteenth in place of the quarter, for instance.

MANIPULATION AND SPECULATION DIFFERENTIATED

The disadvantage of these conditions lies in the liability to a debacle if there is a sudden contingency which leads to the calling in of bankers' money lent on stock pledged for the financing of speculation. This not unfrequently happens. But the total elimination of the speculative factor is impossible and, in fact, unthinkable. At the same time it would be unscientific and futile to deny that it occasionally becomes a real menace to the market. In 1899, for instance, there was a case of a " hammered " member, whose liabilities on differences aggregated £36,000, though his balance at the bank was only £600. Speculation of that type comes within the scope of Marshall's observation that " many of the largest fortunes are made by speculation rather than by truly constructive work ; and much of this speculation is associated with anti-social strategy." The bulk of this class of speculation, however, discovers its opportunity in securities of a youthful type, which in a few years may become " respectable," and take their place among " first class industrials." But the elimination of speculation—say by the extension[1] of Leeman's Act to all securities—would be a far greater peril. Banish speculation, and the work of the manipulator would be infinitely easier for him, and more dangerous to the economic fabric, than is the case where the bull and the bear are allowed to range. Further, the illusion produced by manipulation is only transient and relatively unimportant : especially as the manipulator generally confines himself to classes of security which are more or less outside the range of the serious and conservative investor. No manipulator can repeal, or suspend, economic law. Its *apparent* abrogation, in rare instances of successful manipulation, depends on the fortuitous concurrence of

[1] The *permanent* extension, that is to say. The reopening of the Stock Exchange after the German war crisis was made by the Government conditional upon the temporary application of Leeman's Act to every transaction.

a multitude of market factors, and, as Emery argues, " requires immense capital, coolness and courage, and the greatest practical skill." Were it not for this ineradicable factor of manipulation, the Stock Exchange itself would be the best " all-round " barometer of existing business conditions. A free market, with a large speculative interest, is the best antidote to manipulation. That is the reason why manipulation, although it cannot be entirely eradicated, steadily dwindles in scope and frequency.

It must be constantly remembered that manipulation and speculation are not the same thing.[1] A speculator in the real sense of the word is simply a sentinel or scout. The word was used exactly in that sense of the spies sent out in advance of the Roman armies. Varro speaks of the *Speculator, quem mittimus ante*—the scout that we send out ahead. So again, Cicero alludes to *physicus, speculator venatorque naturae.* The speculator only anticipates the market movement; he does not produce it. The market concentrates all the influences, and he tries to read their unified index in the effort to minimise the factor of Uncertainty. If his judgment is wrong, he pays the penalty of his error. A manipulator tries to *make the stock move* the way he wishes it to go. The

[1] It would be a great mistake to suggest that the manipulation is always initiated from the inside of the Stock Exchange, or by the professional class. The rubber share mania of 1910—largely a manipulated movement—was worked up by the public itself. Probably nobody was more surprised than the Stock Exchange at the ultimate enormous development of the boom. The mere fact that thousands and tens of thousands of speculators and punters were involved in this affair did not in the least alter its character as being essentially manipulation. Social psychology would tell us that mob suggestibility is quite as capable of manipulation as the insidious scheming of a small syndicate. As a matter of fact it was the jobbers' refusal to carry-over which ultimately put the brake on the mania.

To the absurd charge that the Stock Exchange section of the Money-Power favours, if it does not actually precipitate, panics there could be no better reply than the argument of Messrs. J. P. Morgan and Co. They pointed out that in order to sustain the theory that panics are engineered " one must attribute to the engineers not only the power, but some motive for their assumed achievements. And by no process of reasoning can such motive be imagined, because of the fact that the men possessing even a fraction of the influence and resources attributed to them are always the ones holding the largest amounts of fixed investments, which, by disturbed financial conditions, always suffer most severely."

THE STOCK EXCHANGE (1815–1915) 607

speculator has no definite design in the matter : he buys or sells on judgment, not inclination, or sentiment. If we eliminate his judgment and its market consequences, we clear the arena for the purely selfish work of the manipulator. Monopoly spells manipulation. When once the whole commodity (or the whole of an issue of stock or shares) is " cornered " the price can be raised to any level which the monopolist may choose, because no speculative seller dare enter the arena where all the sources of supply are under rigid restraint. Statutory elimination of speculative sales would yield exactly the same result. The German prohibition of dealings for future delivery in grain and flour produced disastrous effects on the trade. Equally unfortunate was the simultaneous attempt at the suppression of dealings for the account in money and industrial securities. Fluctuations became more violent and the tendency to inflation more pronounced in the absence of the bear. As was said in 1907, the power of the market to resist a " one-sided movement " was dangerously weakened. The new legislative obstacles drove business abroad, and diminished the relative importance of Berlin among the world's financial centres. London especially benefitted by the wholesale emigration of German capital, whether for investment or speculation.

SPECULATION A STEADYING FORCE

Public sentiment with regard to speculation is seldom hostile to the bull. It concentrates upon the bear. Yet there may be times when the bear is the only buyer left in the market. " The prices of all industrial securities have fallen," said the Deutsche Bank in 1900, " and this decline has been felt all the more because, by reason of the ill-conceived Bourse Law, it struck the public with full force without being softened through covering purchases," i.e. by the bears. Further, the bull is, after all, only a voluntary holder. He buys the stock, but he is under no compulsion to retain it. On the other hand, the bear assumes the position of an ultimate *compulsory* buyer, no matter what the state of the market may be. The bull has the option of shifting the burden from his shoulders at any moment. The bear has no corresponding choice, but *must* buy sooner or later. Speculation acts like the anti-rolling tanks fitted to some of the newer ocean liners. If the boat rolls to starboard, the contents of the tanks move to port, and vice-versa, thereby mitigating the violence of the movement by setting an opposing force in operation. The bull checks undue depression and the bear is the automatic counterweight of inflation. Both types of operation make for steadiness :—

" The result of regular speculation is to *steady* prices. . . . Speculation tends to equalise demand and supply, and by concentrating in the present the influences of the future it intensifies the normal factors and minimises the market fluctuation. . . . Speculation so far as it has become the regular occupation of a class, differentiated from other business men for this particular purpose, subserves a useful and in modern times an indispensable function."[1]

" The elimination of speculation by laws, if that were possible," said the Committee of the New York Stock Exchange in reply to the Money Trust Committee, " would result in periods of extraordinary inflation of prices, followed by their rapid fall and disastrous panics. No legislation can prevent, or even effectively restrain, speculation and inflation." Discretion is not a commodity which governments can supply. In fact, " no public legislation, consistent with the liberty of the subject, can protect ignorant dabblers in inferior securities from the effects of their wilful blindness ; an attempt at anything in that direction can only end by further compelling outsiders to trust the more implicitly in market price as a guide to value."[2] " On se plaint," as Leroy Beaulieu says, writing with regard to this very factor of speculation, " des maux qu'elle entraine mais ceux qu'elle épargne seraient beaucoup plus grands que ceux qu'elle cause." When it can be affirmed—and no such affirmation can at present

---
[1] Seligman, *Principles of Economics*, p. 365.
[2] Ellis, *Rationale of Market Fluctuations*, p. 126. For instance, " You are of opinion that no law can put an end to dealing in stock and shares before allotment, if the public are inclined to do it ?—Yes." H. Rokeby Price, Stock Exchange Commission, 1878, Question 1726.)

be made—that the evils arising from speculation are too great a price to pay for the advantages of a free market, the time will have come to reconsider the possibility of legislation. Meanwhile, as the credit of an enterprise is largely measured by the stability of its securities, the force which makes for steadiness is a social gain. This is true, whether the force is operative, by the closing of a bear, to check an otherwise disastrous slump; or through the enterprise of a bull, in reinforcing the price of a security against unjustifiable downward tendencies.

" WEEDING OUT " IRRESPONSIBLE SPECULATION

The Stock Exchange, be it emphatically said, has co-operated loyally and efficiently with other factors of the financial hierarchy in the relentless eradication, as far as it was feasible, of the elements of venturesome weakness and undisciplined irresponsibility which form the snags in the stream of modern civilisation. This has been done, externally, as we shall see in due course, by the creation and enforcement of a high standard of responsibility, especially in the case of public borrowers, whenever the use of Stock Exchange facilities is sought, and the parties are consequently compelled to place themselves within the range of its powerful jurisdiction, at present the only existing instrument of international discipline in the sphere of ethics. The same duty has been performed internally by an inexorable insistence—in many cases contrary to the interest of the Stock Exchange itself—upon the sanctity of bargains, and by the stern discouragement of any opportunities for illicit and imprudent gambling.[1] Genuine speculation is concerned to antici-

---

[1] The suggestion was made in the 1878 report that the Committee of the Stock Exchange should " hold the restraining hand " over those of their own members who should be found to have lent themselves to facilitating extravagant speculation, " or any speculation by those who had no adequate means." There is the same discrimination in New York. " Speculation by those who should not speculate, because without either the means or the intelligence to do so, is," says Mr. J. E. Milburn, " properly called unwholesome speculation. The volume of this sort of speculation on the Exchange has been constantly diminishing. It is business that the broker avoids, because of the risks it involves in rapid changes of price and the doubtful ability of his customer to meet his obligations. The Exchange prevents it to the utmost limit of its powers."

pate, and to profit by, the inevitable economic risks arising from changes in value; but gambling is a mere artificial dealing, often with an artificially created risk—as in the case of bets upon the " tape " in the unwholesome atmosphere of the bucket-shop. The speculator contemplates the obligation to deliver or take up, though he may ultimately settle the " difference " only. But the gambler is only interested in the " difference." The recommendation to brokers by the Hughes Commission in the United States, that they should insist upon a 20 per cent. margin on speculative transaction, was simply a recognition of the fact that speculation should be limited to experts and to those who can afford to face its risks.

THE GAMING ACT

Our own Gaming Act (8 and 9 Vict. c. 109 s. 18) is a statute which (whether originally aimed at Stock Exchange gambling or not) has done nothing to check rash speculation. Dealings for differences are only within the Act if it can be shown that gambling for such differences (and not the actual delivery and acceptance of the stock) was contemplated by the parties :—

" What are called time bargains are, in fact, the result of two distinct and perfectly legal bargains, namely, first, a bargain to buy or sell ; and, secondly, a subsequent bargain that the first shall not be carried out : and *it is only when the first bargain is entered into upon the understanding that it is not to be carried out*, that a time bargain, in the sense of an unenforceable bargain, is entered into. Such bargains are very rare."[1]

In one direction the Gaming Act is positively mischievous. Scores of touts invite ignorant persons, by circular, to " open " various stocks for the rise or fall, on the deposit of " cover." If the stock moves against the client, the tout pockets the money : if the client wins, the tout declines to pay, and will be upheld by the court in his plea of the Gaming Act. Utilised in this manner the

[1] Lindley, J., in Thacker *v.* Hardy, 4 Q.B.D., at p. 689. Affirmed on appeal by Bramwell, Brett, and Cotton, L.JJ.

THE STOCK EXCHANGE (1815–1915)   611

Act is worthy of its name of the " Swindler's Charter." The man crossing Niagara on a tight-rope is hardly in a more perilous position than he who swallows the bait of an assurance that " £5 controls £500 stock " and forthwith sends the money. Still, Discrimination is one thing, and Elimination another. The total exclusion of the public by the prohibition of non-professional speculation, would mischievously narrow the market :—

> " The question must be faced of the effect of eliminating the public from the speculative market even if it could be accomplished. It is supposed sometimes that such a result would be all benefit and no injury. On the contrary, the real and important function of speculation in the field of business can only be performed by a broad and open market. Though no one would defend individual cases of recklessness or fail to lament the disaster and crime sometimes engendered, the fact remains that a ' purely professional market ' is not the kind of market which best fulfils the services of speculation. A broad market with the participation of an intelligent and responsible public is necessary. A narrow professional market is less serviceable to legitimate investment and trade and much more susceptible of manipulation."[1]

STATUTORY REGULATION FUTILE

Here the immediate allusion is to the abortive German attempts to eliminate speculation. Conversely, the absence of government-control is one of the reasons for the predominance of London, as well as for the vast business that has concentrated in Wall Street. On the Continent there is sometimes municipal supervision of the Bourse, as in Belgium, and sometimes Imperial control as in Austria. In some countries, e.g. Holland—a theoretical government-control amounts in practice almost to non-interference ; whereas in Paris the agents de Change are nearly, if not quite, government officials. The free, non-government-controlled Stock Exchange might almost be described as a characteristic Anglo-Saxon institution. The task of incessant care and vigilance in the management

[1] Emery, " Ten Years' Regulation of the Stock Exchange in Germany." *Yale Review*, May, 1908.

of these elusive forces is too huge, too subtle, for the statutory mandate to encompass it. " Any attempt to reduce these (Stock Exchange) rules to the limits of the ordinary law of the land, or to abolish all checks and safeguards not to be found in that law, would, in our opinion," said the Stock Exchange Commission of 1877, " be detrimental to the honest and efficient conduct of business." They had declared that " the existing body of rules and regulations have been formed with much care, and are the result of long experience and the vigilant attention of a body of persons intimately acquainted with the needs and exigencies of the community for whom they have legislated." Speculation in some form is a necessary incident of productive operation and cannot be legislatively controlled :—

" When carried on in connection with either commodities or securities it tends to steady their prices. Where speculation is free, fluctuations in prices, otherwise violent and disastrous, ordinarily become gradual and comparatively harmless. . . . For the merchant or manufacturer speculation performs a service which has the effect of insurance. . . . The most fruitful policy will be found in measures which will lessen speculation by persons not qualified to engage in it. In carrying out such a policy exchanges can accomplish more than legislatures. . . . We are unable to see how a State could distinguish by law between proper and improper transactions, since the forms and mechanisms used are identical. Rigid statutes directed against the latter would seriously interfere with the former. . . . Purchasing securities on margin is as legitimate a transaction as the purchase of any property in which part payment is deferred. We, therefore, see no reason whatsoever for recommending the radical change suggested, that margin trading be prohibited."[1]

Corporate regulation, such as the Stock Exchange species, is dependent largely for its application upon the esprit de corps of a professional body. It is much more psychological in operation and sanction than the clumsier mandates and prohibitions of a public statute, backed merely by physical force. A Government might

[1] Hughes Commission Report, 1909.

prepare a system of ethics for the Stock Exchange, and enact it as a statute, but it could not procure its acceptance and observance. Psychological influence and the mysterious energy which we call esprit de corps can penetrate where statutory and mechanical pressure would be easily excluded. That is why the greatest religions have depended on the psychological sanction. Economic reform must depend largely on the employment of the same subtle and penetrative force. But economic reform, whatever shapes it may take, is not likely to extend to the abolition of speculation.

SECTION VI

THE INVIOLABILITY OF CONTRACT—INTERNATIONAL FINANCIAL CENSORSHIP

As we saw at an earlier stage, the fundamental principle on which the Stock Exchange Committee acts is the inviolability of contracts.[1] As the stern exponent of this

[1] Save where their enforcement would itself be a violation of honour, or would aid the success of a fraud. On May 5, 1803, a notice was posted at the Mansion House stating, on what appeared to be first-class authority, that the negotiations between Great Britain and France had been brought to a successful conclusion. Consols rose from $63\frac{3}{4}$ to $71\frac{1}{4}$. By next morning it was more than suspected that the statement was quite baseless. Although there were sanguine people who insisted on its truth, the Stock Exchange Committee refused to open the doors of that institution until the truth was definitely known. As a matter of fact, they were opened shortly after twelve o'clock, and Consols immediately relapsed to 63. (This, by the way, is the example of an earlier closure of the Stock Exchange than that of 1914. Refusing to allow the " House " to be opened is equivalent to closing it.)

In view of the falsity of the news, the Stock Exchange Committee declared void all bargains effected in Consols as a result of it. But it was held, in the case of Doughty v. Axe, which arose out of this affair, that a jobber was not entitled, as against a non-member of the Stock Exchange, to repudiate a bargain in Consols, done during the currency of the rumour, with an innocent seller. Plaintiff's counsel said the case was a conflict between the laws of England and the law of the Stock Exchange.

In the much later case of the Peruvian Railway, six members of Parliament were concerned. The directors bought more shares in the market than they had allotted, but they obtained a settlement after having assured the Committee on their honour that there had been a fair allotment. When the time for the settlement came, it was found that there were no shares to be delivered. The rest of the story may be told in the words of Mr. H. Rokeby Price (Stock Exchange Commission, Question 1867): " Having given a settlement the Committee could not revoke it ;

principle in the financial sphere, it wields unique authority. The premonitory expostulation conveyed by a sharp fall in a group of securities, on the report of attempted tampering with the rights of their holders, or of possible default on the next coupon, is far more effective than legislation. This may be predicated with the greater confidence because the caution is operative in an arena where legislation is impotent—to wit, that of international relationship. The royal autocrat may be beyond the reach of public opinion; but the quotations of his bonds are not, and these are the measure of his credit in the Money Market. He may command armies, but credit is not within his military jurisdiction. " The missionaries of Gregory could penetrate where the legions of Augustus had been destroyed."[1] The influence of finance can reach where law is impotent. City sentiment was sternly opposed to the scheme for the partial repudiation of the British debt, or the deliberate depreciation of the currency, which was urged in 1822. Sir Francis Burdett argued for paying the public creditor £5 instead of £4, since he had lent the money when bank paper was legal tender, and could not expect to be paid in gold. Western, who represented Essex, proposed the depreciation of the currency so that £4 nominal should represent £3 actual. These proposals were not acceptable to a nation already schooled in stern principles of public credit. Dishonesty and default were reprobated, even in the twenties and thirties of the last century. The publicity given, through the embryo City articles, to the misdeeds

[1] Marvin, *Living Past*, p. 125.

---

but, according to our rules, if shares are not delivered within a specific time after the account day, ten days, the parties who have bought those shares can instruct the official broker to buy in those shares against the person who has failed to deliver them. As these directors had the shares in their own hands, they would have supplied them through their brokers to the official broker at any price they chose, which would have brought ruin, not only upon members of the Stock Exchange but upon their principals as well.

" What did you do ?—We . . . resolved that the suspension of the buying in of shares in the Peruvian Railways Company be continued until further notice, and it has been suspended until this day.

" Then practically the contracts for the sale of these shares have never been enforced ?—They have never been enforced."

THE STOCK EXCHANGE (1815-1915)

of Latin-American defaulters led to offers of arrangement, to fundings, and to compromise. " As the medicine operated," observed a City critic of those days, " so the disease began to disappear." More than fifty years ago, City men pointed to the overdue coupon as the brand of shame upon the face of a bond.[1] The Stock Exchange itself initiated the enunciation of regulations, and the creation of a sentiment, which should be fatal to international financial trickery. The effort primarily took the form of the rules, dating from 1847, with regard to Special Settlements. Partial settlements, with undue preference, and the possibility of no settlement at all, were thus, to a great extent, excluded, with a consequent appreciable addition to the responsibility of those who dealt in freshly issued bonds, or the shares of new undertakings. The principle rapidly extended to the field of a cosmopolitan stewardship, where the Stock Exchange realised its firm possession of a weapon that no Government was capable of grasping. " Representations have been made by our Government upon more than one occasion to the foreign Governments," said Mr. H. Rokeby Price to the Stock Exchange Commission of 1877-1878,[2] " and they have got no redress ; but directly a Government comes for money, we have that power which no Government has." The diplomatic weapon, in fact, was early recognised as inefficient. In 1873 the Corporation of Foreign Bondholders indicated their desire to refrain from any such intervention as might result in creating antagonism between Her Majesty's Government and that of any other country. Doubtless the Corporation realised that its power was not of a diplomatic order and that its exercise would not be furthered by diplomatic assistance. At the first meeting of the Corporation (November 27, 1873), it was stated that part of its programme was to prepare archives tracing the history of every foreign loan and that 230 books had already been collected on the subject. In these, and in the utilisation of a defaulter's " record "

---

[1] *City Men and City Manners*, p. 26.
[2] Minutes, Question 1666.

for the protection of short-memoried investors, were to be found (by means of collaboration with the Stock Exchanges) the deadliest missiles against international dishonesty.[1]

The truth is that the world is moving too fast for merely *political* evolution to keep pace with it. Some more rapidly-adaptive capacity is required if international good faith is to be widely inculcated. It is discoverable in finance simply because the rivalry of the twentieth century is, at the root, less a struggle for a chance to sell than for an opportunity to lend. The conflict is quite as much an effort to buy bonds as to sell commodities. The transaction is, in effect, an endeavour by a more advanced community to buy a claim upon the produce of a less-advanced community's prosperity, for the development of which the former provides the means. The borrower enjoys a widened opportunity, the lender an enhanced income; and the " deal " is a true economic bargain, for both are the gainers by it. Firm and consistent relations of this character, involving the creation of the fraternity of confidence and the maintenance of good faith, over extensive areas and among peoples in all stages of social evolution, cannot be conceived save as the result of compact control, itself concentrated upon a small area, and maintained by means of a recognition of

[1] A typical recent protest by the Corporation of Foreign Bondholders may be found in the *Financial News*, December 4, 1912 : " The Council of Foreign Bondholders are informed that certain of the defaulting Southern States of the American Union are again endeavouring to borrow money. For instance, North Carolina, with defaulted obligations amounting without accrued interest to over $12,000,000, is appealing for a loan of $550,000 based on the credit of the State. Mississippi, also, with a repudiated debt of $7,000,000, is anxious to borrow, but this is being done through the medium of some of the counties into which the State is subdivided, the superior Government being quite aware of its own want of credit. About eighteen months ago efforts were made by these two States to obtain loans amounting to upwards of $4,000,000, but strong opposition was encountered and protests were lodged with the Committee of the New York Stock Exchange against any official recognition of their bonds. . . . The Council cannot see what valid excuse these prosperous and wealthy communities can put forward to justify their attitude towards their creditors, and so long as they decline to enter into a reasonable arrangement with the holders of their defaulted obligations, there is no course open but to offer an uncompromising opposition to their attempts to obtain new money."

THE STOCK EXCHANGE (1815–1915)

common honesty and equally common responsibility for its enforcement. " The modern market is based on good faith."[1] This, as a psychical fact, introduces a new and wholesome element into the affinities of mankind. " Among unmitigated rogues, mutual trust is impossible. Among people of absolute integrity, mutual trust would be unlimited."[2] The business of finance is to penalise the first class, and to expedite the transformation of society into the second.

THE NEW POWER WIDELY UTILISED

The existence of this financial prerogative was soon widely understood. " There is only one course of policy open to us," said the late Sir Henry Drummond Wolff at the General Credit and Discount meeting (July 22, 1869), " and that is to oppose, tooth and nail, any loan brought out by the Portuguese Government upon the Stock Exchange."[3] At a meeting of the holders of Mexican bonds in 1870 a speaker said he had caused the protest to be circulated to forty-four bourses in Europe, so it would be utterly impossible for Mexico to borrow a single shilling upon the European markets without first settling with her English creditors.[4] In 1859 a Russian loan was issued here, with the promised provision of a stipulated sinking fund. As the subscription was very meagre, the Russian Government appropriated the sinking fund to the unissued portion of the loan. This was resented by the Stock Exchange Committee, which ultimately, in 1866, took the drastic step of refusing a quotation to the latest Russian loan, and thus compelled the acceptance of its views with regard to the impropriety of dealing with a sinking fund in the manner already described. At the Bank of England meeting in March, 1865, objection was taken to certain of the directors of the Bank being connected with the provision of loans to Spain, at that time

[1] Banks, *Ethics of Work and Wealth*, p. 75.
[2] Spencer, *Essays*, Vol. III. p. 326.
[3] The allusion was to certain claims against the Government by the company with regard to which the former was alleged to have acted in a treacherous and deceitful manner.
[4] *Bankers' Magazine*, July, 1870.

a defaulter and excluded from the *Official List.* The Deputy Chairman declared that the Bank itself had nothing to do with the loan, but did not deny that some of the directors, in their personal capacity, might be associated with it. The most significant incident, however, was the declaration by a shareholder—a plain voucher of ripening financial sentiment—that the advance of money to a defaulting Government was " condemned by the majority of the monetary and commercial world," and that " those directors ought not to remain connected with the Bank." In 1867 the Stock Exchange Committee refused a quotation for a Massachusetts loan which was wholly held by Barings'. But when, a few years later, the bonds were in the hands of investors the quotation was granted. Shortly after the Franco-German War a settlement and quotation were granted to the scrip of the German loan. The definitive bonds contained the condition that the principal should be forfeited after thirty years from the date of its falling due, and that the coupons should be void four years after the date of maturity. The Committee strongly objected to these stipulations, and refused a quotation for the bonds. The quotation was ultimately granted, however, on representations that the condition was a compliance with an old Prussian law. But the Committee declared, in very strong terms, that the existence of this law and the resulting condition should have been disclosed in the prospectus. The refusal of a quotation of the converted Austrian Debt because the conversion had been made compulsory and the sinking fund suppressed are other instances at this period of the exercise of the same disciplinary power. In this latter case insult was added to injury because Internal Bonds were given in place of the old External holdings, and an income tax of 16 per cent. imposed. Ultimately Austria gave way, entered into an arrangement acceptable to the bondholders, and the stocks were reinstated in the list. Where certain members of the Stock Exchange had taken £86,000 out of the total of a £99,000 loan by the City of London (Ont.), settlement and quotation were refused, and only given when, several months afterwards, the firm could certify that the bonds were entirely off their hands. In 1875 the alleged allotment of a certain part of a New Zealand issue, at a preferential price, to favoured individuals was the reason for the refusal of a quotation—subsequently granted, however, on the offer of satisfactory explanations.

EFFECTS ADMITTEDLY SALUTARY

Even the critics and opponents of the powers of the Committee have been compelled to admit that its powers in this direction have had a salutary effect. For instance, Mr. C. Branch before the Commission of 1877,[1] said that he objected on principle to the interference of the Committee. If a foreign Government, notwithstanding its being bankrupt any number of times, wanted to borrow " then I say it is not for the Committee to step in and say that people shall not trust that Government."

Mr. Scott. Practically does not it have this effect : that a foreign Government, knowing that this rule is here, is induced to do the right thing sometimes before coming here ?—I believe that the Stock Exchange have in several instances coerced foreign Governments into a compromise.

Chairman. Not merely a compromise, but into doing partial justice ?—Yes, doing partial justice, certainly.

There was a good actual instance quoted by Mr. H. Rokeby Price to the Commission :—[2]

" Messrs. Knowles and Foster brought out the second Costa Rica loan ; Messrs. Bischoffsheim had brought out a previous one. They opposed a settlement and quotation before the Stock Exchange Committee, saying that the Costa Rica Government had not complied with the agreements of the previous loan. Messrs. Hichens and Harrison appeared before us on behalf of Messrs. Knowles and Foster, and they undertook and gave a pledge on behalf of Messrs. Knowles and Foster, and an undertaking from the Finance Minister, and they handed to Messrs. Bischoffsheim in bank-notes the whole amount. Messrs. Bischoffscheim had said, ' You have not

[1] Question 3902. More recent instances have been avoided, for obvious reasons.   [2] Question 2074.

complied with the condition of the previous loan.' Messrs. Hichens and Harrison referred to Messrs. Knowles and Foster, and Messrs. Knowles and Foster then referred to the Costa Rica Government, and they admitted that Messrs. Bischoffsheim had some ground for complaint and they paid the money.

"Through Messrs. Bischoffsheim's intervention, the Costa Rica Government were obliged to fulfil their previous obligation?—Yes."

STEWARDSHIP NOT UNIVERSALLY EFFECTIVE

These efforts at the creation and enforcement of responsibility were by no means as thorough as they might have been, or so effective at every point. The long series of scandals detailed in the report of the Select Committee of the House of Commons on Loans to Foreign States, 1875, undoubtedly generated doubts whether the supervision of the Stock Exchange Committee was as adequate as it ought to be. The report pointed out that the Committee of the Stock Exchange " gives, by granting a quotation, a certain prestige to a loan, which neither the very slight and superficial investigation on which the grant of a quotation is founded nor the nature of the tribunal seems to warrant." The main defect revealed in the case of such issues as the Costa Rica, Honduras, and Paraguay loans was the ineffectiveness of the power of inquiry into the real circumstances. The Committee had been accustomed, so it was said, to accept the assurances of the issuing houses that all its requirements had been complied with, although, as a matter of fact, thorough investigation would have shown that this was not the case. Moreover, it was clear from the evidence adduced that loans had frequently been introduced to the market without the slightest regard to the ability of the borrowing State to meet its obligations. Loans raised for one purpose had been applied to another. There were even cases where the borrowing Governments had themselves contracted, through intermediaries, to make large purchases of their own issue, merely in order to give a fictitious appearance of cordiality to the reception of the transaction. That is to say markets were made in order, either to induce public subscriptions, or to sustain the price until the balance of the loan had been sold. In some instances, these operations were conducted with funds deducted from the proceeds of the loan itself. One jobber alone had bought and sold the entire Honduras issue of 1870 to the extent of £2,500,000. These markets were "made" by syndicates—as indeed, though to a much less mischievous extent, they are still. "It was stated to your committee that if a law were passed making the action of the syndicates public, it would drive all transactions in public loans to foreign countries. Your committee do not hesitate to say that if these are the only terms on which the profits arising from such loans can be retained in England, they will be too dearly earned at such a price." Moreover, the amounts received by the borrowers were in some cases almost incredibly small in comparison with the nominal aggregate of the issue. The Santa Domingo loan of July, 1869, was for £757,700, of which, according to the report, the amount actually received by the Government was probably only £38,000 and certainly not more than £50,000.

NO FIXED DATE OF LOAN-MATURITY

Worst of all, there were none of the strict provisions, nowadays insisted on, for the repayment of loans within a given time. The natural consequence was that the borrowers, having got the money, ceased to trouble themselves about the existence of the indebtedness, or the means of liquidating it. That abuse has been sternly repressed in later years. Nowadays, the charmed circle of the Money Market is closed to the man or the nation of whom it can be truly said that il n'a pas le sens de l'échéance.[1] Never again will systematised modern

[1] This absence of le sens de l'échéance was doubtless a legacy from the age of irresponsible debt creation. The seventeenth-century law reports abound with cases where debts upon bonds (i.e. personal bonds, not negotiable securities) were allowed to run for forty and fifty years, and then enforced, to the great inconvenience of the defendants. (See an instance in Winchcomb v. Winchcomb—2 Rep. Ch. 53—where the bond ran from 1625 to 1674.) D'Avenant argues that one of the influences contributing to "sink" the Spanish monarchy was the payment of interest on the money borrowed one hundred years ago.

finance tolerate the issue of public securities which are
minus a definite date of redemption at a price determinable
within comparatively narrow limits. A distant date is
no objection, nor yet an alternative date. The earlier
date does but confer an option on the borrower, which
will be exercised if Money Market conditions be favourable. The later date, however, must be definite.[1] Its
fixation puts some check upon depreciation. That is to say,
it adds materially to the element of stability in price. If
there had been a fixed date (not later, say, than 1960)
for the redemption of Consols, the disastrous fall in them
would have been reduced to the extent, probably, of
10 per cent. at least. In the twelve years to the end of 1914
it was estimated by the *Bankers' Magazine* that the banks
of the United Kingdom had written off quite £23,000,000
against depreciation of their securities—mainly Consols
and stocks which have Consols for their bell-wether.
All the recently-issued public stocks of the Imperial
Dominions, provinces, and municipalities (now including
the British War Loan of November, 1914) have been made
with a fixed redemption date. Their section of the
Official List bristles with twentieth-century dates.[2] And
it must not be overlooked that while, as we have seen,
this acts as an automatic check upon depreciation, it
also enforces responsibility upon the borrowers. Nothing
is more likely to breed financial recklessness than the
ability to borrow by drafts upon indefinite futurity. It is
a reasonable and legitimate arrangement that posterity
should bear part of public expenditure the benefit of
which it will inherit as a portion of its legacy from ourselves—especially in the case of a war for national existence, such as that with Germany in 1914. But, obviously,
this principle is inapplicable to public works whose utility
will not outlast the present generation. The shifting of

---

[1] These words had been written, and published, long before the British Government admitted the validity of the reasoning by fixing a short redemption date for the war loan of November, 1914.

[2] As a curiosity it may be worth while to mention the Union Pacific Four per Cent. First Lien bond which has a redemption date as remote as 2008!

such burdens to the shoulders of posterity is neither sound finance nor fair play, since it amounts to a demand that our descendants shall pay for what is already on the scrap heap. Against that policy the Money Market (inspired by its hard lessons in the matter of depreciation) has resolutely set its face. Any attempt in the direction of overborrowing by State, municipality, or company would nowadays be met either by the exaction of so high a rate as would operate in the nature of a severe discouragement, or by an absolute refusal to consummate the transaction. This is not mere theory. Twice during the year 1913, largely in consequence of the glut in Canadian municipal issues, there was a definite refusal by underwriters to enter into any further commitments. The underwriters were subject to two restraining influences—the one arising out of the impossibility of further absorption through the channels of the Stock Exchange (i.e. the Stock Exchange check), and the other a consequence of a hint from the banks that they were loaded up with securities of the class whose issue it was sought to restrain for the moment (i.e. the banking check). This stricter supervision will augment the financial freedom of future generations, in addition to enforcing a greater circumspection upon that of which we ourselves are members. Thanks to the self-restraint of disciplined finance, they will receive the inheritance without the mortgage, or at all events, subject only to a reasonable charge upon it.[1]

[1] The abuse exists in America to a far larger extent than here. "All bonds of municipalities," said J. J. Hill at St. Paul in 1913, "are now refunded, instead of being paid when due. The excuse for a bond issue is always that posterity ought to bear part of the cost of public improvements. But we, as posterity comes along, not only repudiate the contract, but add new burdens to the old and shove both of them on to the future, in the shape of new and refunding bonds. It is perhaps the meanest form of stealing ever invented, because it adds to the criminality of breach of trust the baseness of embezzling the future resources of our own children, who, since there must come an end to borrowing some time, will have these debts to pay." Charles Whiting Baker, of the American *Engineering News*, has warned his American compatriots against the danger that lurks in the over-mortgaging of the resources and products of posterity. "It is of interest," he remarks, "to see what are some of the purposes for which cities at the present day are borrowing money on bond issues. New York leads the way with the issue of bonds to pay for the fireworks burned to celebrate the opening of a new bridge, and other bonds to pay

The Foreign Loans Committee recognised that the Stock Exchange Committee was the best supervisory and disciplinary tribunal that could be found, and that it had, on the whole, done its duty. " We think it is well that the Committee should have and exercise the power of refusing to allow a new foreign loan to be quoted in the *Official List* until the obligations incurred by the same foreign Government in respect of former loans have been either discharged or arranged with its creditors. This power the Committee have hitherto exercised, we have been informed, with great advantage."[1]

The provincial Exchanges manifest exactly the same capacity of resentment, against what they consider unfair treatment, as their London prototype. In July, 1912, the Manchester Stock Exchange took objection to the practice of the City Corporation, in conducting direct negotiations for the renewal of loans to the Corporation, originally arranged through stockbrokers. The Stock Exchange view was that the lender was the broker's client, and could not fairly be approached direct, to the exclusion of the broker who originally introduced him and secured the loan. On July 13 the chairman of the Manchester Stock Exchange announced that

" As the Corporation, after some negotiations, continued to refuse to consent to communicate with the agent at the same time as they communicate with his principal, the Committee as a protest ordered the quotation for Manchester Corporation Stocks to be removed from the Official List.

[1] Report, p. 19.

---

for the music furnished on its amusement piers." The critic admits that the mere size of the existent debt is not disquieting. It is rather the tendency to regard debt as a permanent necessity, and to postpone indefinitely the discharge of the obligation, which requires to be discouraged. Only organised finance, acting unitedly, can discourage it. The disciplinary weapon can only be wielded by a united Money Power. If the imprudent community, finding itself rebuked and discouraged in its prodigality by the financial institution A, is able to play off financial institution B against the original censor, there can be no effective check. And yet, when an attempt is made to unite the Money Power in the exercise of a wholesome restraining influence, the United States Government declares that a Money Trust has been created, and forthwith creates a Pujo Commission to analyse its alleged iniquities !

THE STOCK EXCHANGE (1815–1915)

This breach of a well-recognised custom of agency by a public body such as the Manchester Corporation is much to be regretted."

The questions at issue had not been adjusted up to the time when the Manchester Stock Exchange was closed on the outbreak of the war of 1914.

THE LIMITS OF SURVEILLANCE

This collective resentment, followed by punitive action in the refusal of settlement and quotation, is probably the limit of possible surveillance for the time being. In this country there has, so far, always been a refusal to adopt any statutory method of creating a tribunal to decide, and pronounce judgment, upon the goodness or badness of a given investment. The Foreign Loans Committee definitely stated that, in its opinion, there was no tribunal, however carefully constituted, which could safely be entrusted with such a critical duty. The majority of the slightly later Select Committee, appointed to inquire into the working of the Stock Exchange itself, took a somewhat modified view. What it said was this :—

" It cannot be denied that the requirements of the [Stock Exchange] Committee, and the investigations to which they have led, have in practice been in many instances the means of either detecting fraud or of rendering fraud which has been subsequently detected more easy of proof. This is a strong argument for the continuance, in some form and by some authority, of these investigations. We think, however, in any case, that the Committee of the Stock Exchange is not the proper authority to undertake such duties. They represent only the controlling authority of the market upon which bonds or shares are sold, and to invest them with the duty of inquiring into matters which concern only the validity of the things bought and sold is, in some sense, at any rate to popular apprehension, to make them responsible for the validity and stability into which they inquire. Upon the whole, we think, therefore, that if any such inquiry into the circumstances of a new loan or company is deemed necessary for the public protection it ought to be undertaken by some public functionary and enforced by law."

Mr. Stanhope, a member of the Committee, added a note to its report, in which he expressed his agreement with the view that the Committee of the Stock Exchange was not a proper body to undertake investigation into the soundness or unsoundness of a given enterprise. He thought, however, that a public official would be quite as unfit. There was always the possibility of corruption. Moreover, the moment that a public official had put his stamp upon the supposed soundness of a given company the public would act upon his opinion to an unlimited extent.[1] Thus his appointment would impair the ordinary individual vigilance exercised by an investor, which is so entirely wholesome, both in its practice and in its effects. " If the public," said Mr. Scott, another member of the Committee, in a reservation added over his own signature, " are prone to fall into the mistake of thinking that the Committee perform the duty of authenticating in any way the schemes to which they grant settlement or quotation, they would be still more prone to err in the same direction with regard to a ' public functionary ' backed by the law."[2] As long ago as 1837 Mr. Villiers told the House of Commons that " the more the public were encouraged to lean on Parliament for the protection of their interests the more careless and incautious would they become." The public must not be " nursed," said Rokeby Price.[3] These conservative views have held the field from the seventies until our own day.

The sound principle applicable here is that the business of the Stock Exchange is to maintain as free a market as circumstances permit in the commodities with which it is

[1] In January, 1915, the Treasury announced that new issues of capital could not be made without its previous permission. To prevent the erroneous inference that Treasury *permission* necessarily meant Treasury *endorsement*, if not a Government guarantee, all prospectuses had to bear some such words as these : " The Treasury has been consulted under the Notification of the 18th January, 1915, and raises no objection to this issue. It must be distinctly understood that in considering whether it has or has not any objections to new issues the Treasury does not take any responsibility for the financial soundness of any schemes or for the correctness of any of the statements made or opinions expressed with regard to them."

[2] Report, 1878, p. 30.   [3] Question 1639.

concerned, not to say whether a given investment is good or bad. Just as a famous bishop preferred England free to England sober, so economic advance is doubtless better bottomed in experience, reinforced by Money Market supervision up to the point sanctioned by its own internal opinion, than dragged by apron-strings. And there, again, the common sense of the last generation of City men is with us. The Foreign Loan Commission even took the view that, except where the scheme was, on the face of it, illegal or fraudulent, an official quotation should almost necessarily follow upon the grant of an official settling day, although the grant of a quotation, as the 1878 Committee said, is occasionally taken as a guarantee that the issue or enterprise is sound. "The result is that a sort of spurious stamp of genuineness or soundness is supposed to have been given where none was intended, and a favourable conclusion of merit arrived at where no conclusion on the subject was undertaken to be formed by the Committee."[1] Yet it is a fact, in our day, that every application for an official quotation implies a keen scrutiny. It means, in effect, that every name added to the *Official List* is that of an authority or company which has passed the censorship—limited but incisive—of one of the most experienced financial tribunals in the world. It does not receive the cachet as an assured profit-producer, but in the matter of the *bona-fides* of its compliance with the rules enacted to protect the public, so far as such protection can be usefully and effectively extended. A corresponding restraint is that which prevents the listing of vendor shares until six months after the admission to the *Official List* of the shares in the hands of the public. That is to say, the vendors are precluded from unloading their holdings until there has been, at all events, a fair chance of forming a judgment upon the merit and prospects of the concern. In Wall Street, as on this side, the conditions governing the admission of securities to the list became constantly more severe. As for the prices of stocks, the 1878 Committee thought it was desirable that the

[1] Report of Committee on the Stock Exchange, 1877–1878, p. 20.

public should know what quotations ruled in the various securities which were dealt in. In fact, such publicity was itself a valuable protection against fraud. There ought to be no secrecy about it. But guarantees of soundness were another matter altogether.[1]

A WHOLESOME DISCIPLINARY INFLUENCE

Admitting that the Manitoba legislation probably goes too far, there can be no doubt that collective resentment, manifested through the Stock Exchange, exerts a wholesome disciplinary influence. It encourages social advance

---

[1] The Manitoba Sale of Shares Act affords a recent instance of a legislative attempt at the supervision of dealings in shares, not from the point of view of the method employed, but with regard to the goodness or badness of the shares themselves. The Manitoba system is intended to provide that sales of shares of foreign companies, not registered or recognised under the law of the Province, shall not take place within its limits. A Manitoba company itself only comes within the Act when there is a systematic offering of its shares, evidenced by what the Act describes as "a course of continued and successive acts," such as circularising. The system will best be understood by giving a few instances of such decisions as have been arrived at by the Commissioner, under the powers which the Act affords :—

(a) Automatic Device for Railways.—Company incorporated in British Columbia. Authorised capital, $1,000,000 ; share's par value, $1 ; $400,000 allotted for patent rights. No satisfactory explanation given that they were worth this sum. The effect of this allotment would be prejudicial to legitimate investors.—Certificate refused.

(b) Rotary Engine Co.—Incorporated in Alberta. Capital, $1,000,000 ; $100 shares ; $800,000 was said to have been paid for patent rights. No way of ascertaining this value to be correct. The company would have to be enormously productive to pay this. The same principle was applied. —Certificate refused.

(c) Placer Mine.—Incorporated in Arizona, U.S.A. Capital $1,000,000 ; shares, $1 each ; 588,000 shares given for this property. Holders would share equally with other investors. A large sum was said to have been expended on the mine, but it had never been shown to be productive.— Certificate refused.

(d) Coal Co.—Incorporated British Columbia. Capital, $2,000,000 ; shares, $1 ; 1,500,000 shares were given for certain licences. The proposition was altogether too imaginative to secure authorisation.

Decisions like this constitute pretty drastic action. The reason given in case (d) demonstrates that a fairly wide discretion is vested in the Commissioner—a discretion, to the present writer's mind, far too wide and far too dangerous to be wielded, consistently with the interests of society at large, by any individual this side of the Elysian Fields. But the Dominion has carried the principle of Government supervision much further than the Mother Country. Under the revised Canadian Bank Act the chartered institutions of the Dominion are compelled to make a return to the Minister of Finance showing the amount of their outstanding loans to cities, towns, municipalities, and school districts.

and fosters responsibility. Barbarous nations cannot obtain loans. There is no continuity of responsibility which can be relied upon to fulfil obligations. Since credit is a peremptory necessity of any modern administration which claims to rank above chaotic and capricious savagery it ,is forced to seek the approbation of those in whose hands the control of the credit system rests. But the favour of the Money Market is only conferred in reliance upon the establishment, encouragement, and steady maintenance of civic order, which it is directly and most profoundly interested in securing. " Constitutional government," said President Jordan, of Stanford University,[1] " gives stability which makes possible deferred payments on a vast scale. The Kings of old had to pay on the spot. Their credit was bad. They were forced to make their way by many devices. . . . They depended on fawning, bluster, sale of favours, debasement of coinage, issue of paper money, ' squeezing ' of taxes, and other methods characteristic of the absolute monarchy." That policy no longer pays. The guerdon of Money Market patronage and succour is bestowed upon the converse plan. Good credit means the opportunity to borrow at the lowest rate, since it tends to diminish the charge for insuring the risk which must, in some degree or another, be added to the pure interest. Credit is " inseparable from confidence in the soundness of the social organism and in the economic virtues of those whose credentials are honoured."[2] Therein lies one reason for the almost total disappearance of that most objectionable type of " security," the flashy bonds of irresponsible republics—wild cats dressed in the skins of the tame variety, 8 per cent. speculations painted to look like investments. Countries which have played these tricks are known and marked. A reckless monarch or an equally careless despot may repudiate once. The Money Power does not give him a second opportunity. The modern burglar does not fear the policeman so much as the judicial power behind the policeman. The modern

---

[1] *Unseen Empire of Finance*, p. 5.
[2] Banks, *Ethics of Work and Wealth*, p. 88.

defaulter does not fear the resentment of the investor so much as the stern judgment, and the crushing and prolonged displeasure, evinced in a fashion which is beyond political control, of the Money Market behind him. It would, perhaps, be difficult to find in South America a public authority which has not, during the last forty years, repudiated, compounded, or suspended the discharge of its obligations. That kind of thing used to be done in mere bravado. With the advent of increased capital supplies and the consequent inexorable and incessant pressure towards order (together with the penalising of the converse state of affairs), responsibility has been quickened. Mexico, maintaining the interest on a gold debt during the prolonged throes of the silver crisis, and paying off £9,000,000 of bonds amid the confusion of a revolutionary struggle, offers a brilliant example of financial constancy where once there had been something very different. Default, or even temporary trifling, is seldom ventured now, save when every expedient has failed to furnish financial relief. If it were the obvious resort of a dishonest borrower, the vengeance of the Money Power would be swift, lasting, and terrible. Till there had been repentance and restitution, there would be no restoration to the confidence of the investor. But while dishonesty is reprobate, misfortune can always rely upon reasonable consideration. Where the inexorable pressure of financial circumstance (as with Brazil in 1914) compels suspension of interest for a time, a funding scheme is proposed as the alternative and an honest offer is accepted in its own conciliatory spirit. In fact, Governments not only recognise the desirability in their own interest of carrying out their bargains, but in their anxiety to conciliate the controllers of credit they occasionally go further. Behind the bond is frequently a fund employed in protecting its quotation against undue fluctuation, caused by the rumours which spring so easily and in such ornate form from the fertile brain of the unscrupulous operator. Many of the powerful foreign Governments make it a practice to maintain large and

THE STOCK EXCHANGE (1815–1915)   631

readily-available balances in London, Paris, and elsewhere. These funds can be used, if the need arise, for protecting the prices of their stocks, and even for " putting them up " in order to give a good send-off to some new financial operation. A capacity to enlist the practical sympathy of underwriters and investors, rather than the cynical irresponsibility which propounded " Morton's Fork," is the characteristic which commends itself to a twentieth-century monarch or Finance Minister.

INTERNATIONAL " PSYCHOLOGICAL RESERVE "

The new spirit is creating an international " psychological reserve," in the shape of the unity of interest which is generated by financial co-operation and inter-obligation. This is being steadily created and augmented as the Money Power brings one State after another within the scope of the financial fertiliser and within the reach of its international financial jurisdiction. Admission to the financial family of the world acts upon the new entrant in the same wholesome fashion as the analogous process of admission to graduation in a university or to fellowship in a learned society. The sense of responsibility is quickened; there is a desire to live up to what is expected; a willingness to be braced up to the common standard. It is with nations as with men. The individual whose credit, thanks to unfailing devotion and punctiliousness, is " good for any amount " cannot fail to be psychologically energised by the knowledge of the estimation in which he is held, and the tonic is equally beneficent when it speeds up a nation instead of a man. The necessity in both cases is the existence of a communal opinion which shall create the standard and enforce the obligation of acting up to it. The sentiment and criticism of immediate business associates supply the one. In the wider arena of world-finance it is the Money Power which sits in solemn judgment and metes out the weighty reprobation or approval that mean so much to-day, and are destined to mean infinitely more as international credit tightens its grip upon the world. A thousand years ago it was the fear of ecclesiastical censure which held the unruly elements in check. The Reformation, and the simultaneous modifications of the political and social fabric, made the civil power into the censor. To-day it is financial opinion which has to be considered and conciliated. The rule of the Money Power is acknowledged, and the policy of nations is shaped to its suggestions, rather than directed to its exploitation. In the words of Cunningham,[1] summing up the difference between the later Roman Empire and the modern State in their respective relations with the sources of credit, the " Byzantine statesmen devised expedients for despoiling the wealthy, while modern potentates [are] reduced to borrowing from them." And, as Li Hung Chang used to say, Eastern statesmen are just as alive as their confrères in the West to the importance of keeping on good terms with accumulated capital. Yet withal there is no oppression and no dictatorship. The policy of the Money Power is freedom, if freedom means the opportunity for *right* development.

FIRST DOLIOGENIC, NOW ORTHOGENIC

At the end of this survey, imperfect as it is, of the functions of the Stock Exchange, it is difficult to avoid the retrospective contemplation of its earlier activities as a self-regardant institution, in contrast with the part which it now plays as one of the most complex functions—or may we say sub-organisms ?—of society as a whole. A gulf separates the two aspects. The ultimate function of the Stock Exchange was not only unrealised, but absolutely undreamt-of by the earlier habitués of 'Change Alley and Garraway's Coffee House. Doubtless it was no more within their conception than was the science of ornithology mused upon by Pterodactyl, when he first parted company from his reptilian ancestry. But the duty is understood in our day, and the responsibility accepted, with an ever-growing sense of its importance and its seriousness. The Stock Exchange becomes every year more closely interlocked, more intimately co-operative, with the other great

[1] *Western Civilisation in its Economic Aspects*, p. 169.

THE STOCK EXCHANGE (1815–1915)

factors of the Money Market. With every year that passes, it is at once more willing and more able to discharge efficiently its share of the functions of the complex money market organism. Even the compulsory suspension of a portion of its activities, such as that which followed the German war crisis of 1914, is a demonstration of its inalienable unity with the other factors. Their own quiescence or restraint enforces the inclusion of the Stock Exchange in the adoption of the common policy. This deliberate and calculated effort towards a better corporate equipment for the discharge of an essential function in the social, as distinct from the merely corporate, interest, is almost an economic portent in the world.

The long divergence completed, we resume the main central pathway of our thesis, now rapidly drawing to its consummation and conclusion.

PART V

CONFEDERACY, THE GREAT AVOWAL AND THE SUPREME TEST

CHAPTER XX

POST-BARING EVOLUTION—BANKERS' COUNCIL AT THE BANK OF ENGLAND

THE Baring crisis brought us within sight of recognised and acknowledged unity, involving both confederate action and conciliar deliberation. It exhibited council and coalition, employed as rapidly-grasped weapons to beat off a sudden onset. But this, the last and most impressive lesson in cohesion, did not share the fate of earlier admonitions. It served a deeper purpose than that of a mere transitory caution. Before its memory had ceased to be vivid in the minds of men the policy which it represented was entrusted to a permanent conciliar jurisdiction, vested in a body of bankers meeting at the Bank of England at the invitation, *mirabile dictu,* of the Bank itself. Within the brief space of seventy years the London and Westminster Bank was refused a drawing account at the Bank, and invited to share, within the very walls of the institution, in shaping the policy of the most tremendous economic prerogative in the experience of mankind.

Naturally, an extremely cautious body of men, such as the heads of the financial hierarchy, are only likely to express themselves, or tacitly to allow their policy to be expressed, in the most guarded language. At the same time, bearing in mind the magnitude of the interests at stake and the publicity in which the banks work, the movement towards the final confederation of the factors of the Money Power may not unreasonably be expected to have been more and more boldly enunciated, in some form or another, as the years rolled on. The definite unity can hardly have come into existence without notice. We have, in truth, been witnessing the increasing closeness of cohesion, and listening to the voices of aspiration and exhortation, ever since the Overend-Gurney crisis. What now remains is to trace their augmented precision of expression, their increasing accuracy of aim, so to speak, until at last the hope is realised and modern finance coalesces into a conciliar jurisdiction wielded from the Bank of England by a representative corporate authority. Corporate in the legal sense it is not, of course. But reasons will be given for the view that it is psychically corporate.

For years it had been felt that the suzerainty of the Bank, exercised from a position of isolation, could be much more effective if the central institution became in a real sense, *primus* INTER *pares*. The financial history of the *post*-Baring period teems with the expression of hopes and suggestions directed to the attainment of that momentous end. To begin with, the minor *post*-Baring crises (and especially the American crisis of 1907, which was only " minor " in Europe) thrust home the lesson of essential unity of interest in the presence of common peril. These minor crises must therefore be the subject of brief examination, concurrently with the history of the struggle towards advanced confederacy.

SAVINGS BANK CONTROL CENTRALISED

By a striking coincidence, the year before the Baring crisis saw the proposal made, in the report of the Select Committee on Trustee Savings Banks, for the formation of an Inspection Committee to supervise those organisations. The project was carried into effect by the Savings Bank Act of 1891. This, in section 2, provided for the establishment of an Inspection Committee. With a significance which requires no emphasis, it was provided that one member of the Committee was to be appointed by the Governor of the Bank of England. Moreover, so as to initiate centralised control, the Savings Banks throughout the United Kingdom were grouped into dis-

THE AVOWAL AND THE TEST

tricts surrounding principal towns as centres. An immediate inquiry was instituted into methods of management. In 1892, the Inspection Committee had to report numerous shortcomings in the methods of the Savings Banks, arising either from ignorance of the law, or as a consequence of general laxity of management. In particular there was a mischievous tendency, contrary to all sound banking principle, to place practically unlimited confidence in single individuals, and to tolerate slackness where the principal officer of the bank was an influential person who was able to make his own convenience the standard of the management of the institution. All these abuses have been sternly taken in hand.

THE AUSTRALIAN BANK FAILURES

Elsewhere, trouble arose among another and totally different class of banks. At the meeting of the Bank of Australasia on October 3, 1889, the chairman had warned his shareholders of the grave danger of unrestricted competition. He said, " There always appeared to be one or two, or three or four, new banks arising on the Australian horizon. In fact, it seemed now to be almost in the nature of a ' fashionable occupation '—to open a new bank in the colonies." This recrudescence of competition in Australian banking was in a large measure the cause of the complication which early eventuated. Every little town was equipped with branches of all the leading banks. Their rivalry led them to make excessive loans on practically dead security, to wit, mortgages. One bank alone sent out no less than £3,000,000 for investment on mortgage in Australia. " Well, the result was that the speculation ran its usual course, and there remained piles—he might say miles—of buildings, thoroughly monumental in their character, but at the present time, he feared, unoccupied."[1] The worst feature of the crisis was the fact that not only was Australian money involved, but the Money-Market machinery on this side had been utilised to obtain deposits from all parts of the United Kingdom. This was done

[1] Sir Thomas Sullivan, at Bank of Australasia meeting, October 5, 1893.

through the agencies of local solicitors or stockbrokers who were paid substantial commissions for what money they could get. When the long sequence of failures ceased in 1893, fourteen banks had gone down with aggregate deposits of £85,000,000, of which £56,000,000 was money from the United Kingdom. But the trouble did not produce the serious effects which in other circumstances, or thirty years previously, would undoubtedly have resulted. There was the demonstrable presence, in the background, of a power which could be relied upon to see that things did not go too far. Although the failures coincided with a minor financial crisis in the United States, the fact that the movements in Consols were restricted between $99\tfrac{5}{8}$ and 97 during the whole year 1893 is an ample demonstration of the confidence already engendered in the power of the financial hierarchy. Further, the veteran Bank of New South Wales fearlessly and disinterestedly threw itself into the work of reconstruction in the eight years of trial which followed the crisis. This involved the reduction of the dividend from $17\tfrac{1}{2}$ per cent. to 9 per cent. But such drastic measures were most prominent among those which saved the colony, though they involved no small amount of self-denial on the part of the shareholders. There was also a reversal of the policy in pursuance of which the Australian banks gathered deposits in London for use in Australia. The crisis of 1893 convinced them of the undesirability of that policy, and precipitated disaster upon those institutions which had most sedulously pursued it. Since then the financial relations of London and Australia have been wholly reversed. The Commonwealth banks keep large balances in London, with a resulting accentuation of their dependence upon the central store of gold and of their susceptibility to be influenced by the opinion of the financial hierarchy which administers and protects it.

BANKING CONSOLIDATION IN CANADA

Almost simultaneously with these misfortunes, steps had been taken in another great Dominion towards further financial solidification. When the Canadian banks met at Ottawa in 1890 to discuss the general revision of bank charters, they formed the Canadian Bankers' Association. This proved so helpful that on the request of the Dominion Government, it applied for incorporation in 1900. By the Canadian Bank Act of that year, it was employed as part of the machinery for widening up insolvent banks. It was given various powers with regard to the making of bank notes, their distribution and disposition and final destruction. Moreover, the Bankers' Clearing Houses in Canada are now under the care of the Association, which is itself controlled by an executive elected from the banks themselves. Unity of policy and sentiment have had the most wholesome results, though they have not always enjoyed the warmest welcome. In the boom of 1907 Western Canadian farmers and storekeepers were indignant with the bankers for keeping such a tight hand on their discounts and overdrafts. Their resentment extended to the same policy when it was applied as a check to undue municipal borrowings. Still more recently, the financial stringency which affected Western Canada in 1912 and 1913 had been anticipated by the banking conclaves of Montreal and Toronto. As they were outside the arena of excitement and inflation, they had pursued lenitive and restricting tactics with regard to the grant of credits in the booming West. They were able to do this because they were in alliance for that purpose under the courageous and vigilant leadership of the Bank of Montreal. In Canada the chartered banks, closely organised as a firmly disciplined whole, can prevent such close cutting of rates as has been witnessed in the United States. Merchants can secure accommodation only from their own banks. There is no open market for commercial paper to promote unwholesome competition among the lenders; nor can the merchants cross the border and avail themselves of the lower rates by floating their paper in American territory. The banks frown on the practice, as Gilbart and Rae did upon the discounting client who tried to exploit two bankers. They have to a large degree eliminated it. They object to their customers going elsewhere for loans at a time when they themselves have surplus funds on their hands, and falling back on them when the foreign source has exhausted itself. They are competent, as a united entity, to make their objections weighty. If they were not, or, if the vigilant watchers, instead of being in the East, had been within the infected area, the events of 1913 might easily have precipitated a huge financial crisis in Canada. These conditions of confederacy, closely paralleling those with which Lombard Street is familiar, tend, as in England, to concentrate a plenary responsibility upon one great institution. Standing, as it does, in the same relation to the Canadian banks as the Bank of England to the British banks, the Bank of Montreal is compelled to keep its resources in a peculiarly liquid condition. This is the reason why it permanently retains large balances in London and New York, earning considerably less than would be the case if they were employed in Canada itself. Its London resources and activities give it an authority there, and bring it into the most intimate contact with the hegemony of Threadneedle Street and Lombard Street. Thus the principle of centralised predominance steadily extends and expands. Unfortunately it has not yet been extended over quite the entire field of banking, as carried on by British capital throughout the world. If it had been, the collapse of the Bank of Egypt in November, 1911, might not have taken place.

AN EPISODE AT THE BANK OF ENGLAND

The irony of fate brought the Bank of England for a moment into unpleasant conspicuousness, just at the moment when it was triumphantly emerging from the great Baring achievement. In November, 1893, it became known to the governors that the then chief cashier had seriously exceeded his authority. He had permitted grave irregularities in connection with advances made by the bank to a certain number of its customers. He had, further, in one case, allowed a considerable overdraft without the knowledge of the Governor. Moreover, he had engaged in Stock Exchange speculations which had placed him in difficulties. These disclosures resulted in the directors requiring the chief cashier's immediate resignation. The untoward incident was at the time the theme of prolonged discussion and intense curiosity in the City. On the whole, however, looking at the episode from this distance of time, there seems little reason to doubt that the loss to the Bank was fully counter-balanced by the bracing effect of this sudden call to minute circumspection. Reading between the lines of the allusions made to the incident at the time, it appears not entirely improbable that the weight of years and the sense of unchallengable respectability had bred some slight degree of laxity in the internal administration. This vanished under the operation of the tonic administered by so unprecedented a discovery as irregularities on the part of one of the highest officials. That there was nothing wrong with the *efficiency* of the Bank's management was shown in another direction. Sir E. W. Hamilton, writing of the conversion of the National Debt under Goschen, said, " The labour which the attainment of such results imposed on the Banks of England and Ireland was, as can readily be imagined, prodigious; and nothing short of perfect organisation and untiring zeal could have enabled those establishments to grapple with it." The total number of holdings at the Goschen conversion was 169,235, " which varied in amount from £5,760,000 to the curiously small sum of one penny." As for the primacy of the Bank, that was unaffected. Nowadays even the customer shares the glamour of it. " There is considerable prestige in banking at the Bank of England."[1]

LONDON AND GLOBE COLLAPSE

When at length the Baring shadow passed away then came another period of wild excitement in the shape of the Kaffir boom of 1895. Mr. Rhodes is always said to

---

[1] Charles Gow, London Joint-Stock Bank, U.S. Monetary Commission, *Interviews on Banking*, p. 86.

have engineered it. As a matter of fact, he did his best to stop it, and cursed it when it came. But it did no great harm. On the whole, the most disagreeable City episode since the Baring affair has been the Stock Exchange collapse following the suspension of the London and Globe Finance Corporation on December 28, 1900. More than thirty members of the " House " were declared defaulters. The London and Globe failure, however, although one of gravity, was a purely Stock Exchange misfortune. It was neither a banking nor a trade crisis. There never was any question of its producing any disastrous effect upon the financial fabric itself.[1]

THE AMERICAN PANIC OF 1907

The 1907 panic was entirely American. It was precipitated by all-round reckless speculation, by no means confined to the Stock Exchanges. " It has been shown conclusively," said Governor White,[2] " that speculation on the Stock Exchange was not the chief contributor to the collapse of 1907, but that speculation on a much wider scale, through the length and breadth of the land, was the exciting cause." There was a simultaneous rush to sell everything, with the result (as in London in 1914) that an institution which exists for the *transport* of securi-

[1] Mr. G. H. Pownall referred to another episode when lecturing at the London School of Economics early in 1914. He alluded to it as having happened during the South African War. He was understood to say that he himself had taken a share in averting it. There were reports, so the lecturer said, that a leading firm was in difficulties, and it was realised that if the suspension actually took place the resulting trouble would be as big a thing as the Baring crisis. A well-known bill-broker, who was on intimate terms with one of the partners of the firm, was sent for, and requested to make a personal call and obtain definite information with regard to the firm's position in the matter of (1) cash at the Bank of England ; (2) cash at call in the market ; (3) holdings in Consols ; and (4) amount of outstanding acceptances. The result of the bill-broker's call was that the firm was able to exhibit figures which put its solvency beyond all challenge. This enabled the mischievous rumours to be authoritatively contradicted and dissipated. " Some of you," the lecturer added, " in the coming years may have to deal with a similar state of affairs, and you should deal with it in the same way, by going direct to the fountain-head for information, as we did when we made the inquiries I have detailed, with the result that what might have been a panic passed away without any trouble whatsoever." The story does not appear in the reprint of the Lectures, subsequently issued under the title of *English Banking*.

[2] Hughes Investigation, *Journal of Political Economy*, October, 1909.

ties was suddenly called upon to become a purchaser on a gigantic scale. Difficulties were increased by the impossibility of collecting " syndicate " loans, which had been advanced to an extent far beyond the limits of legitimate banking, and employed in speculation on the Stock Exchange. That kind of thing could not happen in London under the vigilant eye of the " financial hierarchy." The then existent American system of a so-called " chain of banks," in which each lent money against the deposit of the shares of the next in the chain, was another of the operative causes of the panic. On this side of the Atlantic bankers realise too well their responsibility to the public to embark upon any such unscientific adventures. It may be added also that the unceasing mutual scrutiny of one another's balance-sheets renders them too acutely conscious of one another's infirmities for any such method to have the remotest chance of imitation. In 1907 London, although no partner in the follies which led to the panic, helped to resist the shock. When the hurricane broke upon the banks of the United States, said Mr. George E. Roberts, director of the United States Mint,[1] they strained every resource to obtain gold from abroad, and succeeded, by great sacrifices, in bringing in about $100,000,000 in the course of sixty days, of which $85,000,000 came from London.

" The Bank of England, which bore the brunt of our demand, raised its discount rate three times within a week, from $4\frac{1}{2}$ to 7 per cent., not with any expectation of checking the outflow to this country, but to set in motion the forces that would replenish its stock. The Bank of Germany within ten days advanced its rate from $5\frac{1}{2}$ to $7\frac{1}{2}$ per cent. The Bank of France, always strong and less exposed to direct demands, contented itself with advancing the rate from $3\frac{1}{2}$ to 4 per cent. Through these institutions the influence spread over Europe, each institution charged with responsibility for a country's reserves taking a similar action. In this way, although the burden of supplying gold for the United States fell directly upon the Bank of England, it was rapidly redistributed over the entire

[1] *New York Times*, January 19, 1913.

financial world. The Bank of England gave a wonderful illustration of its ability to recoup itself. On October 29, when the Bank rate was first advanced from 4½ per cent., the Bank held £30,420,000 of gold and the percentage of reserve was 39$\frac{15}{16}$. On December 26, after the flood had passed, it held £29,753,000 and the percentage of reserve was 45·90."

No wonder the *Economist*, reviewing the record on March 14, 1908, declared that " the crisis showed, much to the relief of experienced bankers, that the raising of the Bank rate is as effective a device as ever it was in attracting gold." Nor was the benefit of the demonstration limited to the bankers on this side of the Atlantic :—

" The unhesitating manner in which the directors of the Bank of England raised the rate in October, November and December from 5½ to 6 and 7 per cent., showed the financial houses in America that whatever rate was necessary to put obstacles in the way of an undue discount of American bills, would be adopted, but it was only fair to say that the larger banks in America showed considerable reticence in unnecessarily disturbing the London money market."[1]

The 7 per cent. rate was in itself, however, a disturbance. It had to be enacted at a time when it was completely unjustified by our own business conditions, and, in fact, inflicted injury upon our trade. Yet there was no panic, or anything approaching it, on this side ; but there was, on the other hand, a magnificent demonstration of the ascendancy of the Western European banks, as represented by the Bank of England and the Bank of France. As an American critic remarked:—

" The way our bankers got down on their knees to London and Paris in that emergency, frankly admitting their inability, under our old flintlock laws, to handle a situation which foreign bankers meet without difficulty, is a subject at once painful and humiliating. Literally our bankers begged for help, and got it. Some day we shall have to beg again."[2]

[1] Chairman at London City and Midland Bank meeting, January 24, 1908.
[2] Van Antwerp, *Stock Exchange from Within*, p. 207

THE AVOWAL AND THE TEST

After the panic was over Commissioners from the United States Government came to the Bank of England, and learned, like pupils sitting at the feet of Gamaliel, how the mighty European Money Power held its own amid the changes and chances of our financial life. They made an apt selection of their tutor, for Sir Edward Holden has declared that 1907 " gave more education to [British] banks than any year he can remember."[1] But the American bankers' quest was the more remarkable because Wall Street is as yet but an outpost of the cosmopolitan Money Market, and takes only an indirect interest in European securities. As Sir F. Williams Taylor said (speaking, of course, before the new United States banking legislation), Canada, with her small group of banks, was better served, in a banking sense, in 1907, than the United States with her banking institutions running into tens of thousands.

THE AMERICAN MENACE

Since the 1907 crisis stern reforms in American banking have brought to an end a financial scandal of the first magnitude—namely, the propensity of large American interests to rush headlong into a position of great speculative peril, in the assurance that if fortune failed to favour them the European Money Power might be relied upon (as in 1907) to step into the breach and save Wall Street from the penalty of this species of folly. Not once nor twice, within the last quarter of a century, has it been necessary for the leadership of the Bank of England to be invoked in order to obviate the desperate consequences of American financial irresponsibility, which has been especially prone to overlook the objections to the " finance bill " from the point of view of so cautious and conservative a critic as Lombard Street. But it is now possible to say of American conditions that

" sound and conservative business is in the forefront, while the exploits of the freebooters of three decades ago have vanished. There is no more trading in New York on customers' deposits or trust funds ; no more putting at risk by bankers of

[1] At London City and Midland Bank meeting, January 24, 1908.

that which is entrusted to them in a fiduciary relation. It seems impossible, as we look back, that there should ever have been in New York City swindlers of the type of the old familiar species, and sharp practitioners like Jay Gould and Jim Fiske. It seems incredible that this staid and conservative financial centre, as we know it to-day, should have given birth to doubtful railroads like the West Shore and the Nickel-Plate, and should have fostered a long record of railway warfare and monetary disturbances. Despite all the vicissitudes of the passing years, it is difficult to believe that only twenty years ago there were 642 bank failures in America in a single year, with liabilities of $211,000,000, 15,242 commercial failures, with liabilities of $347,000,000, and railway receiverships for 32,379 miles of road, capitalised at $1,651,116,000."[1]

In plain English, the United States is gradually qualifying for membership of the cosmopolitan financial hierarchy.

CONFEDERACY THE CENTRAL ASPIRATION

These recurring " shivers," if they did nothing else, helped to keep the mind of the City fixed upon closer confederacy. Towards that stately consummation its leaders yearned unceasingly. *Pars sanitatis velle sanari fuit.* The graphic lesson of the Baring crisis began to be driven home long before its echoes had died away. There had been ample demonstration of the potency and advantage of united action. There was no doubt—in fact it had been explicitly declared—that in the presence of similar peril there would again be the same rally round the Bank of England. But that was not enough. The organisation should be permanent, not spasmodic. Finance required a definite and lasting compact, not a temporary colligation. " Our bankers," said Mr. J. G. Kiddy, " have stood bravely by Messrs. Baring in and since the crisis of two years ago ; is it a ridiculous thing to suggest that they should make a compact to stand by each other ? "[2] An equivalent suggestion had been made by the great protagonist of the crisis himself. " I feel," said Lidderdale on one occasion, speaking with special reference to the

---

[1] W. C. Van Antwerp, in the *Financial News*, February 6, 1914.
[2] *Bankers' Magazine*, January, 1893, p. 90.

gold reserve, "that the one thing needful is the concentration, in their various degrees, of all banks, and not merely the Bank of England." At the Bankers' Dinner in 1896 the Governor of the Bank of England (Sandeman) declared that "The bankers and merchants were associated in one great brotherhood, and they all joined with the Bank of England in maintaining the resources which were necessary for carrying on the affairs of this great Empire." The share of the Bank in wielding so wide a sway had been compared to that of a constitutional monarch who reigns but does not govern.[1] And just as the constitutional monarch (whether called king or president) is essential to the working, and even to the existence, of a constitution, so is it with the Bank. "The work which the Bank of England performs here in our community is so absolutely necessary that it is unthinkable how we could get on without it or without some other institution exactly taking its place."[2] The speaker (Mr. Gow) frankly expressed his recognition of the suzerainty in Threadneedle Street :—

"The Bank of England is our ally and our best possible ally and, speaking for myself, I will do nothing contrary to the general desires of the Bank of England. I work in harmony with the Bank of England, and am in no respect hostile to it. It is too indispensable a friend."[3]

THE BANKERS' BALANCES AS A FACTOR

The old problem of the bankers' balances at the Bank of England (*ante*, p. 503) was revived at the meeting of the Institute of Bankers on November 4, 1903, by Mr. J. Herbert Tritton. The speaker elaborated a detailed proposal for closer co-operation between Threadneedle Street and Lombard Street. He said :—

" I would strongly urge two or three modifications in the present returns [of the Bank of England], weekly and monthly.

---

[1] *Bankers' Magazine*, 1889, p. 395.
[2] Charles Gow, London Joint-Stock Bank, U.S. Monetary Commission *Interviews on Banking*, p. 87.
[3] U.S. Monetary Commission, *Interviews on Banking*, pp. 87 and 91.

Let the Bank of England adopt Mr. Inglis Palgrave's suggestion, frequently made before, and show, in their weekly statement, once again the bankers' balances. . . . Let the bankers, at any rate the clearing bankers, also adopt another of his suggestions, and make a weekly return, for publication of Thursday morning, of the amount of their cash resources—Bank of England balance, notes, and coin, and articles in course of collection, as on the previous evening. This should be done to the Chief Inspector of the Clearing-house, under strictest privacy, and he would then publish the aggregate with the clearing-house returns of the week. Lastly, I should like to suggest that all bills drawn on places abroad, instead of being, as at present, sold to the exchange houses, should be held—that is, purchased by the banks, and the aggregate amount of these should also, in like manner, be published with the amount of "domiciled" bills, that is, bills drawn on foreigners, but made payable in London, added. This would, of course, involve co-operation of houses other than bankers strictly so-called. We should then have before us on Thursday afternoon week by week :—

"I. The reserve of the Bank of England itself, distinguished from that held against bankers' balances.

"II. The bankers' balances at the Bank of England.

"III. The special bankers' reserve of gold.

"IV. The ordinary cash resources of the clearing banks, unaffected by 'embellishments.'[1]

"V. The record of our power over foreign capitals in the concrete shape of bills of exchange.

"To accomplish these things, if they be considered desirable to initiate, and then to obtain the full benefit of such records in estimating the true position of the market, would require co-operation to a hitherto unknown extent between the Bank of England and the clearing bankers. The latter would doubtless meet weekly, and would receive letters and telegraphic reports from all the chief monetary centres of the world,

---

[1] Less elegantly denominated "window-dressing." In the same year that Mr. Tritton spoke, the London and County (now amalgamated with the London and Westminster) began to print the amount of its daily average cash holding throughout the month, so as to demonstrate that its preparedness was continuous, and not spasmodically coincident with the dates when publicity had to be given to the figures. In 1914 Sir Edward Holden declared his intention of publishing the actual figures of the London City and Midland gold holding. This he did in a balance sheet issued on January 12, 1915—"gold coin, £8,000,000."

THE AVOWAL AND THE TEST

written by the best men to be secured, as to monetary and financial matters. It will probably be found that as a condition precedent of effective co-operation between the Bank of England and the banks, the latter should have their representatives on the Bank Court, and the former should regularly send a representative to the committee of clearing bankers."

ACTION AS WELL AS PROFESSION

Mr. Tritton did not stand alone in his hopes. From every quarter came the expression of equally fervent desires. They were accompanied, as occasion arose, with demonstrations of willingness, and even eagerness, to *do* that which should evidence goodwill, and not only to talk about it. The Bank frankly confessed its duty. " The duty of the Bank is to mitigate the effects of crises, if not to avert them," said the Governor at the Bank Court in January of 1904. In his address to the Institute of Bankers in the same year, the late J. Spencer Phillips urged the desirability of strengthening the *entente cordiale* among the banking community. December, 1905, brought a plethora of money in the market. A simultaneous fall in the French Exchange created considerable danger of heavy withdrawals of gold, which would have depleted the already low reserve of the Bank of England. " Upon this, however," said Mr. Spencer Phillips, in reviewing the circumstances,

" the Bank of England took a new departure. They approached the principal clearing bankers and asked them to co-operate with the Bank to take the surplus money off the market and place it on deposit with the Bank at a low rate of interest. The Bank then charged 5 per cent. on their advances, and the effect was electrical. No bills were discounted under 4 per cent., the French exchange accordingly rose, and the danger of the withdrawal of gold ceased. This precedent has been followed again during the present month [January, 1906] by the Bank.

" I think I may state for ourselves that we welcome, and cordially welcome, this new departure of the Bank ; and, although I have no authority for saying so, I am perfectly certain that I am voicing the opinion of the rest of the bankers in stating that they are equally pleased. *The more the Bank co-operates with the leading bankers the better for everybody.* We are in a certain way inter-dependent upon each other, although, as long as the Bank of England retains its present privileges and is also the ultimate keeper of the reserve—and the system is not likely to be changed in our time—*I think we perfectly recognise that they are the predominant partner.*"[1]

This was plain English. We said that the Bank had frankly confessed its duty. Here was the confession of the bankers. Opinion became every year more definite. In urging the formation of a small permanent committee to consider the question of gold reserves, Sir Felix Schuster went to the root of the matter. He said, in 1906,[2] that

" such a committee would form a nucleus of *a general consultative committee with the Bank of England,* the want of which has long been felt, and thus a step would be taken to bring about that co-operation between the banks that so many have advocated for years past. With the management of the affairs of the Bank of England itself the committee would have no concern whatever; it would only meet for purposes of consultation and co-operation on questions of general interest."

CENTRALISATION IN THE UNITED STATES

Meanwhile, the arguments in favour of a central banking power were being marshalled on the other side of the Atlantic. As enunciated by the New York Chamber of Commerce in November, 1906, they took this shape :—

" The operations of central banks in Europe, especially in France, Germany, Austria-Hungary and the Netherlands, make it impossible to doubt that the existence of such a bank in this country would be of incalculable benefit to our financial and business interests. Such a bank in times of stress or emergency would be able by regulation of its note issues to prevent those sudden and great fluctuations in rates of interest which have in the past proved so disastrous. Furthermore, it would have the power to curb dangerous tendencies to speculation and undue expansion, for by the control of its rate of

[1] Lloyds Bank meeting, January 26, 1906.
[2] Paper read at the Institute of Bankers, December 19.

THE AVOWAL AND THE TEST

interest and of its issue of notes, it would be able to exert great influence upon the money market and upon public opinion.

"Such power is not now possessed by any institution in the United States. Under our present position of independent banks, there is *no centralisation of financial responsibility*, so that in times of dangerous over-expansion *no united effort can be made to impose a check which will prevent reaction and depression*. This is what a large central bank would be in a position to do most effectively. A central note-issuing bank would supply an elastic currency, varying automatically with the needs of the country. This currency could never be in excess, for notes not needed by the country would be presented for deposit or redemption."[1]

COUNCIL AND AGREEMENT

Sir Felix Schuster, in his interviews with the American Monetary Commission, again urged the necessity for periodical meetings. The speaker was not concerned with the fact that for many years a committee (composed of representatives of the London joint-stock banks) had been accustomed to meet on the occasion of a change in the bank rate, and fix the percentage to be allowed on deposits, as well as the charge for Stock Exchange accommodation. Sir Felix meant something much more ambitious than this. Mr. F. Huth Jackson came nearer to a precise promulgation of the essential need in his inaugural address, as president of the Institute of Bankers, on November 10, 1909. Mr. Jackson said that it would, in his opinion, be a good thing if the developed uniformity of action already existing were carried a stage further, so that "London bankers could meet together occasionally, when abnormal conditions prevail in the Money Market, and agree on a definite course of action." The ultimate outcome of these long aspirations and strivings was better than Mr. Jackson hoped. Regular and not occasional meetings were resolved upon; and these councils are not limited to periods characterised by abnormal conditions, but now take place at fixed three-monthly intervals. These gatherings are the Inner Cabinet of finance, as truly as the London

[1] *Bankers' Magazine*, 1911, p. 45.

Clearing Bankers' Committee represents the financial Cabinet in its entirety. But as we pass to the historic circumstances of their definite establishment, and to an attempt at the exposition of their profound significance, a problem blocks the way. Why should not the centralised control of finance be undertaken by the State, on terms, and subject to regulations and principles, embodied in a statute ? Why create a separate financial Cabinet when the ordinary administrative Cabinet—so the question may be posed—might discharge, with all the prestige attaching to its position as the delegate of the sovereignty, the functions attaching to the predominant power in the economic field ?

LEGISLATION WOULD BE FUTILE

The answer is that in the face of the melancholy manifestations of panic and derangement, the best financial authorities of a given period were always fain to confess that " no wisdom of the Legislature, no regulation of the currency," could prevent such misfortunes as those of 1847 and 1857. So said the Select Committee which reported upon the crisis in the latter year. The Money Power must be left to go its own way, employing its own characteristic experience and circumspection in the guardianship of the vast interests entrusted to it. When " Bob " Lowe said, " the Money Market must look after itself," he was not far wrong if he meant that the control of the Money Market must be left to those who have the specialised capacity and experience for the task. Neither then nor now has the remedy been within statutory scope. Lord Haldane admitted as much at the Bankers' Dinner in 1907. At no time were the cheers more cordial than when he gave an assurance that the Government " were not likely to introduce any measure interfering with the Bank of England or with the management by bankers of their own affairs." No legislation can prevent, or even effectively restrain, speculation and inflation. Sound credit and not statute-regulation makes solid finance. Good banking, as Mr. Hartley Withers so well said, is produced, not by good laws, but by good bankers. " Our paper is of value in commerce," declared Burke, " because in law it is of none. It is powerful on 'Change, because in Westminster Hall it is impotent. In payment of a debt of twenty shillings, a creditor may refuse all the paper of the Bank of England."[1] Statutory impotence has been recognised in quarters even more authoritative. " Financial complications," said the King's Speech in February, 1826, " lie without the reach of direct Parliamentary interposition." As the Chancellor of the Exchequer said, in the debate on the Address, they are " beyond the control of any Government." Ministers themselves admitted that Government was going out of its sphere when it intermeddled in finance " and became a liberal banker, as it were, or a generous and not very inquisitive lender." That policy involved the offer of a premium upon improvidence. The State cannot, by statute, provide the lithe solidity which is the guerdon of successful management and unceasing vigilance on the part of the personnel of the banks themselves. Restraint must be imposed " from within, whether by a common purpose, or by the predominant will of the leading partners, or by something of both." The imposition of control postulates a power capable of enforcing its will by methods far too subtle to be capable of definition by statute or of utilisation under statutory authority. Finance is of all businesses in the world the least adapted to run automatically. Its methods depend upon judgment ; and judgment being uncontrollable by the will, is also uncontrollable by the Legislature :—

" The Bank of England knows how to manage [the note issue in times of panic] because it is a trader in the market ; but if the Government once began to lend I do not know whether it would have the same discretion. . . . The Prime Minister or the Chancellor of the Exchequer might be a member for a great commercial community—for London or Liverpool— and the public would never believe that his constituents did not get a benefit."[2]

[1] Burke, *Reflections on the French Revolution, Works*, Vol. IV. p. 342. This was, of course, before Bank of England notes were made legal tender.
[2] Bagehot, 1875 Committee on Banks of Issue, Q. 8186.

These doctrines remain sound, even if we attach no great importance to Bagehot's hint of possible public distrust.

MISCHIEFS OF LEGISLATION

The objections to legislative control are, in fact, axiomatic in their impregnability. Senator Aldrich himself, discussing his own banking plan before the American Bankers' Convention at New Orleans, said that it would " never be successful and never could be successful unless it was kept out of politics." The reason is that " Legislation in the economic field requires . . . in an especial degree, along with a delicate and just appreciation of all economic requirements, the greatest impartiality and freedom from political agitation."[1] German opinion, which in banking carries great weight, in spite of the contrast between Teutonic and British banking methods, has emphasised the essential weakness of the statutory implement in language admirably precise and picturesque. In January of 1914 the New York State Bankers' Association entertained Professor Dr. Riesser (president of the Hansa League), Mr. Robert Masson (of the Crédit Lyonnais), and Mr. J. H. Simpson (general manager of the Bank of Liverpool). Allusions were made to the relationship of banks with the State. Dr. Riesser delivered a notable utterance on the subject of German banks and German industry, in the course of which he said :—

" A banking law is doomed to failure if it gives any power in any important part of the management, except in supervision, to politics, or to leaders in politics, who generally lack banking experience. Politics may sometimes spoil the character —they will always spoil business. We are further convinced that all banking legislation must, in the long run, suffer shipwreck, if, perhaps with an eye on popular currents of opinion, it excludes the expert elements—banks and bankers—from the management of the central note bank, or if, in other words, it treats them as enemies, instead of friends. Such a bank can only fulfil its duties to the nation when working hand in hand

[1] Dr. Wachler, *German Bank Enquiry*, of 1908–1909, U.S. Monetary Commission, p. 72.

THE AVOWAL AND THE TEST

with the other banks. When I want to build a house I call in architects and bricklayers—not fiddlers—not even good fiddlers. The present wonderful prosperity of German industry is, to a very high degree, due to the faithful support which it has at all times received at the hands of the banks and bankers. Any desire on the part of inexperienced professional or habitual saviours of the country to disturb or weaken this close fiduciary relationship as it has developed, to the practical benefit of both parties, in Germany, and to sacrifice the same for the sake of any preconceived notions or pressure from anti-capitalistic sources, would equal the wisdom of the man sawing off the branch of the tree on which he was sitting."[1]

Banking sentiment against fixed reserves (i.e. reserves amounting to a minimum percentage, fixed by statute, of the liabilities at any given moment) is largely a product of this distrust of Government control. Speaking especially with reference to this question of gold reserves, Mr. Cecil Parr, the Chairman of Parr's Bank, said to his shareholders in 1907 :—

" Direct legislation is, in my opinion, greatly to be deprecated. Not only does the expert knowledge necessary to the proper solution of the problem reside chiefly in bankers themselves, but banks have fully earned the right to have a preponderating voice in the settlement of any regulations which are to affect them so nearly."

Mr. Parr's views are those of the whole financial world. " The supremacy of British trade," declared Mr. J. Spencer Phillips,[2]

" is in no small degree owing to the fact that it has been left to the enterprise of individuals untrammelled and unfettered by legislative enactments. In America the banks are bound to keep a certain fixed percentage—15 or 25 per cent., according to the size of the town—of their deposits in cash, with the result that whenever this limit is approached, the price of money is raised to a point which we in this country have never heard of, much less experienced."

[1] Reported in the *Financial News*, February 3, 1914.
[2] Institute of Bankers, November 7, 1906.

The same antipathy to legislative fetters, in the case of another great factor of the Money Market, inspired Mr. Stanhope, as a member of the Stock Exchange Commission of 1877, to object to the incorporation of the institution. " To attempt to regulate the manner in which business is done in the great Money Market of England," said he, " is going far beyond the province of the State, nor is any Government Department in any way qualified to undertake it." For instance, in banking, what legislation could check, with quiet authority and with an utter absence of ostentation or alarm, the circulation of too much paper by a given accepting house ? Conversely, what statute could define the moment, and the manner, suited to the administration of a guarded hint to a bank which is prone to overdo this discrimination ? The external authority cannot effectively wield that jurisdiction. Only collective action based upon inherited specialised corporate experience can protect collective interest. We have built the legal and the moral faculties into the body politic. Enactment and tradition, statute and precedent, unite in a vast and ever-growing aggregate of jurisprudence. But the operative principles are discerned, deduced, defined, and interpreted in application, by trained experts. The economic faculty requires just the same fostering care, just the same expert cultivation. Only in that direction lies our escape from the sway of the wayward, the whimsical, the conjectural, the capricious, and the panicky, into a state of society where sober judgment will reign supreme. " Popular government, or any other, for that matter," Lord Morley has said, " is no chronometer, with delicate apparatus of springs, wheels, balances, and escapements. It is a rough, heavy bulk of machinery, that we must get to work as we best can." But a " rough, heavy bulk of machinery " is surely not the thing by means of which to manipulate the fine-spun fabric of the Money Market, or prescribe its modes of action ? You might as well set a ploughman to regulate your repeater. A Government, as Professor Marshall says, could print a good edition of Shakespeare's works, but it could not get them written. Even so may

THE AVOWAL AND THE TEST

it recognise and encourage, though it can by no means control, a financial mechanism whose combined delicacy and solidity could never have been the progeny of statute.

UNITY OF EXPERT RESPONSIBILITY

Unity and independence of policy are peremptory where there are not only such gigantic resources, but such overwhelming responsibilities to the community at large. Available balances — six times greater than a year's revenue of the United Kingdom, dwarfing into a mere fistful the whole resources of many a mediæval potentate — are now so huge that the policy of the State might be influenced, or the course of social evolution entirely deflected, by their misuse.[1] There is the gravest objection to the financially-unskilled opportunist politician (however great his capacity in other fields of endeavour) getting control of these engines of social advance, as he must do if they pass under State control. But there is equally grave and peremptory reason why their management should be in the hands of a body profoundly conscious of its responsibility, actuated by motives of the highest possible type, entirely distinct from a mere passion for financial aggrandisement.[2] The effect of unskilled empiricism, imposing the rigidities of legislation on an evolving organism like that of finance, would be just as injurious as the attempt to provide a new-born child with a suit of clothes which should last him all his life and never be a misfit. Even where the circumstances of the case are

---

[1] Permanent State-control, which is the subject of the present argument, is, of course, a totally different thing from an *ad hoc* collaboration of Government with finance, such as that which was effected in the presence of the German war crisis of 1914.

[2] "Let it not be thought," said Lord Goschen (Anniversary Dinner, National Discount Co., July 11, 1906), "that the City was composed simply of a group of rich and grasping men, who were endeavouring to accumulate those vast fortunes which figured in the annals of other countries. They were at their posts in order to promote the prosperity of trade and finance in the country at large. By their wisdom as they were wise, by their prudence as they were prudent, by their capacity as they had the capacity, they would help to mould to a great extent the course of business in the country at large, and to maintain by sound, orthodox, and unfantastic measures the prosperity of the great structure of British trade and finance."

such that legislation must be attempted, it frequently happens that the lapse of a few years (and possibly an intervening judicial decision) renders the rigid law of the land and the flexible practice of bankers absolutely irreconcilable. As statutory amendment is a very difficult thing to obtain, the bankers are forced by their public duty into a disregard of the law. Thus, in the Gordon case,[1] " if bankers had acted on the strict letter of the law as thus laid down by the House of Lords," said Mr. J. Spencer Phillips,[2] " the entire business of the country would have been paralysed." In this instance the trouble was remedied by the Bills of Exchange (Crossed Cheques) Act, 1906. Still, there are many other cases in which the rapidity of financial evolution has carried the circumstances completely out of the scope of a statute originally intended to compass them, and has consequently forced the banker to make law and practice for himself in the public interest.

THE BARING PRECEDENT RE-INVOKED, 1911

To confederated finance, thus distrustful of external interference, yet courted by all the world, and drawing yearly into more intimate consolidation, there came in 1911 the consummation of its hopes. The invocation of the Baring precedent, in the handling of a much smaller affair than the crisis of 1890, was—for us, at all events—the Omega of the process whereof the commutation of the feudal dues, five centuries before, had been the Alpha. In the middle of the year 1911 it became known that united action, of the type which had surmounted the Baring crisis, had again been silently and successfully undertaken.

---

[1] Capital and Counties Bank *v.* Gordon and London City and Midland Bank *v.* Gordon, 1903, Ap. Cas. 240. The appellant banks had credited a customer with the amounts of cheques as soon as they were paid in (not waiting for clearance), and had allowed him to draw against such credits before the effects were actually received. Held (the endorsements of the cheques being forged) that this procedure deprived the banks of the protection of s. 82 of the Bills of Exchange Act which protects a banker who receives payment of a crossed cheque for a *customer*. The banker, when he had credited the amount before clearance, ceased to be a mere agent for the collection of the money on behalf of his customer, and was transformed into a holder for value (per Lord Macnaghten, at p. 245).

[2] Institute of Bankers, November 7, 1906.

The Yorkshire Penny Bank, which held assets to the balance-sheet value of £19,023,122, had long been hampered by the necessity of dealing with this money in the manner permissible to a savings bank, while at the same time paying 2¾ per cent. interest on the deposits. The difficulty of maintaining this policy under such conditions at length produced a state of affairs which attracted the attention of the great joint-stock banks. Ultimately it was decided to transform the institution from its original status as a company by way of guarantee into a reorganised undertaking as a company by way of capital. For this purpose a sum of £2,000,000 was subscribed in order to form a new company, called the Yorkshire Penny Bank, Ltd. The subscribing banks were Barclay's, Beckett's, the Lancashire and Yorkshire, the Bank of Liverpool, Lloyds, the London City and Midland, the Manchester and County, the Manchester and Liverpool District, the Union of London and Smith's, and Williams-Deacon. Further, in order to provide against possible future depreciation of the securities held by the bank, a second group of banks had undertaken to give individual guarantees for a substantial amount. This second group comprised the Bank of England, the Capital and Counties, Glyn-Mills, the London County and Westminster, London and South-Western, Martin's, the National Bank, Robarts-Lubbock, the United Counties, the Metropolitan Bank (of England and Wales), and the London and Provincial. The net result of the arrangement was to transform the Yorkshire Penny Bank from an institution struggling with adverse economic conditions into one of the strongest banks in the country. As its deposits represented nearly 600,000 individual accounts, handled at over 100 daily branches and sub-branches, and over 800 smaller branches open on various days of the week, it needs no argument to demonstrate the service rendered to the community by consolidating the position of such an institution and obviating even the bare possibility of trouble. The whole of the arrangements were completed with such caution and celerity that it was not until every adjustment had been made that the public woke up to the real facts of the case and to their tremendous significance.

THE GREAT AVOWAL

The pregnant revelation that the financial organism had "found itself," and was prepared to avow its own existence, arose out of this episode. Avowal was made at the Bankers' Dinner at the Mansion House, on July 1, 1911, in the presence of the Chancellor of the Exchequer (Mr. Lloyd George) and the late Lord Avebury. The presence of the Chancellor was by no means the least happy feature of the occasion, though not one of those who saw him there suspected how intrepid and distinguished a part he was to play, within the next few years, as the protagonist of consolidated finance in its conflict with the machinations of German barbarism. "It is now my privilege," said Mr. A. C. Cole, the Governor of the Bank of England,

"to refer to a matter which I feel is of considerable interest to all the members of the banking community. I am one of those who have always refused to believe that the interests of the bankers are opposed to the interests of the Bank of England. While the Bank of England naturally keeps in view the interests of its shareholders, still, the first consideration of the Bank, in its decisions as to the Bank rate, is the welfare of the trade of the country. We reduce our rate so far as we can, keeping in view that the gold reserve at the Bank must be maintained. In the prosperity of the trade of the country every banker is directly interested, and all bankers are also interested in the maintenance of the gold reserve. There is no conflict of interest between the bankers and the central institution, and I have hailed with the utmost satisfaction a proposal that has been made unanimously by the representatives of the London Clearing Bankers that will bring the Governor of the Bank into more direct personal relations with the Clearing Banks. The resolution is that there should be quarterly meetings of the representatives of the London Clearing Banks at the Bank of England, and, as the outcome of this resolution that was passed yesterday, I hope the first meeting will be held at the Bank next week. While it will probably only be on rare occasions that important matters will come up for discussion, still, I believe the proposed meetings will prove beneficial to the Banking interest."

Twelve months later, at the next Bankers' Dinner,[1] Mr. Cole drove home the lesson of unselfish corporate trusteeship. " Our system of English banking," said he,

" is so largely founded upon credit that the machine must necessarily be, and is, a very delicate one. We are all part of the machine . . . and it is most essential that all bankers, especially the London bankers, should be very careful not to have commitments in other centres which might reflect disadvantageously upon the community of bankers in general."

The epoch-marking importance of these words, as a declaration of policy, is not minimised, but rather emphasised, by the fact, which has long since become public property, that the selection of that particular moment for the announcement was partly a tactical move. It was designed to draw public attention away from certain incidents, then the subject of investigation by the banking community. These, it is perhaps superfluous to add, were the affairs of the Yorkshire Penny Bank. But there was instant public recognition of the momentous character of the announcement. " It is evident," said the *Standard*,[2] " alike from the tone of the Governor's speech this evening and the manner of its reception by those present, that bankers and business men are alive to the importance which attaches to the close co-operation at all times between the Governor of the Bank and the representatives of the various institutions in Lombard Street." It was the City recognition of the soundness of Hobhouse's dictum that " elements of energy originally foreign to the organism " must be " absorbed and arranged so as to subserve the organic movement." Mr. Cole's own announcement was but the expression of a biological principle in the language of finance. A few of the City veterans who heard his voice

[1] May 9, 1912.
[2] At that time the City editorship of the *Standard* and the editorship of the *Bankers' Magazine* were united in the same capable hands—those of Mr. A. W. Kiddy.

may almost, if not quite, have recalled the age when the "elements of energy" were not only "foreign," but hostile, to the organism. And now these former things were done away, and all were to be made new! Within a year it was possible to say that in meeting the gigantic emergency created by the coal strike of 1912 the new conditions of unity and conciliar co-operation had already justified themselves. Within little more than three years from the original announcement came the overwhelming vindication of the immeasurable utility of banking unity which was afforded by the German war crisis of July-August, 1914.

UNITED STATES BANKING REFORM

The process of rehabilitating the banking system of the United States, which was first mooted in 1910, rapidly took a course towards precisely the same goal as that which had already been attained by the financial hierarchy of England. At the very outset of the movement Senator Aldrich urged the necessity of " more complete reorganisation, more thorough association of the banks of the country." He complained that whatever might have already been done, its " beneficial results have been local, and not general, in their character." He proceeded to define, in language which might have come directly from the mouth of an English banker, the purpose for which a financial hierarchy exists. He said that what banking required was

" an organisation that will, as far as possible, ensure reasonableness and steadiness of rates of discount throughout the country ; that will prevent the possibility of bank suspensions in the future ; that will extend to a bank in any part of the country, in proper circumstances, facilities which will enable it to afford relief at all times to those who are entitled to credit. It must provide against any possible disruption of domestic exchanges. *It must be an organisation which will have both the power and the purpose to maintain at all times, in all circumstances, the credit of the great people whose interests it is bound to serve.*"

THE AVOWAL AND THE TEST

In 1914 the United States banking and currency were at last placed upon a unified scientific basis by the establishment of a system of central banks at financially-strategic points throughout the country. Sound banking ideals found a transatlantic, as well as a British and West European, vogue and acceptance.

" A CORPORATE BODY "

In the interval which separated the consummation of confederacy from its subjection to an unprecedented and supreme test, the new conditions were everywhere recognised and avowed. They were an advance upon those which Giffen had originally called a hierarchy. " If there were no such hierarchy as what actually exists," said he, " each bank, whether in the country or in London, would have to stand by itself."[1] When Giffen wrote it was only possible to say that the leading banks of the Metropolis made up the hierarchy under " a supremacy or suzerainty lodged with the Bank of England." It could not be described as a formally recognised alliance. But nowadays the recognition is complete. " We do not," said Viscount Goschen, " regard the London County and Westminster Bank as a separate entity, but as a unit in a corporate body of great financial institutions."[2] They constitute a unity reinforced and consolidated by diversity. The attitude of the confederacy[3] is not patronal, but co-operative; it is that of the organiser, not the exploiter; of captain, not slave-driver. In Lord Milner's words :—

" Great indeed is the responsibility of those who, like the modern kings of finance, have it largely in their power to decide into what channels the streams of capital shall flow. Yet it is not fair, either, to put it all upon them. They are not demigods,

---

[1] Giffen, *Essays*, II. p. 110.
[2] *County and Westminster Magazine*, March, 1914.
[3] It is unfortunate that we have no single term for the financial confederacy. Democracy, aristocracy, ochlocracy, and monarchy we know as scientific terms of clear-cut significance; but the Money Power has no such recognised name. " Plutocracy " is useless for the purpose, since its connotation is riches rather than wealth. " Creditocracy " would be the word if it were not ruled out by the fact of its being, philologically, a mongrel.

but men, and they cannot escape from the influence of the atmosphere by which they are surrounded. It is the temper of the whole community which is the most decisive factor in the case."

This last is an extremely important consideration. At all events, during the last two periods of nineteenth-century finance (1866–1890 and 1890–1915), finance has done its utmost to train the public in the maintenance of a cool head. Steady itself, finance has tried to steady all the rest. Herein the national temperament is an invaluable auxiliary. " The ages of [our] isolation had their use, for they trained us for ages when we were not to be isolated."[1] When we have said all in favour of the British banking system, and the confederacy which directs it, we have still to remember how large is the contribution of the nation itself. The banks owe about £1,200,000,000 to their clients. If they were asked for it in a day, a week, or a month, they could not pay it :—

" The right of every individual to judge for himself is like the right of every man who possesses a balance at his banker's to require its immediate payment in sovereigns. The right may be undoubted, but it can only be safely enjoyed on condition that too many persons do not take it into their heads to exercise it together."[2]

The Bank of England and the confederacy around it have been able for the last half-century to rely more and more upon the solid common sense of the British people—a fact never more conspicuously exemplified than in the war crisis of 1914. For

" just as a man cycling through a crowded street depends for his life not only on his own skill, but also on the care with which the rest of the traffic is driven, so the English banking system is dependent on the sanity and sense of the public as much as on its own soundness."[3]

The foreign banks, especially the Bank of France, have to deal with more emotional people, and, consequently,

---

[1] Bagehot, *Physics and Politics*, p. 40 (slightly modified).
[2] A. J. Balfour, *Defence of Philosophic Doubt*.
[3] Withers, *Meaning of Money*.

THE AVOWAL AND THE TEST 667

cannot take things for granted to the same extent as the Bank of England.

RING OF FORTRESSES COMPLETE

Happily for the Empire, when the supreme test came every weak point of the defences had been eliminated. The ring of credit-fortresses was complete. The mere handful of sickly and weather-beaten "banks," some of them falsely so-called, which existed, or sprang into existence, after the date of the Baring crisis, had either been extirpated by August, 1914, or else went down at once before the storm. In the years preceding the crisis we had seen the last of such financial anachronisms as the Economic "Bank," the London and Universal "Bank," the London and General "Bank," the Charing Cross "Bank," and the Birkbeck Bank. Their fates showed what inevitably happens when the management of money is undertaken on unscientific principles, even though the institution which is active in the matter should have the temerity to call itself a "bank."[1] The London and Universal and the Charing Cross Banks were only money-lenders thus disguised. Disaster was not wholly confined to banks falsely so-called. Between 1866 and 1915 a few "survivals" vanished from the scene, for reasons familiar enough in the mid-Victorian period, though they had almost the smack of antiquity to us. When Greenway's of Warwick and Leamington went down in 1887, it was found that they had been financing tramways, even foreign tramways. They had, moreover, found the money to "run" a tannery. This latter proved a veritable quicksand, as might have been expected, and sucked down all the money thrown into it. Jarvis and Jarvis, who went into the hands of a receiver in December, 1888, had locked

---

[1] They also indicated, in no half-hearted fashion, the urgency of legislation to restrict the use of the word "bank" to thoroughly responsible institutions which can properly be so described. At present a greengrocer can open a "bank" with £5—or even with nothing—in the till. The statutory limit for every new bank should be (a) a minimum capital of £1,000,000, (b) paid up in actual cash to the extent of £500,000, no business to be done until the Registrar of joint-stock companies certifies that the £500,000 has actually been paid.

up their assets in docks and local improvements. Finally, the shock of the German war crisis destroyed the National Penny Bank, the Civil Service Bank, and the small Naval Bank at Plymouth. They were not, and never had been, banks in the strictest sense of the word, nor were they within the charmed circle of the hierarchy. The first was a semi-philanthropic institution. The second disclosed loans and overdrafts which included £5577 to the chairman, £1600 to a director, £8708 to the auditor and £5450 to the manager and secretary. The third was an isolated survival from earlier banking conditions. These small banks cannot exist, however tenacious their struggles. If we take the expression " small bank " in the sense in which it is used by the *Bankers' Magazine*—namely, as meaning an institution which has total assets amounting to less than £1,000,000—we shall find that in 1893 there were 42 such banks, in 1906 16, and in 1913 12. The figures rose from 42 in 1893 to 44 in 1894, and from 16 in 1906 to 27 in 1907. But this spasmodic attempt at revival, followed by a further decline, and then by the hurricane of 1914, only proves that the pressure of the *status quo* is too strong, and that the small bank cannot survive in an age of big banking. It cannot vary into correlation with its environment, and the resistless fiat of its doom goes forth.

EARLY " SHIVERS " IN 1914

The early months of 1914 were marked by occasional " shivers " and by co-operative effort to obviate or minimise them. Severe stringency made its appearance not only in the affairs of Brazil itself, but as affecting certain large enterprises operating in that Republic. The persistent and, in some cases, calamitous, fall in prices produced a state of apprehension which effectually checked the boom in gilt-edged stocks that had manifested itself immediately on the appearance of cheap money towards the end of January. But, although no official statement on the subject has ever been made, it is an accepted fact that powerful interests met and agreed upon a common policy, the effect of which was to assure certain financial assistance in quarters where it was necessary, so as to prevent the actual occurrence of crises. In the case of Brazil, however (largely owing to the German war crisis), the funding of the interest for three years had ultimately to be adopted. But neither when war broke out, or before, was the affair allowed to assume serious dimensions. In May of 1914 the commitments (including, so it was said, Trunk Ordinary to the extent of some millions) of a large City house were stated to have been taken over by a private syndicate, under the guidance of the Bank of England, and the spread of the trouble in that way stopped for a time. Circumstances arose, however, which led to the decision that it would be better to let events take their course; and on June 6 Chaplin, Milne, Grenfell and Co. and the Canadian Agency suspended payment.

THE GERMAN WAR CRISIS

The German war crisis of 1914 was entirely political.[1] Neither in banking, industry, nor commerce had anything been done which would have created any crisis. The Bank rate stood at 3 per cent. as late as July 29. If the war had not supervened, financial affairs, for all that we can see to the contrary, would have pursued their normal course, and all the various functions of the Money Market would have continued to subserve their normal purpose. What happened, however, was that the Government, with the unanimous support of the nation, considered it desirable to declare war on Germany. That act, justifiable and statesmanlike to the last degree, must nevertheless have produced an unprecedented convulsion in the Money

---

[1] The detailed treatment of this crisis forms no part of the plan of the present essay. I shall briefly argue that the total absence of panic, and the demonstrated adamantine strength of the banking confederacy, completely confirm, as I hope, the thesis which I have endeavoured to establish. There I shall stop, having brought the analysis of the Evolution of the Money Market practically to the end of the first century of its definitely separate existence. The German war crisis of 1914 requires a treatise to itself. But that treatise cannot be written yet, for the simple reason that we are too near the events for anything like an adequate scientific judgment to be passed upon them. Mr. Withers, however, in his *War and Lombard Street*, has made an admirable beginning.

Market if instant and drastic steps had not been taken to avert the calamity. That was why the Government intervened. There was nothing whatever wrong with the financial system. In fact, events between the declaration of war and the end of the year showed that it had never been in a state of greater efficiency. But the Government, having in the national interest provoked the crisis, was bound to confer upon the banks the special powers, shaped to the unprecedented exigencies of the occasion, which should enable them to meet the shock. None of the previous financial crises since Waterloo had been produced by the crash of war, unless, indeed, we attribute to the South African war the minor and purely local Stock Exchange crisis precipitated by the London and Globe crash at the end of the year 1900. With that very slight exception every crisis since Waterloo has been either financial or commercial. Every crisis and " shiver " from 1867 to June, 1914, was met and fought by finance alone without any assistance whatever from the Government. Perhaps it is going too far to employ such an expression as " every " crisis. There was only one that really touched London— the Baring episode of 1890. So far as the English credit fabric is concerned the old sequence of an approximate ten-year cycle, from crisis to crisis, is at an end. Whatever may have been the influence at work, solar or terrestrial, the ten-year cycle is obvious enough in the crises of 1825–26, 1837, 1847, 1857, 1866, 1878, and perhaps 1890. After 1890 twenty-four years had elapsed without crisis— for the stringency of the early years of the present century was the result of the Boer war, and was in no sense crisis, while the American panic of 1907, as we have seen, left London intrinsically unscathed, if sympathetically affected.

So well had the iron bastions of modern finance been built and bolted together. Nor did the public, educated for half a century to be steady in the presence of financial menace, fail to justify the teaching in the presence of the most stupendous of all trials. The author of the present essay, who had heard from many a departed City veteran the story of the scenes in the cataclysm of 1866, tested

THE AVOWAL AND THE TEST 671

his own conclusions, with regard to the unshaken confidence of the business public in the almost omnipotent grip of the Money Power, by an observant walk through the banking quarter at noon on Friday, July 31, 1914, when war was a certainty and the Stock Exchange had just been closed. At the London City and Midland Bank, in Cornhill, he counted five persons at the counter. At the head office of the London and South-Western he enumerated six persons, two of whom were engaged in paying money in. Barclay's appeared to be empty, but a customer was just entering it. There were a mere handful of people carrying on leisurely transactions at Martin's. There was, in fact, not the slightest sign of excitement in the whole banking quarter. An ordinary day in the middle of a normal holiday season could not have been quieter. One might almost have characterised the position of affairs as exhibiting the proverbial coolness of the cucumber. A tour of the same district on the stroke of four yielded similar results. The banks presented the same appearance as they always do at the closing hour, without the slightest manifestation of disquietude. To give a specific instance, the number of persons at the paying desks of the London and South-Western head office on the stroke of four was six, of whom one was a girl, apparently delivering a message, and the other five were drawing small amounts.

A SHORTAGE OF CURRENCY

By this time, however, some precautionary expedients had already been adopted. The Bank rate had gone to 4 per cent. on July 30, to 8 per cent. on July 31, and to 10 per cent. on August 1—mainly as a result of the calling of loans from bill brokers and discount houses, who were driven, as usual, to the Bank of England for assistance in their emergency. When war was finally declared there was seen to be lacking one factor of preparedness, and this the banks, in the absence of legislative authority, were incompetent to supply. There was no elasticity in the *standardised* (note) currency, as distinguished from the *unstandardised* (cheque) currency. The latter, which depends entirely upon confidence and credit, must naturally tend to shrink—primarily, at all events—in the presence of events that enforce extreme circumspection. Unless replaced by the other species, monetary stringency must eventuate. But bankers, while they can supply unstandardised currency to any amount, cannot legally create the other type at all :—

" Bankers have for years seen this weakness. For a considerable time before this [German] crisis, a small Committee consisting of three bankers had been sitting week by week with the object of deciding on some satisfactory scheme. They agreed that the [Bank Charter] Act should be amended to the effect that if one-third of gold and two-thirds of securities were placed by the banks in the Issue Department, a corresponding amount of notes might be issued. The scheme, which was to come into operation only when a crisis was at hand, was submitted to the Gold Committee presided over by Lord St. Aldwyn, and was approved by them. It was then submitted to the representatives of the Clearing Banks and was also approved by them. To increase the currency, the only alternative to this scheme was a suspension of the Bank Act, which meant an issue of notes without any gold cover at all. The scheme submitted by the Committee would form an inducement for bankers to hold more gold, inasmuch as, when a crisis was imminent, they would be able to get more currency.

" This scheme was submitted to the Chancellor of the Exchequer, but strong opposition to it was shown by the Bank of England. The bankers persisted, and they understood that the opposition either was or would be withdrawn, but it was too late. Friday, August 7, 1914, was approaching, when the banks were to be reopened. It was deemed advisable for the present to drop the scheme, and they then made another suggestion which was adopted, viz. that the banks should give security for an issue of notes to be made to them by the Government ; and the issue was made in the shape of Treasury Notes. . . . On Friday the banks all over the country reopened, and as they had been closed for five days, people naturally wanted a little additional money, but by Friday night all difficulties were past."[1]

[1] Sir Edward Holden, London City and Midland Bank meeting, January 29, 1915.

THE AVOWAL AND THE TEST

Thus was the "expansive theory" justified again.[1] In plain English, the leaders of the banking hierarchy had foreseen the difficulty. If they had been free to act "on their own" they would have been ready. Hampered by the necessity of statutory authorisation, they were like a man swimming in a sack.

But, after all, the main point is that the financial confederacy met the shock as a single solid mass, not as a random congeries of disunited interests. On Bank Holiday, August 3, a meeting of the bankers and merchants of the City was held at the Bank of England. A resolution was passed petitioning the Government to proclaim Tuesday, Wednesday, and Thursday as additional holidays, the banks to reopen on the Friday. The Government, on its own side, "called into council representatives of the Bank of England, of the great joint-stock banks, of the Stock Exchange, of the accepting houses, of the traders, and, in fact, of all interests principally concerned."[2] The "Committee of Bankers was in constant session throughout and rendered great service, in an advisory capacity, to the Treasury, as well as in guiding the business of banking, upon which our trade and business credit almost entirely depend."[3] A moment's cogitation upon the potentialities of this colossal emergency, if it had burst upon the separate, isolated and conflicting factors once called a "banking system," will confront the imagination with something like an economic Inferno.

LONDON WAS TOO STRONG FOR THE EXCHANGES

But fact, replacing imagination, assures us that so mighty were the united and confederated forces that until

---

[1] "We acted on the lessons which every crisis has taught—be liberal in your lending and meet every legitimate demand if you can. We hav· over 1000 branches, and the managers of those branches were instructed to refuse nothing to their clients without referring to head office, and head office gave every assistance that it possibly could." So said Sir Edward Holden at the London City and Midland Bank meeting, *supra*.

[2] Lord St. Aldwyn, London Joint Stock Bank meeting, January 28, 1915.

[3] Sir John Bethell, London and South-Western Bank meeting, January 28, 1915

674 EVOLUTION OF THE MONEY MARKET

1914 London did not know how strong it was.[1] The colossal strength of London was so overwhelmingly demonstrated that, in the words of Mr. Withers,[2] "it put the rest of the economically civilised world into the Bankruptcy Court." It was able to claim something like £200,000,000 of short money. The rest of the world could not pay. Cosmopolitan financial sentiment, now schooled in the most exalted of modern ideals, did its best.

[1] This point is opportune for a review which may give some idea how colossal were the forces which the confederate financial power controlled. In December, 1844, the deposits of the joint-stock banks in London— London and Westminster, London Joint Stock, Union, Commercial, and London and County—totalled £7,984,305. The united capital was £2,062,900. These figures are relative to the time. In 1851 the London and Westminster had only five branches besides the head office. The London Joint Stock had one City and one West End Office, while the Union of London had one City office and two in the West End. Lloyds in 1865 had 16 offices. At the end of 1913 it had 679. Precise statistics are not easily obtainable when we are concerned with the number of customers rather than with the aggregate balances. But at the London and County Bank meeting on February 2, 1865, the chairman said that they had 41,767 customers, an increase of 2623 on the year. At the half-yearly meeting six months later the number had advanced to 44,616, and at Christmas 1866 it had reached 50,389. In the great crisis year of 1847 the aggregate deposits of the public in the joint-stock banks of London were less than £9,000,000. In 1874 the corresponding group (consisting of 11 institutions) of the leading banks held £96,900,000 of deposits, their total liabilities being £110,800,000, with aggregate capitals and reserves of £12,500,000. The Right Hon. James Wilson, in his speech during a debate on the 1847 crisis, estimated that the total deposits of the banks of the United Kingdom were from £200,000,000 to £250,000,000. In 1851, Mr. Newmarch put it at £260,000,000, including deposits at bill brokers not received from bankers. Palgrave in 1872 estimated it at £616,000,000, or, adding the amounts belonging to foreign and colonial banks with offices in London and estimated at £152,000,000, the grand total of £768,000,000. The late John Dun in 1876 put the total for the United Kingdom at £782,000,000–£934,000,000, including the estimated money in the hands of foreign and colonial banks. Between 1894 and the end of 1912 the "deposits, current accounts, and notes in circulation" of the banks of the United Kingdom increased by £401,000,000, i.e. from £679,000,000 to £1,080,000,000. The precise proportion attributable to deposit accounts, if it be desired to divide them from current accounts, is not ascertainable. During the prolonged period of market quietude —and, towards the end, of falling trade as well—which began about May, 1912, the existing deposit accounts increased at the rate of about £50,000,000 a year. A separation of the deposits from the current accounts is not practicable with exactitude, because the two items are not divided in the majority of published accounts. But a conjecture which has the weight of great experience behind it would allocate 45 per cent. to deposits and 55 per cent. to current accounts. This, taking in the total of current and deposit accounts at £1,200,000,000, would give about £540,000,000 as the amount on deposit with the banks of the United Kingdom in the spring of 1915.

[2] *The War and Lombard Street*, p. 99.

But its best broke down the whole machinery of the foreign exchanges. Mr. Withers (who has exceptional sources of information) insists that even the German bankers paid all their London debts as long as they could buy sterling. "At a point their exchange broke down, like all the others." The United States, in a noble struggle to meet the exigencies of the situation, bought sovereigns as high as $7—the normal figure being about $4·85!

PROTECTING THE ACCEPTING HOUSES

The breakdown at once produced the necessity for ameliorative strategy. Inextricably woven, as they are, into a single seamless texture, the various factors of the Money Market all depend upon one another for their efficient and wholesome functioning. In the Money Market organism, as in its physical analogue, the healthy activity of the whole cannot subsist coincidently with the atrophy or dislocation of any of the parts. Therein lay the justification for the first proclamation, issued on Monday, August 3, which enabled any accepting house to postpone for one month the payment of any bill accepted before August 3, and falling due within such month, subject only to the payment of interest at the rate of 6 per cent. The importance of the protection granted to the accepting houses lies in the fact that their actual resources at any given moment form only a small proportion of their outstanding commitments by way of acceptance. We have seen that it has, for more than a century, been the practice of leading London mercantile houses to sell the use of their credit, in return for a commission, to people whose paper, in the absence of such an acceptance, would only take a relatively low rank. But in carrying on this very high-class credit business the accepting houses obviously rely, and must rely, upon an uninterrupted stream of remittances to meet the various obligations as they mature. In a word, they undertake, for a commission, to assume a responsibility which, in fact, seldom or never falls upon them; and, by a paradox familiar to all students of English banking, their responsibility in this respect is frequently, if not always, far in excess of their capacity to discharge it, if, as a matter of fact, they were actually called upon to do so. Now, clearly, if a whole class of accepting houses are relying on foreign remittances to meet obligations for which they have rendered themselves ultimately responsible, a situation of the very gravest character must arise if all these remittances are suddenly stopped by the breakdown of Exchanges. That was actually the case during the first week in August. The accepting houses saw themselves confronted with a sequence of maturing obligations quite beyond their power to meet in the absence of the remittances which would in the ordinary course have provided for them; while they knew, at the same time, that these remittances were impossible, owing to the sudden stop of the whole financial mechanism, as a result of the declaration of war. In an admirable review of the situation, contributed by Professor Keynes to the *Economic Journal* for September, 1914, it is pointed out that there are four ways in which a foreign creditor may expect to remit funds to meet his obligations: (1) by sending goods, (2) by sending gold, (3) by selling securities, and (4) by discounting bills and thus raising fresh short credits. Every one of these expedients was put out of gear by the outbreak of the war. Consequently, in the absence of the proclamation of August 3, the accepting houses must have been left naked to every wind that blew.

A still further expedient consolidated the work already done. On the evening of Wednesday, August 12, it was announced that the Government had completed arrangements with the Bank of England under which, in the words of the official announcement, " the Bank of England are prepared, on the application of the holder of any approved bill of exchange accepted before August 4, 1914, to discount at any time before its due date at Bank rate, without recourse to such holder; and upon its maturity the **Bank of England** will, in order to assist the resumption of **normal** business operations, give the acceptor the opportunity until further notice of postponing payment, interest being payable in the meantime at 2 per cent. over Bank rate."

THE AVOWAL AND THE TEST 677

The result of this striking offer was a rush to the Bank of England of such volume as to make it a physical impossibility to keep pace with the bills presented. But the announcement was not only an evidence of the impregnable strength of the modern Money Power centred in the Bank itself, but was also a demonstration of the confidence with which the British Government entered into a financial alliance involving a responsibility of absolutely unprecedented magnitude.

CLOSING OF THE STOCK EXCHANGE

Another factor of the mechanism—the Stock Exchange—had perforce to suspend operations on July 31. This, however, was no admission of failure. It meant, as we have already seen,[1] that an institution designed to perform, and capably performing, a certain well-defined function cannot be expected instantly to undertake the fulfilment of another, a totally different, and a gigantic obligation. In the closing of the Stock Exchange would be another justification, if it were needed, of the bankers' claim to the most generous statutory co-operation. Sound banking depends, and legitimately depends, upon liquidity of assets. But liquidity of assets is an impossible state of affairs in the presence of a closed Stock Exchange—the market which alone provides the means of realisation for many of them. That the closure, at the time of the German war crisis, was peremptorily essential, no sane critic would venture to deny. Yet if the Government and the menace of events intervened—the former courageously, legitimately, inevitably—to take away one of the main auxiliaries of the banking mechanism, the operators thereof cannot be reproached for expecting certain ameliorative measures. That a man cannot survive in a vacuum is not a proof of his physical degeneracy or intellectual incapacity, but a demonstration that nature has inviolate laws. The reproach is not with the man, but with the circumstances that force him into collision with the adamantine fiat that has made the supply of oxygen a

[1] *Ante*, p. 587.

condition of human existence. Liquidity is the oxygen of banking.

THE NEED FOR A MORATORIUM

Therefore—if we may pursue the metaphor—when the supply was cut off, further Government co-operation became necessary. Obviously, if depositors became alarmed and peremptory, the closing of the Stock Exchange and the sudden stoppage of all remittances from abroad had cut off two of the main sources from which funds might otherwise have been drawn to meet the needs of the bankers. Moreover, there was the almost certain prospect that numbers of persons upon whom the banks had relied to pay all maturing bills would be unable to discharge their obligations. This would not happen because they were unwilling, but because they could not themselves collect money due to them. D expects to receive money from C, which C is perfectly willing to pay. But he relies for the funds upon a certain debt due to him from B; and B, in his turn, is expecting a remittance from A. If A does not send the money, B finds himself in a position of financial stringency. He cannot pay C, and consequently C cannot discharge his obligations to D. Obviously, when there is a risk of a catena of embarrassment such as this, the only thing to do is to give each man time to turn round by postponing the maturity of the obligation which is the cause of his anxiety. That was exactly what the proclamation of August 6 did. It went right to the root of the matter, by recognising and providing for the relationship of debtor and creditor between banker and customer. With unprecedented boldness, it conferred upon the banker the power of postponing for a month the settlement of his obligations to his creditor, although these, in ordinary banking practice, must be settled on demand at any moment across the counter. There was a similar extension for one month of the moratorium in its application to other debts, with certain exceptions. The closing of the Stock Exchange as a protective expedient was further fortified on September 14 by the issue of a list of official minimum prices for all the first-class securities, with the announce-

THE AVOWAL AND THE TEST 679

ment that no member of the Stock Exchange would be permitted to do business in them below the prices thus officially fixed. The list remained in force till March 18, 1915, when it was slightly revised downwards.

NO SUSPENSION OF THE BANK ACT

There was no suspension of the Bank Charter Act.[1] At an early stage of the crisis an attempt was made to put upon a statutory basis, so to speak, the emergency machinery for the suspension of the Bank Charter Act. Instead of the Treasury being left to its traditional, but irregular, exercise of the power of suspension, and the Bank itself to a subsequent Parliamentary indemnity, authority to suspend was deliberately conferred upon the former by section 3 of the Currency and Bank Notes Act, August 6, 1914 (critical words italicised) :—

" (3) The Governor and Company of the Bank of England and any persons concerned in the management of any Scottish or Irish bank of issue, *may, so far as temporarily authorised by the Treasury and subject to any conditions attached to that authority,* issue notes in excess of any limit fixed by law ; and those persons are hereby indemnified, freed, and discharged from any liability, penal or civil, in respect of any issue of notes beyond the amount fixed by law which has been made by them since August 1, 1914, *in pursuance of any authority of the Treasury or of any letter from the Chancellor of the Exchequer,* and any proceedings taken to enforce any such liability shall be void."

This section puts into regular statutory form the power thrice irregularly exercised on the part of the Treasury, by the suspension of the Bank Act in 1847, 1857, and 1866. On those three occasions the Treasury, acting " on its own," authorised the Governor of the Bank of England to disregard the provisions of the Bank Act. It undertook to procure legislative indemnity for him and his co-directors, so as to legalise their illegal action. What section 3 now does is to regularise this method. It enacts that, instead of the Treasury being compelled to go to

[1] But see *ante*, p. 352, on the question whether the issue of Treasury notes was a constructive suspension or not.

work on its own initiative, and to take the risk (albeit a small one) of Parliamentary displeasure, it shall be legislatively endowed with the power to suspend the Bank Act. The Bank of England may, " *so far as temporarily authorised by the Treasury*, and subject to any conditions attached to that authority," issue notes in excess of the legal limit. The power which the Treasury snatched, so to speak, in 1847, 1857, and 1866 is now placed in its hands by statute. It will remain there till Parliament sees fit to withdraw it—unless, indeed, there is to be a permanent delegation of this authority. The power thus conferred was never used. The issue of Treasury notes satisfied the needs of currency expansion, and the Bank always had gold against every note issued above the statutory limit of £18,450,000.

Thus the confederate Money Power held the situation as in the grip of a gigantic vice. The bank rate was at 10 per cent. for six days and then returned to 5 per cent. within a week of a crisis the like of which the world had never seen before. It was the Sixteenth Decisive Battle of the world. All the old mischievous elements of isolation had gone down before the onset of organised finance. They finally vanished from the scene. There was no suspension of the Bank Act, no panic, no excited throng, no catena of catastrophe. No single institution might have withstood the strain, but the combined confederate factors of the financial organism were impregnable. The searching test discovered no weak place in the entire banking system—except the shortage of currency. And that was the fault of the legislature, not of the banking hierarchy. We may doubtless see crises again in the years to come. Credit with active expansion must perforce go on, and a cycle of movement will doubtless be more or less clearly traceable. But conditions will no longer, in the lands controlled by the banking hierarchy, swell into panic as of yore.

Writing in 1908, Riesser thought that there would probably never be a permanent cessation of crises.[1] Prophecy in such a field is dangerous ; and of *crisis*, perhaps,

[1] *Great German Banks*, U.S. Monetary Commission, p. 15.

THE AVOWAL AND THE TEST 681

the present century may not see the last. But of panic it may well believe itself rid for ever, in the light of the experience gained in the German war crisis of 1914. Lord Goschen[1] has summed up the work of the financial hegemony in this respect :—

"There is one feature to which we may look with satisfaction. Last century we were accustomed, on an average, to a financial crisis every ten years, always attended by some failures; but is it not a little remarkable that, although we have passed through times of trouble since then—times when it appeared as if Europe were on the brink of war, and stocks from abroad have been thrown on this market to be sold at panic prices, yet they have not been attended by any serious failures? May not this be largely attributed to the financial institutions, which have acquired such power in the world of finance that at the moment when credit appears to be inflated and speculation unhealthy, they are able to restrict credit for other than legitimate trade purposes, and so compel those disturbing forces to mark time, if not to halt, until equilibrium is once more established?

"It is a fact that some months ago the English banks generally shut their eyes to any but the most pressing needs, and this attitude produced a most salutary effect on the overstrained market. It is, then, a source of congratulation if the periods of crises are less frequent—in other words, that the gap between each crisis grows wider—and I think that the excellence of our present-day banking institutions may take credit for much of the improvement. As years pass, the influence of finance on 'world politics' greatly increases, and imposes upon us corresponding obligations, which we must recognise, and be prepared to assume."

Remembering the innumerable instances where the group has held its own in circumstances where the divided units must have gone down, one is tempted to wonder whether civilisation is destined to face its foes on one last field of Armageddon; and whether the compact financial organisation will provide, in that last dour conflict, the staying power that shall win the day.[2]

[1] Addressing the Institute of Bankers in November, 1913.
[2] These words were in type before the outbreak, or even the approach of the German war. They are advisedly left as originally written.

CHAPTER XXI

SUMMARY AND CONCLUSION

THE waves of more than five centuries roll between the commutation of the feudal dues, with its resulting embryonic money-economy, and the emergence of the Inner Cabinet of British banking as the mind of a puissant financial organism, a hierarchy over other hierarchies. They have been five centuries of ceaseless evolution. " It is at least evident," remarks Haldane, " that the extension of biological conceptions to the whole of Nature may be much nearer than seemed conceivable even a few years ago."[1] This essay will have been written in vain if it fail to convince its reader, even at the point which he has now reached, of the substantial validity of the argument for continuous development as connecting the lowest with the highest orders of being in the financial as well as in the biological world. What now remains is to survey, as succinctly and yet as adequately as may be, all that is involved in the scheme which we have seen unfolding, and to state what results may be postulated for it thus far. A retrospect of three centuries and a quarter carries us to the first definite statutory recognition of that differentiation and specialisation of function which marked the beginnings of complexity in the developing financial organism. We encounter the Broker, " Driver of Bargaynes," and " Shyfter " in Tudor loan transactions. Homogeneity begins to vanish and heterogeneity takes its place. Interplay and interdependence begin, experience accumulates, and the rudiments of an organic tradition, leading to a keener circumspection and a unity of sentiment

[1] Haldane, *Mechanism, Life and Personality*, p. 101.

SUMMARY AND CONCLUSION 683

(already ripe and keen in the presence of peril), subtly reinforce the psychic equipment of the embryo organism. Though as yet almost unconscious of its own existence, it acts as an integrity in self-defence and self-preservation against royal or statutory aggression. It scans the environment and becomes more daring in the presence of conditions which it judges to be auspicious. This is the stage at which banking in the modern sense—the borrowing of money to lend it again, or to employ it as the basis of credit-creation—displays itself as an inchoate art. But although we may speak of finance, even at this stage, as an organism, we must remember that it is as yet only embryonic. It is so far incapable of the permanent co-ordination of its functions. There is a lack of that mysterious influence, living and moving behind the physical manifestations, which differentiates personality from mere existence.

CALCULATED CO-ORDINATION

" Perhaps the most striking fact with regard to physiological phenomena," remarks Haldane,[1] " is the evidence they present of activity co-ordinated in such a manner as to conduce towards the survival of either the individual or the species. Co-ordination of a similar striking kind is not found anywhere outside the organic world. The mere existence of it has been taken as strong evidence for the presence in living organisms of some co-ordinating influence apart from blind physical and chemical forces." Apart from this guiding and governing influence the organism will never grapple on terms of equality, and ultimately of predominance, with its environment. " The mere organism," as Haldane tells us, " is at the mercy of the physical environment: it is helplessly swept hither and thither and learns nothing from experience." Therein lies the supreme importance of the establishment of the Bank of England. It provided the dominating intellectual nucleus around which the subordinate ganglionic centres could gradually be clustered, to which they could report and from which receive their mandates. Simultaneously with

[1] *Mechanism, Life and Personality*, p. 8.

its establishment, banking itself became (in London, but not yet in the country) a specialisation, distinct from its old alliance with the goldsmith's business, or the keeping of a shop. In its new shape, it was the stronger as an anabolic force, capable of the liberation, by katabolism, of kinetic energy. But the great institution at the centre, as it grew in years and wisdom, became an object to itself, permanently self-identical, the depositary of an ever augmenting aggregate of tradition and experience. Just as " a pigmented spot has slowly become an organ of vision," just as a few specialised hairs have been developed into a recipient organ for variations of pressure, a rudimentary organ of touch and of hearing,[1] even so this centre of financial force, originally intended as a mere temporary auxiliary for an impecunious administration, became every year more capable of correlating the act of the moment with permanent interests and general principles. It grasped the continuity running through its experience, focussed it in generalisations, and became ambitious and capable of wielding authority over less circumspect and less abundantly endowed entities. Thus we are led to the period of Waterloo, when the financial organism has developed far enough for us to attempt the analysis of its further evolution on lines precisely parallel with those discernible in the history of a physical analogue. We are able to place in juxtaposition (*ante*, p. 266) the three stages of physical and financial evolution respectively, and to see how apt the analogy is. But in both cases we are driven to ask in what, after all, and essentially, the process of development consists. We are led to accept the conclusion of Hobhouse that it " consists in the growth of Mind." That proposition we may unreservedly accept in its application to the process of physical development which has culminated in the ascent of man. But can we speak of mind in relation to a financial organism ? Dare we suggest that such an organism is actually capable of accumulating tradition, of storing experience ? Must we not rather admit that instead of a corporate memory and

[1] McKendrick, *Principles of Physiology*, p. 217.

SUMMARY AND CONCLUSION

experience, stretching across the centuries, we have only the laboriously acquired knowledge of each generation of bankers, existing isolated, and unrelated, save in approximate coincidence of purpose and endeavour, to the generations that have gone before ?

IS THERE A CORPORATE HERITAGE ?

On the contrary, all the most daring modern speculation points to corporate continuity, persistent corporate consciousness, and a constantly widening and deepening corporate experience, unbroken in entail from age to age :—

" We cannot suppose that those relations of facts or objects in consciousness, which constitute any piece of knowledge of which a man becomes master, first come into being when he attains that knowledge : that they pass through the process by which he laboriously learns, or gradually cease to be as he forgets or becomes confused. They must exist as part of an eternal universe—and that a spiritual universe, or universe of consciousness — during all the changes of the individual's attitude towards them, whether he is asleep or awake, distracted or attentive, ignorant or informed. . . . We must hold, then, that there is a consciousness for which the relations of fact, that form the object of our gradually attained knowledge, already and eternally exist ; and that *the growing knowledge of the individual is a progress towards this consciousness.* It is a consciousness, further, which is itself operative in the progress towards its attainment, just as elsewhere the end realised through a certain process itself determines the process : as a particular kind of life, for instance, informs the processes organic to it."[1]

But this reasoning, it will be said, applies only to the individual mind. It has no cogency where the alleged consciousness is that of a legal corporation, or where, even in the absence of the legally corporate personality, there is a sufficient identity of interest, ideal, and endeavour to create a common cause and the closest of association, as in the instance of the financial hierarchy. These are objections which cannot prevail in the light of advancing

[1] T. H. Green, *Prolegomena to Ethics*, p. 80.

realisation of the subtlety of psychic forces. "Deeply convinced though our lawyers may be," remarks Maitland,[1] "that individual men are the only 'real' and 'natural' persons, they are compelled to find some phrase which places State and Man upon one level. 'The greatest of artificial persons, politically speaking, is the State'; so we may read in an excellent First Book of Jurisprudence.[2] Ascending from the legal plain, we are in a middle region where a sociology emulous of the physical sciences discusses of organs and organisms, and social tissue, and cannot sever by sharp lines the natural history of state-groups from the natural history of other groups. Finally, we are among the summits of philosophy, and observe how a doctrine, which makes some way in England, ascribes to the State, or more vaguely the Community, not only a real will, but even '*the*' real will: and it must occur to us to ask *whether what is thus affirmed in the case of the State can be denied in the case of other organised groups*: for example, that considerable group the Roman Catholic Church "

—or that other considerable group, the financial hierarchy. It is not likely to be contended that a corporate will can only exist by strictly *legal* procreation. If the will to be corporate makes the corporation, then the financial hierarchy possesses a distinct corporate individuality, and, as such, may be the subject of every predication made by Green with reference to the " real " individual.

Thus we are brought face to face with Gierke's theory of the corporate will, in its application to the grouppower which controls the financial mechanism. Gierke's term is Genossenschaft. Maitland, casting about for a translation, avoids " partnership," urges that " company " is too specific and technical; that " society " also is dangerous; and ultimately falls back upon " fellowship " —which is, in truth, the most felicitous word that could be applied to that form of association which gives us the financial supremacy of the Bank of England and the intimate confederacy of the allied interests :—

" Our German fellowship is no fiction, no symbol, no piece of the State's machinery, no collective name for individuals, but a

[1] *Political Theories of the Middle Age*, Intro., p. xi.
[2] Pollock, *First Book of Jurisprudence*, p. 113.

SUMMARY AND CONCLUSION

living organism and a real person, with body and members and a will of its own. Itself can will, itself can act ; it wills and acts by the men who are its organs as a man wills and acts by brain, mouth, and hand. It is not a fictitious person : it is a Gesammtperson, and its will is a Gesammtwille : it is a groupperson, and its will is a group-will."[1]

This is the scientific form of the "organic idea," in its application to the group-power that rules finance. Is it too much to say that, if these theories be sound, we have a developed "group-will" in the financial sphere—that finance itself is an evolved organism, possessing " a consciousness for which the relations of fact that form the object of our gradually attained knowledge, already and eternally exist," as an increasing corporate inheritance, swelled by memory and experience, which has come down to us from days of humbler achievement and less vivid self-realisation ?

If—to go a stage beyond the postulation of an organism —personality is the " spiritual inheritance of ages," a new and deeper significance attaches to the words of Mr. Withers when he observes that " this psychological reserve [of British bankers][2] is the priceless possession that has been handed down through generations of good bankers, and every individual of every generation that receives it can do something to maintain and improve it." The psychological factor is ineluctable, peremptory. Finance, as we see it around us to-day, can no more be surveyed, analysed and accounted for in terms of physics and paper, ledgers and gold, than art can be dissected into the chemistry of colour or religion into the minute textual criticism of the Sacred Deposit. The sum of the components discovered by chemical and physical analysis is less than their whole resultant as revealed in a vital action. The physical world is "only the appearance of a deeper reality which is as yet hidden from our distinct vision, and can only be seen with the eye of scientific faith." Even so is the visible financial mechanism the premonstration of a higher reality, now becoming visible to the

[1] Maitland, op. cit., Intro., p. xxvi.   [2] *Meaning of Money*, p. 286.

discerning scientific vision, which may hope in future years, perhaps, somewhat to pierce the veil hiding the Master of the tireless strategy that moves the panorama of the ages. When we add up the components revealed by economic analysis, in the shape of money, credit, and all the machinery for distributing and utilising them, they do not amount to the whole resultant of the modern Money Market. The factors of human energy and foresight, of moral force, and of an aggregate corporate power which is far greater than the sum of its components, have yet to be taken into consideration. There remain to be added those characteristics of the living sentient creature which are manifest in a " persistent unified behaviour, a power of profiting by experience, a creative capacity as a genuine agent." Together, the factors constitute an organic unity of attributes, faculties and functions, capable of self-determination towards a deliberately-selected aim. The conception of organised correlation of function, lofty as it is, becomes incapable of fully accounting for the phenomena, almost simultaneously with their clear emergence among the higher manifestations of the super-organic world into distinct actuality. We are compelled " to have recourse to another conception—that of personality." This is the reason why, at an earlier stage of the present essay (p. 219) so great stress was laid, in the case of the Bank of England, upon the continuity of corporate consciousness, capable of " correlating the act of the moment with permanent interests and general principles." When not only the act of the moment but a whole class of elements, previously separate, are united in a synthesis of correlation, and inspired by a common purpose, an organic determination; and when the purpose itself is found to contemplate achievement in fields so elevated as hitherto to be regarded as closed to human effort, any hypothesis short of a deathless corporate personality will fail to account for the facts. Physical science, or legal enactment, is incompetent to soar into the region dominated by a corporate consciousness. " In self-diremption, its combination of unity with plurality, of identity with difference, separates it *toto cœlo* from the material order, and therefore from the jurisdiction of the sciences which deal with that order."[1]

THE SELECTIVE PROCESS

We turn to scan the *agents* of the corporate personality. Over the wide arena of modern financial interests, and among all the minds of varying calibre, experience, and outlook which occupy themselves in them, a selective process is incessantly going on, analogous to that which in earlier ages preserved the species best adapted to its environment. The banker is naturally its primary product, for upon his capacity, responsibility, loyalty and skill the solidity of the whole fabric depends. He cannot, as in former times, divide his energies between banking and some other business. Banking is a profession which must stand alone in the devotion of its practitioners. The capable man moves towards the centre. He becomes in course of time a picked specimen—an " artist in credit," as Sir Edward Holden once said—the finest that contemporary banking science can produce. The best financial talent from the country, and especially from Scotland, is recruited for Lombard Street. Ultimately there is evolved the unseen but potent unity that forms and focuses prevailing financial sentiment, and—more exclusive still—its visible representatives who can confer at the Bank of England :—

" The normal expansion and contraction of bank credit are of such vital importance to the whole business community that their regulation ought to be entrusted to those who have been chosen by a process of natural selection to manage the banking business, and not subjected to administrative rules of thumb."[2]

As all the higher types of life begin in a unification of two inheritances, so, it may be, the higher types of banking evolve from the unification of varying business experiences. In the shape which the central and dominant conclaves of the banking hierarchy have now assumed

[1] Illingworth, *Personality, Human and Divine*, p. 107 n.
[2] Seager, *Introduction to Economics*, p. 337.

they constitute, in its widest aspect, " association without presence." They are the capitalisation of three centuries of experience in the observation of the phenomena of credit. They are guided by a profundity and scope of knowledge quite unattainable by the mere capitalist of earlier ages, because it has to do with forces, tendencies, and potentialities utterly out of the range of his perception. The hegemony correlates scientific order with uninterrupted and resistless movement. The title to membership of its Inner Cabinet at the Bank of England is not based upon the possession of an argumentative talent, but on the utilisation of a practical and practised intellect. Entrance to the ancient social hierarchy was effected by the sole qualification of landed possessions. The new financial hierarchy requires only intellect, capacity and experience as the price of membership. A share in the control of untold millions is open to the man who does not possess £10,000 of his own. The individually-hereditary and semi-hereditary factor is almost . gone. Its absence is a gain, in spite of Bagehot's half-regretful reflection that the democratic structure of English finance prevents " the long duration of great families of merchant princes, such as those of Venice and Genoa, who inherited nice cultivation as well as great wealth, and who, to some extent, combined the tastes of an aristocracy with the insight and verve of men of business." These are idealistic conditions, as we saw when we were studying the antique type of private banker. But they cannot survive profitably to an evolving organism. Recruiting for modern financial leadership is selective by demonstrated ability, and consequently excludes a former source of weakness, waywardness, and lack of adaptation, sinister in operation and wide in scope. The leaders inherit a corporate, as distinguished from an individual, equipment. The knowledge that qualifies for promotion to conciliar dignity is not the doubtful product obtained from second-hand sources, and achieved, may be, in the discharge of a family duty, but the weapon that is only to be won upon the world's broad field of battle. The banking experience

SUMMARY AND CONCLUSION

and acumen of the age are concentrated in a few brains. Each, in the quietude of the council room—be it at the board table of the individual bank or finance company, or at the meetings of the Inner Cabinet of finance in Threadneedle Street—interprets to the rest the meaning of the contemporaneous phenomena as they present themselves to him. The collective judgment, based on vast stores of accumulated corporate experience, is a thing apart, far above the capacity of separate intellects which coalesce to shape it. Soundness of information, combined with the sense of a common interest, and with allegiance to an elevated ideal, creates a community of sentiment which has been called a " bankers' opinion," and is a far more efficient force than the " opinions of bankers." Its influence elevates the *morale* of the whole organism. The branch manager knows the "bankers' opinion" as formed by the central Mind and enunciated in the policy of his bank. The possession of the knowledge makes him something more than a mechanical money-lender. He is energised because " the banking world has, without conscious search, found its common brain."[1] The " pivotal points of social ethics "—independent personality and common collective responsibility—are also the pivotal points of banking organisation. Its moving principle is within and not without. It is a self-conscious evolution, struggling towards an ascertained, though not fully definable, goal. It " lives, and grows, and develops character," but keeps its identity . . . " being never[2] a disconnected aggregate, but always an organic whole." The fact that it can (and frequently does) choose the devious route in preference to the direct, the long road as against the short, is itself a demonstration of the selective and purposeful corporate intelligence that controls and guides.

STEADINESS THE CONSTANT AIM

The acceptance by this central conciliar jurisdiction of a corporate responsibility for the protection of the vast

[1] Pownall, *English Banking*, p. 50.
[2] In the stage which it has now attained, that is to say (Illingworth, *Personality, Human and Divine*, p. 27).

and far-flung financial interests of the Empire—and almost of the world—is an obligation which no law could impose or enforce. The power has not been sought for its own sake. The purpose was to get rid of evils which, if uncontrolled by the only authority which possessed the capacity for discipline, must have wrought untold evil. Corporate responsibility, reinforced by inherited experience and developing an extraordinary precision of judgment, alone is competent for such delicate tasks as confront those to whom is committed the care of the modern credit fabric. " While there would almost seem to be no limit to the expansion of credit, the limit is there all the same, though not the greatest monetary scientist can define it, or can determine the precise moment when that limit is about to be reached."[1] The " fatal facility of credit," denounced in 1866, must be controlled, difficult as it is to define the point where, and the moment when, restraint becomes imperative. " One day there is a surplus to lend and the next day there is not, just because somebody has changed his opinion "[2] of the safety of the transaction in existing circumstances. Every movement toward systematisation, every increase in the equipment of a centralised and disciplined professional experience and opinion, tends to reduce the scope of this element of caprice, with resulting greater *steadiness*—Spencer's ideal once again!—in the running of the machine. Conciliar quietude and restraint are all the more imperatively needed when the closeness of international business intercourse tends occasionally to produce a species of neurasthenia very much akin to that with which town-dwellers are affected in consequence of the incessant pelting of sense-impressions, never for a moment intermitted, upon the personality. The swift circulation of news among a cosmopolitan business community may become a peril in itself if there be no steadying influence to minimise the shock upon the financial nerve-centres. On the one hand (as we saw with especial vividness in our analysis of the functions of the Stock

[1] Kiddy, Address to Chartered Institute of Secretaries, February 12, 1914. [2] Giffen.

SUMMARY AND CONCLUSION

Exchange) is the delicate susceptibility of the fabric to the slightest breath of danger, and on the other the disciplined central rule which instantly braces it up to meet the oncoming shock. The greater the velocity of transmission in the case of the disturbing factor, the more urgent the necessity for a central source of cosmopolitan consolidation and restraint, capable of exerting its authority over the whole of the seething area. The serene self-confidence engendered by this consolidation of credit resources and by the cognate possession of a capacity to grapple with all and every circumstance, is in itself no mean asset. London's prestige rests as much upon its ability to withstand financial shocks, to ward off panics, to continue payments in gold at any and all times, as it does upon its great resources.[1]

London is the stronger for its task because of the incessant intimate association of a corporate intellectual entity like the Inner Cabinet of finance, and its immediate coadjutors, with the working of the machine which it controls. The intimacy prevents the gaping of any chasm between the theory of the governors and the actualities of the sphere of government. The hierarchy is the brain of the organism, not an external authority wielding an alien sway. The nervous system of the whole economic fabric converges upon the unpretentious central conclaves. The men who compose them are lifted, by a sense of their tremendous obligation to society, above their individual level of intellectual outlook and unselfishness, so that they are capable, in their fiduciary capacity, of a toil, a sacrifice, a daring, otherwise beyond achievement, and even beyond contemplation. This is a psychic replacing of physical governance and military aggression by a supremacy of infinitely more subtle character. Development is an extension of harmony in activity, without excluding the tendency to variability; and the " harmony involves mutual furtherance of the development "[2] with an advantage over the unharmonious and

[1] L. M. Jacobs, *Banking Problems* (American Academy), p. 515.
[2] Hobhouse, *Development and Purpose*, p. 363.

incoherent, until " the whole field of reality is subdued to the needs of a single organic whole." And the organic whole of finance, in its nervous contact with the entire social fabric around it, answers completely to the evolutionary law, in that it stands for a ceaseless transition of financial power from a diffused to a concentrated state. It is, in the Spencerian system, a *compound* evolution, because the normal process is modified, both as to rate, course and mode, by the existence of other and reacting aggregates tending constantly to become larger, such as society in the mass, large social interests like the trade unions, new political doctrines like socialism, new international relationships, such as those which gave us our Allies in the German war, and so forth.

" AWARE OF ITS AWARENESS "

Thus the whole financial organism becomes acquainted with itself. It has at last learned the conditions of its own evolution, and the true goal of its action. It becomes aware of itself; and, by a still more subtle psychological refinement, is aware of its awareness. It realises itself, it knows what are the fundamentals of its structure, the goal of its struggles. " It discovers a unity underlying the differences and divergencies " of life, and a plan containing the possibilities of a future. It has recognised, as biologists have, that the study of the individual is useless for broad scientific purposes. Finally, it understands that world-finance is a woven fabric, a cosmopolitan entity which is not susceptible to injury at any spot without instant injurious reaction upon all the rest. If the highest ideals are to be realised, the power must not remain diffused anywhere. " Has not the time arrived," asked Sir Felix Schuster,[1] " when the whole of Europe should stand together ? Grave problems are arising from day to day in many parts of the world which will have to be faced, and which only a united, not a divided, Europe can solve." Towards a world control, therefore, the ambitions of finance already turn, sighing for fresh worlds to conquer.

[1] Bankers' Dinner, May 21, 1913.

SUMMARY AND CONCLUSION 695

Cosmopolitan finance, centralised in London, is developing at breathless speed. Theories that only a few years ago commanded the allegiance of the best financial intellects are already out of date because of the rapid change in the environment. The late Mr. Luke Hansard once suggested that Consols and first-class Colonial securities might to some extent be replaced among bankers' investments by good international stocks, such as Egyptian, Spanish, and Turkish. Hansard's theory was that, as these securities command an international market, they might be saleable at a time when Consols and first-class Colonials were difficult, if not impossible, of realisation, all the more so because the pressure to sell them must fall entirely on one market, namely, the London Stock Exchange.[1] Hansard declared that he had known times of pressure in the Money Market when it was as easy to sell Turkish stocks as Consols, though, of course, there can be no comparison as to the relative merits of the securities. Moreover, he argued that if English bankers held securities upon which they could raise money abroad they could render great assistance to the Bank of England at a time of foreign drain, and so facilitate its efforts to control the stock exchanges. Since then, however, cosmopolitanism has proceeded apace. As the war crisis of 1914 demonstrated, none of the great stock exchanges—even New York itself, away on the other side of the Atlantic—could escape the pressure of any grave emergency. Certainly, in 1914, the events which rendered it difficult to realise Consols and first-class Colonial securities had precisely the same effect in the international market. The foreign Bourses, indeed, were closed before London. Finance has turned the whole world into a single market. You can no longer have crisis here and normal conditions there.

PRINCIPLES OF WORLD-WIDE VALIDITY

Certainly a cosmopolitan *financial* control can attempt that which would be impossible to cosmopolitan *political*

[1] Address to the Manchester and District Bankers' Institute, January 18, 1901.

ambition. The reason is that the fundamental postulates of sound finance are the same in all lands, whereas political principles, at all events in their contemporary application, change at every frontier :—

"The banking profession follows the same principles all over the world. It depends upon industry, upon honesty, and upon a broad view of what happens in human affairs. Therefore, there are no people who can feel the pulse of the nation— the pulse of the world—better than bankers. They know better the rise and fall of political temperature than any political physician. They feel the advent of peace—they pay out on the threatened prospect of war, they have no small interests or small aims of separating one nation from another. If there is one bond that ties together the whole civilised world, it is the bond of the great moneyed interests whereby bankers preserve, guard, and utilise the earnings and savings of private men."[1]

Money will collect where it is safe, hide itself in hoards if it be menaced, occupy itself where the largest return is available, and command a higher rate contemporaneously with an augmented risk, whether the government be a monarchy or a republic, and whether the dominant religion be Christianity, Mahommedanism, or the worship of the sun. International finance, entering one field after another, acts upon principles and by means of methods which commend themselves instantly to every enlightened business mind. If they fail at first to do so, the fault is in the mind, not in the methods. The attempted application of a given political system in the same sphere would probably arouse the bitterest and the most unreconcilable antagonism. This is no mere fanciful generalisation. Mr. Justice Story, in his judgment in Swift v. Tyson,[2] saw plainly a tendency which has become tenfold more manifest since his day. Said he :—

"The law respecting negotiable instruments may be truly declared, in the language of Cicero, adopted by Lord Mansfield in Luke v. Lyde,[3] "to be in a great measure, not the law of a

[1] Professor Mahaffy, Institute of Bankers in Ireland, October 29,1898.
[2] 16 Peters 1.   [3] 2 Burr. 887.

SUMMARY AND CONCLUSION 697

single country only, but of the whole commercial world, non erit lex alia Romæ, alia Athenis, alia nunc, alia post hac, sed et apud gentes et omni tempore una eademque lex obtinebit."

Finance, as the Paris meeting of the British, French and Russian Finance Ministers in 1915 clearly demonstrated, is a mode of pacific assimilation. Spreading ceaselessly over the whole cosmopolitan area, it becomes correlated with every department of human activity and experience. As a process which is the sum of a thousand subordinate processes, it is subjected to, and stimulated by, the constant impact of new ideas from all parts of the arena over which it ranges. The wider diffusion of economic opportunity, which notoriously diminishes the tension between classes in a given nation, has exactly the same effect in the international arena. Under financial inspiration we think internationally. The ancient ideal represented by the Law Merchant as a code of international jurisprudence is again, as we have seen (*ante*, p. 562), attracting us. That famous system was capable of application in days when transport was slow and communication supremely difficult. Under modern conditions its utility of operation and facility of application would be multiplied a thousandfold in comparison with the mediæval environment in which it originally subsisted ; and for that reason its re-attainment is worth struggling for. But its re-attainment must subject cosmopolitan relationships to a higher control than the commercial. Finance is the power which is taking us from the national to the cosmopolitan. Our English statecraft, originally adjusted to an isolated agricultural community, has, in turn, been adapted to a pelagic-mercantile and an oceanic-manufacturing nation. It is now, perforce, being again transformed and reorganised under the influence of a confederate financial power which grows stronger every year. For if he has sufficient financial backing, man can go anywhere on enterprise and profit bent. The organic appliances of animals, developed over immense periods of time, have not enabled any animal greatly to expand its territorial range, or to migrate far from the region to which it was originally adapted. Man, as Mr. Ward says,[1] is the only animal whose habitat is not circumscribed. Finance enjoys the same ubiquity.

That is the reason why it is scientifically inaccurate to speak of capital going abroad. The real fact is that for capital, as directed by finance, there is no such place as " abroad." As long as money flows from land to land simply to seek a wider opportunity and a better return, and carries out its programme with reasonable vigilance, the phenomenon is wholly satisfactory. But, of course, when its departure is a consequence of fear of taxation, or dread of raids, we are in the presence of a sinister economic manifestation. Otherwise, the whole world is the home of finance. " The Latin author who said ' I am a man ; nothing that is human is outside my province,' was obviously thinking specially of bankers," once remarked Sir Felix Schuster. Finance, in directing and managing capital, is as cosmopolitan as the sun and the atmosphere. Physical frontiers have no meaning for it. To speak of it as going " abroad " is to revert to the primitive phraseology of the Heptarchy, when Wessex was " abroad," from a Northumbrian point of view. It does not go " abroad." It makes a wider arena for its own activity, and rejoices at the larger liberty and scope that it has won. The capital of the bank, or the resources of the trust company, may be the same in a cosmopolitan as in a national or even municipal economy ; but the opportunities in the former are enormously wider than those in the latter. The financial mechanisms of England, France, and Russia, respectively, each working as an isolated factor, would produce immensely less beneficial results for the world than when these three co-operate and become, in effect, parts of a gigantic cosmopolitan system, whose services and facilities are available to the whole of humanity. Co-operation on such an unprecedented scale is what we were privileged to see when the Finance Ministers of the three Great Powers met in conference in Paris in February, 1915. Only *national*

[1] *Psychic Factors of Civilisation*, p. 257.

SUMMARY AND CONCLUSION 699

finance was within their contemplation. But the confederacy neither originated there, nor will it be confined within those boundaries. Not only will the public finance of three nations co-operate in the presence of war, but the entire financial mechanisms of the world are destined to coalesce for the furtherance of peace. Instead of financial principles being, as it were, a mere island in a sea of disorder, they are destined to exert a unitary and integrating force operative over the entire area of civilisation.

RESULTS ALREADY ACHIEVED

England was the first—or one of the first—countries to display such economic phenomena as a money market, and a competing trade based upon large capital, " in such vigour and so isolated as to suggest a separate analysis of them ; but as the world goes on, similar characteristics are being evolved in one society after another."[1] The dreams of cosmopolitan financial ambition had begun to take definite shape before the war. Difficulties which arose in 1910 with regard to cotton bills of lading were met by the formation of a bankers' committee. This organisation formed a smaller committee within itself, on cosmopolitan lines, representing the following institutions :—

Banca Commerciale	Comptoir National
Crédit Suisse	Société Générale
Swiss Bankverein	Lloyds Bank
Deutsche Bank	London City & Midland Bank
Dresdner Bank	Parr's Bank
Russo-Chinese Bank	Bank of Liverpool
Austrian Laender Bank	Baring Brothers & Co.
Crédit Lyonnais	Kleinwort, Sons & Co.

A better initiatory demonstration of the cordiality of cosmopolitan finance could hardly be desired. We even got within sight of an Imperial banking conference when the Institute of Bankers, in 1911, held a special meeting in honour of Sir Edmund Walker, the distinguished chairman of the Canadian Bank of Commerce. Sir Edmund

[1] Bagehot, *Economic Studies*, p. 20.

Walker stated the necessities of the case in admirable terms (which he at the time intended to be more especially applicable to Canada) when he said that "there should be a committee of bankers, possessing the respect of the bankers as a whole, having authority to confer with the heads of any bank which seemed to be getting into bad courses." That tribunal, as we have already seen, is now in being. But it is only the forerunner of an international prerogative, wielded for a world-economy. The proposal has been made in terms. In 1912 Dr. Julius Wolf, Professor at Breslau University, writing in the *Neue Freie Presse*, proposed an international gold reserve. It had, he argued, become a recognised fact that when one country is in urgent need of gold other countries must be prepared to lend their assistance, and all the more willingly because they may some time or other be, in their turn, in the position of seeking help from others. Dr. Wolf thought that the nomination of a permanent international committee of banks, prepared to meet at a moment's notice, would be a remedy for the existing circumstances under which only the extreme consequences of financial disturbance are avoided. As things are, said Dr. Wolf, the embarrassed bank raises its rate of discount to attract foreign gold; commerce and industry suffer and the Bourse is disturbed by the doubt whether foreign assistance will be available, and must, therefore, be prepared to fight the battle for gold. To have the matter discussed at the very moment when the need arises must be a great advantage. The war has checked, but by no means destroyed, these international aspirations. In fact their realisation was attempted in spite of the dislocation resulting from hostilities. During the war, to take only one example, it was announced in London that if the exchanges between Great Britain and the United States became such that gold exports from either country to an unreasonable amount might result, committees of bankers should be appointed in the United States and in the United Kingdom respectively to consider plans for dealing collectively with the situation. Again, at the Ionian Bank meeting (April, 1915), the

SUMMARY AND CONCLUSION 701

Chairman outlined a scheme for a system of international clearing-houses to adjust the commerce of the world.

FINANCIAL DIPLOMATS IN LOMBARD STREET

Modern governments themselves bow to the new cosmopolitan sway. Lombard Street, like the Court of St. James's, receives ambassadors from all parts of the world. As there is scarcely a spot on the globe which is not being scientifically exploited, it follows that the necessity for the favour and countenance of scientific finance is equally ubiquitous. A financial diplomacy, centred in Lombard Street, is the immediate consequence. In order to explain details and negotiate terms, it is necessary for the world's men of action, its statesmen and industrial pioneers, to visit personally the centre of financial influence. If it be a Dominion loan, the arrangements will often be made in London, on the spot, by the Finance Minister himself. The Premier of Alberta will personally come to London to adjust the final details of a provincial loan. The Mayor of Gisborne travelled all the way from the Antipodes to place a corporation issue. But these are comparatively minor results. The concentration of cosmopolitan finance in London has brought about the necessity, on the part of borrowers who seek its assistance of Great Britain, to maintain financial and propagandist organisations at the Court of Money Power. Brazil and Mexico, for instance, have Financial Delegations in this country. How extensive are their operations may be gathered from the fact that Mexico has paid off, at one time, as many as 91,025 drawn bonds,[1] representing a total sum of over £9,000,000. How rapidly these organisations act may be inferred from the instant appearance of a contradiction, by them, of any misstatement with regard to the credit, or the resources, of the Governments which they represent. The same principle of action has been adopted by the Overseas Dominions of the British Empire, whose High Commissioners and Agents-General carry on an unceasing propa-

[1] The advertisement of the numbers occupied ten whole pages of the *Financial News*!

ganda, designed to attract the careful attention, the patriotic sympathy, and the financial co-operation of the Money Market. There is now no British Dominion Beyond the Seas which does not possess, in London, an elaborate official mechanism specially designed and created to wrestle strenuously with the modern Money Power. This is not only true of the Dominions in their federal capacity, represented by their High Commissioners. It is equally true of the constituent Provinces, with their interests in the capable hands of the Agents-General. Quebec and Queensland, as well as those larger entities the Dominion of Canada and the Commonwealth of Australia, carry on their propaganda in search of the investor. They keep him constantly supplied with the latest information about their products, progress, and population. If he will visit the office which is the centre of the propaganda he will be shown the corn and wine and oil, the fruit and the mutton, the gold and the diamonds, which the Province produces. If he contemplate the purchase of real property, or a share in some undertaking, large resources of experience and information will be placed at his disposal. Week in and week out official news of the progress of the Dominion or Province is widely circulated, even to the remotest parts of Great Britain.

The High Commissioner who is the centre and leader of this crusade will be a statesman of rank and experience, specially instructed to make himself and the Dominion popular at the centre of financial force. The Agent-General will be a gentleman with an inexhaustible knowledge of provincial policy and resources, skilled to plead its cause with those who can be persuaded to provide capital for the financing of its needs. These standard-bearers of the Great Dominions are nowadays to be found everywhere. You cannot even dine out without noting a High Commissioner among the distinguished guests, and without hearing the roar of welcome which greets him as he rises in response to a toast. The offices, the *personnel*, the advertising, and the social amenities which are a part of the plan, all combine to render this an expensive propa-

ganda. At least, it is expensive from the point of view of
the money that goes out, though it is dirt cheap if we
contemplate what it brings in. But its significance lies
in the fact that it is deliberately aimed at enlisting the co-
operation of Money Power for Imperial purposes. It is
an exhaustively-planned campaign, conducted with the
greatest dexterity and circumspection, for diverting the
money-force into Imperial channels. Its organisation, its
skill, its enterprise, its patience, and its persistence are
worthy of all praise. But above and beyond all praise is
its success. Looking at the finance and credit of the great
Dominions, as well as of their states, provinces, municipalities and public authorities, to-day, it is difficult to
believe that their unchallengeable position as trusted
borrowers, with their stocks in the Trustee List, is the
creation, almost entirely, of the last half-century. The
Bank of British Columbia had to admit, in 1866, that it
held £15,800 of 6 per cent. British Columbia bonds for
which there was no market, although they were redeem-
able at as short a date as 1872. Nowadays there is hardly
a public security in the whole Imperial list which ranks
below first class. The Dominions have paid court to
finance, and it has energised and steadied them at every
point. If the co-operation had not been ready to their
hand, the present year of grace in the great Overseas
Dominions would be nearer 1860 than 1915.

THE WORLD AS ONE

In every direction the inscrutable control and supervision
spread—often without the public obtaining the merest
inkling of the policy elaborated and pursued for its protection. The whole of the keenness, the talent, the enterprise, the foresight, once invested in merely aggressive
and destructive war, are destined to be devoted—and the
time draws very near—to the peaceful service of humanity,
under the leadership of correlated and co-ordinated international finance. In Dr. Bosanquet's phrase, the permanent nucleus in the material sphere which is possessed
by the individual man is amplified by an equally per-

manent nucleus of credit, possessed and administered on behalf, not merely of the community, but of civilisation in the aggregate. Everywhere, in the fine words of Lord Bryce—[1]

"The world is becoming *one* in an altogether new sense. . . . More than four centuries ago the discovery of America marked the first step in the process by which the European races have now gained dominion over nearly the whole earth. . . . As the earth has been narrowed through the new forces science has placed at our disposal . . . the movements of politics, of economics, and of thought, in each of its regions, become more closely interwoven. . . . Whatever happens in any part of the globe has now a significance for every other part. World History is tending to become One History. . . ."

Credit and freedom have reached their zenith together, as if they were a kind of double star, each the satellite of the other. The worlds of leisure and learning are more and more dependent upon finance, which keeps in motion, and guides in operation, the forces upon the harvest of which leisure and learning depend. It disciplines that which is material, compelling it to subserve the intellectual and spiritual while these latter work out their own destiny. " Social sustentation," said Spencer, " is essential to social evolution."[2] When the work of social sustentation throughout the world is guided, co-ordinated, energised, and uplifted by a central financial hegemony inspired by the loftiest aims, what may not man attempt ? At the end of the first century of the Money Market he is but at the beginning of his task, ready and eager to conquer the realm of " unending and infinitely varied originations " which lies before him. Finally let us remember that " the Purpose operating in evolution is itself not fully defined from the beginning, but susceptible of development."[3] So that " beyond us still is mystery : but it is mystery lit and mellowed with an infinite hope. We ride . . . at the

[1] Address on April 3, 1913, as President of the International Congress of Historical Studies.
[2] *Fragments*, p. 195.
[3] Hobhouse, *Development and Purpose*, p. 370.

SUMMARY AND CONCLUSION

haven's mouth."[1] The centenary of the Money Market sees us conscious of the achievement that lies behind and of the mystery that looms before. The main outlines of the Design are there, though we shall never see its complete elaboration. Yet those who follow us in the coming centuries may perhaps envy our lot as witnesses of the end of the First Century of the Money Market, and as contemporary observers of the gigantic upheaval, fraught with infinite blessings to generations yet unborn, which marked the opening of the Second.

[1] F. W. H. Myers.

INDEX

INDEX

"ABROAD," unknown to finance, 698.
ACCEPTANCE, vogue and importance of, 374.
ACCEPTING HOUSES, develop into issuing houses, 386; protection of, in crisis of 1914, 675; Bank of England board recruited from (1825), 332; banks as acceptors, 520.
"ACCOUNTABLE RECEIPT," 99.
AGRA AND MASTERMAN'S BANK, suspension (1866), 401.
AGRICULTURAL AND COMMERCIAL BANK OF IRELAND, 288.
ALBERTINES, failure of, 18 and 18 n.
AMALGAMATION. See BANKING.
ARBITRAGE, 567.
ASSIGNABILITY (see CHOSES IN ACTION), distinguished from negotiability, 20 n.; shares endowed with, by charter, 169, 173; unchartered companies' shares not assignable, 177; and brokers to be prosecuted for treating them as such, 177, 185 n.; huge importance of, 177; hostility to, partly due to fears of seizure of "control," 178; purported, of shares, could not be an offence at common law, 183 and 183 n., 184.

Law Cases cited :—
Blundell v. Winsor, 1837 (assignable shares illegal), 182.
Harrison v. Heathorn, 1843 (late arguments against full assignability of shares), 145, 177, 183.
Garrard v. Hardey, 1843 (assignment of shares not an offence at common law), 144, 182.
ASSOCIATED GURNEY BANKS, 462.
ATTWOODS, SPOONER AND CO., 288.
AUDLEY, HUGH, seventeenth-century money-lender, 106.
AUSTRALIAN BANK FAILURES, 1892-3, 639.

BACKWELL, great seventeenth-century banker, 95.
BACON, on usury, 53, 83.
BAGEHOT, on private bankers, 420; on responsibilities of Bank of England, 502; on directors of Bank of England, 512.
BANK CHARTER ACT, 345 ff.; provisions of, 345; history of renewals, 228 n., 300; silver bullion not now held under, 345 n.; securities in Issue department, are they ear-marked ?, 346; criticism of, 348 ff., and see 352; suspension of, now on statutory basis, 351; suspension of, 1847, 360; suspension of, 1857, 368; actually infringed in 1857, as distinct from 1847 and 1866, 368; suspension of, 1866, 403; text of letter to Government in 1866 and reply, 403; War Loan of 1914

710 EVOLUTION OF THE MONEY MARKET

loans upon, are they a constructive breach of the Bank Charter Act ?, 351; not suspended in 1914, 679; modified by Currency and Bank Notes Act (1914), 679.

BANKER AND/OR BANKING (see GOLDSMITHS, ACCEPTANCE, BRANCH BANKING, PRIVATE BANKERS, PROVINCIAL BANKING, NOTES, BILLS OF EXCHANGE), makes for public stability and quietude, 63; transformation of the banker from bailee to debtor of his client, 63 ff.; present relationship as defined by Lord Cottenham, 73 n.; early methods, as described by Malynes, 75; bankers' censorship of customers' affairs, beginning of, 77; later, 435; banking economises currency, 78 and 78 n.; enables swift transmission of money, 78 n., 79; rapid growth of influence of financial community (seventeenth century), 91; mentioned in the statute 22 and 23 Car. II. (c. 3), 94; alleged to be branded with republicanism, 207; Sir James Scarlett on early meaning of the word "bank," 94; Sir Josiah Child on "bankeering," 96; Duncombe, successful goldsmith-banker, 96; Rev. David Jones (1692) attacks bankers, 96; Backwell, Alderman, his large banking business, 95, 96; Francis Child specialises as banker, and abandons the goldsmith's business, 112; so does Smith, founder of Smith, Payne and Smiths, 117; banking since 1844 confined to banking *alone*, 113, 433; in the eighteenth century, errors of, 123; a bank could originally be started by anybody, 127, 129; local, as distinct from national, in eighteenth century, 127; speculation, practised by early bankers, 129, 234; Newcastle discriminates against guilty banks, 234; speculation still occasionally practised where discipline loose, 129; though condemned by Gilbart and since, 234 and 234 n.

Principles of, early ignorance of, and attempts to enunciate, 130 ff.; banks may sue or be sued in name of public officer (1826), 184; after 1844, banking companies must have Crown grant of incorporation, 185; lofty motives of, formulated, 223; co-operative self-protection among merchants and bankers, 231 ff.; Bagehot's definition of, 249; draws money out of hoards, 274 ff.; great extension of (1810), 275; democratisation of the note issue, 276; troublous period of inexperience and experiment, 1815–57, 283 ff.; singular laxity of early bank trust deeds, 284; Thomson Hankey's relative on the essentials of, 292; unlimited liability on shares, evils of, 293, and steps taken to abolish, 302 and 302 n.; survival of obsolete conditions down to 1858, 296 ff.

Joint-stock banks, rise of, chapter x.; Acts permitting joint-stock banks, 300 ff.; Baring, Adam Smith and Lord Liverpool on joint-stock banks, 302; joint-stock banking, did not originally involve limited liability, 302; limited liability, brings in better class of bank shareholder, 294, 304 n., 465 n.; "spiritual persons" as shareholders, 304 n.; joint-stock, prejudice against, illustrated, 308 ff., 333; joint-stock, figures as to its increase, 310; utterly unsystematised in 1826, 334; joint-stock, large increase of, in provinces, and danger thereof (1834), 338; joint-stock, 1836 Secret Committee's hostility to, 339; joint-stock, Bank of England discriminates against, 333, 339; joint-stock banks, association of, (1838), 343; legislation, 1697 to 1844, summarised, 353; colonial origins of, 312.

Widespread utilisation of banking facilities between 1815 and 1858, 312 ff.; socially elevating influence of a bank account, 315; social influence of, 521; Scottish, in England, 353 n.; obvious solidification around London, 370 ff.; increase in number of bank accounts, 370; Scotland feels the "pull" of London, 373; foreign banks come to London, 388; higher ideals of personal conduct

among bankers, 392; companies, a special feature, 1862–1866, 396; capital and reserve, small proportion to liabilities in the 'sixties, 397; public confidence in banks in 1866, 408.
Natural selection among banks, chapter xv.; amalgamation and absorption process analysed, chapter xv.; absorption, real cause and significance of, 418 ff.; the typical record of Parr's Bank, 419 n.; complete change in environment of, 423; is not partnership, 432 ff.; shareholders as customers, 439; continuous distribution of capital by, 441, 444; (*see* CAPITAL); competition not ended by amalgamation, 448; limits of rivalry, 454, 457 n.; balance-sheets, publicity for, 449 n.; "up to the hilt," 455; elevated modern ideals of, 458, 689 ff.

How banks withstood German war crisis, 459; federation plan, how far realised, 462; co-operation in 1866, acknowledged by Bank of England, 487; (*see* CONFEDERACY); deposits, growth of, summarised, 674 n.; foreign banks in London, 387, 494 ff.; new scheme for co-operation with Bank of England (1876), 508; (bankers' balances at Bank of England, *see* that head under BANK OF ENGLAND); hierarchy, its existence obvious, 522; value of Stock Exchange securities to, 574 ff.; depreciation of securities 1900–1914, 622; Canadian hierarchy, work of, 641; American, reforms in, 647, 664; not manageable by legislation, 654 ff.; in no sense plutocratic, 659 n., 690; confederacy, avowed at last, 662 ff.; confederacy is corporate, 665; ring of fortresses complete for 1914, 667; "banks," failures of petty concerns so-called, 667; abuse of the title "bank," 667 n.

Unmoved steadiness of, in German war crisis 1914, 670 ff.; bankers had foreseen need of war-currency, 672; co-operation with Government in crisis of 1914, 673; inter-relationship with Stock Exchange, 677; cosmopolitan principles of, 695; work of, in diminishing intensity of crises, 681; supreme tribunal of, how selected, 689 ff.; agreement as to cotton bills of lading, 699; Imperial banking conference ?, 699; international gold reserve, 700; international clearing-houses, 700.

Law Cases cited :—

Mayor of London *v.* Bennet (early use of word "bankers,"), 95.
Rivers and Pudsey's case (early instance of apprentices entrusted with master's money), 59.
Talbot *v.* Godbolt, 1609 (apprentices entrusted with master's money), 59.
Core's case, temp. Henry VIII. (money bond to bearer, 21; and bailment of money), 65.
Lyte et Ux. *v.* Perry (early bailment of money), 65.
The King *v.* Sheriff of Hertford, 33 Car. II. (bailed money in a bag), 66.
Higgs *v.* Holliday, 42 Eliz. (property in loose money, when bailed, is in the bailee), 67.
Bretton *v.* Barnett, 41 and 42 Eliz. (property in loose money, when bailed, is in the bailee unless the coins are identifiable), 67.
Moorwood *v.* Dickens (assignment of money), 67.
Wilshalge and Davidge's case, 28 and 29 Eliz. (settlement in sterling of bargains made in other coinages), 70.
Rastall *v.* Draper, 3 Jac. I. (ditto), 70.
Heydon *v.* Godsole (dispute as to value of a besant), 70 n.
De Acuno *v.* Gifford (value of a "ducket"), 70 n.
Kendar *v.* Millward, 1702 (money has no Ear-mark), 64, 98.
Hartop *v.* Hoare, 1743 (property in money follows possession where the coins are loose and unidentifiable), 68.

712 EVOLUTION OF THE MONEY MARKET

Giblin v. M'Mullin, 1820 (bailment of gold in a cask), 68.
Devaynes v. Noble, 1816 (banker is the *debtor* of his client), 72.
Foster v. Essex Bank, 1820 (banker has right to the *use* of clients' money), 71, 72.
Potts v. Clegg, 1833 (deposits are really loans to banker), 72.
Re Agra and Masterman's Bank, 1866 (banker a debtor, not a trustee), 73.
Foley v. Hill, 1848 (definition of relations between banker and customer), 73.
Capital and Counties Bank v. Gordon, 1903 (cheques credited before cleared), 660 n.

BANKER AND MONEY-LENDER, difference between, 58 n., 105.

BANK NOTES (*see* NOTES), are really impersonal bills of exchange, 100 n.

BANK OF ENGLAND, refuses to handle alien coins, 69 n. ; its advent, a necessity of financial organisation, 110 ; dependence of provincial banks upon, 126 ; refuses to open country branches (eighteenth century), 126, 127; bears and Bank stock, 147 ; policy, summarised by Harman, 201 ; varied experience of, 203 ; establishment of, involves a new relationship between organised finance and society at large, 204 ; not to lend to the Crown without authority of Parliament, 206 ; disregard of this prohibition, 238 ; directors ask Pitt for an Act of Indemnity, 239 ; directors' " serious and solemn resolution " on this subject, 239 ; early nervousness about possible seizure of control of, 178 ; alleged to be a Republican scheme, 207 ; and also a " Royal Bank," 208 ; a bulwark of the Whigs, 207 ff. ; fears that it will govern the whole kingdom, 207 ; early loan and discount rates, 209 n. ; unprejudiced religious attitude of, 210 ff. ; early services to the State, 212 ff. ; early cash balance 2 per cent. of liabilities, 213 ; gradually becomes banker to the Government, 215 ; but enjoys no " privileges," 216 ; still, the fact of being banker to the Government confers enormous prestige, 217 ; though there is no partnership or alliance with the Government, 217 ; but the prestige confers power, 219 ; Peel indeed wanted a State Bank, 347.

Persistence and continuity of the Bank as social forces, 220 ; the Bank as a conscious permanent *self,* 221 ff. ; realising its duty to society, 223 ; its prestige early recognised and its leadership visible, 200 ff., 224 ; early tributes to, 225 ; credit of, originally superior to that of the nation, 225 ; but only " equal " in Adam Smith's time, 237 ; new stock, at 15 prem., 226 ; Queen Anne favours, 226 ; prestige of monopoly of, 226, 229 ; its note issue as a source of monopoly, 226, 228, 299 ; but a note issue not essential to banking, 299 ff. ; monopoly of note issue broken, 300 ; Charter of, history of its renewals, 228 n., 300 ; (*see* BANK CHARTER ACT); Bank stock, once a market bell-wether, 229 ; Bank stock movements, their record a brief history of England, 230 ; Bank stock bought by Forbes, and his reasons, 236 ; confers a status upon its holders, 555 ; City merchants rally around (1745), 232 ff. ; and again in 1796, 240 ; takes disciplinary action in the Neal-Fordyce failure, 233 ; regarded as a model (1782), 236 ; acts with over-eagerness in crisis of 1792–93, 237 ; suspends cash payments (1796), 237 and 237 n. ; foreign observers alarmed at prospect of embarrassment of, 238 n. ; directors decline to meet except on their regular day (1790), 238 n.

Steadily asserts its independence, 238 ff. ; liberality of, 239 ; its dominance assured, 240 ; doors unhinged by rush of crowd for loan (1818), 254 ; pays no interest on deposits, 270 n., 344 ; its own views on this topic, 271 n. ; now accepts " special deposits " for use

INDEX 713

in the market, 272 n.; finances an iron concern, 289; lends on permanent mortgages, 289 and 317, 289 n.; and Northumberland and Durham Bank, 291; opens branches, 300 n.; and is therefore compared to Sarah, 301 n.; private bankers' protest against branches, 333; the "right hand of the State," 322; makes "common cause with the country" (1825), 331; psychological reserve of, 323; assured prestige of, after Waterloo, 323; prestige even becomes embarrassing, 491; Ricardo's hostility to, 324; not quite strong enough to ride the storm of 1825, 327; but nevertheless acted with intrepidity, 331; borrows from Bank of France (1825), 329; borrows again (1839), 340; this borrowing criticised (1846), 341; directors of, "staid old merchants" (*circa* 1825), 332; refuses to discount bills drawn by bank of issue, joint-stock or private, 333, 339.

Alleged to be *imperium in imperio*, a "petty state" and a conspirator with the Government (1834), 335; "hourly intercourse" with bankers (1832), 337; statement, March 6, 1832, 337; statements, 1844 and 1914 compared, 355; in 1836-37 "pressure," 338 ff.; assists Barings, 1836-37, 340; helped by Bank of France (1839), 340; financial prestige of, 343; strict practice of, and suzerainty of provincial branches over joint-stock banks, 344; example of methods of Liverpool branch, 344; Paul Moon James on sound rules of, 345; unselfish public spirit of (1844), 347; and Scottish banks, 354 n.; and railway boom, 358; intrepid policy (1847 panic), 361; also in 1857 panic, 366; "everything depended on it" (1857), 367.

Increasing influence of, in the discount market (1844 onwards), 381 ff.; bank rate, attempt by joint-stock banks to break away from, 381; *moral* primacy, as distinct from *financial*, 384, 487; policy as to checking outflow of gold, 384, 645; policy in 1866 panic, 403 ff.; saves District Bank of Newcastle (1847), 427 n.; supervisory rôle of, 436; originally published no accounts even to its directors, 449 n.; acknowledges banking co-operation (1866), 487; in metaphor (1858-1878), 489; and Gledstane's failure, 491; "Old *Woman* in Threadneedle Street," 492; John Jones at meetings, 495; its authority invoked against its own branches, 493 n.; calm confidence of public in (1873), 500; dependence of all of institutions on, 502; Thomson Hankey wants a Bank, not a Financial Suzerainty, 502; joint-stock banks became financially greater than, 503.

Bankers' balances at, 337; exceed Bank reserve, 503; proposal to constitute a separate bankers' reserve, 504; Bank's caustic hint, 504; Bank ceases to state amount of, 504-505; Mr. J. H. Tritton's scheme, 549; publication of, Sir Edward Holden on, 506; Bank's official view, 506; Lord Aldenham's opinion, 507.

Fresh plan for co-operation with other banks (1876), 508; directors of, "new blood" among, 511; governorship and reinvigoration of, 512; permanent sub-governor suggested, 514; never gratifies curiosity, 513 n.; assists Bank of Ireland (1883), 515; master of the situation, (1878), 516; discount policy of, 516; summed up by Mr. Weill, 518; (*see* BARING CRISIS, chapter xviii.); leader of a colossal agglomeration of financial power, 528; the unpleasant episode of 1893, 642; conversion of National Debt by, 643; and American panic, 1907, 645; United States Commissioners visit, 647; its rôle absolutely essential, 649; INVITES JOINT-STOCK BANKS TO QUARTERLY COUNCILS, 662; and scheme for issue of bank-notes against one-third gold and two-thirds securities (1914), 672.

BANK OF FRANCE, assists Bank of England, 1825, 329; assists again, 1839, 340; these transactions criticised (1846), 341; assists in Baring crisis, 524.

BANK OF IRELAND, started, 116 n.

714   EVOLUTION OF THE MONEY MARKET

BANK OF LONDON, 288.
BANK OF MANCHESTER, 449 n.
BANK OF MONTREAL, disciplinary policy of, 416; wide distribution of capital by, 445, 447; Canadian leadership of, 641, 642.
BANK OF SCOTLAND, started, 116 n.
BANK OF UPPER CANADA, collapses (1866), 416.
BANK POST BILLS, origin of, 105.
BARCLAY AND CO., John Tritton's evidence before Bullion Committee, 1810, 118; their two classes of share, 304 n.
BARINGS, origin of the firm, 128; one of the "six great powers" of Europe (1819), 340; difficulties of, in 1836-1837, 340; their part in borrowing from Bank of France, 340.
BARING CRISIS, chapter xviii.; early prototype of policy then adopted, 232; method of handling, foreshadowed in 1837, 339; causes of, 523; story of, as told by Mr. Lidderdale, 524; Lidderdale's policy in, 526 ff.; guarantee, arrangement of, 524, 525; guarantee, text of, 525 n.; criticism of, 529 ff.; guarantors, their identity, 525; localisation of, 526 ff.; close of liquidation, 530; the precedent reinvoked, 1911, 660.
BARNARD'S ACT, 154.
BARNED'S BANK, failure, 399.
BEAR (*see* SPECULATION), earliest recorded operation in England by a, 89 n.; of Bank Stock, 147, 230; stock-jobbers as bears, 155 n.; the *bête noire* of early critics of the Stock Exchange, 157; attacks on bank shares, 294; stopped by Leeman's Act, 295; Napoleon and the bear, 603 n.
BEARER BONDS. See STOCK EXCHANGE.
BEARER, PAYMENT TO. See NEGOTIABILITY.
BERLIN, cannot rival London and why, 497.
BILL-BROKERS, early, 46, 80, 82; at the Restoration period (" scriveners " and " money-scriveners "), 80; attempted statutory regulation of, 135; their function in the modern money market, 377 ff., 511; keen vigilance of, 596.
BILLS OF EXCHANGE (*see* also FINANCE BILLS), the early history of, 21 n.; evolution of, sketched by Treby, C.J., 104 n.; swift recognition of utility of, 24; first decision on, 26; for foreign remittances, 77; dishonoured, damage to Cardinal Archduke's credit (1596), 88; bank-notes are impersonal bills of exchange, 100 n.; dealt on an early Stock Exchange, 145; huge modern importance of, 376; "as good as Government securities," 486; how dealt with, in 1914 crisis, 676.

Law Cases cited :—
Martin *v.* Boure, 1603 (first case in Bill of Exchange), 26.
Hodges *v.* Steward (drawing a bill makes the drawer a merchant), 104.
Bromwich *v.* Lloyd (legal evolution of bills of exchange), 104 n.
Jenny *v.* Heale, 10 Geo. I. (Bill of Exchange not payable out of particular fund), 102.

BIRKBECK BANK, reason of failure, 472.
BIRKBECK, HENRY, 531.
BIRMINGHAM BANKING CO., 291.
BIRMINGHAM JOINT-STOCK BANK, 291 n.
BIRMINGHAM PENNY BANK, 281.
BLACK DEATH and successive epidemics, economic results of, 14.
BLACK FRIDAY (*see* OVEREND, GURNEY), 400.

INDEX

715

BONDS, earliest instances of, 20 n., 21 n. ; seventeenth-century issues of five per cent., at Siena, 26.

  Law Cases cited :—
  Winchcomb v. Winchcomb (fifty-year personal bonds), 621 n.
  Popham v. Aylesbury, 1748 (bonds and securities are not "money"), 142.

BOURSE (see STOCK EXCHANGE), name of portreeve in 1158 may indicate one in London, 40 ; none in early sixteenth century, 40, 41 ; Royal Exchange originally called the, 41.

BRADFORD OLD BANK, 331.

BRANCH BANKING, early experiments in, 289 ff. ; risks of, in early days, 290 ; distance of branches from head office, curious fears as to, 290 ; branches of Bank of England, 300 n., 333, 493 n. ; increase of branch banking, 310 ff. ; in the 'sixties, 431; development of, reasons for, and wholesome effect of, 431.

BRICKYARDS, a banker's bogey, 286 and 286 n., 289 and 289 n.

BRISTOL OLD BANK, 117.

BRITISH LINEN BANK, 128 ; co-operates with Forbes in crisis of 1793, 235.

BROKER (see BILL-BROKERS and STOCK EXCHANGE), traceable as early as Edw. I., 147 n.; in the fifteenth century, 39 ; in the seventeenth century, 82 ; [stock] broker's oath, text of, 147 ; [Stock] Broker's Relief Act, 1844, 148 ; stockbrokers, not originally essential to the conduct of dealings, 156 n. ; distinction between, and jobber, how it arose, 157 n. ; not to deal in assignable shares (Bubble Act), 177 ; supposed illegality of such dealings, curious case of broker, 185 n. ; provincial stockbrokers organised, 540.

BULL, early market operator always a, 89 n.

BULLION DEALERS, only one firm in 1810, 119 n.

BURGESS, WM. AND CO., failure (1825), 329.

BURKE, on provincial banks, 117 ; on commercial paper, 655.

CABLE TRANSFERS, beginning of (c. 1876), 601.

CALVIN, recognised fairness of interest, 49.

CANADIAN AGENCY FAILURE (1914), 669.

CANADIAN BANKING CONSOLIDATION, 640.

CANALS, eighteenth-century bankers' finance, 124.

CAPE OF GOOD HOPE BANK, suspends (1890), 416.

CAPITAL AND/OR CAPITALISM, played off against landed interest, 12 ; becomes mobile, 13 ; modern mobility of, 585 ; ventures abroad, 18 ; whence came early accumulation ?, 14, 16 ; foreign trade aids aggregation of, 15 ; foreign capital comes to England, 40 ; foreign, influx of to Stock Exchange in eighteenth century, 157 n. ; instances of immigrant capitalists' loans to Queen Elizabeth, 42 ; foreign, further influx of, 93 ; English, in seventeenth century, largely local, 121 ; as a stimulus to industry, 123 ; borrowed, social stimulus from, 123 and 123 n. ; aggregation of, its social utility, 219.

  Capitalism, distinguished from finance, 248 ff. ; capitalism supreme in immediate post-Waterloo era, 255 ; must elevate its ideals, or relative social power will decline, 257 ff. ; continuous spatial distribution by banks, 440 ; continuous re-distribution of, Sections V. (a) and V. (b) of Stock Exchange, pp. 574 ff. ; cheapened by Stock Exchange, 586 ; seasonal distribution of, 444 ; this illustrated from Dominion Banking, 444 ; distribution now becoming cosmopolitan, 446.

CAPITAL, NEW ISSUES OF, subjected to Treasury permission (1915), 626 n.

716   EVOLUTION OF THE MONEY MARKET

CECIL (Burghley), a shareholder in Mines Royal, 169.
CENTRALISATION OF FINANCIAL AUTHORITY IN LONDON, the final influences which assured it, 240 n., 493 ff.
CERTIFICATE, SHARE-, and the STOCK-, fifteenth-century instance of, 19.
'CHANGE ALLEY. See STOCK EXCHANGE.
CHAPLIN, MILNE, GRENFELL AND CO., failure (1914), 669.
CHARLES II., raid on goldsmiths by, 97.
CHARTERS, of corporations, 168.
CHEQUE BANK, 352 n.
CHEQUES, origin of, 101; modern definition of, 101 n.; early specimens, 101; not originally appreciated as currency, 102; early vogue of, limited by legal prejudice, 102 ff.; earliest *printed* (1762), 103; earliest cheque *books* (1781), 103; dated more than fifteen miles from bank on which drawn, must be stamped, 291 n., 317 n.; crossed, origin of, 306 n.; huge increase in utilisation of, between 1815 and 1858, 312 ff.; cheque currency, immense public utility of, 316 ff.; cheque currency, is its own guarantee, 317; cheque currency, Pownall's statistics as to, 318; cheque currency, is automatically regulated, 319.
CHILD, FRANCIS (" Father of the Profession " of banking), devotes himself to banking alone, 112 (*see* 270 n.).
CHOSES IN ACTION (*see* STOCK EXCHANGE and ASSIGNABILITY), bills of exchange an early exception to non-assignability of, 25; choses in action, shares, debentures, bonds and securities as, 142; rights to a dividend are, 143; not originally assignable, 143, 177 ff.; but King, by prerogative, may make them so, 144; non-assignment of, hampered early Stock Exchange, 146.

Law Cases cited :—
Breverton's case, 1537 (King's grantee of chose in action may sue upon it in his own name), 144 and 144 n.
Gorge and Dalton's case, 1587 (royal prerogative competent to assign a chose in action), 144.
Duvergier v. Fellows, 1828 (assignee of chose in action cannot sue on cause accruing before assignment), 145, 177, 180.
Dalton v. Midland Counties Railway, 1853 (right to a dividend is a chose in action), 143.

CHOSE IN SUSPENSE, 142 n.
CIRCULAR NOTES, origin of (1770), 103 n.
CITY ARTICLE. See NEWS SERVICE.
CITY OF GLASGOW BANK, appalling liability on shares, 304 n.; [first] failure, 1857, 366; [second] failure, 1878, 430, 510, 515.
CLEARING-HOUSE, origin and history of, 305 n.; Metropolitan Clearing, 307 n.; Country Clearing, 307 n.; clearing principle applied to Stock Exchange, 307 n.; the system in the United States, 308 n.; striking figures (1872), 395; proposed international, 700.
" CLOG " ON THE EQUITY OF REDEMPTION, 107; used against royal borrowers, 107; equity's repulsion for, 107.

Law Cases cited :—
Newcomb v. Bonham, 1681 (" clog " on equity of redemption), 107.
Jennings v. Ward, 1705, do., 107.
Vernon v. Bethall, 1761, do., 108.
Samuel v. Jarrah Timber, 1904, do., 108.
De Beers v. British South Africa (equity doctrine of the " clog " probably has no application to floating charges), 109.

INDEX 717

CLYDESDALE BANK, 354 n.
COLE, MR. A. C. (Bank Governor, 1910), on bankers' balances at Bank of England, 506; announces the arrangement of quarterly meetings of bankers at Bank of England, 662.
COLEBROOK, SIR GEORGE, aided by Bank of England, 233.
COLLECTION FOR THE IMPROVEMENT OF HUSBANDRY AND TRADE, 146.
COLLIE FRAUDS, 430.
COLONIAL BANKING, rise of, 312; absorption process in, 415; Australian bank crisis (1892–1893), 639; Canadian banking consolidation, 640; Canadian Bankers' Association, work of, 641.
COMMERCIAL BANK OF SCOTLAND, origin of, 440.
COMMUTATION OF FEUDAL DUES (see MONEY-ECONOMY), date and results of, 5 ff.
COMPANIES, joint-stock and corporations (see LIMITED LIABILITY and UNLIMITED LIABILITY, ASSIGNABILITY, CHOSES IN ACTION), chapter vi.; corporation, theory and origin of, 163 n.; six types of commercial corporation, 164 n.; is the company *really* "persona ficta"?, 165 n.; or is there a reality underlying corporateness?, 686; Gierke on real individuality of, 165 n., 222 ff., 686 ff.; regulated companies, what they were, 166; originally concerned with foreign trade, 163; and ultimately almost monopolised it, 171 (see Kinder v. Taylor, 180); the company or corporation is a single legal entity, 166; Merchant Adventurers, mode of incorporation of, 167; amalgamation of, early instance of, 168; Charters of, early, remain as precedent, 168; at home, activity of (*circa* 1561), 169; with transferable shares, first case of, 169; generally sought monopolies, as reward of enterprise (*circa* 1603), 171; monopolies abolished, 172; reconstruction of, early instance, 173; meetings of, early case of notice of, 173.
Declared by Ellenborough to be partnerships only, 1808, 178; (see 176 n. 2); African Company, 1682 (early reconstruction), 173; as "nuisances," 176; "Bubble Act" to suppress, 176; "Bubble Act" repealed, 1825, 179; judicial criticism of, 177 ff.; Crown receives new powers of incorporation, 184; may sue or be sued through a "public officer" (1834), 184; discrimination against their bills, as late as 1870, 186; rush of new, in 1825, 326; rush of, again after 1862, 395; recent change in types of shareholders in, 465 and 465 n.
Law Cases cited:—
Rex v. Webb, 1811 (attempt to suppress companies), 178.
Pratt v. Hutchinson, 1809 (building societies not within "Bubble Act"), 179.
Josephs v. Pebrer, 1825 (illegality of companies, especially as to premiums on share-issues), 179.
Kinder v. Taylor (joint-stock companies likely to discourage small traders), 180.
See also cases cited under ASSIGNABILITY and CHOSES IN ACTION.
CONFEDERACY OF FINANCE (see BANK OF ENGLAND, BARING CRISIS, FINANCE), in fighting crises, beginnings of, 231 ff., 328, 332; merely temporary at first, 333; earliest signs of deliberate unity, with examples, 336; Association of Joint-Stock Banks (1838), 343; does not efface banking competition, 448; Confederacy "in a Flood," chapter xvii.; Arthur Crump's suggestions, 488; lessening violence of crises, in presence of, 498; diminishes intensity of crises (and ultimately abolishes them?), 681; Stock Exchange powers in the enforcement of international honesty, 613 ff.; Corporation of Foreign Bondholders, work of, 615, and 616 n.; fresh plan for, between Bank of England and other banks (1876), 508; general movement towards, after 1866, 509; Arthur Ellis on necessity for, 510; banking hier-

YY

718 EVOLUTION OF THE MONEY MARKET

archy obvious to Giffen, 522 ; in the Baring crisis, chapter xviii. ; a vast agglomeration of financial power, 528 ; international finance, 631 ff. ; work of Canadian Bankers' Association, 641 ; resumed movement towards, after Baring crisis, 648 ff. ; American arguments for, 652 ; legislation cannot produce, 654 ff. ; Baring precedent re-invoked, 1911, 660 ; banking, avowed at last, 662 ; corporate, of banks, 665 ; ring of fortresses complete for 1914, 667 ; demonstration of its potency (1914), 680 ; operative agents of, 689 ff. ; cosmopolitan results already achieved, 699 ; international gold reserve, 700 ; survey of whole subject, chapter xxi., p. 682.

CONSOLIDATED BANK, 288.

CONSOLIDATED DISCOUNT, suspension (1866), 401.

CONSOLS, in 1847 panic, 361 ; alleged unsaleable in 1857 panic, 367 ; also in 1866, but this denied, 402 ; their primacy among investments challenged, 331, 556 n. ; absence of fixed date of redemption, mischievous influence of, 622.

CO-OPERATION (see CONFEDERACY), co-operative movement among working classes, 489 n.

CO-ORDINATION, of financial functions, the whole argument summarised, chapter xxi., p. 682.

CORPORATION OF FOREIGN BONDHOLDERS, 615.

CORPORATIONS. See COMPANIES.

COSMOPOLITAN FINANCE, beginnings of, 41 ; London as a centre (but not yet the centre) of (1669), 93 ; cosmopolitan currency, London cheques becoming a, 320 ; obvious about 1836, 340 ; cosmopolitan financial censorship, chapter xix., sec. vi. (p. 613) ; cosmopolitan securities, 567 ; Hansard's theory as to, 695 ; financial principles, 695 ; gold reserve scheme, 700 ; clearing-house. 700.

COUNTRY BANKING. See PROVINCIAL BANKING.

COUNTRY CLEARING, origin of, 307 n.

COUTTS AND CO., early partnership with Carr, 120 ; last firm to issue bills on demand, 229 n. ; Thomas Coutts and George III., 282 n. ; lent on permanent mortgages, 317 ; John, only once drunk in his counting-house, 393.

CREDIT, growth of the sense of, 85 ; good, value of, evidenced, 87 n. ; damage to (1596) from dishonoured bills, 88 ; extending facilities, 99 ; involves new relationship with the State, 205 n.

Public, advent of, 206 and 206 n. ; Addison's allegory on, 206 n. ; "cradled in bankruptcy and beggary," 213 ; national, at one time inferior to that of the Bank of England, 225.

Law Cases cited :—
Leycroft v. Dumkin (early attacks on credit), 85, 86.
Selby v. Carrier (do.), 86.

CRÉDIT LYONNAIS, 388, 417.

"CREDIT SHOP," three types of, 471.

CRISIS (see PANIC), difference between panic and, 324 n. ; minor, of 1822, 324 ff. ; cyclic sequence of, 501 and 501 n. ; of 1878, 515 ; Baring, chapter xviii. ; London and Globe affair, 643 ; anonymous crisis averted, Mr. Pownall's story of, 644.

German War (1914), 669 ; unique character of, 670 ; banking steadiness and solidity in, 670 ff. ; protecting accepting houses, 675 ; steadily diminishing violence of, as Money Power tightens its grip, 681. Possible entire cessation of, 680.

"CRISISOMETER," 261.

CROMWELL, OLIVER, banked with Hoare's, 95.

INDEX 719

CROMWELL (Thomas), financial experiences of, 17 and 17 n.
CROSSED CHEQUE. *See* CHEQUE.
CURRENCY. *See* MONEY, CHEQUE.
CUSTOMS, MERCANTILE (*see* LAW MERCHANT), early recognised by the Courts, 30; instances of, 30 n.; *see* Sheldon *v.* Hentley, 103.

DARWINISM (*see* ORGANISM), principles of, unconsciously applied by Lord Liverpool to early banking, 302; Natural Selection among banks, 320 and chapter xvi.; enters scientific field, 392; *see* pp. 258 ff., especially 266, and chapter xxi.; cosmic process deflected in the case of finance, 482.
DEBENTURES, rudimentary form of, 170; are choses in action, 142 n.
DENNISTOUN AND Co., stoppage of (1857), 367.
DEPOSITS, INTEREST ON, 269 n.
" DEPOSITORS' LIST," 100; developed into pass-book, 102.
DEPRECIATION of bankers' securities, 622.
DEUTSCHE BANK, 388.
DIPLOMACY, FINANCIAL, in Lombard Street, 701.
DISCONTO-GESELLSCHAFT, 417.
" DISCOUNTING " events in advance, market habit of. *See* STOCK EXCHANGE.
DISTRIBUTION, of money. *See* MONEY, CAPITAL.
DISTRICT BANK OF NEWCASTLE, 427.
DOCK WARRANT FRAUDS, by Cole, 364.
" DOLIOGENIC," sense in which the word is used in this essay, 224 n.
DOLLAR, " COMPENSATED," scheme for, 564 n.
DOUGLAS HERON AND Co., rash discounting policy of, 123; prolonged liquidation of, 304 n.
DRUMMONDS, " near failing " (1772), 233; lent on permanent mortgages, 317.
DUN, JOHN (Alliance Bank), 348; on publicity for bank reports, 450 n.
DUNDEE BANKING Co., early speculation by, 129.

EAST OF ENGLAND BANK, 288.
EDWARD I., dealings with the Frescobaldis, 240 n.
EDWARD VI., borrows from the Fuggers on City security, 50; " clogs " on his loans, 107.
EDWARD VII., King, visits the Stock Exchange (as Prince of Wales), 156 n.
EMBRYOLOGY OF THE MONEY MARKET, chapter i.
ENGLISH JOINT-STOCK BANK, losses at branches, 289; spends £13,000 in fighting bears of its own shares, 294; " temporary " suspension of (1866), 401.
ESDAILES, helped by Bank of England, 338.
EXCHANGES, FOREIGN, beginnings of, 24 n.; Exchange houses, transformation of, 386; policy of modern banks as to, 338; foreign banks in London, 387, 494 ff.; breakdown of, 1914, 673.
EXCHEQUER, the seventeenth-century bankers' bank, 97.
EXCHEQUER BILLS, origin of, 213 and 213 n.; further issues of, 215; Gurney on, 331 n.
" EXPANSIVE " POLICY. *See* PANIC.

720 EVOLUTION OF THE MONEY MARKET

FAIRS, 29; decline of, 38 n.
FARM MORTGAGES, as bankers' security, 122; as an investment trust security, 473.
FAUNTLEROY, HENRY, 289.
FEUDAL DUES and services (see COMMUTATION); feudal relationships, in contrast with financial, 245 ff.
FINANCE (see CONFEDERACY, ORGANISM, ORGANISATION), meaning and history of the word, 201 n.; distinguished from capitalism, 248 ff.; misconceptions as to, in early nineteenth century, 255 ff.; methods of, utilised by working classes, 489 n.; . as a confederate force, chapter xvii.; deflecting the cosmic process, 482; unmanageable by legislation, 654 ff.; avowal of confederacy, 662; a corporate entity, 665; solidly organised and confederate, 680; its co-ordinated functions surveyed, chapter xxii. (p. 682); corporate heritage of, 685 ff.; supreme tribunal of, how composed, 686; steadiness the constant aim of, 691; the most potent cosmopolitan force, 695; receives ambassadors from all the world, 701; destined to make the world one, 703.
FINANCE BILLS (" open credits "), origin and vogue of, 378.
FINANCIER ?, what is a, 202 n.
FORBES, SIR WILLIAM, and the Scottish crisis of 1793, 235.
FOREIGN AND COLONIAL GOVERNMENT TRUST, 469.
FOREIGN BANKS, their advent to London, 387, 494 ff.
FOREIGN BONDS (see LOANS, FOREIGN), ostracised by Bank of England, 513 n., 514; special Exchange for, unsuccessful, 159 n.
FOREIGN LOANS, Stock Exchange censorship as to, chapter xix., sect. vi. (p. 613).
FOREIGN LOANS COMMITTEE, 620.
FOREIGN POLICY, City influence over, a result of early royal borrowings, 91; new nationalities financed, 326.
FORGED TRANSFERS ACT, 365 n., 540.
FRANCE, bank amalgamation in, 417.
FRANCO-GERMAN WAR, financial influence of, 494 ff.
FRESCOBALDIS, Edward I. and the, 240 n.; Thomas Cromwell and the, 17.
FUGGERS, financed Edward VI., 50; and Elizabethan business, 171.
FUNDS, BRITISH (see CONSOLS), largely held abroad (1718), 219 and 219 n.

GERMAN WAR CRISIS. See CRISIS.
GERMANY, bank amalgamation in, 417, 424, 460, 463; banking in, differs widely from English, 433 ff.
GIERKE, theories of, as to reality behind corporateness, 165 n., 222, 686.
GILBART, J. W., discovers that note issue is not essential to banking, 300; opens London and Westminster Bank, 304; on banker's care of his own health, 393.
GLEDSTANE'S FAILURE, and Bank of England, 491, 499.
GLYN, MILLS, CURRIE AND Co., have never absorbed any other bank, 415; and the People's Trust, 474.
GOLD, mode of checking outflow of, 384, 645.
GOLDSMITHS, their early clients were fifteenth-century vendors of land who bought jewellery, 11; specimen purchases, 32, 33; not originally money-dealers at all, 57; as trustees, 50 n.; established position of, and importance, in later sixteenth century 53; concentrating in Lombard Street, 54, 96; this produces some pride in the appearance of the street, 55 n.; prestige enhanced as assayers of coin, 56.

INDEX 721

Affected by reduced demand for plate and jewellery, 57; and consequently take to banking, 58; become goldsmith-bankers, 53, 55; this variation necessary to ensure survival, 58; "Mystery of the New-Fashioned Goldsmiths," 58; definitely transformed into bankers, 59; originally bailees: how did they become debtors of their clients?, 63; effect upon this transformation of the alien element in our coinage, 68; supremacy of goldsmith-bankers, chapter iii.; Covill, goldsmith, dies (1670) worth £400,000, 95; raid on, by Charles II., 97; their " running caskes," 99; Tassel v. Lewis, 7 Wm. III. (goldsmiths' notes are money), 99; necessity for organisation of, 109; Francis Child specialises as banker, and abandons goldsmiths' business (1690), 112; goldsmith-bankers survive till 1790, 128. See Hartop v. Hoare, p. 113.

GOSCHEN, MR. (Lord) (the late), suggests scheme for checking outflow of gold, 384.

GOSCHEN, LORD (the present), on finance as the averter of crisis, 681.

GRESHAM, SIR THOMAS, invests money in gold chains, 33; Cecil's reliance on his " advertisements," 598.

GURNEY's (Associated Gurney Banks), 462.

HALLETT, OMMANNEY AND CO., 288.

HAMMOND, WILLIAM, founder of present Stock Exchange, 159.

HANKEY, THOMSON, protests against Financial Suzerainty, 502.

HANSARD, LUKE (Martin's Bank), on 1866 panic, 402; theory of, as to value of international securities as bankers' reserve, 695.

HANSEATIC LEAGUE, 165.

HARRIS, C., H. AND A. AND CO., 331.

HENRY VI. and the Albertine failures, 18 and 18 n.

HENRY VIII., borrows in the City, 50; " clogs " on his loans, 107.

HERRIES, FARQUHAR AND CO., 103 n.

HIERARCHY, FINANCIAL. See CONFEDERACY.

HOARDING, early examples of, 31 ff.; deadening influence of, 32; Richard III. hoards money in bed, 33; hoards of jewellery, 32, 33; these employed in aid of Parliament in Civil War, 34; extraordinary sixteenth-century instances of, 74 and 74 n.; in the seventeenth century, 98 n.; encouraged by the raid on the goldsmiths, 97; superseded by the deposit account, 269, 371 n.; some revival of in Waterloo period, 272; instinct of, still prevalent on the Continent (1914), 297; slight recrudescence (1857–1866), 371.

HOLDEN, SIR EDWARD, quoted, 506; decides to state gold resources of London City and Midland, 650 n.; on new bank-note scheme, 672; on banking policy in German War crisis, 673 n.

HUDSON, GEORGE, and the railway boom, 357.

HUDSON's BAY COMPANY, 173.

IMPERIAL MERCANTILE CREDIT, suspension (1866), 401.

INDUSTRIAL REVOLUTION, 122.

INSURANCE, money market, function of, 188; Lloyds, origin of, 188 ff.; services of, as part of the protective resources of the Money Power, 192; principle of, utilised by the Investment Trusts, 470 ff.

INTEREST ON CURRENT ACCOUNT discontinued (1877), 272 n.

INTEREST (see USURY), quoted rate includes three factors, 106 n.; and six rates of, always current, 106 n.; high, no prejudice to trade, so Locke thought, 134.

722 EVOLUTION OF THE MONEY MARKET

INTERMEDIARIES, money market, enumerated in 13 Eliz. c. 8, 46 ; classes of at Restoration period, 80 ; and in Queen Anne period, 136.
INTERNATIONAL FINANCIAL SOCIETY, 468.
INTERNATIONAL MARKETS. *See* COSMOPOLITAN.
INVESTMENT, originally in jewellery and luxurious garments, 31 ff. ; Gresham invests in gold chains, 33 ; sixteenth - century examples including Shakespeare,¶ 43 ; INVESTMENT TRUSTS, *see* that head ; in mortgages, prevalence of (1825), 464 ; extension of, 465 ff. and 465 n. ; by Trustee Savings Banks, 279 ; *see* Hawkins v. Parker, 44.
INVESTMENT TRUSTS, chapter xvi. ; unknown to early Money Market, 467 ; principles of, defined (1868), 469 ; distribution of risks, 470 ; increase in number of, 1884 to 1890, 472 ; insurance, principle utilised by, 470 ff. ; and speculative securities therefore included in holdings, 472 ; limitation of holdings in any given investment, 473 ; as " relief funds," 473 ; and the " people," 474 ; functions of, modified in recent years, 475 ; German form of, 478.
IRELAND, early banking in, 117 ; Munster Bank failure (1883) and consequences, 515 ; Bank of, models its system on Bank of England, 236 ; Bank of, assisted by Bank of England, 516.
ISSUING HOUSES, origin of, 386.

JACKSON, MR. F. HUTH, on banking consolidation, 653.
JAMES, PAUL MOON, on Bank of England, 345.
JEVONS, theory as to periodicity of crises, 501.
JEWS, influence on early development of negotiability, 21 n. ; originated news-services, 27, 589 n. ; return to England, 88 ; their characteristic financial talents, 89 and 89 n.
JOBBERS, origin of, 157 n.; distinction between brokers and how it arose, 157 n. ; functions analysed, 581.
JOINT-STOCK BANKS. *See* BANKING.
JOINT-STOCK DISCOUNT CO., failure, 399.
JONES LOYD AND CO. (Lord Overstone's firm), origin of, 122 n.
JOSEPH JONES AND CO., later Jones Loyd and Co., 122 n.

KING, the (*see* also under LOANS), borrows from the trading classes, 35 ; instances of loans, 35 ; (James I.) pawns the Crown jewels, 4 3 borrowing by, mitigated sentiment against usury, 49 ; his loans required City security as collateral, 50 ; veto on foreign loans, 149 and 149 n. ; Gresham objects to forced renewals of loans, 86 ; City attitude towards, 87 ; lost financial prerogative of, 205 ff.

LABOURERS, STATUTE OF, origin and results of, 7 *et. seq.*
LANCASHIRE AND YORKSHIRE BANK, 462.
LAND, sold by retail, causes of such a tremendous innovation, 9 ff. ; not bought by capitalists for investment till Tudor epoch, 10 ; proceeds of fifteenth-century sales, invested in plate and jewellery, 11 ; slackening of sales, and effect on goldsmiths, 57 ; money diverted from, in eighteenth century, 209 n. *See* MORTGAGES and INVESTMENT.
LANE, SON AND FRASER, failure of, 237.
LAW, ECONOMIC, not within human control, 82 n.
LAW MERCHANT, necessity for and history of, 28 ; originated in Mercantile Custom, 28 ; becoming a modern ideal, 562, 697.

Law Cases cited :—
Brandao v. Barnett, 1846 (recognition of the Law Merchant), 30.

INDEX 723

Luke v. Lyde (universality of mercantile law), 696.
Sheldon v. Hentley, 1680 (custom legalises payment to bearer), 103.
See also cases cited under NEGOTIABILITY; and observations of Cockburn, C.J., in Goodwin v. Robarts, 30.

LEEMAN'S ACT, origin of, 295 and 295 n.; practically extended to *all* securities (1915) for a time, 295 n.

Law Cases cited:—

Perry v. Barnett, 1885 (Stock Exchange practice as to Leeman's Act), 295 n.
Neilson v. James, 1882 (ditto), 295 n.

LEVIATIONS, an early form of "calls," 166.
LEX MERCATORIA. *See* LAW MERCHANT.
LIABILITY, LIMITED. *See* LIMITED LIABILITY.
LIDDERDALE, MR. WILLIAM. *See* BARING CRISIS.
LIMITED LIABILITY, peremptory necessity for, on shares of companies, 174 ff.; early efforts to defeat limitation, 174; a "mischievous delusion," 178; *see* cases cited under COMPANIES; certificate of, specimen, 1843, 183 n.; conferred generally (1855), 185; survival of prejudice against, down to 1851, 186; has always characterised the three great "national" banks of the Kingdom, 303.

Law Cases cited:—

Salmon v. Hamborough Co. (early unlimited liability), 175.
Rex v. Dodd, 1808 (limited liability a "mischievous delusion"), 178.
Walburn v. Ingilby, 1832 (transferable shares not necessarily illegal, but limitation of liability "entirely nugatory"), 182.
Agriculturists Cattle Insurance *ex parte* Baird, 1870 (duration of unlimited liability), 187 n.

LIVERPOOL BOROUGH BANK, rash methods of, 292; collapse (1857), 367.
LLOYDS, origin of, 188 ff.
LLOYDS BANK, illustrative list of absorptions by, 132; has never sought amalgamation, 425 n.; an early experiment of the method successfully adopted in Baring crisis, 531.

LOANS, early (*see* under "CLOG" and KING; also Hill v. Snow, 82), Gresham's objections to forced renewals of, 86; City criticisms of royal borrowings, 87; royal requests for, give City an increasing influence on foreign policy, 91; on East India stock (1676), 107; on lottery tickets 123 and 123 n.; first foreign loan dealt in on the Exchange, 149; royal veto on foreign loans, 149 and 149 n.; this precedent invoked in 1915, 149 n.; foreign, numerous issues of (1825), 326; foreign bonds, mania for (1860–1875), 500; foreign, Stock Exchange censorship of, chapter xix., sec. vi. (p. 613); Government and public, nature of the security for, analysed, 553; enemy holders of, their position, 553 and n.; necessity of fixed dates of maturity, 621.

LOMBARD STREET, concentration of goldsmiths in, 54, 96; their pride in appearance of street, 55 n.; enhanced value of property in, 495.

LONDON, flow of capital to, 236 n.; money "gravitates" to, 370 ff.; assured financial predominance of (1800), 240; financial supremacy, sketch of evolution of, 240 n.; financial supremacy, 1815, 254; its "names" universally known, 376; centralisation of financial authority in, final influences which assured it, 493 ff.; country bankers' dependence on, 126.

LONDON AND COUNTY BANK, bear raid on shares of, 294; originally hampered by having only one class of clientele, 443.

LONDON AND EASTERN BANK, 289 and 289 n.
LONDON AND GLOBE collapse, 643.

724 EVOLUTION OF THE MONEY MARKET

LONDON AND PROVINCIAL BANK, admitted to clearing, 307 n.; triple grouping of branches, 442.

LONDON AND SOUTH AFRICAN BANK, 415, 441 n.

LONDON AND SOUTH WESTERN BANK, described (1862) as "only a twopenny ha'penny company," 309; purpose of its establishment, 314.

LONDON AND WESTMINSTER BANK, establishment of, 300, 304; refused admission to Clearing-house, 305; refused an account at Bank of England, 306; enters Clearing-house, 1854, 308.

LONDON ASSURANCE CORPORATION, origin of, 170.

LONDON CITY AND MIDLAND BANK (see HOLDEN, SIR EDWARD), bold policy of, 430, 453; decides to state gold-holding, 650 n.

LONDON EXCHANGE BANKING CO., 103 n.

LONDON FINANCIAL ASSOCIATION, 468.

LOTTERIES, once a regular source of national revenue, 151 and 151 n.

LOTTERY TICKETS, as a banker's security, 123 and 123 n.; "known" to early Stock Exchange, 146.

MANCHESTER AND LIVERPOOL DISTRICT BANK, proposed amalgamation with Lloyds, 425 n.

MANITOBA legislation on new issues, 628.

MARKETS, early examples of, 38.

MARSH AND CO. (Fauntleroy's firm), 289.

MARTIN'S BANK, early attempt to enunciate banking principles, by partner of, 131.

MAYNELL, seventeenth-century goldsmith, 106.

MERCHANT ADVENTURERS. See COMPANIES.

METROPOLITAN CLEARING, 307 n.

MINES ROYAL, 169.

MINING EXCHANGE, 159 n.

MOCATTA AND GOLDSMID, bullion dealers, 119 n.

MONASTERIES, Henry VIII.'s thefts from, 34.

MONEY (cash), extraordinary scarcity of, in fifteenth century, 35; curious examples of scarcity, 35, 36; foreign element among English money (fifteenth and sixteenth centuries), 68; early and clumsy modes of transmitting, 78 n., 79; (credit) re-distribution of, by banks, in accordance with local and seasonal demands, 121, 440 ff.; lack of facilities for this in eighteenth century, 127; (cash) value of, originally estimated in relation to land purchase, 134; currency reform of 1696, 214; "gravitates" to London (1858), 370.

MONEY-ECONOMY, obvious in reign of Richard II., 4; advent of, accelerated by epidemics, 4; capitalists played off against the landed interest, 12.

MONEY-LENDER (see USURY), and banker, difference between, 58 n., 105; in Tudor times, 73; in seventeenth century, 105; Money Lenders Act, 1900, a failure, 139.

MONEY MARKET (see MARKETS, BROKERS, BILL-BROKERS, BANKER, GOLDSMITH, INTERMEDIARIES, CREDIT, STOCK EXCHANGE, FINANCE), components of, 140; essentials of, 258 ff.; modern, dates from 1815, 243; factors of, 467 n.; their close inter-relationship, 593 ff., 679; sensitiveness of, 589 ff.

MORATORIUM (1914), 678.

MORGAN, J. PIERPONT, personal power of, 251 and 251 n.

MORRIS, PRÉVOST AND CO., 128.

INDEX 725

MORTGAGES, as bankers' securities, 284, 289, 317; their inferiority as credit instruments to Stock Exchange securities, 575; extensive investments on (1825), 464; companies formed to invest on, 471; losses on Australian (1892–1893), 639.

MUNSTER BANK failure (1883), 515.

MURRIETAS, collapse of, 526.

NATIONAL DEBT, creation and function of, 212, 218, 219 ff.; conversion, 643.

NATIONAL PROVINCIAL BANK OF ENGLAND, kept out of London by its note issue, 300, 354 n.; forfeits issue to come to London, 373; early amalgamation by, 425.

NATURAL SELECTION (see DARWINISM), as operative upon banks, chapter xv. (p. 411).

NEAL, FORDYCE AND Co., failure, 233.

NEGOTIABILITY (see CHOSES IN ACTION and BEARER BONDS, under STOCK EXCHANGE), principle of, 19 ff.; early history of, and of negotiable instruments, 19 n. ff.; difference between negotiability and assignability, 20 n.; a development of the impersonal obligation, 21 n.; and of the renunciation of all technical defences in advance, 22 n.; early bribes paid by negotiable instruments, 23 n.; immense utility of the principle, 26; as operative in the case of bank-notes, 100 n.; challenged, 103; usury laws employed to defeat, 138.

Law Cases cited :—

Higgs v. Holliday, temp. Eliz. (negotiability of lost note), 104 n.

Clerke v. Martin (Holt's mistaken judgment as to negotiability of goldsmith's note), 31.

Horton v. Coggs (negotiability of goldsmith's deposit note), 104.

Crowley v. Crowther (full negotiability of bill to bearer), 104.

Grant v. Vaughan, 1764 (full negotiability of bill to bearer), 104.

Miller v. Race, 1791 (leading case on full negotiability of bank notes), 105.

Goodwin v. Robarts, 1875 (Foreign Government Scrip negotiable by Stock Market custom), 30 and 105 n.

Colonial Bank v. Whinney, 1886 (negotiability generally), 20.

London Joint-Stock Bank v. Simmons, 1892 (negotiability by custom), 30.

NEWCASTLE JOINT-STOCK BANK, suspension (1847), 361.

NEWCASTLE MERCHANTS, co-operate with banks, 234.

NEWS SERVICE, early forms of, 27; originated by Jews, 27; bankers and their correspondents, 76; first financial weekly, 146; development of, to modern times, 598 n.; City article, history of, 600 n.; cable news begins, 601 n.; financial journalism, modern, 601 n.; quotations, supply of, 602 n.; financial influence of, 602 n., 614; in New York, 602 n.

NEWTONIAN THEORY OF GRAVITATION, coincidence of discovery with earliest organising movement in finance, 111.

NEW YORK STOCK EXCHANGE, crisis of 1873, 499; wide interests of, 541.

NONCONFORMITY as a financial factor, 210.

NORTH AND SOUTH WALES BANK, suspension (1847), 361.

NORTHERN AND CENTRAL BANK, 293; difficulties of, 338.

NORTHUMBERLAND AND DURHAM BANK, loaded with local paper, 286; finances the Derwent Iron Co., 291.

" NOTE ACCOUNTABLE," 100.

NOTES, originated in " Running Cash Notes," 99; their negotiability challenged (*see* Law Cases cited under NEGOTIABILITY) ; early mistakes in management of note issues, 125 ; with an option between eight and six months, 125 ; early utility of, where cheques would have been useless, 126 ; issuable by anybody down to 1775, 127 ; all notes under £5 abolished (1777), 127 ; this prohibition temporarily relaxed, 127 ; originally considered essential to banking, 227 ; that idea exploded by Gilbart, 300 ; issue by corporate bodies (or partnerships of more than six) prohibited (15 Geo. II. c. 13); give place to cheques about 1772 in London, 229 n. ; suspension of cash payments by Bank of England, 237 and 237 n. ; democratisation of, 276 ; forgeries of, 276 n.

Generally superseded by cheques, 1815–1858, 314 ; and now a matter of secondary importance, 317 ; centralisation of issue of, under Bank Charter Act, 348 ; criticism of this, 348 ; Bank of England, become mere bullion certificates under Bank Charter Act, 350 ; suggested discretionary power of issue by Bank of England, 350 ; Treasury (1914), 348, 349 ; events leading up to issue of, 671 ; bankers had foreseen need of larger supply in war emergency, 672.

OHIO LIFE AND TRUST CO., stoppage, 366.
" OMNIUM," meaning of, 160 n.
" OPEN CREDITS." *See* FINANCE BILLS.
OPTIONS. *See* STOCK EXCHANGE.
ORDINARY SHARES, are parts of ownership, 167 n. ; participating, first case of, 167.
ORGANISATION OF FINANCIAL FORCES (*see* CONFEDERACY), peremptory necessity of, (seventeenth century), 109, 197 ff. ; the Nucleus of, Part II. ; financial, more closely related to biological sciences than to the mathematico-physical group, 252 ; financial, not advanced enough to check the crisis of 1825, 327.
ORGANISM (*see* CONFEDERACY), MONEY MARKET AS AN, beginnings of development in that direction, 110 ; the process, outlined by Hobhouse, 224 ; physiological analogy between evolution of Money Market and the process of organic development, set forth in detail, 258 ff. ; parallel " sets of conditions " on lines laid down by Hobhouse, 266 ff. ; the whole argument summarised, chapter xxi. (p. 682).
OVEREND, GURNEY AND CO. and dock warrant frauds, 364 ; helped weak firms in 1857, 366 ; money in foreign land, 288 ; their failure (1866), 395 ff. ; Black Friday, 400 ff. ; assets, compared with Barings', 529.
OVERSTONE, LORD, odd idea about banking capital, 286 n. ; prejudice against joint-stock banks, 309 ; on the gold supply (1857), 316.

PALGRAVE, on bankers' balances at Bank of England, 503.
PANIC (*see* PRESSURE, CRISIS), difference between crisis and, 324 n. ; early experiments in " expansive " treatment of, 233 ff. ; in the eighteenth century, 231 ff. ; " restrictive " treatment in 1793, is changed to " expansive " policy, 237 ; of 1825, 324 ff. ; fatuity of restrictive treatment, 330 ; of 1847, 355 ff., 491 ; three modes of dealing with, 359 ; of 1857, 364 ff. ; " most unjustifiable panic of the century," 368 ; Stock Exchange crisis of 1859, 369 ; of 1866, 395 ff. ; " expansive " policy in 1866, 407 ; in 1914, 673 ; steadily lessening violence of, 498, 528, 680 ; American, of 1907, 644 ; probably non-recurrence of, 680 ; Stock Exchange dislike of, 606.
PARIS, why its financial influence declined in comparison with London, 494 ff.
PARR, MR. CECIL, on banking confederacy, 657.

INDEX 727

PARR'S BANK, absorption process illustrated by record of, 419 n. ; value of northern connections as a means for profitable employment of money, 443.
PARTNERSHIP, distinguished from corporation, 174.
PASS-BOOK, origin of, 102.
PAWNBROKING, originally a department of the goldsmith's business, 112.
PEABODY, GEORGE AND CO., apply for assistance (1857), 367.
PEEL, SIR ROBERT (see BANK CHARTER ACT), favoured a State Bank, 347.
PEOPLE'S TRUST CO., LTD., 474.
PERPETUITIES, judicial misgivings as to, 109 n.
PERSONALITY, theory of, as applied to financial organism, 686 ff.
PETO AND BETTS'S SUSPENSION (1866), 401.
PHILLIPS, J. SPENCER, on banking consolidation, 651.
PINTO, PERCY, ASHBY AND CO., failure, 399.
POLE, SIR PETER AND CO., failure of, 328 ff.
POLITICAL ECONOMY, unfamiliar in 1818, 256.
PORDER, RICHARD, on foreign exchange business, in sermon in 1570, 25 ; on usury, 52.
POSTLETHWAITE, MALACHY, on stock dealings, 156.
" PRESSURE " of 1836–39, 337 ff. ; of 1875, 500.
PRICE (SIR C. R.), MARRYAT AND CO., 288.
PRICES (stock and share), first regular list of 1714, 149 ; list in *Gentleman's Magazine* (1802), 161. See STOCK EXCHANGE.
PRIVATE BANKERS, early, each was " on his own," 130; their character and early mistakes, 281 ff. ; specimen list of assets of Wood of Gloucester, 285 n. ; protest against Bank of England branches (1826), 333 ; decline of, in consequence of the joint-stock banks, and reasons for it, 412 ff. ; personality of the private banker, 420 ff.
PRODUCE WARRANT SYSTEM, 604.
PROMISSORY NOTES, supposed origin of, 100.
PROSPECTUS ADVERTISING, originally (1825) on a small scale, 326 n.
PROVINCIAL BANKING, origin of, 116 ; Smith, Payne and Smiths an example of, 116 ; Dr. Bisschop's theory as to origins, 119 ; Burke on, 117 ; originally a mere " side-show " in a draper's or grocer's shop, 117, 128 ; " in every market town by 1796," 118 ; Tritton, John (Barclay and Co.) on, before Bullion Committee (1810), 118 ; Stuckey, Vincent, on extension of, in West of England, 118 ; social significance and influence of, 120 ; mistakes of, 124 ; failures, 1814–1816, 124 ; "local" paper, danger of, 124, 125; dependence on Bank of England, 126.
Contribution of, to banking system, illustrated from history of Lloyds Bank, 132 ; development of, crippled by monopoly of Bank of England, 228 ; typical " run " (" John Halifax, Gentleman "), 287 n. ; and Bank of England branches, 334 ; influence of amalgamation upon, chapter xvi. ; must be *sui generis*, 442 ; its utility as a means for the effective redistribution of capital, 442 ff.
PROVINCIAL STOCK EXCHANGES, 538, origin of, 538 ff., their capacity of resentment, 624.
" PUBLIC OFFICER," right of banks (1826) and companies (1834) to sue or be sued in name of, 184.
PUGET, BAINBRIDGES AND CO., 288.
RAE, GEORGE, on unlimited liability, 303 n., 304 ; on country note issues, 348 ; nearly caught in Overend-Gurney collapse, 398 ; on publicity for bank reports, 450 n. ; sceptical about confederacy, 510.

RAILWAY MANIA, causes 1847 panic, 356; scandals of, 359; effect on Stock Exchange membership, 535.
READING BANK, 426 n.
REAL PROPERTY (*see* MORTGAGES), as an eighteenth-century banker's security, 123, 124; bankers refuse to lend on, 124 n.; mortgage companies, 471; mortgage investments by the trusts, 473.
REDPATH, LEOPOLD, frauds of, 365.
REGULATED COMPANIES. *See* COMPANIES.
"RESTRICTIVE" POLICY. *See* PANIC.
REVELSTOKE, LORD. *See* chapter on Baring Crisis (xviii.).
RICARDO, hostility to Bank of England, 324; issues Greek loan (1825), 326.
RICHARD II., possibly behind the Peasants' Rising of 1381, 11.
RICHARD III., hoards money in bedstead, 33.
RIESSER, DR., on inapplicability of legislation to finance, 656; and *see* chapter xv. for numerous quotations from.
ROBSON, W. J., frauds of, 365.
ROSKEL, ARROWSMITH AND KENDAL, 289.
ROTHSCHILD[S], "stand" of, on Royal Exchange, 146; Nathan Meyer originally a capitalist, 255; and helps slumping market in crisis of 1825, 327; gave assistance in 1857, 366; the late Lord, in 1878 crisis, 515; their aid to the Government in Egyptian finance, 522; and the Suez Canal share purchase, 522.
ROYAL BANK OF LIVERPOOL suspension (1847), 360.
ROYAL EXCHANGE, sixteenth-century assemblages on, 41; original house of Stock Exchange, 146.
ROYAL EXCHANGE ASSURANCE CORPORATION, origin of, 170.
RUBBER SHARE mania (1910), 606 n.
"RUNNING CASHES," 99; represented by Running Cash Notes, 99; these became currency, 99; and perhaps originated promissory notes, 100.

SADLEIR, JOHN, M.P., frauds of, 365.
SAFE CUSTODY, deposits with bankers for, 65 ff. *See* Hartop *v.* Hoare, 113; Pitt diamond deposited with Bank of England, 231. *See* Giblin *v.* M'Mullin, 68.
SANDERSON, SANDEMAN AND CO., SUSPENSION (1857), 367.
SANDERSON'S, SUSPENSION OF (1847), 360.
SAVINGS, begin to be banked, 269; banks, classes who originally patronised, 271 and 271 n.; lack of facilities for investing, and its ill results, 273 ff.; banks, origin and development of, 277 ff.; control centralised, 638; Post Office Savings Bank, origin and real purpose of, 281 n.; Trustee Savings Banks, given power to invest, 279, but Gladstone thought they "smelt of class," 271 n.; resistance to reform of Savings Banks, 293.
SCHUSTER, SIR FELIX, on banking consolidation, 652, 653; on banking without statutory interference, 657; on necessity for international financial unity, 694.
SCOTLAND, BANKING IN, 118; centred in Edinburgh, 118; judicial misgivings about, 118; early co-operation among Scottish bankers, 235; position of Scottish banks in England, 353 n.; banks of, in 1847 panic, 362; feels the centripetal influence of London, 373; solidity of Scottish banks (1876), 511.
SEAMEN'S TICKETS, "known" to early Stock Exchange, 146.

INDEX

SECURITIES, TYPES AND GRADES OF (see STOCK EXCHANGE), cognoscibility of, 574 ; liquidity of, 574.
SHAKESPEARE, as investor, 43.
SHARES, are choses in action (see STOCK EXCHANGE); transferable, first case of, 169 ; calls on, in shape of leviations, 166 ; calls on, in shape of power to assess, 170 ; calls on, early forfeiture of shares, for non-payment of, 173 ; forged, early scandals, 364–365 ; transfers of (see ASSIGNABILITY.)
SHEFFIELD AND HALLAMSHIRE BANK, 291 n.
" SHOP," the word, why employed to describe a bank, 471 n.
SILVER BULLION, now no part of metallic basis of Bank of England note issue, 345 n.
" SLUMP," first appearance of the word, 521.
SMITH, PAYNE AND SMITHS, origin of the firm, 116 and 116 n.
SOUTH EASTERN BANKING CO., 414.
SOUTH SEA SCHEME, 152 ff.
SOVEREIGN, the, as an international coin, 493.
SPANISH ARMADA, Sutton's daring operation to delay, 53 n.
SPECIAL SETTLEMENTS. See STOCK EXCHANGE.
SPECIALISATION AND DIFFERENTIATION of financial functions (see INTERMEDIARIES), in sixteenth century, 46 ; biological significance of, 46, 682 ; essential to efficiency, 92 ; and therefore conferring great influence, 92 ; Francis Child specialises in banking only, 112 and see 433 ; provincial banking, a case of, 116, 117 ; instance of Ralph Carr, 120 ; general lack of, a fruitful source of early trouble among bankers, 128 ; Bagehot on, 136 ; " Money'd Men " and " great bankers," 207 n.
SPECULATION, early bankers guilty of, 129. See STOCK EXCHANGE.
STAMFORD, SPALDING AND BOSTON BANKING, 286 n.
STANDARD BANK OF SOUTH AFRICA, 415 ; enterprising policy of, 441 n.
STANDARDISATION, ideals of, as regards the creation of an unwavering measure of value, 221 n., 563 ; Professor Irving Fisher's scheme, 564 ; of balance - sheets, 565 n. ; of commodities, 565 n., 604 ; of interest rates, 565 n. ; of prices, 566.
STOCKBROKER. See BROKER.
STOCK-JOBBER AND STOCK-JOBBING. See JOBBERS and STOCK EXCHANGE.
STOCK EXCHANGE, chapters v. and xix. ; early tendency of financial business towards site of, 17 n. ; embryo of, in sixteenth century, 40 ; Gresham's servant (Clough) on absence of a Bourse, 41 ; nature of early dealings on, 43 ; wherein it differs from other markets, 142 ; it deals in choses in action (q.v.), 142 ; it " knows " tallies, bills of exchange, lottery tickets and probably tulips, 146 ; the Royal Exchange original home of, 146 ; statutory description of, temp. Wm. III., 147 ; broker's oath, 147 ; broker's conduct subject, under 8 and 9 Wm. III. c. 32, to minute regulation, 148 and 148 n. ; options, over three days, void, 148 ; Broker's Relief Act 1844, 148 ; dealings spread to 'Change Alley and South Sea House, 149 ; first regular list of prices, 1714, 149.
Already a political barometer in 1722, 150 ; early services to Government in the matter of the National Debt, 151 ; South Sea scheme, 152 ; contemporary list of " bubbles," 153 ; discounting events in advance, early case of, 153 ; Sir John Barnard's Act, 154 ; stock-jobbing, " infamous practice of," 154 ; stock-jobbers, early allusions to, 154, 155 ; their present functions analysed, 581 ; eighteenth-

EVOLUTION OF THE MONEY MARKET

century distrust of, 155; not altogether dissipated in nineteenth, 536; not recognised by Adam Smith, 156; early dealings were between actual holders, 156 n.; first royal cognisance of, 156 n.
Definitely located at Jonathan's Coffee House, 157; legislative attempt to extirpate (1773), 157; removes to Stock Exchange Coffee House (1773), 157; already known as the "House" (1773), 157; admission, sixpence, 157; committee established, 159; removes to present site (1802), 159; Deed of Settlement (1802), 159; obsolete slang of, specimens, 160; investment and speculation focussed in, (1801) 160; its real functions not completely understood by its founders, 161; and Leeman's Act, 295; crisis of 1859, 369; London, plain predominance of, 374; mutual aid among members (1859), 486; and Baring crisis, 529.

History 1815-1915, 534 ff.; railway boom and membership, 535; *Official List*, evolution of, 537; closing of (1803), 613 n.; (1915), 538, 587, 677; provincial Stock Exchanges, 538; Manchester Stock Exchange, 538; dispute with Manchester Corporation, 624; discipline of, 543 ff.; law as to, 543 n.; incorporation of, objections to, 544 ff.; open Stock Market, impossibility of, 547 and 547 n.; rarity of disputes, 549 n.; stands for "inviolate faith," 549; and a high standard of conduct, 551, 613 ff., 629 ff.; Gaming Act, 610; plea of, would not be allowed by Stock Exchange, 551.

Securities, types and grades of, 551; *qualitative* standardisation, 552 ff.; objective and subjective security, 554; *quantitative* standardisation, 559 ff.; bearer bonds, their origin and utility, 560; necessity for international rules as to, 562; prices, fixation and standardisation of, 566; arbitrage, 567; securities, cognoscibility of, 574; liquidity of, 574; is concerned with the *transport* of capital to the point of maximum utility, 580, 587; social advantages of its expensive mediumism, 579 ff.; cheapens capital, 586.

Closing of, in 1914, 587; sensitiveness of market, 589; "discounting," habit of, 589 ff.; indicates and records, but does not cause, disturbance, 591; intimate contact with all other money market factors, 593 ff., 677; speculation, chapter xix., section v. (p. 599); speculation and manipulation distinguished, 605; hatred of panic, 606; speculation is a steadying force, 607 ff.; speculation cannot be regulated by statute, 611; international financial censorship of, chapter xix., section vi. (p. 613); illustrated, 617 ff., 631 ff.; special settlements, disciplinary use of, 613 ff. and 613 n.; Foreign Loans Committee, 620; now insists on fixed dates of loan maturity, 621 ff.; surveillance by, limits of, 625, 628; official quotation, significance of, 627; and vendors' shares, 627; London and Globe collapse, 643.

Law Cases cited :—
Mitchell v. Broughton, 1702 (stock-jobbing), 148 n.
Dutch v. Warren, 1721 (early stock-dealing), 150 n.
Renaux v. Ferres, 1762 (Jonathan's Coffee House a stock market time out of mind), 158.
Doughty v. Axe, 1803 (bargains done in reliance on false rumours), 613 n.
Grizewood v. Blane, 1851 (gambling for differences is within the Gaming Act), 550.
Grissell v. Bristowe, 1869 (functions of jobber and broker), 583.
Thacker v. Hardy, 1878 (time bargains), 610.
Brown and others v. Committee of Stock Exchange, 1892 (Stock Exchange power of expulsion), 543 n.
Harker and another v. Edwards (scope of Stock Exchange rules), 544 n.

STRAHAN AND CO., 288.

INDEX 731

"STREET" dealings, in sixteenth century, 40 ; dealers decline to use Leadenhall, 40 ; Gresham's servant (Clough) on their refusal, 41.
STUCKEY, VINCENT, on provincial banking extension (1810), 118 ; on bills of exchange v. Government securities, 331 n.
SUEZ CANAL SHARES, purchase of, 522.
SUN SPOTS AND CRISIS, 501.
SUPREMACY, FINANCIAL, sketch of evolution of, 240 n.
SUSPENSION OF CASH PAYMENTS. See BANK OF ENGLAND.
SUTTON, THOMAS, financial operation by, to delay Spanish Armada, 53 n.
SWORN BROKERS, 147 ff.

"TAPE," 602 n.
"TICKER," 602 n.
TRANSFERABILITY. See NEGOTIABILITY AND ASSIGNABILITY.
TREASURY, receives statutory suspensive authority in relation to Bank Charter Act, 679 ; note issue by, 348, 349, 671.
TRITTON, JOHN. See BARCLAY AND CO.
"TRUST," English sense of the word, 467 n.
TRUST AND AGENCY CO. OF AUSTRALIA, genesis of, 471.
TRUSTEES, early difficulties of, as to investments, 34 ; Goldsmiths' Company as, 50 n. ; seventeenth-century need of trust investments, 84 ; see Glide v. Wright, 84.
TRUSTEE SAVINGS BANKS. See SAVINGS BANKS.
TULIPS, once " known " to Stock Exchange (probably), 146.
TURKEY MERCHANTS, 168.
TWININGS, 128.

UNION BANK OF CANADA, 445.
UNION BANK OF LONDON, directors of, and bears of bank shares (1866), 295 ; first meeting of, 309.
UNITED STATES BANKING REFORM, 647, 664.
UNLIMITED LIABILITY (see LIMITED LIABILITY), power to limit granted 1879, 187 ; instances of loss, and prolonged claims, under, 187 n. ; of bankers, in contrast to limited, of Bank of England, 226 ff. ; on bank shares, evil results of, 293 ff. ; banking with, history of, 302 and 302 n. ; drives investors into foreign loans, 500 ; see Law Cases cited under LIMITED LIABILITY.
USURY, sixteenth-century legislation as to, 44 ; 10 per cent. maximum, 44 ; all usury abolished, 45 ; 10 per cent. re-enacted, 46 ; legislation only permissive, 47 n. ; liberalisation of sentiment with regard to, 48 ; this change largely influenced by Puritans, 48 ; Calvin, for instance, 49 ; royal loans had the same effect, 49 ; so had the views of merchants who originally started on borrowed money, 51 ; so had the declining authority of patristic opinion, which was hostile to usury, 51 ; widespread practice of, in Tudor period, 52 ; Bacon on, 53, 83 ; 10 per cent. maximum reduced to 8 per cent., 80 ; beneficial results of reduction, 80 ; 6 per cent. enacted by Cromwell, 80 ; concurrent power to reduce in exceptional cases, 80 ; 6 per cent. fixed by Restoration Parliament, 81 ; outstanding mortgages excepted, 81 ; reduction of interest alleged to be subversive of monarchy, 82 ; Petty on, 83 ; arguments in favour of interest from the existence of helpless beneficiaries of deceased estates, 84 and 84 n. ; revival of mediæval hostility to (end of the seventeenth century), 133 ; David Jones's denunciation, 134 ; Bastwick's conclusive reply, 134 ; 5 per

732 EVOLUTION OF THE MONEY MARKET

cent. enacted by 13 Anne c. 15, 135; usury laws suspended as regards Bank of England, 137; and not applicable (in equity) where original bargain made abroad, 137; this confirmed by 14 Geo. III. c. 79, 137; endeavour to employ usury laws against the principle of negotiability, 138; this defeated by 58 Geo. III. c. 93, 138; mischievous working of usury laws in Waterloo period, 246; and in 1825, 329; anti-usury laws a failure and why, 138; and totally repealed in 1854, 139; revived by Money-lenders Act, 1900, 139; Ruskin on interest, 140; attempt to create anti-usury laws in Canada, 140.

Law Cases cited :—
Fountain v. Grymes, 1611 (purchase of annuity not a usurious transaction), 43.
Porter v. Hubbart, 1672 (interest during the Civil War), 81.
Barnet v. Tompkins, 1694 (illustrative case on usury, 136 and 136 n.).
Thompson v. Barclay, 1828 (Foreign loans not within the usury laws), 138 and 138 n.

VALUE, standardisation of (gold), 563 ff.
VENETIAN ADVENTURERS, 168.

" WALKS " in the Royal Exchange, 146.
WALPOLE, alleged to be an operator in Bank Stock, 230 and 230 n.
WAR, City dislike of, 391.
WAR CRISIS (1914), 669 ff.
WAR LOAN, 1914, and Bank Charter Act, 351.
WATTS, WALTER, frauds of, 364.
WEST END, banking in the, 117.
WESTERN BANK OF SCOTLAND, loose method of, 288; applies for assistance (1857), 366; collapses, 367.
WEST OF ENGLAND BANK FAILURE, 515.
WEST SURREY BANK, 414.
WILDES, WIGGINS AND WILSON, failure of (1837), 339.
WILTS AND DORSET BANK, 452.
WOOD'S BANK, GLOUCESTER, 117; specimen list of assets of, 285 n.

YORKSHIRE PENNY BANK, beginnings of, 281; Baring precedent reinvoked to protect, 661 ff.

ZACHARY LONG AND HALDIMAND (Morris, Prévost and Co.), 128.